Beginnings *of* Interior Environment

Beginnings *of* Interior Environment

Sixth Edition

Phyllis Sloan Allen

Miriam F. Stimpson

MACMILLAN PUBLISHING COMPANY
NEW YORK

Production Supervisors: Janice Marie Johnson and John Sollami
Production Manager: Richard C. Fischer
Text and Cover Designer: Patrice Fodero
Cover photograph: Norman McGrath
Photo Researcher: Lucy Barber

This book was set in Palatino by Waldman Graphics, Inc.,
and printed and bound by Von Hoffmann Press, Inc.
The cover was printed by The Lehigh Press, Inc.

Printed in the United States of America

Macmillan Publishing Company
866 Third Avenue, New York, New York 10022

Collier Macmillan Canada, Inc.

LIBRARY OF CONGRESS CATALOGING-IN-PUBLICATION DATA
Allen, Phyllis Sloan.
Beginnings of interior environment/Phyllis Sloan Allen, Miriam F. Stimpson.—6th ed.
p. cm.
Bibliography: p.
Includes index.
1. Interior decoration—Handbooks, manuals, etc. 2. Interior environment. I. Stimpson, Miriam F. II. Title.
NK2115.A59 1990
728—dc19 88-38818
ISBN 0-02-301811-9 CIP

Printing: 2 3 4 5 6 7 Year: 0 1 2 3 4 5 6

Dedicated to all beginning interior designers, professional and nonprofessional, on whom the quality of America's future interior environment depends.

Phyllis Sloan Allen

Dedicated to my mother and father.

Miriam F. Stimpson

1 Our Domestic Architectural Heritage

Tudor Half-Timber

Contents

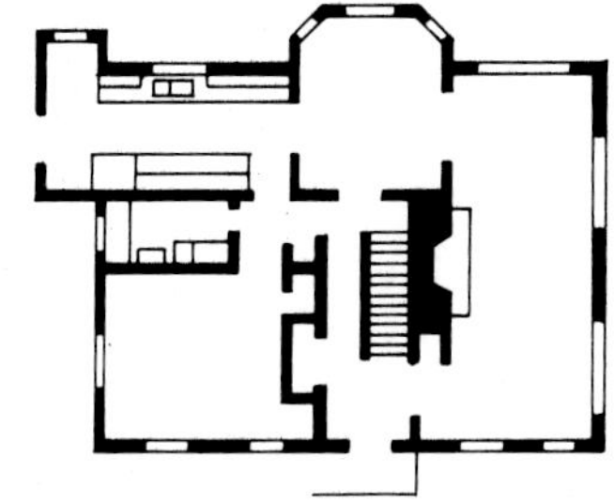

5 Color

6 Fabrics

7 Floors, Walls, and Ceilings

8 Windows, Doors, Stairways, and Fireplaces

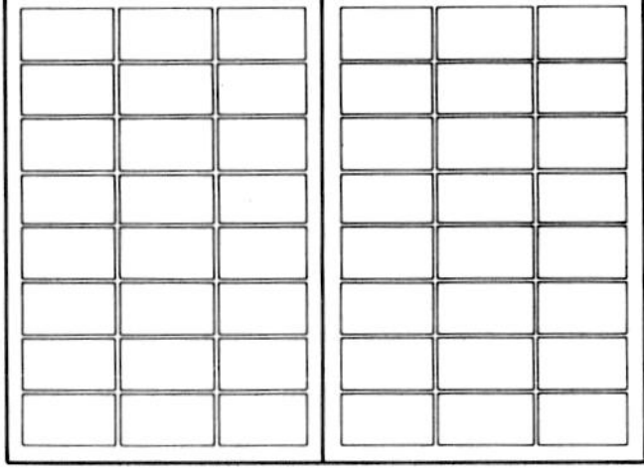

Shoji screen

9 Furniture

10 Furniture and Wall Arrangement

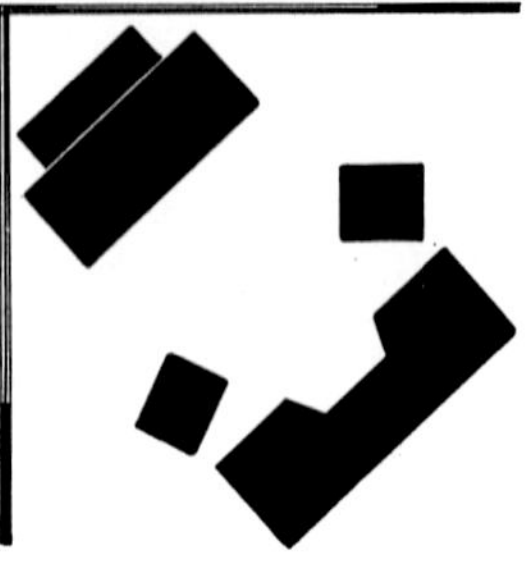

11 Unifying the Interior Environment

12 Interior Design as a Career

Preface

The sixth edition, like the previous editions of *Beginnings of Interior Environment,* covers a broad survey of related subjects for an introductory course in interior design. The goal in this new edition is to acquaint the reader further with basic design elements and principles and provide helpful information on how to integrate these timeless concepts into today's living spaces and life-styles. Although the book has served instructors and students for more than sixteen years with its practical approach to design and furnishings, the new edition recognizes new design expressions, technology, and materials, as well as the changing ways of American life in contemporary terms.

Today, convenience and efficiency are essential to life-styles, and space is often limited; so more people are choosing to live in apartments, condominiums, co-ops, or mobile homes. The need for energy conservation affects many aspects of the home or commercial setting. In addition, the products of our newest technologies are being accommodated in the process of interior planning. With these changes in mind, the sixth edition of *Beginnings of Interior Environment* helps design students, consumers, and professional designers enrich interior spaces both practically and aesthetically. The growing field of professional interior design will be well served by this book of "beginnings," which helps establish a framework for future career studies. Information on how to be creative within the bounds of good taste and sound design principles is presented in a somewhat structured fashion in the belief that a solid foundation in these principles and guidelines is necessary before a designer can depart from them with success.

The new edition has been considerably rewritten, expanded, and updated to encompass historic residential architecture, interiors and furnishings, space planning, principles and elements of design, materials and components, interior design as a profession, computer-aided design, and an accompanying glossary.

A particular effort has been made to present updated photographs and illustrations to acquaint students with timeless design executed in a variety of styles and price ranges and demonstrating the creative efforts of many professional designers across the nation.

The new edition offers the instructor and student added flexibility with the inclusion of Chapters 1, 2, and 9. These chapters, which deal with the history of the American home and furniture, provide an excellent reference even if not included as an integral part of the course, or they can serve as an introduction suitable for incorporation into the course material. Since *Beginnings of Interior Environment* is intended as an introductory text, all pertinent facets of the field are presented. Chapters 1, 2, and 9 provide the student with an appreciation and understanding of the development, challenges, limitations, and human and physical considerations in the evolution of the most important home and furniture styles in America. They substantiate the contention that the design expression of the exterior and interior of a house is inseparable from the total design concept. If these chapters are not included as part of the course outline, they can be drawn upon for use and application when presenting other chapters in the text.

At the end of Chapters 3, 4, 5, 6, 9, 10, and 11, specific projects have been assigned to test the student's competency in those particular areas. The worksheets for these assignments are located in the Student Packet prepared to accompany the text. The *Instructor's Guide,* coordinated to the new edition, includes a daily schedule for the entire course based on 43 class periods of 50 minutes each. It contains suggestions and supplementary materials for class demonstrations and projects, outline forms for correcting projects, a number of quizzes, a midterm examination, and a journal or file assignment.

Other supplementary items accompanying the text include a *Lecture Outline/Student Workbook,* which provides students with a course guide, additional activities, and review material. A slide package of 250 color slides keyed to the chapters is available from the publisher to professors who have adopted the book for their courses. A test bank is also available.

Chapter 1, Our Domestic Architectural Heritage, presents an overview of the history of the American home that has emerged from the early Settlement period during the sixteenth and seventeenth centuries to the Victorian Era. This chapter is planned to heighten the student's appreciation for the timelessness of historic residential architectural and interior design—knowledge that will be a valuable foundation for future architectural or design studies. The student of design is better equipped to select a personal style preference or adaptation from the most prominent styles in America for present or future application.

Chapter 2, The Modern House and Future Trends, briefly outlines the development of the modern house and major design directions currently popular. The chapter also surveys various options for homes that are available, from the traditional or modern custom-built house to dwellings designed to conserve energy.

Chapter 3, Floor Plans, focuses on determining the most suitable arrangement of a given space considering pertinent criteria employed by professional designers. The goal is to provide comfort, financial efficiency, and a pleasant environment for the occupant based on an analysis of individual needs.

Chapter 4, Design Theory and Application, is concerned with the development of good taste, and it helps the reader develop a sensitivity for discriminating between poor and effective design. It does so through discussion of accepted and time-proven principles and elements of design and their application to our physical surroundings.

Chapter 5, Color, explores the power of color, considered the single most stimulating element in home design.This chapter informs the reader concerning prominent aspects of color, including its use throughout major historic and contemporary periods, the psychology of color, and its theory and application. Hands-on projects help students discover important color concepts and create livable color schemes.

Chapter 6, Fabrics, concentrates on the various uses of fabric in creating interiors. Through study and practical projects, students learn that with skillful handling, fabric can establish beauty, comfort, mood, style, and a unity in designing interiors.

Chapter 7, Floors, Walls, and Ceilings, is a survey of the most up-to-date treatments for floors, walls, and ceilings, with charts showing characteristics and uses of each treatment; a discussion of the boom in the carpet industry, with a focus on fiber characteristics and their uses for beauty, function, and durability; and a study of wallpaper with its many practical and creative uses in today's interiors.

Chapter 8, Windows, Doors, Stairways, and Fireplaces, outlines various types of windows and methods of treatment. Emphasis is given to the importance of windows in today's smaller living spaces, and suggestions are given for ways of treating them in conserving energy. The design and materials employed for doors, stairways, and fireplaces are presented to familiarize the reader with the importance of these interior details.

Chapter 9, Furniture, is divided into two sections for the convenience of the instructor and student. The first section deals with basic furniture categories, materials employed, quality, finish, and additional consumer information. The second section presents a concise introduction to the principal furniture styles prevalent in America today. The complete history of furniture styles in America, of course, is beyond the scope of this beginning text. The material contained here, however, is a valuable resource and reference for both the instructor and student as it relates to the other chapters in the book. Especially helpful in Section 2 are single pages of precisely drawn illustrations for each style—providing the student with an overall visual concept of principal furniture periods. Included are sketches of the most common furniture pieces with accompanying identification.

Chapter 10, Furniture and Wall Arrangement, treats the arrangement of furniture to achieve the most efficient use of interior space and the design of pleasant and successful wall compositions.

Chapter 11, Unifying the Interior Environment, brings together the principles and elements of design and applies them to the problems of designing specific rooms of a dwelling to create a workable and unified whole. The challenge of effective planning for the handicapped and elderly is outlined here. Also included is an expanded survey of decorative and functional accessories that provide an enduring aesthetic and practical element to the home.

Chapter 12, Interior Design as a Career, explores the field of interior design, considering the classifications of the profession, qualifications and responsibilities, preparation, working procedures, opportunities, and future challenges for the professional interior designer. The topic of the significance and application of computer-aided design is a timely addition to this chapter.

Acknowledgments

Two years ago, Phyllis Allen approached me with the idea of writing a revision for *Beginnnings of Interior Environment,* a text she originated almost 20 years ago. I want to express my warm gratitude to Phyllis for extending complete confidence in my ability to revise her well-written and -organized text. It has been a pleasure to work closely with her from the first drafts to the completion.

Special appreciation is extended to the many architects, designers, manufacturers, museums, and galleries who contributed photographs of architecture, interior design, and products for this text. These photographs have provided most effective support to the written material.

I am particularly grateful to Sally Sharp, who works for an architectural firm in Phoenix, Arizona, for her precise and engaging illustrations throughout the text—especially the skillful drawings in the section on furniture styles in Chapter 9.

Thanks also are extended to the following reviewers for their helpful comments and suggestions: Kay Alger, Southern Utah State University; Cindy Armold, Bassist College, Oregon; Susan M. Coleman, Orange Coast College, California; Catherine C. King, Campbell University, North Carolina; Kyung J. Lee, West Virginia University; Karlene Morris, San Antonio College, California; Diane Richardson, Olivet Nazarene University, Illinois; Patricia T. Stealey, Shepherd College, West Virginia; Gretchen Steensen, Kent State University, Ohio; and Shawna Stroebel, Ricks College, Idaho.

I also wish to thank my editor, Julie Alexander, and the staff at Macmillan for their confidence in the project, attention to detail, and valuable professional advice.

Finally, to my family and my colleagues and students at Brigham Young University I express my love, gratitude, and appreciation for their wholehearted support and encouragement.

M.F.S.

Introduction

Since prehistoric times, when primitive drawings decorated the walls of caves, human beings have been concerned with the embellishment of their dwellings. Throughout history, people have considered their home as their castle, and the pride they have taken in its beautification is well known.

A major event in the development of interior design in its contemporary sense began in 1897 when Edith Wharton and Ogden Codman wrote a book entitled *The Decoration of Houses,* which they claimed was the first book on decoration to be published in 50 years. In the early twentieth century, Elsie de Wolfe's book, *The House of Good Taste,* published in 1913, gave respectability and great impetus to the relatively new profession of decorating. For several decades, however, interior decoration was to a great extent unattainable for most people, because only wealthy clients could afford the services of the interior decorator. Today, reputable furniture and department stores generally have on their staff one or more interior designers whose services are available free of charge to clients who make their purchases through the store.

For years the "decorator" too often applied modern materials and technology in creating interiors that expressed personal taste with little regard for the client's preferences and needs. This practice also has changed. The new emphasis in interior design, especially during the past decade, is on people.

A major challenge for the contemporary interior designer is to use materials and technology to create environments that are responsive to the needs of people—environments that are efficient but flexible and concerned not only with function and efficiency, but also with psychological and spiritual needs. A professional interior designer generally does not encourage clients to adjust their lives to the designer's notion of what an environment should be. Rather, the designs of environments are planned to grow out of the needs of people who inhabit them.

Because of current complex social and economic problems, the high cost of leisurely pursuits, the need for energy conservation, and changing life-styles, the home—although becoming increasingly smaller—is rapidly evolving into the center of people's lives. Benefits deriving from this change can be many and positive if the home is given top priority and household values are reordered for home-centered living. The home environment can be substantially improved to meet total needs, thereby adding to the pleasure and quality of life.

Homeowners today are demonstrating an unprecedented interest in interior design. Never before has there been such an abundance of materials from which the designer and consumer may choose, nor in such a wide price range. Articles for function and beauty from the past and present and from all countries are readily attainable. Additionally, today's market abounds in dirt-defying materials and soil-preventive devices unheard of a few years ago. Through these, the common problems of maintenance have been cut to a minimum.

A life worth living should have beauty, and beauty is everywhere. We need only to learn to see and appreciate it. Elizabeth Gordon, former editor of *House Beautiful,* said of beauty, "If you can't afford it when you are poor, you won't likely have it when you are rich." Acquiring the ability to see beauty means developing an acute awareness of the world around us, an awareness of color, texture, pattern, light, and form as they relate to each other and to other objects. It means learning to see beauty in simple and commonplace things, such as the subtle coloring in the bark of a tree and in the softness of new moss, the exquisite form of a simple well-designed glass vase, or the wealth of color in a flower garden. It means enjoying the feel of soft wool and the mellow patina of well-cared-for wood or sensing how filtered light through sheer curtains can relax the nerves. The therapeutic value of seeing beauty in everyday life is worth any amount of effort.

In recent years much has been said about a return to elegance. What is true elegance? Is it reserved for only the wealthy? The answer is no. True elegance is not a matter of a price tag; it is not a show of affluence nor a superficial display. Elegance is a certain refinement that comes from understanding the lasting beauty of simplicity. Because the physical environment has such a subtle but powerful influence on one's personal life, care should be taken in designing and arranging daily surroundings in the best and most satisfying manner. Great comfort and reassurance are often derived from seeing familiar things such as the same rooms, furniture, paintings, books, and personal belongings. Through day-to-day observation of these elements, values and attitudes are established that are often difficult to change.

Shaping the environment with good taste and a discriminating eye is a desirable goal and these aspects have little to do with cost. Through the knowledge and application of timeless principles of art and design, good taste may successfully be cultivated. Many individuals are surrounded by so much luxury that they can lose sight of the importance of little things that frequently make the difference between a house and a home. Finding a room that cannot be improved in some way is uncommon. The smallest change may correct an irritating problem or add a touch of beauty and enjoyment, making a major contribution to the ease and pleasure of daily living. With mounting pressures and stress of modern life, it is increasingly important that living spaces provide feelings of serenity and well-being. True peace may come from within, but a well-planned environment can nurture and preserve that peace.

Studies show that human beings function at their best in an atmosphere free from irritation and frustration. Conscious and constant refining in daily life can contribute immeasurably to feelings of repose and well-being. As people change, their needs change, and finding solutions to these needs is a constant challenge for the professional designer. Design within the home can reflect the occupant's varied interests in books, music, hobbies, religion, and other elements. Maintaining a sense of appropriateness for individual life-styles is a worthwhile goal. Someone once said people's homes are reflections of the way they live and think. Could it also be said that a home shapes the way that its occupants live and think?

P.S.A.
M.F.S.

Our Domestic Architectural Heritage

Chapter One

(continued)

Other Foreign Influences

The French House

The Norman Cottage

The French Plantation House

The Gallery House

The French Town House

The Dutch House
The German House
The Swedish House

Interiors of Dutch, German, and Swedish Houses

The Victorian Era (circa 1845–1900)

The Gothic Revival (1840s–1880s)
The Italianate Style (1830–1890s/1920s)
The Mansard, Second Empire, or General Grant Style (1850s–1880s)
The Queen Anne Style (1870s–1880s)
The Octagonal (1850s–1870s)
The Exotic Revival (1835–1890)
The Stick Style (1860–1890)
The Romanesque Revival (latter half of nineteenth century)
The Shingle Style (1880–1900)
The Beaux Arts Mansions
The Traditional Styles Revived

Preserving Our Architectural Heritage

How a nation lived in its homes is now recognized as having far greater importance than facts as to how many of the same people perished and how.

—Anonymous

The history of the American home is the history of our nation. Where did that history begin? Although some claim the first Europeans settled in what is now New Mexico in 1536, the general agreement is that the mainstream of American culture stems from those English colonists who founded Jamestown in 1607 and landed in Plymouth in 1620.

The dwellings of the earliest colonists were merely crude shelters against the elements. Soon, however, settlers in divergent areas ranging from New England to Louisiana, living under particular circumstances and using ***indigenous*** materials, constructed houses that filled their individual needs and expressed their distinctive characteristics. Through this process a variety of architectural styles evolved gradually and naturally. Because speed was necessary in providing all settlers a suitable shelter, it was an important factor in determining a principal characteristic common to early ***colonial*** architecture—simplicity.

An understanding of the traditional styles of American architecture is necessary to the interior designer and should be of interest to the home owner. This knowledge can deepen an appreciation of our architectural heritage and provide a foundation for better understanding the present. Rarely are the colonial styles copied precisely today, but many individual elements such as roofs, doors, windows, and other architectural details may be used to give a feeling of a historical style. Exteriors of a particular period may be adapted to fit today's floor plans and yet retain the desired *traditional* appearance. One advantage of a well-designed period house is that as current trends come and go, it is always in style.

Of equal necessity and importance to the interior designer and home owner is an appreciation for the background of modern architecture, with its roots beginning as early as the late nineteenth century. Just as the well-designed *period style* will endure, so also will the well-designed modern structure. (See Chapter 2.)

Figure 1.1 Parson Capen House (1683), Topsfield, Massachusetts. A garrison or jetty style and a superb example of medieval framing in America. *(Photography by J. Jan Jansen.)*

The Spanish Influence (circa 1565 to twentieth century)

Where did the history of American houses begin? The earliest explorers to land on American soil are believed to have been the Spaniards, who established the first permanent European settlement in Florida. As early as 1565, the Spaniards built a military garrison in St. Augustine. Soon, early settlers introduced the Spanish style of architecture into the South. Of homes from this period, practically none remain. Damp climate, frequent hurricanes, persistent fires, and the ravages of war have destroyed these first dwellings. One house in St. Augustine, Florida, however, still stands on its original foundation. It was built in the late 1500s and was restored in 1888 and again in 1959. This house is claimed by some to be the oldest in the United States and is called **Oldest House.** By the first part of the eighteenth century, a style known as the "St. Augustine look" emerged with homes featuring a definite Spanish feeling including balconies, ***loggias,*** and wooden gratings over the windows. The Spanish tradition further spread when explorers, politicians, the Catholic clergy, and others settled in what is now New Mexico, Texas, Arizona, and California. The Spanish home as we know it today falls into four distinct categories: the **Spanish Colonial/Mission, Southwest Adobe, California Ranch,** and **Monterey** styles.

Figure 1.2 Oldest House (1565), St. Augustine, Florida. This Spanish house rests on its original foundation. Some historians claim this is the oldest house in the United States. *(Courtesy of the St. Augustine Historical Society.)*

The Spanish Colonial/Mission Style

In the sixteenth century, Cortez introduced the Spanish influence into Mexico, where it took on a colonial atmosphere unique to the area. The early Spanish Colonial style was simple because of unskilled Indian labor and crude materials. The style was further influenced by a chain of Catholic missions built along the California coast in the early nineteenth century. Most of these missions have been restored and are now open to the public. Spanish architecture has had a romantic appeal for Americans, and when well designed, this type of home has a definite charm. It is especially favored for practical use in warm, dry climates, restricting its practical use to the southern and western areas of the United States. From time to time—during the 1920s, for instance—the Spanish Colonial and Mission styles have been actively revived, and characteristics of the two styles have often been combined. Numerous examples of this style are found in southern California, especially in the Santa Barbara area, where many Spanish-style buildings, both residential and commercial, have been authentically restored and opened to the public. (An example is **Casa Covarrubias.**)

The following are general characteristics of the Spanish Colonial and Mission house.

Exterior

- Blending of the Mexican, Indian, and Spanish cultures
- Stucco-covered walls, whitewashed or tinted, often with a crude finish
- Low-pitched tile roof with broad overhang
- Heavily carved doors in geometric patterns used throughout

Spanish

Figure 1.3a Santa Barbara's Street in Spain, built around an adobe hacienda dating from 1827. The tile-roofed adobes bring to life the Spanish influence of Old California. *(Courtesy of the Santa Barbara Chamber of Commerce.)*

Figure 1.3b Elements of the Spanish Style are evident in this contemporary room. They include dark exposed beams, white plastered walls, a crude archway, a Spanish chest, Mexican tile, the religious painting, and other Spanish accessories.

- *Arcaded* porches surrounding an inner court (frequently)
- Intricate wrought-iron designs employed for interior and exterior
- **Reja,** or wooden grating, typical on windows of original houses
- Balconies and terraces occasionally employed

Interior

- Floors of plain wood or paved with Mexican tile or brick
- Whitewashed stucco walls, often with a crude finish
- Colorful painted tile trim around doors and on stair *risers*
- Chandeliers of handwrought black iron
- Heavy masculine furnishings with deep geometric carvings
- Accessories and artifacts depicting religious themes, especially in Catholic and Indian relics

(See Chapter 9 for additional information on Spanish furniture.)

The Spanish home has been a favorite in warm areas of the United States. During the 1920s the Spanish style particularly had an active revival. During the 1960s, with the popularity of the Mediterranean influence, Spanish colonial architecture again found favor in many parts of the country. Spanish homes created today often express a sense of the criteria just described, interpreted in contemporary terms. Great flexibility and freedom to combine various elements are employed. The result may display only a few ideas from the early Spanish influence, but the feeling of the culture is evident.

Figure 1.4 Palace of the Governors (1610), Santa Fe, New Mexico. The oldest public building in the United States. *(Courtesy of the New Mexico Department of Development.)*

The Southwest Adobe House

In 1605, Southern colonists traveled to the area that is now New Mexico, where they found Indians living in ***pueblos.*** Taos Pueblo, first visited by Captain Pedro de Alvarado in 1540, is considered the oldest and perhaps the largest continuously occupied apartment dwelling in the United States. Today it houses about 1,500 Pueblo Indians, whose way of life has changed little in 800 years.

Figure 1.5 Old House, Santa Fe, New Mexico. Considered by some to be the oldest house in the United States. *(Courtesy of the New Mexico Department of Development.)*

Dominated for about 300 years by Spain or Spanish Mexico, a unique vernacular architecture evolved incorporating elements of the native Indian, Spanish, and Mexican cultures. In 1610, Santa Fe became the capital for Spain, later for Mexico, and finally for New Mexico. In that same year, **Palace of the Governors,** which is the **oldest public building in the United States,** was built on the site of an old Indian pueblo. An ancient ***adobe*** structure known as **Old House,** near the San Miguel Mission in Santa Fe, is claimed by some historians to be the oldest house in the United States. Whether the structure is older than Oldest House in St. Augustine has not been definitely established. The adobe houses built today, mainly in Arizona and New Mexico, follow the same basic style as the early adobes. Santa Fe, more than any other city in the Southwest, has admirably preserved the heritage of the early adobe dwelling, with structures in this style dominating both residential and public buildings. From the 1920s to the present, a unique style based on the Southwest Adobe has emerged known as ***the Santa Fe Style***—and remains popular. This style incorporates many of the original concepts of the early exterior and interior features. (See Chapter 9.)

Pueblo or Southwest Adobe

General characteristics of the Southwest Adobe house are as follows.

Exterior

- Thick adobe brick construction providing good insulation against heat
- Flat roof and deeply set windows and doors
- Exterior finished with a thin coating of mud
- Sculptured contoured exterior and interior corners
- Rough-hewn pole ***beams*** projecting through walls
- Rectangular plan with one or more stories
- Pole ladders on exterior in place of interior stairs
- A courtyard-centered arrangement surrounded by a Greek Revival ***colonnade*** was a typical later feature

Interior

- Informal feeling
- Backgrounds of plastered surfaces with exposed ceiling beams
- Rounded, molded, plastered fireplace
- Tile or wood floors
- Furniture and accessories a blend of Spanish, native Indian, and Mexican pieces
- Colors that reflect the desert landscape

Figure 1.6 Interior reflecting the Santa Fe Style. A molded corner fireplace, exposed pole beams, Mexican tile, plastered walls, equipale leather chair, and other Mexican, Indian, Spanish, and contemporary furnishings are typical elements of the current Santa Fe Style. *(Photograph by Peter Aaron/Esto Photographics.)*

Adobe structures of particular interest are Old House, Santa Fe, New Mexico; S. Parson's House, Santa Fe, New Mexico; Palace of the Governors, Santa Fe, New Mexico; and the University of New Mexico, Albuquerque, New Mexico.

The California Ranch House

The California ranch house is a mixture of the Spanish style and the old western farmhouse. The low, rambling structure developed from an informal life-style and simple building space. This style originally emerged from the old adobe home with its flat roof; but considering the rainy California climate, a pitched roof was more practical and was added to the structure in the early 1800s. Often a three-sided fence enclosed and defined the outdoor living space—the beginnings of what we now regard as the ***patio.*** This type of house is currently popular among many families in the West. The term ***ranch style*** has been used so freely that individuals tend to believe it means merely a long, low house. An authentic California ranch house, however, has several identifying characteristics.

California Ranch House

Exterior

- Structure hugging a relatively flat terrain
- Long, low roofline; roof originally of tar, then tile; today tile or shingles used
- Wide, low overhangs supported by posts
- Indigenous materials used for construction, such as adobe, wood, stucco, or brick
- Wing-sheltered patio easily accessible from most rooms

Interior

- Similar to interior details described in Spanish Colonial section (today, great freedom of style is incorporated)

The Monterey House

The Monterey house is a blending of the Spanish, French, and New England architecture that had its birth in California when that state was a colony of Spain and Monterey was the most important seaport on the West Coast. Since lumber was plentiful but workers scarce, builders employed Indians, skilled in the use of adobe, for constructing the thick walls. The Spanish influence was seen primarily in the red tile roofs. The overhanging ***balconies*** with their wrought-iron railings reflected the French houses of New Orleans. The basic style had already been established when the settlers arrived from New England with their English ideas; but they contributed doors, windows, and moldings, some of which they brought with them. **Thomas Larkin,** of Boston, Massachusetts, contributed significantly to the original Monterey style when he combined these various cultural details in his own home in Monterey (which was completed in 1837 and is now open to the public). He even introduced the use of wallpaper and applied it to the plastered walls. In fact, many historians believe Larkin built the first Monterey home and thus influenced others to build their homes based on the same principles. The result of this happy blend was the Monterey house, which after more than 100 years continues to be a popular style of architecture in some areas of America, particularly in California.

The following are general characteristics of the Monterey house.

Exterior

- Adobe, stucco, or whitewashed brick walls, sometimes tinted
- Flat-pitched tile roofs
- Wide overhangs to shade windows
- Second-story balcony

Monterey

- Woodwork showing New England influence

Interior

- Walls, floors, and other backgrounds incorporate English and Spanish influences, as does the exterior
- Furnishings and accessories can either be elegant or simple English or Spanish or a combination. However, one style generally will dominate, depending on the tastes of occupants.

Our English Heritage—Medieval and Renaissance Influence

Although the history of American architecture began with the Spanish who set up a garrison in Florida, the mainstream of American culture began at Jamestown, Virginia, and Plymouth, Massachusetts, in the seventeeth century. The culture British colonists brought to the new land when they settled along the Atlantic seaboard had a far greater influence on America than all other cultures combined. Technically, American houses built during the seventeenth century and based on historic English prototypes fall under the category of "English Medieval." However, styles that have emerged from this period, although displaying many overlapping characteristics, are quite distinctive and are popularly known under particular names. The most prominent of these English Medieval styles include THE HALF-TIMBER, STONE, OR BRICK TUDOR HOUSE, THE ELIZABETHAN OR JACOBEAN MANOR, THE COTSWOLD, THE SALTBOX, THE GARRISON, THE GAMBREL, and THE CAPE COD.

The Early Half-Timber, Brick, and Stone House

The first permanent dwellings constructed by British settlers who landed in **Jamestown** in 1607 were initially little more than caves dug in the earth or crude thatched huts. Some huts for survival were copied from native Americans. As soon as initial hardships were overcome, however, settlers began building more substantial houses based on those they had known in England. Early structures were patterned after the ***half-timbered*** one-room Tudor and Elizabethan "hall" familiar in England at the time. These simple one-room spaces were quite small, with a high pitched roof of thatch and a side chimney. The half-timber house was constructed of massive wooden frames employed for the structural components, with sections in between filled with plaster or masonry. An early filling material was called ***wattle and daub***—interlaced boughs covered with clay and mud. (When used in America today, half-timber construction is usually simulated by placing boards on the surface, which gives the appearance of the original construction.) Another popular filling material of the period was ***brick nogging***—bricks arranged in a pattern in between the half-timber exterior framing. Of the many thatched half-timber English cottages, the charming **Anne Hathaway's Cottage** (home of William Shakespeare's wife) outside of Stratford-upon-Avon, England, is perhaps the most fa-

Figure 1.7 Agecroft Hall (sixteenth century), a handsome half-timber Tudor manor house, formerly stood in Lancashire, England. In 1925 it was transported to Windsor Farms near Richmond, Virginia, where it was reconstructed. *(Photograph by Miriam Stimpson.)*

Tudor Half-Timber

Virginia House

Figure 1.8 Interior with rich wood paneling, carved chairs, chandelier, and fireplace typical of the English Tudor home. *(Courtesy of Stuart Interiors, England.)*

mous. One picturesque half-timber house built in England in the sixteenth century and relocated in America in 1925 is **Agecroft Hall** in Windsor Farms, Virginia. These two half-timber houses were built in England, however, and serve in this text to demonstrate the building technique. Often the half-timber stone or brick medieval English house is referred to as ***Tudor,*** but in fact, the English Tudor period officially ended with the death of Elizabeth I in 1603, a few years before Jamestown was settled. The influence, however, of the Tudor style continued during the seventeeth century in both England and America. (Although the earliest homes of the colonists employed this building technique, the real

Figure 1.9 Adam Thoroughgood House (ca. 1636), Norfolk, Virginia. The oldest brick house in America, with a style reminiscent of its English ancestry. *(Courtesy of Haycox Photoramic, Inc., Norfolk, Virginia.)*

influence of the Tudor home in America has been particularly evidenced from the Beaux Arts period to current times.)

Having come primarily from the upper classes, the Jamestown colonists preferred brick, the material to which they were accustomed, and there was an abundance of clay in the Jamestown area. Although almost nothing remains of the earliest dwellings around Jamestown, one extant brick structure, the **Adam Thoroughgood House** (circa 1636) Norfolk, Virginia, reflects its English prototype. It features brick construction, sharp gables, massive buttressed chimneys, small diamond-paned windows, and a simple doorway typical of the medieval tradition of English houses. Many historians believe that the Adam Thoroughgood House is the oldest brick residence in America.

The Medieval English Tudor house is characterized by the following features.

Exterior

- Two to three stories
- Rambling design
- Half-timber most common construction (stone or brick optional), with **wattle and daub** or **brick nogging** (***clapboard*** used in New England often covered half-timber because of severe climate); stone or brick construction optional and often simplified versions of the style
- Use of the ***Tudor arch*** over doorways and fireplaces
- Second-story overhang or ***jetty*** frequently used
- Sharp ***gables***
- Clustered or columned chimneys
- ***Oriel*** and ***bay windows***
- Small-paned leaded windows, often diamond shaped
- Chimneys: ***buttressed,*** stone-end, or simple unembellished
- Projecting porch or doorway optional

The Elizabethan Manor House

During the reign of Elizabeth I (who was also a Tudor), the Gothic and Medieval English design in architecture merged with the new Dutch influence, resulting in the great ornate-gabled house known as the ***Elizabethan.*** Although elements of the Elizabethan style continued to be popular through the following centuries in England, especially during the ***Jacobean period*** (the reigns of James I, Charles I, Charles II, and James II in the seventeenth century), the style had little long-lasting influence in America. A fine example of medieval architecture in the Elizabethan style is **Virginia House** in Richmond, Virginia, a majestic structure once the county seat of Warwick, England. Virginia House was moved to America in 1925 and now stands reassembled at Windsor Farms near Richmond, Virginia. Another excellent example of the English manor house, reflecting both Elizabethan and Jacobean influence in America is **Bacon's Castle** (1665) in Surrey County, Virginia, with its typical ***cross-plan.*** The English manor house built in the colonies follows the same general style as its prototype in England, with the following features.

Bacon's Castle

Exterior

- Rambling design, often E shaped or employing the English cross-plan, with the two-story projecting entrance
- Large house with two or three stories
- Stone or brick structures most typical (half-timber construction, a carryover from the earlier Tudor period, optional)
- **Flemish gables** and ***parapets*** reflecting Dutch influence; especially popular in Jacobean England
- **Balustrades** often used on roof line or above windows and edging balconies and terraces
- **Bay** and **oriel** windows with small leaded panes
- Doorways recessed; round or **Tudor arch** framing; Tudor arch, also ***Gothic arch*** (optional)
- Numerous clustered chimneys and exterior chimneys common

Interior

- *Simple Tudor homes:* plain plastered walls, sometimes with simple vertical wood paneling; half-timbering often exposed inside
- Large fireplace with heavy wood mantel or Tudor arch and brick interior
- Wide plank wood floors; Tudor arch over doorways optional
- Heavy wood-beam ceilings
- Furniture often handcrafted and simple; some pieces brought from England with typical English carvings.
- Simple and informal fabrics, typically homespun, cottons, and wools
- *Elizabethan and Jacobean manor homes:* more elegant interior details; wood paneling, bay windows, leaded panes; Tudor arch over doorways
- Wood or stone fireplaces with Tudor arch
- Gothic detailing (optional)
- Wood or stone floors
- Elizabethan and Jacobean furniture and fabrics; some Gothic furniture (see Chapter 9 for furniture and fabric details)
- Fabrics: tapestry, crewel embroidery, chintz, leather; rich colors; flame stitch and large flower motifs popular

(See Chapter 9 for additional information on furniture.)

The Cotswold House

A sixteenth-century English cottage typical of houses in the ***Cotswold*** area can be seen in Dearborn, Michigan, where it was relocated. These stone houses are often characterized by a front attached chimney, an asymmetrical arrangement, dormer windows, and a low cottage

Cotswold (English Cottage)

Thatched Cottage

Figure 1.10 Old Cotswold Cottage, sixteenth-century English Medieval. Reassembled in Dearborn, Michigan. *(Courtesy of the Henry Ford Museum, Dearborn, Michigan.)*

look. Construction of stone in gray and gold tones is typical, although some houses have a light-colored stucco applied over the stone walls. The Cotswold house is a **simplified interpretation of the Tudor and Elizabethan styles.** Houses of this type and others of English origin have had an important influence on American domestic architecture from its beginning and from time to time have had a resurgence.

New England Saltbox, Garrison, Gambrel, and Cape Cod

The **Pilgrims** who first landed at Massachusetts Bay were for the most part from a low economic class and were seeking political and religious freedom. Although ill-equipped to meet the hardships that awaited them, they were courageous, vigorous, and devout zealots who responded to the challenge of establishing a home in a harsh and unknown land. The Pilgrims' first shelters were similar to those of the Jamestown settlers—little more than dugouts or crude huts of boughs covered with clay (wattle and daub); yet by the middle of the seventeenth century their homes had a surprising degree of comfort.

Because the land was heavily wooded and had to be cleared for dwellings, wood was the logical choice for construction material. In addition, adequate tools were in short supply, and speed in construction was a necessity. These two factors accounted for distinctive characteristics of the seventeenth-century New England house: **wood construction** and **simplicity.** Early houses, which were built from memory, were derived from English folk architecture of the late Medieval and Elizabethan period. Through the forthright use of local materials and necessary ***adaptations,*** the result was a unique provincialism expressing the vigor of the early colonists. Fortunately, the sharp gables, steep roofs, large chimneys, and small-paned windows, to which the colonists had been accustomed, were practical for the severe New England climate.

The strong Tudor and Elizabethan influences in early New England architecture can be seen in many of the seventeenth-century houses that are still standing. A New England parsonage in Springfield, Massachusetts, built in 1639 of half-timber construction and with a projecting tower, reveals its English ancestry.

A unique example of a stone house in the medieval tradition is **Old Stone House** in Guilford, Connecticut (see Figure 1.11). Built in 1639, its 2-ft-thick walls are made of local stone and mortar mixed with yellow clay and pulverized oyster shells. The simple facade with its tiny windows and large exterior chimneys are typical of the English Medieval influence. Stone construction was rare in the area

Figure 1.11 The oldest known stone house still standing in what was once colonial America. Built in 1639 for Reverend Henry Whitfield in Guilford, Connecticut. The Old Stone House remains today a glimpse of seventeenth-century America. *(Photograph by Elliott Erwitt, courtesy of Magnum.)*

Figured 1.12 Witch House (ca. 1642), restored, Salem, Massachusetts. An architectural treasure with distinctive medieval features. *(Courtesy of the Chamber of Commerce, Salem, Massachusetts.)*

due to a lack of materials. This house remains the oldest stone house in New England and is open to the public.

A notable architectural treasure of the seventeenth century is **Witch House** in Salem, Massachusetts, built circa 1642 and now restored. Owned by Jonathan Corwin, a judge in the witchcraft court, Witch House is believed to have been a site for some of the witch trials of that century.

Other important seventeenth-century New England houses reflecting the English Medieval tradition are **House of Seven Gables** (1668), and **John Ward House** (1684), Salem, Massachusetts; **Whipple House** (1638), and **Strawberry Hill,** or Proctor House (circa 1670), Ipswich, Massachusetts; **Fairbanks House** (1636), Dedham, Massachusetts; and **Ironmaster's House** (1636), Saugus, Massachusetts.

Because of the circumstances peculiar to the environment, homes of the New England settlers, although still retaining medieval features, took on characteristics that became uniquely American.

The Half-House

The first houses were but a **single room** (half-house) with the chimney on the side wall. The door opened into a tiny entrance that abutted the chimney; from there, steep stairs rose to an attic.

The Two-Room or Double House

Soon a **second room** was added on the other side, and the fireplace became the central core of the house. **John Howland House,** built in 1666 in Plymouth, Massachusetts, the only extant house in which Pilgrims once lived, shows the original medieval-like half-house and the 1750 addition. **John Alden House,** built in 1653 (now restored), is an example of a two-room house in the medieval tradition.

The Saltbox

To provide additional space, a **lean-to** that usually became the kitchen was added to the two-room house.

Saltbox

Figure 1.13 Howland House (1666), Plymouth, Massachusetts. The only house still standing in Plymouth in which Pilgrims once lived. *(Courtesy of the Pilgrim John Howland Society, Plymouth, Massachusetts.)*

Late in the century, the lean-to was often part of the original plan. This type of house, called a **saltbox** because the shape resembled the boxes in which settlers stored their salt, became the most characteristic silhouette of many early colonial houses. Three noteworthy examples extant today are **John Quincy Adams House** (1675), Quincy, Massachusetts; **Jethro Coffin House** (1686), Nantucket Island; and **Ogden House** (1690), Fairfield, Connecticut.

Development of the New England house

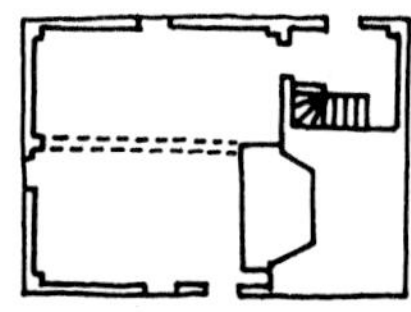

Half-House – 1650

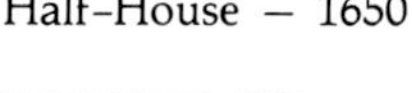

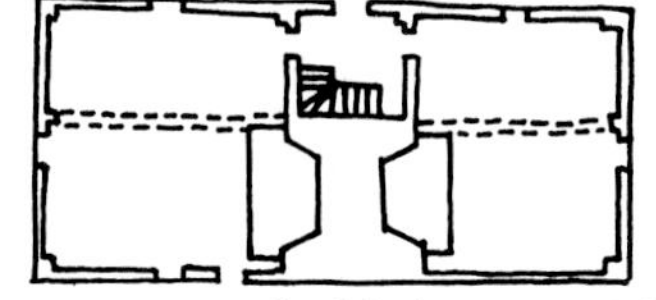

Two-room or double house – 1675

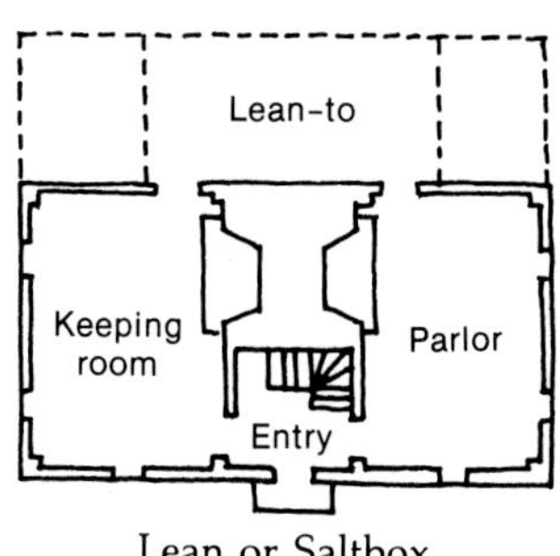

Lean or Saltbox

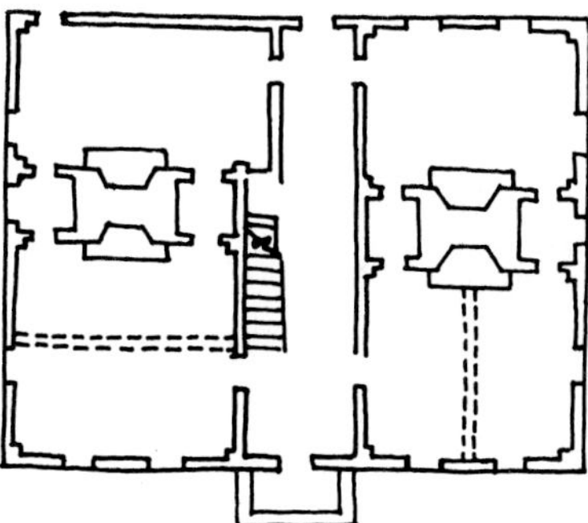

Early Georgian – 1750

The Garrison

In many houses, the second story extended beyond the first floor, a carryover from medieval England. The overhang, or **jetty,** had end brackets with hand-carved ***pendants.*** This house is commonly called a **garrison.** The garrison-styled **Parson Capen House** in

Garrison or Jetty

Figure 1.14 Simple, sturdy living room of the Parson Capen House (1683), Topsfield, Massachusetts. Notice the date, 1708, carved on chair back. *(Photography by J. Jan Jansen.)*

Figure 1.15 Brick-lined fireplace of the Parson Capen House, with authentic cooking accessories displayed. *(Photography by J. Jan Jansen.)*

Gambrel

Topsfield, Massachusetts, built in 1683, is a superb example of medieval framing in America. Three garrison houses of particular interest are **Paul Revere House,** 1650, Boston's oldest house; **John Ward House** (1684), Salem, Massachusetts; and **Scotch-Boardman House** (1651), Saugus, Massachusetts.

The Gambrel

Another modification had a **double-pitched roof** made of two sections of rafters. This roof style was inexpensive to build and permitted more headroom in the attic. The ***gambrel roof*** is often incorrectly called Dutch colonial. Seventeenth-century examples of the gambrel-roof house are **Fairbanks House** (1636), Dedham, near Boston; **Harlow-Holmes House** (1649), Plymouth, Massachusetts; and **Glebe House** (1690), Woodbury, Connecticut.

The Cape Cod (Transitional)

During the final decade of the seventeenth century, one of America's best-loved houses made its appearance. This style was an outgrowth of the half-house and the two-room or double house. What has come to be known as the **Cape Cod** was a humble cottage that retained much medieval character. Covered with *clapboards* or shingles, the structure had a *central chimney,* a simple *plank doorway,* and *small-paned windows*—often two on one side of the entrance and one on the other. The Cape Cod derived its name from the great number of these houses built on Cape Cod.

Cape Cod

Early in the eighteenth century, the Cape Cod house took on some of the features of early ***Georgian*** architecture, such as ***dormers, dentil-trim, cornices,*** impressive end-chimneys, and symmetrically arranged ***double-hung windows.*** A paneled central doorway had a ***transom*** (small window above a door or window) of small glass panes topped by a flat cornice. Later in the century, a ***pedimented*** doorway was sometimes added. The Cape Cod has been one of the most widely copied and adapted houses in America and has proven appropriate for almost any area in the country. Although the style often took on a more formal aspect in the eighteenth century, the quaint seventeenth-century form with the low roofline has persisted virtually unchanged to the present. Two seventeenth-century Cape Cod houses of particular interest are **Jabez Wilder House** (circa 1690), Hingham, Massachusetts, and **Jonathon Kendrick House** (late seventeenth century), South Orleans, Massachusetts. Two **transitional structures** built early in the eighteenth century showing the Georgian influence that followed are **Brush-Everard House** and **Raleigh Tavern,** both in Colonial Williamsburg, Virginia.

Along with their own distinguishing characteristics, the four seventeenth-century New England houses share a number of features.

Exterior

- Rectangular plan
- Wood or shingle construction
- Central chimney
- Small casement windows
- Asymmetrical and symmetrical arrangement
- Simple English medieval character

Figure 1.16 Jonathon Kendrick House (late seventeenth century), South Orleans, Massachusetts, an early Cape Cod style. *(Photograph by Arthur Haskell, courtesy of the Library of Congress.)*

Figure 1.17 Brush-Everard House (1717), an early eighteenth-century transitional style. Tall windows, dormers, and dentil trim show Georgian influence. *(Courtesy of the Colonial Williamsburg Foundation.)*

Interior

- Plain plaster walls or ***palisade*** wood paneling common; ***wainscoting*** employed
- Small-paned casement windows, often double-hung
- Wide plank floors (later, Oriental rugs popular)
- **Furniture** often homemade; **Windsor** chairs; furniture with Elizabethan and Jacobean influences, including the **Elizabethan court cupboard,** the **Carver chair,** and the **Hadley chest.** Later, furniture became more elegant (See Chapter 9.)
- **Fabrics** similar to those employed in Elizabethan and Jacobean manor home typical

Numerous seventeenth-century houses have been restored and can still be found throughout New England, many furnished in the manner of the period and open to the public. Massachusetts particularly boasts numerous homes of this period.

The English Heritage—The Georgian Period

The period when England was ruled by the Stuarts, roughly the seventeenth century, is divided into three subperiods: (1) **Jacobean** (1603–1689), (2) **William and Mary** (1689–1702), and (3) **Queen Anne** (1702–1714). For the first 40 years in the seventeenth century there was little change in English architecture inside or out. Many houses that were started during the Elizabethan period were not completed until well into the seventeenth century and incorporated Jacobean influences. Then **Inigo Jones** (1573–1652), the prominent English architect of the early seventeenth century, revolutionized English architecture when he introduced the ***Renaissance*** and ***Palladian influence*** into England. When Inigo Jones built his **Queen's House** in Greenwich, England, with its unique square plan (the English had been used to the rambling design), a new style evolved. **Sir Christopher Wren** (1632–1723), the great English architect responsible for rebuilding much of London after the Great Fire of 1666, became its foremost exponent. In his capable hands, Wren developed the ideas of Inigo Jones into a gracious architectural style (called Queen Anne Style in England) adaptable to both manor house and modest dwelling. Because this style flourished during the reigns of **George I, George II,** and **George III,** it became known as **Georgian.** Although Sir Christopher Wren never came to America, his influence was the dominant force in American architecture during the early Georgian period (circa 1720–1750). The

Wren–Georgian

later part of the Georgian period was dominated by the ***Palladianism*** of another eminent English architect, **James Gibbs** (1683–1754).

By the second decade of the eighteenth century, the colonies had grown and the people prospered largely because of the expansion of shipping and commerce. English craftspeople and builders, laden with tools and architectural drawings, arrived in the colonies. There they worked with local craftspeople, and the rugged simplicity of the earlier houses soon gave way to the new and grander Georgian style. At the time of the American Revolution, the new style had become familiar in American facades from Jamestown to Portsmouth.

The Early Georgian or Wren-Georgian Style (circa 1720–1750)

The Early Georgian house in America retained the basic elements, fine proportions, and symmetry of its English prototype, but it took on local differences.

The following are general characteristics of the **early Georgian–Wren baroque style.**

Exterior

- Influence of English Baroque and Sir Christopher Wren
- Symmetrical facade with a general feeling of dignity and formality
- Two to three stories—rectangular block
- Symmetrically placed double-hung (sash) windows with small panes
- Central doorway flanked by ***pilasters*** and crowned by one of the four pediment forms
- **Hipped roof**, often with a balustrade protecting a ***captain's*** or ***widow's walk;*** **dormer windows** typical, often with **shutters**
- Tall end chimneys
- Brick, clapboard, or stone construction
- Cornice with ***dentils*** or ***modillions***

PEDIMENT FORMS

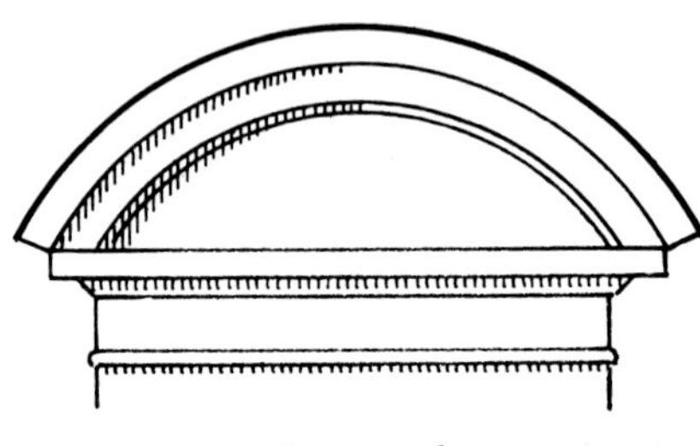

Segmental

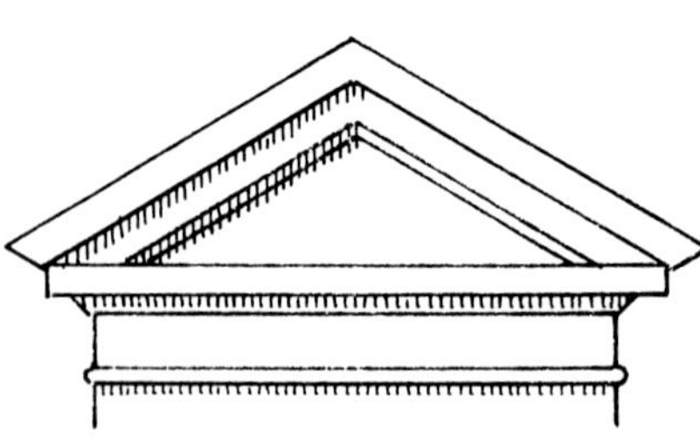

Triangular

Broken

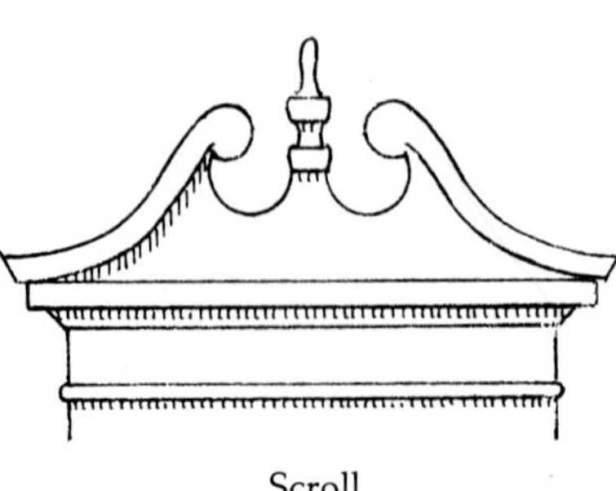

Scroll

- Stringcourse (bands of stone or brick between stories) (optional)
- Corner ***quoins*** (optional)
- ***Cupola*** or ***belvedere*** (optional)
- Gabled or gambrel roof (optional); gambrel roof typically employed in New England

English craftspeople who arrived in the colonies in the eighteenth century brought with them **handbooks for builders,** filled with uniform structural information and carefully drawn decorative detail. The widespread dissemination of these manuals accounts in large measure for the similarity seen in the architecture of the period. This style of architecture, commonly known as Georgian, was first seen in the colonies in Virginia, and the earliest structure was the **Wren Building** at **William and Mary College** in Williamsburg. (According to some, it was designed by Wren himself or by someone in his office, but this has not been documented.) The Wren-Georgian style, however, reached its greatest refinement in the gracious mansions plantation owners built along the lower James River in Virginia. On the banks of the James River are three splendid and thoroughly English examples of these early eighteenth-century houses, all extant and in a remarkable state of preservation: **Westover** (1730–1740) and **Carter's Grove** (1750–1753), both of which have side wings that were later additions, and Berkeley

Carter's Grove–Wren influence. Wings added later show Palladian influence.

Figure 1.18 Carter's Grove (1750–1783). One of the most beautiful Early Georgian houses in America. The side dependencies, built at a later date, show the Palladian influence. *(Courtesy of Colonial Williamsburg Foundation.)*

(1726). Another notable example is the **Governor's Palace** in Williamsburg, Virginia (1706–1720).

As the new style spread, great brick and wood mansions were built in the new Georgian manner, but with regional differences. Rooflines varied from the hipped styled to sharp gables and gambrel. Since wood was plentiful, it continued as the common building material in New England. Although Georgian houses in the North lacked some of the formal elegance of southern mansions, they reflected the formal

New England Early Georgian Style

Figure 1.19 Hunter House (1746), Newport, Rhode Island. Typical of the Wren-Georgian style in the North, it ranks among the ten best examples of colonial residential architecture in America. *(Photograph by John T. Hopf, courtesy of the Newport County Chamber of Commerce.)*

grandeur of the Wren-Georgian style. New Englanders also favored the gambrel roof. Some examples of **Wren-Georgian architecture in the North** are **MacPheadris-Warner House** (1718–1723), Portsmouth, New Hampshire; **Ropes Memorial** (1719), Salem, Massachusetts; **Hunter House** (1746), Newport, Rhode Island; and **Wentworth-Gardner House** (1760), Portsmouth, New Hampshire.

The Late Georgian or Gibbs Palladian Style (circa 1750–1790)

The Roman Palladian style (developed by **Andrea Palladio** (1518–1580), an Italian Renaissance architect), which became popular with the English aristocracy in the early eighteenth century, was introduced into America near the middle of that century, primarily through books. Among the many builders' manuals that made their way to the colonies, perhaps most important was **James Gibbs's *A Book of Architecture,*** first published in England in 1728 and believed to have reached the new land in 1751. Intended as a pattern book, its simple and conservative style had an immediate appeal to the colonists and exerted a powerful influence on American architecture. Although buildings retained the basic Wren-Georgian style, Gibbs's new Palladianism offered a more monumental quality and greater degree of formality than did earlier buildings.

The following are general characteristics of the **late Georgian Palladian style** in America.

Gibb s style pedimented pavilion

Exterior

- Features of basic structure essentially Wren-Georgian
- Classical details such as pilasters and pediments
- Central section of facade emphasized by pedimented ***pavilion*** or ***breakfront*** extending above the roofline

Figure 1.20 Mount Pleasant (1761), Fairmount Park, Philadelphia, Pennsylvania. The imposing mansion with its formal Gibbs-style facade was considered one of the grandest in the colonies. *(Courtesy of the Convention and Tourist Bureau, Philadelphia, Pennsylvania.)*

Figure 1.21 Contemporary interior with Chippendale chairs reflecting the eighteenth-century Georgian influence. *(The British National Trust Collection.*™ *Courtesy of Century Furniture Co.)*

- Pavilion sometimes flat, sometimes projecting ***portico*** form
- Side dependencies or wings connected to the main block, often by open ***colonnades***
- ***Palladian window*** prevalent
- ***Quoining*** (optional)

Interior—Early Wren and Late Georgian Palladian

- Cornices with dentil trim
- Pediments over doorways and mantels
- Painted wood paneling or plaster; stained wood paneling; late Georgian featured more Palladian interior details
- Wallpaper above a ***dado;*** late Georgian favored ***continental*** or Chinese wallpaper
- Wood plank floors with Oriental rugs
- Brass or bronze **baroque** chandeliers
- William and Mary, Queen Anne, and Chippendale furniture; Chippendale especially popular in late Georgian interiors (see Chapter 9)
- Elegant and formal fabrics: damasks, velvets, brocades, etc.
- Prominent colors: rich golds and reds, Williamsburg green, deep gray-blue

In the South the Palladian influence was seen in the symmetrical villalike plan with its central block and side dependencies extending on either side. Early Georgian structures, like Carter's Grove in Virginia, later often featured wings added when the Wren or Palladian style was in vogue. Some outstanding Palladian houses in the South are **Tyron Palace** (1760), New Bern, North Carolina; **Hammond-Harwood House** (1773–1774), Annapolis, Maryland; and **Miles Brewton House** (1765–1769), Charleston, South Carolina.

In the Middle Atlantic states, side dependencies (when used) were usually detached from the central block. **Mount Pleasant,** built in 1761 in Fairmount Park, Philadelphia, was the most imposing house of the area. Another great mansion with a formal Gibbs facade in Fairmont Park is **Woodford** (1742–1756).

In the North after 1750, wood continued as the principal material used for construction and side dependencies were rarely added. Only the facades revealed Gibbs's Palladianism with their triangular-topped pavilions, the ***classical*** detail of which was more authentically done than anywhere else in the colonies. Examples of particular merit are **Longfellow** (vassal) **Home** (1750), Cambridge, Massachusetts; **Lady Pepperell Mansion** (circa 1760), Kittery Point, Maine; **Shelton's Tavern** (1760), Litchfield, Connecticut; and **Jeremiah Lee House** (1768), Marblehead, Massachusetts.

Neoclassicism in America (circa 1790–1845)

Neoclassicism in America, which covered the last decade of the eighteenth century and the first four decades of the nineteenth century, is made up of two periods: ***Federal*** and ***Greek Revival.*** Between Georgian Palladianism, Federal, and Greek Revival, however, no clear lines of demarcation exist. Rather, one style gradually blends into the other. Much neoclassicism was communicated to the colonies through books, but also, young men were encouraged to go abroad and study classical architecture. This effort resulted in a group of trained and highly motivated American-born architects. In the early nineteenth century, British and French architects began arriving on the scene—among whom English-born **Benjamin Latrobe** (1764–1820) was the first—and European ideas were further infused into American architecture.

Figure 1.22 Longfellow House (1750), Cambridge, Massachusetts. Its classical detail with the triangular-topped pavilion reveals Gibbs's Palladianism. *(Courtesy of the U.S. Department of the Interior, National Park Service.)*

The Federal Period (circa 1790–1825)

The decades following the revolutionary war were eventful for America. The tendency was to break with anything reflecting English dominance, and interest in French ***modes*** grew. Consequently, when the excavation of ***Pompeii*** captured the interest of French designers during the reign of Louis XVI, as well as the interest of the brothers Robert and James Adam in England, the new classical style rapidly superseded the Georgian. Although America was reluctant to adopt this style from England, the neoclassic designs of English architects and cabinetmakers exerted great influence during the period following the adoption of the Dec-

Figure 1.23 Monticello (1769–1809), Federal "Palladian" home of Thomas Jefferson, Charlottesville, Virginia, reflects the Federal-Roman influence. *(Courtesy of the Thomas Jefferson Memorial Foundation.)*

Figure 1.24 The dining room at Monticello in the Federal style, featuring Hepplewhite furniture and typical woodwork of the period. *(Courtesy of the Thomas Jefferson Memorial Foundation, Inc. Photograph by James Tkatch.)*

CLASSIC GREEK ORDERS

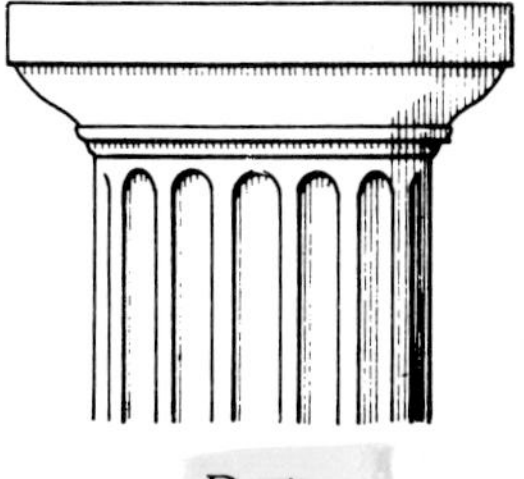

Doric

Ionic

Corinthian

laration of Independence. The architectural style of the early Federal period, influenced primarily by the designs of the Adam brothers, was concentrated in the North; but the later phase, dominated by **Thomas Jefferson,** occurred in the South.

Two main factors brought about this change in America: (1) the **need for an official architecture** and (2) Thomas Jefferson's enthusiasm for the new classicism, together with his distaste for English-Georgian architecture. Jefferson was a scholar and skillful architect, and his designs for the new **Capitol of Virginia** at Richmond, inspired by the **Maison Carée** in France, established the columned portico as the essential motif of American official architecture. His home, **Monticello,** strongly influenced the design of domestic buildings. Jefferson's support of architects such as Latrobe, who was trained in the new classicism, enabled the classical revival to attain a greater vogue in America than it did in England. Young architects traveled to Greece and Rome, where they took exact measurements of Greek temples and adapted them to American buildings. Throughout the colonies buildings had columns capped with one of the three famous Greek orders (i.e., ***Doric, Ionic,*** or ***Corinthian***). Columns also appeared inside, separating rooms and supporting mantels. Triangular pediments were placed over doorways, windows, and fireplaces; ***reeding, bead-and-reel, egg-and-dart,*** the urn, and all manner of classical decorations were employed both inside and out. Around 1820, Jeffersonian classicism had developed into a full-blown Greek revival. The Wren-Georgian style was not immediately discarded, however. The basic style of the Georgian house continued to be used, and only the details, particularly the addition of the pillared portico, indicated the postrevolutionary date.

In residential work of the Federal period, four names stand out as representing the best American architectural design: **Samuel McIntire** (1757–1811) of Salem, **Charles Bulfinch** (1763–1844) of Boston, **John McComb** of New York, and **Benjamin Latrobe** in the South. Among these architects, the first is probably the best known. McIntire planned three-story, square, dignified mansions with exquisite detail and simplicity. McIntire's influence was largely responsible for transforming the small seaport town of Salem, Massachusetts, into the city that became known as the New World Venice. The elegant three-story porticoed homes he designed for well-to-do citizens have been considered as representative of one of the purest styles of architecture ever developed. Salem remains today the most typical example of an American city of the Federal period.

The following are typical characteristics of the Federal-English and Federal-Roman period house.

Exterior—Federal-English Influence

- Influence of Robert Adam and English Georgian architecture
- Influence of ancient Grecian and Roman architecture and detailing
- Three stories high, with smaller third story
- A columned portico in front
- Doorway sidelights (frequently); entrance topped by ***elliptical fanlight***
- Delicate classical detail
- Windows crowned by pediments or ***jack arch lintels*** (optional)
- Stringcourse (optional)
- Flattened hipped roof with balustrade above cornice concealing roof (optional)

Exterior—Federal-Roman Influence

- A rejection of the mannered delicacy of the Adam style associated with the English Georgian architecture
- Expresses qualities of strength and dignity based on architecture of Republican Rome
- Influence of Andrea Palladio

Federal

Interiors

- Classical detailing from ancient Greece, Rome, and Pompeii; Adamesque motifs; plaster ceilings with Adam motifs an important feature
- Woodwork usually painted white. Wallpaper above a dado (optional)
- Adam mantels
- Crystal chandeliers
- ***Parquet*** or wood plank floors; Oriental rugs
- ***Hepplewhite*** and ***Sheraton*** furniture; ***Martha Washington chair*** (See Chapter 9.)
- Fabrics: formal and elegant; damasks, silks, velvets, brocades; motifs from ancient Greece and Pompeii and from Democratic America
- Colors: muted blues and greens; soft pinks, yellows, and peaches popular

Excellent residential examples of the Federal period extant today are the **Pierce-Nichols House,** 1782, and **Pingree House** (1804), Salem, Massachusetts; **Harrison Gray Otis House** (1796), Boston, Massachusetts; **Monticello** (completed 1769–1809), Charlottesville, Virginia; **Homewood** (circa 1800), Baltimore, Maryland; **Nathaniel Russell House** (1809), Charleston, South Carolina; and the **White House** (present structure completed 1829), Washington, D.C.

The Greek Revival Period (circa 1825–1845)

Although the Neoclassic Style reached the South later than the North, the style of the Greek Revival period—the final phase of neoclassicism—perhaps became more predominant in the South than anywhere else. The size and elegance of the plantation mansion, the ample space for expansion, and

Figure 1.25 Pingree House (1804), Salem, Massachusetts. A dignified Federal-period mansion designed by Samuel McIntire. *(Courtesy of the Chamber of Commerce, Salem, Massachusetts.)*

Figure 1.26 Dunlieth (1847), Natchez, Mississippi. Two-story columns surround this southern Greek Revival mansion of exceptional beauty. *(Courtesy of the State of Mississippi Department of Economic Development.)*

the luxurious manner of living lent themselves well to the new style. The architects in the South did not merely build ***replicas*** of Grecian temples, but adapted the ***classic*** style to meet the needs of the hot climate. Two-story columns framed the cool ***verandas,*** often encircling the entire house.

Greek Revival—isolated temple form

Greek Revival—short end to the street

On a more modest scale, the Greek Revival house was a simple pitched-roof structure much like earlier houses, but the short end faced the street (such houses are especially found in Charleston, South Carolina). Authentic Greek details were applied to the front corners. The house had Doric pilasters topped with a flat ***entablature*** and pediment displaying a full entablature around the cornice. The door was usually asymmetrically placed, and the entire structure was painted white.

The Greek Revival house is characterized by the following features.

Exterior

- Continued use of Georgian, Federal, and French forms
- Precise adherence to Greek proportions, orders, and ornaments
- Isolated temple form

Figure 1.27 Shadows-on-the-Teche (1830), New Iberia, Louisiana. A fabled and beautiful southern Greek Revival mansion. *(Photograph by Gleason, courtesy of the National Trust for Historic Preservation, Washington, D.C.)*

- Profuse use of two-story columns on more pretentious houses; columns often continue on all sides. Second story balcony (optional)
- White exterior
- Many or a few steps leading up to the veranda or porch; in damp climates, house raised to accommodate a high basement
- House often built with gable end to street, with or without proper colonnaded portico attachment
- In absence of a portico, placement of pilasters, frieze, and classically framed doorway
- French doors and shutters often employed, especially in South

Interior

- Grand treatment of classical orders (columns and pilasters)
- Elegant crystal or oil-vessel-type chandeliers; ceiling fan (**punka**) found in South
- Continuation of scenic wallpaper
- Dominant masculine feeling; ***Empire*** and ***Duncan Phyfe*** furniture; harp a favorite piece; some use of English ***Regency*** (See Chapter 9.)
- White ivory button on ***Newel post*** signifying paid mortgage
- Colors: Empire green, gold, black and white, rich reds and blues; colors and motifs popular with Napoleon copied
- Fabrics: elegant and formal; velvets, damasks, and brocades

Some examples of Greek Revival houses are **Andalusia** (1836), Bucks County, Pennsylvania; **Wilcox-Cutts House** (1843), Orwell, Vermont; **Alvin T. Smith House** (1850s), Forest Grove, Oregon; **Stanton Hall** (1852–1857), Natchez, Mississippi; and the **Mississippi Governor's Mansion** (1841), Jackson, Mississippi.

Figure 1.28 Greek Revival interior. A strongly patterned carpet, the grand use of columns, a crystal chandelier, and chairs with scroll arms are typical elements of the Greek Revival Style. *(All rights reserved. The Metropolitan Museum of Art.)*

Other Foreign Influences

The French House

The heartland of America—the area between the Allegheny and the Rocky mountains, from Canada to the Gulf of Mexico—was controlled by France for over a hundred years; yet during this time, little of the area was colonized.

The Norman Cottage

French colonists who came to America in the seventeenth century settled mainly along the St. Lawrence River and in the South along the Mississippi River. The houses they built in the North often had high hipped roofs and rounded corner towers with whitewashed exteriors, reminiscent of the ***châteaus*** and manor houses the colonists had known in France. In 1678 French ***Huguenots*** founded a settlement in New Paltz, New York. Five of the original stone houses built there are standing today, along what is called Huguenot Street. One of these houses is the **Abraham Hasbrouck House** (1692–1712).

Early Norman cottage in the north

The French Plantation House

In the South the basic structure of the northern cottage was retained and adapted to the climate by adding an encircling ***galerie*** or porch covered by a broad ***bonnet roof.*** The roof provided shelter from frequent rains and gave a

Figure 1.29 Abraham Hasbrouck House (1692–1712). One of the original stone houses still standing along Huguenot Street in New Paltz, New York. *(Courtesy of the Huguenot Historical Society, New Paltz, New York.)*

pavilionlike appearance. Another practical adaptation was raising the house to allow an air passage underneath, which helped to keep the house dry and cool. Because of the high water table, use of basements was impossible. A further variation was the raised cottage, in which the ground floor was built of brick or stone, topped by a white plastered wooden pavilion. ***French doors*** opened on all sides onto the porch, which served as a hallway.

With the passage of time, new architectural influences were evidenced in the evolution of the French house. The masonry wall of the lower floor was replaced by posts that supported an encircling balcony. When neoclassicism swept the country, posts gave way to classical columns on both upper and lower stories and windows were surmounted by pediments.

Pavilion house with bonnet roof

Pavilion house with stone foundation

Posts and an encircling gallery replace stone foundation

The zenith of the French plantation house during the Greek Revival

Antebellum Mansion

During the prosperous decades that preceded the Civil War, the Greek Revival period reached its zenith in the great plantation mansions of the South. Two-story Greek columns swept from ground to roofline. Delicate wooden balustrades enclosed upper galleries and rooftops. Graceful fanlights crowned the doors. What had begun as a modest French farmhouse had blossomed into the ***antebellum*** mansion of exquisite beauty and grandeur.

The Gallery House

The tiny French Cajun cottage, with its front porch protected by an overhanging roof, was the original gallery house. As the Cajun cottage evolved, it was enlarged and a second-story gallery was added on the front. As it was further embellished, it developed into the full-blown Greek Revival characterizing many southern mansions. Some of the magnificent antebellum mansions that have survived are **Shadows-on-the-Teche** (1830), New Iberia, Louisiana; **Oak Alley** (1836), St. James Parish, Louisiana; **San Francisco** (1849), Lower Mississippi, Louisiana; **Dunlieth** (1847), Natchez, Mississippi; and **Houmas** (circa 1840s), north of New Orleans, Louisiana.

The French Town House

The galleries of the French town house faced away from the street onto a private courtyard. The ground floor was used for shops or utilitarian purposes; the family quarters were above. Lacy cast-iron balconies facing the street were added in the nineteenth century, which gave the **Old French Quarter of New Orleans** a flavor of French architecture found nowhere else in America.

American 20th Century adaptations of the French house

Louisiana French–raised basement

French City House

French Manor

French Cottage

Over the years, houses recalling original French city houses, manors, and cottages have been built in America adopting various prominent features and even combining characteristics from originals to suit contemporary needs and tastes. In more recent years, many distinctive American modifications of the French house have been developed, and this style direction continues to be popular.

Four general French styles based on original prototypes have emerged and are known under the following names:

Louisiana French—Exterior

- High raised basement to protect from floods and dampness
- High steep hipped roof with or without dormers
- Tall decorative chimney on each end
- French windows and shutters
- Porch with one-story columns
- Lacy ironwork (originally added during the Victorian era)

French City House

- Formal, dignified, bisymmetrical design
- High hipped roof
- Windows breaking line of eaves
- Delicate stucco or painted brick
- Lacy ironwork (frequently)
- Central doorway, often recessed
- Quoining (frequently)

French Manor House

- Style a combination of simple chateau and glorified farmhouse, usually built like shallow horseshoe around three sides of courtyard
- ***Dovecote roofs*** on wings
- ***Mansard roof*** with dormers on central structure
- French windows on main floor; use of shutters
- Beautifully symmetrical
- Brick painted in delicate colors
- Quoining (optional)

French Cottage

- Low hipped or dovecote roof (or both)
- Asymmetrical design
- Recessed double doors (frequently)
- French windows and shutters
- Small U-shaped courtyard at entrance
- Quoining (frequently)
- Lacy wrought-iron work (optional)

Interiors—Eighteenth-Century Court Style (typical for all French variations employing this design)

- Elegant paneling, gilt moldings, dainty classical detailing from Pompeii and Greece
- Influence of the court of **Marie Antoinette** and **Louis XVI**
- Painted walls in pastel colors
- Fireplace with shell motif; gold-fan fire screens
- Parquet floors; ***Aubusson, Savonnerie,*** and ***Oriental rugs***
- **Louis XVI** furnishings most dominant; some Louis XV (see Chapter 9)
- Elegant brocades, velvets, damasks, silk, etc.; classical motifs; pastel colors; ***toile-de-Jouy*** fabrics (see Chapter 9)

Figure 1.30 French Louis XV furniture combined with modern pieces complement a contemporary living room. A large dhurrie rug provides a unifying base and focus for the room's decor. *(Photograph by Alex Groves.)*

Interiors—Country or Provincial French Styles (typical for French variations employing influence of both styles; particularly known in America as "French Provincial")

- Adaptation of Court French, but in simpler terms
- Painted or wood paneling for wall treatment—not as ornate as Court French; plain plaster walls for a typical country feeling
- Fireplace similar to Court French, but not as decorated
- Floor treatment same as Court French; braided rugs typically employed for a country look
- Use of simplified **Louis XV** furniture most popular; wood finishes; ***armoire*** important piece; ***salamander ladderback chairs***
- Cottons, linens, and informal textiles; motifs associated with French themes; checks and stripes; small quaint prints; toile de Jouy (See Chapter 9 for a discussion of typical French fabrics and furnishing details.)

Currently there is great flexibility and freedom in designing American homes employing French styles. The characteristics just listed can be incorporated into today's French-style home to provide an authentic feeling of original treatments. Contemporary French homes often employ only a suggestion of authentic French structures, interior backgrounds, and furnishings to reflect the owner's personal preferences and living style.

The Dutch House

In 1650, Dutch settlements were well established throughout the regions of Manhattan Island (which Dutch settlers named New Amsterdam), New Jersey, and Delaware. Although Dutch domination was brief, Albany, New York, still reflects ***Flemish*** influence in the few remaining houses with ***stepped gables*** (or **crow-stepped gables**) and ***Flemish gables.*** Some early Dutch homes had a distinctive

Dutch Farmhouse

Figure 1.31 Van Cortlandt Manor, a restored Revolutionary War estate in Croton-on-Hudson, New York. Built of fieldstone with characteristic long, sweeping Dutch roofline extending over full-length porch. *(Courtesy of Sleepy Hollow Restorations, Tarrytown, New York.)*

patterned brickwork on one or both sides of the structure. Dutch houses built in the countryside were usually constructed of fieldstone, shingle, or clapboard and typically had high gable ends with a long sweeping roofline extending over a full-length porch (the flowing eave). The early Dutch gambrel, or **bell gambrel,** had a high breaking point just below the ridgeline; later it was dropped to its final position. Four notable examples of the Dutch house in America are **Van Cortlandt Manor,** Croton-on-Hudson, New York, begun in 1665, now authentically restored; **Van Rensselaer Manor** (1650), Hudson River, opposite Albany; **Dyckman House** (1783), New York, New York; and **Richard Vreeland House,** Leonia, New Jersey, built circa 1786.

The German House

German colonists who settled in Pennsylvania built a variety of homes reflecting medieval features, ranging from simple log cabins to half-timbered homes (called ***Fachwerkbau***) to large stone manors. Structures most identified with the German contribution during the eighteenth century are homes built of local fieldstone with 2-ft-thick walls. The typical roof was steeply pitched, but the gambrel was sometimes used. A distinguishing feature found in some German houses was a sheltering hood between the first and second stories, known as a ***pent roof.*** Often the owner's place of business or the barn was integrated into the home. Examples of stone houses built by the Pennsylvania Germans, mistakenly referred to as Pennsylvania Dutch (Deutsch), are **Ingham Manor** (circa 1750), Bucks County, Pennsylvania; **Thompson-Neeley**

Pennsylvania German stone house with sheltering hood (pent roof)

Figure 1.32 Thompson-Neeley House (1701), Washington Crossing, Pennsylvania. An example of a Pennsylvania Deutsch (German) home. *(Courtesy of the Washington Crossing Foundation.)*

House (1701), Washington Crossing, Pennsylvania; **Squire Boone House** (home of Daniel Boone), Baumstown, Pennsylvania (circa 1735); and the **Georg Mueller House,** Milbach, Pennsylvania (1752).

The Swedish House

Swedish colonists who settled in the Delaware Valley in 1638 introduced the **log cabin** to America, although it was also familiar to the German settlers. Log construction, however, was borrowed to only a limited extent on the eastern seaboard. With the opening of new wilderness areas for colonization, particularly with the westward movement, the log cabin, with its numerous adaptations, became the standard dwelling. Swedish colonists also built stone houses, often with gambrel roofs, large end-chimneys, and dormers. Three of the few authenticated early Swedish houses extant are **John Morton Homestead** (log; 1654), New Prospect Park, Pennsylvania; **Hendrickson House** (1690), Delaware Valley, Pennsylvania; and **Keith House** (1722), Graeme Park, Pennsylvania. In the twentieth century the log cabin has enjoyed a revival. This method of log construction has been employed for everything from simple vacation homes to millionaires' cabins. One example of an extravagant log cabin is **Sagamore Lodge,** vacation home of Alfred Gwynne Vanderbilt, Adirondack Mountains, New York (1893).

ROOF TYPES

High-pitched gable

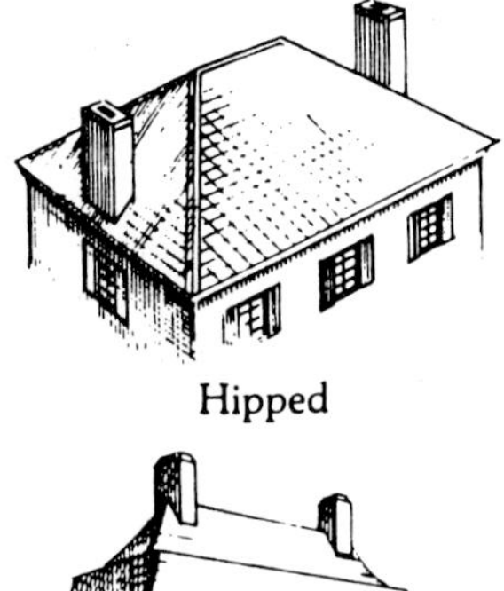

Hipped

Low-pitched gable

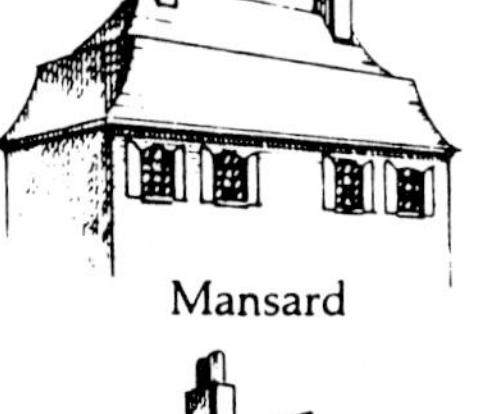

Mansard

Gambrel

Dovecote

Figure 1.33 Keith House (1722), Graeme Park, Montgomery County, Pennsylvania. Representative of the work of Swedish artisans, who built this structure from native fieldstone. *(Courtesy of the Pennsylvania Historical and Museum Commission.)*

Figure 1.34 A contemporary log-constructed home reflects the building style of our Swedish and German ancestors. *(Photograph by Michael Skott.)*

INTERIORS OF DUTCH, GERMAN, AND SWEDISH HOUSES

Dutch, German, and Scandinavian settlers' crafts contributions were perhaps more influential than the various homes they built. Handcrafted furniture was often painted with delightful and colorful motifs from the homeland. Tole painting, handmade quilts, stenciling, glass design, pottery, and other decorative crafts were beautifully designed and today have become an important inspiration for the current Crafts Revival in America.

The Victorian Era (circa 1845–1900)

Architecture of the Industrial Age coincided with the reign of **Queen Victoria** and bears her name. Nostalgia for buildings of the past pervaded America during this time, expressing itself in an unprecedented monopoly over other architectural styles. The revival of interest in Victorian architecture led to years of harsh criticism. The style has long been maligned and held in disrepute, having been referred to as the "battle of the styles," among other derogatory terms.

In recent years, however, many authorities have regarded Victorian architecture as inventive, full of vigor and diversity, and representative of a coherent and unified course of development. Today many individuals believe architecture of the nineteenth century is particularly American and represents the most significant style in our nation's history. Americans throughout the country have rediscovered these picturesque yet long-neglected Victorian dwellings and have remodeled or restored them for private or commercial use. Numerous Victorian homes have also been restored and opened to the public. The heritage of Victorian houses has again gained nationwide appreciation.

During the second half of the nineteenth century, through a rapid succession of overlapping modes, four major architectural styles emerged: **Gothic, *Italianate,* Mansardic (Second Empire),** and **Queen Anne.** Five additional Victorian designs popular during the period were the **Octagonal, Exotic, Stick, Romanesque Revival,** and **Shingle** styles.

(1) The Gothic Revival (1840s–1880s)

Andrew Jackson Downing (1803–1892) is considered the **father of the Gothic Revival in America.** Since stone, the material used in English Gothic, was costly and stonemasons were few, Downing translated the English stone Gothic into wood, and the style became known as **Carpenter Gothic.** Thousands of these houses, many of which are still standing, were built throughout the country from the 1840s to 1860s. The Gothic Revival also includes houses built of stone employing Gothic detailing.

The following are general characteristics of the Gothic Revival and Carpenter Gothic styles.

- Broken, picturesque exterior, planned from inside out
- Steep gables
- Porches leading to informal gardens
- Lofty windows, often pointed
- Carpenter Gothic: wood sheathing, often board and batten (vertical boards)

Carpenter Gothic

- Carpenter Gothic: **bargeboard** or **vergeboard** (shaped wooden edging) under gables
- Carpenter Gothic: **"Gingerbread"** decoration in gables (from stone ***tracery,*** which consisted of ornate patterns in the pointed arches of Gothic architecture)

One famous Gothic Revival structure from the period is **Lyndhurst,** built from 1838 to 1841 in Tarrytown, New York, overlooking the Hudson River. A well-known Carpenter Gothic structure is now a bed-and-breakfast establishment: **The Abbey** in Cape May, New Jersey.

Figure 1.35 Lyndhurst (1838–1841), Tarrytown, New York. America's most distinguished Gothic Revival mansion. *(Photograph by Frohman, courtesy of the National Trust for Historic Preservation, Washington, D.C.)*

(2) The Italianate Style (1830–1890s/1920s)

In the 1830s, America's admiration for the Italian arts resulted in popularity for the modified Italian ***villa.*** Used for both urban and suburban dwellings, including town houses, the Italianate style remained popular for 100 years and left a lasting imprint on American architecture. A later development was a cube-shaped house, but the tower—called a cupola, belvedere, or observatory—continued as the most distinctive feature. A wealth of Italiante dwellings are found in northern California, the Midwest, and the Northwest.

Italianate Victorian

Figure 1.36 Dining room at Lyndhurst with carved Gothic style furniture and detailing. *(Courtesy of the National Trust for Historic Preservation, Washington, D.C.)*

The following are general characteristics of the **Italianate style.**

- Stately structures with vertical emphasis
- Low-pitched or low-hipped overhanging roof supported with large decorative **brackets**
- Free arrangement of bold square or rectangular blocks; structure topped by a **square tower,** built for pleasure rather than utility
- Easy access to outdoor ***terraces***
- Windows topped with pediments, fanciful **crowns, hoods,** or **"eyebrows"**
- **Cupolas** or **belvederes**
- Small entry porches (optional)
- Use of the **Italian arch** and **columns**

(3) The Mansard, Second Empire, or General Grant Style (1850s–1880s)

The mansard roof, which François Mansart introduced in France in the 1600s, was the answer to many architectural problems. The roof was adaptable, took a variety of shapes and sizes, and provided more efficient use of space. The style is also known as the General Grant style, after Ulysses S. Grant. An excellent example of the French Second Empire style is the **Governor's Mansion,** 1871, in Jefferson City, Missouri.

The **Mansard** or **Second Empire house** is characterized by the following.

- Stately structure, rectangular or square form, towers (optional)
- Tall **French windows** opening onto deep porches; windows often topped with decorative **pediments** or **crowns**
- Crowned by a steep sloping **mansard roof;** massive cornices with brackets smaller than Italianate; roofline frequently topped by iron cresting and finials; colored-tile patterns (optional)
- Quoining and stringcourse (belt course) typically employed

Mansard or Second Empire Victorian

(4) The Queen Anne Style (1870s–1880s)

The most whimsical of the Victorian era's *eclectic* styles was the so-called Queen Anne. This style had no relationship to Queen Anne of England and was a deliberate imitation of many defunct architectural styles. Two examples are the **Clevenger-McConaha House** (circa 1887) in Centerville, Indiana, and the **Whitmore Mansion** (1898), in Nephi, Utah.

The **Queen Anne style,** with its full range of architectural detailing, has some identifying features.

- All manner of decorative wood and plaster detailings, including gingerbread, ***festoons,*** spindles, brackets, vergeboards, patterned shingles, and belt courses
- Variable heights and shapes; sometimes built on grand scale
- **Fish-scale shingles** common (in the form of overlapping fish scales)
- Numerous steps leading up to porch; porches often circular with ***colonnettes*** and turned railings

Queen Anne Victorian

- Windows grouped in banks, with upper panes often colored
- Most distinctive feature is **circular or square tower** extending from ground level to all floors, topped with a **cone-shaped roof;** many other projections including bay windows, balconies, porches, and turrets

In addition to the four major Victorian styles, another five design directions were prevalent during the period: the **Octagonal, Exotic, Stick, Romanesque Revival,** and **Shingle** styles.

(1) The Octagonal (1850s–1870s)

Only a few hundred homes remain standing today employing the octagonal plan. The **Orson Squire Fowler House** (1848–1858), Fishkill, New York and the **Dewey-Jenkins House** (1855), Milwaukee, Wisconsin are two good examples of the Octagonal style. Outstanding features of the Octagonal style are

- An eight-sided architectural form (sometimes either fewer or more sides used)
- Topped with a cupola

Figure 1.37 Whitmore Mansion (1898), Nephi, Utah. An example of the Queen Anne Victorian style. *(Courtesy of Don and Darlene Bendoski.)*

- Accompanying features: a high basement, a low-hipped roof topping the octagonal, quoining, porches, balustrades, and decorative features found on other Victorian styles

(2) The Exotic Revival (1835–1890)

In the 1830s to 1890s, some architects and builders were fascinated with "exotic" styles from "exotic" places. The most prevalent revivals in America include the Middle-Eastern influence and Swiss Chalet. One of the best known of Exotic-style Victorian mansions is **Alana** (1872), a majestic Persian castle on the Hudson River in New York, and the **Vedanta Society Headquarters** (turn of the century) in San Francisco, California. Features include the following.

- **Swiss Chalet:** Extravagant use of gingerbread; porches; balustrades; steeply pitched roof (Swiss style often used for resort homes on the eastern seacoast)
- **Middle-Eastern:** Particularly Turkish and Moorish themes; onion domes; mosque arches; intricate oriental detailing

(3) The Stick Style (1860–1890)

The Stick Style is easily recognizable by the decorative stickwork applied to the walls of the structure. With its half-timbered effect, the Stick Style comes close to being identified as a Tudor Style. This type of house was built particularly in the northeastern and northwestern parts of the United States. The **J. N. A. Griswold House** (1863), in Newport, Rhode Island, is a fine example of the Stick Style. Often the **William Carson House** (1885), in Eureka, California, is labeled by historians as the "stick style" and sometimes as "Queen Anne" and "High Victorian Eclectic." Regardless of its label, the Carson House is one of the most delightful Victorian homes in the nation. Typical distinctive features include the following.

- Horizontal, vertical, or diagonal **wood strips** applied on top of exterior walls of plaster, shingles, or clapboard
- Porch, often with **Y-shaped supports;** turned column supports (frequently)
- **Steeply gabled roof** with clustered chimneys
- Brackets, balustrades, pendants, dormers, and decorative trusses
- Towers (optional)

(4) The Romanesque Revival

The Romanesque Revival style was introduced by **Henry Hobson Richardson** (1838–1886), who is considered one of the most important early modern architects in America (see Chapter 2). He borrowed features from the Medieval Romanesque period and incorporated them into his clean structural (simple, devoid of historic details) buildings. One of his finest residential works is the **John J. Glessner House** (1885–1887), in Chicago, Illinois, recently restored and opened to the public. The Romanesque designs of Richardson were widely copied during the Victorian period by numerous architects employing the following features:

- **Massive stone masonry** with a **rusticated surface**
- Use of the heavy ***Roman arch,*** especially over the doorway
- Emphasis on the **horizontal line**
- Strong, solid, and simple structure with no ornamentation

(5) The Shingle Style (1880–1900)

The Shingle Style is considered to be the last of the Victorian styles and is recognized by shingles everywhere on the exterior. The style originated in New England, but soon the approach was used across the nation. Henry Hobson Richardson also was a prominent exponent of the Shingle Style. The **John Bryant House** (1880), Cohasset, Massachusetts; **Kragsyde** (1884), Manchester-by-the-Sea, Massachusetts, and the **William Low House** (1887), Bristol, Rhode Island, are three outstanding examples. Features of the Shingle Style include

- **Exterior of shingles,** usually found on all wall surfaces and either stained dark brown, painted white, or weathered gray
- Simple structure with little or no decoration
- Roofs include hipped, steep-pitched, turrets, and other styles
- Porches extend across front and often wrap around sides
- Romanesque arches, bays, towers, dormers, and balustrades optional

Interiors during the Victorian period varied from region to region in the United States, but generally the feeling was similar and included the following characteristics.

Victorian Interiors

- A variety and profusion of patterned wallpaper, fabrics, carpets, and rugs fashionable; flower motifs particularly favored; velvets, damasks, brocades, and

Figure 1.38 The Abbey, a restored 1869 Gothic Revival home of a coal baron, now functions as a bed and breakfast inn in Cape May, New Jersey. The Parlor has rich pattern and detailing with Eastlake furniture pieces. The arched Gothic windows are treated with lace curtains. *(Courtesy of Jay and Marianne Schatz.)*

other formal fabrics; rich gold, mauve, red, and purple especially popular

- **Windows** often with lace casements, elegant tied-back side draperies; topped with an ornate metal crown or valance

- **Fireplaces** ornately designed; marble and round-headed fireplaces popular; mirrors with gold glided or large carved wooden frames found over fireplace

- **Furniture** massive and heavily carved, drawing themes from Gothic, French, Italian, and other styles of the past; marble tops on casepieces; Belter and Eastlake designs (see Chapter 9)

- **Accessories** everywhere; wax flowers under glass, stereo viewers, family portraits and other pictures (often hung on long cords), knickknacks and personal collections of all kinds displayed

- **Lighting:** heavy chandeliers of crystal, heavy brass, colorful tinted glass, and white opaline glass balls typical; electrified gasolier in many designs

Figure 1.39 The Breakers (1892–1895), in the foreground of an aerial view of the Cliff Walk, which depicts the concentration of palatial Beaux Arts residences in Newport, Rhode Island, at the turn of the century. *(Photograph by John T. Hopf, courtesy of the Newport County Chamber of Commerce.)*

The Beaux Arts Mansions

Beginning in the early 1880s, a **revival of Old World styles** left a legacy of Victorian extravagance in many areas of the country—concentrated especially in New York State; Newport, Rhode Island; and Florida. **William Kissam Vanderbilt**'s elegant **château** on Fifth Avenue in New York City, built in 1881, triggered a new extravagant architecture promoted by a few powerful wealthy American families. Most notable was the Vanderbilt family.

The name **Beaux Arts** was applied to this style after the world-famous design school, **L'École des Beaux Arts in Paris,** a school dedicated to promoting architectural styles of the past. **Richard Morris Hunt** (1827–95), one of the first American architects to train at L'École des Beaux Arts, was the most prominent designer of this opulent style. The architectural firm of **McKim, Mead & White** soon followed Hunt as popular designers in this direction, creating fabulous mansions employing magnificent use of past styles. The rage for palatial mansions was also inspired by flamboyant Victorian architecture and the influence from world-traveling Americans who wanted to imitate the castle-lined Rhine River in Germany and the Loire River in France. On every eminence was erected a Greek temple, an Italian villa, a medieval fortress, a Tudor manor house, a French château, or a dwelling with Near Eastern influence. Soon the Beaux Arts mansions inspired further building in other metropolitan areas of the United States, especially in Chicago, Philadelphia, Washington, D.C., and southern California.

The style remained popular in America during the jazz age but generally died out with the stock crash and Great Depression in the 1930s. Many structures in this style have been victims of twentieth-century "progress." Others, through the concerned efforts of many dedicated individuals and organizations, remain today as monuments to Beaux Arts architecture. A few of the best-known Beaux Arts palaces are

- **The Breakers** (1892–1895), Newport, Rhode Island; Richard Morris Hunt, architect; an enormous Italian villa known as the "summer cottage," the palatial home of Cornelius Vanderbilt II

- **Marble House** (1892), Newport, Rhode Island; Richard Morris Hunt, architect; a French Neoclassically

Figure 1.40 Lavishly decorated dining room at The Breakers, the summer "cottage" of the Vanderbilt family in Newport, Rhode Island. *(Courtesy of The Preservation Society of Newport County, Newport, R.I. Photograph by John T. Hopf.)*

Figure 1.41 Marble House (1892), Newport, Rhode Island. A lavish Beaux Arts mansion modeled after the Petit Trianon in Versailles, France. *(Photograph by John T. Hopf, courtesy of the Newport County Chamber of Commerce.)*

designed "summer cottage" patterned after the Petit Trianon at the Palace of Versailles; the residence of William Kissam Vanderbilt

- **Elms** (1901), one of the finest examples of an eighteenth-century French château in the United States; summer home of coal magnate Edward Berwind

- **Viz-Caya,** Miami, Florida; a splendid Italian mansion built of some pieces from original Italian villas; residence for James Deering

- **Ringling Mansion,** Sarasota, Florida; a pink mansion for the owner of the Ringling Circus, patterned after the Doges' Palace in Venice

- **Biltmore** (1890–1895), Asheville, North Carolina; Richard Morris Hunt, architect; an extraordinary French château built for George Washington Vanderbilt

- **Hearst Castle** (1919), San Simeon, California; home of the publishing magnate William Randolph Hearst; a grand Hispano-Moresque palace filled with European treasures

(*Note:* All of the Beaux Arts mansions just listed are open to the public.)

The Traditional Styles Revived

Although the palatial Beaux Arts homes were suitable for the very wealthy, they were hardly affordable for the rest of America. Many beautiful traditionally styled homes were also built during the Beaux Arts period capturing styles of the past interpreted in simpler terms. These smaller and more affordable homes were introduced in 1886 when McKim, Mead & White designed a formal Georgian Revival home for H. A. C. Taylor. Traditional styles particularly popular

Figure 1.42 Biltmore House, (1888–1895), the Beaux Arts mansion built by architect Richard Morris Hunt for George W. Vanderbilt and patterned after a French Renaissance château. *(Courtesy of Biltmore House and Gardens.)*

Figure 1.43 In the opulent Banquet Hall at Biltmore House, the ceiling arches rise 70 ft above the 72′ × 42′ room. *(Courtesy of Biltmore House and Gardens.)*

were Spanish Colonial, Georgian Colonial, Greek Revival, English Tudor, French Colonial, and Italian Renaissance. The trend toward and preference for traditional styles continue today throughout the country, as interpreted in countless variations. For example, since the years when colonial architecture was developed and refined, its popularity has never ceased throughout the United States, especially with respect to the small home. Although building materials may vary in different areas, this need not alter the inherent charm found in the original styles. Because colonial styles depend so little on ornamentation and so much on proportion and scale for their beauty, they must be expertly designed and built.

When confronted with designing contemporary traditional homes, the architect today is generally influenced by features of original prototypes but will often reinterpret and adapt a style in numerous ways suitable for current living conditions. Well-designed homes based on styles of the past are appropriate for many areas of the country and never seem to become outdated.

Preserving Our Architectural Heritage

Only during the past 20 to 30 years has the preservation of our architectural heritage generated widespread interest. Some earlier reconstructed villages—notably **Colonial Williamsburg** in Virginia, **Sturbridge Village** in Massachusetts, and **Strawberry Banke** in Portsmouth, New Hampshire—have for some Americans created a nostalgic curiosity about the legacy of our nation. Many houses, some of which are featured in this chapter, have been authentically restored and made available to the public. Hundreds of homes have been preserved, but thousands have been destroyed. Magnificent structures built to stand for hundreds of years have fallen before the bulldozer.

Perhaps the most important towns surviving today with much of their early architecture extant are **Ipswich** and **Salem, Massachusetts; Portsmouth, New Hampshire; Newport, Rhode Island; Williamsburg, Virginia; Charleston, South Carolina; Savannah, Georgia; Natchez, Mississippi;** and **New Orleans, Louisiana.** Ipswich, Massachusetts, probably has the most seventeenth-century houses. **Salem** is well known for its imposing Federal-period mansions. Many designed by McIntire border the famed Chestnut Street, once reputed to be the "handsomest street in America." **Newport,** once known as the "Athens of the New World," claims the distinction of having more prerevolutionary buildings (about 300) than any other community in the United States. In **Portsmouth,** however, the most complete and well-preserved record remains. The houses range from simple structures with weathered siding and shingles to large elaborately designed and decorated houses of the Georgian and early Federal periods. **Charleston** has preserved more of the beauty of its rich historical background than perhaps any other colonial city on the continent. In no other city in the United States are there so many superbly built and exquisitely decorated southern-style homes. Once every year the **Charleston Historic Foundation** sponsors Open-House Days, during which many private homes are open to the public. Every March, **Natchez,** a romantic antebellum city, recreates the charm of plantation living by opening some 30 of its great houses to the public.

In the past, individuals interested in old structures were sometimes looked on as eccentric and somewhat anomalous. This attitude is changing, however. Throughout the country, **organizations have been established to locate, research, and preserve old buildings in local communities.** The concern of these organizations is not limited to impressive public buildings and distinguished mansions; their interest extends to all structures—old mills, candy factories, even whole neighborhoods—provided that these buildings have documented historic value. Many of these organized groups are made up of young people who are finding in their architectural heritage a sense of permanency and a connection to the past.

The **National Trust for Historic Preservation in Washington, D.C.,** founded in 1949, is the largest organization in the country devoted to the preservation of historic buildings, districts, and neighborhoods. A private entity sustained by public and private contributions, the National Trust, maintains historic buildings as museums, disseminates information about preservation to property owners and to the public at large, and assists in a variety of preservation, restoration, and rehabilitation efforts around the country. Local chapters have been organized in cities and counties throughout the country. Many sites continue to be designated as historic landmarks for preservation and restoration.

The **Victorian Society of America,** founded in the late 1960s, has local chapters from coast to coast. Members of this organization are dedicated to preservation of the architecture and decorative arts of the nineteenth and early twentieth centuries. Their efforts are predicated on the belief that the Victorian era was the most typically American era in our country's history.

The present trend of preserving America's past continues to gain momentum. Although thousands of impressive historic buildings have needlessly been destroyed, many others can and have been saved. Restoration involves experts in many areas including research, history, design, and craftsmanship. Of course, adequate funding is necessary to execute each project.

Enthusiasts of American architectural history, those interested in America's cultural heritage, and casual observers can view houses from every period today thanks to the efforts of many organizations and individuals. A considerable number of these houses are in their original form, and others have been restored. Many are furnished in the authentic style of the time in which they were built and are open to the public.

The Modern House and Future Trends

Chapter Two

(continued)

The Energy-Efficient House

The Solar House

The Passive Solar Energy System
The Active Solar Energy System

The Earth-Sheltered House

Looking to the Future

Ornament should take architecture to a higher expression—or be left out altogether.

—Frank Lloyd Wright

Beginnings of Modernism

During the 1880s, many designers in the United States rebelled against nineteenth-century eclecticism and enslavement to the past—a reaction first seen in Europe—and a completely new house form evolved. Previously, however, the **Shakers,** a religious order in America during the latter half of the eighteenth century, felt decoration was wicked. Their structurally simple houses and furnishings reflected this philosophy, although the clean lines of functionalism would not be fully developed until the twentieth century. The influential roots of modernism in the United States and Europe can primarily be traced to the **Industrial Revolution** (late 1700s to early twentieth century), an era that introduced the use of the machine, as well as new technology, materials, and design philosophies. The study of the modern movement in Europe and America is extensive, and many significant contributions were made on both continents. For the intent of this introductory text, however, only major developments in the evolution of modern architecture and design can be highlighted.

Principal Early Modern Movements (latter half of nineteenth century)

- **The Arts and Crafts Movement** (circa 1860s to 1890s), founded by **William Morris** (1834–1896) in England, rejected the machine and modern society. The design group found the handcrafted ideals of the Middle Ages a perfect model for their own handcrafted furniture and decorative objects. This philosophy was reflected in simple unadorned architecture and furnishings that ironically are considered early beginnings of modernism. Other Arts and Crafts leaders in England included **Charles Francis Annesley Voysey** (1857–1941) and **Philip Webb** (1831–1915), who designed simple and well-planned houses.

Figure 2.1 Richard Meier's Douglas House, set on a steep wooded site, makes a striking contrast with its natural surroundings. The clean white planes and structural design are a good example of current expression of the International Style as developed during the 1920s and 1930s. *(Photograph by Ezra Stoller.)*

Figure 2.2 "Less is more" and "form follows function" were battle cries of pioneer modernists of the twentieth century. The extremely simple and unadorned homes and furniture of the Shakers were developed through a sense of religious obligation, but the result was clean and finely crafted design still admired by modernists today. *(Courtesy of The Metropolitan Museum of Art, Emily C. Chadbourne Fund, 1972.)*

Figure 2.3 Timberpeg has created a living room inspired by the Arts and Crafts Movement of the late 19th century but interpreted in contemporary terms. Simple handcrafted oak furniture and pattern details drawn from original motifs add to the authenticity. *(Courtesy of Timberpeg. Photograph by Keith Scott Morton.)*

- **The Arts and Crafts Movement in America** (circa 1860s–1920s) was the counterpart of the English movement. The foremost exponents were **Gustav Stickley** (1848–1942) in New Jersey and the brothers **Charles Greene** (1868–1957) and **Henry Greene** (1870–1954) in Pasadena, California. Stickley published his advanced design ideas in a periodical called *The Craftsman.* Greene and Greene designed handsome handcrafted furnishings for their new residential architecture. They helped develop the ***bungalow*** and ***shingle-styled*** homes in southern California that, in turn, influenced the nation. These homes featured wood construction with handcrafted finishing, wide overhanging roofs, stained glass, shutters, and low horizontal lines. The fresh "modern" approach of all these craftsman-designers had a tremendous impact on the design world.
- Boston-based designer **Henry Hobson Richardson** (1838–1886) is considered America's father of modern architecture. He looked to the Romanesque churches of the Middle Ages for inspiration, using heavy rusticated stone, round arches, towers, and horizontal lines in his work. The structural and simple aspects of his architecture were combined with the latest advancements in technology. Richardson's vigorous Romanesque-styled homes are early examples of "modernism."
- **Art Nouveau** (circa 1890–1910) was a completely new decorative style considered modern at the time. It was based on nature and employed organic and animal motifs of all types, including flowing vines, flowers, stalks, reptiles, peacocks, and the female form. Belgian architect **Victor Horta** (1861–1947) built his exquisite Tassel House in Brussels (1893), which has become a symbol of Art Nouveau architecture. The sinuous curves of Art Nouveau were found in his architecture, furniture, and accessories. The style was popular throughout Europe

Figure 2.4 The Gamble House in Pasadena, California, is now the headquarters for the Greene & Greene Foundation and remains the finest example of their craftsman approach to architecture. *(Courtesy of Esto Photographics; © Peter Aaron.)*

Figure 2.5 This interior view of the Gamble House reveals exquisitely handcrafted wooden architectural members and handcrafted furnishings. *(Courtesy of Esto Photographics; © Peter Aaron.)*

Figure 2.6 The Tassel House in Brussels, Belgium (1892–1893), is one of Victor Horta's best-known town houses and one of the earliest private residences designed in the Art Nouveau style. Swirling organic forms decorate the interior of the entry. The graceful stair railings and supports are fashioned in iron. *(Photograph courtesy of the Museum of Modern Art, New York.)*

Figure 2.7a Henry Hobson Richardson employed rusticated stone, horizontal lines, and heavy Romanesque arches and columns, which are evident in his last work—the Glessner House in Chicago. *(Courtesy of the Chicago Architecture Foundation.)*

Figure 2.7b An interior by Henry Hobson Richardson conveys the elements of the Romanesque approach preferred by the architect through the use of wood paneling, beams, and horizontal emphasis. *(Courtesy of Esto Photographics; © Wayne Andrews.)*

Figure 2.8 The white studio drawing room in the Mackintosh House (1900) at the Hunterian Art Gallery at the University of Glasgow. All furnishings were designed by Charles Rennie Mackintosh and his wife, Margaret, at the turn of the century. The Mackintosh rose motif is found on the back of the chair in the foreground and on the doors of the bookcase on the right of the fireplace. *(Courtesy of the Hunterian Art Gallery, University of Glasgow.)*

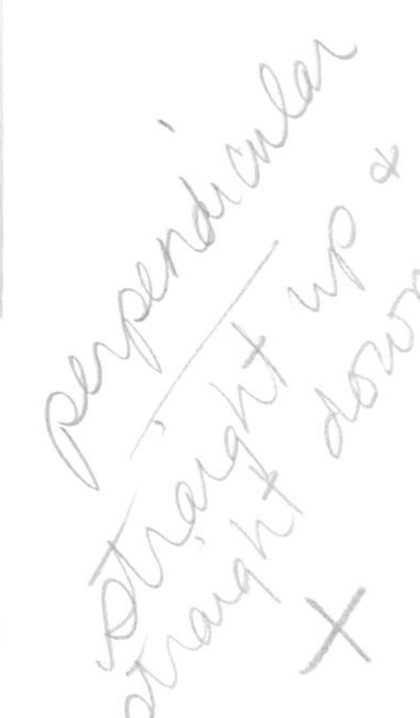

Figure 2.9 Louis Comfort Tiffany was both an interior designer and industrial designer. His best known works are his beautiful stained glass pieces. This Tiffany lamp (c. 1900) shows organic motifs, a favorite of the Art Nouveau period. *(Courtesy of The Metropolitan Museum of Art, Gift of Hugh Grant, 1974.)*

and America, with various designers interpreting the style in their own manner. Other important contributors were the French architect and furniture designer **Hector Guimard** (1867–1942) and the whimsical and imaginative designer **Antoni Gaudi** (1852–1926) in Spain.

A titan of the modern movement, active during the Art Nouveau period, was **Charles Rennie Mackintosh** (1868–1928) in Glasgow, Scotland. He combined aspects of Art Nouveau with a new direction he developed called the **perpendicular style.** His houses and furniture displayed graceful Art Nouveau motifs side by side with strong geometric forms. Mackintosh exerted tremendous influence on other architects on the continent and in America.

Louis Sullivan (1856–1924), of the Chicago School in America, is considered one of the foremost exponents of Art Nouveau in America. He employed organic motifs for architectural detailing on his buildings.

Another designer, **Louis Comfort Tiffany** (1848–1933), is considered one of America's greatest designers in the Art Nouveau style and is especially known for his exquisite stained-glass windows and lamps.

- **The Chicago School** (1870s–circa 1910) claimed as its principle members early modern architects **Louis Sullivan** and **Frank Lloyd Wright** (1867–1959), two leaders among a group of innovative designers who introduced new ideas for home and commercial design that were extraordinary for the time. The most important member of the Chicago School in the development of the modern American home was Wright, who worked for a few years as a draftsman for Sullivan.

Principal Modern Movements (early twentieth century)

Organic Architecture (circa 1894 to present)

In 1892, Frank Lloyd Wright broke with Sullivan and set up his own practice in Oak Park, Illinois, where he designed over 35 homes in his ***prairie style*** employing ***"organic architecture,"*** a term he formulated. His revolutionary work was soon recognized in Europe and by the turn of the century was well known in the Chicago area. His innovative techniques eventually won acclaim throughout the United States, and in 1936, Wright won the American Institute of Architects (AIA) Gold Medal Award for the Kaufmann residence, **Falling Water,** built in Bear Run, Pennsylvania, and con-

Figure 2.10 Falling Water (1936), Bear Run, Pennsylvania. The best-known house among those designed by Frank Lloyd Wright. *(Photograph by Michael Tedison, courtesy of the Western Pennsylvania Conservancy.)*

sidered his residential masterpiece. The fundamental principles of organic architecture continue to be a prominent modern design direction and include the following characteristics.

- House and site coexist harmoniously; "a house should grow out of the land"; natural materials compatible with site employed
- Frankly revealed structural members; simple geometric ornamentation, if any
- Planning arranged from inside to outside with spatial flexibility ***(open planning);*** fireplace functions as heart of home
- Large spacious balconies and terraces with wide overhanging eaves incorporated into design
- Horizontal emphasis and asymmetrical composition

Figure 2.11 A reconstructed Frank Lloyd Wright room at the Metropolitan Museum of Art. *(Courtesy of The Metropolitan Museum of Art, Purchase, Bequest of Emily Crane Chadbourne, 1972. [1972.60.1] Installation through the generosity of Saul P. Steinberg and Reliance Group Holdings, Inc.)*

Figure 2.12 Dining room of the Palais Stoclet (1905–1911), in Brussels, Belgium, with all furnishings executed by Josef Hoffmann and the Secessionists. This private home is a hallmark of this design direction. *(Photograph courtesy of The Museum of Modern Art, New York.)*

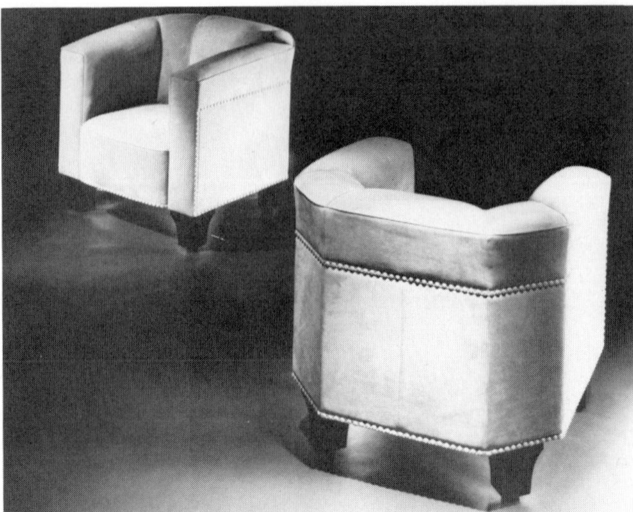

Figure 2.13 The Palais Stoclet chairs, remarkably modern for the period, were designed for the Stoclet home by Josef Hoffmann. *(Courtesy of ICF.)*

The International Style (turn of century to present)

At the turn of the century, roots of the International Style—a style entirely contrary to Wright's organic architecture—were evidenced primarily through the efforts of a few major design groups. ***The Secession*** in Austria and Germany and ***De Stijl*** in Holland made contributions to the style early in the century. During the 1920s, design concepts put forth by ***Bauhaus*** members in Germany, **Le Corbusier** in France, and various designers particularly in Scandinavia and America led to the fully developed International Style.

- **The Secession** (circa 1897–1903) was a radical design movement founded by **Otto Wagner** (1841–1918), **Josef Maria Olbrich** (1867–1908), **Josef Hoffmann** (1870–1956) and others in Vienna, Munich, and Berlin at the turn of the century. Their motto was "to each time its art, and to each art its freedom." In 1903, Hoffmann and others set up a more formal workshop named ***The Wiener Werkstatte*** in Vienna (see Chapter 9). The structural and geometrical architecture and furnishings of this group highly influenced the International Style. The most important work by this group was the **Palais Stoclet** (1911) in Brussels.
- **De Stijl** (1917–1931) in Holland was a group of extremists who felt all design should be reduced to basic design elements: the use of only red, blue, yellow, black, gray, and white; total abstraction; smooth shiny surfaces; and compositions at right angles—ideas what would help establish the International Style. Leaders included **Theo van Doesburg** (1883–1931), the founder; **Piet Mondrian;** and **Gerrit Rietveld** (1888–1964), whose **Schroeder House** (1924) in Utrecht is a landmark.

Figure 2.14 The angular interior of the Schroeder House in Utrecht, Holland (1924), designed by Gerrit Rietveld, exemplifies the theories of the De Stijl movement. *(Photograph courtesy of The Museum of Modern Art, New York.)*

Figure 2.15 The abstract red, yellow, blue, and black Schroeder table (1923), was designed by Gerrit Rietveld to complement the interiors of the Schroeder House. *(Courtesy of Atelier International.)*

Figure 2.16 Exterior of the revolutionary Bauhaus experimental design school in Dessau, Germany (1926). *(Photograph courtesy of The Museum of Modern Art, New York.)*

Figure 2.17 The Farnsworth House, Plano, Illinois by Mies van der Rohe (1946–1950). The architect's philosophy of "less is more" is expressed in this glass and metal domestic project in the International Style—designed after he became the director at Illinois Institute of Technology. *(Photograph by Bill Hedrich, Hedrich-Blessing.)*

Figure 2.18 Classic Bauhaus furniture designed by master architect and furniture designer Marcel Breuer. From *left to right*, the Cesca chairs, Laccio table, and Wassily lounge, designed by Breuer while he taught at the Bauhaus. The Isokon lounge, *far right*, was designed in 1935 in England. *(Courtesy of Knoll International.)*

- **The Bauhaus** (1919–1933) was an experimental design school founded by architect and designer **Walter Gropius** (1883–1969) in 1919 in Weimar, Germany, for the purpose of unifying art and technology. The Bauhaus concentrated on applying practical artisanship to solve industrial problems characterized by an economy of design and geometric proportion. The school, however, met with vigorous opposition from the German government. It was moved twice, and finally Hitler's stormtroopers closed the Bauhaus in 1933. In the meantime, Gropius, **Marcel Breuer** (1902–1981), **Ludwig Mies van der Rohe** (1886–1969), and other great Bauhaus faculty members fled to America, where they gave impetus to the new movement. Mies's **Farnsworth House** (1947) in Plano, Illinois, became an important prototype of the International Style.
- **Le Corbusier (Charles-Edouard Jeanneret-Gris)** (1888–1965) worked out of his Paris studio during the 1920s until his death. Considered a giant of modern

architecture, he built in Poissy, France, his famous **Villa Savoye** (1930), a home that has become an important residential example of the International Style.

The ***International Style,*** a term coined by **Philip Johnson** (b. 1906), one of America's best-known modern architects, and architect and writer **Henry-Russell Hitchcock** in the 1930s, firmly established a discipline based on functionalism and purity of line for a new generation of architects. After the Bauhaus closed in 1933, Mies van der Rohe, Walter Gropius, and Marcel Breuer, in particular, further developed their ideas on modern architecture in the United States. Gropius and Breuer assumed teaching positions at Harvard University, and Mies van der Rohe became the director at the Illinois Institute of Technology in Chicago. The formula set down for the new International Style had features conflicting with Frank Lloyd Wright's "organic architecture," although some features were similar. Today, the style, developed by many individuals and design groups through the years, continues to be interpreted and reinterpreted. Major features include

- Basically simple design; ornamentation, if employed, generally geometric or abstract
- Flat roof; emphasis on the horizontal line; today, vertical, curved, and diagonal lines often used
- Common materials: reinforced concrete, stucco, steel, and glass; exterior and interior walls usually have stark white finish
- House designed to *contrast* with nature rather than blend with surroundings
- Asymmetrical composition usually dominant
- Continuous wall surfaces, often combined with large openings and panes of glass

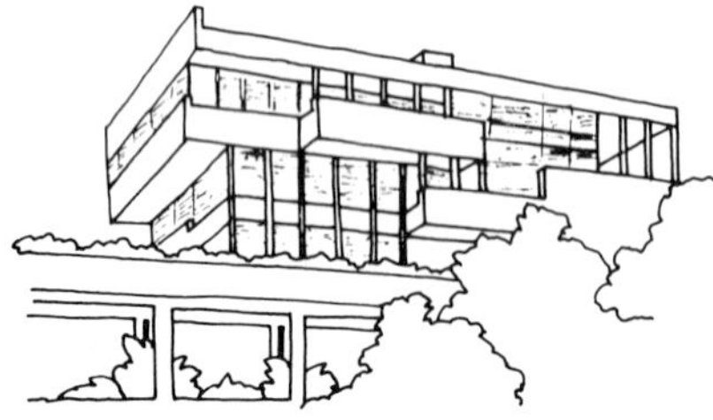

The International Style
The Lovell House (1929)
by architect Richard Neutra

Figure 2.19 Villa Savoye (1929–1931), Poissy, France, designed by Le Corbusier in the International Style. Raised on a dozen freestanding columns, the stark, white, flat-roofed structure seems to float in space. *(Photograph by Miriam Stimpson.)*

Figure 2.20 Architect Philip Johnson's "Glass House" in New Canaan, Connecticut (1949), with glass walls and Barcelona furniture by Mies van der Rohe. Johnson was an early follower of Mies van der Rohe. *(Courtesy of Ezra Stoller.)*

- Open floor plan
- Clearly expressed function

Some notable homes in America designed in the International Style are the **Lovell House** (1929) in Los Angeles by **Richard Neutra** (1892–1970); the **Farnsworth House** (1949–1951) by Ludwig Mies van der Rohe in Plano, Illinois; the **Walter Gropius House** (1938), in Lincoln, Massachusetts, and the **Glass House** (1949) by **Philip Johnson** in New Canaan, Connecticut. The **Douglas House** (1975), designed by prominent American architect **Richard Meier** (b. 1934), is a good example of the International Style applied in a contemporary manner.

Art Deco (circa 1920s–1940)

During the 1920s and 1930s in America, a new decorative style flourished based on numerous design influences including the International Style, the ancient Egyptian and Aztec cultures, the jazz age, the glamorous cinema, the fashion world, the new industrial age, and other aspects of modern society. Architecture reflected motifs from many of these influences while incorporating the latest materials and techniques. The Art Deco style was sophisticated, yet naive in expression. Strong geometric forms including the pyramid, zigzag, and sunburst motifs were popularly employed.

Figure 2.21 The Blue chair, designed by Eliel Saarinen in 1929, was designed at the Cranbrook Academy of Art. The Art Deco piece has a blue lacquered frame accented with gold leaf. *(Courtesy of ICF.)*

Post–World War II

After World War II, although the Organic and International Styles continued to be popular, new architectural directions emerged as a number of individualists in America and Europe inspired new designs for the modern house. Some primary directions and current expressions include the following.

- **Classic Modernism.** This style of home incorporates simplified and elegant structural designs influenced by ancient Greece and Rome and interpreted in modern terms. This approach is usually delicate and "pretty," often with lacy concrete blocks, slender columns, and a white finish. American architect **Edward Durell Stone** (1902–1978) spearheaded this direction.

Figure 2.22 A contemporary interior reflecting the Art Deco period. The room's design combines a tiered fireplace (a favorite Art Deco treatment), uplighting, and Le Corbusier's tubular steel Grand Confort furniture collection. *(Photograph by Norman McGrath.)*

Figure 2.23 A striking bathroom is treated in the Art Deco expression with typical outlining in black; ziggarat forms over the mirrors; the use of tile and marble; and a pink, black, and gray color scheme. *(Courtesy of Kathy Andrews and Mark Kaufmann.)*

Figure 2.24 The stately "New American Home '89," designed by Charles Moore Associates, incorporates elements of the Classic Modern Style. Georgian and Greek Revival features are simplified and updated in a contemporary expression. *(Courtesy of Charles Moore Associates. Photograph by Gabriel Bensur, Inc., Atlanta, GA.)*

- **Scandinavian Style. Alvar Aalto** (1898–1976), Finland's master architect and furniture designer, was particularly influential in spreading modern ideas from Scandinavia to the United States. This style of home is a compatible blend of Organic and International Styles. Simple structural white surfaces complemented with the use of natural materials are typical.
- **Industrial Style "High Tech." Charles Eames** (1907–1978), America's great furniture designer and architect, was one of the first to employ industrial components for home design. Later, the "High Tech" style of home employed more frankly exposed industrial units and construction elements. This style is often punctuated with bright primary colors.
- **Post-Modern.** By the late 1960s, Post-Modern architecture began to borrow from the early modernists, whose principles were combined with new creative designs and modern technology. In many respects Post-Modern architecture rejects the International Style and borrows freely from the past, but in extreme contemporary terms. The style has continued to be popular during the 1980s. Some historians feel that the Post-Modern style today is simply an update of the old Art Deco style; and, indeed, many similar motifs are employed. Major exponents of this style are **Michael Graves** (b. 1934), designer of the Portland Building in Portland, Oregon, and **Philip Johnson,** responsible for Post-Modern buildings in cities across the nation. Their works have sparked numerous architects to follow similar design principles for both residential and commercial projects.
- **Freestyle Movement** (1980 to present). Freestyle, one of the most significant recent trends in residential architecture, emerged

Figure 2.25 The Scandinavian influence in the American home shows a congenial combination of the Organic and International Style. Clean white walls with wood detailing are typical. The classic modern Scandinavian chairs on the right were designed by Poul Kjaerholm of Denmark in 1956. *(Photograph © Ezra Stoller Associates/ESTO.)*

Figure 2.26 Charles and Ray Eames designed their Case Study House in Santa Monica in 1949. With its prefabricated components and modular arrangement, the house is a good example of the Industrial Style. *(Photograph by Julius Shulman.)*

Figure 2.27 Michael Graves designed this Post-Modern residence in New Jersey in 1986. Tall, slender pedestals are capped with Egyptian-like capitals, and walls are painted soft peach. *(Photograph by Norman McGrath.)*

Figure 2.28 In an extravagant Post-Modern masterbath, structural columns support a pyramidal-type roof. The bold use of tile and lighting also contribute to the style. *(Courtesy of Kohler Co.)*

Figure 2.29a A powerful use of art by Frank Stella, Ellsworth Kelly, Donald Judd, and Robert Rauschenberg in this gallery-like living room mixes with an antique table and comfortable sofas. The use of the Freestyle expression is uniquely evident. *(Photograph by Tim Street-Porter.)*

Figure 2.29b Frank O. Gehry's own house in Santa Monica, California. The architect has embellished an old 1930s house with chain link, glass, corrugated metal, and other materials in a design reflecting the controversial Freestyle direction. *(Photograph by Tim Street-Porter.)*

in California during the 1980s. Architects with very diverse—and often contradictory—approaches are involved in the movement, all expressing their own personal interpretations. The basic elements of Freestyle seek (1) to combine American and European architectural styles with local California design to create a livable environment and (2) to enrich the routine of daily living through various textures, colors, and expressive form. One outstanding leader of this design direction is **Frank O. Gehry.**

The Traditional Japanese House

Interestingly, the *traditional* Japanese house has contributed much to the modern style of architecture in America, especially to the mass-produced ***prefabricated*** house. Frank Lloyd Wright, who greatly admired the Japanese house and design philosophy, was instrumental in introducing this style to the United States. The classic Japanese house was constructed of wood; and although many of the houses built today use concrete, steel, masonry, and stucco, the classic Japanese form is very prominent. In recent years, many architects, particularly in California, have adapted Japanese ideas to meet American needs.

The following are general characteristics of the traditional Japanese house.

- Simplicity in line and form
- Most often constructed of wood and other natural materials
- Close connection to outdoors; garden (often several small gardens) is an integral part of the house
- Open planning with ***fusuma screen*** partitions
- Materials left in natural state; little, if any, ornamentation
- Predominance of horizontal lines
- Unpretentious facade with frequent retaining walls
- Sloping, protective overhangs with hipped and gable roof
- Natural stone foundation supporting post and roof
- Avoidance of symmetry
- Honest expression of basic structure
- Feeling of serenity and refinement
- Universal use of a uniform module and the 3-by-6 foot ***tatami mat***
- Window treatments is the ***shoji screen***
- Both house and garden elements symbolic, incorporating basic Oriental philosophies

Oriental House

Figure 2.30 The Jack Lenor Larsen apartment is an excellent example of the Japanese influence in the American home. A rock steps up to a Japanese-styled dining area complete with low table and legless chairs. In the living room area "fusuma" screens with a subtle pattern are the focus. A simple treatment of textures and a *shubui* color scheme add to the feeling. *(Photograph by Norman McGrath.)*

Figure 2.31 The Chinese influence in the American home (see Chapter 9) is employed in this living room with a bright lacquered red coffee table and chairs. A Chinese rug and accessories further provide a suggestion of the style. *(Courtesy of Gayl Baddeley/Associates. Photograph by Richard Springgate.)*

Current Trends

A 1980s survey of population shifts revealed that since the peak of metropolitan growth during the mid-1970s, a definite move to small communities has occurred. This survey done by Professor Harley Johansen, University of Idaho and Professor Glen Fuguitt, University of Wisconsin was the first systematic analysis of American villages (population 2,500 or less) done on a national scale since the late 1920s. The findings of the survey were published in *The Changing Rural Village in America: Demographic and Economic Trends Since 1950.*

The latest home-ownership survey (1983) by the U.S. League of Savings Institutions show that condominiums are not the wave of the future. Although still favored by retirees, condominiums are in excess supply. When lower interest rates and prices provided the opportunity, the baby-boom generation chose single-family houses on their own lots. Condominiums in most cases were considered as temporary accommodations.

Despite a nationwide trend in the early seventies toward simplification to provide affordable housing, most people still want the amenities they have come to expect in today's housing, particularly in the kitchen, family room, bathroom, and master bedroom.

Market Demands

Because of inflation, high interest rates, the need for energy conservation, smaller families, and changes in life-styles, a number of significant changes in the demands of the building market have occurred. For example,

- Buyers are better educated than in the past and are asking more questions.
- Important to buyers is the optimum balance of value and cost—a concept known in the building market as "value effectiveness." In other words, people want their money's worth when buying a home.
- Buyers are interested in saving energy.
- Buyers place a high value on prestigious locations.
- Living units must suit a variety of life-styles.
- Buyers place a high priority on security.
- Buyers want homes with low maintenance, labor-saving devices, and water-saving appliances, especially dishwashers, toilets, and shower heads.

Trends in Home Design

To anticipate market needs, architects and builders are forecasting the following trends for the near future.

- Fewer single-family homes will be built in conventional subdivisions.
- Living spaces in both attached and detached housing will be smaller than those to which Americans are accustomed.
- The enclosed architectural area (or volume) will be utilized to make spaces more flexible and give them a larger appearance.
- Although rooms will be fewer, they will be larger and have more flexibility.
- Floor plans will be influenced by changing life-styles and will be more expandable.
- More industrialization and factory-made parts will be used, with on-site building techniques joining with prefabricators.
- Buyers will have more options, such as the capacity to add or subtract walls and choose or refuse luxury appliances.
- Security will be given a high priority.
- New product advances will be used to save labor, cut down on maintenance, promote luxury and convenience, save energy, and save space while retaining the appearance of spaciousness. (Also see "Looking to the Future," page 64.)

Options for Prospective Home Owners in the 1990s

A wide variety of options are available for the prospective home owner today. Consumers can choose a custom-designed, predesigned, shell, mobile, factory-built, or tract home; a condominium; an apartment; or an older home to remodel. Each of these options has various advantages and disadvantages. The buyer's **household size, life-style,** and **economic capability** will determine what the choice will be.

Although increasingly fewer buyers are able to build the home of their dreams, some are able to plan and build single-family detached houses. Three building options are available: (1) the custom-designed plan, (2) the predesigned plan, and (3) the factory-built (prefabricated) package and shell home (factory built with no interior fittings). Carefully examining each option to determine which one most closely meets the household's physical and economic needs is beneficial. Problems involved in building will be solved differently, depending on which building option the buyer selects. Before making the final decision to build a home, the buyer must accept the fact that many problems may arise. Building a home requires much planning, numerous decisions, and indefinite patience; but the final product can bring many rewards.

The Custom-Designed House

The buyer who selects a custom-designed plan hires an architect, who generally first works out a personalized style and floor plan. The floor plan indicates room arrangement, traffic lanes, storage, wall space, doors, and windows. When the design and plan have been finalized, the architect makes rough drawings for the buyer's approval. After approval is obtained, the architect prepares final working drawings and aids the buyer in selecting materials. Additionally, the architect obtains contract bids, acts as a liaison between buyer and builder, and oversees the construction to ensure that the home is built according to the buyer's specifications. A custom-designed plan is the most expensive procedure available to the prospective home owner.

Two alternatives to working with a professional architect are available: (1) hire an architectural designer, whose work is often comparable to that of a professional architect, but whose fee is less, or (2) let a local architect at a reputable building firm draw up plans and supervise the building. Most lumber companies have such drafters on their staff, and the charge for their services is minimal if the buyer purchases materials through the company.

The primary problem in custom design is cost. When building for the first time, the consumer is seldom prepared to cope with the unexpected costs that inevitably arise. Too often the consumer has an unrealistic notion of what the desired home will cost and fails to get a firm estimate on the finished project. Doing extensive planning and research is the best assurance of satisfaction. A wise house plan for a young family is one that is expandable. A basement or an upstairs can be roughed in (i.e., the necessary construction for walls, floors, and ceilings can be installed) and converted to usable space at a later time. If planned initially, walls can be added later to the main floor with a minimum of expense.

Figure 2.32a A custom-designed home in northern Delaware by Venturi, Rauch and Scott Brown expresses the architects' personal and expressive design approach. *(Photograph by Tom Bernard/Venturi, Rauch and Scott Brown.)*

Figure 2.32b Interior of Figure 2.32a. A fanciful ceiling treatment with a painted design complements the employment of traditional and modern furnishings in this music room. *(Photograph by Tom Bernard/Venturi, Rauch and Scott Brown.)*

The Predesigned Home Plan

Some buyers consider the cost of an architect's services prohibitive and choose a predesigned plan instead. Thousands of plans are available today, and a set of complete working drawings is moderately priced, depending on the designer and the size of the home. These drawings can be purchased directly from the plan service, from the individual designer, or through building magazines.

Studying many plans carefully can enable the buyer to select a suitable plan that most closely approximates personal needs and design preferences. Making minor alterations is possible, and the cost savings will justify making some personal compromises. Some plans include a complete materials list, detailing the quantity and size of lumber, doors, windows, and many other items that will be used in the construction. After selecting a plan, the buyer hires a contractor and discusses any minor changes desired. Any modifications can usually be incorporated with little or no expense if done during the initial planning stage. Once the building has begun, any construction change becomes expensive, in this or any other type of plan. When the details have been worked out, the project should proceed much the same as with a custom-designed plan, except that an architect will not be supervising unless the buyer makes special arrangements for this service. Developing the competency to do the supervising personally may be time well spent for the buyer. Concern for every detail can often compensate for lack of technical knowledge, and this concern can be conveyed to the contractor or designer.

The Factory-Built (Prefabricated) House

The use of industrialized building techniques is no newcomer to the United States. Many of the early settlers built their homes from panelized parts shipped from England. Since the colonial period, technology has greatly advanced, and today a well-constructed factory-produced house can hardly be distinguished from its counterpart of traditional construction methods. Unfortunately, the term ***prefab*** has for too long carried the stigma of inexpensive inferior housing. As a result, a prefab house is often regarded as a home built only as a last resort. Public resistance to factory-built homes has changed during the past decade, mainly because of improvements in design, materials, and construction. Currently, many consumers are purchasing and enjoying the benefits of the prefab house.

Factory-built houses come in three basic types: (1) the ***modular*** house consisting of various elements made and put together at the factory and shipped for immediate assembly on a permanent site; (2) the ***component unit,*** a precut house in which all materials are cut, sized, and labeled in sequence for fast erection; and (3) the ***mobile home,*** also a modular house, but put together at the factory and shipped in one or two units to be placed on a temporary foundation. Today, however, mobile homes are being placed in permanent communities planned and landscaped only for this home type.

Buying a factory-built house has a number of benefits. Because these homes are built in quantity, less waste occurs, quality can be controlled (which many manufacturers claim produces a higher quality home), and inspection is less expensive. All these factors add up to a quality home for less money. Another item to be considered is time. Building a custom home can take months—even years—to plan and execute. The factory-built home can be ready for occupancy in a fraction of the time it takes to construct a house by traditional methods. Moreover, the conventional route to building is fraught with uncertainties and hazards. Scarcity of available skilled labor, along with vandalism and undetermined costs, may contribute to delays. A definite price established at the outset for the factory-built homes precludes these concerns. In addition to these advantages, factory-built homes can be just as energy efficient as their site-built counterparts.

Mobile homes began as makeshift shelters in the housing-shortage days of the 1940s. The term *mobile home* is a misnomer, because these homes usually spend only a short time on the move. The Mobile Home Manufacturers Association calls a mobile home a "transportable structure built on a chassis and designed to be used as a dwelling unit with or without a permanent foundation when connected with the required facilities." When mobile homes were first put on the market, they were looked on as a poor relation of conventional hous-

Assembling a modular home at the site

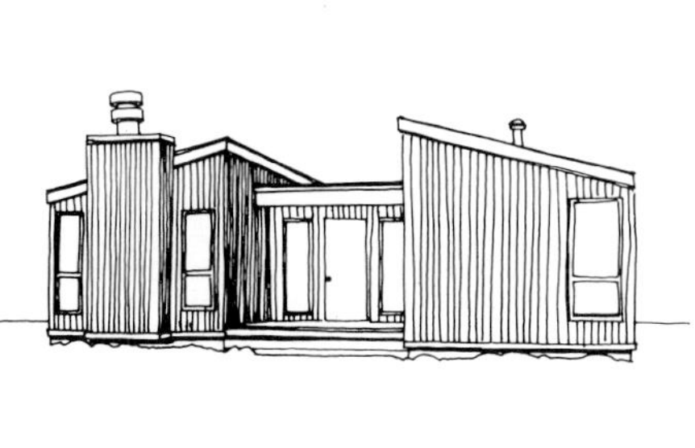
Exterior

Interior

Figure 2.33 Thoughtful placement on the site and use of exterior elements and planting can comfortably integrate the mobile home into a traditional neighborhood.

ing, and mobile-home parks (trailer courts) were a dreaded neighborhood liability. Today, their role in the housing market is of increased importance. Radical changes have taken place in the homes themselves and in public attitudes. In general, the public today is better informed on housing at all levels, and a growing awareness of and demand for better quality and design are bringing about improvements in the mobile home. Evidence of these changes is seen not only in the recent alliance between industry and architecture but also in the increased sophistication in technology and in a growing belief that good design need not be costly.

With skyrocketing prices, the need for manufactured housing has increased, with the greatest demand coming from the young and old. With the current increase in the number of people between ages 55 and 75, the demand is increasing dramatically. With a lessening of the concern that mobile-home parks are harmful to the aesthetic environment, mobile-home subdivisions have increased. Most are attractively landscaped and with new zoning laws are located in nice areas of the community. With government financing available for mobile homes, the poor image of trailer courts eliminated, and better designed structures available, the mobile home has become a practical alternative in affordable housing.

Figure 2.34 A classic 1½-story Cape Cod style factory-built house. A basic affordable home designed to grow with the family. *(Courtesy of National Homes.)*

Shell Framing

One concept having moderate success is shell framing, in which the builder constructs, on the owner's foundation, a bare frame with doors and windows. Finishing of the roof, interior walls, plumbing, electricity, and all interior fittings is left to the owner. The result of this type of construction depends on the ingenuity and business acumen of the owner. Shell-framing components are also available from various manufacturing concerns.

The Tract Home

The term *tract home* refers to a house that is one of a group of dwellings in which only a few alternative plans are used. Mass production allows the builder to offer such a house at a price considerably lower than for a custom-built one. If the location of the tract is wisely chosen with future area growth in mind, and if the house is well designed and constructed, the value of a tract house should keep pace with inflation and bring a higher price than the buyer initially paid. A completed tract home is offered at a set price "as is." If the buyer contracts with the builder before construction has begun, however, minor changes can be made at little or no extra cost. The buyer is also permitted to select paint colors and have some choice in the selection of floor coverings and appliances.

During the 1950s and 1960s, tract developments created neighborhoods in which row upon row of look-alike houses presented an atmosphere of total anonymity. Individual families were hard put to give their homes a distinct personality. This trend is being reversed today as more planned communities with houses of varying styles are clustered to take advantage of natural surroundings and create a feeling of individual living. Today, however, the tract house is to a great extent being replaced by the condominium.

The Condominium

Another alternative in the choice of a home is the condominium or town-house apartment. **Condominium** is a Latin word dating back to the sixth century, meaning "joint dominion" or "joint ownership." Such an arrangement does not specify a type of housing; instead, it is a financial governance commitment that may involve any type of housing. The occupant is the sole owner of an apartment or housing unit in a multifamily project, but shares with other co-owners common areas and elements of the property, such as gardens, swimming pools, recreation rooms, and lobbies. All owners share in making the rules and governing the project, and in many places they also share responsibility for enforcing the rules.

The **co-op** is a variation of the condominium. In the co-op, the resident owns a share in the corporation that owns the building. Co-op residents have a long-term proprietary lease on their units but often must get approval for a would-

Figure 2.35 Town house condominiums. Attractive two-story multifamily town houses provide convenient living for a variety of life-styles. *(Courtesy of Kinateder and Smart Associates.)*

Figure 2.36 Clustered condominiums have the charm and individuality of custom-built homes, plus the advantages of a planned community. *(Courtesy of the Irvin A. Blietz Organization.)*

be buyer from the board of directors. Condominium owners may sell to whomever they wish and have their own mortgage on their individual unit. Co-op tenants might share the mortgage of the entire project.

Once thought of as places for weekend retreats, condominiums are now being used year round. Many refinements have been added, but the main advantages seem to be good security and freedom from maintenance worries. All mechanical conveniences that contribute to creature comforts, such as utility centers, electrical apparatus, and heating and air conditioning units, are taken care of. Some disadvantages are present, however. Yards are usually small, and storage space is often limited. Because of the necessary cooperative nature of these communities in solving common neighborhood problems that arise, living happily in such close proximity is often difficult for families with children. Nevertheless, many first-time home buyers—singles (young or elderly), elderly couples, busy professionals, small families with one or both parents, couples whose grown children have left home, and many others—find the condominium the best answer to their housing needs and the best buy per square foot.

Condominiums are designed in two basic styles: (1) the conventional **row house** or **town house** and (2) the **cluster.** Town-house condom-

Figure 2.37 Reston, Virginia (1960s), was one of the first clustered housing townships of its kind in the United States. A variety of styles are pleasantly arranged around a lake, shops, and other facilities. *(Courtesy of Ron Molen, architect.)*

iniums are usually two or three stories and are made up of similar attached units. **Cluster planning,** which has more of the appearance of the single-family dwelling, represents a more enlightened attitude about today's environment. Detached and attached single-family houses are clustered around culs-de-sac with a central recreation area and are separated from each other by green belts.

The Apartment

In the past, many people—particularly singles, students, and newly married and mature couples—have chosen the apartment as their home. Apartment dwellers pay a monthly rent, which sometimes includes the cost of utilities and use of laundry facilities. Renters are free from obligations outside of the apartment itself, and privacy is usually a sought-after advantage. Apartment living for families with children, however, is usually not the most desirable, because many apartment houses do not allow children and facilities are not planned for, nor do they function for, children's activities and well-being.

Remodeling and Restoring a House

Two strong trends in the United States are to buy a "fixer upper" or to stay in a dwelling and make modifications to suit personal needs or desires. With soaring housing costs, families and individuals are seeking more affordable alternatives, and finding an older or used home to remodel can be both a challenging and rewarding task. In some cases the older home may date back to a particular period. Victorian homes, for example, are particularly popular. These homes cannot be reproduced today without incurring great expense; but many Victorian homes built during the latter half of the nineteenth century are being purchased at a lower price, saved from destruction, and lovingly restored. In some areas of the United States entire deteriorated neighborhoods are being revived through the efforts of concerned and dedicated citizens in the community. In most cases the homes in these areas are exceptionally inexpensive. Additionally, older neighborhoods are drawing younger families and singles who are revitalizing the homes and area. Whether restoring a period home, fixing up a run-down home, or staying in a current home and remodeling, it is wise to consider advantages and disadvantages:

- **Advantages:** Low cost, individuality of an older home (especially in the case of a period home), satisfaction that comes from creating and restoring a home
- **Disadvantages:** Possibility of considerable repair work, including new wiring, plumbing, roofing, and other interior and exterior replacements; termite problems; unexpected and considerable costs for restoration and remodeling

The Energy-Efficient House

A principal challenge that architects and builders have faced in the 1970s and 1980s and will continue to face in the 1990s (although to a lesser degree) is the conservation

Figure 2.38 An old Queen Anne Victorian home has been carefully remodeled to meet contemporary requirements and taste. *(Photograph by Julius Shulman.)*

of energy. In meeting this challenge, the heat from the sun, or solar energy, is being harnessed successfully and used to supplement dwindling and progressively more expensive energy supplies.

The Solar House

Solar houses come in a variety of guises and may be large or small, but all have one common attribute: they are built to capture the sun's energy and conserve conventional fuel. Solar energy is used by way of two major systems: **passive** and **active.**

The Passive Solar Energy System

The passive system is a nonmechanical method relying on the house itself to absorb and store the sun's heat. The system uses indoor thermal masses of air, as found in garden rooms, greenhouses, and indoor pools, and masses of masonry, such as walls and floors, that are directly penetrated by the sun's heat. In each case, heat is absorbed during the day and radiated at night.

The **envelope** house, a self-cooling and self-heating unit, is a unique concept in passive thermal regulation. By this method the house is encircled by a continuously circulated envelope of air. Excess heat is stored in a layer of insulated earth beneath the house. An integral part of the envelope house is the greenhouse, which acts as the solar collector. This system works in any climate and can be adapted to any style of house.

Waterwall space heating is a passive method in which a water-filled panel installed between the wall studs acts as a solar-powered radiator storing and releasing the sun's heat. Many innovations are being tried in which simple applications that do not require any moving parts work very well. The passive solar energy system has a number of advantages over the active system: (1) it allows more design freedom, (2) it is simpler to operate, (3) it is silent, and (4) it is more economical.

The Active Solar Energy System

The active system relies entirely on mechanical means—collector panels, fans, pumps, and a storage area—to trap the heat and distribute it throughout the house. Some disadvantages of active solar systems at present are that (1) the collector panels are expensive, (2) the panels limit the house design, and (3) the indispensable photovoltaic cells, used to generate electricity from solar energy, are in a semiexperimental stage and need perfecting for the residential market.

The Earth-Sheltered House

The idea of homes inside the earth dates back to prehistoric times when earth dwellings protected humans from the elements. The earth is a natural temperature moderator that keeps temperatures fairly constant, and the darkness and dampness formerly associated with earth-sheltered living have been overcome by today's sophisticated weatherproofing and lighting

Figure 2.39 A passive solar energy exterior. The lean-to greenhouse is designed to fit against the house, extend living space, and serve as a passive solar collector to help reduce fuel bills. *(Photograph by Robert Perron, courtesy of Lord and Burnham.)*

Figure 2.40 A passive solar energy interior. The solarium is weather tight, totally insulated, and ideally suited to serve as an energy-efficient solar collector. *(Photograph by Robert Perron, courtesy of Lord and Burnham.)*

Figure 2.41 Decade Eighty Solar House, an active solar energy structure, is highlighted by a copper roof of which solar collectors are an integral part. Dozens of technical features and design innovations create a comfortable and convenient solar home. *(Courtesy of the Copper Development Association, Inc.)*

Figure 2.42 Both active and passive solar energy systems are used in this charming gambrel. The roof panels provide active solar energy, and the solarium provides passive solar energy. *(Courtesy of Timberpeg.)*

(see Figure 2.43). Although the earth-sheltered house has many possibilities and holds great promise for the future, it is still in the experimental stage and has some definite disadvantages. This type of dwelling requires a large tract of land, the floor plan requires particular attention, and at present its use is severely hampered by building code restrictions.

Figure 2.43 An earth-sheltered house, planned for maximum energy conservation. The greenhouse provides passive solar energy. *(Courtesy of Milliner Construction, Inc., Frederick, Maryland.)*

Looking to the Future

Housing alternatives during the past few decades have encompassed many new design expressions, building materials, technological advances, and creative solutions to housing requirements (see Chapter 3). Many architects and designers across the nation foresee a number of trends in housing during the 1990s, including (1) a continuing preference by home owners for authentic historical styles; (2) new materials, technology, and adaptations incorporated into period home styles; (3) a demand for homes with more open and livable spaces; (4) a decrease in the popularity of solar homes (however, better materials will be utilized for this home type); (5) new expressions of the modern style in form, color, and materials, but continuing popularity and development of the basic directions of Organic or International Style; (6) prevalence of a vigorous direction in home restoration and renovation; (7) a challenge to architects to design more affordable homes; (8) smaller but more efficiently planned homes; (9) incorporation of better insulation elements; (10) more two-, three-, and four-plex houses massed together to give the image of semidetached houses, with owners willing to share this type of mass housing if it is in a pleasant location and attractively designed with a personal identity to satisfy the American dream of private ownership; (11) a larger condominium market; and (12) a strong move to suburban areas, although regional differences may alter this trend, and some metropolitan centers will encourage development of new housing or restoration and renovation in urban areas.

The Department of Housing and Urban Development forecasts a continuation of current efforts to meet the challenges of providing suitable and efficient housing for all members of society regardless of their socioeconomic status and lifestyle. Also, during the 1990s the commitment to pursue creative and affordable solutions to existing housing problems will be a high priority.

Chapter Three

Floor Plans

Initial Planning Stage—The Program

Functional Needs
Occupants
The Site
Economic Considerations
Beauty
Individuality

The Floor Plan

Fundamental Requirements for the Completed Floor Plan
Well-Designed Basic Areas
Efficient Traffic Lanes
Well-Placed Openings
Adequate Space
Well-Arranged Floor and Wall Space
Ample Storage Space
Economic Considerations
Projected Changes and Remodeling
Analyzing Basic Types of Floor Plans

The Rectangular Plan
The Square Plan
The Multistoried Plan
L-*Shaped Plan*
T, U, *and* H *Plans*
The Atrium Plan
The Circular Plan
The Closed Plan
The Open Plan
A Poorly Arranged Floor Plan
A Well-Arranged Floor Plan

Attached and Multifamily Plans

Houses are built to live in and not to look on; therefore, let use be preferred before uniformity, except where both may be had.

—Sir Francis Bacon, 1612

One of life's great challenges is creating a desirable home. The need for adequate shelter is only the beginning. The worthy endeavor of creating a refuge, an environment in which to promote the growth and development of a household—not only physically but also intellectually, morally, and spiritually—merits dedicated study and application. The graphic details of a floor plan indicate the spatial boundaries of the home that strongly influence the occupants' life-style and well-being. Becoming acquainted with reading and evaluating a floor plan is essential for both the occupant and the professional designer.

Initial Planning Stage—The Program

The ultimate goal of planning a home should be the integration of the basic requirements for an efficient and attractive home: (1) functional needs, (2) economic considerations, (3) incorporation of beauty, and (4) individuality.

Functional Needs

Occupants

To be livable, a house should fulfill its intended function: to satisfy the needs of the people for whom it is designed. Careful consideration of functional needs should commence in the initial planning stage—before a purchase has been made. Members of each household should ask numerous questions concerning their life-style, design preferences, and requirements. With deep and costly regrets, many owners have been influenced by others' advice rather than considering their own everyday living concerns. This pitfall may be avoided if the homeowner carefully and accurately assesses

Figure 3.1 Space is allowed to freely flow throughout the interior space of this dynamic contemporary home designed by architect Ralph Edwards. *(Courtesy of Ralph Edwards.)*

immediate and future household needs. A part of the early planning phase, or program, involves completing a personal profile for each occupant. Spatial requirements should be planned after insightfully evaluating this information. Special design requirements may be necessary for children, the elderly, or handicapped occupants. Currently, information is readily available to the designer regarding efficient planning for the handicapped.

The Site

Selecting the site is probably the most important—and the most difficult—project decision. Before making the selection, the prospective home owner should have the general plan of the house in mind. Not until the site has been analyzed and decided upon, however, should that plan be finalized. Many factors should be considered before the building site is purchased, including such things as schools, transportation, availability of police and fire protection, the quality of the neighborhood, utility availability (water, power, sewage disposal, garbage collection), taxes, and building restrictions.

The safest topography is a gently sloping lot that provides good natural drainage and allows sewer lines to be connected easily. A steep lot may cost less initially but may require expensive retaining walls and other hidden costs. Selecting the best house design for the lot is essential through evaluating the various types of plans available. Effective positioning of the house on the lot and orienting of the structure to take advantage of solar properties are also important criteria.

Figure 3.2 This brick and wood modern house is integrated to its mountain site with soaring vertical sections that reflect the nearby majestic peaks. *(Courtesy of Ron Molen, architect.)*

Economic Considerations

A home is probably the largest single investment a consumer will ever make. Receiving the best value possible for every dollar spent is, therefore, highly important. The owner should study costs on paper and look carefully at available resources, abilities, time, and energies. The initial cost of buying a home is only the beginning; payments and upkeep must continue. According to most home-financing agencies, the monthly payment should not exceed 40 percent of monthly *take-home* pay. The percentage may vary in different parts of the country, but 40 percent is the amount generally approved.

Before the overall expense of the house is determined, the buyer may wish to investigate ways of limiting building costs. A reputable architect or contractor can be helpful, but in most cases the buyer should take the initiative and assume most of the responsibility for keeping costs down. The following suggestions concerning methods and materials can help minimize building costs and upkeep and add to the resale value of the house.

- *A well-designed house plan:* The services of a reputable architect are invaluable, but if the buyer cannot afford such services, a wide selection of excellent architect-designed stock plans is available.

- *A simple house plan:* You can maximize space and minimize cost by using a simple plan. Most houses are based on one of six basic plans: the rectangle or square and the H, U, T, L, and E shapes. Of these plans, the rectangle, the L, and the U are most common. Regarding cost, the nearer to a square shape the exterior walls are constructed, the less will be the cost per square foot. Cost does not increase in direct proportion to a home's square footage; jogs and angles drive the construction costs higher. Two stories cost proportionally less than a low, rambling plan, because the roof and foundation

Figure 3.3 An L-shaped interior plan allows one functional area to lead into another. In this home, the living room area is at a right angle to the dining area, providing adequate separation of spaces. *(Courtesy of Peter Paige.)*

can serve twice the space, heating can be more centralized, and the second story provides extra ***insulation*** against summer heat and winter cold.

- *A unified theme:* Unnecessary mixing of materials should generally be avoided. Any building material, no matter how old or new, should be used appropriately. Simplicity is most often the key to a well-designed home.
- *Adequate insulation:* Insulation should be adequate to reduce heating costs. In regions where wood is readily available, the buyer might consider installing a wood- or coal-burning stove (a trend popular in many areas) to cut heating costs, if pollution is not a concern.
- *Solar orientation:* Locating the house to take the best advantage of the climate can save on heating and air-conditioning bills. The winter sun should strike long walls and large windows, but large areas of glass should not face the afternoon sun in the summer. Passive solar energy systems might be incorporated. A wise positioning

Figure 3.4 A solar-oriented house is designed to take full advantage of the sun's rays, which can contribute to effective heating and cooling of interior spaces. An effort has been made during the past decade to make the solar-oriented house more attractive.

The three enclosures below, each requiring the same amount of wall surface, illustrate the way in which the price per square foot increases as the space deviates from the square.

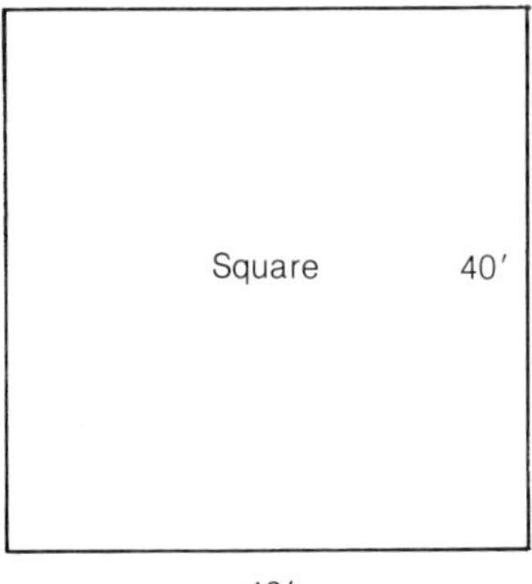

= 160 ft wall surface
= 1600 sq ft floor space

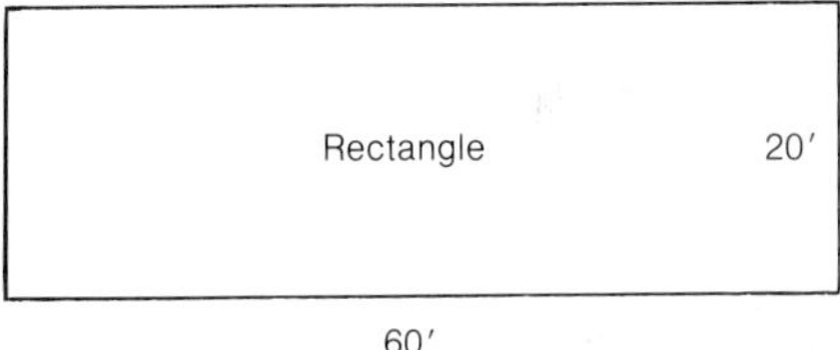

= 160 ft wall surface
= 1200 sq ft floor space

(A loss of 400 sq ft of floor space with the same wall surface)

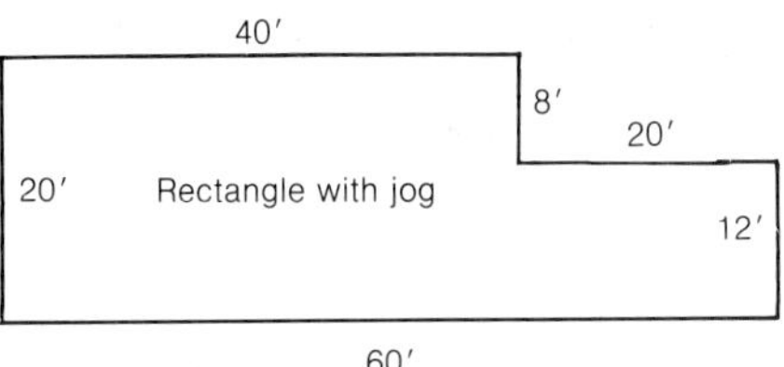

= 160 ft wall surface
= 1040 sq ft of floor space

(A loss of 160 sq ft of floor space plus the extra expense of the jog)

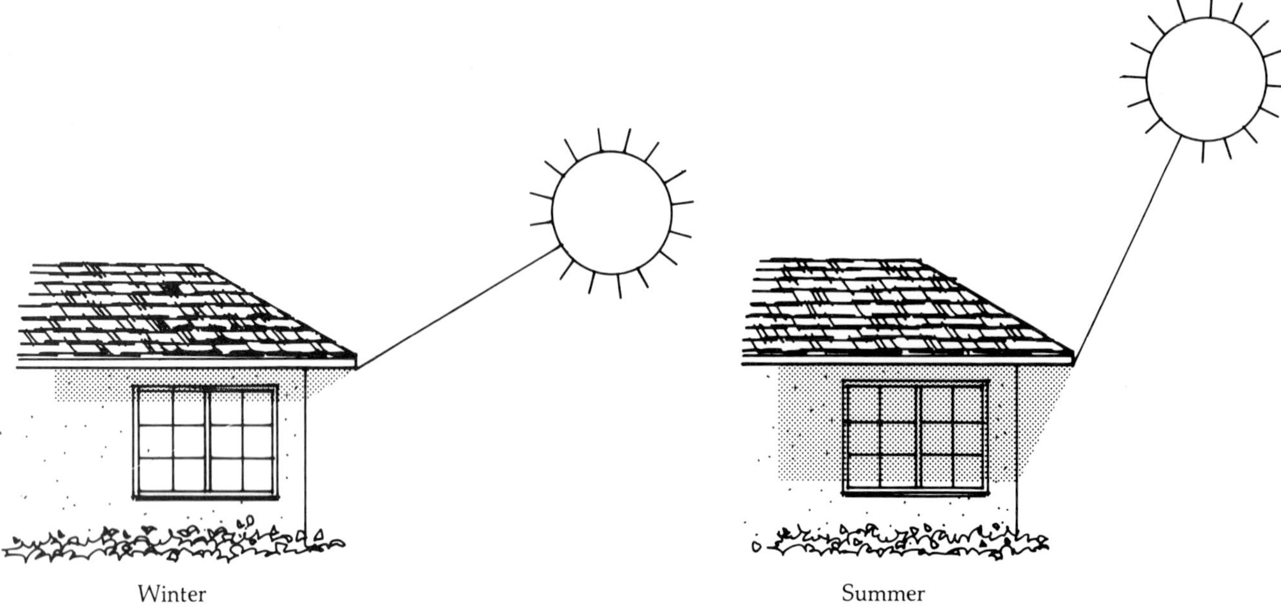

A well-designed roof can permit the warm winter sun to flood the interior spaces in December and block out the hot summer sun in June.

of the house can reduce the cost of utilities. The cost of connecting water, gas, and electricity to the main line depends on the distance from the house to the road.

- *Centralize:* Money can be saved by using centralized plumbing. Bathrooms can be placed back to back or one above the other.

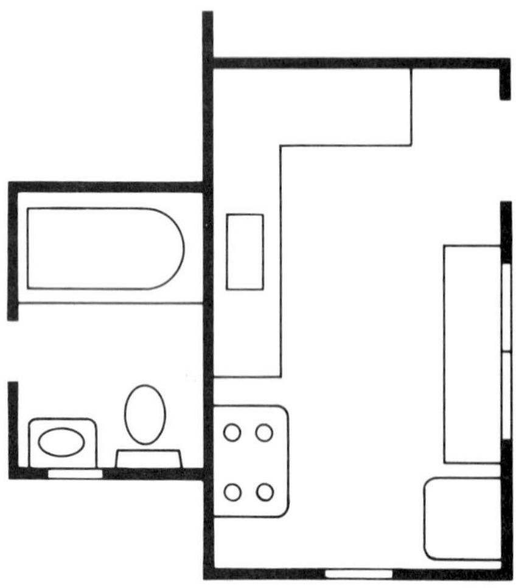

Back to back plumbing

Figure 3.5 Centralized plumbing can help cut down building costs by taking advantage of a common wall for water pipes. In this bath, pipes for the tub, sink, and toilet are located on the right wall. *(Courtesy of Kohler Co.)*

FIREPLACES

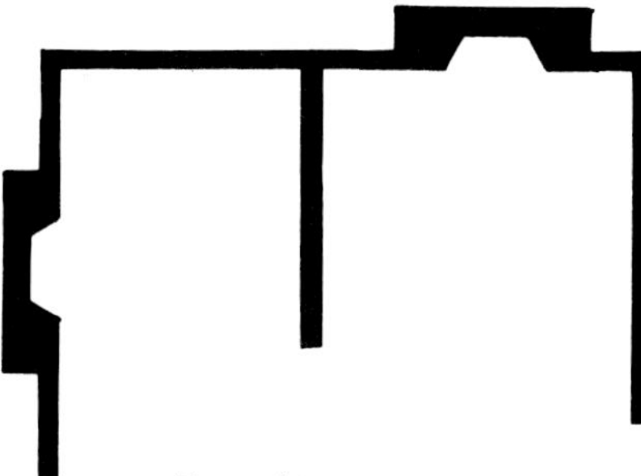

Two chimneys create extra expense.

Two fireplaces can be combined to share the same chimney.

Figure 3.6 This standard milled fireplace is machine processed out of hardwoods that provide the consumer with an economical price as well as durability. Milled items often can replace hand-carved processes and still not sacrifice the beauty achieved from age-old styles of authentic woodwork. *(Courtesy of Driwood Ornamental Wood Moulding & Millwork.)*

Kitchen and utility room plumbing can be located to take advantage of the same major drains. Fireplaces can be planned to take advantage of a common chimney.

- *Plentiful indigenous materials:* Materials found on-site in the construction area can offer great savings. Flawed materials may cost less and character can be gained by making a feature out of a fault.
- *Standard milled items:* These include doors, window frames, cabinets, stairways, mantels, and wood trim. Milled items can be well designed and are readily available at factory-built prices. In some areas plastic plumbing pipe can be used instead of copper pipe.
- *Consideration of long-term upkeep:* Before making the final decision on any item that goes into the completed house, the buyer might consider the upkeep over a long period of time. Some things that are more costly initially are the most economical in the long run. For example, the best heating plan for a particular house in its particular locality is the most economical. In some areas brick may cost more than frame construction or facades, but it never needs painting and the resale value is usually higher than that of wood. A lifetime roof will cost considerably more than one of plain cedar shingles, but the latter may need repair through the years and is more of a fire hazard. Hardwood ***balusters*** are more costly than pine, but pine balusters are easily broken and replacement may soon add up to more than the cost of the hardwood.
- *Do-it-yourself possibilities:* The buyer may wish to negotiate with the contractor and complete some tasks on his or her own, such as painting, finishing cabinetry, and laying flooring. Planning for expansion can save money when more space be-

comes necessary and can enhance the resale value of the house. Once the design is completed and construction has begun, making further changes should be avoided, because they are expensive at this stage.

Beauty

A house, to be a satisfactory home, should appear pleasing to those who live in it and ought to have a certain intrinsic appeal. What is beauty, and what makes a home appear beautiful?

Beauty has been described as that quality which pleases the senses and lifts the spirits. Authorities in the interior design field generally agree that beauty in any object is achieved through the application of the principles of design and a skillful use of the elements, unified by a basic theme. A home designed with these principles and elements in mind, regardless of style, should appear pleasing and have resale value.

Individuality

Individuality is an elusive quality, particularly when considering its properties in a home. It often develops slowly and naturally, revealing the personality of the household. In custom-built homes this development is perhaps easier to achieve. In look-alike subdivisions and mobile-home areas, for example, the challenge to express a personal statement is more difficult.

The Floor Plan

Few prospective home owners are aware of the impact the physical home environment has on the occupant's life. In the plan of a house both exterior and interior considerations are important. Well-arranged floor space should be given top priority to assure a home planned where many household activities can be carried on with a minimum of frustration. Having the valuable space needed is possible, even on a limited budget, if there is a willingness to forego expensive frills. Building a house with a good plan costs no more than building one with a poor plan—and sometimes actually costs less. As noted earlier, the buyer's input is invaluable to the architect when finalizing the home design.

Experience has proven that the intelligent application of basic design requirements to the general floor plan is conducive to the smooth working of a home and contributes immeasurably to the daily enjoyment of household life. Styles and personal preferences have changed through the years; however, certain desirable features have remained constant. Surveys indicate that the home owner continues to appreciate good traffic patterns that preserve a sense of privacy, a private dining area, a fireplace, a place to study or to work at hobbies, a separate entrance hall, a pantry, adequate spaces for bedrooms, a special living room area, conveniently placed laundry rooms, and spaces for casual family living.

In recent years, skyrocketing building costs and interest rates, along with dramatic changes in the family structure, have forced people to live in smaller spaces, making multipurpose areas a necessity.

The prospective home owner who is planning to build, either working with an architect or from a predesigned plan, should be able to read and understand an architect's working drawing of a floor plan. This graphic design is referred to as the ***blueprint,*** since the old

Figure 3.7 In keeping with the trend of combining various functions, a dividing peninsula serves both kitchen and dining areas while providing privacy for the dining area's wide range of activities. *(Courtesy of Wilsonart Products.)*

printing method employed white lines on a bright blue ground. The standard today, however, is to use blue lines on a white ground. The floor plan is a two-dimensional drawing indicating the walls, floors, partitions, windows, stairs, cabinets, and other structural components of the home that outline the available space. Floor plans are drawn to ***scale*** precisely indicating size relationships. The most commonly used scale is ¼ in. equals 1 ft. This scale reduces the size of the plan, allowing the designer to represent the outline of the home on paper. To understand the blueprint, the home owner should become familiar with basic architectural symbols, which include room dimensions, closets, openings, stairways, bathroom fixtures, kitchen appliances, electrical outlets, and heating units. With this knowl-

ARCHITECTURAL SYMBOLS

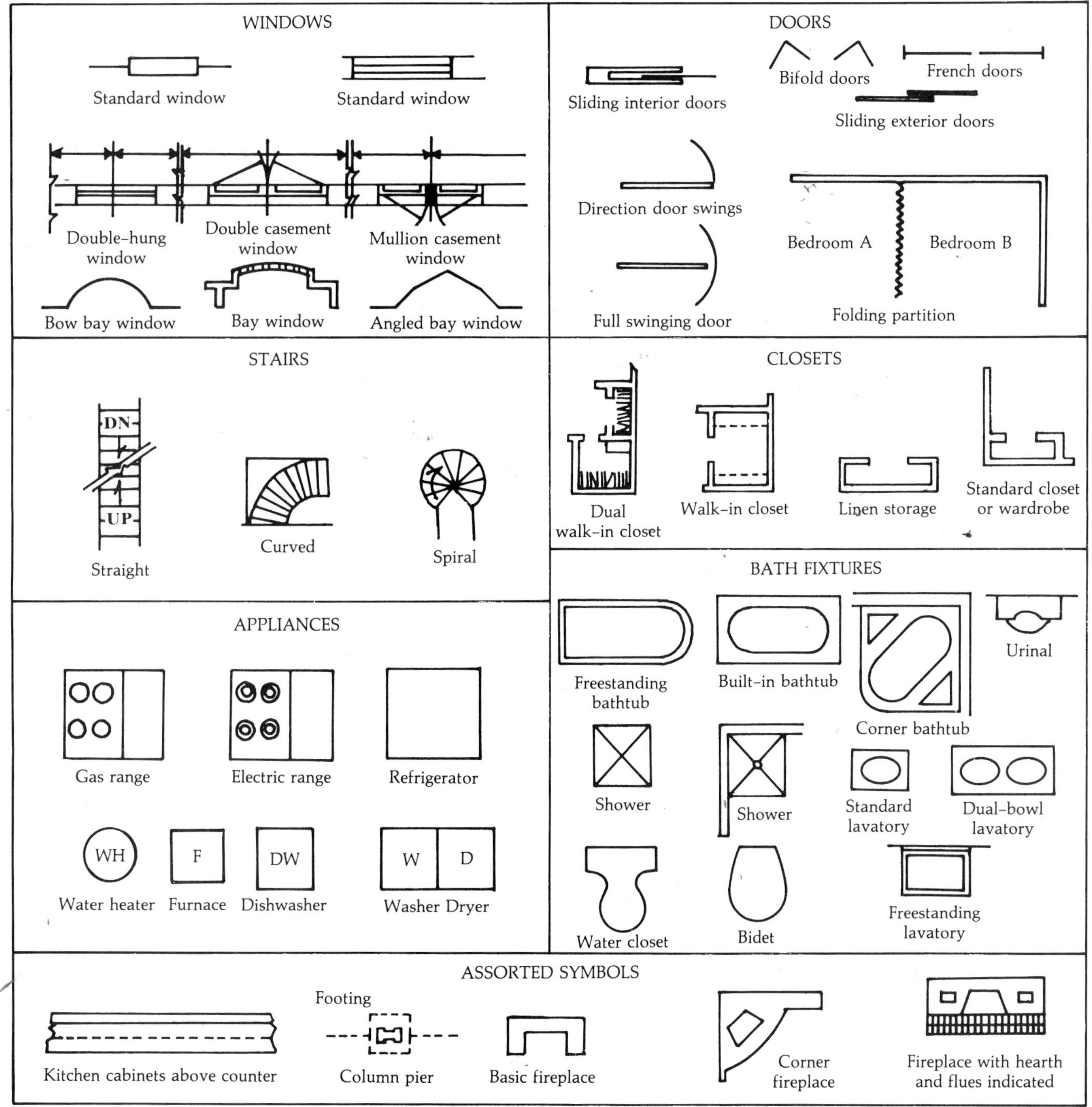

edge, the home owner can intelligently examine the blueprint while "moving" from room to room. Although this evaluation does not provide a three-dimensional understanding, it will reveal any objectionable features, which can be changed before the plan is finalized. Familiarization with a graphic floor plan is an essential step for the professional designer, the builder, and the buyer.

Figure 3.8 Open planning expands visual space in this eclectic living space and allows for casual living. The high ceiling directs the eye upward and the view of the landscape from the windows provides a link to the outside adding to the feeling of spaciousness. *(Courtesy of Kirkwood Shutters, Phoenix, AZ.)*

Fundamental Requirements for the Completed Floor Plan

Although individual differences in life-style should be taken into account when planning a home, basic time-tested features should also be considered if the home is to function efficiently. The following features and considerations can aid the home owner.

Well-Designed Basic Areas

Working areas for kitchen activities, laundering, ironing, sewing, hobbies, and so forth should be conveniently located with well-arranged space and adequate lighting.

Informal eating areas for quick snacks and informal family meals are most conveniently located in or near the kitchen. More formal dining areas need privacy from the front door, with provision made to shut the eating area off from the clutter of the kitchen. A pleasant atmosphere and effective lighting are also important. When not being used for meals, dining areas can be used for activities such as studying, sewing, and playing games.

Informal family and recreation rooms should be convenient to the kitchen and outside. More formal areas should be placed away from major traffic lanes and planned for privacy and relaxation.

For maximum quiet and privacy, sleeping and dressing areas should be away from the public areas of the home, with easy access to bathrooms.

Efficient Traffic Lanes

Well-planned traffic lanes are convenient and adequate in size without being wasteful. A central entrance hall should channel traffic to all areas of the house. From the kitchen, easy access to the front door, back door, utility room, service area, garage, and all areas of the home is desirable. Direct access to the outside service area from the utility area is also a convenient feature. At least one living area should have easy access to the outside living area. An access door—other than the large garage doors near the front of the house—leading directly into the kitchen is a valuable feature. All major traffic lanes should generally be routed to avoid going through any room to reach another.

Well-Placed Openings

Doors and windows should be conveniently located to preserve functional wall space. Well-designed windows and the placement within the wall area can make the task of window treatment more pleasing and efficient.

Adequate Space

Allowing enough space for each member of the household is essential. Many personal preferences for space arrangement and needs vary, but generally, 200 square ft of space per person in the household is a minimum; 500 or more square ft per person provides added luxury. Additionally, each room of the

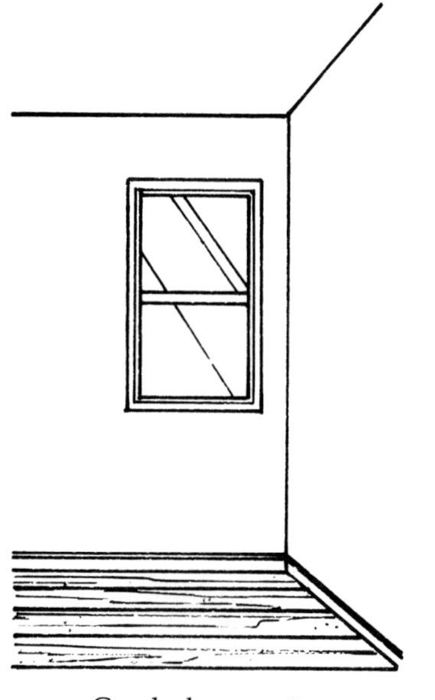

Good placement

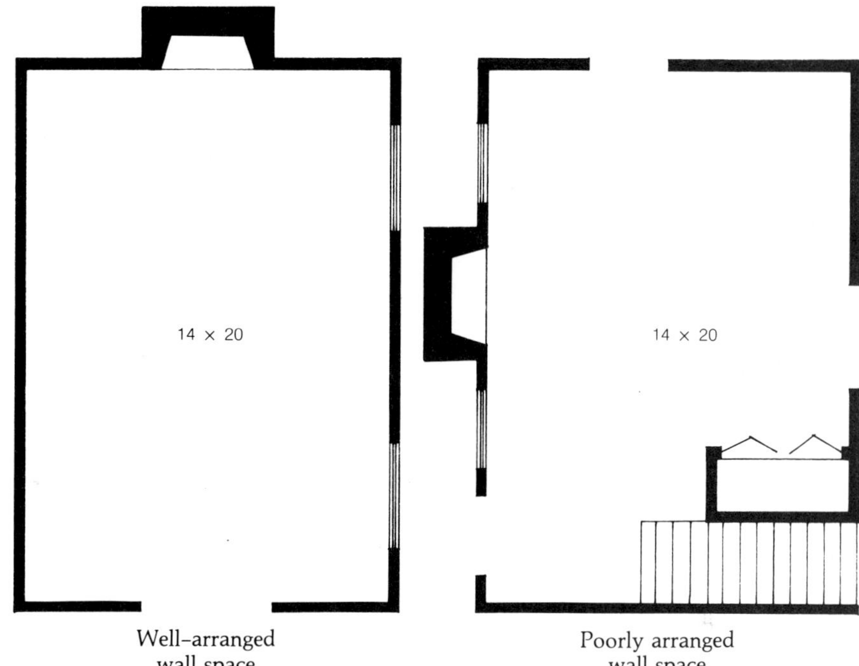

Well-arranged wall space

Poorly arranged wall space

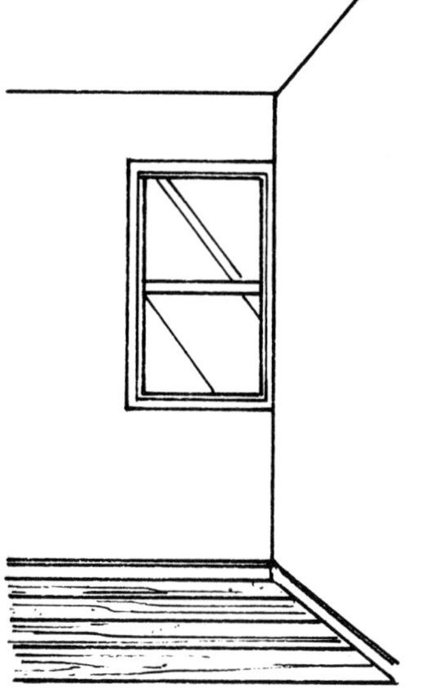

Poor placement

home requires special consideration for functional and pleasant living with space appropriate for household activities.

Well-Arranged Floor and Wall Space

Adequate wall and floor space providing necessary square footage for each member of the household is important, to accommodate large and necessary pieces of furniture and other requirements for the occupant.

Ample Storage Space

Sufficient storage space should be conveniently located throughout the house and garage. Providing sufficient storage within the home is a major concern, and needs may differ according to various lifestyles and household situations. Attics and basements provide added storage space.

Economic Considerations

The final plan meets the criteria outlined on pp. 68–72 incorporating available economic advantages.

Projected Changes and Remodeling

Through the years household needs may fluctuate, and remodeling may become necessary. A good plan can effectively accommodate projected revisions. For example, an initial kitchen plan may have a

EXPANDING A SMALL HOUSE

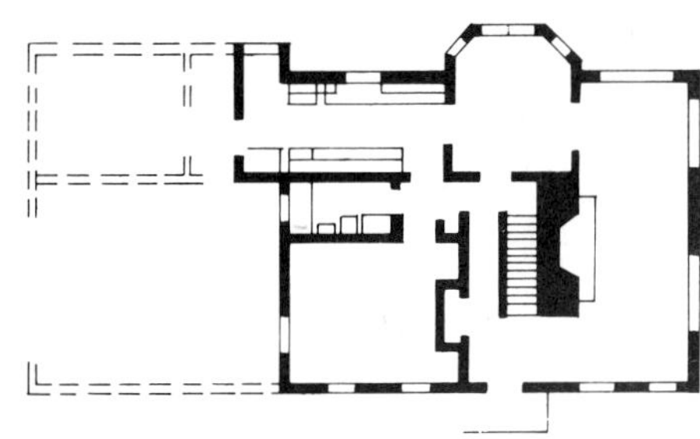

Add walls to the main floor

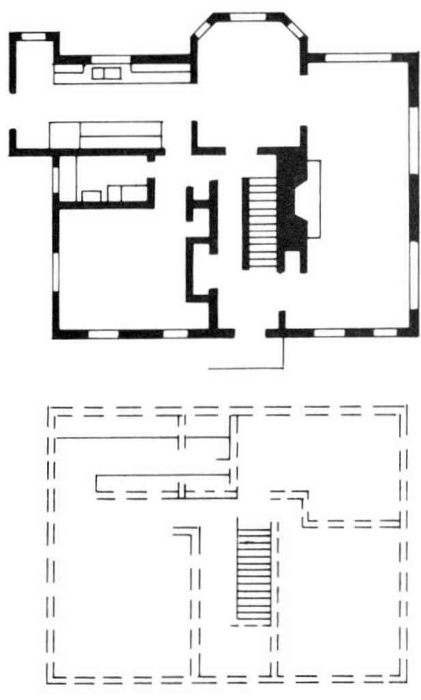

Add a second story

wall that could easily be expanded for added space or a family room window removed for an additional living area.

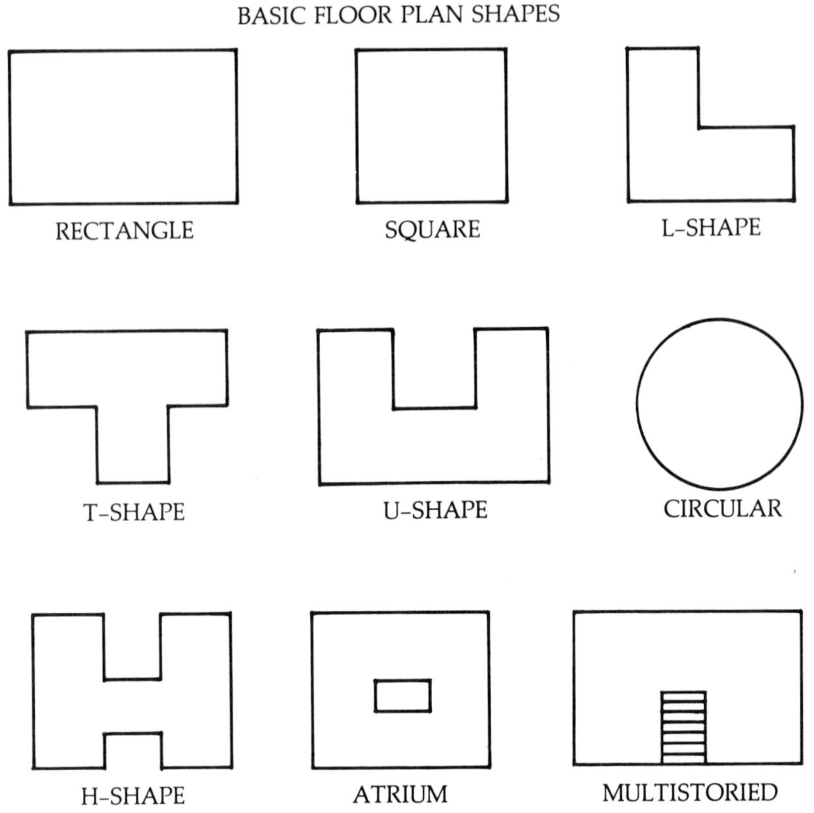

Analyzing Basic Types of Floor Plans

The Rectangular Plan

The simplest floor plan is the rectangle. The further the plan departs from this shape, the more complicated and costly it becomes. Each jog and additional roof angle means added expense, and thus more dollars per square foot of floor space. The rectangular plan is readily adapted to both traditional and contemporary exteriors. The plan shown is particularly well arranged and meets the necessary requirements.

- An ample entrance hall routes traffic to all areas of the house.
- Basic areas are well defined and conveniently located. Plumbing is

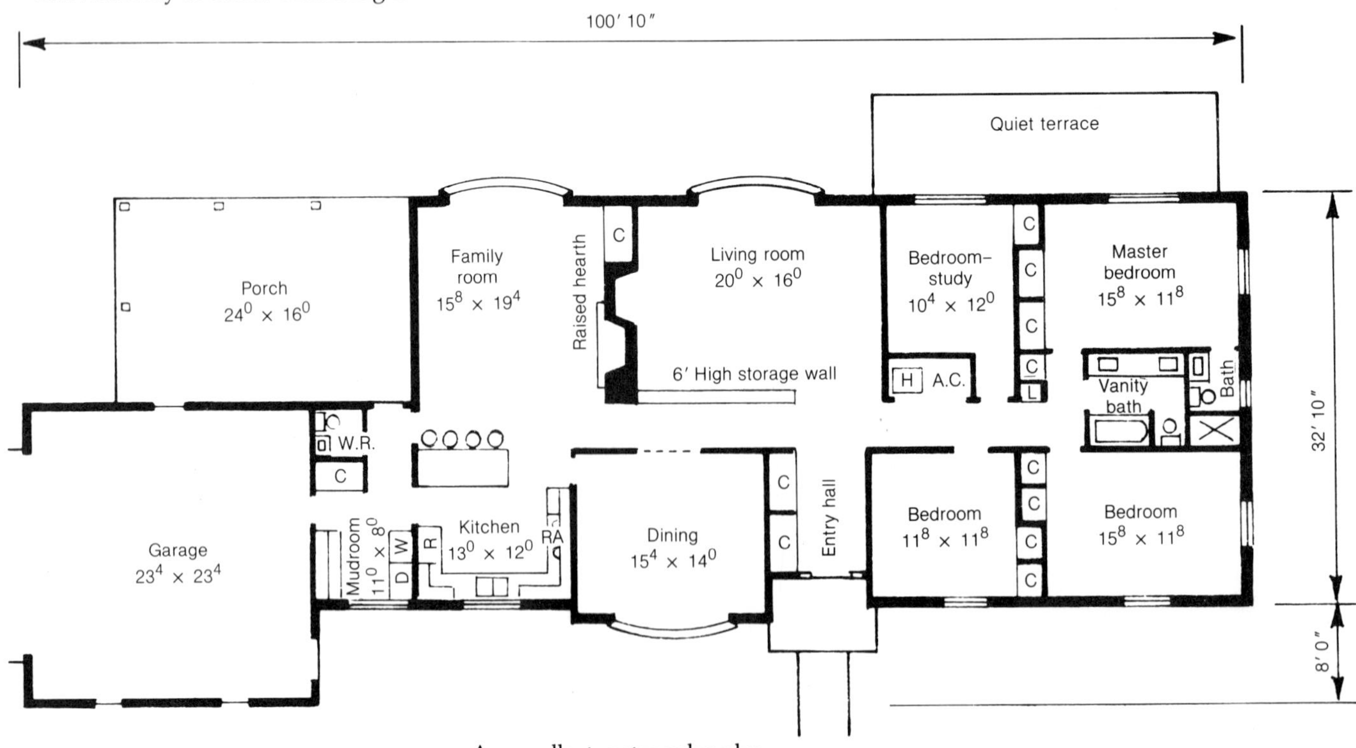

An excellent rectangular plan.
(Courtesy of Home Building Plan Services.)

back to back in the bedroom wing and in the work area.

- Large windows looking onto a private garden create a pleasing indoor–outdoor relationship.
- The family room has easy access to the outside.
- Access from the kitchen and utility rooms to the outdoors and to the garage is convenient.
- The garage faces away from the street.
- The access door opens from the front yard into the garage.
- Ample space is provided for informal and formal eating.
- Fireplaces in the living and family rooms use the same chimney.
- Storage is adequate and well placed.
- Openings are placed for convenience.
- Wall space is adequate throughout.

The Square Plan

The square plan is also a simple and inexpensive arrangement of space with distinct advantages and disadvantages similar to the rectangular plan. Many homes employing this basic shape were built after World War II to accommodate the need for efficient and low-budget housing. As a result, many subdivisions throughout America have rows of small homes built utilizing the square plan. Most designers try to minimize or even change this boxy shape—both for interiors and exteriors—through creative manipulation of the elements of design to achieve a more pleasing shape. Some considerations when employing the square plan include the following.

- The square plan is one of the least expensive to build because

Basic Kitchen Arrangements

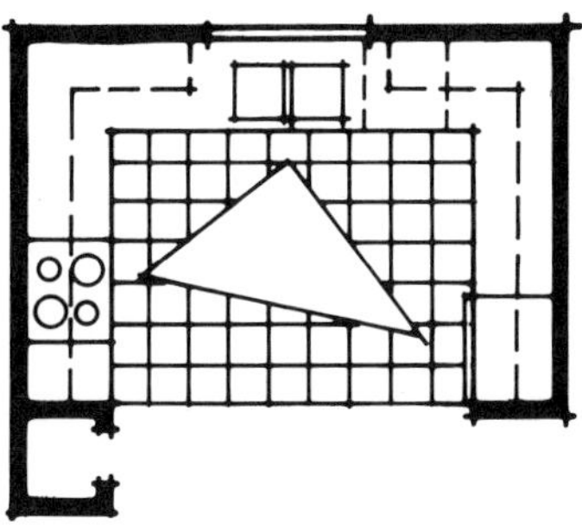

U-SHAPE KITCHEN
U-shape kitchens are generally considered the most comfortable and efficient. Work centers are out of the way of traffic and more conveniently located.

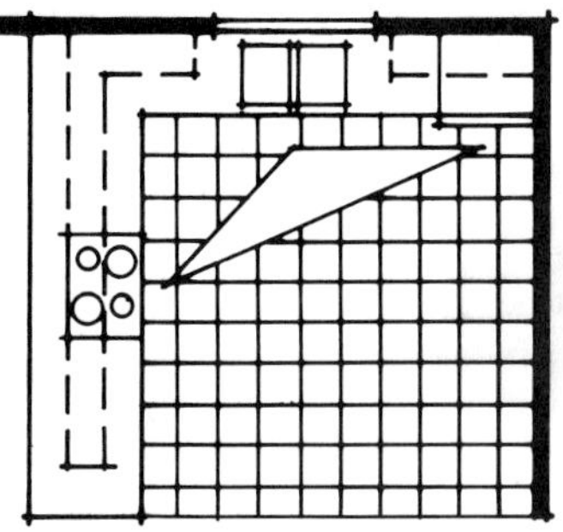

L-SHAPE KITCHEN
L-shape kitchens are a little more efficient than the parallel since traffic lanes do not intrude into the space. Work centers are conveniently located.

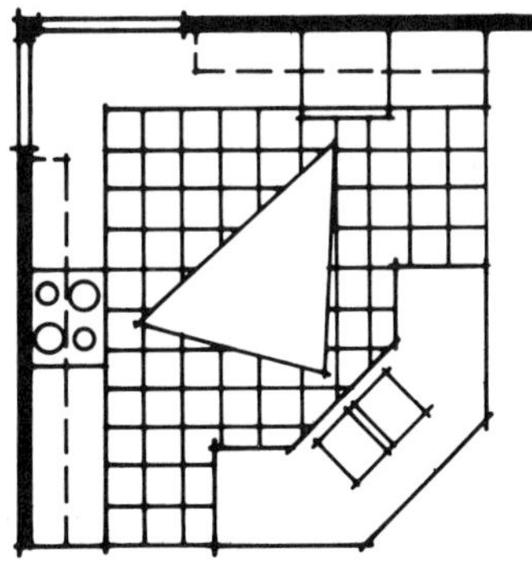

ISLAND KITCHEN
The island kitchen has similar qualities as the U-shape, but with the unwelcome addition of possible traffic through the space.

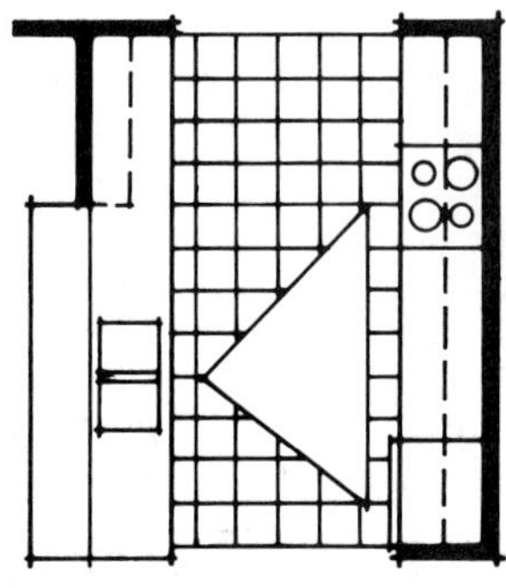

PARALLEL KITCHEN
Parallel kitchens provide undesirable traffic, especially when doors are located at each end. Work centers are more convenient than one-wall kitchens.

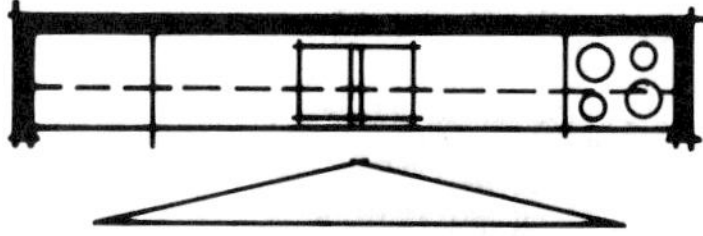

ONE-WALL KITCHEN
One-wall kitchens economically use one plumbing wall, can be concealed with folding doors and do not take up much space. They are usually most suitable for apartments and small living spaces. They have very little counterspace and work space pattern is long.

corners are limited to four. It requires only a basic and simple roof and foundation—generally the most costly elements of all house construction.

■ Care should be taken to arrange rooms so traffic can flow freely. Placement of an entrance and hallways can be a challenge in the square plan.

■ Good planning should provide adequate light and air circulation—often a problem with the square plan. The center may be poorly lit. A centrally located skylight is one method of eliminating this condition.

■ The square plan generally does not provide interesting and inviting outdoor living spaces; however, through skillful landscaping this problem can be eliminated. Sometimes the square plan is turned on an angle to the lot, thus providing a unique diagonal or diamond shape.

■ Good separation of interior living spaces is more difficult to arrange in the square plan (for example, with the sleeping and activities centers).

The Multistoried Plan

Multistoried plans provide living space on two or more levels. This two-story arrangement allows versatile living. Desirable features of this plan include the following.

■ A rectangular plan eliminates most unnecessary jogs.

■ All basic areas are well defined on two levels for convenient living.

■ An entry hall channels traffic throughout the house.

■ Traffic lanes are economical and permit easy access to basic areas.

■ Doors and windows are well placed.

■ Plumbing is back to back on

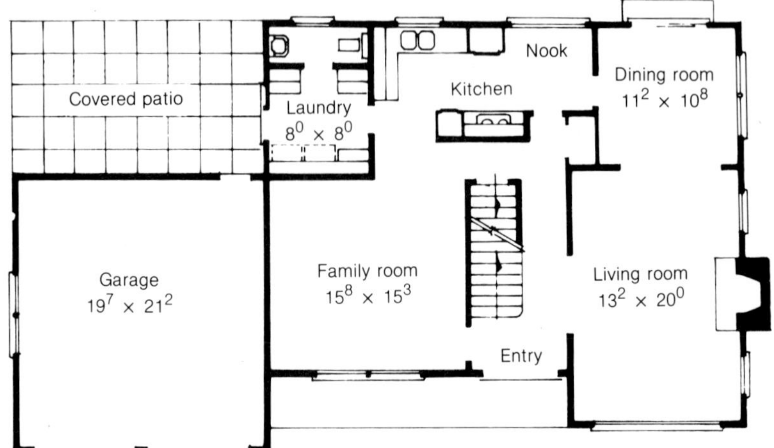

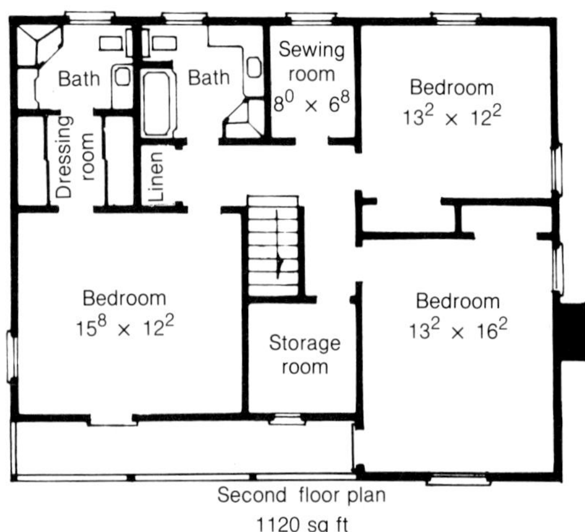

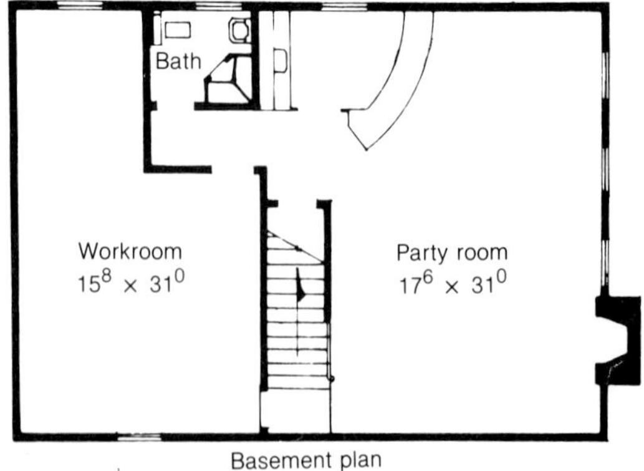

A well-arranged two-story plan. (*Courtesy of Home Building Plan Services.*)

each floor, and second-story and basement plumbing is directly above and below the main-floor plumbing.

■ The full basement may be roughed in and finished at a later date.

■ An undesirable feature is that the front of the garage has no smaller access (entry) door.

L-Shaped Plan

The L-shaped plan allows variety in space planning through an extension from the rectangular shape. Well-designed features of the L-shaped plan are that

■ The plan incorporates the basic requirements for functional space allocation.

■ A central entrance hall routes traffic directly to living, sleeping, and work areas without cross-circulation.

■ Large glass doors open onto a private garden away from the street, giving an indoor-outdoor openness.

■ The family room is conveniently combined with the kitchen for informal activities.

■ The garage has an access door.

■ The service area between the kitchen and half-bath is out of the main line of traffic yet convenient to the kitchen and the outside.

■ The bedroom wing is away from the work and living areas.

■ The family and private baths are back to back.

■ The closet space is well placed in the bedrooms. Three closets open to the main entrance hall.

■ The bar in the family room is handy for quick snacks. The separate dining room invites more formal meals.

■ The rooms are well planned with well-placed openings and ample wall space, with the exception of the two front bedrooms, which have an added window for cross-ventilation.

T, U, and H Plans

These shapes allow additional space extensions, with advantages including more variety in room arrangement, easy division of noisy and quiet areas, effective traffic lanes, opportunity for more efficient natural lighting and cross-ventilation, and more interesting landscaping possibilities. Disadvantages might include the cost involved for heating and cooling; added expense for foundation, roof, and jogs; and the need for a larger lot to accommodate the T, U, and H forms.

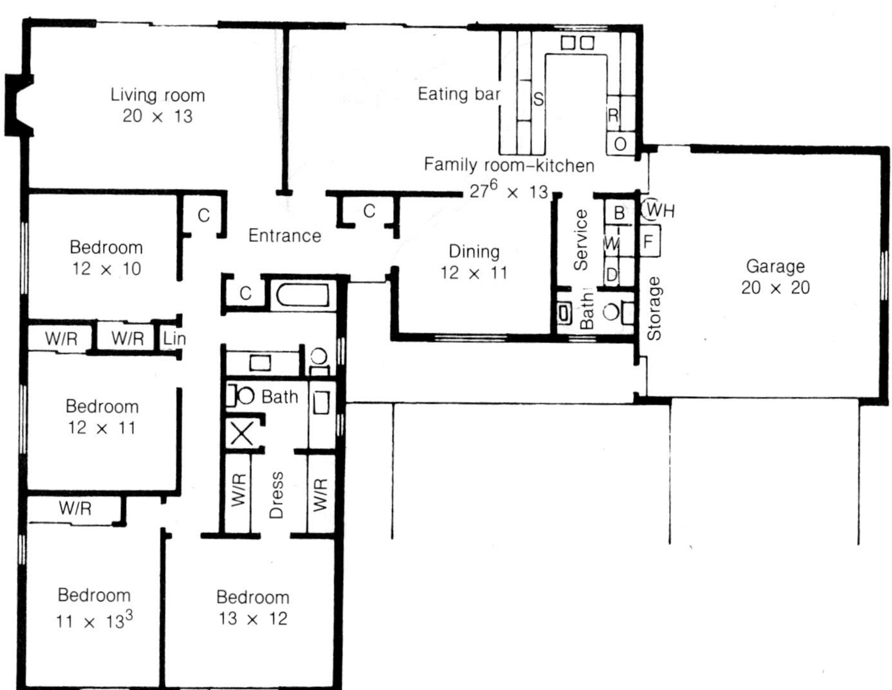

An efficient L-shaped plan

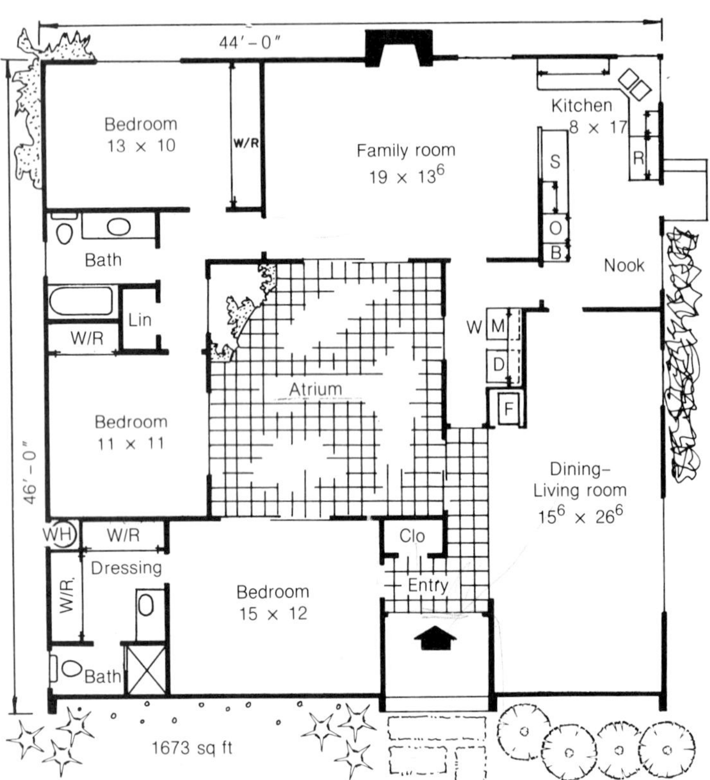

The atrium plan. (*Courtesy of Hiawatha Estes.*)

Figure 3.9 An interior with an atrium plan brings privacy to the central area of the home. The glass ceiling covering this atrium in a private mountain residence designed by Walter Cowie allows light to flood the area and provides a pleasant living space. *(Photograph by Lincoln Allen, Salt Lake City, Utah.)*

The Atrium Plan

The ***atrium plan,*** an inner courtyard arrangement, was used by the ancient Romans and has become a desirable feature in many contemporary homes, particularly Spanish-style ones. This inner courtyard can be either completely enclosed as the central focus of the entire house or built within a U shape or to one side. The atrium can also be either open to the sky or topped with a skylight.

With the increasing importance of solar energy, the atrium can function as a sun room and be incorporated into a passive solar house design. The atrium plan has advantages and disadvantages similar to those for the other plans described thus far, but it has the added feature of the inviting interior private living space.

The Circular Plan

The circular plan is often considered the least preferable shape because of problems involved with decorating and living in a circle. The lot is difficult to landscape and allows very little natural private living areas. An advantage is its unusual design which can provide a unique living dimension when well planned.

The Closed Plan

The arrangement of floor space over the years has fluctuated between two basic schemes: the ***closed plan*** and the ***open plan.*** The closed plan, as seen in the preceding illustrations, provides separate rooms for specific activities and allows more individual privacy. Many people, particularly large families, often prefer this plan.

The Open Plan

In the open plan, space for various activities flows from one area to another, broken by few wall barriers. One advantage of this plan is that it seems to expand space, which may be left entirely open or partially isolated for freestanding partitions. The open plan has particular appeal to people with an informal life-style.

Open planning has been used in this spacious U-shaped design to enlarge two areas visually. The living and dining rooms are combined, and for additional space the master bedroom can be opened. Visual space is further provided by sliding-glass patio doors. The kitchen and family rooms are also one open unit for informal living.

A Poorly Arranged Floor Plan

Careful examination and comparison of the two floor plans on page 82 can help the student in reading and critically evaluating a plan. Undesirable features of the plan are as follows:

- Poor arrangement of space; square footage would be unnecessarily costly and living spaces inconvenient and frustrating; also, too many costly jogs
- Poorly planned traffic lanes
- Lack of entrance way, making living room a major traffic lane
- Poorly located front door prevents a private conversation area around fireplace due to traffic-pattern problems
- No privacy in eating areas
- Inconvenient placement of garage makes transporting of groceries a chore
- Necessity of crossing through a bedroom to reach half-bath from kitchen
- Uneconomical placement of plumbing
- Inconvenient location of washer and dryer in kitchen
- Window size and placement undesirable; window in small corner bedroom abutting the wall; windows in living room too small, providing inadequate light
- Insufficient storage in garage and throughout home
- Noisy and quiet areas not adequately separated
- Private informal living space ignored; for example, television set would have to be placed in living room

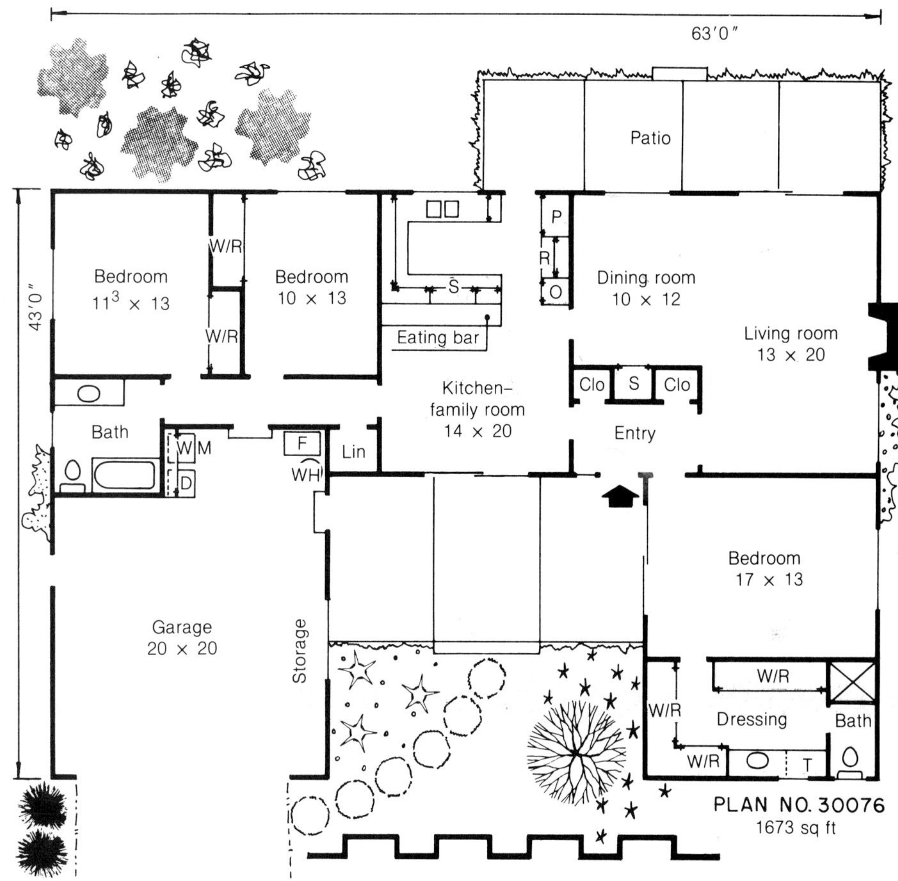

Open planning. (*Courtesy of Hiawatha Estes.*)

A Well-Arranged Floor Plan

Compare the well-organized, easy-to-live-in, and economically designed plan on p. 82 with the one above it. This plan has more living space and could be built for the same amount or less than the poorly arranged plan. Improved features of the plan are as follows.

- Eight costly jogs eliminated
- Family room and separate dining room added
- Traffic lanes well planned with (1) entrance way directing traffic throughout house, allowing privacy for living and dining rooms, (2) outside entrance into family room, (3) acccess door into front of garage and from back of garage to backyard, and (4) convenient traffic lanes from kitchen to outside
- Plumbing centralized; bathrooms, kitchen, and utilities back to back
- Washer and dryer out of kitchen but nearby in utility area
- U-shaped kitchen compact and efficiently arranged
- Windows provide sufficient light and permit easy draping
- Convenient storage planned in garage
- Two fireplaces use same chimney
- Quiet and noisy areas well defined and separated

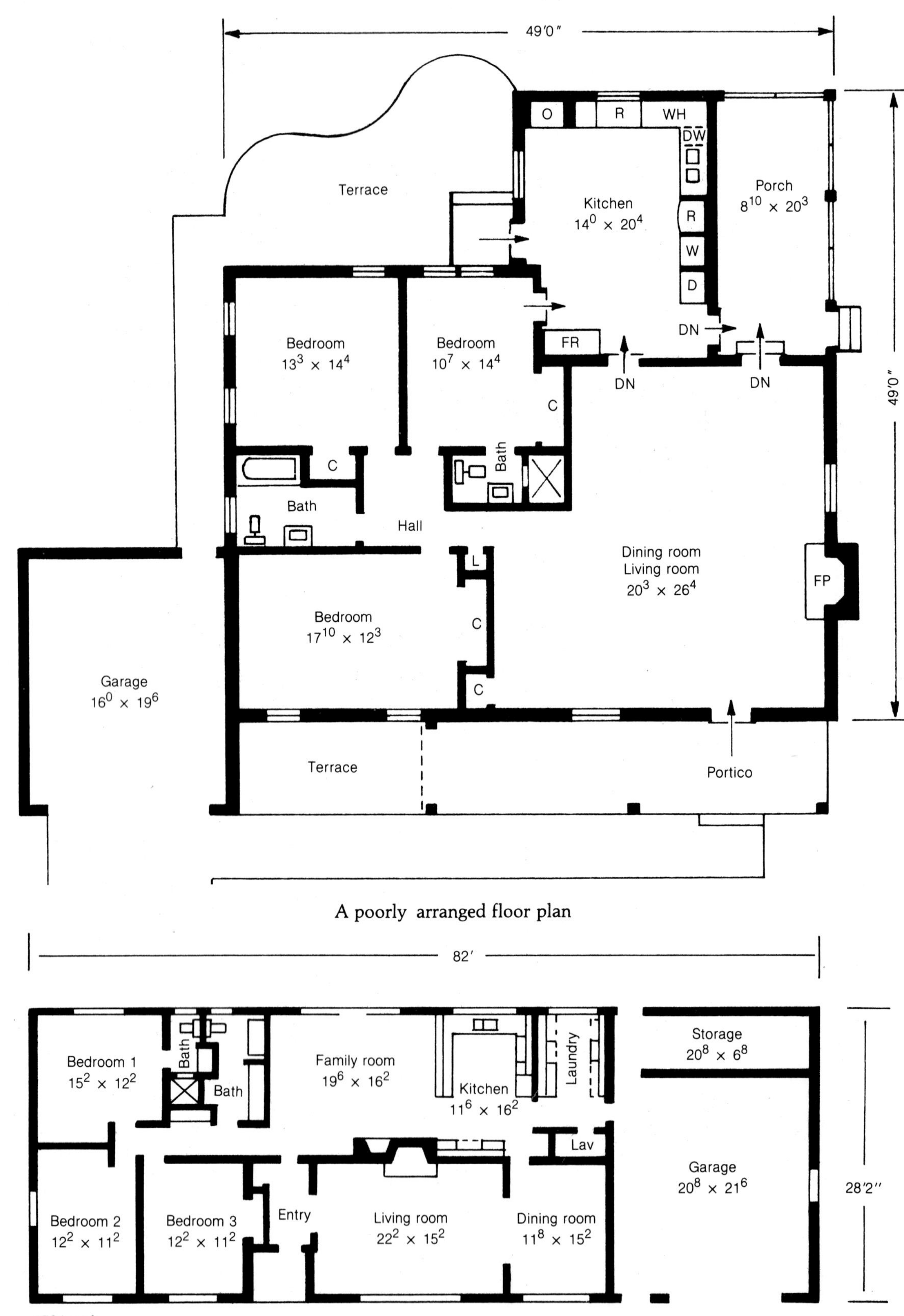

A poorly arranged floor plan

Well-arranged floor plan

Attached and Multifamily Plans

Architects are currently designing high-density housing units accommodating a variety of life-styles and tastes. In all cases, main concerns include efficient use of space, privacy, easy upkeep, security, and energy conservation. **Apartment houses, duplexes, garden apartments, clustered condominiums,** and **town houses** are planned inside much like single detached houses. Floor plans for attached and multifamily housing may vary from large two-level multiroom units to compact one-room arrangements. For example, the following three compact town-house condominiums are designed for particular life-styles.

The one-bedroom unit has a conventional plan for a tandem buyer. Well-arranged space is convenient and adequate for a couple or for a single person. A **tandem arrangement** is one in which individual units are placed side by side or one behind the other.

The **compact studio** shows how to make the most of limited space. The living room includes above-the-sofa storage, a dining room table that can be used for work or

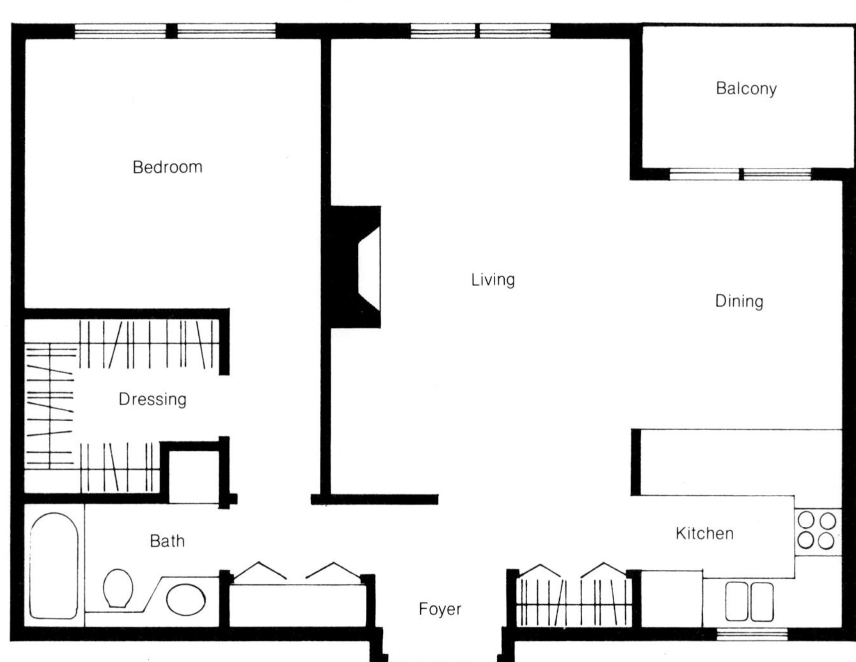

One-bedroom unit

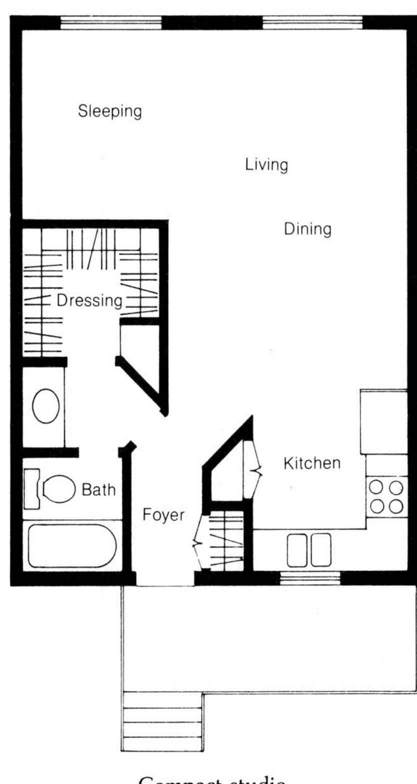

Compact studio

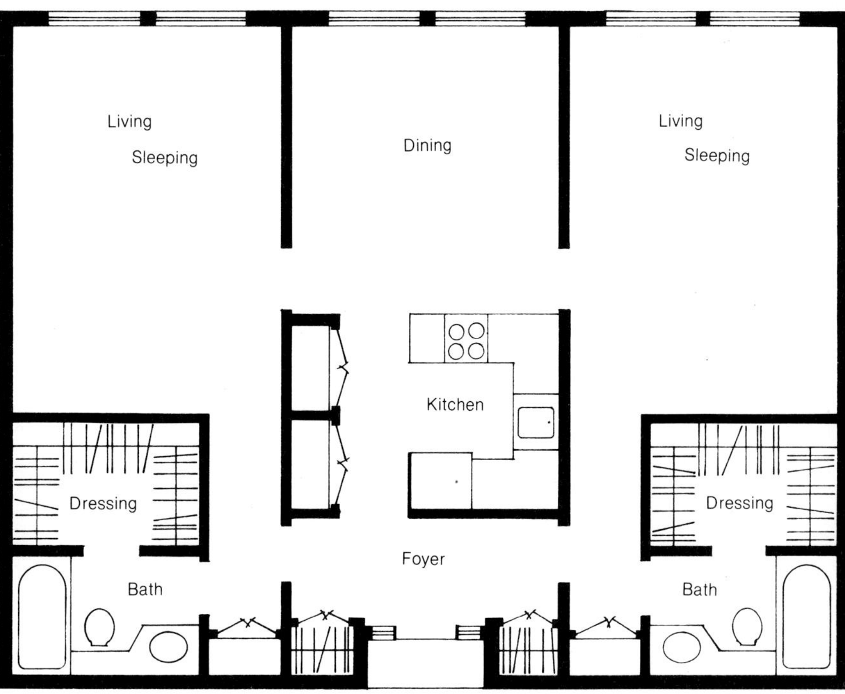

Mingles unit

hobby space, a queen-sized bed that folds away during the day, and a compartmentalized bathroom.

The **mingles unit** has two separate but equal living spaces. The unit has mirror-image sleeping and living spaces and equal-sized baths with shared kitchen and dining areas sandwiched between. Access is by a single-entry unit.

ASSIGNMENT

The following assignment is outlined to demonstrate competency in selecting an economical and efficiently designed floor plan.

1. Select a floor plan that meets the requirements described in this text, keeping in mind that this plan must be for a *year-round family dwelling.* Do not attempt to draw a plan, because this requires special training and skill beyond the scope of this course.
2. Submit your plan, mounted on black, white, or gray paper, with an accompanying critique considering all features discussed under "Fundamental Requirements for the Completed Floor Plan" (p. 74).
3. In addition to the critique, compute the total cost of the chosen house by multiplying the total number of square feet by the *current* cost per square foot in your particular locale. If the plan has a basement or a second story or both, costs should be checked with a builder or architect. Building costs vary regionally and can even change from month to month.

Design Theory and Application

Chapter Four

Basic Guidelines for Design
Basic Design
- Structural Design
- Decorative Design

Elements of Design
- Texture
- Pattern
- Line
- Form or Mass
- Space
- Light

Natural Lighting
Artificial Lighting
- Lighting Sources
  - *Combustion*
  - *Incandescence*
  - *Fluorescence (or Luminescence)*
- Types of Lighting
  - *Ambient or General Lighting*
  - *Task Lighting*
  - *Accent Lighting*
- Methods of Artificial Lighting
  - *Architectural Lighting*
  - *Portable or Nonarchitectural Lighting*
- Direct and Indirect Lighting
- Switches and Outlets
- Lighting for Specific Areas
- Light Control
- Lighting for Energy Conservation
- Measuring Light
- Color

Principles of Design
- Proportion and Scale
  - *Proportion*
  - *Scale*
- Balance
  - *Bisymmetrical, or Formal, Balance*
  - *Asymmetrical Balance*
  - *Radial Balance*
  - *Other Considerations Involving Balance*
- Rhythm
- Emphasis
- Harmony

Poverty is a poor excuse for ugliness, and one can never get rich enough to purchase good taste.

—Alice Merrill Horne

People are not born with that elusive element called "good taste"; it is a capability for making **aesthetic judgments** that develops over years of learning and experience. Anyone can express personal preference, but the acquisition of good aesthetic judgment requires a **knowledge of the elements and principles of design.** This knowledge can serve as a basis for an understanding of the qualities of design and for **visual appreciation** and **intelligent selection.** Although acquiring this knowledge informally or through exposure is possible, more formal training is usually required. Once knowledge of the basic principles is established, new media and modern technology can be applied in original and creative ways to produce appropriate solutions to current situations. To the person trained to discern good and poor design, the use of innovative forms and proportions can be not only favorable but desirable. Attempting innovative applications without first having an understanding of the basic principles of design, however, would be folly.

Basic Guidelines for Design

Good design has no absolute formula. However, the successful employment of aesthetic principles—scale and proportion, rhythm, balance, harmony, and emphasis—will enhance the designer's skill and provide a sound background for decision making. Integrity and simplicity are important ingredients in good design, along with consideration for the design's function and its relationship to the environment and to people. Whatever the design, its basic intention should be to enrich people's lives and enhance the human experience. Good design is a long-term investment; although at times expensive, it is often worth the cost. Mediocre design will always be mediocre, and good design will always be good, no matter what the change in fashion. The best design should be demanded and expected in all areas.

For the student anticipating a career in interior design or for those desiring to increase design awareness, certain guidelines can help in ac-

Figure 4.1 Skillful use of texture, pattern, line, form, space, color, and lighting has created an eclectic room of elegance and warmth. The traditional architectural background of this brownstone home has been contrasted with the use of contemporary furniture, fabrics, and accessories. *(Photograph by Norman McGrath.)*

quiring the capability to choose design of lasting beauty and enjoyment.

- **Acquiring knowledge** of the principles and elements of design is fundamental. Deliberate application of these principles will enable them to become part of the aspiring designer's consciousness.
- **Carefully and constantly observing objects in nature**—light and shadow, shape and texture, and pattern and color—can develop personal awareness. These elements can be viewed not only in and of themselves but also with respect to how they interrelate. Looking for balance, rhythm, emphasis, scale, and proportion in nature can help you develop a sense of the harmony these principles produce.
- **Studying and researching historical, modern, and contemporary architecture and furnishing styles** will provide the design student with a knowledgeable background for current application.
- **Critically examining the excellent design periodicals** available on the market is beneficial.
- **Asking questions of experienced professionals** in furniture stores and design studios is invaluable.
- **Acquiring knowledge of accessories** is important, particularly with regard to items appropriate for each style of furniture, as well as their use for enhancing rooms.
- **Realizing that fashion is not a good criterion of design is vital.** Like fashion in clothes, fashion in home furnishings may often become outdated. Individual taste can be influenced by national trends, events, and celebrities. For example, over the years, world fairs have had a great effect on public taste. Trendsetters like famous designers, political figures, actors, rock stars, and others have inspired novel ideas in many mediums and residential and contract design in varying degrees.

Applying knowledge of what constitutes good design enables consumers to make purchases wisely. Each purchase, no matter how small, is of utmost importance. Whether the purchase is a crystal goblet, a chair, or a house, good taste is not determined by cost alone. Ultimately, taste is a sense of what is appropriate to a particular life-style, and the success of interior design depends on the choice of ingredients and the way they are blended together.

Basic Design

Webster's Dictionary defines design as "the arrangement of details which make up a work of art." As defined in the *Encyclopaedia Britannica,* design is "the arrangement of lines or forms which make up the plan of a work of art with especial regard to the proportions, structure, movement, and beauty of line of the whole."

In any well-planned and well-executed design—whether a silver spoon, a rug, or a complete house—carefully considering the principles of design can lead to a successful solution. Becoming familiar with the two basic types of design, **structural** and **decorative,** is a helpful introduction to the section dealing with the principles and elements of design.

Structural Design

Structural design relates to the size and shape of an object; the design is an integral part of the structure

DESIGN IN NATURE

Gradation

Asymmetrical balance

Bisymmetrical balance

STRUCTURAL AND DECORATIVE DESIGN

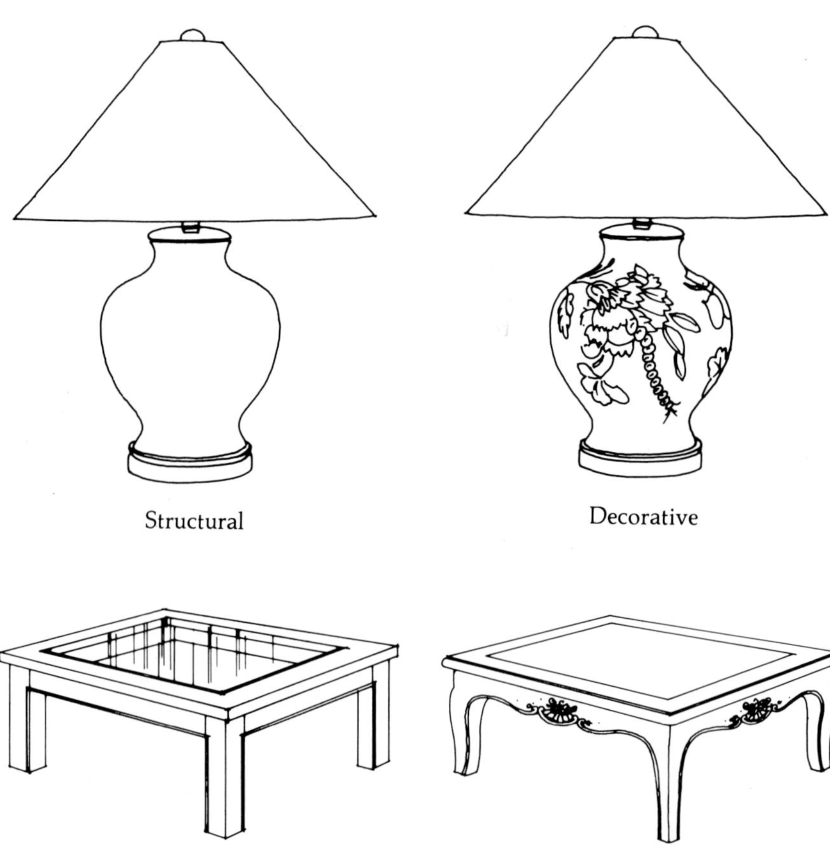

itself. For example, the ancient pyramids of Egypt are structural design because they expose the stone blocks from which they were made. Contemporary architecture, both inside and out, frankly reveals the materials that make up the basic structure, such as wood or metal beams, brick, stone, and concrete. The design of modern furniture is seen in the form itself, such as the metal frame of the Barcelona chair and the molded plastic of a ***pedestal*** table.

The attributes essential to successful structural design are **simplicity, good proportion,** and **appropriateness of materials used.**

Simplicity. Whether the structure itself is to stand as the finished product or is only the supporting element for design, it should be kept simple. If the basic structure—a house, a room, or an accessory—is badly designed, the finished product will not be pleasant. For example, a room with too many or poorly placed openings, arches, and niches will seldom be pleasing until some elimination or simplification has been accomplished.

Good Proportion. Any object that is structurally well proportioned will be intrinsically pleasing, whether it remains plain or is appropriately decorated. When a room is well proportioned, it is a pleasure to plan the interior; one that is badly proportioned is difficult to correct. An upholstered chair with armrests that overpower the rest of the design must often be completely rebuilt for a pleasing effect.

Appropriateness of Materials. Different materials lend themselves to various objects and construction methods. Glass may be blown and intricately decorated by skilled craftspeople, and molded plastic chairs may be turned out by an assembly-line method. Interchanging the procedures and materials for producing an object may not be feasible or may fall short of the desired result. Material selected for a design can contribute to or destroy the success of the finished product. Suitable materials should be selected for the intended purpose without sacrificing the aesthetic outcome.

Decorative Design

Decorative design relates to the ornamentation of the basic structure, which may be achieved through the selection and placement of color, line, and texture. For example, the exterior surfaces of the East Indian temples are completely covered with embellishment. Victorian-style houses often display fanciful decoration added to the structure. Furniture may be handsomely carved to add charm and dignity. In addition to furniture and architecture, fabrics, wallpapers, rugs, accessories, and other furnishings can be attractively enhanced by decorative design.

Four classifications apply to decorative design: **naturalistic, conventionalized** or **stylized, abstract,** and **geometric.**

- **Naturalistic,** realistic, or photographic—in this type of design the motif is reproduced from nature in its natural form. For example, flowers look exactly like flowers as they are seen in the garden.
- **Conventionalized** or **stylistic** design creates a motif taken

Figure 4.2 This room is entirely structural, or devoid of ornamentation—including the tile floor, furniture, architectural background, window treatment, and accessories. *(Courtesy of Thayer Coggin.)*

from nature but adapted to suit the shape or purpose of the object to be decorated. In this case, flowers are recognizable but are modified or slightly changed. This type of design is particularly employed for interior furnishings.

- **Abstract** design departs from nature. The elements, which may or may not be recognizable, are transformed into nonrepresentational design.
- **Geometric** design is made up of geometric motifs such as stripes, plaids, chevron patterns, and zigzags.

The attributes essential to successful decorative design are **suitability, appropriateness,** and **placement.**

Suitability. The purpose for which any item is intended should be immediately recognizable. A lamp should be designed to look like an object for giving light and not like a ***Dresden*** doll holding an umbrella. A salad bowl should look like an article to contain something.

Figure 4.3 In contrast to Figure 4.2, this bedroom has a large-scale floral design with bouquets of day lilies, marigolds, dahlias, and sunflowers that surrounds the room, categorizing it as a primarily decorative interior. *(Courtesy of Van Luit & Company.)*

Appropriateness. Any decoration added to the basic structure should accent its shape and beauty. For example, vertical ***fluting*** on a supporting column will make it seem higher, but crossbars will appear to cut the height and reduce its dignity. Classic figures on a ***Wedgwood***

TYPES OF DECORATIVE DESIGN

Naturalistic

Conventional

Abstract

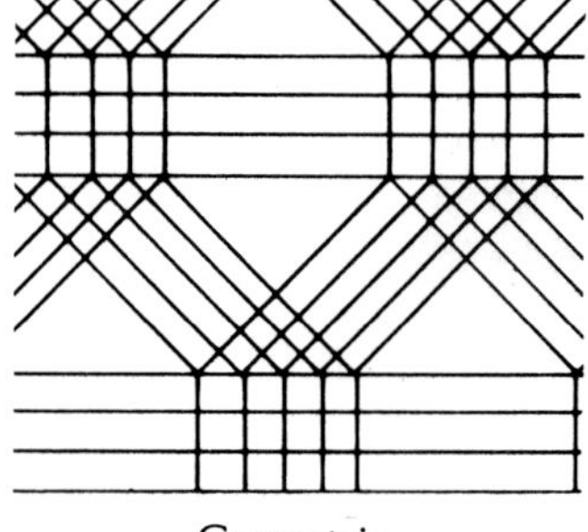

Geometric

DECORATIVE DETAILS

Swag
Antefix
Modillion
Linenfold
Arabesque
Husks
Griffin
Tudor Rose
Volute
Lunette
Wheat
Honeysuckle
Strapwork
Rosette
Quatrefoil
Trefoil
Rinceau
Cartouche
Shell Carving
Diaper Work
Laurel Leaf
Dentil Molding
Spool Bead
Lozenge
Cornucopia
Guilloche
Escutcheon
Urn
Palmette Band
Acanthus
Lotus
Fret
Festoon

(Courtesy of the Seng Company.)

Figure 4.4 A bed framed by bold square pine posts, with a tailored laminated deco-sculptured headboard is an example of structural design. *(Courtesy of The Naturalist.)*

Figure 4.5 With traditional carvings from the Tudor period in England, this bed is an example of decorative design. *(Courtesy of Stuart Interiors.)*

vase will emphasize its rounded contour, but harsh lines will destroy its beauty.

Placement. The embellishment of any item should be placed with purpose in mind. ***Bas-relief*** on the seat of a chair is uncomfortable to the occupant, but such carving on a wall plaque can be attractive, and is more suitable.

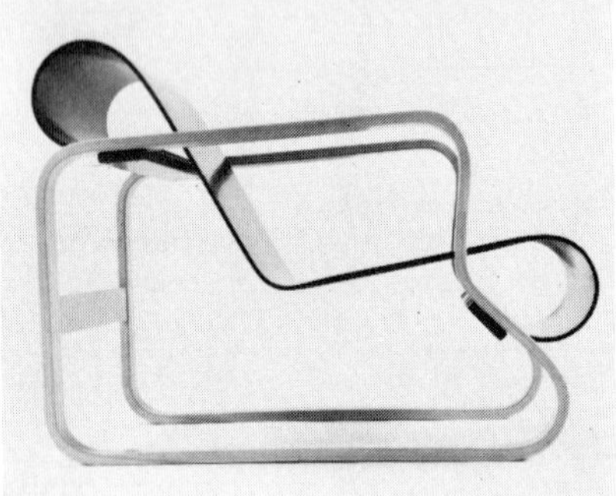

Figure 4.6 The beautifully proportioned Paimio "Scroll" chair of bent laminated wood designed by the Finnish architect Alvar Aalto is an excellent example of structural design. *(Courtesy of ICF.)*

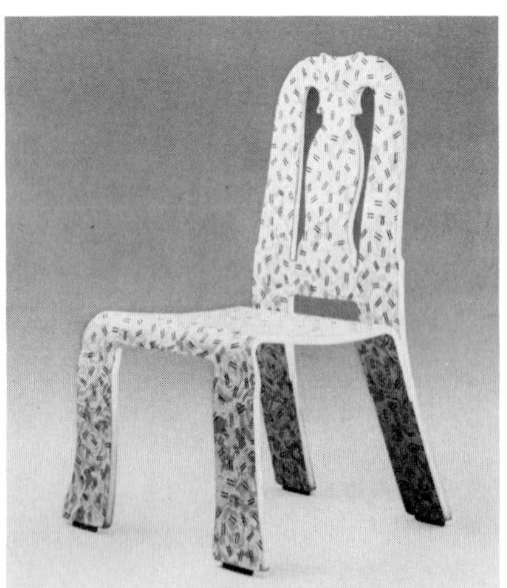

Figure 4.7 An example of a decorative contemporary design is the Queen Anne chair in the Post-Modern style designed by architect Robert Venturi and covered with a quaint all-over pattern. *(Courtesy of Knoll International.)*

The amount of surface decoration should be placed with great care, while keeping the basic structure in mind. The Greek proportions of 3:5, 4:7, and 5:8 are wise to follow (see pp. 111–114). It is usually unwise to embellish exactly half the surface of an object.

Elements of Design

The basic components that make up a total design are known as the elements of design: **texture, pattern, line, form** or **mass, space, color,** and **lighting.** The elements aid the designer when creating a visual environment and are often referred to as *tools.* Organization and arrangement of these elements or tools relate closely to the principles of design.

Texture

Texture refers to the surface quality of objects—the quality that not only can be seen and touched but also can be sensed through memory. For example, the roughness of sandstone, the softness of a deep-pile rug, the smoothness of glass, and the shininess of growing leaves all produce for each of us a peculiar sensation because of our previous associations with these textures. Basically, textures fall into the following categories: **soft, smooth, shiny, dull,** and **rough.** Throughout history, smooth, highly polished surfaces, lustrous metals, and fabrics of satin, silk, and fine linen have been symbolic of wealth and high status, whereas rough, hand-hewn textures and homespun fabrics have characterized homes of peasants and others in lower economic classes. Today this is no longer the case. Many wealthy individuals prefer the handcrafted look, which may well cost as much

Figure 4.8 The dull and rough wood texture of this wall provides an outstanding background for other furnishings. A variety of textures including shiny and smooth surfaces provide variety to the room. *(Courtesy of Gayl Baddeley/Associates.)*

as the most refined look. Additionally, smooth and shiny surfaces have been reserved for formal interiors, while dull and rough textures have been associated with informal treatments. Regardless of style, a knowledgeable use of texture is a sure way to bring character to a room. Textures in the interior environment can often combine several characteristics. For example, a wool carpet can have a soft and dull texture. Properties of and considerations regarding texture include the following.

- **Visual interest, beauty, and character.** Texture has added much visual interest in the environment through the ages. Cave dwellers enjoyed the feel of animal skins under their feet. The early Greeks delighted in the smoothness and beauty of mosaic floors. The people of Persia have always taken pride in the fine texture of their hand-knotted rugs, and the Japanese enjoy the freshness of grass mats called ***tatami.*** Modern interiors particularly depend on the physical impression of texture to create variety and interest. The texture of a certain surface reflects a particular character and unique beauty that provides a physical or psychological impression.
- **Light reflection.** Each texture has a surface quality that affects light reflection. Smooth, shiny surfaces like glass, mirrors, satin, porcelain, and highly polished wood reflect more light than rough and dull textures like brick, concrete, stone, and coarse wood.
- **Maintenance.** Surfaces in the home require upkeep, and a particular texture determines the amount of maintenance.
- **Acoustics.** Textures can absorb or reflect sound. Smooth and hard surfaces tend to magnify sound, and soft and rough textures have a tendency to absorb sound. The sensation of walking through a completely unfurnished room with hard floor surfaces demonstrates a high level of sound. When the same room is furnished with rugs, fabrics, draperies, and other furnishings, the sound is greatly muffled. Designers can control the acoustics of a particular space with wise textural combinations.
- A **combination of textures.** The dominant texture of a room is often established by the architectural background. For example, a room paneled in fine-grained and polished wood or papered in a traditional formal wall covering generally requires furniture woods and fabrics with a smoother and shinier texture than that required of a room paneled with natural coarse-grained wood or constructed of masonry. Contemporary use of texture may break these traditional rules, providing an element of surprise. A combination of textures, whether employed for an avant-garde or conservative environment, will enhance the total visual experi-

Figure 4.9 The primary textural emphasis in this large entry is a shiny and smooth tile floor. Other compatible textures include glass, painted walls, plants, and flowers. *(Courtesy of Arizona Tile.)*

ence. For example, a room may contain the textures of glass, wood, stone, plants, and fabrics, thus providing variety, interest, and character.

Pattern

Pattern is a decorative design, figure, or motif created through the use of line, form, space, light, and color. Pattern, or decorative design, falls into four categories: naturalistic, stylized, abstract, and geometric (see pp. 89–90). Pattern, as opposed to undecorated or plain design, can be effectively employed to create interest in the environment. Too much pattern can make a room too "busy" and uncomfortable, and a room devoid of pattern may be stark and uninviting. The total arrangement of the various components of a room creates an overall pattern, but the more obvious patterns are seen in fabric and wallpaper. Understanding the use and effect of pattern and pattern combinations is more thoroughly covered in Chapter 6.

Figure 4.10 With a profusion of pattern ranging from geometrics to florals, this small sitting room sets the mood for casual country living. *(Courtesy of Country Life Designs.)*

Line

Line is the **direction** of an art creation and is particularly dominant in contemporary art and interiors. The feeling of a composition—a room—is established by the lines that give it motion or repose. Skillful use of line is therefore of utmost importance.

Line can seemingly alter the proportion of an object or of an entire room. For example, in the accompanying illustration, two identical rectangles are divided, one vertically and the other horizontally. The eye travels upward along the vertical line, and the area is made to seem higher. Along the horizontally divided area, the eye is directed across, making the rectangle appear wider. Each kind of line has a particular psychological effect on a room. To achieve the desired result, the interior designer should keep in mind the distinct effects of each line.

- **Vertical lines** tend to provide a feeling of height, strength, and dignity. These lines are particularly evident in the exterior of a building where columns are used and in the interior where upright architectural members are conspicuous, in high pieces of furniture and in the long straight lines of vertical louvres or folds of drapery.
- **Horizontal lines** create a feeling of repose, solidity, and strength. These lines are often seen in cornices, ***dadoes,*** bookshelves, and long low pieces of straight-lined furniture. Falling Water, a famous Frank Lloyd Wright house, is an excellent example of horizontal architecture.
- **Diagonal lines** give a room a feeling of action and movement. They are evident in slanting ceilings, staircases, Gothic

Figure 4.11 A two-story living room has a catwalk that breaks through the space. The emphasis is on the vertical line focusing on the vertical wooden supports on the railing, protruding vertical brick detailing on the fireplace, vertical wood strips on the walls, and the arrangement of upright books. *(Courtesy of Ron Molen, architect.)*

LINE

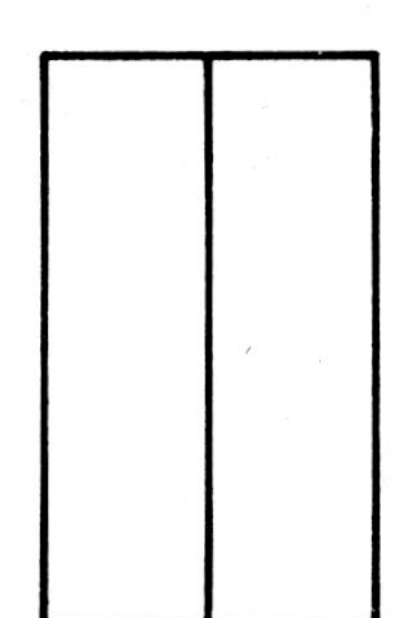

When two identical rectangles are divided differently – one horizontally and one vertically – the proportion seems to change.

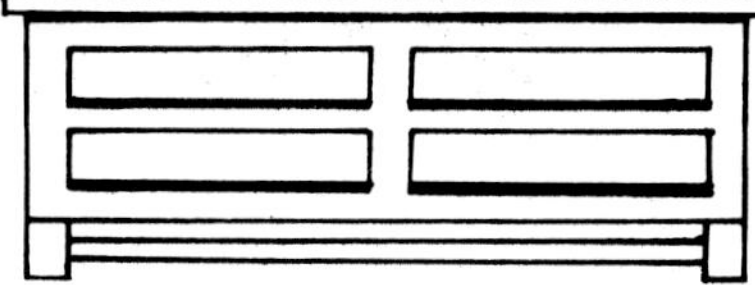

Horizontal lines give a feeling of repose.

Diagonal lines are lines of movement.

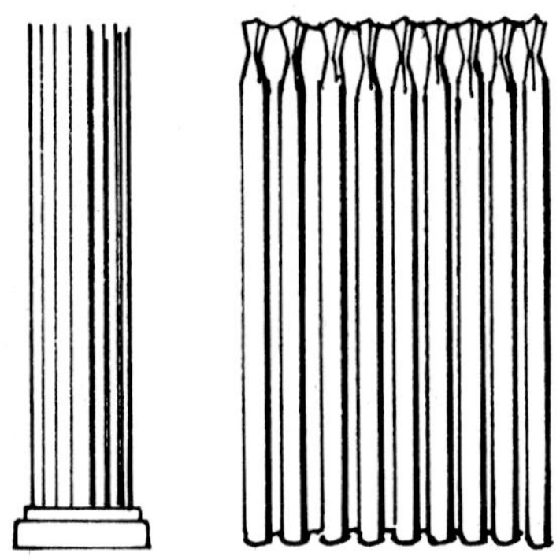

Vertical lines add height and dignity.

Vertical lines emphasize and enhance the basic structure.

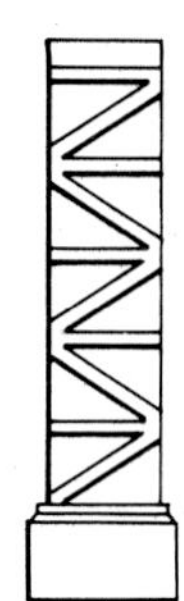

Zigzag lines detract from the basic structure.

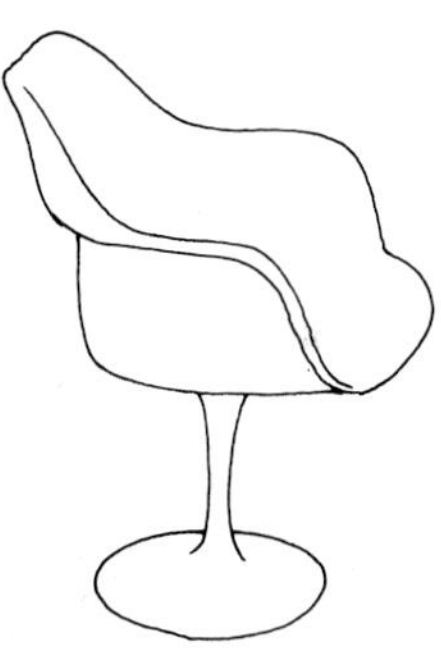

The curved line was employed by Eero Saarinen to create the classic pedestal chair.

Figure 4.12 Strong horizontal forms dominate this living room designed by architect Kevin MacCabe, especially as seen in the window design, fireplace projections, and long, low sofa. These lines are tempered through the use of a few vertical, curved, and diagonal lines. *(Photograph by John Rees.)*

arches, and sloping furniture. Too many diagonals may give a room a feeling of unrest.

- **Curved lines** have a graceful and delicate effect on a room. They are found in arches and other curved architectural treatment, drapery ***swags,*** rounded and curved furniture, and rounded accessories. The ***Taj Mahal*** is a supreme example of graceful architecture primarily employing curved lines. Curved lines fall into four general categories: (1) Large upward curves tend to provide an uplifting feeling. (2) Large downward curves often give a feeling of solidity or even sadness. (This line has been employed by artists to evoke a feeling of mourning or unhappiness). This line may also be very dramatic, especially when used in modern

Figure 4.13 Curved lines are evident in this living room and entry as the eye travels particularly to the circular stairway and rounded sofa. Diagonal lines are embossed into the carpet and seen on the tile, and a few horizontal lines are found on the shutters and accessories. *(Courtesy of Gayl Baddeley/Associates.)*

Figure 4.14 The unusual curving shape of the Pop Ionic chair, formed of soft polyurethane foam, was designed by Studio 65 in Italy and inspired by the ancient Greek Ionic column with the ram's horns or scroll top. *(Courtesy of Gufram.)*

design. (3) Horizontal curves can imply restfulness. (4) Small curves often express lightness and merriment.

Too much line movement in a room may evoke instability. A careful balance of line is essential to the feeling of comfort and harmony in a room. Vertical, horizontal, diagonal, and curved lines with their various psychological and physical properties, as just described, can be employed throughout the home and working environment to provide interest, comfort, and unity.

Form or Mass

The contour of an object is represented by its shape, which is made up of lines. When a two-dimensional shape takes on a third dimension, it becomes form or mass. In the planning of interiors, mass is perceived as objects of furniture that require space and may be moved to various locations. The arrangement of form within a room—furniture arrangement—is discussed in Chapter 10.

Basic forms or shapes fall into three basic categories:

- **Rectangular and square forms** are the most dominant shapes employed for architecture and interior design. They provide a sense of unity and stability, are easy to work with, and may be arranged to conserve space. The use of too many rectangular and square forms may result in severe monotony. By introducing circular and angular forms into the space, this effect can be altered.
- **Triangular forms** have a pointed shape. The diamond shape results when triangles are arranged base to base. Also, a variety of other shapes using the diagonal line may be created and fall into this category. These forms are often seen in sloping ceilings of contemporary homes and motifs applied to fabrics and wallpapers. Also, triangular, diamond, and other diagonal shapes may be used for flooring materials, furniture, and accessories, providing a dynamic effect.
- **Curved forms** include sphere, circle, cone, and cylinder shapes. Curved forms are found everywhere in nature. Even our own bodies are curved. This form is constant, unifying, and pleasing. When used in the home environment, circular forms may be dramatic, like a sweeping curved staircase or domed ceiling or a shape used for accessories like a piece of pottery, a plate, a lamp, a round table, or a sculpture. Curved forms may also give relief and variety to a room with a predominance of angular and rectilinear forms.

Very few homes employ only one shape or form. The environment is most often enhanced by skillfully combining the three basic forms for architecture and furnishings. However, too much variety of form and shape may produce a room with a feeling of confusion. The transition from one object to another as the eye moves about the room should be easy and pleasurable. The emphasis created when a curved form is placed against a rectangular panel, however, may produce a pleasant diversion. For example, a pair of ornately carved Belter chairs against a plain paneled wall in a modern room may provide unexpected and agreeable relief to the otherwise severe lines of the room. The sophisticated combination of forms is currently evident in both modern and traditional styles.

Space

Space is perhaps the most important element of domestic architecture. *Funk & Wagnalls' Dictionary* defines *space* as "an interval or area between or within points or objects." Space may be characterized as the opposite of form or mass. Well-planned and well-organized space makes for a smooth-working home. When walls are erected for a living area, space has been defined—a particular space that can be articulated to create a functional and livable environment for the occupants. Today, most homes lack adequate space, and the challenge of making the most of available space is a prime concern for the designer. By utilizing all the elements of design—line, form, color, light, pattern, and texture—available space can be utilized to create rooms that are physically and psychologically pleasing. Following are some suggested guidelines for achieving this goal.

- Arrange space so the eye can easily travel throughout a room to outside areas like a garden, terrace, or view.
- Employ unobtrusive patterns and textures.
- Use few pieces of furniture, ones that are lightly scaled and placed close to walls.
- Employ colors that are light in value, muted, and cool and that blend with each other. This treatment can visually increase space.
- Use artificial lighting around the perimeter of the room both on the ceiling and with uplighters on the floor. This treatment enhances a small space, giving the illusion of depth.
- Employ wall-to-wall floor treatment and ceiling-to-floor window treatment. Consider simple window treatment that omits heavy draperies, like shutters, shades, and blinds.
- Create the illusion of more space through the use of mirrors.
- Explore the possibilities of open planning, a projecting window, or a skylight.
- Select furnishings with a "see-through" look, like pieces with clear glass, plastic, or caning components. Avoid furniture with bases that are flush with the floor. Instead, select furniture that is up off the floor supported by legs or pedestals or is wall-hung.
- Keep rooms free of clutter, with an occasional empty corner.
- Use a few well-chosen accessories.

When the designer is faced with the problem of space that is too expansive and lacks definition, the preceding guidelines may be effectively reversed. Again, the elements of design may be the tools to achieve the desired outcome. Furnishings can be grouped to provide a pleasing division of space. The challenge of working with a vast space is to create a visually pleasing composition providing a sense of comfort and security suited to human scale.

The arrangement of space within the interior framework of the home

Figure 4.15 A stunning view of the living room from an upper balcony in the Massico Vignelli apartment, designed by Vignelli, provides a vivid impression of the use of space and form. Two classic Barcelona chairs, two large sofas, and a coffee table and freestanding sculpture/dividers are dramatically placed within the space. *(Photograph by Norman McGrath.)*

and working environment is discussed in Chapters 3 and 10, which deal with floor plans and furniture arrangement.

Light

An essential element of interior design for both function and beauty is lighting, which merits special consideration from the initial planning of the house until placement of the last accessory. The lighting needs of each room can most satisfactorily be determined by drawing a floor plan and indicating the location of built-in overhead and wall fixtures, switches, and flexible outlets for portable lamps. **Light for function** is lighting for specific activities like sewing, reading, playing the piano, and typing. This category includes task lighting of all kinds, and the lighting needs of each activity require special attention. **Light for safety** is also an important consideration. Stairways, hallways, basements, attics, porches, and patios all present hazards if not provided with adequate and strategically placed lighting.

Besides lighting for particular tasks and safety, lighting for other household activities deserves thoughtful planning. For example, conversation, dining, and television watching require only a low level of ***diffused light.*** In areas where a large group gathers, light must be at a high enough level to enable the group to see clearly about the room, yet not be so brilliant that it is aesthetically unpleasant.

Light for beauty is a magic tool, and the ways in which today's versatile lighting can be used in beautifying a room are limited only by the extent of the interior designer's ingenuity. The art of decorative lighting can provide warmth and exciting visual interest throughout interior and exterior spaces.

Furnishings and spaces can be specifically defined through **natural** and **artificial lighting,** which ultimately affect our perception of all objects.

Natural Lighting

The source of natural light is the **sun.** Its properties, including ultraviolet light, warmth, and radiant energy, are of utmost importance to people's health and well-being. Today's designer is trained in controlling natural light within a living space to contribute to the occupant's comfort and aesthetic sense. Natural light changes from morning to evening, with light shifting from soft to bright rays. A designer may therefore treat a south- and west-facing room with muted, cooler, and darker colors to counter the sun's afternoon warmth and glaring rays. The designer can also determine the most suitable window treatment for a particular structure considering its position on the site, geographic location, or climate, allowing natural light to enter a space in a manner that will enhance the environment and minimize glare.

Artificial Lighting

Artificial lighting is a man-made source for illumination. With today's versatile artificial lighting created for both function and beauty, designers can fully employ all aspects of ingenuity in illumination. Through the art of lighting, space can be modified; structural elements can be emphasized or subordinated; color and texture can be enhanced; plants, paintings, and other art objects can be brought into focus; and an atmosphere of

Figure 4.16 A large, soaring window over the tub area allows natural light to flood the bathroom, giving a pleasant, livable, and functional element to the room. *(Courtesy of Eduard Dreier, architect, and Guy Dreier and Associates. Photograph by Richard Springgate.)*

cool formality or warm intimacy can be imparted to a room. To accomplish this, the designer should have an understanding of both the aesthetics and techniques of lighting. In most rooms incorporation of a variety of lighting is desirable, because comfort, beauty, and general mood are influenced by the source, amount, and quality of illumination.

Lighting Sources

The term *lamp* is a generic name for a man-made source of light. A lighting unit consisting of a lamp with a shade or reflector (or both) enclosing a light is also called a lamp. The light source within the unit is the globe or bulb. A ***luminaire,*** which is a complete lighting unit such as a ceiling fixture, wall bracket, portable lamp, or a built-in or an applied unit, is also referred to as a lamp. Although light is the illumination or density of luminous flux on a surface, a complete fixture is sometimes referred to simply as light. Artificial light is produced in three basic ways: (1) ***combustion,*** (2) ***incandescence,*** and (3) ***fluorescence*** (or **luminescence**).

COMBUSTION

Combustion is the oldest known method of producing light. Fire used by ancient tribes, oil lamps, wax candles, and gaslights are all methods of combustion. Candles are still widely used, but only as supplementary lighting. Their main value is in the soft glow that sheds a flattering light and bestows an atmosphere of warmth and intimacy.

INCANDESCENCE

Incandescent light comes from the familiar light bulb, in which is sealed a tungsten ***filament*** that glows when heated through the passage of electricity. Incandescent light sources—the most common type—are small, adaptable, and easily controlled. They do not flicker, hum, or cause significant interference with radios or televisions. Although not the most efficient light source, incandescence is the basis of the most effective accent and task lighting, because it permits precise optical control (see illustrations).

REPRESENTATIVE INCANDESCENT SHAPES

General service

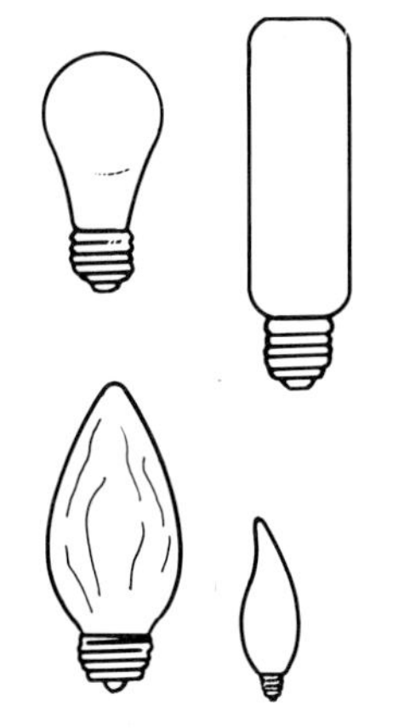

Decorative

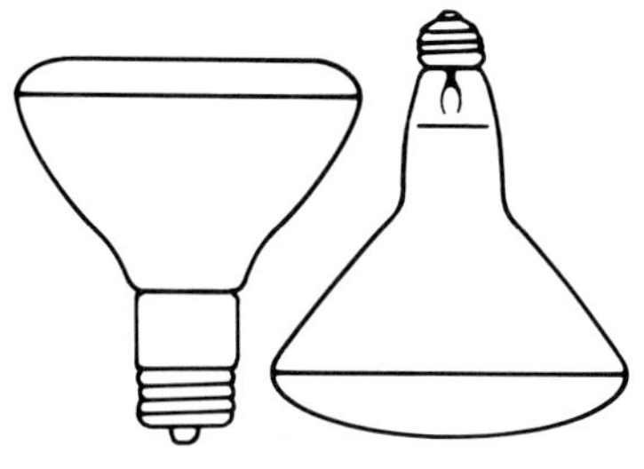

Reflectorized

FLUORESCENCE (OR LUMINESCENCE)

Fluorescent light, the luminescent light most often used in homes, is produced in a glass tube lined with a fluorescent coating, filled with mercury vapor and argon, and sealed at the ends by cathodes. When gases are activated by an electric current, ultraviolet rays stimulate the phosphorous bulb coating, which in turn emits visible light. Fluorescent lamps emit less heat, use less energy, and last longer than incandescent lamps. Their sources are also larger and create broader areas of light. The most commonly used cool white lamp produces a cold light many people consider unflattering. Tubes are available in other fluorescent colors, however, including warm white and warm white deluxe, which blend with incandescent light to create a more inviting atmosphere. Fluorescent tubes are made straight, U-shaped, circline, and ciclete (see illustrations).

Fluorescent lighting can be used successfully for ambient lighting, and incandescent lighting can be

FLUORESCENT TUBES

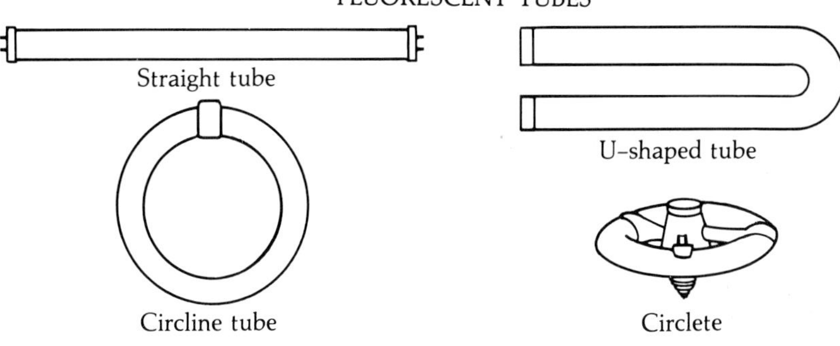

Straight tube

U-shaped tube

Circline tube

Circlete

FLUORESCENT SHAPES

Outdoor light

Bug light

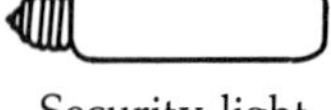
Security light

Night light

DIFFUSERS

Bowl

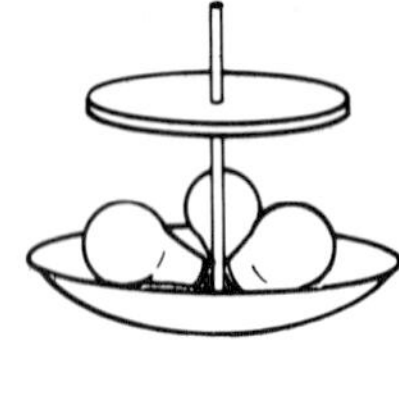
Shallow dish

Figure 4.17 Ambient (or general) lighting in this living room is provided by recessed ceiling lamps that illuminate the entire room, reduce sharp contrast between task lights, and bring a comfortable level of lighting. *(Courtesy of General Electric Company.)*

used effectively for specific locations and decorative accents. When mixing incandescent and fluorescent lighting, a warm white or warm white deluxe fluorescent should be used. Built-in lighting can be direct or indirect, warm or cool, harsh or soft, bright or dim. With strategically placed hanging fixtures and an occasional floor or table lamp, harshness, glare, and strong contrasts of light can be avoided and comfort can be achieved.

Types of Lighting

The three main types of lighting are (1) **ambient** (or **general**), (2) **task,** and (3) **accent.** A fourth type—**mood lighting**—can fall within the accent and ambient categories.

Ambient or General Lighting

Ambient lighting spreads an overall luminosity and reduces harsh contrasts between pools of concentrated light. Ambient lighting can be produced by large area light sources; by a number of small sources focused to ceilings, walls, and drapery brackets; by direct or indirect light; or by chandeliers, downlights, and reflected light from portable lamps. Soft general lighting may be relaxing, but too much indirect or reflected light can be harsh and uninviting. When recessed lighting is used for general illumination, lamps with aluminum reflectors will provide almost twice as much light as ordinary "white cans."

Task Lighting

Task lighting is functional and localized for a particular activity such as sewing, reading, writing, preparing food, or grooming. Task lighting is usually placed near the activity, but aimed to avoid glare and distributed evenly over the working surface to minimize shadows. Most tasks of a concentrated nature, especially when prolonged, require a high level of illumination. This can be achieved by the use of pendants, recessed lights, track-mounted fixtures, and shielded fluorescent tubes either hanging,

Ambient lighting

Task lighting

Figure 4.18 An over-the-sink lighting design, consisting of exposed bulbs within a custom-designed upright case in this bathroom, provides efficient task lighting and casts a warm glow on the bronze mylar patterned wallpaper and other surfaces. *(Courtesy of The Jack Denst Design, Inc.)*

TABLE 4.1 *Recommended ranges of light levels for some activities*

ACTIVITY	PROLONGED DURATION	INCANDESCENT	FLUORESCENT
Craft work	Moderate to high	75–200 w	30–55 w
Dining	Low	40–60 w	16–22 w
Entertaining	Low to high	40–200 w	16–55 w
Grooming	High	150–200 w	40–55 w
Hand sewing	High	150–200 w	40–55 w
Ironing	High	150–200 w	40–55 w
Kitchen and laundry	High	150–200 w	40–55 w
Machine sewing	High	150–200 w	40–55 w
Reading musical scores	Moderate to high	75–200 w	30–55 w
Reading	High	150–200 w	40–55 w
Television viewing	Low to moderate	40–100 w	16–44 w
Writing	Moderate	75–100 w	30–44 w

placed under shelves or cabinets, or wall mounted above and on each side of a mirror. Placement, shade design, socket location, and shielding all contribute to controlling glare and supplying good light. Additionally, the choice of lamps or tubes will determine the quantity of light (see Table 4.1).

Figure 4.19 Artistic placement of accent and ambient lighting in this Brooklyn, New York apartment, designed by Stanley Jay Friedman, highlights the conversation area. Pools of light wash the walls, and interestingly placed art brings life to an achromatic gray scheme. *(Courtesy of Stanley Jay Friedman. Photograph by Peter Vitale.)*

Accent Lighting

Accent lighting employs a concentrated beam of light focusing on a particular object or area. A highly flexible lighting tool, accent lighting can be placed at any angle and be controlled precisely to provide the desired amount of intensity and color to emphasize one area and subordinate others. This type of lighting can separate one area from another, highlight a treasured item, establish a focal point, and create a touch of drama. Accent

Accent lighting

lighting, which is often combined with ambient lighting, can be produced by recessed, surface-mounted, track-mounted, or portable fixtures.

Methods of Artificial Lighting

The two basic methods of artificial lighting are (1) **architectural** and (2) **portable,** or **nonarchitectural.**

Architectural Lighting

Architectural lighting is closely correlated with the structure of the room and should be included in wiring plans of the original house as an integral part of the complete design. This method supplies lighting fixtures or ***luminaires*** for both function and beauty and is particularly suited for contemporary living. The flexibility of architectural lighting, however, can be fairly limited, considering the various functions that take place in a room. In terms of general types, **wall lighting** includes a variety of fixtures permanently located on a wall surface. Other fixtures are mounted and attached at the **ceiling.**

Wall Lighting

- ***Valance lighting*** is positioned over windows. A horizontal fluorescent tube is placed behind a valance board, and the light reflects off the ceiling and also shines on the drapery, thus producing both direct (downlight) and indirect (uplight) lighting.
- ***Bracket lighting*** is similar to valance lighting, but it is placed either high on the wall for general wall lighting or low for specific tasks such as washing dishes, cooking, or reading in bed. When used in living areas, the length of the bracket should relate to the furniture grouping that it serves.
- ***Cove lighting*** placed near the ceiling directs all the light upward and gives a feeling of height.
- ***Canopy lighting*** is a canopy overhang providing general illumination. This lighting is most applicable to bath and dressing rooms, but it may be

SIX TYPES OF ARCHITECTURAL LIGHTING

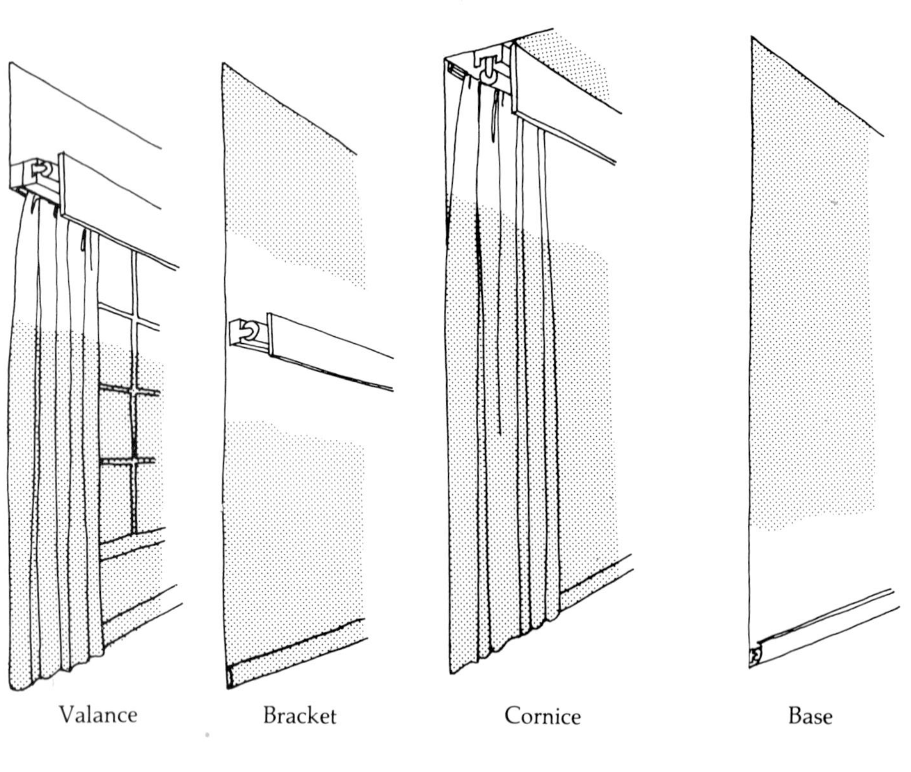
Valance Bracket Cornice Base

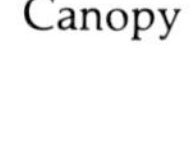
Canopy

Cove

used for a particular purpose in other rooms.

- ***Sconces,*** or lighting fixtures permanently attached on the wall, may be modern or traditional in style and can provide direct or indirect lighting. Sconces can substitute for lamps that require floor or table space.
- ***Luminous wall panels*** are a type of recessed lighting inside the wall that can be purely functional or used to create a dramatic effect.

Luminous wall panels create pleasant vistas.

Ceiling-Mounted or -Attached Fixtures

- ***Cornice lighting*** is usually installed at the ceiling and directs the light downward only. This lighting can provide a dramatic effect for drapery, wall covering, and artwork. When used over a window, it eliminates the black mirror effect at night.
- ***Soffit lighting*** consists of enclosed light attached to the ceiling and designed to provide a high level of light directly below. Excellent for bathrooms, this light is also effective in niches, such as over built-in desks and sofas.
- ***Luminous panels*** consist of recessed light diffused through ceiling panels and used primarily in kitchens, utility areas, bathrooms, and office spaces. They may partially cover the ceiling or extend over the entire ceiling area.

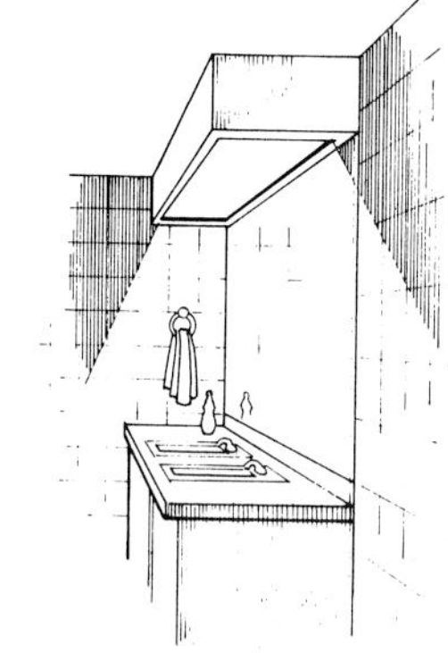

Lighted soffits provide high-level light wherever needed.

Figure 4.21 Functional task lighting for grooming is amply furnished by a well-placed soffit. *(Courtesy of General Electric Company.)*

Figure 4.20 Custom-designed cornice lighting in combination with architectural fixed ceiling downlighters focuses attention on a unique wood bed and cabinet arrangement. A wall downlighter accents an abstract painting over the bed. *(Courtesy of Ron Molen, architect.)*

Luminous ceilings provide a skylight effect.

Figure 4.22 A luminous ceiling casts a diffused light throughout the room and illuminates shadows, which makes this lighting particularly efficient for kitchen use. *(Courtesy of General Electric Company.)*

- ***Recessed downlights,*** including eyeballs and wall-washers, may spotlight a definite object or produce general lighting when used in sufficient numbers (see Figure 4.23). The eyeball type is adjustable and can be focused in any direction.
- ***Track lighting*** consists of a track mounted to the ceiling (also may be mounted vertically to a wall) and comes in a broad array of sizes, shapes, and finishes. Fixtures clip anywhere along the track to create a precisely designed optical system with a vast range of lighting effects. Layout configurations are infinite, and consumers can choose from an abundance of fixtures that are economical, easily installed, and highly energy efficient. Track lighting is a total lighting system that is virtually unlimited in flexibility and versatility to meet the needs of contemporary homes, whether traditional or modern in style.
- ***Suspended fixtures,*** which are suspended or dropped down from the ceiling, are available in numerous flexible designs. This lighting type can be effective when ceilings are particularly high or designed simply for

Figure 4.23 In this spacious private residence, designed by Gayl Baddeley and William Fleming, recessed architectural downlights are placed at appropriate intervals to illuminate the entire area. *(Courtesy of Gayl Baddeley/Associates.)*

Figure 4.24 Designer Robert Brain has run a track with lighting fixtures over a long dining table that is reflected in a mirrored wall butted up against the table's end. The adjustable fixtures cast light down upon the table where needed. *(Courtesy of Robert Brain.)*

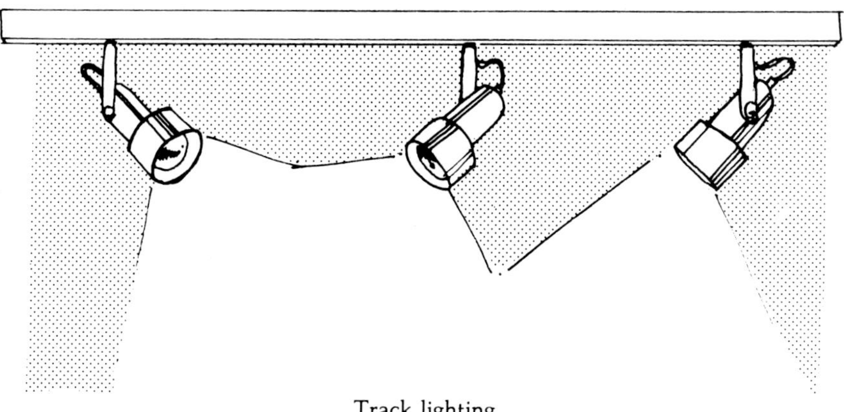
Track lighting

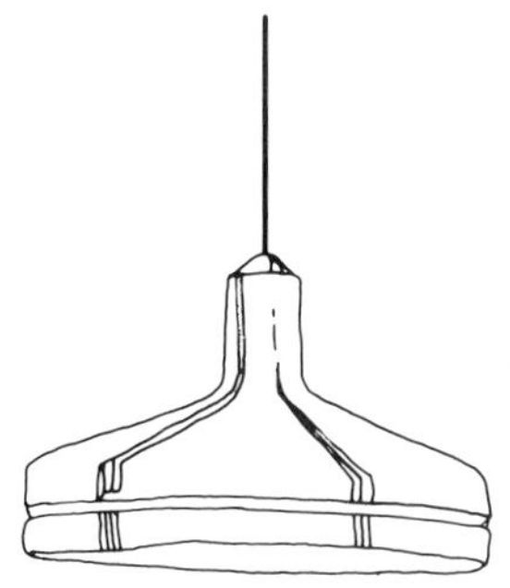

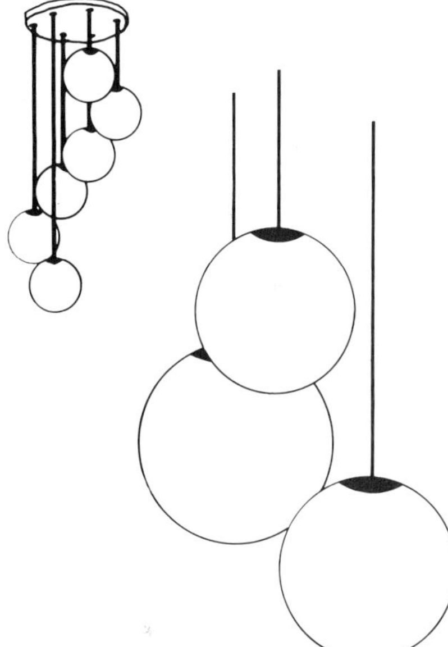
Pendant lighting

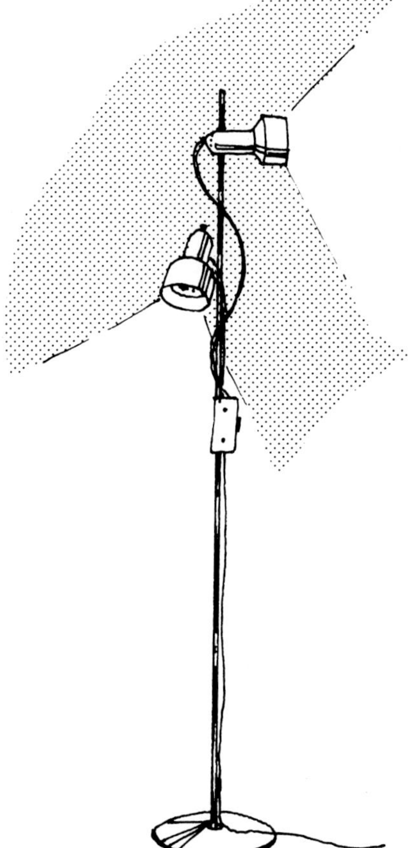
Vertical track lighting

Wall light
or bracket

function and visual appeal. One popular type of suspended fixture is the ***chandelier.*** When hung in an 8-ft-high dining room, a chandelier should be suspended approximately 30 in. above the table and raised 3 in. for each additional foot of ceiling height. Chandeliers must be high enough for clearance if they are hung in rooms in which people move about.

- ***Flush-mounted lighting,*** as opposed to recessed, refers to surface-mounted fixtures that may project a few inches into the room and that reflect direct or indirect lighting, depending upon the design and use. The most common flush-mounted fixtures are simple glass shapes

Figure 4.25 The famous Artichoke hanging light fixture was designed by a pioneer of lighting design, Poul Henningsen, in Denmark. The fixture has a layered design of projecting forms that allow the light to filter through in a fascinating manner. *(Courtesy of Poulsen Lighting Inc.)*

Figure 4.26 The large, adjustable curve of the Arco floor lamp, designed by Achille Castiglioni in 1967, allows light to focus downward wherever the lamp is placed. The dramatic effect has been favored by designers for use in various interior spaces. *(Courtesy of Atelier International.)*

Figure 4.27 Another classic lamp is the Tizio, designed by Richard Sapper in Germany during the 1970s. The flexible lamp—which is available in a floor or table model—can be adjusted to a number of positions and is a popular choice for both contract and residential design. *(Courtesy of Artemide.)*

Figure 4.28 The Nesso lamp, sometimes called the "mushroom" because of its distinctive form, was designed in Italy. It is made of plastic and comes in a variety of colors and in two sizes. The graceful lamp sheds a soft light from four small interior bulbs. *(Courtesy of Artemide. Photograph by Aldo Ballo.)*

Figure 4.29 The jar form of swelling proportions is based on one from the Six Dynasties period (265–617). Like the original, it is hand thrown with bands that accent the shape, is incised with flowing lines, and has freely modeled lugs. *(Courtesy of Design-Technics.)*

centered on the ceiling, but other such figures include wall-washers, eyeballs, and numerous modern styles.

Custom-designed architectural lighting is lighting created for a particular purpose or design effect. Often this type is incorporated into built-in or stationary furniture and architectural features in a unique manner. ***Base lighting*** is a type of lighting that may be used in dark hallways and in the base of steps as a safety device.

Portable or Nonarchitectural Lighting

The term *portable lighting* indicates the ability to transport lamps from location to location as desired, considering the purposes they serve and the area in which they are used. Portable lamps (both table and floor models) are the oldest forms of interior lighting. They provide flexible lighting in the residential or working environment and may be purely functional, decorative, or both.

- Although portable lamps often function as a secondary light source, their **placement** in the room is important. They generally should be positioned as part of a furniture grouping, near an electrical outlet, and out of the line of traffic.
- Lamps for **function** should be chosen with the definite task in mind. For example, a table lamp used for reading is most effective when the bottom of the shade is at eye level of the person seated—38 in. to 42 in. above the floor. The **shade** works well when at least 16 in. across the bottom so that the lamp will shed light on more than just the reading area and thereby prevent eyestrain caused by a sudden change from light to dark. When the shade is lined with white, maximum light is provided and glare is eliminated when the shade covers the bulb and fixture.
- A soft white bulb will provide the best **light diffusion.** An opal glass diffuser bowl will also improve the quality of light, and a flat dishlike diffuser can soften and mask direct light from horizontal bulbs.
- The **scale and proportion** of a lamp should be considered in relation to other furnishings and to the size of the room and the lamp itself.
- **Decorative lamps** generally work best when the design is simple, unobtrusive, and enhancing to the room's style and design. Overelaboration in both the base and shade often attracts more attention to the lamp than desired.
- **Structural lamps** devoid of ornamentation are popularly employed by both professional designers and home owners. A room's success is enhanced when structural lamps are (1) simple, (2) well proportioned and suitably scaled, and (3) constructed of materials and textures that complement the room's style.

Direct and Indirect Lighting

Direct lighting is light thrown directly onto a particular area, resulting in shadows and sharp contrast between dark and light. Downlights of all kinds yield direct lighting. They may have an ambient glow over a large area or may be concentrated on a specific object.

Indirect lighting is a luminaire directed from a source that is usually hidden on the ceiling or another surface and that reflects the light back into the room. Indirect lighting tends to expand space visually and when reflected from the ceiling provides general illumination, resulting in few if any shadows. Like the sun at midday, however, indirect lighting tends to be flat and in most cases needs to be supplemented by portable lamps. Indirect lighting can also be used to dramatize a particular area or object and create a soft and exotic mood. Concealed floor spotlights placed behind grilled windows or directed upward on a plant can create fantastic shadows.

Direct and indirect lighting can be produced by portable lamps with open tops, particularly those with ***opaque*** shades that direct light both upward and downward. Some fixtures are specially equipped to direct most of the light upward, some direct most light downward, and still others distribute the light more evenly.

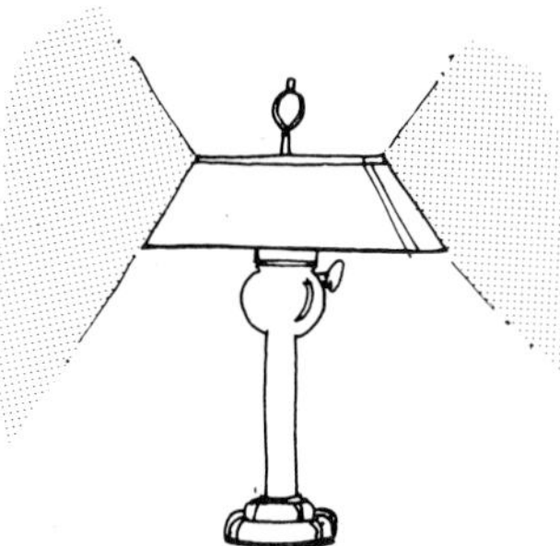

Portable lamps; direct and indirect light

Indirect lighting for a touch of glamour

Switches and Outlets

The convenient location of switches and outlets is essential and must be indicated on the blueprint and electrical plan of the structure. Each room requires a light switch which may or may not control both built-in and portable lamps. Switches may conveniently be placed on the latch side of each access door to provide immediate illumination on entering and serve as a reminder to turn them off when leaving. Switches are also necessary at both ends of hallways and at the top and bottom of stairways. Where task lighting is necessary, switches placed within easy reach are practical. Dimmers on switches allow great flexibility for various levels of lighting—ideal for creating a preferred mood.

Throughout interior spaces, outlets should be ample and suitably installed for specific tasks. Easily accessible outlets for appliances in kitchens and utility areas and electrical equipment in bathrooms require special attention. When a room's function is determined, outlets can be conveniently located. Outlets placed at regular intervals, approximately 3 to 6 ft apart between doorways and floor-length windows, will decrease the need for hazardous extension cords. Outlets mounted 12 in. from the floor and switches located 50 in. high provide a workable placement. Where heavy mechanical devices are power driven, special heavy-duty outlets should be provided. It is necessary for outdoor outlets to be weatherproofed, made ground-fault interruptible, and situated safely.

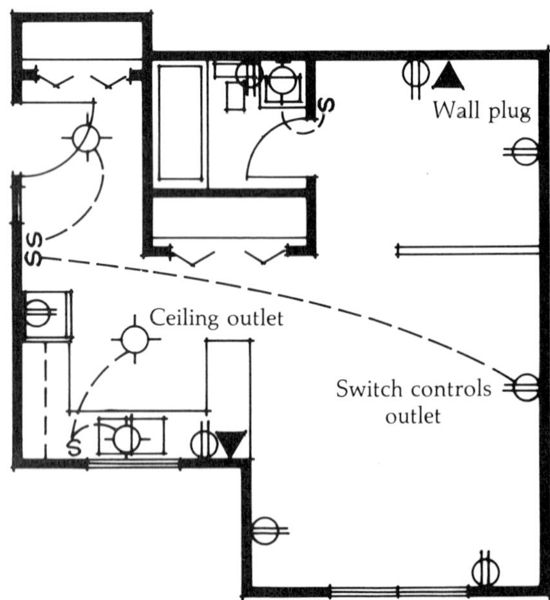

A floor plan indicating the wiring and location of electrical outlets and switches. This information aids the designer in determining functional furniture arranging.

Lighting for Specific Areas

Through the art of creative lighting, aided by today's new and wondrous technology, one can bring light to everyday activities and endow various areas of a house with safety, efficiency, beauty, and individuality.

- The **entrance hall,** as the keynote to the decor of a home, can provide a cordial air of hospitality where lighting plays an important role. During the day, the entry hall should be bright enough to allow a reasonable transition from the bright outdoors to the darker interior. Illumination need not be a high level at night, but it should be strong enough to enable entering guests to see and be seen. Modern or traditional ceiling-mounted luminaires plus suitably placed wall sconces or portable lamps that diffuse light will provide adequate lighting and a pleasant atmosphere. Staircases should be well lit so that treads and risers can be distinguished clearly. The entrance is an ideal place to try a dramatic lighting effect such as an accented art object or plant.
- **Living rooms** need soft general lighting supplemented by special area lighting. Both direct and indirect lighting sources are desirable, although an excess of indirect lighting may result in a washed-out appearance. Well-chosen lamps at necessary locations will add a feeling of comfort and hospitality conducive to pleasant conversation. When accented by downlights, built-in shelving, display cases, and art objects help to personalize a room and establish its focal point. For reading, studying, playing the piano, and other similar activities, lighting should be direct and combined with general lighting to avoid strong contrast (see Figure 4.28).
- **Family and recreation rooms** accommodate a variety of activities and thus require particularly flexible lighting. General lighting is essential, with area and task lighting supplied for specific activities. Television viewing is most comfortable when lighting is general and at a low level with no strong con-

Figure 4.30 Planning for lighting in a kitchen demands adequate light sources for such tasks as preparing and serving meals and cleaning up afterward. In this stimulating red, black, and natural wood kitchen, recessed lighting in the ceiling faced with red strips provides good overall lighting for the function. *(Photograph by Norman McGrath.)*

trasts or glare. The television screen itself reflects light and contributes to the total lighting effect. In a recreation area planned for table games, Ping-Pong, dancing, or other physical activities, a high level of illumination that does not interfere with these functions is preferable.

- **Dining areas** deserve versatile lighting around the table area that can be adjusted for a variety of functions in addition to formal and casual dining, such as studying, sewing, and playing games. A low-level background can be provided by general lighting techniques. A chandelier or pendant using incandescent globes and hung over the table about 22 to 30 in. above the table will add sparkle to silver and glass at formal meals. Dimmer controls will allow for a change of mood, and added light from candles will shed a flattering glow to skin tones. Today, there are other modern—and often dramatic—lighting alternatives designed for use over the dining-table area. Dining rooms can display added lighting interest through lit china closets, built-in niches, or uplighters spotting plants and art objects. If the dining space is part of or open to other areas, ingenious lighting can successfully set it apart.

- **Kitchens and utility rooms** function best when generous overall lighting for safety and efficiency is planned. Ceiling or close-to-ceiling fixtures such as recessed or flush downlights, track lighting, or illuminated ceiling panels will give adequate general light and eliminate shadows. Recessed or shielded fluorescent tubes over work areas and under top cabinets will help prevent accidents, speed up food preparation, and enhance the decor. Task lighting is especially necessary in the mixing, cooking, and sink centers. Warm white or warm white deluxe tubes will give red objects and meat a pleasing color. The table area should have pleasant and adequate lighting for eating and possibly studying activities.

- **Bedrooms** should have comfortable and pleasant general lighting with appropriate task lights for reading, desk work, grooming, and other activities, depending on the uses of the space. Direct lighting is also efficient when placed over chests of drawers, in closets, close to seating, and over beds. Dim circulation lighting for safety at night is a basic requirement.
- **Bathrooms** require shadowless lighting for shaving and grooming, which can be supplied by light from overhead and from both sides of a mirror and by light reflected upward from a light-colored basic or counter top (see Figures 4.16 and 4.18). Mirror lighting is usually sufficient to illuminate an average-sized bath or powder room; however, general lighting overhead and over tub areas is preferable.
- **Halls and stairways** require overall illumination for safe passage. Fixtures may be recessed in or hung from the ceiling, attached to walls, built in near the baseboard for hallways, or supplied by a combination of two or more of these methods. Stairways should have a lighting source clearly visible at the top and bottom areas as a safety factor.
- **Outdoor lighting** at night enhances gardens, decks, patios, walkways, and other outdoor living areas and can bring visual pleasure from the interior. Additionally, outdoor lighting helps alleviate the black glass look inside by balancing and extending the lighting to the outside. Weatherproof luminaires of all types for outside use are available and can be attached under the eaves and on exterior walls. Custom lighting often includes exposed and concealed fixtures, placed at various important areas of the garden, that throw light upward, downward, or in both directions on trees, plantings, a garden sculpture or fountain, a gazebo, and other garden features to create a visually exciting experience. Since the front door conveys the first impression of a home, exterior lighting can be set off by fixtures that have eye appeal and conform to the style of the house.

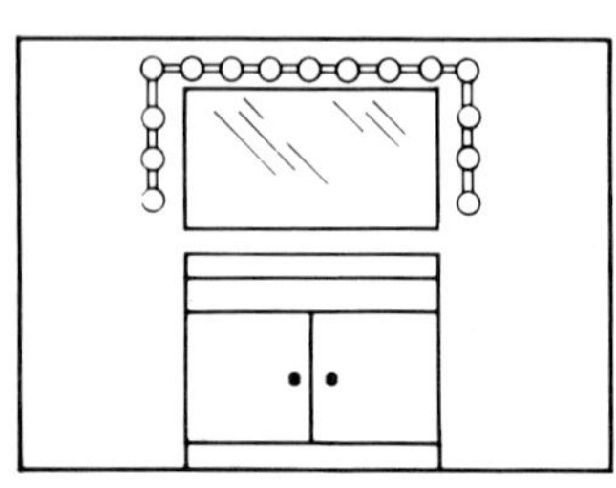

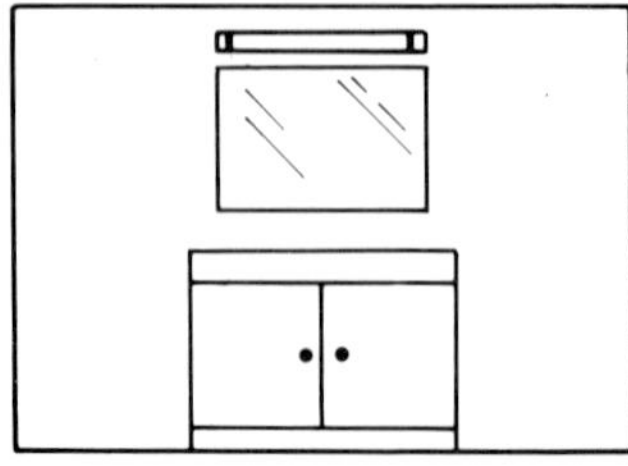

Bathroom light for grooming

Light Control

Since humans are psychologically and physically affected by light, it is an important factor when planning interior spaces. A designer has the means available to control natural and artificial light through a variety of resources. Glaring light is disturbing and hampers most activities within an interior area, and bland or inefficient light can actually result in physical fatigue. Designers can alleviate lighting problems by controlling the light source and causing the light to be reflected, absorbed, or redirected. This goal is achieved through consideration of all aspects of lighting and other elements and principles of design.

Lighting for Energy Conservation

Knowledgeable planning and purchasing can give a home sufficient lighting and still save watts and dollars. The following guidelines can help conserve energy in lighting.

- Lighting should fit specific needs. Since task areas such as kitchen counters require more light than nonworking areas such as circulation space, lighting should be chosen accordingly. Sufficient light is important, but using more light than necessary wastes electrical energy.
- Dimmers that lower the voltage are useful in adjusting light levels.
- Installing multiple switches makes it possible to use only the amount of light required in a specific area.

- Fixtures should be energy effective. Light should be placed where it is needed, instead of trapped or scattered wastefully. Fixtures that can be adjusted and moved when necessary are a wise choice. Track lighting has great flexibility and permits the light to be directed where it is wanted.
- A reflectorized lamp is good for accent or task lighting. Low-voltage spotlights are especially effective where a tightly controlled beam is required.
- Light sources should be efficient. Light output is measured in ***lumens*** or ***footcandles*** per watt, and each type of light source varies in efficiency according to wattage and color. Fluorescent lamps use as much as 80 percent less energy, produce 5 to 30 times as much light, and last 20 times longer than incandescent lamps.
- Three-way incandescent lamps allow for selectivity in the amount of light needed.
- Where appearance is not a consideration, as in garages and basements, industrial reflectors are an economical option.
- Ceilings, walls, floors, and furniture should have light-colored finishes. Rooms done in dark colors absorb light and may require much more lighting than those done in light-reflecting colors.
- Keeping reflectors, diffusers, and lamps clean will help to maintain lighting equipment.
- Lights should be turned off when not needed.

Measuring Light

Light is measured four different ways, which should be considered when planning lighting needs for a specific area.

- **Footcandle:** the unit of measure for the amount of light falling on a particular surface
- **Lumen:** a measure of light flow produced by one lamp—for example, a new 75-watt incandescent bulb produces 1,180 lumens.
- **Footlambert:** the unit of measure of the amount of light perceived as coming from a surface
- **Candela:** the unit of measure for the intensity of light or brightness coming from a particular light source

The topic of light is discussed further in Chapter 5.

Color

Color, considered the most important element of design, is covered in detail in Chapter 5.

Principles of Design

The goals of a successful design, whether for a single object or a total exterior and interior environment, include function or utility, economy, beauty, and character (discussed in Chapter 3). Through the centuries certain timeless principles have evolved through careful observation of both nature and art. When these principles of design—balance, rhythm, emphasis, scale, proportion, and harmony—are thoughtfully considered and sensitively applied, they contribute to achieving the goals of design. The elements of design discussed in the first part of the chapter are the "tools" employed by the designer to accomplish the desired outcome.

Although there are no absolute rules when creating a design project, most interiors are enhanced by adhering to these basic guidelines. Understanding these principles is one means through which a designer can achieve excellence, whether the design involves a painting, a room, or an entire house. Although some successful contemporary designs violate these time-tested principles, understanding them is central to the interior designer's creativity and is essential for a beginning designer.

Proportion and Scale

visual weight

Proportion

Proportion encompasses both the relationship of one part of an object to the other parts or to the whole, and the relationship of one object to another—both aspects involving shape or form. Proportion has been a major concern to creative minds through the ages. Although no absolute formula for good proportion works in all design projects, the early Greeks over 2,000 years ago discovered some secrets of good proportion and set down rules that students of design have accepted and incorporated into their art compositions for centuries.

Figure 4.31 The exquisite proportions and refined decoration of Flight crystal from Block China Corporation are well suited to the material. *(Courtesy of Block China Corporation.)*

- The Greeks found that the square was the least pleasant proportion for an enclosure and that the rectangle was better. Their standard for good proportion was a rectangle or oblong with its sides in a ratio of 2:3. This shape is called the ***golden rectangle.*** The ***golden section*** involves the division of a line or form in such a way that the ratio of the smaller portion to the larger is the same as that of the larger portion to the whole. The progression 2, 3, 5, 8, 13, 21, 34, and so on, in which each number is the sum of the two preceding numbers, will provide a close approximation to this relationship. For example, 2:3 is roughly the same ratio as 3:5, 5:8 is roughly the same ratio as 8:13, and so forth. Another pleasant space relationship is 4:7. By multiplying any of these combinations of figures, the interior designer can plan larger areas with similar relationships.

Perhaps the most important application of these proportions in house planning and furnishing lies in the relationship of sizes or areas. These proportions can be applied when planning the dimensions of a room or when selecting a piece of furniture for a particular area. For example, if the length of the living room measures 25 ft, a desirable width would be 15 ft. This measurement is determined by using the following process. Since the length of the living room (25 ft) is divisible by 5, the 3:5 ratio may be used. If

$$\frac{\text{width}}{\text{length}} = \frac{3}{5} = \frac{W}{25'}$$

then W would equal 15.

In another example, a piece of furniture 4 ft long would be a good size to place against a 7-ft wall space. These dimensions have the desirable ratio of 4:7.

GREEK PROPORTIONS

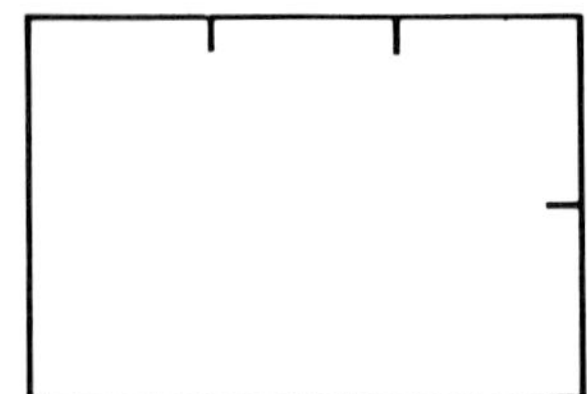

The golden rectangle. The Greek standard for good proportion is a rectangle with its sides in a ratio of 2:3.

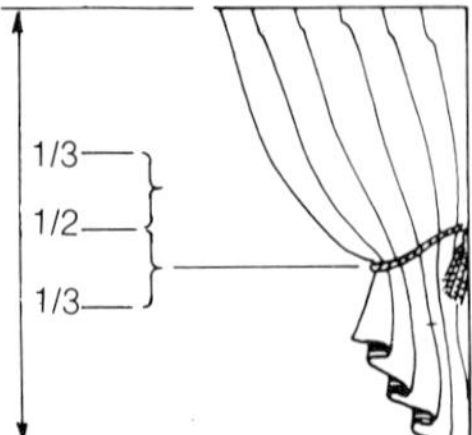

The golden mean. The division of a line somewhere between one half and one third is the most pleasing.

The Parthenon at Athens—based on a mathematical ratio of 1:1.6—fits almost precisely into a golden rectangle. Because of the frequency with which it occurs in the arts, the golden rectangle has mystified experts for centuries.

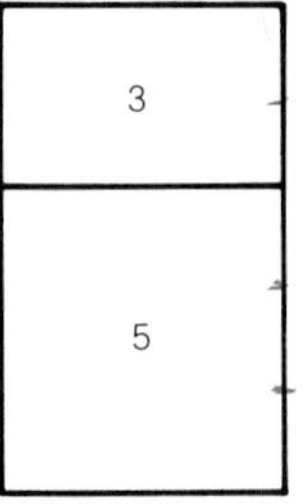

The golden section. 3:5 is roughly the same ratio as 5:8.

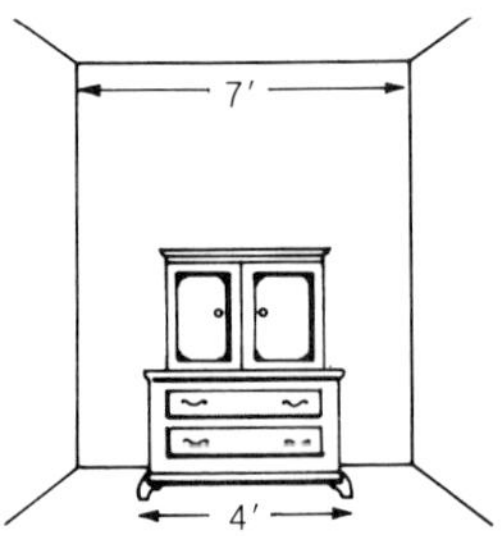

4:7 is a pleasing proportion.

- Another Greek discovery was that the division of a line somewhere between one-half and one-third its length is the most pleasing. This division is still retained as a ***golden mean*** and can be applied when planning any wall composition, such as determining the height for a mantel, tying back drapery, or hanging pictures, mirrors, or ***wall sconces.***
- The Greeks also discovered that odd numbers are more pleasing than even ones. A group of 3 objects to 3 is more pleasing than 2:2 or 4:4, and 2:3 is better than 2:4. An application of this might be when selecting pillows for the sofa or arranging pictures on a wall.

Scale

Scale refers to the overall **size** of an object or its parts compared with other objects or their parts, regardless of shape. A house is large, but it may be large or small in scale. A table is a smaller item, but

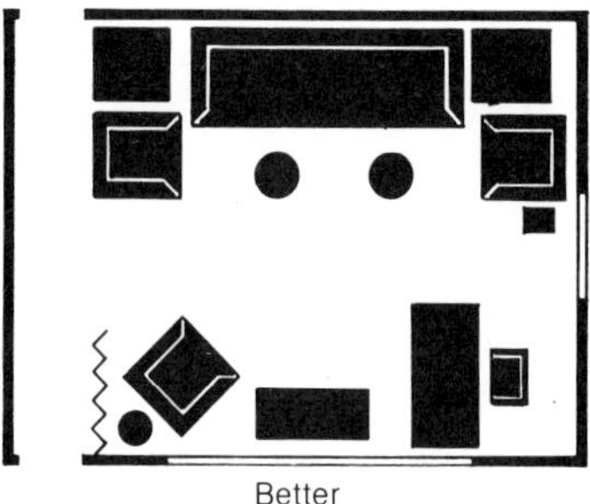

Furniture should be in the right scale for a room.

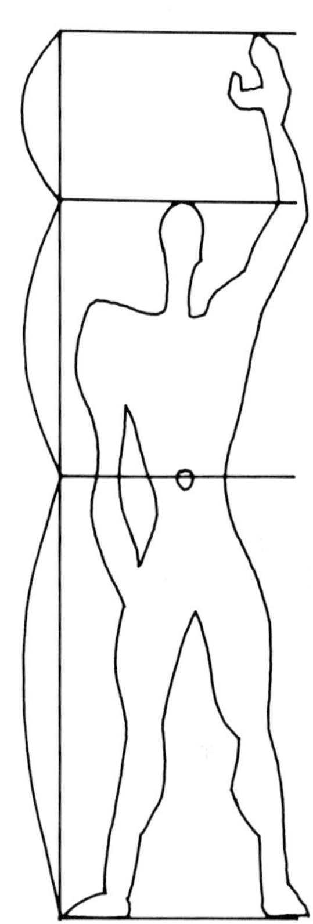

Le Corbusier planned his architectural projects to be consistent with the proportions of his human Modular (*right*). The same ideal proportions can be applied to the famous marble statue of the Apollo Belvedere of ancient Greece or Rome (4th or lst Century B.C.) (*left*).

it may be large or small in scale. It is only large or small when compared to another object.

- The correct use of scale and proportion is important to the success of a house and its furnishings. Yet, because scale is a relative quality, mathematical correctness is not the solution, because weight and measurement will not always produce a feeling of rightness. For example, two love seats may have the identical overall dimensions, yet may not look compatible if one has heavier arms and shorter legs than the other.
- Interior design deals with size relationships geared to human scale, which determines the design of homes and furnishings. Considering that human beings usually weigh between 100 and 200 pounds and are between 5 and 6 ft in height, an interior environment can be planned and scaled accordingly. Successfully scaled rooms and furnishings make adults and children feel comfortable—they are not too large or too small, but well suited to the occupants.
- Good scale and proportion begin with the choice of the house on the lot and must be taken into account until the last accessory is chosen and put in place. A tiny house on a spacious lot will look lost, and a large house will look cramped and uncomfortable on too small a plot of ground. The size of trees and shrubs, carefully selected, can complement the overall plan.
- The material used in construction should be in scale with the house itself. For example, a Cape Cod cottage would not look right made of large cinder block. The heavy material is not compatible with the refined scale of this particular home style.

Figure 4.32 The beautiful lines and proportions of the highly acclaimed Barcelona chair, designed by Mies van der Rohe in 1929 for the Barcelona Exhibition, has made the modern piece a timeless classic. *(Courtesy of Knoll International.)*

Figure 4.33 The proportions of this room are well suited to the scale of furniture, large patterns, and other elements used to enhance the size relationship of each item to the whole. *(Courtesy of Gayl Baddeley/Associates.)*

PERCEPTION

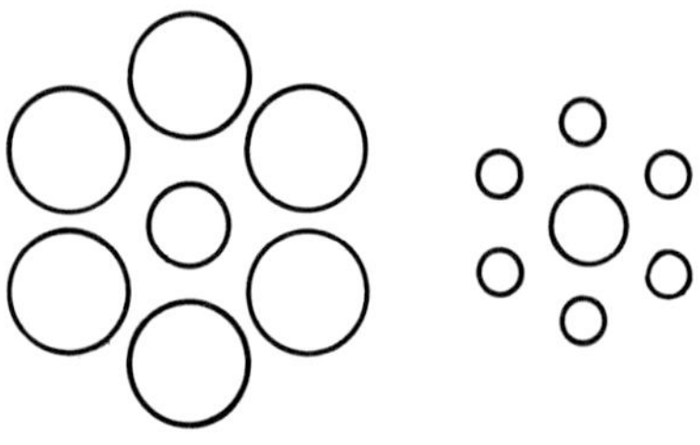

The center circles in the above diagrams are identical. The apparent change in size is due to the difference of the surrounding circles.

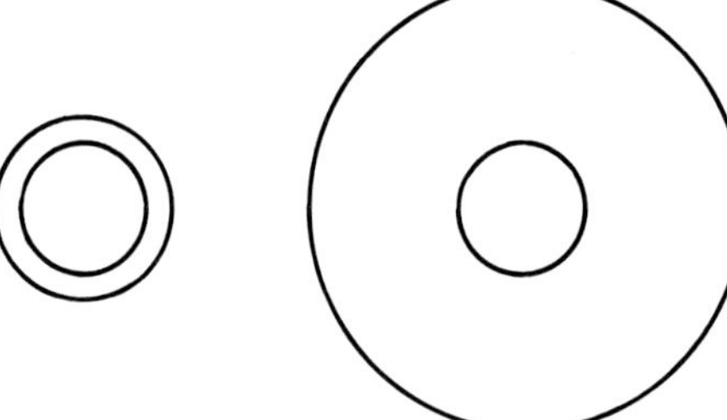

The center circles above are identical. The apparent change is due to the difference in size of the surrounding area.

- Architectural features on the exterior of the house should be carefully designed and located. Because the door is the focal point of the facade, perfect scale is of utmost importance. Windows that are carefully positioned and suitably scaled and proportioned will provide an overall pleasing effect.
- An object is perceived in relation to the area around it. Objects that are too large will crowd a small room and make it appear smaller; furniture that is too small will seem even smaller in an oversized room. When surrounded by small-scaled furniture, a large piece of furniture will appear larger than when surrounded by large-scaled pieces. A small table with spindly legs placed at the end of a heavy sofa or chair will look out of place, and a large-scaled table placed near a dainty chair will not be enhanced. Combining large and small components in a room can often enhance all of the components through the effective use of contrast.
- Accessories such as mirrors, pictures, and lamps need to be scaled for the items with which they are to be used. A lamp generally must not overpower a table, nor should it be so small that it looks ridiculous. The lamp shade also requires a suitable scale for the base.
- Not only form but also color, texture, and pattern are important in the consideration of scale and proportion. Coarse textures, large patterns, and bold colors will cause the object on which they are used to appear larger than an object with smooth textures, small patterns, and soft, light colors. Whatever attracts the eye seems larger. Through the skillful use of these and other principles, the apparent size and proportion of rooms and objects may be altered. The decor of a room succeeds largely through knowledgeable use of the principles of design.

Balance

Balance is that quality in a room that gives a sense of equilibrium and repose. It is a sense of weight as the eye perceives it. Generally, human beings have a need for balance in many aspects of their lives, and in the interior environment, balance is necessary to achieve an atmosphere of comfort and pleasantness. The three types of balance are ***bisymmetrical, asymmetrical,*** and ***radial.***

Bisymmetrical, or Formal, Balance

Bisymmetrical balance is that in which identical objects are arranged equally on each side of an imagi-

BALANCE

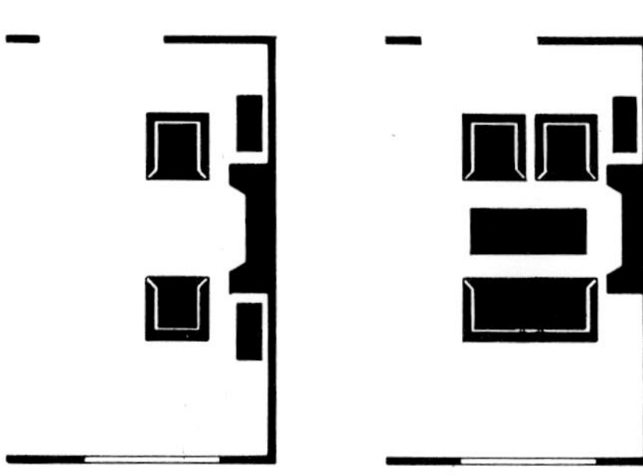

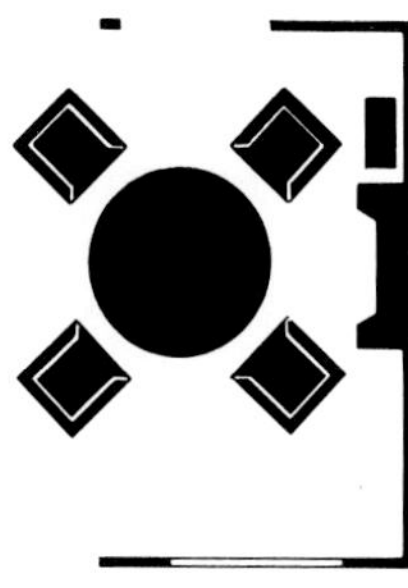

Figure 4.34 The shuttered windows, sofas, and pillows designed for this seaside dwelling are placed bisymmetrically around an Oriental carpet. Accessories on the coffee table are arranged asymmetrically, providing variety to the composition. *(Courtesy of Pinecrest, Inc.)*

nary line. This type of balance has the following characteristics:

- Often employed in traditionally styled environments
- Predominantly formal and dignified in feeling
- Contrasts with nature, since much in nature is asymmetrical
- Conveys a restful and peaceful sensation, since this type of balance is easily perceived and appreciated

Asymmetrical Balance

Asymmetrical balance is more subtle than bisymmetrical balance, and it is often referred to as occult or optical. It requires more thought and imagination, but once achieved, remains interesting for a longer time. In this type of balance objects of different sizes, shapes, and colors may be used in an infinite number of ways. Two small objects may balance one large item, a small, shiny object may balance a larger dull one, a spot of bright color may balance a large area of neutral color, and a large object moved closer to a central point may balance a smaller one pushed farther away. No measurement will indicate at what point these different items must be placed. The point at which balance is achieved must be sensed. General aspects of asymmetrical balance include the following:

Figure 4.35 Asymmetrical balance is seen in this bathroom with the countertop placement of a box, soapdish, sculpture, and plant. *(Courtesy of Gayl Baddeley/ Associates.)*

- Predominant in modern interiors
- Tends to be informal
- Generally more active than symmetrical balance
- Is more compatible with nature
- Provides a more spacious appearance

Radial Balance

With radial balance all elements of the design radiate from a central point like the spokes of a wheel radiating out from the hub. This balance is most often seen in a room where chairs surround a round table, in flower arrangements, and in chandeliers. Radial balance is often a visually pleasant

Figure 4.36 Radial balance is seen in the design of the hanging lamp—radiating outwards from the top of the cord. Five chairs around a circular table and five table settings placed around a central bowl are excellent examples of this type of balance treatment. *(Courtesy of Atelier International, Ltd.)*

alternative and combines effectively with the other two types of balance.

Other Considerations Involving Balance

The architectural background including doors, windows, paneling, and fireplaces, along with all accompanying furnishings, can be effectively arranged to provide a feeling of equilibrium. Some considerations include the following:

- Opposite walls and interior spaces and objects should have a comfortable feeling of balance through the pleasant distribution of high and low, and large and small objects.
- Most rooms need both bisymmetrical and asymmetrical balance.
- When furnishings are positioned above eye level, they will appear heavier than items positioned below.
- Bright colors, heavy textures, unusual shapes, bold patterns, and strong lighting will readily attract attention and can be manipulated to achieve balance within a space.
- Large furnishings in a space can be complemented by placing them by small items, and vice versa, creating a refreshing contrast.

Rhythm

Rhythm is an intangible component of a composition. Rhythm to most people suggests a flowing quality, but in interiors it is something that assists the eye in moving easily about a room from one area to another. This principle can be achieved through ***repetition, opposition, transition, gradation*** or ***progression, radiation,*** and ***contrast.*** By effectively creating rhythm, a room can have continuity and interest.

Repetition is rhythm established by repeating color, pattern, texture, line, light, or form. For example, in a particular room a color in the upholstery fabric of a sofa can be repeated on a chair, the drapery, and a pillow, thus introducing rhythm. Too much repetition—or in some cases too little repetition—can produce confusion, monotony, or a lack of stability. Repetition is a common means of achieving rhythm in a room because it is a relatively easy approach.

Opposition, a type of repetition, is found in a composition wherever lines come together at right angles (as in the corners of a square window frame). Other examples might include where a straight fireplace lintel meets an upright support or wherever a horizontal line of furniture meets a vertical architectural member.

Transition, still another type of repetition, is rhythm found in a curved line that carries the eye easily over an architecture element, such as an arched window, or around items of furnishings, like drapery swags or a circular chair.

- **Gradation or progression** is rhythm produced by the succes-

TYPES OF RHYTHM

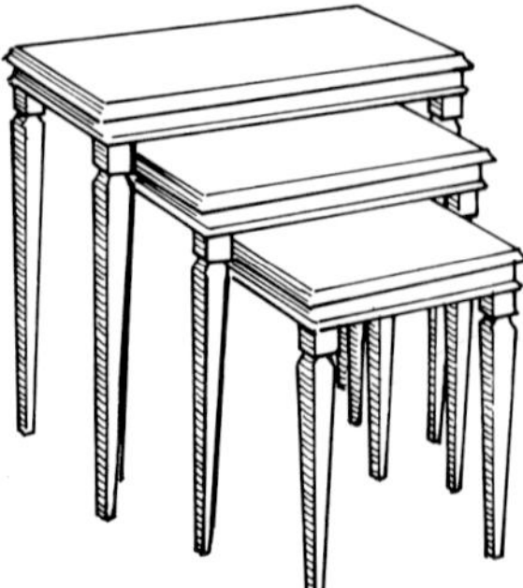

Gradation

Repetition

Transition

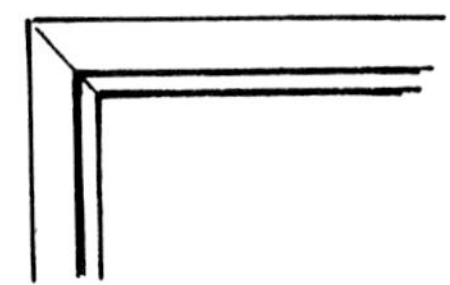

Opposition

Radiation

Figure 4.37 Rhythm is particularly achieved in this living and dining area through the repetition of color, rectangular forms, and the diagonal line. The lamps, chandelier, and plants all radiate outwards from a central point, providing a continuing rhythm in the room. *(Photograph by Lincoln Allen.)*

Figure 4.38 A contemporary Santa Fe Style house features a prominent fireplace brought into focus through the use of form, color, texture, and space. *(Photograph by Peter Paige.)*

sion of the size of an object from large to small or of a color from dark to light. Examples include the progression of one step up to another step; the gradation of a small salt container to a medium-sized sugar container up to a large flour container; and a rug that might have a dark border, a medium inner border, and a light interior area.

- **Radiation** is a method of rhythm in which lines extend outward from a central axis. This pattern is usually found in the accessories of a room, such as in lighting fixtures or a bouquet of flowers, but it also may be seen when furnishings or architecture radiate outward from a central core.
- **Contrast** is achieved when opposites are placed in close proximity, arousing the visual senses; for example, placing white against black or a rough texture against a smooth one, or putting a square glass piece on top of a cylindrical coffee-table base. Contrast can also be achieved by putting an ornately carved antique against a simple structural wall—currently a popular treatment in the contemporary home.

Emphasis

Emphasis in a room refers to the **dominant** and **subordinate** components of a room or to the focal point and supportive furnishings of this center of interest. In every well-planned room, it is effective to have one feature repeatedly draw the eye. This emphasis or focal point can bring a feeling of order and unity into a room, with all other groupings subordinated to it. When a lack of emphasis in a room exists, boredom and an uninteresting space can result. When there is too much emphasis (i.e., more than one or several centers of interest), chaos and unrest can result. Analyzing a room and determining what components to emphasize and subordinate can be a challenging task. A general approach includes viewing the room in four basic levels of emphasis and then determining what components will be featured.

- **Emphatic.** These features may include a dramatic view, fireplace, or architectural feature. For example, if a fireplace is very prominently placed and designed, it naturally becomes a focal point; in addition, a burning fire radiates warmth, movement, color, and hospitality—a natural site for a main seating arrangement. Many rooms may not have an emphatic feature.
- **Dominant.** In many instances, this is the level where most

Figure 4.39 Emphasis in this modern living space is centered around a comfortable conversation area and a soaring fireplace with a recessed niche. *(Courtesy of Ralph Edwards, architect.)*

designers begin. In the absence of dramatic features in a room, a dominant focal point may exist or be created. A fireplace in this case may not be an architecturally dramatic feature, but it certainly can be played up and designed to dominate a room. Other dominant features might include a wall of books, a composition of paintings, a beautiful piece of furniture, or a garden view.

- **Subdominant.** This category includes the level of furnishings that support the focal point and might include large pieces of furniture or the window, ceiling, and floor treatment. Of course, if the designer has elected to have the window or floor coverings and furniture treated so that they dominate a room, these items would move up to the dominant category.
- **Subordinate.** This level will most often include accessories in a room like lamps, plants, art objects, and small furnishings. Accessories chosen with discrimination can be artistically arranged and can give importance and individuality to a room in a unique and supportive way.

This method of analyzing a room and breaking it down into various levels of importance can aid the designer; however, great flexibility is possible. Furnishings and architectural features can be rear-

EMPHASIS

The fireplace in a room becomes the natural focal point. When the television is placed in the same wall, it utilizes the convenient furniture arrangement.

A corner window with a pleasant view may be the room's focal point.

ranged within this framework depending on the desired outcome—in other words, the designer can determine what components will be emphasized and subordinated.

As emphasis in a room is planned and even manipulated through the use of the elements of design, it is essential that a pleasing relationship exist between all the parts and that one supports the other. Whatever the choice for a focal point, it can be important but not overpowering. Although some elements dominate, it is necessary that the eye be allowed to move easily about the room without one aspect completely controlling the environment. The room is enhanced when the elements are linked to other furnishings within a space.

Color is probably the most important element by which a grouping may be brought into immediate focus. Color can be used artfully in achieving the desired amount of emphasis.

Form usually involves arranging of furniture within the space—placing furnishings so they focus on the point of emphasis. Also, unusual or strong form employed for furnishings or architectural background can be dominant or even dramatic.

Texture—whether rough, smooth, shiny, or dull—can help draw the eye to a particular item. The designer may employ this tool to create dominance or to allow a component in the room to blend into the background.

Lighting can be used creatively to tie the group together, dramatize, attract attention, or create a focal point.

Harmony

Harmony is an essential ingredient in any well-designed room. A unifying theme—a **common denominator**—should run through all the component parts and blend them together. Two goals are combined to create harmony: **unity** and **variety.** Exteriors and interiors are pleasing when there is a pleasant relationship that provides unity, yet the aspect of variety is essential to provide interest. **Harmony results when all other principles of design come into play, aided by**

Figure 4.40 A harmonious neutral color scheme is used for the sofas, ceilings, and carpeting, contrasted by two French chairs covered in a blue and white checkered fabric. Light and dark blue pillows, flowers, and ceramics artfully accent the design. *(Courtesy of Gayl Baddeley/Associates.)*

Figure 4.41 The elements and principles of design have been thoughtfully combined in this family room. The texture of wood, stone, leather, and pebble concrete is especially effective, and the accessories are conveniently and aesthetically placed. *(Courtesy of Ron Molen, architect.)*

the basic elements of design. Following are some of the most common and important considerations when seeking a harmonious living environment:

- In every room, the **interior architecture** is a determining factor. Just as the exterior and interior architecture should be consistent, the furnishings of a room must also be in harmony with the background. For example, molded plastic chairs do not especially belong against formal eighteenth-century paneling, nor is a classic Louis XVI chair particularly pleasing against a heavy block wall. A surprising juxtaposition of seemingly unrelated objects may occasionally add relief, but this practice requires sophisticated judgment.

- **Furniture** in the room should seem to belong there. Whether the room is large or small, furniture should be scaled accordingly. Whether the architectural background is strong—perhaps with exposed beams and masonry construction—or more formal and refined, the furniture should reflect the same feeling.
- **Colors** appropriate to the style and scale of furnishings should be considered; however, great flexibility in color usage is prevalent in today's interiors, creating a refreshing alternative. A sensitive approach to color harmonies in relationship to furnishings, background, and style is of utmost importance in achieving a unified result.
- The **texture** of surfaces (i.e., smooth, rough, shiny, or dull) is a determining factor in the success of a room's harmony. Textures should be compatible with the design and style of all furnishings. For instance, a heavy homespun fabric is generally not suitable on a highly formal Queen Anne chair, nor is delicate silk damask usually at home on rough-hewn ranch oak.
- A **window treatment** can contribute to the room's total harmony, and planning a hard or soft line treatment suitable for the theme and style is essential. For example, ruffled cottage curtains are out of place in an Oriental-style house, and elegant silk damask swags are inappropriate for a rustic cottage.
- Carefully selected **floor coverings** help unify the scheme. Hard floor surfaces like wood, tile, and stone are extremely versatile and enhance most living areas. Area rugs, such as Persian Orientals, are at home in any decor, and wall-to-wall carpeting can tie an entire room together. The designer is wise to consider the resilience, texture, color, style, and pattern, if any, when selecting the most harmonious floor treatment.

  Additionally, hard and soft floor coverings should be chosen with purpose in mind. If a room does not function well for the occupants, it cannot be considered harmonious. For example, white wall-to-wall carpet seems inappropriate for a well-used family room, and a heavily textured stone in a bedroom would be uncomfortable for most occupants.
- Consistency or harmony is best achieved by carrying out a basic **theme** or **style.** The basic style need not be followed slavishly, but an effort to maintain a general feeling of unity throughout is wise. Basic themes usually fall into the categories of **formal modern, informal modern, formal traditional,** or **informal traditional.** This allows the designer to combine good design from many periods with one theme dominating. Within this overall theme, an occasional surprise to give variety and interest can provide charm and individuality.
- **Accessories** can pleasantly enhance a room or completely destroy the desired effect. If an accessory is not beautiful, useful, or meaningful to the person using it, it does not belong. The final touches added to a room reveal individual personality more readily than any other items of furnishing and cannot be overlooked in creating rooms of beauty and interest. Items that are essentially good, however, can lose their charm when not well used. For example, a gracefully scrolled wrought-iron wall sconce can add much to a room of Spanish or Mediterranean styling but would look heavy and out of place in a pastel room with delicate furnishings (see Chapter 11).

ASSIGNMENT

The following is an assignment aimed at promoting an awareness of the many principles and elements involved in the complete design of a room.

Select a *clear colored* picture of a living room. The view should be complete, not just a corner view. Mount the picture on white paper, allowing a margin sufficiently wide for answering question 1. Write the answers to the remaining questions below the picture.

1. Point out the following by drawing a line from the correct object or objects in the picture to the explanation in the margin:

An example of structural design
An example of decorative design
The use of the golden mean (explain briefly)
A vertical line
A horizontal line
A curved line
A diagonal line
An example of bisymmetrical balance (explain briefly)
An example of asymmetrical balance (explain briefly)
Rhythm by repetition
Rhythm by gradation
Rhythm by opposition
Rhythm by transition
Rhythm by radiation
Rhythm by contrast

2. Is there a predominance of one line, or are lines pleasingly distributed?

3. Are the elements of the room more strong or more delicate—or is neither effect predominant?

4. What kinds of designs are used in the fabrics in the room (e.g., naturalistic, conventional, abstract, geometric)? If the fabrics have no design, point out two specific textures used.

5. What is the focal point of the room? Point out four ways through which elements were used to bring this area into focus (see the section on emphasis).

6. Does the room have a feeling of unity and harmony? Examine the room carefully: backgrounds, furniture, fabrics, and accessories. Point out six specific elements of the room that contribute to the overall feeling of unity (see the section on harmony).

7. Does the lighting appear to be adequate? Are lighting fixtures and lamps artfully and conveniently located?

Make comments specifically related to picture submitted. Selection and presentation will be considered in evaluating this project.

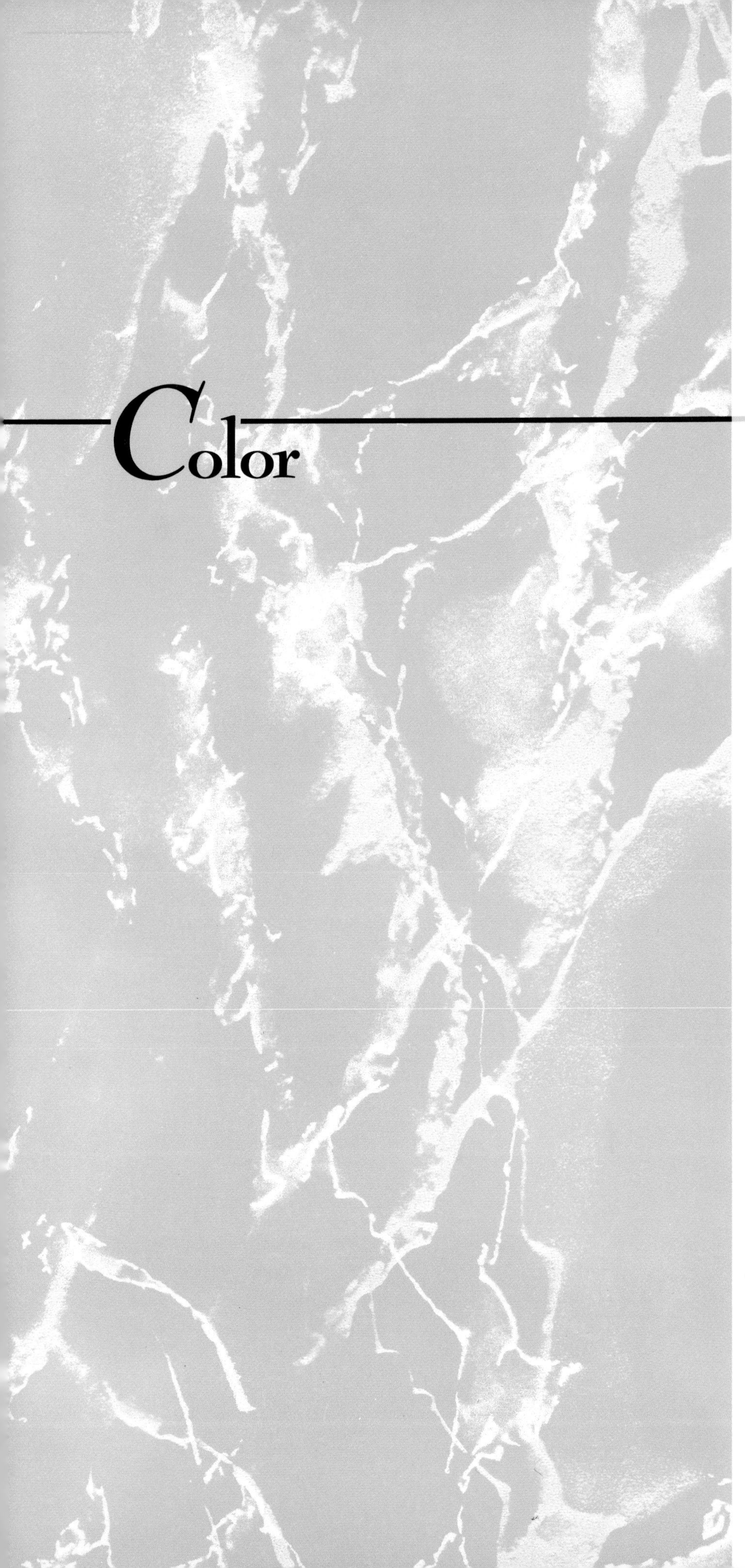

Color

Chapter Five

Color, like music, is an international language. Throughout the world, birds, animals, trees, flowers, jewels, signals, and many other objects are identified by their coloring. The red-breasted robin, the green pine tree, and the blue sapphire look much the same wherever they are found. A red signal is recognized everywhere as a warning of danger, a green signal as an assurance of safety.

Color has always had symbolic importance. In early China, yellow had religious significance and remains today the imperial color. In early Greece and Rome, red was believed to have protective powers. Purple was the imperial color of the ancients and was restricted for the use of nobility—hence the term *royal purple.* When the remains of Charlemagne (742–814) were disinterred in the middle of the twelfth century, the coffin contained robes of sumptuous purple velvet. To the present time, purple is identified with royalty.

Among English-speaking people, many colors signify certain character traits, and expressions using color names have specific meanings commonly used and understood. When someone has the blues, the interpretation is that the person is unhappy or depressed. When a person has a green thumb, the meaning is an unusual ability to make plants grow. Other common color expressions and descriptive associations include

yellow	cowardice, deceit
blue	honesty, masculinity, loyalty
pink	femininity
red	courage, martyrdom, anger, danger
white	purity, cleanliness, sterility
gray	penance, gloom
black	mourning, sorrow
green	envy, peace, security, safety
gold	royalty, wealth
purple	royalty, nobility, opulence, worship
brown	masculinity, stability, warmth, security

Figure 5.1 Soft blue-green and mauve walls provide a stunning background for the owner's art collection. The antique bronze European chandelier dates back to the eleventh century. Deep tones of the Oriental rug provide a rich color base. *(Courtesy of Walter Cowie, designer. Photograph by Lincoln Allen.)*

Color in History

Color has revealed much about the civilizations of people in both primitive tribes and highly developed cultures, but perhaps the greatest value of color is its power to create beauty. Since the dawn of history, humans have toiled to bring beauty into their environment through the use of color. Following are some of the most important cultures that have had a significant influence on color use through the centuries:

- **Ancient Egypt.** The ancient Egyptians adorned the walls of tombs and temples with brilliant hues of blue, tangerine, green, and ***carmine.***
- **Ancient Greece and Rome.** The great temples and dwellings of Greece and Rome were decorated with colored marble and mosaic floors, brightly painted walls and ceilings, and richly colored tapestries and silks. Particularly associated with ancient Italy are gold, blue, and a dull red called Pompeian red.
- **Medieval Europe.** The great cathedrals of medieval Europe, with their gloriously colored stained-glass windows, brought beauty into the drab lives of a downtrodden people and remain today as supreme creative achievements of Western culture.
- **Renaissance.** During the Italian Renaissance, the vibrant reds, greens, golds, and blues used by the master artists were carried into the sumptuous villas of the reigning families in Italy and later into the great palaces of France, Germany, and England.
- **Louis XV and *Rococo.*** With the rococo extravagance of Louis XV in France, where feminine tastes had a great influence, colors became less vibrant. Madame du Pompadour and Madame du Barry highly influenced the use of lighter colors. During the latter part of the eighteenth century, when Marie Antoinette dominated the court of **Louis XVI,** colors became even more delicate and softly pastel. Throughout the late seventeenth and eighteenth centuries, when France dominated the arts of the Western world, French colors were in vogue wherever beauty and luxury were cherished.
- **Eighteenth-Century England and America.** This elegant period in England is well known for its great cabinetmakers—Chippendale, Hepplewhite, Sheraton, and the Adam brothers. The first half of the century witnessed the Chinese influence in the use of rich reds and golds, particularly found in the work of Thomas Chippendale. Both in England and America this period became known as **Georgian**—named after the English kings George I, II, and III (see Chapter 1). Toward the latter part of the century, the excavation of Pompeii in Italy inspired the Brothers Adam in England, and Thomas Jefferson and others in America, to introduce the neoclassic style. Colors became more delicate, with Adam green (a sharp, light green), peach, pink, soft yellow, and blue as favorites. In America the style was known as **Federal** (see Chapter 1).
- **Empire and Greek Revival.** A grand use of classic architecture and furnishings particularly inspired by ancient Greece and Egypt was popular during the first half of the nineteenth century. Napoleon in France promoted the colors black, white, Empire green (a deep emerald green), gold, and blue which in turn influenced both

Figure 5.2 Pastel colors popular during the latter half of the eighteenth century help establish an authentic atmosphere in this drawing room of a Southern Colonial mansion. The white painted moldings, mantel, and paneling enhance the delicate blue, rose, and peach scheme. *(Courtesy of Driwood Mouldings.)*

European and American interiors.

- **China.** Colors used in China for centuries have had a tremendous impact on the Western world that continues today. They include blue, white, gold, red-orange, red, and black.
- **Japan.** The complex color theory called ***shibui*** employs colors derived from nature. American architect Frank Lloyd Wright was one of the first designers to introduce this color concept to the Western world.
- **Spain and Mexico.** Vivid colors—blue, red, gold, pink, and orange—coupled with white and black have long been expressive of the Spanish and Mexican cultures, and such colors contribute to this style in traditional and contemporary Spanish American homes.
- **Victorian Period.** The Victorian Era was a period of eclecticism known for its abundance of furnishings and accessories in the home. Colors were predominantly dull reds, greens, browns, and mauves, which prompted use of the term *the Mauve Decades* to refer to this era.
- **Arts and Crafts Period.** From about 1860 until the turn of the century, the Arts and Crafts Movement was popular in England and America. The movement, founded by William Morris, advocated a return to handcrafted articles for home use inspired by medieval times. Popular colors were rich greens, reds, blues, and golds (see Chapter 2).
- **Art Nouveau.** During the opening decades of the twentieth century, the revolutionary ideas of Art Nouveau introduced plant forms and other influences from nature interpreted in exaggerated flowing forms. Soft afternoon colors of apricot, greens, and golds were made popular by French graphic designer Alphonse Mucha and others. Stained glass in rich colors was used by Louis Comfort Tiffany, and Charles Rennie Mackintosh in Scotland introduced the "modern" use of white, rose, pink, purple, and black for furnishings and interiors.

  Other avant-garde designers in Europe and America involved with Art Nouveau also combined unusual color schemes considered innovative for the time.
- **Bauhaus, International Style.** The famous Bauhaus experimental German design school, which flourished from 1919 to 1933, Swiss/French modern designer Le Corbusier, and others in Europe and America advocated clean, simple white color schemes. This movement introduced modernism on a grand scale (see Chapter 2). In 1917 the modern Dutch group De Stijl introduced the use of white interiors accented by red, blue, yellow, gray, and black furnishings.
- **Art Deco.** A decorative style of the "Roaring Twenties" and thirties in America and Europe, Art Deco employed inspiration from many sources including the cinema, new modernism, ancient Egypt, and new technology. Colors included white, black, gray, silver, red, purple, chocolate brown, turquoise, gray-blue, gray-green, peach, and pink. The style remains popular today, interpreted in contemporary terms.
- **Post-World War II.** Light colors were generally preferred through the fifties; particularly popular were beige or off-white walls. Turquoise, orange, brown, rose, and blue were also popular for furnishings. American interest also turned to Mexico, and a shift to brighter colors with more contrast occurred. This shift paved the way for a shocking palette of color which found favor with lovers of Spanish colonial. Scandinavian modern design and colors were introduced in America during this time, and the use of blue and green and other "new" color combinations arose. Other modern movements with new color possibilities were generally accepted during the 1950s and 1960s. Particularly in the 1960s, a renewed interest in English furnishings of the sixteenth and seventeenth centuries brought with it rich, blended color schemes employing blue, green, gold, and red. French country and Court style furnishings and colors continued to be popular in America during the postwar period.
- **The 1970s.** The decade of the seventies witnessed a wide range of color fashions. One direction had to do with the patriotism generated by the American bicentennial, producing a renewed interest in the ever-popular combination of red, white, and blue. These colors were used not only for color schemes in many rooms of the house but also for many areas of industry and the arts. Dramatic use of color in both hue, value, and chroma was also prominent. For example, three extremes were fashionable: one employed shiny black walls with strong colors throughout the room, another used a silvery look on all furnishings and backgrounds, and still another was the all-over white look.
- **The 1980s.** With the advent of new architectural and design styles such as Post-Modern, Memphis, High Tech, and other directions (see Chapter 2), color trends have increasingly incorporated many choices for both contract and residential design.

Figure 5.3 Inspired from the romantic settings of ancient Rome, this contemporary dining environment was created by designer John Saladino for the Italian Tile Center in New York. A pink and blue-green color scheme supports the Post-Modern style. *(Courtesy of Italian Ceramic Tile.)*

For example, the Memphis influence incorporates strong vivid primary and secondary colors. Post-Modernism has popularized muted purples, blues, pinks, greens, and peach. A great freedom in the use of color in the home and working environment is evident. Although they stay in vogue for only a short time, color fads and trends continue to influence designers and consumers. One trend that has remained strong throughout the 1980s is the use of gray, pastel hues, and muted colors made popular by the Post-Modern style and neutral schemes.

The Psychology of Color

The knowledge of color and its relationship to people is basic to the interior designer, but industry also recognizes its importance in advertising, manufacturing, and packaging. The significance of color in the physical environment is generally well established. Experiments have shown that workers function more efficiently in surroundings of pleasant colors than they do in drab environments. Young people in detention homes have been found to respond more positively when dull-colored walls have been repainted with a bright color. Also, pink has been found to have a soothing and calming effect.

Responding to the generally accepted notion that red will excite one to action and blue will calm one's nerves, some athletic directors have painted their players' dressing rooms in bright reds and oranges and visitors' dressing rooms in pale blues. The directors claim that it works.

Emotional reactions associated with color are spontaneous. The reaction is often due to the perception of a color rather than to the color itself, and the reaction produced may be positive or negative.

One such situation occurred in a meat market in Chicago, which, when painted a bright and cheerful yellow, lost business. A color consultant quickly informed the owner that the yellow walls caused a blue afterimage. It gave meat a purplish cast, making it appear old and spoiled. The walls were repainted bluish green, creating a red afterimage that enhanced the appearance of meat and sales zoomed (John Dreyfuss, *Los Angeles Times,* 1977).

Some other popular color studies have indicated that

- Drivers of brightly painted sports cars have higher insurance premiums and receive more traffic tickets than drivers of cars painted in more conservative colors.
- Most people prefer to eat from a white dinner plate rather than a colored one.
- Most flags of the world employ red, white, and blue because of the admirable associations of these colors.
- Color-blind bulls react to the movement of the matador's cape rather than the color red—the crowd reacts to the excitement of red.
- Doctors today tend to paint the walls of their offices soft calming colors, as opposed to the traditional stark white walls, which used to have a frightening and cold effect on patients.
- Factory workers complained how heavy their black boxes were to carry. After a color expert painted the boxes light blue, the workers congratulated the administration on making the boxes lighter.

Information thus far obtained, however, often indicates the superficiality of the knowledge on which popular assumptions about color are based. Serious research on the subject is inconclusive and often contradictory, and wide gaps between laboratory studies and their applications are frequent. Authorities in the field generally agree that color and emotion are closely related and that people react differently to color. They do not, however, agree on the emotional effects of color, nor do they know whether emotional reactions to colors are inherent or learned.

That individuals have definite color preferences is common knowledge. Almost every person has a favorite color that they find invariably attractive and comfortable. Because of this, it is advisable to fashion a personal environment with colors that are pleasurable, thus alleviating unnecessary mental discomfort.

The simplest psychological division of color results in two major areas or groups: **warm** and **cool,** with **neutral** in between. A line drawn through the standard color wheel will approximate the division between cool and warm colors.

A number of characteristics peculiar to these color groups should be understood and considered when choosing colors for decorative purposes.

Color Groups

Warm Colors

Warm colors of a strong intensity are generally

- Active
- Cheery
- Advancing
- Somewhat informal, tending to blend objects together (soften outlines)

If used in strong intensity in large areas, warm colors may cause psychological irritation.

Cool Colors

Particularly in tints, cool colors are generally

- Restful
- Soothing
- Receding
- Somewhat formal, tending to make individual objects stand out (reinforce outlines)

Rooms done in cool colors may be too cool and unfriendly and may lack unity.

Neutral Colors

Colors falling midway between warm and cool are called neutrals. Neutral colors are important to

Figure 5.4 A warm color scheme of red, yellow, and orange is found in the use of fabrics, the wall treatment, and accessories. *(Courtesy of Laura Ashley. © Laura Ashley/ Weidenfeld & Nicolson.)*

Figure 5.5 A cool color scheme of blues and lavenders was developed around a geometrically designed dhurrie rug. Lavender umbrellas suspended from the ceiling provide a dramatic effect. *(Courtesy of Robert Brain.)*

Figure 5.6 A neutral color scheme establishes a warm and inviting mood in this eclectic room in Colorado. The appeal of neutral colors is timeless, providing a livable environment for many years. *(Courtesy of Gayl Baddeley/Associates. Photograph by Richard Springgate.)*

every color scheme. A warm neutral is a tint, tone, or shade of a warm color, and a cool neutral is a tint, tone, or shade of a cool color. Warm neutrals are easier to work with than cool neutrals. Large background areas of warm neutral tones tend to produce the most livable and lasting color schemes.

Psychological Effects of Individual Colors

In addition to the division of colors into warm and cool, each color contains peculiar properties that produce certain psychological effects.

- **Blue** is cool and soothing, recalling sky, water, and ice, but it is difficult to mix and varies greatly under different lighting. More than any other color, blue is affected by the different materials it colors. Lacquer and glass, for example, have a reflective quality that intensifies blue. In deep-pile carpet, blue has great depth. Nubby fabrics soften blue. Shiny materials make blue look frosted.
- **Green** is nature's color and is serene and friendly. It is a good mixer, especially yellow-green. White brings out green's best qualities. Green is a great favorite and when grayed, warmed, or cooled, makes an excellent background.
- **Red** is conspicuous wherever it appears and, since it is lively and stimulating, should be used with care. Red mixes well, and most rooms are enhanced by a touch of one of its tones.
- **Yellow** is the sunlight color. High-noon yellows are the most revealing and demanding and merit careful attention. Gray-yellows of early dawn are *foils* for more fragile colors—pinks, blues, pale greens. Warm afternoon yellow is a foil for rich, warm woods. Burnished yellows of brass give a cast of copper gilt and bring life to a room. All yellows are reflective, take on tones of other colors, and add flattering highlights.
- **Gold** is the symbol of affluence and when used well adds style to most rooms. On large areas it may appear brassy or garish unless neutralized.
- **Pink** is delicate and flattering to almost everyone. Add a little yellow, leaning toward peach, and pink becomes warm. Add a little blue, leaning toward violet, and it becomes cool. Pink is often enhanced by a stronger contrasting color. It especially blends well with grays, browns, greens, and sharp blues. Combined with purples and lavenders, pink takes on a fresh look.
- **Violet** can be a dramatic color. When pink is added, it becomes warm, and a touch of blue makes it cool. It combines well with both pink and blue. A light value of violet produces lavender, a popular pastel employed in today's interiors.
- **Orange** has similar stimulating properties as red, but is not as demanding. When lightened and muted, orange becomes a peach tone. Orange mixes well with cool colors.
- **Brown** is warm, comfortable, and earthy. The homeyness of brown tones makes them universal favorites. Ranging from pale cream beige to deeper chocolate brown, these tones, tints, and shades can be used together in a room to give infinite variety. Browns are particularly easy to work with.
- **Gray** is cool and formal in light tones. If light and slightly warmed, it makes an excellent background; if too heavy, it can be oppressive. Grays are easy to work with and generally are compatible with most colors.
- **White and off-white** have the psychological quality of making all colors in a room look cleaner and livelier. Warm off-white is considered unequaled as a mellow background color and works wonders in blending furniture of different woods and styles. Changes of light from day to night are kind to off-white and give it quiet vitality.
- **Black and off-black** (rich black-brown) in furniture finishes, small areas of fabric, or accessories add an important accent that tends to make other colors crisp and clear. When used for larger areas, black can be extremely dramatic but can be oppressive.

Color and Pigment

Ever since Sir Isaac Newton, over 300 years ago, began a series of experiments that provided the foundation for our modern knowledge of color, scientists have been developing new color theories and systems. Many different scientific approaches to color exist. The **physicist** works with colors in **light,** the **chemist** is mainly concerned with the production of **pigments,** and the **psychologist** has theories based on **visual perception** and the effects of color on the emotions. The artist—and particularly the student of interior design—will benefit from an understanding of all three approaches, especially regarding color in pigments.

The most practical approach to the understanding of color derives from personal experience. Individuals are constantly surrounded by color, in light and objects. The colors in objects are referred to as pigment colors and the colors from the sun and from lamps are called light colors.

The process of combining primary colors (red, green, and blue) is said to be an **additive** one (i.e., the sensations produced by different wavelengths of light, or ***spectral*** colors, are added together). When pigments are mixed, however, the resulting sensations differ from those of the spectral colors. In this case, the method is a **subtractive** one, since subtraction or absorption of the wavelengths of light occurs.

In reality, **a ray of light** is the source of all color, for without light, color does not exist. Color is light broken down into ***electromagnetic*** vibrations of varying wavelengths, which cause the viewer to see different colors. This phenomenon can be demonstrated by passing a beam of light through a glass prism. The beam divides into the colors of the spectrum, proving that white light contains these colors. The longest wavelength is perceived as red and the shortest as violet. Everyone has had the experience of seeing these rainbow colors in a variety of places. A bright beam of light striking a soap bubble or the ***bevel*** edge of a mirror reflects the spectrum hues.

Since the pigment colors are more commonly used, however, this text will limit its study primarily to these colors. What is meant by pigment in relation to color? Certain pigments are said to be combined to get certain colors, such as red and yellow to obtain orange, or blue and yellow to obtain green. Pigments are substances of various kinds that can be ground into fine powder and used for coloring dyes and paints. Before people learned how to produce pigments by chemical means, they were derived from **animal, mineral,** and **vegetable** sources. The ***Mayans*** in Central America extracted purple from shellfish. The highly prized Tyrian purple, which was used to color the robes of early Roman emperors, was obtained from shellfish found in the Mediterranean Sea by the Phoenicians. Another important dye of the Near East was a red dye extracted from kermes, the dried bodies of scale insects.

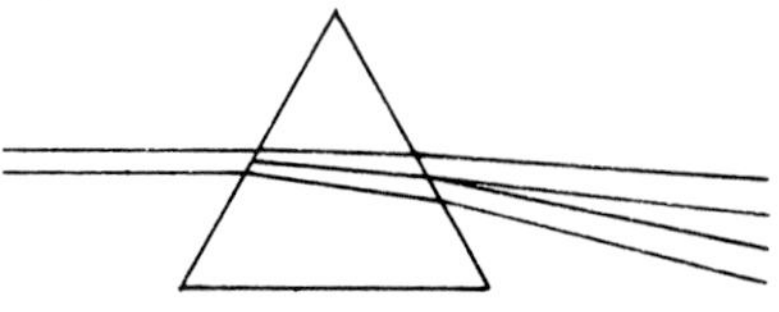

A beam of white light passing through a glass prism.

The East Indians, who are usually credited with having first developed a thriving dyeing trade, were skilled in securing dyes from many plants, such as ***madder*** for red and ***indigo*** for blue. The ancient Chinese and Arabs were also familiar with natural sources of various pigments. For hundreds of years nature was the only source of dyes, many of which did not hold up well. Modern technology has improved the sharpness of color and the fastness and durability of dyes.

A basic understanding of the derivation and development of color pigments is essential and rewarding to the interior designer, and a wealth of excellent books on the subject are available for further in-depth study.

Color Systems

A number of color theories, or systems, have developed and are in use today. Some incorporate psychological as well as physical factors. A variety of color wheels have been produced, each based on a different group of basic colors. For example, the Ostwald color wheel, developed by Wilhelm Ostwald, is based on four principal hues: yellow, red, blue, and green, plus black and white; the Munsell begins with five hues: yellow, red, blue, green, and purple; and the Brewster system is based on the three primaries: yellow, red, and blue. This chapter will consider the Brewster and Munsell theories.

The Brewster System

Developed by David Brewster, the **Brewster system** is the simplest and best known of all the color systems. (It is often referred to as Prang, or the **standard color wheel.**) This is a pigment theory employing the familiar color wheel based on **three *primary* colors: yellow, red,** and **blue.** ***Primary*** means the colors cannot be mixed from other pigments, nor can they be broken down into component colors. Theoretically, with five tubes of paint—the three primaries, plus black and white—one could produce the entire range of colors, although the degree of precision needed makes this almost impossible. By using the 3 primaries, however, the 12 colors of the complete wheel can be derived.

By adding equal amounts of any two of the primary colors, the result is a ***secondary*** color. The Brewster wheel has three such colors: green, which is produced by mixing yellow and blue; violet, by mixing blue and red; and orange, by mixing red and yellow. In each instance, the secondary color lies midway between the primary colors from which it is formed.

In similar fashion, ***tertiary,*** or ***intermediary,*** hues are composed by mixing equal amounts of a primary color and a secondary color. These hues are also situated midway between the two hues that produced them and are identified by hyphenated names such as blue-green, red-orange, and red-violet. The last one, red-violet, is a combination of the two extreme hues of the spectrum. These 12 hues make up the full color wheel and include all of the spectrum colors plus red-violet. The Brewster Color Wheel is a simple and useful tool for the designer.

Figure 5.7a The standard Brewster Color Wheel.

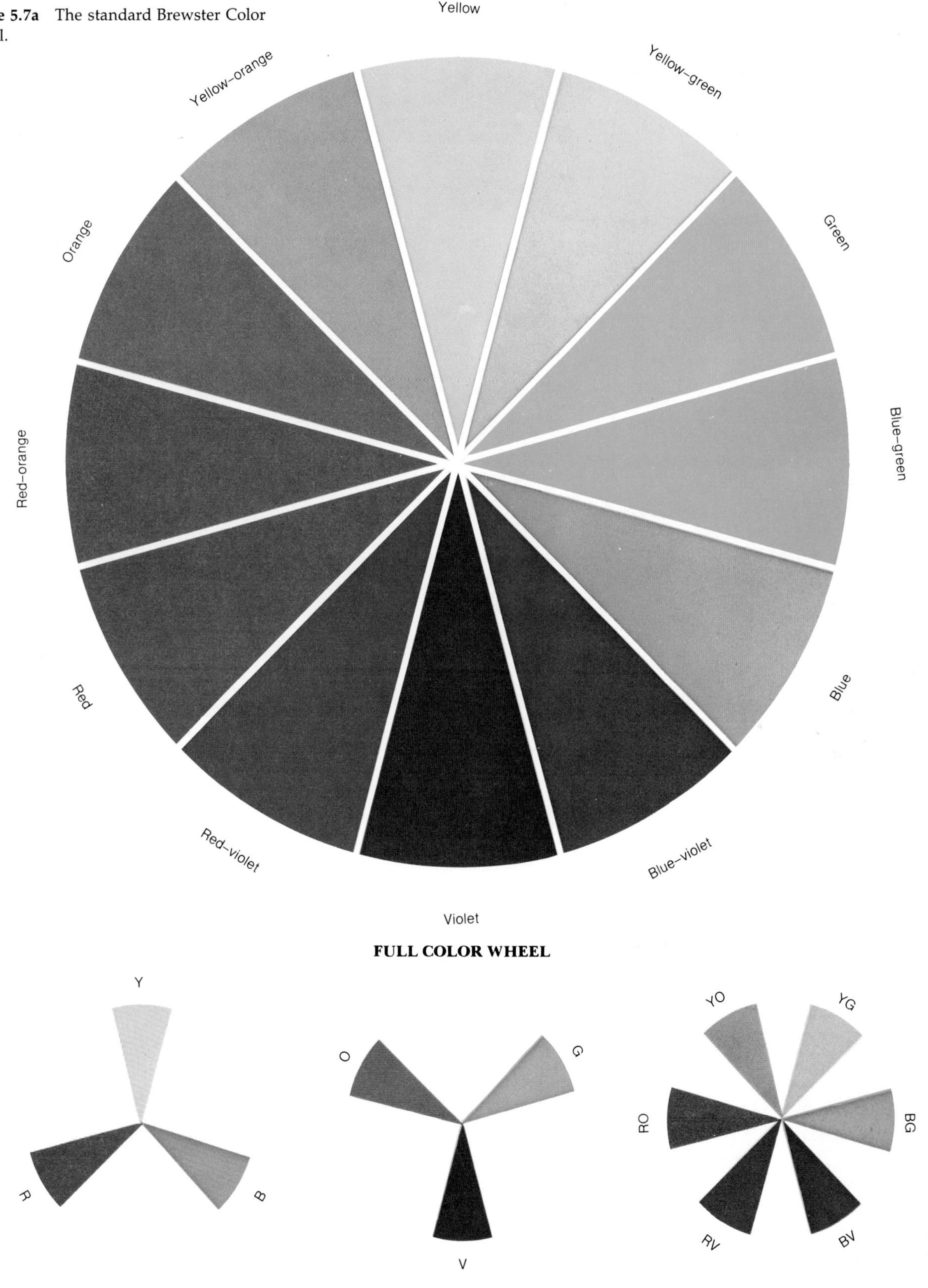

The Munsell System

The **Munsell system** of color notation is essentially a scientific concept of describing and analyzing color in terms of three attributes: **hue, value,** and **chroma.** The designation of each color is written as **H v/c.**

- **Hue,** or the color name, is indicated by the capital letter *H*, followed by a fraction in which the numerator represents the value and the denominator indicates the chroma. In the diagram, hue is indicated by the circular band.
- **Value,** or the lightness and darkness of a color, is indicated by the central axis, which shows nine visible steps, from darkest value at the bottom to lightest value at the top, with 5/ for middle gray. Pure black would be designated as 0/ and pure white as 10/.
- The **chroma** notation is shown by the horizontal band extending outward from the value axis. It indicates the degree of departure of a given hue from a neutral gray of the same value. Since hues vary in their saturation strength, the number of chroma steps also varies. For example, yellow has the smallest number, and red has the greatest number. Since yellow is nearest to white, it is placed nearest the top of the color tree at step 8; thus, normal yellow is Y 8/chroma. Other hues are placed at their natural values' levels, such as 5 red in natural at R 4/. Thus, the value of 5R and step 4 on the value scale are equal, designated as R 4/c. Purple is the darkest hue and is normal at step 3 on the value scale: P 3/c. Thus, the complete notation for a sample of vermillion might be 5R 4/14, meaning that 5R = pure red, 4/ = natural value, and /14 = strongest chroma (see figure).

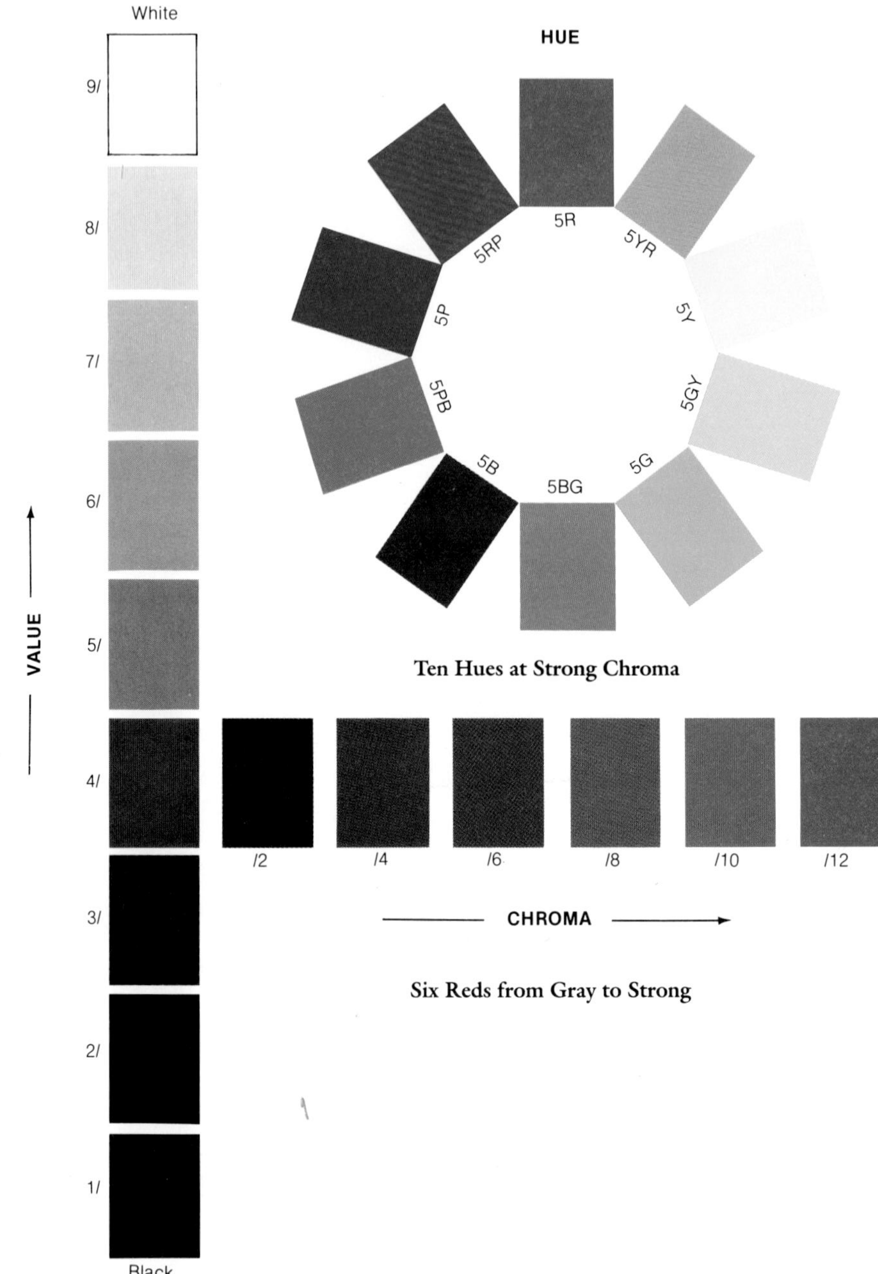

Figure 5.7b Munsell Color System, including hue, value, and chroma relationships. The circular band represents the hues in their proper sequences. The upright, center axis is the scale of value. The paths pointing outward from the center show the steps of chroma increasing in strength, as indicated by the numerals. *(Courtesy of Munsell Color Company, Inc.)*

In the Munsell system, **chroma,** the Greek word for "color," is used instead of intensity. In this system, the chromatic colors are based on the three primary colors, as is the case in the Brewster system, but they are divided into **five principal hues: red, yellow, green, blue,** and **purple.** The five intermediate colors that lie between these hues are yellow-red, green-yellow, blue-green, purple-blue, and red-purple,

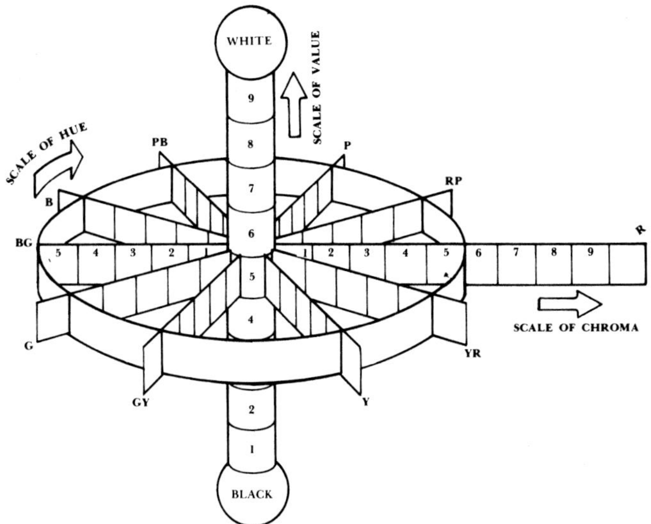

Hue, value, and chroma in their relation to one another. The circular band represents the hues in their proper sequences. The upright center axis is the scale of value. The paths pointing outward from the center show the steps of chroma, increasing in strength as indicated by the numerals. *(Courtesy of Munsell Color Company, Inc.)*

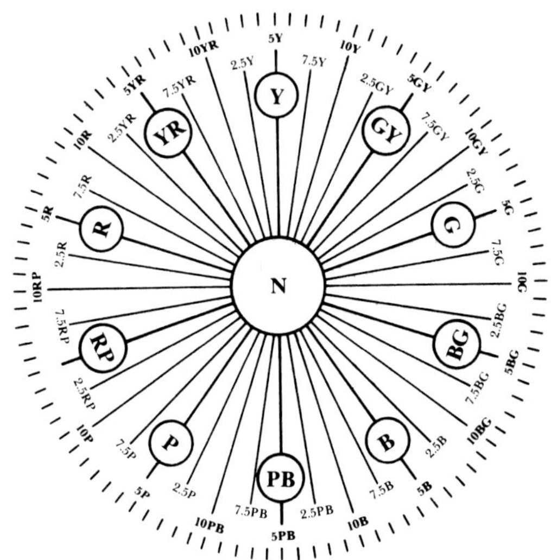

Hue symbols and relationships. Hue notations of the five principal and the five intermediate hue families are encircled. A breakdown into 100 hues is indicated by the outer circle of markings, and the breakdown of each hue family into four parts (2.5, 5, 7.5, and 10) indicates the 40 constant-hue charts appearing in the *Munsell Book of Color. (Courtesy of Munsell Color Company, Inc.)*

these being combinations of the five principal hues. Each of these 10 hues is subdivided into four parts, indicated by the numerals 2.5, 5, 7.5, and 10. These hue names are symbolized by capitalized initials, such as R for red or YR for yellow-red. When finer subdivisions are required, these 10 hues may again be combined, such as R-YR, which may be combined into still finer divisions.

The segment lying between each of the 10 color hues is divided into 10 color steps (see figure). In each case, the basic and intermediate color is in the center and is marked by the number 5, which indicates it is the strongest degree of pure color of that particular hue. Each of the 10 different hues, such as red, is designated by a number using the decimal system to indicate its degree of redness or intensity. For example, 2.5R has more red than 10RP, but both have much less red than 5R. Because this designation is done with the 10 color segments, the Munsell Color Wheel has a total of 100 different colors.

By using the correct letters and numbers, one can describe any given hue and locate it on the color tree. Through this practical method colors can be identified and standardized for professional purposes. This system of color notation is scientifically related to the Inter-Society Color Council, making it extremely useful in science and industry. This notation is also useful to the interior designer, because it makes it possible to communicate color information in a precise manner.

Color's Three Dimensions

The three dimensions of color have already been referred to in the Munsell notation. These major characteristics, basic to all colors, can accurately be measured and are essential in visualizing and describing any color. These qualities are hue, value, and intensity (or chroma).

Hue

Hue, or the **color name,** is that singular characteristic which sets each color apart from all the others.

A color may be lightened or darkened, made more intense or less intense. If blue is the hue used, the result will be light blue, dark blue, bright blue, or gray-blue, but each will be of a blue hue. In all, about 150 variations of full chroma of hue exist, of which only 24 basic hues of full chroma have enough variation to be of practical use.

When neighboring hues on the color wheel are mixed, they produce new hues that are harmonious and closely related. When hues opposite from each other on the color wheel are mixed, the result is a neutral hue. In beginning a color scheme for any room, generally one dominant hue is the starting point against which all other colors are gauged. The choice of color is personal, but in each case the room's size, proportion, function, style, and mood and the exposure and amount of light should be taken into consideration. Since color frequently produces the first and most lasting impression on those entering a room, selecting and combining hues is probably the greatest challenge to the interior designer.

Value

Value is the degree of **luminosity,** or **lightness and darkness** of a hue in relation to black and white. Nine such gradations are easily visible to the eye (see Munsell illustration).

The value of any hue can be raised by adding white and lowered by adding black. When black or another darkening agent is added to a hue, the value is lowered and the result is a ***shade*** of that particular hue. When white is added to a hue, the value is raised, and the result is a ***tint.*** Many value steps may be created in any hue between normal value and black and white.

Tints, either clear or neutralized, are most frequently used for large background areas such as walls and ceilings. When mixing tints, it should be taken into consideration that certain pigments are not perfect, that is, they contain other hues. For example, white contains blue and a little violet, orange contains too much red, and blue has some violet. Making a correction for these imperfections is therefore necessary to get a perfect tint of the desired hue. Table 5.1 points out the procedure for mixing tints by correcting imperfect pigments.

In the nine gradations of value from white to black, the small circles are identical in shade, demonstrating that the eye perceives color not in itself but in relation to its environment.

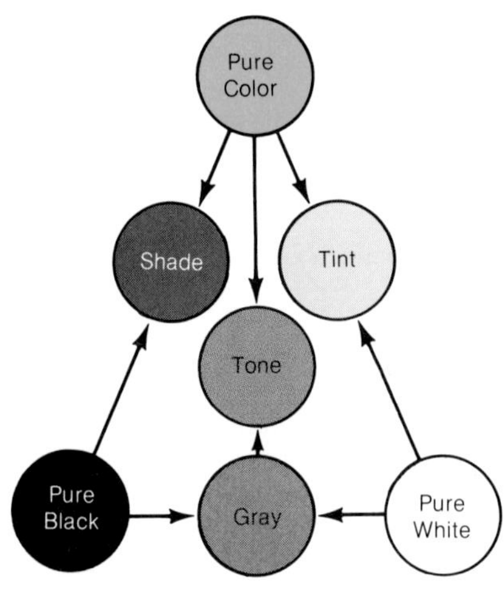

Although black and white pigments are not considered true colors, their addition to colored pigments produces tints, shades, and tones. Adding black to a pigment color produces a shade; adding white produces a tint. When gray (a mixture of black and white pigments) is added to a color, a tone is produced. *(Courtesy of General Electric Company.)*

In addition to shades and tints, a third classification is ***tone.*** A tone is formed by adding both black and white to the hue or a pigment of the color directly opposite from it on the standard color wheel. These grayed hues are extremely useful in working out color schemes in which muted colors are necessary to tone down the brighter hues. Any tint may become a tone with the addition of a touch of black or of some of the hue's complement.

Value may be applied in many ways when designing and furnishing a house. As an object is raised in value, apparent size increases. A fabric colored in low value will make a chair seem smaller than one in light or high value. Since light colors recede and dark colors advance, one may, with skill, alter

TABLE 5.1 *To get a clear tint of a color*

BASIC HUE	RESULTANT COLOR	CORRECTION	TINT
white + red	= light blue-pink	+ yellow	= red tint
white + yellow	= light violet-yellow	+ orange	= yellow tint
white + blue	= light violet-blue	+ yellow	= blue tint
white + green	= light blue-green	+ yellow	= green tint
white + orange	= light red-orange	+ yellow	= orange tint
white + violet	= light blue-violet	+ orange	= violet tint

Note: To get a clear tint of a color, yellow should be used to correct the color. When using yellow or purple, however, orange should be used to correct the color.

the apparent size and proportion of individual items or of an entire room. In small rooms, light values will expand walls and ceilings. In long narrow rooms, colors in darker value will pull in end walls and make the room appear shorter. Value may be used to conceal or emphasize objects. The use of sharp value contrast will emphasize an object. For example, the fine lines of a dark piece of furniture will be accentuated if placed against a light background. The dark will seem darker and the light background will seem lighter. A piece of furniture will seem unobtrusive if it is the same value as the

Figure 5.8 Light, medium, and dark values have been effectively distributed throughout this study area. The dark rugs with light borders make a striking contrast and focus. *(Courtesy of Kirkwood Shutters, Phoenix, Arizona.)*

Walls in light value tend to recede.

Walls in strong value tend to advance.

Color can conceal and emphasize. The bright-colored shutters against the white siding create a definite contrast and call attention to the windows. The bright door attracts instant attention, and the windows and shutters blend into the walls of the house.

background. Black and white have a strong visible effect on other colors when brought into juxtaposition. Black tends to make adjacent colors look richer. White reflects light into adjacent colors. Rooms that seem lifeless may often be given sparkle and interest by the addition of black, white, or both.

The manner in which tonal value is distributed throughout a room is of major importance. Each room usually contains three tonal values: light, medium, and dark, with varying amounts of each. The amounts of light and dark should not be equal. In most cases, having large areas of light set off by small areas of dark is wise. When colors for backgrounds and furnishings are selected, a careful consideration of value distribution will contribute to the success of the environment.

Intensity (or Chroma)

Intensity, or **chroma,** is the **degree of saturation of pure color.** It describes the brightness or dullness and strength or weakness of the pure color that a hue contains. As any color may be raised and lowered in value by the addition of white or black, so the intensity may be strengthened by the addition of pure chroma or lessened by the addition of that color's complement, which is the color directly across from it on the standard color wheel. The more of the color's complement that is added, the less pure color the original hue contains. Two colors may have similar hue (both blue) and the same value (neither darker nor lighter), yet may be markedly different because of the different color strength or intensity.

A color is visually made more intense by adding more of the dominant hue to it. A color may be made to appear more intense by placing it against its complementary color, whether of the same intensity or neutralized. For example, a painting with predominantly orange hues will seem more orange if hung against a blue wall.

When two complementary colors are mixed in equal amounts, they tend to neutralize each other. Therefore, to decrease the intensity of a color, some of that color's complement, black, black and white, or another neutralizing agent should be added. The degrees of neutralization are many, the number varying with different hues. A color will *appear* more neutral or less intense if placed against an object that is of the same hue more saturated in chroma. For example, a muted green vase placed against a bright green background will appear even more muted.

When planning color schemes for rooms, one should keep in mind that strong chroma is conspicuous and size-increasing. Furniture will seem larger and will fill up a room more if intense colors are used. Walls in strong chroma, as with dark value, will seem to advance and make the room appear smaller. Since rooms are backgrounds for people, color is generally most pleasing when not too demanding. The psychological effect of large areas of intense color can be irritating and have undesirable emotional effects. A wise choice, therefore, is to select colors in softly neutralized tones for large background areas in rooms where the occupants spend considerable time. Intense colors can work well when reserved for small areas and accents. A safe guide in planning a color scheme is the ***law of chromatic distribution:*** "The large areas should be covered in the most neutralized colors of the scheme. As the areas reduce in size, the chromatic intensity may be proportionally increased" (Whiton, *Interior Design and Decoration,* 1963).

Color is a great mood setter. Strong chroma tends to create a feeling of informality, and soft neutralized tones are generally reserved for a more formal atmosphere. In today's interiors, when design rules are often considered and then broken, the opposite treatment may prevail.

Creating Livable Color Schemes

Planning and organizing color schemes for the home can be a challenging and satisfying task. Endless color possibilities are available to the designer and consumer, derived from traditional organized methods or sparked by original ideas. Individual color preferences are naturally a consideration coupled with the preferences of other occupants who may be living within the interior spaces. Harmonizing colors employing the standard color wheel is a popular approach and may aid the individual in color selections. In general, color schemes derived from the color wheel fall into two categories: **related** and **contrasting.** Within these categories the variations are endless. Related colors produce harmonious schemes that may be cool, warm, or a combination. Contrasting schemes have great variety and tend to be more exciting, particularly if strong chroma is used. In any scheme, black, white, or neutrals may be added without changing the scheme.

The basic color schemes are **monochromatic, achromatic, neutral, analogous,** and **complementary.** Although professional interior designers seldom select a specific scheme initially, the final scheme often falls into one of these categories.

Monochromatic

Monochromatic color schemes are developed from a **single hue,** but with a range of values and different degrees of intensity (see Figure 5.6). Unity is probably the most notable element in this type of scheme, and if light values predominate, space will be expanded. A danger in the one-color scheme may be monotony; however, if one looks to nature, where monotony is never present, the guidelines are clearly apparent. By examining the petals of a rose, one may determine the shadings from soft, delicate pink, to deep red. The variety of tones, tints, and chroma of the green leaf can be combined in a room using the subtle neutralized tones for large wall areas, slightly deeper tones for the carpet, medium tones for large furniture, and vivid chroma for accents.

Monochromatic schemes are often further enhanced by the use of textures such as fabrics, woods, stones, metals, and glass, which aid in bringing life and interest to the room. Pattern can also add variety and character to the one-color scheme. Black and white may be employed without changing the character of the plan and in fact may help sharpen the scheme and add interest.

Figure 5.9 A vivid monochromatic color scheme of a rich red wallcovering is seen in this stimulating dining room. The floral outline and border of gold and white provide variety and interest, which are often needed to make a one-color scheme successful. *(Courtesy of The Jack Denst Designs, Inc.)*

Figure 5.10 Sleek formality pervades this all-white kitchen. *(Courtesy of Allmilmo Corporation.)*

Achromatic

Achromatic color schemes, which are basically monochromatic in nature, are those that possess **no hue, only values.** They are created utilizing **black, white,** and variations of **gray.** Small amounts of hue used for accents or small furnishings can enhance the achromatic approach and do not change the basic scheme. Like monochromatic schemes, the achromatic approach is often enriched with the introduction of interesting textures and pattern.

Neutral

Neutral schemes employ colors that fall **midway between warm and cool colors** (see page 129), and they can be categorized as a type of monochromatic scheme. Neutral colors can be employed as tints,

Figure 5.11 When bright color is added, the room assumes a different aspect. Forms are emphasized and the room becomes less formal. *(Courtesy of Allmilmo Corporation.)*

tones, or shades, or combinations of the three. These schemes are easy to live with and relatively simple to create; therefore, they naturally are popular across the nation. Accents of stronger chroma may be used for smaller furnishings and accessories without changing the neutral scheme and can add visual interest.

Analogous

Analogous, adjacent, or **related** color schemes are produced from any segment of colors that are in juxtaposition but contain no more than half the colors on the standard color wheel. This color scheme has much interest, is widely used, and is easy to achieve, with successful results. The colors may be warm, cool, or a combination. Harmony is easily established with analogous colors because they usually have one color in common. Yellow, for example, is the common factor in orange and green, and by using the intermediate colors of yellow-orange and yellow-green, an interior designer may achieve a close relationship with a great variety of values and intensities. Generally, one dominant color should be present.

Complementary

Complementary, or **contrasting,** color schemes are probably the most widely used of all the color schemes because they have more variety. These may be developed in a number of ways, but each scheme uses colors of contrasting hues. In each case, values and intensities may vary depending on the use and amount of area to be covered. All contrasting hues placed side by side enhance each other, and if they are in the same intensity, each makes the other seem more intense. When added together, however, contrasting hues will subtract from each other, as in color neutralization. When equal amounts of two complementary colors are used, they produce a neutral. Complementary schemes always have some warm and cool colors, since they are opposite on the color wheel. These schemes can work well for either traditional or modern interiors. In strong chroma they are lively and vigorous; in grayed tones they may be subtle and restful. In each case, one dominant hue is usually employed to set the mood.

Six types of complementary schemes are direct complement, split complement, triad, double complement, alternate complement, and tetrad.

Direct Complement

The **direct complement,** the simplest of the contrasting color schemes, is formed by using any two colors that lie directly opposite each other on the color wheel. In each case, one of the hues should dominate. Used in equal amounts and in strong intensity, complementary colors will clash, thus creating an unpleasant element in a room. The secondary color, therefore, may work best when neutralized or used in small areas.

Split Complement

The **split complement** is a three-color scheme composed of any hue plus the two hues next to its complement. For example, if yellow is selected as the dominant color, red-violet and blue-violet will be the complementary colors. These colors contrast less than the direct complement, which is violet. Red has been added to one and blue to the other, giving a softness to the scheme and at the same time adding variety and interest.

Figure 5.12 A subtle analogous color scheme is employed through the use of violets and blues in this sophisticated contemporary living room. *(Photograph by Peter Paige.)*

The **triad complement** is another three-color contrasting scheme (see below). The triad is made up of any three colors that are equidistant on the color wheel. These colors may be sharp in contrast, using strong chroma such as the three primaries—red, yellow, and blue, or red-orange, yellow-green, and blue-violet—or they may be neutralized, raised, or lowered in value to produce a tranquil scheme or any variant.

Double Complement

The **double complement** is a four-color scheme in which two pairs of complementary colors are used. This scheme doubles the possible combinations of colors, offering a wide variety of decorative effects.

Figure 5.13 The Tenenbaum House in Columbia, South Carolina, designed by Alan Buchsbaum, displays a bright red and soft green complementary color scheme on wall surfaces and furnishings enhanced by additional walls in crisp white in the living room. *(Photograph by Norman McGrath.)*

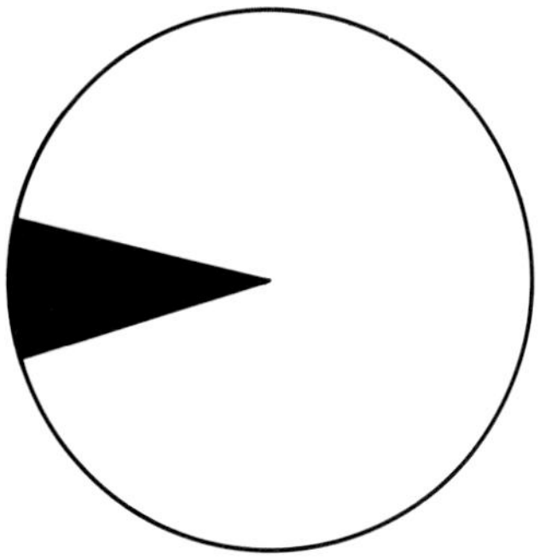

Monochromatic
(one-color plan)

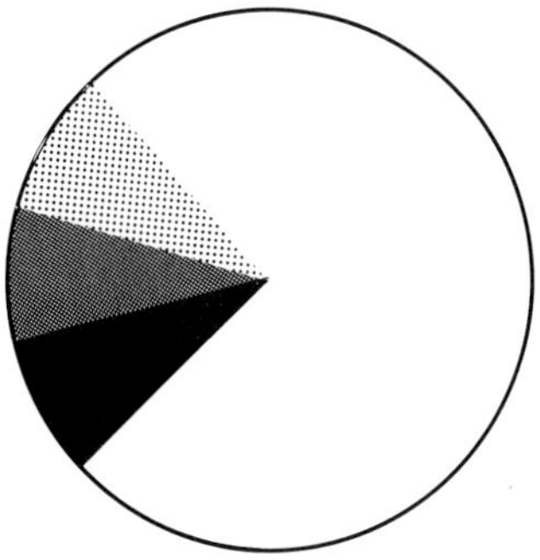

Analogous
(three- to six-color plan)

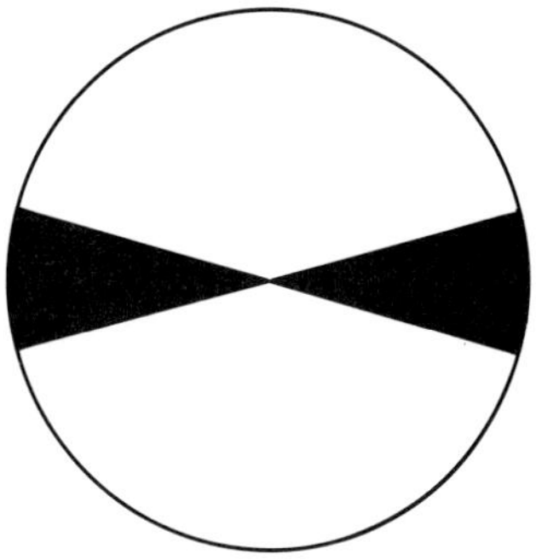

Direct complement
(two-color plan)

Split complement
(three-color plan)

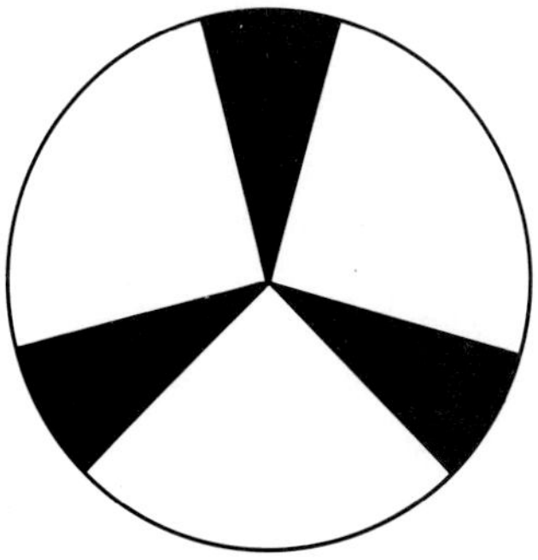

Triad complement
(three-color plan)

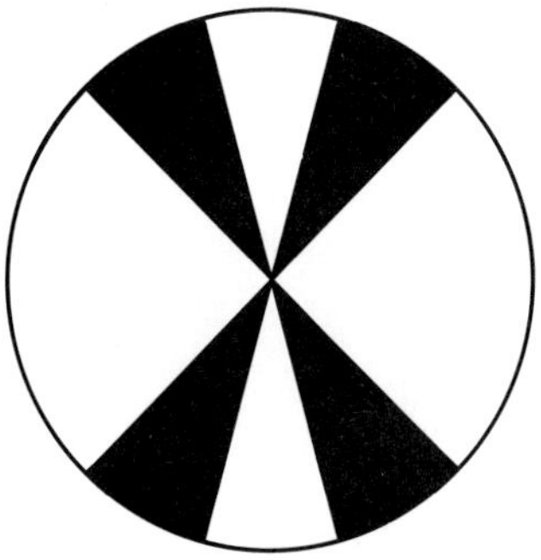

Double complement
(four-color plan)

Alternate complement
(four-color plan)

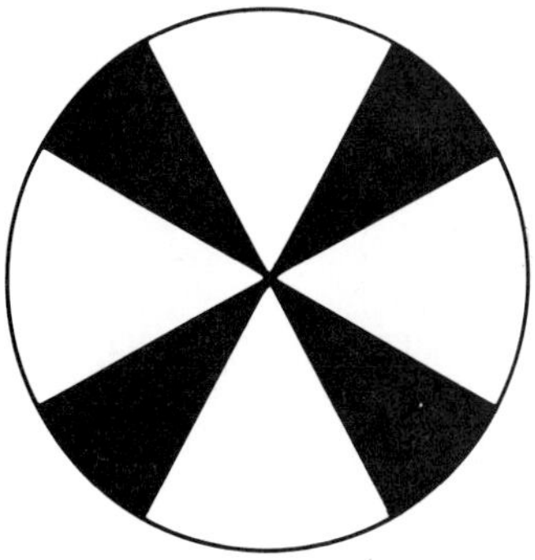

Tetrad
(four-color plan)

Figure 5.14 A pink and green complementary color scheme was inspired by the wallpaper and coordinating fabric. The rug, painting, and other accessories unify and support the scheme. *(Courtesy of Country Life Designs.)*

Alternate Complement

The **alternative complement** is another four-color scheme combining the triad and the direct complement. The possibilities of creating interiors from this scheme are numerous.

Tetrad

The **tetrad** scheme combines any four hues that are equidistant on the color wheel. An example would be the combination of orange, yellow-green, blue, and red-violet. This grouping of unexpected colors can add excitement and variety to the decor.

Creating Livable Color Schemes—Additional Methods

In addition to employing the basic color schemes, other methods can inspire a room's color combinations.

- An attractive **fabric** might be a starting point for a color scheme. Following the law of chromatic distribution, for example, one of the lightest and most neutral colors can be selected for the room's background, and other colors from the fabric can be used for various objects in the room. The most intense colors might be reserved for accents.
- A color scheme can be established drawing colors from a favored **wallpaper.**
- An **area rug, art rug,** a **custom rug,** or **wall-to-wall carpeting**—patterned or plain—can be the inspiration for a room's color scheme.
- A prized **painting, print,** or **art object** can determine a color scheme.
- **Nature** can provide an unlimited number of color schemes. One popular color theory is called ***shibui*** (or ***shibusa***).

The Shibui Color Scheme

Shibui (or **shibusa**) expresses in one word the **Japanese approach** to beauty as well as the intrinsic nature of their culture. No single

Figure 5.15 In this assemblage of fabrics and carpets, textures and colors are drawn from nature to create the essence of shibui. *(Courtesy of Rosecare Carpet Company.)*

word in the English language precisely describes ***shibui,*** an elusive Japanese adjective (***shibumi*** is the noun). The word *shibui,* however, suggests an appreciation of **serenity** and a protest against ostentation. Belief in the power of the **understated and unobtrusive** dominates the sophisticated philosophy of the Japanese, who have an uncommon sensitivity to and awareness of beauty.

The color scheme essential in producing a shibui effect is one in which colors are brought together to enhance each other in a harmonious whole that will be quietly pleasing to live with for a long time. To be deeply satisfying for an extended time, livable schemes must have depth and complexity, or they will soon become tiresome. A shibui color scheme possesses such qualities. The following ideas are incorporated in achieving a shibui effect.

- Understanding the shibui concept of color scheming requires *looking to nature, on which the color scheme is based.* Shibui uses colors found in nature, combining them in the same ratios. Colors found in the largest areas are quiet and undemanding (neutralized). Bright, vibrant colors are found in a small proportion.
- *Nature has thousands of colors, but none of them match or are uniform.*
- In nature the darker, more *solid colors occur underfoot.* As one looks upward, colors become lighter and more delicate.
- Most of the natural landscape is a *matte finish with little high shininess or glitter,* such as the sun sparkling on a ripple in a stream.
- *Pattern and texture in nature are everywhere*—in every stone, leaf, and tree trunk—but they have to be discovered through close examination. This subtleness accounts for the absence of uniformity and the dimension of nature's colors.
- *Pattern in nature is not uniform.* No two patterns are identical, yet unity prevails throughout. Nature's colors, textures, and patterns appear simple and natural, but on close scrutiny prove highly complex.

Translating the shibui concept into today's decorating means following principles found in nature and applying them to the interior. American architect Frank Lloyd Wright greatly admired the Shibui

Figure 5.16 The Oriental shibui concept of color scheming is translated into an American interior by Jack Lenor Larsen with an emphasis on texture and simple colors. Small areas of brightness are found in the floating flowers and flowers in baskets. The effect is subtle and unpretentious. *(Photograph by Norman McGrath.)*

design philosophy and incorporated its concepts into many of his works. In recent years Americans have come to recognize the value of this Eastern influence, and interest in Japanese design has been gaining momentum. New expressions of old Oriental themes and soft, earthy colors mix pleasantly with today's contemporary furnishings, producing depths of beauty and an atmosphere of serenity essential to contemporary homes.

An atmosphere of long-lasting **repose and tranquility** can be achieved by emulating the Japanese, whose homes are most notable for a **feeling of serenity** with an **absence of pretentious display and clutter.**

Whatever method of creating a color scheme is followed, the result should be a livable color scheme appropriate for the particular **function** of a room and for the **people** who will use it.

Other Considerations in Color Application

The Effect of Adjacent Colors on Each Other

Perhaps the most significant thing to remember about color is that a color is not important in itself. What is important is what happens when different colors are brought together. The eye perceives color not in and of itself, but in relation to its environment.

Physiologists have shown that people are not color blind to one color only but to two or four, and the eye is sensitive to colors not singly but in pairs. The familiar afterimage demonstrates this perception. If a person looks at any one color for about 30 seconds, then looks at a white page, the complement of that color will appear. Also, when the eye sees a colored object, it induces that color's complement in the environment. For example, when a green chair is placed against a light neutralized background, the eye sees a tinge of red in that background.

When two primary colors are placed side by side, they appear tinted with the omitted primary; for example, when placed near blue, red will take on a yellow tinge. When contrasting or complementary colors in strong chroma with the same value are used against each other, they will clash, producing a vibration that is fatiguing. When contrasting colors with strong differences in value are used side by side or one against the other, the colors will stand out but will not clash. Harmoniously blended colors of middle value used against each other will tend to blend together, and at a distance, the difference will become almost indiscernible (see Figure 5.22). The latter combination is the basis for most Japanese shibui color schemes.

The juxtaposition of colors

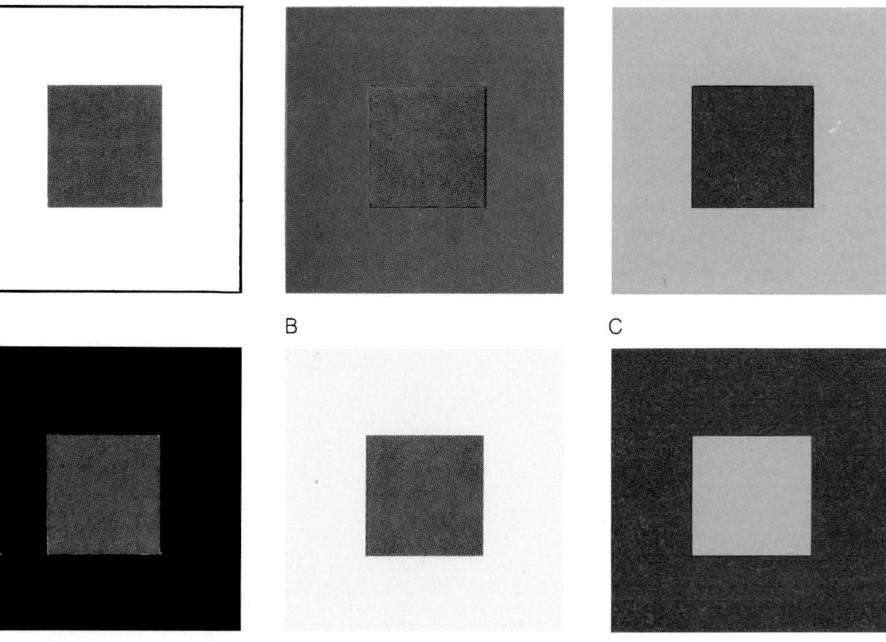

Figure 5.17 These diagrams illustrate the effect of adjacent colors: *A,* gray looks much darker against white than it does against black; *B,* a gray or neutral against a colored background appears to be tinted with the complement of the color; *C,* when placed side by side, complements of equal intensity create visual conflict. Complements of varying intensities enhance each other. *(Courtesy of Large Lamp Department, General Electric Company.)*

A chair in light value blends into a similar background.

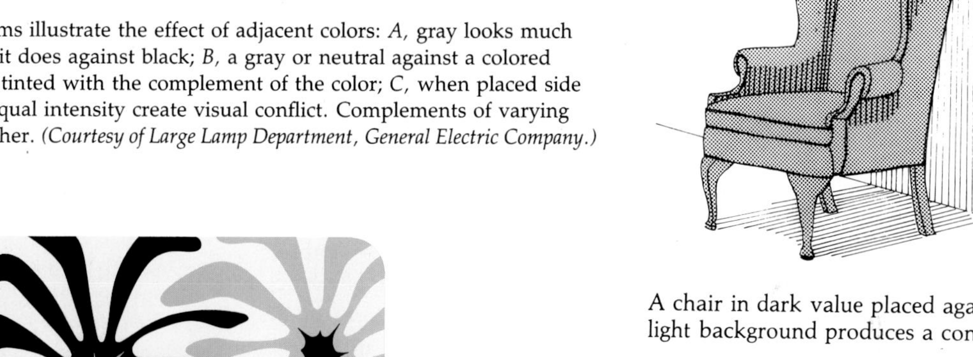

A chair in dark value placed against a light background produces a contrast.

Figure 5.18 Complementary afterimage. Stare at the black dot just below center for 30 seconds, then look at the black dot in the white space at extreme right. Prolonged concentration on any color will reduce eye sensitivity to it, and the reverse (complementary) color, remaining unaffected, will dominate the afterimage for a brief period until balance is restored. *(Courtesy of Large Lamp Department, General Electric Company.)*

Figure 5.19 Clashing colors. Complementary colors of strong chroma and similar value will clash in juxtaposition, causing line vibration. *(Courtesy of Large Lamp Department, General Electric Company.)*

A chair in light value placed against a dark background creates a more pronounced contrast.

Figure 5.20 Chameleon effect. Colors of medium value and chroma will appear to change in the direction of the lighter, brighter colors—or the darker, duller colors—surrounding them. *(Courtesy of Large Lamp Department, General Electric Company.)*

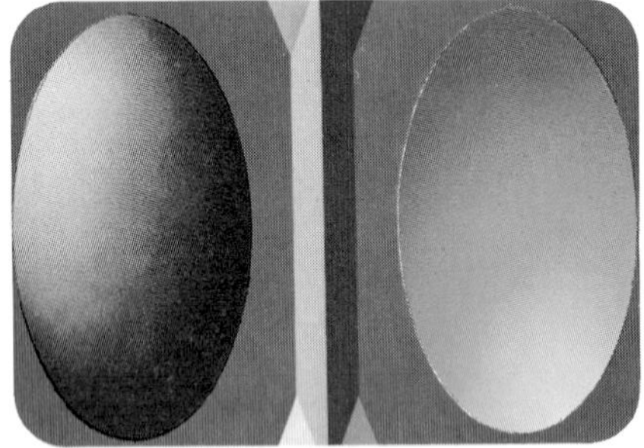

Figure 5.21 Advancing and receding colors. Warm colors and light grays appear to advance toward the eye; cool colors and dark grays appear to recede. *(Courtesy of Large Lamp Department, General Electric Company.)*

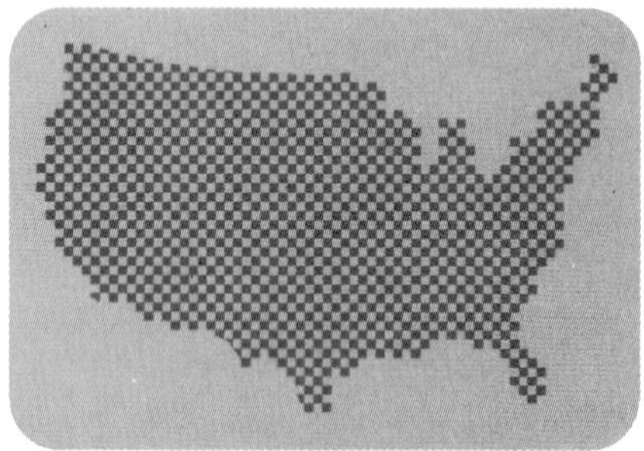

Figure 5.22 Additive spatial fusion. The green dot pattern in the shape of the United States will merge into solid gray when viewed from a distance of 6 to 8 ft. At that distance, the eye no longer distinguishes the individual colors. *(Courtesy of Large Lamp Department, General Electric Company.)*

affects not only hue but also value. The change of value may be seen when a gray circle is placed on a white background. As black is added to the background, which becomes progressively darker, the gray circle appears progressively lighter, showing that colors may be made to appear either lighter or darker according to the tonal value of the adjoining or background color. When black and white are placed side by side, the white looks whiter and the black looks blacker. Colors closely blended will conceal an object, and contrasting colors will emphasize an object. These facts about color have numerous applications in decorating.

The Effect of Natural and Artificial Light on Color

Without light, color does not exist. Both natural and ***artificial light*** are important elements in any room composition. Light can be used to make rugs look deeper, fabrics more luxurious, metals exotic, and woods softer. The mood of the room can become dramatic or warm and intimate.

The first consideration in planning the color scheme for a room should be the quantity and quality of natural light entering the room. The amount of natural light depends on the number, size, and placement of the windows. A room with few or small windows, and hence a small amount of light, is enhanced by light-reflecting colors. A room with large areas of glass may be more pleasant with a predominance of darker light-absorbing colors that will reduce glare. The percentage of light reflected by some of the more common colors is as follows:

White	89%
Ivory	87%
Light gray	65%
Sky blue	65%
Intense yellow	62%
Light green	56%
Forest green	22%
Coconut brown	16%
Black	2%

To assure the necessary amount of natural light and still avoid glare, it is wise to plan the color scheme for each room in relation to the **reflective characteristics** of the large elements in the room—particularly the backgrounds. For example, dark walls will absorb most of the light, and light walls will reflect most of the light. The effect of the floor covering will be the same. A dark carpet that has a ***matte*** finish will make a room much darker than a light-reflecting vinyl.

The quality of **natural light** depends on the direction from which it comes and the time of day. Light from the north is cool. Light from the east is warmer than northern light but cooler than the warm afternoon light from the south and west. The quality of light varies not only from different points of the compass but also at different times during the day. Western light during early hours of the day is neutral, but in later afternoon it contains much red. Because of these differences, generally a wise choice is to use warmer colors in rooms with cool light and cooler colors in sunny rooms with south and west exposures. Because the quality of light also varies during the day, testing colors by carefully observing them during different hours is advisable.

Understanding the interrelationship of color and artificial light is necessary to achieve beautiful color schemes. ***The color of artificial light is determined by*** (1) the source of light, (2) the surface reflecting it, (3) the type of diffusion, and (4) the amount of diffusion. ***The color of an object is the result of*** (1) the spectral qualities of the light source,

Figure 5.23 A room in the natural light of day. *(Courtesy of Louverdrape and Steve Chase Associates.)*

Figure 5.24 The same room as in Figure 5.23 is illuminated by artificial light. *(Courtesy of Louverdrape and Steve Chase Associates.)*

(2) the reflective traits of surface materials, (3) the level of illumination, and (4) the method of lighting.

The Light Source

The three sources of **artificial light—combustion, incandescence,** and **fluorescence**—have already been discussed in Chapter 4, with an emphasis on methods of lighting. This chapter is concerned with the light source and its effect on color.

- Ordinary incandescent light casts a warm glow but can be varied by tinted globes.
- Fluorescent tubes come in white, warm, and cool tints. White light is the most natural and emphasizes cool colors.
- Warm light is most flattering to skin tones and is usually preferred in areas where lower levels of illumination are involved.
- Review of the color wheel demonstrates that to gray or neutralize a color, some of its complement must be added, and to intensify a color, more of the basic hue must be added. Colored light will produce the same effect. Warm light accentuates warm colors and neutralizes cool colors. Cool light intensifies cool colors and deadens warm colors. Warm light is friendly and tends to unify objects. Cool light expands space, produces a crisp atmosphere, and tends to make individual objects stand out.
- Both single and mixed colors take on a different look when subjected to artificial light. For example, a yellowish light will bring out the yellow in yellow-green and yellow-orange. A cool light will bring out the blue in blue-green and blue-violet. Under a warm light—regular incandescent or warm fluorescent—greens will tend to be unified, but blues, which may be pleasantly harmonious in natural light, are thoroughly undependable.

The Surface that Reflects Light

As with natural light, absorptive and reflective surfaces of the room should be planned and observed under artificial light.

The Level of Illumination

The level of illumination will also affect the appearance of color. Quantity of light is measured in **footcandles:** one footcandle provides the amount of light produced by one candle at a distance of 1 ft. Experts have established minimum standards of illumination for various purposes, and these can be measured with a light meter. The effect of color in a room when the light is bright can be stimulating, and a relaxing feeling can be experienced when the light is low. Color, however, may become dull, lifeless, and dreary with insufficient light. As illumination increases, color becomes more vibrant.

The Methods of Lighting

Color is also affected by the method of lighting. Light rays that fall directly from the source onto the surface are **direct lighting.** Light directed upwards and reflected from another surface, usually the ceiling or wall, is known as **indirect lighting.** The direct method, used often for task lighting, may also be effective in creating a warm glow over any area. An indirect light reflecting from a cove onto the ceiling produces an overall light resembling the light of midday. This method of lighting is practical for kitchens and work areas, but it is unflattering for living areas because it tends to give a feeling of flat monotony. When used alone, it can produce a commercial feeling. Portable lamps give direct light, indirect light, or both. With a diffused effect they can produce soft shadows that alter colors, adding interest and attractiveness to a room. Portable lamps can light any area and serve multiple purposes, creating a variety of decorative effects.

Artificial light, when understood and used with skill, may alter, subdue, highlight, or dramatize the colors of a room in a way that no other decorative medium can. Because any situation has many variables, setting down definite rules for the use of light and color is impractical. Therefore, before making a final choice, it is advisable to try each color in the environment for which it will be used, observing it during different hours of the day and after dark.

The Effect of Texture on Color

Color appears different when the texture is varied. Because smooth surfaces reflect light, fabrics with a deep, textured surface, such as pile carpet, velvet, and all manner of nubby weaves, cast tiny shadows. These materials will appear darker than a smooth fabric that is dyed with the same hue and is of the same value and chroma. A rough-textured wall may appear grayed or soiled under artificial light because of shadows cast from the uneven surface. A smooth, shiny surface will reflect light and provide the opposite effect of a rough texture. A dull or matte surface will absorb color, and if it is also dark, may absorb much of the color.

The Effect of Distance and Area on Color

Near colors appear darker and more brilliant than the same colors at a greater distance. Brighter and darker colors used in large rooms will therefore seem less demanding than the same colors used in small rooms. Colors appear stronger in chroma when covering large areas. For example, a small color chip may be the exact color tone preferred for a room, but when that tone is painted on four walls, it looks much darker and brighter because the area of that color chip has been multiplied many thousands of times. When selecting a wall color from a small color chip, it is best to choose one several tints lighter than the color desired for the completed room. A good approach is to paint a sizable area of color on walls in opposite corners of the room and observe them in the light at different times of the day and night before making the complete application.

The Effect of Color on Temperature

Some evidence indicates that color can alter the apparent temperature of a room. When used in large amounts, colors such as red, orange, yellow, and brown tend to make a room feel warm. Colors such as blue, lavender, and gray tend to make a room feel cooler.

Some Uses of Color for the Interior

Off-White

A common notion among many untrained individuals is that off-white in itself is a specific color and complements any decor. This idea is far from the truth. Off-white is white tinted with a hue—any hue. To be compatible, however, off-whites must contain only the same hue. For example, off-white walls, ceilings, glass curtains, and fabrics work best in a room when tinted with the same hue. Value and intensity may vary, but the hue must be the same. Warm off-whites are more easily blended than cool off-whites, recalling a basic characteristic of warm and cool colors.

For Wood Trim

The color of wood trim around doors, ceilings, floors, and other architectural features is important to the general color scheme of the room. When painted, it may be (1) the same hue, value, and intensity as the wall; (2) a darker shade of the wall hue; or (3) a color that contrasts with the wall—if it is pleasantly related to some other major colors in the room. Many professional designers maintain the same wood trim color throughout the home—or at least on each floor—for an effective color transition from room to room (see p. 155).

On the Ceiling

The ceiling is the largest unused area of a room, and the color is important to the general feeling. If the objective is to have the wall and ceiling look the same, the ceiling should be a tint of the wall, since the reflection from the walls and floor tends to make the ceiling look several shades darker than it actually is. If the walls are papered, the ceiling may be a tint of the background or the lightest color in the paper. If walls are paneled in dark wood, the ceiling can be effective if painted white or a light tint of the wood color. If the wood trim is painted white, a white ceiling is advisable. When the ceiling is too high, a darker shade or brighter hue will make it appear lower. If the ceiling is low, the opposite treatment can help make the ceiling appear higher. Often ceilings are painted white or off-white regardless of the respective wall treatment.

When Selecting a Window Treatment

The success of any room is largely dependent on the window treatment and the color used for curtains, draperies, blinds, screens, shades, shutters, or other window decor (see Chapter 8). Windows can be the room's most conspicuous and decorative element or simply be treated as functional. If the objective is to have a completely blended background, the hard or soft treatment should be the same hue, value, and intensity as the wall. If a contrasting effect is desirable, a color that contrasts with the wall can be employed, but it must relate well with other colors used throughout the room. When glass curtains are employed in the treatment, they are usually more pleasing when white or off-white. If the window treatment employs wood, metal, or materials other than fabrics, remember that the color of these materials is also a

A light ceiling expands space.

A dark ceiling feels lower.

consideration in the room's total color effect.

When Walls Are Paneled

Where dark wood paneling is used, colors of intense chroma can be used in the room, since deep wood tones tend to absorb color. If paneled wood walls are light, colors may be light and less intense if a blended effect is desired. If wood paneling is more formal, colors employed for furnishings should complement this feeling. If wood paneling is informal in appearance, colors should enhance that casual effect.

In Altering Apparent Size and Proportion

An object that attracts the eye usually seems larger; therefore, items of furniture may be made to appear larger if painted or upholstered with colors in strong chroma. A small room may be made to seem even smaller if demanding colors, which are space-filling, are used on backgrounds and furniture. On the other hand, light, blended, and receding colors will expand a room and seem to create more space. Through the skillful application of color, a room's dimensions may be altered significantly, and architectural features and furnishings can be highlighted or minimized, depending upon the desired finished effect.

In Bringing Balance to a Room

Since that which attracts the eye seems larger and therefore appears heavier, a small area of bright color will balance a large area of softly muted color, and a small area of dark color will balance a larger area of light color. For example, a small bouquet of bright flowers placed near one end of a long table will balance a large lamp of soft color placed near the other end. A small bright-blue chair will balance a much larger gray-blue sofa. Entire areas of rooms may also be balanced through the use of color. A large end wall treated with bright or dark colors may be balanced on the other side of the room with a similar treatment.

In Transition from One Room to Another

Whenever two rooms adjoin, the colors in them should have a pleasant relationship. One or more colors carried from one room to the other—but not necessarily used in the same manner—will make a pleasing transition. For example, the accent color in the wallpaper of an entrance hall may be neutralized and used on the walls of the adjoining living room or may be emphasized in a piece of upholstery fabric.

Whenever one room may be seen from another, like dining and living rooms, closely related colors will establish a color unity. Following are some of the most common and successful methods of achieving color transition.

- Many professional designers prefer to keep the **floor covering** consistent from room to room. For example, a gray carpet might be employed for all rooms with the exception of hard floor surfaces for entries, bathrooms, and utility areas.
- Similar or matching **wall and ceiling colors** from room to room will create a continuity of color transition.
- The consistent use of **moldings and architectural trim** throughout the home helps provide unity.

Figure 5.25 Color transition from a seating area into an executive board room is accomplished by artfully repeating the blue and green scheme in various ways on walls, upholstery, and custom-designed carpets. *(Courtesy of Dan River/Wunda Weve.)*

- Related colors employed on various pieces of **furniture** and for **window treatments** should be considered for effective color transition.

- **Accessories** that carry colors from one interior space to another can aid in creating an effective flow of colors.

In Period Rooms

Particular styles and periods of furnishings have appropriate colors that reflect their character and set the feeling of authenticity (see Figure 5.2). Colors should be chosen with discrimination when designing period rooms. Many excellent sources are available providing full information on the subject for the designer trying to create color schemes for a style actually employed during a particular period. This approach is particularly useful for restoration projects. Many designers today, whether creating traditional or modern styles, approach the design program with complete flexibility in color usage.

In Hue Distribution

The distribution of color has already been discussed under hue, value, and intensity, but a brief reiteration by way of emphasis can be helpful. Color is the most unifying element available to the interior designer, and its skillful distribution is essential to the feeling of unity. Color distribution can be achieved in various ways.

1. First, planned value distribution is a necessary step. Each room can be enhanced with some light, some dark, and some medium tones used in varying amounts according to the effect desired. In most cases, the darkest tones are used in the smallest amounts, although in special rooms the reverse may be employed with dramatic results. When applying the law of chromatic distribution to a room, backgrounds will be in the most neutralized tones, large pieces of furniture will have more intensity, and accents such as small chairs and accessories will be in the strongest chroma. This procedure in distributing color produces rooms with a feeling of serenity and lasting comfort.
2. Second, many successful rooms are planned around one dominant hue. This color need not be repeated on all major pieces of furniture, but it should be repeated at least once to give a feeling of unity. Unity may also be achieved by using colors containing one hue common to all. For example, hues on the color wheel going clockwise from orange to blue-green all contain yellow and combine pleasantly together. The color that is common to all—yellow—will recede and the other colors will stand out.

Although the preceding is the safest way to color scheme a room, deviating from these guidelines is possible and in some instances desirable. For example, dark walls can create a feeling of comfort, warmth, and security and unify the room's furnishings. A light floor will visually expand space and when adjacent to dark walls will create a dramatic effect. Seldom, however, is a dark ceiling advisable. In the search for space, a common need today, a light ceiling seemingly provides space by visually extending the room's height. Under most conditions, dark ceilings can decrease the feeling of space and be oppressive. On the other hand, depending on the architecture, a ceiling may be painted a dark value and provide a feeling of the infinity experienced from viewing a nighttime sky. This approach is often effectively employed in commercial spaces like restaurants, museums, and exhibition areas.

Many individuals have difficulty visualizing a completed room. This capability develops through experience. Forming a mental picture of how colors appear when juxtaposed is not easy, and students and clients may need visual aid. This procedure requires preliminary planning.

- One way to envision a completed room is to make a chart using approximate proportions of various elements such as walls, floor, ceiling, furniture, and accents. Fabric, paint, and hard material samples can then be attached to the chart. This method will not show exactly how the completed project will appear, but it will be helpful.
- Another method is to assemble a setup with actual samples of all items to be used. Students often use this procedure in a design lab or in the classroom employing an **A frame.** A designer can create this grouping of colors and materials for furnishings in a professional setting for the client. Samples are presented of all materials to be used in approximate proportions. This method will most closely approximate the look of the completed room.
- Additionally, professional designers can create a rendering of a particular space that indicates the planned color scheme. This allows the client to visualize on a small scale the projected idea.

Reflecting the Mood of the Room

More than any other element, color is capable of setting the general mood of a room. For example, various hues, values, and intensities can create a restful or stimulating feeling. Rich, muted tones most often produce a mood of tranquility, and lively, contrasting colors create an informal mood. General color moods can be evoked for specific areas of the house.

- The **entrance hall** is a room that introduces the home. The entrance area can effectively emphasize the theme chosen for major rooms. Color in this space can be somewhat dramatic and daring or simple and unobtrusive, depending on the occupant's taste.
- **Living areas** for more formal purposes generally have neutralized color schemes that tend to produce an atmosphere of tranquility. If a more lively mood is desired, colors of stronger intensity can achieve this effect.
- **Informal living areas** such as family and recreation rooms are often treated with stimulating color schemes that can create a cheerful and casual environment.
- **Dining rooms** are at their best when the color schemes are unobtrusive, permitting a variety of table decorations as well as a serene dining atmosphere.
- **Kitchens** and other work areas are usually more desirable when large areas of color are light, fresh, and clean looking. Often, bright accents of strong chroma can enhance these areas. Personal color preferences can help dictate a suitable color scheme for the occupant who will work in the space.
- **Bedrooms** are private areas of the house, and personal preference should be the determining factor in the choice of colors. As a general rule, the master bedroom should be done in restful tones pleasing to the occupants. Children are often given the opportunity to select colors for their own spaces. These colors may only be employed for accents and small furnishings, but the satisfaction of providing some color input can be very satisfying for a child.
- Color schemes for **bathrooms** are probably the most flexible. Colors may be stark white or dark in value, muted or intense, with any hue employed. The colors for this private area can work well by reflecting the style and mood of adjoining rooms.

Reflecting Personality

Color is a valuable design tool for reflecting the personality of the individual for whom it is chosen. Although there is little research to substantiate the theory that personal color preferences are related to certain personality characteristics, general associations are often suggested. For example, outgoing, informal, and friendly individuals are thought to prefer warm and bright colors, and more formal and private individuals, cool and more subdued colors. Colors selected may be any combination of hue, value, or chroma if they are personally pleasing and livable. The problem of selecting colors that reflect personality is compounded when a number of individuals are involved. Hopefully, input from all occupants will be considered before final color decisions are made. In the selection of colors, current trends may be taken into account but need not be the determining factor. Regardless of what colors are

Figure 5.26 Cinnamon brown walls and a pastel Kirman rug, from which the scheme was taken, unify furnishings and provide a warm, cloistered atmosphere. *(Photograph by Mark K. Allen.)*

Figure 5.27 Color use reflecting a comfortable and relaxing mood is conveyed in this bedroom combining a soft blue carpet, neutral walls, a white bedspread, and limited use of unobtrusive patterns. *(Courtesy of Gayl Baddeley/Associates.)*

in fashion, the personal preferences expressive of the occupants should always be the main consideration.

Color in Wood

Since wood has color and each type of wood has a particular beauty, wood should not be overlooked when planning a color scheme. Heavily grained woods generally call for heavier textures and stronger colors than do fine-grained woods. Mixing woods can add interest to a room, but it is wise to use woods in close proximity that are similar in feeling. For example, rough-grained golden oak and formal reddish-brown mahogany are not particularly good companions, but finely grained light-brown maple and brownish walnut usually combine well. Of course, style and design of a partic-

Figure 5.28 Each wood type has a particular color characteristic considered when color scheming a room. A room with all the same wood tends to be monotonous, and a room with too much variety of wood can be confusing. In this mountain residence the dark reddish tones of the wood used for architectural detailing nicely contrast with the light-colored lodge-pole pine furniture. *(Photograph by Lincoln Allen, Salt Lake City, Utah.)*

ular wood item must be considered when selecting various components for an interior space. A vast selection of woods, each with unique color variations, is available for furniture, paneling, moldings, cupboards, flooring, and other furnishings and architectural details. Becoming familiar with the particular colors and characteristics of wood can help provide confidence and success in selecting pleasing combinations for interiors. (See Chapter 9 for information on wood types, color, characteristics, and uses.)

Color Forecasts for the 1990s

When reviewing color forecasts made by various professional sources, it is important to remember that there are no absolute color rules that can be applied at any particular time. An awareness of color fashions is advisable, but, ultimately, personal preferences for comfortable and pleasing colors are the most valuable consideration. The interior designer's responsibility is to help the client select colors that are right for a personal environment, regardless of trends. The greatest challenge—and possibly the most satisfying reward—to any designer is to achieve beautiful and livable schemes for every room in a house through the knowledgeable use and distribution of color.

Organizations that help determine color preferences for American residential and contract design include the following: (1) the Color Association of the United States, (2) the Home Fashion's League, (3) the International Colour Authority, (4) the National Decorating Products Association, and (5) Colorcast. Color forecasts are drawn from the latest research conducted by color stylists and authorities, and they provide fairly accurate annual predictions that help consumers, professional designers, and merchandising experts.

Forecasts for 1988 indicated a strong color shift toward the warmer palette, darker values, and tones that contain gray and black. Popular colors include yellowed taupes and warm yellows, black accents, colored neutrals, pinks, peaches and corals, earthy colors, tans, lavenders and plums, gray-blues, corals and reds, blue-greens, and a wide variety of greens—from warm to cool and from light to dark.

As more consumers and professionals design with personal style in mind, the more difficult the task becomes to make color forecasts for the future. It is predicted by many color experts in the field that colors preferred during the next decade will be selected on the basis of individual taste preferences of the client and homeowner without being influenced to a great extent by colors promoted by professionals.

Since color guides are only published annually by various color organizations to aid the interior designer, fashion designer, and industrial designer, information on trend predictions for the 1990s is limited. However, many color experts expect some general trends for the 1990s. It is predicted that warm desert hues and coppertones will be employed. Many colors available will be mixed with gray, and the use of light, medium, and dark values will be seen. Green will be one of the most popular colors ranging from soft muted greens to apple greens and to deep forest greens. Yellows will make a fresh appearance. White, off-whites, and taupes will gain in popularity. Blues will mostly be muted whether it be a light value or a dark indigo shade. Blued greens and turquoise will continue as preferred interior colors as well as rich reds and deep plums. Pink in both warm and cool hues will continue as an annual favorite.

To sum up trend predictions for the 1990s, the consumer will have a wider range of hues from which to select with the home furnishings industry offering colors to suit a variety of tastes. Colors are generally expected to be richer and muted, although pastels will continue in use. Bright colors will be limited in use and whites, grays, and taupes will regain popularity.

ASSIGNMENT

In the Student Work Packet are 10 color plates. By applying the principles discussed in this chapter, complete the 10 color plates according to the following directions and submit them to the instructor for evaluation.

Note: In doing all color plates, paint neatly and creatively using paint *only*, except for plate 8. In planning color schemes for the rooms in plates 6 through 10, first establish the dominant color you desire, then choose subordinate and accent colors. Keep the law of chromatic distribution and the criterion of livability in mind when planning each room.

PLATE 1 (Process for Mixing True Tints)

After carefully studying the lesson material on mixing tints, proceed as follows:

1. Paint the six circles in the left-hand column with white.

2. Paint the second vertical group with the hue indicated.

3. Starting at the top, from left to right, add a *small* amount of red hue to white and paint the circle labeled "Result." Notice that the result is a bluish pink. This is because white is an imperfect pigment and contains blue. To correct this, add a *small* amount of yellow (paint the fourth circle yellow). The final result on the far right (which will be made up of white and red plus a touch of yellow) should be a clear light tint of the red in the second column.

4. Continue this procedure until all six tints are completed. To determine the proper hue to add for each correction, refer to the section on value. (*Note:* Access to Munsell color chips for result comparisons is helpful.)
5. *Caution:* Be certain that the tint results at the far right are *clear* and *light* and that all final tints are as near the same value as possible.

PLATE 2 (Process for Mixing Tones and Shades)

1. Begin with the top line and paint the first circle red.

2. Add a touch of black to the red to produce a *shade,* and fill in the middle circle.

3. Add a touch of white to the shade to produce a *tone,* and fill in the third circle. For a lighter tone, add a touch of the shade mixture to white.

4. Continue in this manner until a satisfactory shade and tone of each of the six hues in the left-hand column have been produced.

5. Each shade should contain the same amount of black and each tone the same amount of white for a consistent result.

PLATE 3 (Value Distribution)

This is an exercise in the application of value distribution in creating two achromatic color schemes.

1. Fill in the circles on the left. Begin with black at the bottom and raise the value of each succeeding circle. The top circle should be white.

2. Using black, white, and values in between, paint the two identical pictures to illustrate the dissimilar effects created when value is varied. Distribute the values differently, keeping in mind that the darkest value works well when used in the least amount. Note the two sets of window drapery: sheers to the outside and drapery against the wall.

PLATE 4 (Color Neutralization Process)

This is an exercise in neutralizing colors.

1. Paint the circles in the left-hand column in the hues indicated.

2. Paint the circles in the middle column with the complementary hue of each.

3. In the third column, make three degrees of neutralization by adding a *slight* touch of the complement to the first section, a little more to the second section, and still a little more to the third section.
Caution: Be certain that all sections in the far-right column remain neutralized shades of the original hue in the far-left column, and *not* muddy browns.

PLATES 5, 6, 7 (Monochromatic, Analogous or Complementary, and Shibui Color Schemes)

These are exercises in planning and executing color schemes.

1. Carefully examine Plates 5, 6, and 7. At the top of each one, the color scheme for the room to be painted is indicated: monochromatic, analogous or complementary, and shibui.

2. Plan each one carefully according to the scheme.

3. In planning the shibui color scheme, select an object from nature such as a leaf, piece of bark, seashell, or stone and use this as the basis for the color scheme. Evaluate the principles of shibui before completing Plate 7.

4. After planning the color schemes for Plates 5, 6, and 7, apply paint to the line drawings.

PLATE 8 (Color Scheme from Wallpaper or Fabric)

This is an exercise in color scheming a room from wallpaper or fabric. Select a piece of patterned wallpaper or fabric and attach it to the entire wall area on Plate 8. Using this pattern as a basis, develop a color scheme for the room using the following procedure:

1. If the wallpaper or fabric will be used on all four walls, cover the entire area indicated. If it will be used on only one wall, cover about two-thirds of the area and paint the remaining area with a color that enhances the wallpaper or fabric.

2. Paint the ceiling a color (preferably a tint of the wall color) that complements the wall.

3. Finish the wood trim in one of the following ways: paint it the same hue as the wall, using the same value and intensity; use the same hue as the wall, but in a deeper value and intensity; use a contrasting color related to one of the room colors; use white (if it complements the fabric or wallpaper); or use a natural wood tone, in which case a picture of natural wood grain is acceptable.

4. Paint the floor a slightly darker shade of the wall hue for a blended effect or use an appropriate color taken from the patterned wallpaper or fabric.

5. If the goal is to blend curtains and drapery with the plain wall or with the wallpaper or fabric background, follow the procedure given for wood trim. If a contrasting effect is desired, select an appropriate color from the wallpaper or fabric. (Note that the drapery is the one against the wall. The glass curtain is the one to the outside.) If you select a hard window treatment (levelors, shutters, screens, vertical louvres, etc.), a picture of this treatment is acceptable.

6. For upholstery fabrics, pick up colors from the patterned wallpaper or fabric. One successful approach is to apply the law of chromatic distribution, in which the most intense colors are reserved for the smallest areas.

PLATE 9 (Color Scheme from a Picture)

This is an exercise in using the colors in a picture to plan a scheme for a room.

1. Find a small picture appropriate for a living room wall.

2. Mount it on Plate 9 over the area indicated. Follow the same procedure for color planning a room, as for Plate 8.

3. *Caution:* Examine the picture carefully and try to interpret the general feeling in the room.

PLATE 10 (Color Transition)

This is an exercise in planning a color scheme for three adjoining rooms to provide a pleasant transition of color. Applying material found in this chapter, artistically paint the entrance, living room, and dining room in a related color scheme.

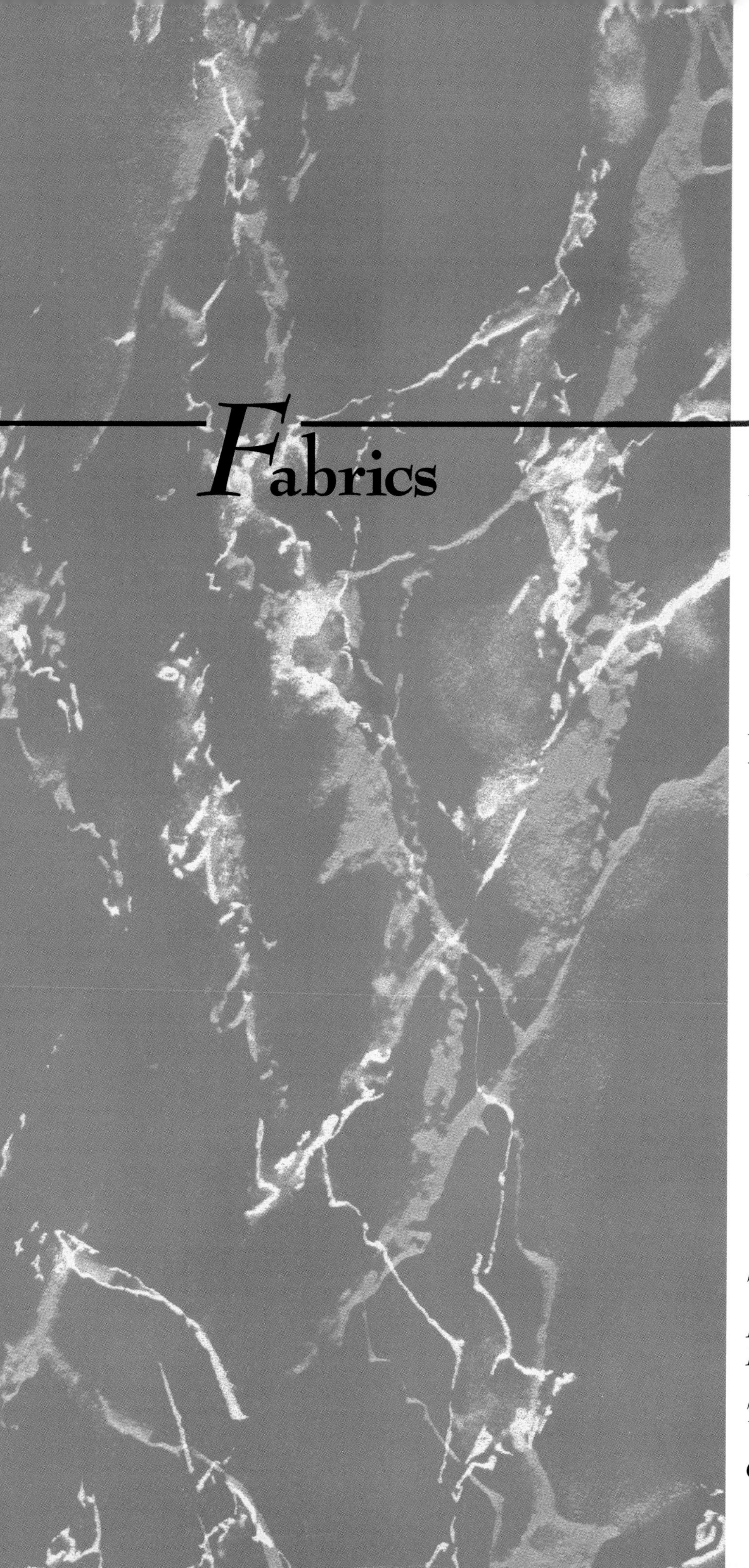

Fabrics

Chapter Six

Authorities in the field recognize that skillful use of fabric with the right color, texture, and design is a sure means to creating a successful room. Throughout history fabric has contributed immensely to the decorative beauty of particular eras. For centuries fabric has been used to cover walls, drape windows and beds, and upholster chairs and sofas. The various components of a room—the walls, floor, and furniture—can be brought into harmonious relationship when fabric is used judiciously. Through knowledgeable use, fabric can serve many functions, add beauty, and establish a unifying element in the total design. Both natural and man-made miracle fibers are woven into fabric for visual appeal and functional purpose. As never before, today's interior designer can satisfy the desire for elegance and practicality at the same time.

The term ***fabric*** is freely applied to textiles or cloth manufactured by machine or by hand, which includes **weaving, knitting, twisting,** ***felting,*** and **lacing,** as well as the **fabrication of plastics.** The appearance and durability of a fabric are dependent on the type and qualities of materials used and the method of construction, as well as the color, pattern, finish, and other surface embellishment.

Fibers

The raw material, either derived from nature or man-made, is the fibers. Silk or man-made fibers can be produced into long threadlike ***filaments,*** sometimes miles in length. A perfect fiber that will adequately serve every general household purpose does not exist. Each fiber has its own desirable properties and limitations. Manufacturers have found that by blending certain fibers, the most desirable qualities of each can be incorporated into a fabric. With today's modern technology, advanced and improved methods are being employed to create new and better synthetic fibers and improve old fibers.

Yarns are made by spinning various lengths of fibers (the raw material) into strands in preparation for fabric construction. Performance and ap-

Figure 6.1 The nineteenth-century documentary pattern in this trio of wall-coverings and fabrics features a small-scale design with sprigs of flowers scattered over a white ground. *(Courtesy of Van Luit & Co.)*

pearance of the fabric are affected by the method and the amount of twisting of the fibers. A high twist produces more strength and durability but takes away some of the luster. Long filaments with little twist will generally maintain a high luster but will lose much of their stability. ***Ply*** is the result of twisting two or more single yarns together before weaving to give added strength or create a novel surface effect.

Natural Fibers

Fibers that come from nature fall into four classifications: ***protein, cellulosic, metallic,*** and ***mineral.***

Protein

The **protein,** or **animal, fibers** of most importance are wool and silk.

- ***Wool*** taken from the fleece of sheep or from Angora goat (***mohair***), camel, and other animal hairs has been used since the seventh or eighth centuries before Christ. In early Egypt, Greece, Asia, and the Middle East, it was used for clothing and some household articles. Wool is resilient, resists abrasion, is a good insulator, is flame retardant, and can be used woven fine or coarse, loose or tight. It can be dyed from palest to deepest colors, cleans well, resists dirt, and can absorb up to 20 percent of its weight without feeling damp. Disadvantages include a tendency to yellow with age, shrink, and be damaged by moths and other insects.
- ***Silk*** is an ancient fiber that, according to legend, was discovered in China about 2540 B.C. The process of producing it from the larvae of silkworms, known as ***sericulture,*** was kept secret for many years but gradually became known in countries around the world. A beautiful long fiber, soft and luxurious, silk is surpassed in strength only by nylon. It takes and holds dye well, but the sun's rays break down the fiber, necessitating its protection from direct sunlight. Raw silk, or uncultivated silk, is a shorter and coarser fiber with less luster. Both types of silk fibers are used for fabric construction and are expensive.
- ***Leather,*** although not a fiber, is an animal product that has long been used for aesthetic and utilitarian household purposes. It is pliable and durable and may be dyed or used in its natural color. Genuine leather is expensive, but it has been simulated to a remarkable degree and currently is available at reasonable prices.

Cellulosic

Cellulosic, or **vegetable, fibers** include stems, leaves, and seed hairs found in cotton, flax (linen), and some minor fibers.

- ***Cotton*** is believed to have been grown in India during the fourth century B.C. and used in Rome before the time of Christ. Cotton is the most plentiful of the natural fibers. It takes and holds color well, washes easily, and can be woven any way—from sheer to heavyweight. Its flexibility allows it to be adapted for such functions as upholstery, floor coverings, and window treatments. Cost varies according to the quality of the fiber, weave, and finish.
- ***Linen*** is made from flax fibers and is the most ancient of all the fibers. It was used for weaving in Egypt as early as 4000 B.C. Linen is strong, pliable, lustrous, and washable, and it takes and holds color. It is absorbent but wrinkles readily unless chemically treated, which then reduces its wear potential.

Other miscellaneous vegetable fibers known and used since prehistoric times are **ramie** (China grass or grass linen, a fiber resembling linen), **yucca, milkweed, hemp, jute, kapok, palm leaves,** and **sisal.** These fibers make their appearance in household materials such as floor coverings, wall fabrics, upholstery, padding, and place mats.

Metallic

- **Metallic fibers** include strips of gold, silver, or copper and are used chiefly as accents in decorative fabrics. Metallic fibers glitter without tarnishing and are washable if used in washable fabrics.

Mineral

- **Mineral fiber,** found in **asbestos,** is difficult to spin without the addition of another fiber. Asbestos is best known for its fire-retardant quality, but it has been found to be unhealthy and unsafe. Another type of mineral fiber, metallic fibers, is made from gold, silver, copper, or other metals. These mineral strips, which technically have to be produced by people in fiber form, are used chiefly as accents in decorative fabrics.

Man-Made Fibers

The increasing use of fabrics made from man-made fibers derived either from chemicals or natural solutions chemically treated is due to new chemical research and advanced technology and research that have resulted in improvements in quality; durability; resistance to soil, mildew, and moths; ease of

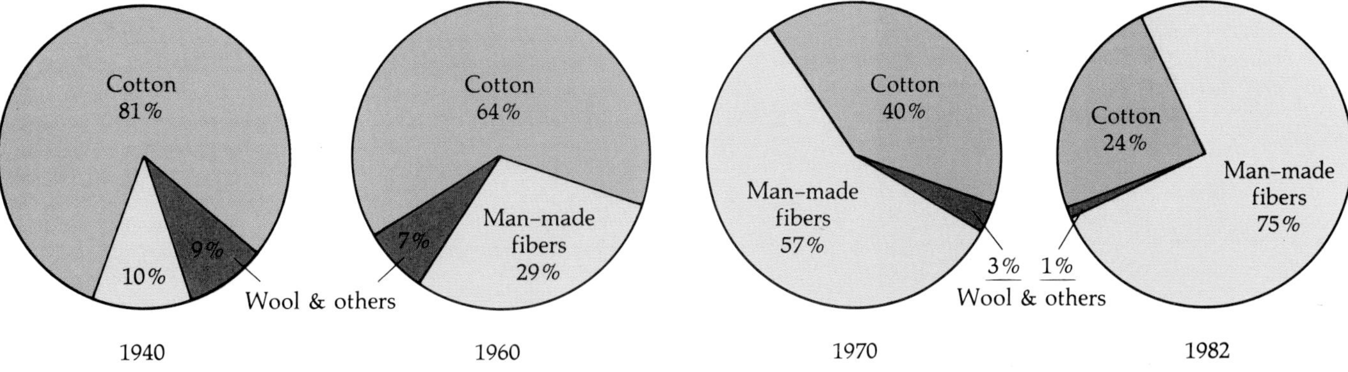

care; and other desirable properties. Although costs vary, these fabrics tend to be less expensive than those made from natural fibers. Man-made fibers fall into two categories: **regenerated cellulosic** and **synthetic.**

REGENERATED CELLULOSIC

- **Regenerated cellulosic fibers** are produced by changing the physical and chemical formation of natural ingredients. Some examples are rayon, acetate, and triacetate.

SYNTHETIC

- **Synthetic fibers** are produced from chemicals and carbon compounds. Some examples are nylon, acrylic, modacrylic polyester, olefin, and glass. In the bewildering array of man-made fibers on the market today, the consumer is often at a loss in making a choice. To alleviate the problem, the Federal Trade Commission (FTC) established rules and regulations under the Textile Products Identification Act. Under these regulations, each manufactured fiber is defined in specific terms and given a ***generic*** name, which along with the company's trade name must appear on the label attached to the fabric. The generic name is the term assigned to a chemical family of which all members exhibit certain traits. For example, all members of the nylon family are characterized by unusual strength and resistance to abrasion, but they will not hold up well under direct sunlight. The polyester family is known for its drip-dry quality and resistance to sun deterioration. The ***trade name*** identifies the manufacturer. Because manufacturers have a practical need to give specific names to their products, hundreds of trade names for man-made fibers exist, making it virtually impossible for the consumer to recognize them all. Familiarity with the general properties of each fiber family, however, and checking of the label to make sure of the fabric content will help one select the fabric that best serves specific needs. The fiber alone, however, will not ensure good performance if the construction, dyes, and finishes are not properly handled.

During the past four decades, the production and consumption of man-made fibers has steadily increased. In 1940, man-made fibers accounted for only 10 percent of the fibers used. By 1960, the usage had increased to 29 percent. Man-made fibers now account for approximately 75 percent of all fibers used by American textile mills, with polyester being the single most widely used fiber. The pie charts show the change in fiber consumption from 1940 to 1987.

Table 6.1 includes the most common man-made fibers, their generic names, an analysis of the qualities characterizing each, their most important decorative uses, and some trade names and their manufacturers.

Construction

The history of textile arts is almost as old as the history of humanity. The exact origin of the loom is not certain, but evidence suggests that it was used in Mesopotamia before 5000 B.C. A remarkable correlation exists between the history of the textile industry and the important economic, political, and social events that have transpired in many areas of the world since ancient times. Although modern mechanization has brought about great changes in textile production, weave structures are much the same as they were at the beginning of the Renaissance, and simple standard weaves are still basic to the industry. More intricate weaves that originated in the Orient, such as damasks and brocades, are now produced on ***Jacquard*** looms.

TABLE 6.1 *Properties of man-made fibers*

GENERIC NAME	APPEARANCE	ABRASION	RESILIENCE	HEAT TOLERANCE	FLAMMABILITY
Acetate (regenerated cellulose)	Smooth; silky; drapes well; holds shape well	Fair	Poor	Poor	Slow
Triacetate a subdivision of the acetate group	Crisp; smooth; silky; drapes well; strong colors	Fair	Good; resists wrinkling; retains pleats	Less sensitive than acetate	Slowly combustible
Acrylic	Wool-like; soft; bulky; warm; may squeak; rich colors; pilling depends on quality	Good; needs treatment for static	Good; holds heatset pleats	Sticks at 450°F	Resists fire; burns with yellow flame
Modacrylic (modified acrylic)	Similar to acrylic; good color retention	Good	Fair to good	Does not melt	Self-extinguishing
Aramid	Stiff and smooth	High; exceptional strength	Excellent; low stretchability	Not affected	Low flammability
Glass	Soapy; lustrous; silky; color range fair; Beta Fiberglas has remarkable sheerness	Strongest of all fibers	Excellent	Fireproof	Nonflammable
Nylon (polyamide)	Squeaky; silky; cold; natural luster; good color range; drapes well	Excellent	Very good; resists wrinkling; can be heat set to hold shape	High resistance	Melts slowly
Olefin (propylene and ethylene)	Waxy; wool-like; color range fair	Good to excellent	Good; resists wrinkling	Poor; heat sensitive	Slow to burn
Polyester	Silky, cotton, or wool-like; drapes well; color range fair	Good to excellent	Excellent; resists wrinkles	Sticks at 400°F	Burns slowly
Rayon (regenerated cellulose)	Soft; drapes well; excellent color range; bright	Fair to good	Low to medium; crease retention poor	Excellent; does not melt	Burns quickly
Saran	Soft; drapes well	Tough	Crease retentive	Shrinks in intense heat	Nonflammable
Vinyl (thermoplastic resins)	Smooth; variety of weights; expanded vinyl; closely resembles leather	Good	Low	Shrinks at 212–230°F in dry heat, less in moist heat	Burns with difficulty

Notes: All man-made fibers are resistant to moths and mildew.
Insulation depends on construction and is primarily a function of thickness. Hollow polyester fibers provide particularly good insulation.
Costs are variable, depending on construction.

LIGHT TOLERANCE	DECORATIVE USES	CARE	SOME TRADE NAMES AND MANUFACTURERS
Long exposure weakens fiber; colors fade unless protected by special finish	Curtains, drapery, upholstery, rugs; for shower curtains in blends with other fibers; moderate cost	Soil resistance fair; wash in lukewarm water or dry-clean, depending on dyes, finishes, decorative designs; quick drying; iron at moderate heat	Ariloft (Eastman); Celanese Acetate (Celanese); Chromspun (Eastman); Estron (Eastman); Lanese (Celanese); Loftura (Eastman); Lanese (Celanese)
More resistant than acetate	Same as acetate	Same as acetate	Arnel (Celanese)
Good	Rugs, carpets, blankets, curtains, drapery, upholstery	Keeps buoyancy when washed with warm water; machine dry; does not shrink, sag, or stretch; steam pressing reduces loft	Acrilan (Monsanto); Creslan (American Cyanamid); Orlon (DuPont); Zefran, Zetkrome (Dow Chemical)
Excellent	Curtains, drapery, in carpet blends, furry rugs, blankets	Similar to acrylic; resists chemical stains; washable; use warm iron; shrinks unless stabilized; does not dry-clean well	Acrilan (Monsanto); Verel (Tennessee Eastman), Dynel (Union Carbide)
Weakens with long exposure	Carpets	Not affected by moisture	Kevlar (DuPont); Nomex (DuPont)
No loss	Curtains, drapery, bedspreads; Beta Fiberglas used for bedspreads	Impervious to moisture; hand wash; drip-dry; needs no ironing	Fiberglas (Owens-Corning); Pittsburgh PPG (Pittsburgh), Vitron (Libby-Owens-Ford); Unirove (Ferro Corporation)
Poor	Upholstery, bedspreads, carpets	Washable; quick drying; use warm iron; resists soil; easy spot removal; static electricity unless treated	Altron (Monsanto); Anso (carpet yarns) (Allied Chemical); Antron Nylon (DuPont); Cadon (Monsanto); Caprolan (Allied Chemical); Cumuloft (Chemstrand); Lusterloft (carpet staple) (American Enka)
Good	Rugs, blankets, upholstery, webbing, seat covers; low cost	Wash or dry-clean; iron at very low heat; good soil resistance	Durel (Celanese); Herculon (Hercules Powder); Marvess (Alamo Industries); Patlon (Monarch Carpet Mills); Marquesa (Amoco Fabrics); Vectra (National Plastic Products); Polyloom (Chevron Chemical)
Loses strength in prolonged exposure	Curtains, drapery, upholstery, carpets and rugs, pillow floss blankets	Soils easily; machine wash in warm water; dries quickly; use warm iron; resists stretching and shrinking	Avlin (American Viscose Division, FMC); Dacron (DuPont); Encron (Enka Manufacturing); Fortrel (Celanese); Kodel (Eastman Chemical Products); Trevira (Hystron Fibers)
Fades when not solution dyed	Curtains, upholstery, drapery, table linen, rugs; relatively inexpensive; probably most versatile fiber	Same as acetate; fair soil resistance	Avril (Avtel Fibers); Coloray (solution-dyed staple) (Courtaulds North America); Enkaire (flat filament staple) (American Enka); Enkrome (American Enka); Fibro (Courtaulds North America); Zantrel (American Enka)
Excellent	Outdoor furniture, upholstery and screening, curtains, drapery, wall coverings	Excellent ease of care; resists wrinkling and stains; water-repellent	Saran (Dow Chemical); National (National Plastics); Rovana (Dow Chemical); Velon (Firestone Plastic)
Weakens with long exposure	Shower curtains, wall coverings, upholstery when backed with fabric	Stain resistant; waterproof; wash and wipe clean	Beautafilm (Hartford); Boltaflex (General Tire and Rubber); Duran (Masland); Fabrilite (DuPont); Ford (Ford Motor); Koroseal (B.F. Goodrich); Lumite (Chicopee Mills); Naugahyde (U.S. Rubber); Rucaire (Hooker Chemical)

Weaving

COMMON TYPES OF WEAVES

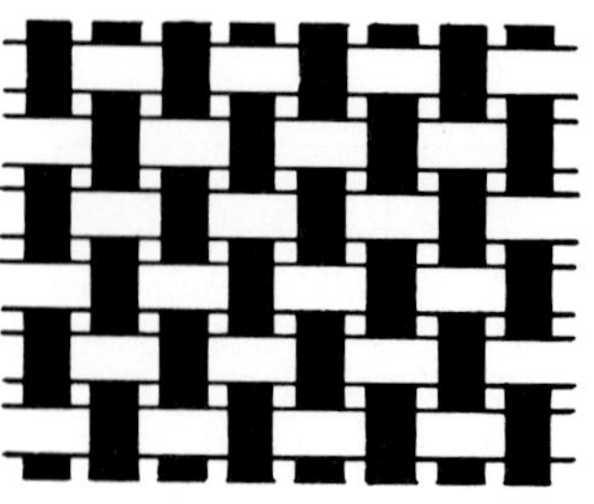
Plain Weave

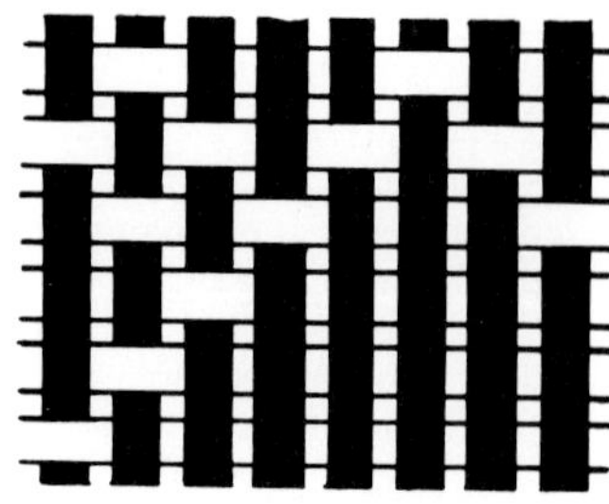
Jacquard Weave

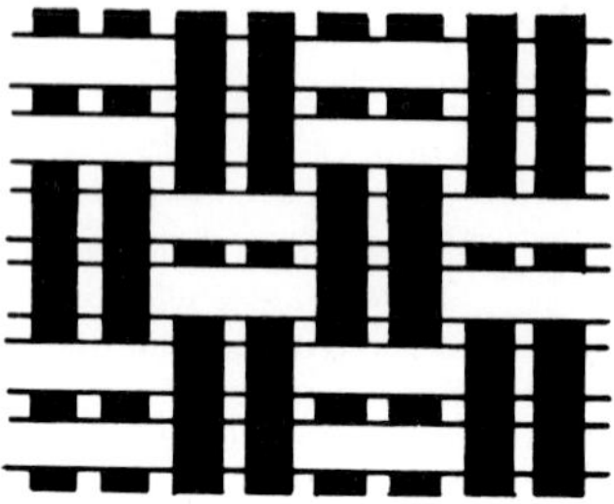
Double (or Basket) Weave

Sateen Weave

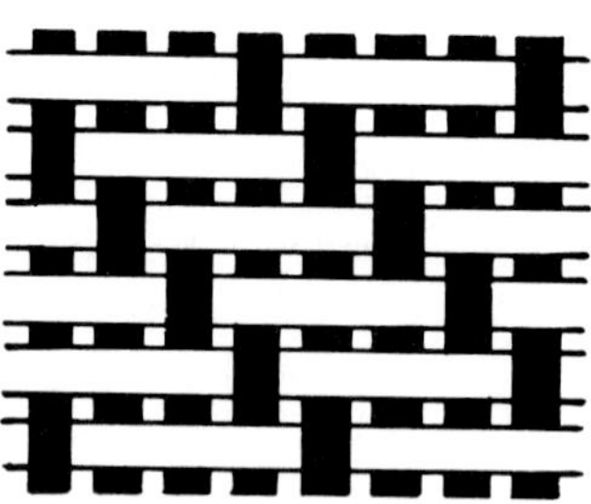
Twill Weave

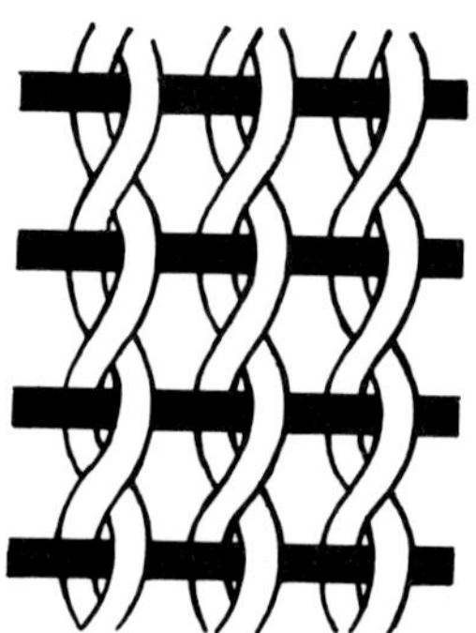
Leno Weave

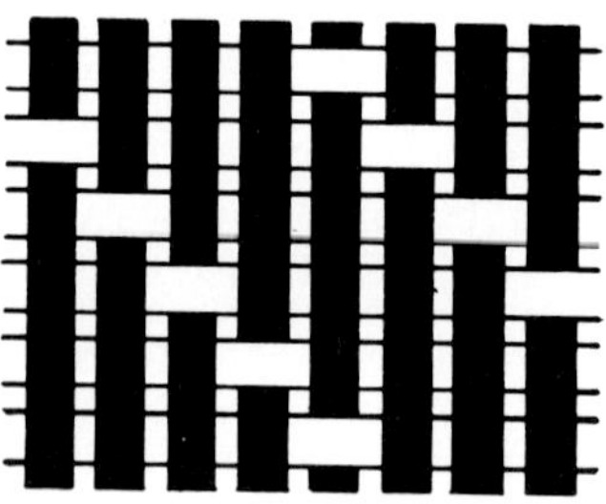
Satin Weave

Uncut Pile

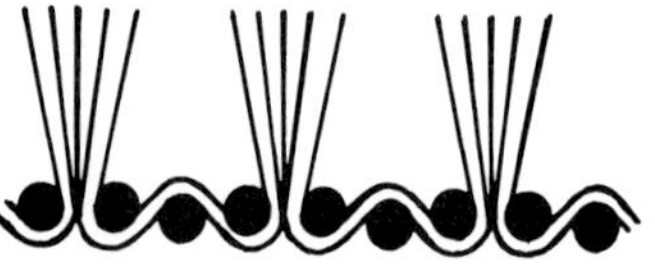
Cut Pile

The following are the most common weaves, as well as some more intricate ones, used in producing today's decorative fabrics, with a brief description of the basic structure of each.

- ***Plain weave*** is made by the simple interweaving of warp (vertical or lengthwise) and weft or woof (horizontal or crosswise) threads, and may be single or double, regular or irregular.

  In the plain ***single*** weave, one weft thread passes over each warp thread. When the weave is balanced in sequence of over and under so that the warp and weft have the same yarn count per square inch, it is called ***regular.*** A plain regular weave is also called a *tabby* weave. When the warp and weft differ because of different weights or textures of yarn, the weave is called ***irregular*** or ***unbalanced.*** Novelty yarns vary in appearance.

  In the plain ***double*** (or ***basket***) weave, two weft threads are interlaced into two warp threads. When the weave is regular, it is called *backed cloth.* This weave may also be irregular due to variations of weight or texture.
- ***Twill weaves*** are those in which two or more threads pass over or under another set of threads, skipping at regular intervals to produce a diagonal effect. Twill weaves may be regular or irregular. In the regular twill, the long threads, or floats, pass over and under the same number of yarns. In the irregular twill, the floats pass over and under a different number of threads. Irregular twills account for many decorative fabrics such as denim, gabardine, and herringbone.
- ***Satin weaves*** have few interlacings or filling yarns with long floats. This combination produces a fabric with luster, softness, and drapability, especially when the fiber is smooth, as with satin and sateen.
- ***Jacquard*** is a revolutionary loom machine system capable of creating multicolored fabrics of intricate patterns. It was invented in France in 1801 by Joseph-Marie Jacquard (1752–1834). Some of the most common woven fabrics created on the Jacquard loom include damasks, tapestries, and brocades.

- *Tapestry* weaving is a great art known since ancient times. It has been said that the history of the world is woven into tapestry. This fabric was originally handwoven and made with bobbins. Tapestry can be woven on practically every type of loom, but the Jacquard is most commonly used. The weave is essentially plain but is made in a special way: across the warp in sections with the weft yarns interlocking around the same warp, into one another, or around adjacent warps, leaving a narrow slit. Tapestry has a rough feel. American Navajo rugs, French Aubusson rugs, and a wide range of upholstery fabrics are made of this type of weave.
- *Pile weaves* are produced by loops or tufts of yarn that stand out from the surface of the fabric. These loops may be cut, uncut, or a combination. The piles may be formed from the warp or the weft threads.

  A great many pile weaves are used in a wide variety of fabrics. The basic weave of the carpet industry is the raised-warp pile. Plush and velvet, originally woven by this method, are generally made today in a double cloth that is cut apart to produce the pile. Numerous household fabrics used for both utility and luxury are produced by one of the pile weaves, including terry cloth towels; corduroy, frieze, and velvet; and shag, velvet, and tufted carpets.
- *Extra warp and weft pattern weaves* are those in which extra warp and weft yarns are added to the fabric during weaving. Inlay pattern weaving was a well-known art in ancient Egypt, China, the Near East, and Peru. Some of the most beautiful decorative fabrics are made by this type of weaving. For commercial distribution, the Jacquard loom is used. Inlay weaves fall into several classifications but are all referred to as brocades.
- *Double-cloth weaves* are woven in two attached layers, often resulting in a quilted appearance. These fabrics, known to the ancient Peruvians, account for many of the durable and beautiful fabrics used today. When these fabrics are woven for commercial use, the Jacquard loom is required. Among the many varieties of this type, warp-faced pile weave and matelasse are two of the most common.
- *Open, lacelike weaves* can be obtained in a number of ways. One is the ***leno,*** a loose weave in which the warp threads are wound in half twists around each other, alternating in position on each row. The ***gauze*** weave is similar to leno but differs in that the warp threads maintain the same position in relation to the weft. Gauze weaves range from simple to complex. Sheers, semisheers, and novelty casements employ these weaves.
- *Tension and texture-treated weaves* are those in which uneven tension in either weft or warp yarns produces an uneven surface effect. This may be accomplished in a variety of ways and with multiple effects. Yarns of various twists, warp yarns held at different tension, floated yarns combined with tightly woven yarns, combinations of yarns that react differently to heat, irregular battening, irregular reeds, and combinations of unusual fibers are all used to produce a variety of surface effects. A commonly used decorative fabric of this type is brocatelle, in which floated and compactly woven yarns are combined to produce the raised effect.
- *Combination weaves* occur in many fabrics used today; they are produced by combining two or more weaves. The weaves combined are often suggested in the name of the fabric, such as brocaded satin and voided velvet.

Knitting

Knitting is a process of interlocking a series of yarn loops by means of blunt needles. Through a variation of stitches, patterns are formed. Knitted fabrics, either hand- or machine-made, range from loose, open construction to close, fine weave. Finely knit fabrics are used for many home furnishing needs because of their desirable qualities of wrinkle resistance, tight fit, and ease of care. The tendency of knitted fabrics to stretch is being overcome by new methods of production.

Twisting

Twisting, interlocking, and knotting of yarns account for various types of mesh construction, such as nets, laces, and macramé, the intricacies of which are unlimited. With the current revival of handcrafts, macramé has become particularly popular.

Felting

Felting is a nonwoven process of subjecting a mass of fibers to moisture, heat, and pressure, which produces a compact sheet that does not fray, absorbs sound, and provides good insulation against heat and cold. Felt was formerly made from wool and hair fibers. Through modern technology, new fibers and fusing methods are employed to produce a variety of nonwoven materials.

when two (or bonded or gether chemically ing methods. By bonding er of fabric to the underside, the face fabric can be stabilized. If care is not taken, however, cleaning may cause a separation of the layers.

Dyeing

Fibers and fabrics are dyed or colored through various processes. These processes include (1) direct physical action, in which the structural elements of the fiber absorb the color; (2) chemical action, in which particular dyes have the ability to unite chemically with certain fibers; and (3) intermediate action, in which a ***mordant*** is used to unite the dye and fiber.

The various methods of dyeing yarns, fibers, and fabrics include (1) ***solution*** dyeing, in which the coloring agent is added to the viscous liquid of the synthetic before it is forced through the spinnerette to be formed into a fiber; (2) ***stock*** dyeing, in which the dye is applied to the fibers before they are processed into yarns; (3) ***yarn*** dyeing, in which the skeins or hanks of yarns are dyed before they are woven into fabrics; and (4) ***piece*** dyeing fabrics after they are woven. Piece dyeing, which usually produces a solid color in fabrics, can be done in several ways. ***Jig*** dyeing passes the open fabric back and forth through a stationary dye bath. ***Pad*** dyeing runs the fabric through the dye bath and then between rollers that squeeze the dye deeper into the yarns of the fabric. ***Winch, reel,*** or ***beck*** dyeing immerses the fabric continuously without strain to the fabric. ***Continuous machine*** dyeing has compartments for wetting out, dyeing, aftertreatments, washing, and rinsing. High-temperature processes are sometimes used for greater dye penetration. These processes are used especially for synthetic fibers.

Finishing

The finish is a treatment that may be applied to the fiber or yarn before or after construction to change the appearance and performance. When the unfinished fabric comes from the loom, it is referred to as ***greige*** or ***gray goods.*** Before the cloth is ready for the market, it goes through a series of finishes: the preparation, the functional finish, and the decorative finish.

Preparation

Preparation of the gray goods consists of a variety of treatments including ***bleaching*** (to whiten), ***shrinking*** (to prevent fiber contraction when exposed to moisture), ***heat setting*** (to add stability), ***beetling*** or pounding (to give luster), ***gigging*** or ***napping*** (to produce a flannel-like texture), ***calendering*** (to provide a smooth finish and tighten the weave), and ***singeing*** (to remove surface fuzz or lint). Following the preparatory finishing, the cloth is ready for the functional and decorative finishes.

Functional Finishes

Functional finishes are applied to improve performance, and they can make the fabric antistatic, soil resistant, crease resistant, fire and flame resistant, water repellent, and insulated against heat, cold, and noise.

Decorative Finishes

Decorative finishes include **printing** and **embroidery.**

PRINTING

Printing may be done by hand or by machine.

Hand Processes. With the exception of warp printing, fabrics are printed in the piece (after weaving). Fabrics done by the hand-printing processes of stencil block, ***batik*** tie-dye, and spray painting are not readily available because they are not produced on a commercial scale. Only the ***silk-screen*** process produces hand-printed textiles on a commercial scale. Some of these prints are so lovely in their design quality that they rival fine paintings. The process is essentially one in which a specially prepared fabric screen resists the color penetration except in desired areas. Dye in paste form is forced through the screen onto the fabric below. A separate screen is prepared for

Figure 6.2 This famous hand-blocked chintz, "Victoria and Albert," was originally designed in 1854 for the first royal yacht of Queen Victoria, and it is still printed from the same wooden blocks. *(Courtesy of Stroheim & Romann, Inc.)*

each color used in the artist's design.

Mechanical Processes. Many prints are produced mechanically by the transfer of color from an engraved copper roller onto the fabric. This process is called ***roller printing.*** A separate copper roller must be engraved for each color of the design, but once prepared, the rollers can be used on a variety of color schemes for thousands of yards of fabric; thus, the cost is greatly reduced. The roller can be adapted to do resist printing, discharge printing, ***parchment*** printing, etching, embossing, and duplex and warp printing. Warp printing is done on the warp yarns of a fabric before it is woven. Printed fabrics come in designs of unlimited styles, including ***documentaries***—designs copied from patterns of a particular historical period. These designs range from historic styles to the twentieth-century modern periods and help establish an authentic feeling.

NEEDLEWORK

Needlework, the embellishing of fabrics with intricate stitchery, is an ancient art form. Part of the current renaissance occurring in all handcrafts is the enthusiastic promotion of a major product of the Handcraft Revival of the 1970s and 1980s—stitchery of all kinds, both hand- and machine-made. A wide variety of handwork, such as embroidery, macrame, needlepoint, candlewicking, appliqué, and quilting, is again embellishing homes across the country.

Principal Uses of Decorative Fabrics for the Interior

Today's interior designer has a wider choice of fabrics than ever before, with new fabrics appearing almost daily. The market abounds with fabrics suitable for every taste, style, and decorative purpose in every price range. Adding to the appeal of new and improved fibers is the seemingly unending variety of designs ranging from folk patterns from around the world to

Figure 6.3 A documentary group of Victoria and Albert chintz fabrics are used to cover the headboard and are used for the bedspread and pillows. *(Courtesy of Stroheim & Romann, Inc.)*

Figure 6.4 "Bainbridge" glazed cotton from Greeff's English Garden Collection features a Victorian floral bouquet design based on an English document circa 1840. *(Courtesy of Greeff Fabrics.)*

Figure 6.5 A combination of complementary designs suitable for a variety of uses is featured in pastel colors. *(Courtesy of David & Dash.)*

traditional and contemporary designs. Selecting from this abundance the right fabric for the purpose at hand may sometimes seem overwhelming. With some study and careful planning, however, fabrics can be selected to create rooms that are pleasant and comfortable, satisfying personal taste and fulfilling individual needs.

The following are the principal decorative uses of fabrics in the home, the purposes each can serve, the qualities necessary for each use, and some fabric examples.

Sheers or Glass Curtains

Sheers or glass curtains may hang permanently over the glass window to filter the light, thereby giving softness to the room and providing daytime privacy.

Fabric should be sheer enough to permit light and frequently a view, should be sunproof as to colorfastness and splitting, and should wash or clean well without shrinkage. Any sheer fabric that has the necessary qualities can be used for sheers or glass curtains. Batiste, ninon, and chiffon are three popular examples.

Casements or Semisheers

Casements or semisheers serve as side drapery during the day and are drawn at night for privacy.

Fabric should be heavy enough for nighttime privacy but should permit some light. The fabric should be drapable, sun resistant, and nonsplitting and should wash or clean well without shrinkage. Leno weaves especially help control sagging. Fabric choice is unlimited. The style of decor will aid in determining the type of weave desired.

Drapery

Drapery serves as stationary side drapery or can be designed to draw for privacy. In addition to function, drapery can add beauty, height, and dignity to a room. When the desired design, texture, color, and method of hanging are employed, drapery can contribute to the style and help set the mood of the room (i.e., formal or informal).

Fabric should drape gracefully, clean without shrinkage, and meet the particular needs of the room in which it is used. Any drapable fabric that is suitable for the style of furnishings, background, and window type can be used. Examples are silk, antique satin, and other medium- to lightweight fabrics.

Upholstery

Upholstery covers furniture permanently, adds beauty and comfort, conceals or emphasizes furniture, and adds to or sets the theme or mood of the room.

Fabric used for upholstery should have a tight weave, be durable, be comfortable, and clean well. Any fabric having the necessary qualities can be used. Common upholstery fabrics include heavyweight fabrics such as matelasse, tweed, tapestry, velvet, bouclé, frieze, and leather; medium-weight fabrics such as damask, brocatelle, and canvas; and lightweight fabrics

Figure 6.6 A contemporary treatment designed by Gayl Baddeley and William Fleming featuring chairs with a small print on a white ground with a coordinating design employed for pillows accenting a white sofa. *(Courtesy of Gayl Baddeley/Associates.)*

such as antique satin, chintz, linen, homespun, and moiré.

Slipcovers

Slipcovers may cover worn upholstered furniture, protect more expensive fabrics, and brighten or change a room's atmosphere.

Slipcovers are generally more efficient when durable, tightly woven, nonsnag, and nonstretch (unless they are of a stretch variety). Pliable or lightweight fabrics make fitting and sewing easy. Indian Head, sailcloth, ticking, chintz, whipcord, and corduroy are all good choices for slipcovers.

Walls

Fabrics can be used on walls to add beauty or to solve a decorative problem. (See Chapter 7 for uses of flexible wall coverings.) The fabric should have a tight weave with firm body. Canvas, burlap, moire, ticking, heavy cotton or linen, velveteen, and damask are often employed for wall coverings.

Framed fabric can add interest and glamour.

Lamp Shades

Lamp shades are used most often to diffuse light. Fabric for lamp shades usually works best when a neutral, white, or off-white color with a texture appropriate for the lamp base and room style is used. Shantung, taffeta, and loose homespun weaves are typical.

Figure 6.7 Peach and neutral fabrics in this bedroom combine comfort, softness, and color. *(Courtesy of Gayl Baddeley/Associates.)*

Use of Pattern, Texture, and Color When Combining Fabrics

Perhaps the most common question clients ask professional interior designers is, What fabric goes with what? This question has no absolute answer. Combining fabrics is a matter of training and skill. Some people seem to have an aptitude for acquiring this skill; others require much patient study and practice. Although an unexpected combination of materials may create a feeling of great interest and charm, some general principles may be helpful to the inexperienced designer when combining colors, textures, and patterns.

Pattern

Pattern indicates that the design has motifs sufficiently large in scale, or with enough contrast in color or tone, to permit the eye to distinguish them clearly. When the parts of the pattern are so subtle or are blended in such a way that they are indistinguishable, the design becomes one more of texture than of pattern.

Many people are afraid of patterned fabrics and avoid them entirely; others use them ineffectively. Although they are not a necessity, well-chosen patterned fabrics can enhance most rooms. The adroit use of pattern can camouflage defects, create beauty and glamour, and perform decorating miracles.

As with color, no absolute dos or don'ts govern the use of pattern. A few general guidelines, however, may be helpful.

- Patterns used within the same room should have a **pleasing relationship** to each other. Common elements such as color, texture, or motif running throughout tie them together and give an easy flow to the entire scheme.
- The **principal pattern** need not be repeated in the room so long as one or more of the colors in that pattern are carried over into another area. The same pattern, however, may with pleasing results be repeated on furnishings or used at the windows or on the walls, depending on the overall effect desired. Odd pieces of furniture

Bold patterns should be used with discretion. Too much pattern becomes overpowering.

can be unified when covered in the same fabric, and repetition of the fabric brings unity into an entire room. When pattern is selected with discrimination, the final product will generally not be too busy, stimulating, or overpowering.

- The use of no more than one **bold pattern** of the same type of design, such as a floral, is usually more effective. Once the dominant motif is established, it may be supplemented by a small pattern, stripe, check, or plaid with complementary plain textures added.
- When combining patterned fabrics, **scale or size** of the pattern should be considered. For example, if a bold floral print is combined with a plaid or a stripe or both, the continuation of bold scale is often most effective. If an unobtrusive floral pattern is used, then accompanying fabrics may blend well in scale and not overpower the principal pattern.
- **Unusual juxtaposition** of fabric may create a dramatic effect, but this kind of carefree sophistication usually develops from knowledge and practice that have produced confidence to do the unexpected. The novice is wise to follow some basic guidelines.
- A knowledge of what makes a fabric **formal or informal** is essential in successfully combining textures and patterns.

Formal Fabrics

Formal fabrics are primarily those with smooth and often shiny textures, typically employing stylized and geometric patterns. Some examples of formal fabrics are velvet, damask, brocade, brocatelle, satin, shantung, and taffeta. Today, formal fabrics can be used in either traditional or modern interiors in a range of colors.

Figure 6.8 Formal and elegant fabrics are used in a traditional setting for the newly decorated Governor's Mansion in Salt Lake City, Utah. *(Courtesy of Gayl Baddeley/Associates.)*

Figure 6.9 Rich royal blue fabrics in a modern setting are seen in this living room, providing a more formal feeling, and are enriched by the use of shiny glass, mirror, and metal materials. *(Courtesy of L. J. Graham Company, Inc./L. Lowenstein Inc.)*

Informal Fabrics

Informal fabrics are generally those with a rougher texture and matte finish, such as burlap, canvas, hopsacking, muslin, tweed, and bouclé. Fabrics with a handcrafted quality often fall into this category. If the informal fabric employs pattern, the design may be bold, naturalistic, abstract, or geometric.

Many fabrics can be used in either category. For example, cottons and linens may have textures, colors, and patterns that fit into a formal setting or may have textures, colors, and patterns that are at home in an informal room. Traditionally, colors for informal fabrics have had a tendency to be bolder; but today white, pastels, and neutrals are also employed in an informal manner. For example, pale pink canvas may cover seating units on informal wicker furniture frames.

Experience in training the eye while trying out innumerable fabric combinations, along with general guidelines, will develop a sense of what fabric selections are complementary and what groupings do not work well together.

Figure 6.10 Informal patterned fabrics employing a simple plaid and a lilac and tulip floral provide a casual look. Three wallpaper patterns contribute to the overall atmosphere. *(Courtesy of The Jack Denst Designs, Inc.)*

Solving Design Problems with Fabrics

Problems can often be solved through the skillful use of fabric, with unlimited possibilities. The following are some ways fabrics may serve many purposes and come to the rescue of the knowledgeable interior designer. A well-chosen fabric can

- **Lighten or darken** a room.
- **Emphasize or conceal** walls, windows, or furnishings.
- **Set the mood** of a room: give it a feeling of formality or infor-

Figure 6.11 An informal treatment of gray fabric is used on the large sofa in a modern room with accents of large plants and flowers. *(Courtesy of Dennis Keehn/Magical Plants.)*

Figure 6.12 Harmony and balance are established in this living room by coordinating a neutral color scheme, compatible textures, and geometric and abstract patterns. *(Courtesy of Gayl Baddeley/Associates.)*

Fabric can solve design problems. Radiator wall can be covered with fabric-sheered shutters, and the same fabric can be repeated on and above the bed.

mality through the use of color, pattern, and texture.

- **Bring harmony and unity** to a room where furnishings previously seemed unrelated by repeated use of the same or complementary fabrics.
- **Provide balance** to a room. For example, a bold-patterned fabric hung at a window or used to upholster a small piece of furniture will balance a larger piece of plain furniture at the other side of the room. A spot of bright color will balance a larger area of muted color.
- **Change the apparent size and proportion** of a piece of furniture or an entire room. For example, a sofa covered in a large pattern or bold-colored fabric will appear larger than if it is covered in a light, plain color or a small unobtrusive pattern. A chair or love seat upholstered in a vertical stripe will look higher

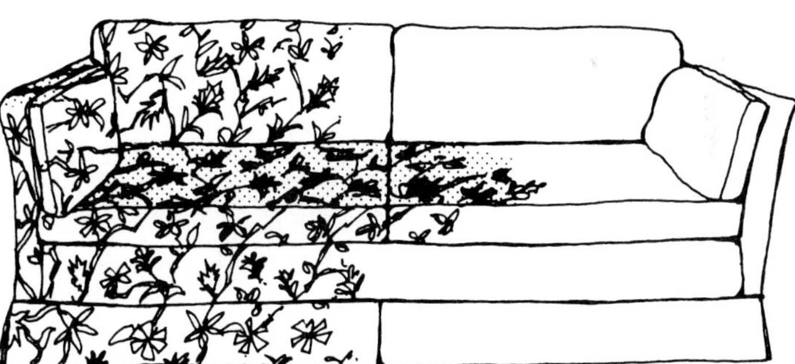

Large or conspicuous pattern tends to make furniture appear larger.

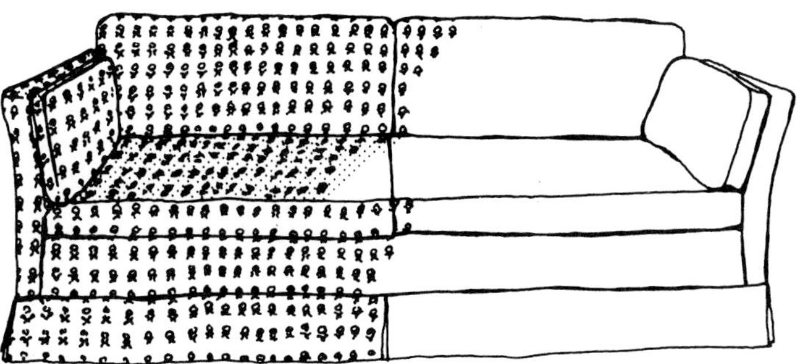

Small pattern diminishes size.

Figure 6.13 This stunning eclectic room was created primarily through the knowledgeable use of fabric. One pearl gray fabric unifies the diverse furniture. Contrasting purple accents contribute to the sophistication of this formal and eclectic setting. *(Courtesy of Mark Epstein.)*

than the same piece covered in a plain fabric.

- Relieve an otherwise monotonous room by adding **interest and beauty.**
- **Establish the room's color scheme.** A successful method of color scheming a room is choosing a favorite patterned fabric as a starting point, which was discussed in Chapter 5.
- **Establish the historic or modern style** of a room. If the room is based on a certain period, the fabric, more than any other item or furnishing, can set the desired feeling. Documentary fabrics can provide historically authentic styles.
- **Change the look of a room for different seasons.** For example, a couch and chairs in deep warm colors may be slipcovered in light-colored ticking for summer. Heavy winter drapery may be changed for light sheer glass curtains to create a cool atmosphere for summer.
- **Add softness and comfort,** providing a uniquely human factor in the home.
- Functionally, the **pliable and flexible qualities** of fabrics allow the designer to use fabrics easily in the home—and in countless ways. Additionally, fabrics are relatively inexpensive and easily replaced.

In the absence of a headboard, fabric can be attached to the wall for height and glamour.

FABRIC CAN CHANGE THE PERSONALITY OF A CHAIR

The floral pattern gives a traditional appearance.

A plaid fabric accentuates the square silhouette and gives the chair a modern appearance.

Fabrics for Specific Areas

Because fabric more than any other element can set the mood and atmosphere of a room, fabric selection requires careful consideration of color, texture, and pattern keyed to specific areas or rooms in which the fabric will be used. In general, a specific mood is appropriate for each room, although this necessarily varies according to individual preference and needs.

Fabrics for Period and Contemporary Rooms

Design in textiles was used in ancient times as a symbolic medium for religious purposes. With the passage of time, fabric became a significant medium for aesthetic expression of people throughout the world. A discernible affinity is present in the primitive designs

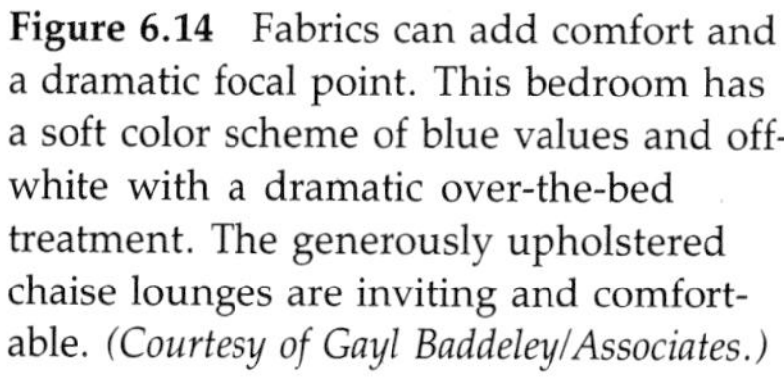

Figure 6.14 Fabrics can add comfort and a dramatic focal point. This bedroom has a soft color scheme of blue values and off-white with a dramatic over-the-bed treatment. The generously upholstered chaise lounges are inviting and comfortable. *(Courtesy of Gayl Baddeley/Associates.)*

in fabrics of all countries. For example, the design motifs used in the early rugs of East Turkistan are much the same as the designs used in the early rugs of the Inca and Navajo Indians, halfway around the world. This similarity is easily explainable. Primitive peoples represented the phenomena of nature in their early art forms. For example, the sun and stars were represented in identifiable form. The difference in early textile weaves is minimized because all were done on simple looms, and primitive cultures used natural fibers and dyes. Although each country developed characteristics peculiar to its origin, a common quality in their early crafts blends them together harmoniously.

A close relationship often existed among the designs of European, Near Eastern, and Eastern countries during the Middle Ages and the Renaissance. A brief look at history reveals the explanation for this relationship. The conqueror of a country imported artisans of all kinds to his homeland, where they continued to carry on their trades. In time, they were influenced by the designs of their new environment, and the eventual blending of different methods and motifs produced art forms with distinct individuality. During the Renaissance and the seventeenth and eighteenth centuries, fabrics from Far Eastern countries, with their unique Oriental motifs and colors, were in great demand and were imported to Europe and America. The individualities of all these expressions differentiate the designs of one country or period from another, making it possible today to give a room a distinctive character through the use of appropriate art forms employed in these various styles, particularly in fabrics.

Figure 6.15 Fabric can set the desired style of a room. "Nobuko" wallcovering and coordinating fabric has a striking pattern of giant peonies, which are among the most popular flowers in Oriental design. *(Courtesy of Van Luit.)*

With the increased sophistication in today's interiors, drawing on historic designs to establish an authentic feeling of a specific period or style that can bestow a dramatic contrast in the home is popular (see Figure 6.16). To accomplish this, documentary fabrics bearing designs from a wide range of historic periods are being produced by the finest manufacturers.

Sophisticated interest in decorative styles of the past continues today, although seldom does a client wish to create an entirely authentic period room; this is usually reserved for projects of restoration. Creating a decorative scheme based on a specific period can easily be achieved today through a vast selection of authentic fabrics.

To serve those clients who prefer the modern look, an abundance of decorative and functional fabrics is also available. Improved production methods and new design techniques are making pos-

Figure 6.16 An eighteenth-century English bed is traditionally draped with a documentary floral print complemented by a coordinating striped fabric used on the Queen Anne chair. *(Courtesy of Century Furniture Co. Photograph by Jonathan Hillyer.)*

Figure 6.17 Jacqueline, a graceful wallpaper, is an adaptation of an 1860 document. The original hand-blocked wallpaper employed 33 colors printed on a polished paper. Scalamandré, honoring modern taste and printing techniques, reduced the palette to 23 colors, providing a bouquet of French blooms. *(Courtesy of Scalamandré.)*

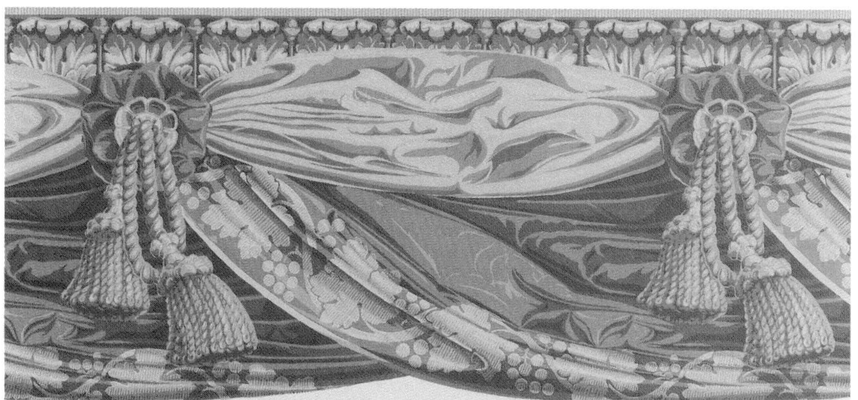

Figure 6.18 A trompe l'oeil wallpaper border depicting swags of fabric held together at intervals by cords and tassels. *(Courtesy of Scalamandré.)*

sible remarkable fabrics to serve the diverse desires of consumers. Current fabric-selection trends in home design employ the use of contemporary fabrics that reflect 1980s techniques and innovations. Many designers may use historic furnishings upholstered in the latest fabrics. For example, an eighteenth-century Queen Anne chair might be covered in a contemporary white wool fabric rather than the traditional damask often employed in the earlier period. In other words, fabrics designed today are flexible enough to be used for all types of furniture—modern or traditional.

The following information can assist the designer—both professional and nonprofessional—in getting maximum service from popular fabrics in use today.

Types of Decorative Fabrics and Terms

The following are the most popularly employed household fabrics and the qualities of each. Fabrics are listed under their common decorative name.

Batiste A fine, soft, sheer fabric of plain weave made of various fibers. Glass curtains.

Bouclé A French word meaning "curly." It indicates yarns are curled or looped in a flat or pile fabric. Heavyweight. Upholstery.

Bouclé marquisette Sheer material of leno weave with a bouclé yarn. Glass curtains.

Broadcloth A lightweight fabric in a plain or twill weave. Cotton, wool, or synthetic fibers popularly used. Draperies, bedspreads.

Brocade A medium-weight fabric woven on a Jacquard loom. An embroidered multicolored pattern stands out in relief against a satin or ribbed background. Drapery and upholstery.

Brocatelle A medium-weight Jacquard fabric with an extra set of wefts for backing, unevenly twisted which results in a high relief ***repoussé*** appearance on the surface. Upholstery and draperies.

Buckram Stiffened material sized with glue. Reinforcement for draperies and valances.

Burlap A medium-weight coarse fabric woven of jute in a plain, loose weave. Wall coverings, drapery, and lamp shades.

Calico A lightweight plain cotton weave with a small all-over print.

Canvas A medium-weight, closely woven cotton. A plain, diagonal weave in plain colors or prints. Upholstery, drapery, walls.

Casement A broad term covering many drapery fabrics. Usually light, neutral colors in plain or novelty weaves.

Challis A lightweight wool, cotton, or synthetic soft fabric in a plain tight weave. Printed designs or plain. Drapery, upholstery.

Chenille A heavyweight fabric woven with chenille yarns. When woven in a fabric, can create a pile similar to velvet; if woven on a Jacquard loom, can look similar to cut velvet. Upholstery, bedspreads.

Chiffon A sheer fabric used for glass curtains. Tight weave, lightweight.

Chintz A plain, tightly woven lightweight cotton fabric with fine yarns. Sometimes processed with a glazed finish. Can be either a solid color or printed. Draperies, slipcovers, bedspreads.

Color flag The series of clippings attached to a purchased fabric sample to show the colorline.

Colorline Refers to the complete color range of a given fabric series.

Colorway Refers to the color of an individual fabric.

Corduroy A heavyweight cotton or synthetic pile fabric, ribbed or corded lengthwise. Drapery, slipcovers, upholstery, bedspreads, and other uses.

Crewel embroidery A heavyweight plain-woven cotton, linen, or wool fabric embroidered with fine, loosely twisted, two-ply worsted yarns. Usually worked by hand in the Kashmir province of India. Drapery and upholstery.

Crocking Rubbing off color from dyed or printed fabrics.

Damask A Jacquard-woven medium-weight fabric with patterns created, providing unique weave effects. Can be woven self-tone, one-color warp, different-color filling, or multicolor in design. Distinguished from brocades because face of fabric is flatter. The color is reversed on the wrong side. Drapery and upholstery.

Denim A medium-weight, tightly woven cotton twill made of coarse yarns. Usually in a solid color, but can be patterned. Drapery, upholstery, bedspreads, walls, and numerous other uses.

Dotted swiss Sheer fabric woven with extra yarns forming dots when clipped. The effect may be produced by flocking. Curtains.

Faille A lightweight, flat-ribbed fabric woven with fine yarns in the warp and heavier yarns in the filling using a plain weave. The ribbed effect is flatter than grosgrain and smaller than rep. Faille can be the base cloth for moire. Drapery, upholstery.

Felt Wools or mixed fibers pressed into a compact sheet. A heavyweight fabric used for walls, table covers, and other uses.

Fiberglass Fibers and yarns

produced from glass and woven into flexible lightweight fabrics. Noted for its fireproof qualities. Beta Fiberglas is a trademarked glass fiber. Curtains.

Film A lightweight thin or thick plastic sheet used for upholstery, shower curtains, or table coverings. Can be textured, patterned, or plain.

Friezé A strong heavyweight fabric with a fine, cut or uncut, low-loop surface woven on a wire loom to maintain an even size to the loops. Upholstery.

Gimp Ornamental braid used to cover upholstery tacks.

Gingham Medium- or lightweight cotton or cottonlike fabric for informal use. Made of colored yarns forming checks, plaids, or stripes.

Grass cloth Coarse grasses glued to rice paper. Used for wall coverings.

Gros point Heavyweight needlepoint embroidery. Upholstery.

Homespun Loosely woven lightweight fabric made to resemble handwoven material. Curtains or drapery.

Hopsacking A rough-surfaced medium-weight fabric loosely woven of various fibers in a plain basket weave. Mainly for drapery and slipcovers.

Insulating Fabrics processed with reflective metallic or foam plastic on one side to provide insulating qualities.

Jacquard Damasks, brocades, tapestries, and all fabrics requiring the Jacquard loom.

Lampas Fabric having a rep ground with satinlike figures formed of warp threads and contrasting figures formed of weft thread. Drapery and upholstery.

Matelassé A double-woven heavyweight fabric with a quilted appearance. Derived from the French word *matelasser,* meaning "to cushion" or "to pad." Upholstery.

Moiré A wavy, watery effect pressed into a ribbed surface such as taffeta or faille. A lightweight fabric suitable for drapery, upholstery, or bedspreads.

Monk's cloth A coarse medium-weight fabric in a loose weave of flax, jute, or hemp mixed with cotton, generally in neutral colors. May have sagging problems.

Muslin Bleached or unbleached plain, lightweight cotton weave. Has many uses in decorating, especially in Early American and modern rooms. Walls, drapery, slipcovers. Solid colors or printed patterns.

Needlepoint A heavyweight handmade or Jacquard fabric. Fine and delicate effect is known as *petit point;* larger needlepoint is known as *gros point.*

Net A sheer lacelike fabric with a consistent mesh texture available in a variety of fibers. Suitable for glass curtains.

Ninon A sheer plain tight weave used for glass curtains. Has a smooth, crisp gossamer appearance.

Organdy A sheer crisp cotton fabric with good pleating qualities. Available plain, embroidered, or printed. Glass curtains.

Osnaburg A light- to medium-weight fabric similar to homespun. A loose, uneven, coarse cotton with solid color or printed motifs.

Oxford A plain-weave fabric. Large filling yarn goes over two warp yarns. An informal fabric with many uses.

Pilling Formation of fiber fuzz balls on fabric surface by wear or friction, encountered in spun nylon, polyester, acrylic, cashmere, or soft woolen yarns.

Plissé A lightweight fabric with a crinkled or puckered effect created by chemical treatment. Curtains.

Plush A heavyweight pile fabric with greater depth than velvet. Usually has a high sheen. Upholstery.

Polished cotton A plain- or satin-weave cotton cloth characterized by a sheen ranging from dull to bright. Polish can be achieved either through the weave or by the addition of a resin finish.

Quilted fabrics A pattern stitched through a printed or plain fabric and through a layer of batting. Outline quilting traces around the pattern of a printed fabric. Loom quilting is a small repetitive design made by the quilting alone. Ultrasonic quilting produces thermally bonded welds in place of stitching threads.

Rep Plain-weave, lightweight fabric with narrow rounded ribs running the width or length of the fabric. Usually a fine warp with heavier filling yarns. Drapery, upholstery, slipcovers, bedspreads, and other informal uses.

Sailcloth A medium-weight fabric in a plain weave similar to canvas. Popular for informal indoor or outdoor upholstery.

Sateen A highly lustrous fabric usually made of mercerized cotton with a satin weave. Drapery lining.

Satin *Plain:* Fine yarns woven in such a manner as to give a more lustrous surface. May be lightweight or heavy enough for upholstery. Has many decorative uses when a formal style of decor is desired. *Antique:* A smooth satin face highlighted by slub (or twisted) yarn in a random pattern. Today it is an important fabric for drapery.

Seersucker A lightweight fabric employing a special weaving process producing a permanently wrinkled or puckered striped effect.

Suede Leather with a napped surface. Polyester suede washes and wears well. Upholstery.

Taffeta *Plain:* Tight and crisp smooth weave with slight horizontal ribbed effect. When woven of silk, it is a luxury fabric for drapery, bedspreads, and lamp shades. *Antique* or *shantung:* A smooth, soft weave with random slub yarn creating a textured effect. A lustrous fabric with many decorative uses, especially drapery and lamp shades.

Tapestry A figured multicolored fabric woven on a Jacquard loom made up of two sets of warp and weft. The design is formed by varying weave effects brought to the surface in combination with colored yarns. The surface has a rough texture. A heavyweight upholstery fabric.

Terry cloth A medium-weight cotton or linen pile fabric. May be cut or uncut. Loops may be on one side or both. Bedspreads, upholstery, and towels.

Ticking A medium-weight tightly woven cotton or linen fabric. A strong, usually striped fabric in a satin or twill weave. Mattresses, pillows, wall coverings, slipcovers, and drapery.

Toile de Jouy A floral or scenic design usually printed on a plain cotton or linen ground. Originally printed in Jouy, France.

Trapunto Quilting that raises an area design on the surface of upholstery fabric.

Tweed Plain-weave, heavyweight upholstery fabric with a tweed texture because of flake (or knotted yarn) in multicolors. Upholstery.

Velour A French term loosely applied to all types of fabrics with a nap or cut pile on one side. Specifically, it is a cut-pile fabric similar to regular velvet but with a higher pile. Heavyweight upholstery fabric.

Velvet A heavyweight fabric having a short, thick warp pile. May be of any fiber. ***Crushed:*** Most often the fabric is pulled through a narrow cylinder to create the crushed effect. ***Cut:*** Jacquard design, usually cut and uncut pile on a plain ground. ***Antique:*** Velvet that has an old look. Upholstery.

Velveteen A heavyweight weft-pile fabric with short pile, usually of cotton. Drapery, upholstery, bedspreads, and innumerable uses.

Vinyl A heavy nonwoven plastic fabric capable of being printed or embossed to produce any desired finish such as a leather, wood, floral, or textured design. Cloth backing prevents tearing. Walls and upholstery.

Voile A fine, soft, sheer fabric in a variety of textures used for glass curtains.

Webbing Heavyweight jute, cotton, or synthetic strips, generally 1 to 4 in. wide. Interwoven and plain or printed. Particularly used for modern seating units. Can also be used to support springs for an upholstered piece.

Caring for Upholstery and Decorative Fabrics

Protecting Fabrics

Many fabrics are susceptible to sun damage, and window glass magnifies the destructive element in the sun's rays. Even the winter sun and reflection from the snow can be harmful. Lined and interlined draperies help protect fabrics from the sun, especially when fragile materials are used. Blinds drawn during the day and exterior awnings also are practical. Trees or shrubbery can also help protect windows. Also, colors can fade by oxidation (gas fading) if unaired in storage for a period of time. Impurities in the air may cause as much fading as the direct rays of the sun. It is helpful to remember that some colors are more fugitive than others.

Cleaning Fabrics

A reputable dry cleaner specializing in home furnishings is preferable for cleaning fabrics. Frequent vacuuming of fabrics to remove dust can help cut down on major cleaning bills, because dust has impurities that affect fabrics. Spots should be removed immediately. Knowledge of the scrubable or washable properties of a particular fabric is essential for upkeep.

Fluctuation in Fabrics

Small fluctuations in length of draperies may occur. No fabric is completely stable. A completely stable fabric would have no textural interest.

Fabrics breathe and absorb moisture, resulting in stretching or shrinking. A reasonable expectation is a 3 percent change in a 108-in. (3-yd) length, which would amount to 3 in., depending on the fabric involved.

Wear in Fabrics

Fabrics wear; they are not indestructible. Wear will vary with the amount of use. A favorite chair will not last as long as a seldom-used showpiece in the living room. Some weaves are stronger than others.

Finishes

Finishes may help fabrics resist spotting, but they are not necessarily the answer to every problem. Light colors are likely to benefit most. Dining room chairs will soil no matter what fabric is used. A finish does not eliminate the necessity of properly caring for fabrics. Spots should be removed immediately.

Man-Made Fibers

Man-made fibers have made an invaluable contribution to weaving technology, but they cannot perform miracles. Performance will vary with the construction of the fabric.

In the final analysis, as is true in every industry, the integrity and experience of the fabric supplier are your best assurances as to the intrinsic value of a purchase, but these factors must be combined with knowledge and understanding on the part of the consumer.

ASSIGNMENT

The following assignment will determine the student's ability to coordinate compatible materials for floors, walls, windows, and upholstery. The pictures of fabric arrangement (Figures 6.19 and 6.20) present the format generally employed by most professional designers when specifying fabrics for a commercial or residential project.

1. Select two neutral, colored, gray, or black mat boards approximately 9 in. by 12 in.

2. Follow the format for arranging fabrics found in the Student Packet.

3. Coordinate background colors,

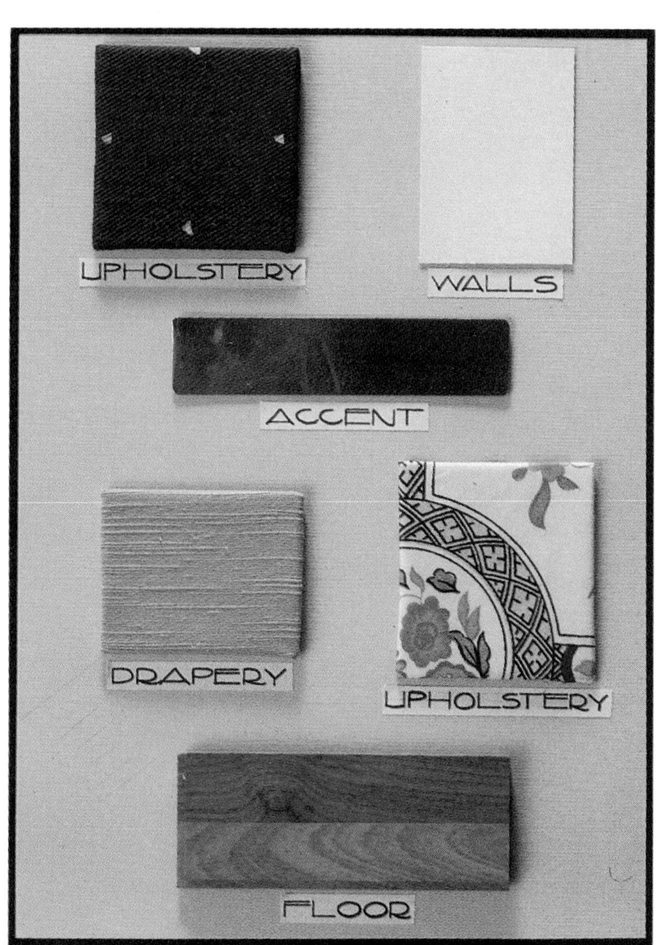

Figure 6.19 Compatible colors, textures, and patterns are coordinated to produce a formal contemporary grouping of fabrics. This format is one typically adopted by professional designers. *(Courtesy of Bengt Erlandsson.)*

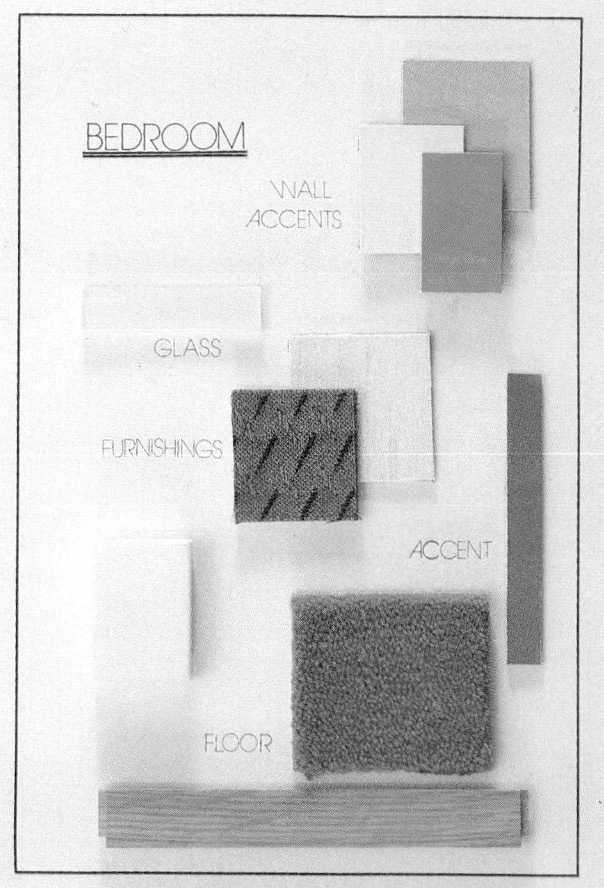

Figure 6.20 Layout with a juxtaposition of fabric samples affixed to a small presentation board indicates application in an interior. *(Courtesy of Paul Edwards.)*

materials, and fabrics for two rooms. Each completed layout should contain the following sample materials:

Ceiling: Usually painted white or an off-white to blend with room

Floor: Sample of flooring or floor covering

Walls: Select wall treatment (paint, paper, fabric, paneling, etc.)

Wood trim: Indicate paint or natural wood sample

Windows: Select and present window treatment (hard or soft line)

Upholstery: Include upholstery fabrics for particular rooms chosen

4. Mount fabric and carpet samples on small scraps of mat board. If the fabric is heavy, it may be cropped to fit the boards. If it is lightweight, it may be better to wrap the board. Mount the finished samples to the mat board in the appropriate space outlined.

5. Use professional lettering to indicate the room type (e.g., informal family room, formal living room). The project should be neatly presented.

Floors, Walls, and Ceilings

Chapter Seven

The general scheme of any room is established by the architectural background: walls, floors, and ceilings, plus such items as fireplaces, doors, windows, paneling, and moldings. The decorative treatments added to these backgrounds, as well as to the movable objects in the room, should be in keeping with the overall feeling if the room is to have an atmosphere of harmony and unity. Since backgrounds are for people, generally a wise choice is to make large areas—walls, floors, and ceilings—unobtrusive.

Floors and Floor Coverings

Because of their function—primarily to be walked on and provide the foundation for other furnishings—floors, more than any other surface, take a great amount of abuse. After the floor's construction is complete, the task of covering this area is a major concern for the designer and homemaker. The last decades have witnessed a renaissance in both hard-surface **nonresilient** and soft **resilient** floor coverings, with the market abounding in a variety of selections for every purpose and decor. Perhaps the most notable characteristic of today's materials is the merging of beauty and practicality due to improved technology, developments in old and new materials, and methods of production. Hard or soft flooring materials are no longer confined to particular areas of the house and may be used in any room. When making a decision on what type of floor covering is most suitable, the following considerations can be helpful. The designer and the consumer need to determine whether the specific room (bedroom, entry, kitchen, family room, etc.) seems to require a hard or soft floor covering. Considerations include:

Figure 7.1 In an architecturally dynamic space designed by architect Eduard Dreier, a pyramidal window ceiling treatment soars above the living areas. Walls are painted white to emphasize form and space. A Moroccan rug contrasts with a dark carpeted floor. *(Courtesy of Gayl Baddeley/Associates.)*

- The intended **function;**
- The **number, age,** and **special needs of the occupants;**
- The **life-style** of the occupants—**formal** or **informal;**
- Considerations concerning the **location** and **climate;**
- Surface quality as a **safety factor** (stairways, nursery, rooms for elderly persons, etc.);
- **Acoustic properties** of a floor covering required for a specific area;
- **Economic considerations**—initial expense plus long-term maintenance;
- **Durability** required for a particular area;
- **Style** qualities for a certain design direction;
- **Personal preferences** of the occupants.

Nonresilient and Resilient Hard Flooring

Nonresilient Flooring—Masonry

Resilient flooring refers to the material's ability to spring back when depressed. Nonresilient flooring is devoid of flexibility. The initial cost of hard-surface nonresilient flooring is generally high. In long-range planning, however, this is more than compensated for by its extreme durability, versatility, ease of maintenance, and timeless usage. Hard-surface masonry flooring such as brick, stone, and tile remains popular, and with improved production, surface enrichment and methods of installation are of finer quality today. New setting methods for all types of masonry allow installation over most surfaces. The durable qualities of quarry, ceramic, and Mexican tile; stone; and wood allow these materials to be employed throughout the home. They may flow from

Figure 7.2 This handsome contemporary room is well planned, comfortable, and uncluttered. The deep-pile rug against the unglazed quarry tile floor and the undraped windows offset by well-placed plants are a fitting background for classic modern furniture. *(Courtesy of American Olean Tile Company.)*

Figure 7.3 Extremely durable, Italian tiles decorate this Greenwich, Connecticut bath by designer Elinor Hirshaft. The tiles, with tiny red flowers and green leaves, cover the walls, floor, steps, shower, and shelves—enveloping this room with a fresh, alfresco appeal. *(Courtesy of Italian Ceramic Tile. Photograph by James Levin.)*

Figure 7.4 Durable Mexican tile in warm earth tones is the perfect flooring for a sophisticated look adaptable to many design approaches. Here the tile adds rustic charm to an American contemporary kitchen. *(Courtesy of Elon Inc.)*

the inside entrance hall or family room out onto the porch or patio, thus expanding space, providing unity and beauty, and providing a practical surface requiring little upkeep.

In every area of hard floor covering, great strides have been made in the improvement of both practical and aesthetic aspects. Tables 7.1 and 7.2 contain information on the most commonly used hard floor coverings—both resilient and nonresilient—regarding their characteristics and uses, plus some suggestions for treatment and care of each.

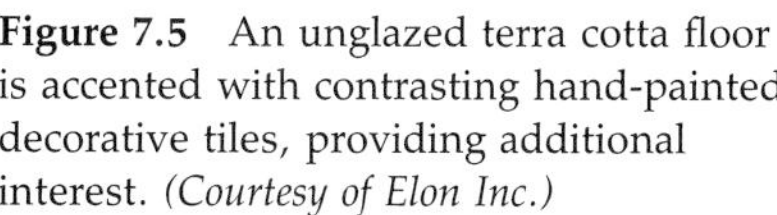

Figure 7.5 An unglazed terra cotta floor is accented with contrasting hand-painted decorative tiles, providing additional interest. *(Courtesy of Elon Inc.)*

Figure 7.6 Dark slate arranged in a circular pattern provides a durable and welcoming floor surface in this Health Spa in Atlantic City, New Jersey. *(Courtesy of The Structural Slate Co.)*

Figure 7.7 Highly worked bricks provide an adaptable transition in a foyer. *(Photograph by Stanley F. MacBean.)*

Figure 7.8 A handsome and durable deep green marble floor and walls with hand-painted foliage set the scene for a luxurious bath. Elegant fixtures in tropical colors add to the opulent bath labeled "Green Utopia." *(Courtesy of The Kohler Design Center.)*

Figure 7.9 This terrazzo floor with marble chips (aggregate) in a matrix (cement mortar) is used in a commercial setting and is an excellent flooring material for heavy use. It also provides an interesting floor texture supportive of the dramatic design. *(Courtesy of the National Terrazzo and Mosaic Association, Inc.)*

Figure 7.10 In a basement family recreational area, the flooring of small pebbles embedded in concrete provides a durable, maintenance-free surface and also provides an interesting textural background for furnishings. *(Courtesy of Ron Molen, architect.)*

Figure 7.11 In an elegant contemporary home in Colorado, smooth cream-colored travertine has been used to tile the floor and raised pond in the formal entry area. A mirrored ceiling doubles the stunning effect. *(Courtesy of Gayl Baddeley/Associates.)*

TABLE 7.1 *Hard-surface flooring: nonresilient*

MATERIAL	CHARACTERISTICS	USES	TREATMENT AND CARE
Flagstone	Any flat stone that varies in size, thickness, quality, and color Versatile, durable, handsome Easy upkeep Colors range from soft grays through beiges and reddish browns May be cut or laid in natural shapes Surface slightly uneven Absorbs solar energy	Walks, patios, foyers, greenhouses, any heavy traffic area May be dressed up or down, making it appropriate for wide range of uses	Careful waxing will soften rugged effect and produce soft patina Coating of vinyl will protect bricks from grease penetration Dust with dry mop, wash occasionally For stubborn stains, use trisodium phosphate
Slate (special kind of stone)	More formal than flagstone Qualities similar to flagstone, except for color, which runs from gray to black Absorbs solar energy	May be used in traffic areas in formal rooms Appropriate for some period rooms—particularly sun rooms and dining rooms—and for greenhouses	May be polished or unpolished, but more often waxed and highly polished
Mexican tile or terra-cotta	Crude base made of clay as it comes from earth Hand shaped and sun dried with smooth surface in limited range of colors Durable, informal, inexpensive Absorbs solar energy	Wherever a hard, cementlike surface is desired or wherever energy storage is desired	Care same as for terrazzo Surface seldom waxed
Concrete tile	May be solid or in squares, smooth or textured, polished or unpolished Color may be added before pouring or after Tile liner may be grouted to give a tile effect Absorbs and stores solar energy	Particularly desirable for some hardwear areas and for support of heavy equipment Tile patterns appropriate for foyers, penthouses, and any area where energy storage is required	Heavy waxed surface necessary for maintenance Do not use lacquer, varnish, or shellac Special finishes available Wet before cleaning and use detergent Easy to maintain
Brick	Durable, little upkeep Comes in many textures, sizes, and colors Transmits moisture and cold readily and absorbs grease unless treated Absorbs and stores solar energy	Walks, patios, foyers, greenhouses, any room where a country look is desired	Treatment and care same as for flagstone
Exposed aggregate	Surface in which stones are laid in concrete and polished to smoothness, but surface remains uneven Absorbs and stores solar energy	Especially appropriate for walks and fireplace hearths	Dust, wash occasionally
Quarry tile	Type of ceramic tile formed and fixed as it comes from earth One of hardest and most durable May be glazed or unglazed Heat and frost resistant, easy upkeep, and durable Both ceramic and quarry tile practically impervious to grease and chemicals Absorbs and stores solar energy	Suitable for many period rooms, especially Italian, early English, and rooms with Mediterranean feeling Can be used wherever hard surface is appropriate, such as in greenhouses Coolness makes it desirable in hot climates	Unglazed: may be waxed to give soft sheen Glazed: dust with dry mop, wash when needed with soap and warm water

TABLE 7.1, CONTINUED

MATERIAL	CHARACTERISTICS	USES	TREATMENT AND CARE
Ceramic tile	Has unique aesthetic quality One of hardest and most durable floor and wall coverings Common type using small squares is called mosaic May be glazed or unglazed, comes in many colors, patterns, and textures Glossy surface squares usually 4½ in. New developments producing handsome tiles 12-in. square with variety of designs, textures, and colors Pregrouted tile sheets up to 2 by 14 sq ft now available Absorbs and stores solar energy	Especially attractive for foyers, sun rooms, bathrooms, but may be suitable for any room, depending on color, texture, and period of room	Care same as quarry tile
Marble	Hardest of nonresilient flooring materials Now available in many varieties Marble gives feeling of elegance More expensive than most other flooring materials, but is permanent New stone-cutting techniques have made marble lighter and less expensive Tiles are reinforced by epoxy–fiberglass coating	Wherever elegant durability is needed Especially appropriate with classic styles of furnishing	Wash with soap and warm water
Travertine	Porous limestone characterized by irregular cavities that should be filled with either clear or opaque epoxy resin Clear resin has three-dimensional appearance	In formal settings where durability is required	Wash with soap or detergent and warm water
Terrazzo	Consists of cement mortar (matrix) to which marble chips (aggregate) are mixed Custom or precast; comes in large or small marble chips Larger chips give more formal appearance Available in limited range of colors Sanitary, durable, and easy to clean	Patios, foyers, halls, recreation rooms, bathrooms, or wherever traffic is heavy	Dust with dry mop, wash occasionally with detergent Some varieties need occasional waxing
Glass tile	Modules 1⅝ in. by 3/16 in. of impervious and homogenous glass Stable, inert, and nonporous with nonslip surface Unaffected by fire, heat, or frost Available in white and some earth tones May be custom colored Easy maintenance	Suitable for dark areas Adaptable for walls or floors	Clean with detergent and warm water
Glass block or vista-brick	Solid glass blocks 8 in. by 8 in. by 3 in. offer excellent light transmission, good visibility, and provide high-impact strength	Used as pavers, covers for light fixtures recessed in floor	Clean with detergent and warm water
Poured seamless vinyl	Plastic from a can Has glossy surface Nonslippery Easy to maintain	Kitchens, bathrooms, family rooms	Does not require waxing Clean with soap and warm water Avoid heavy detergents

Wood Flooring

Wood is considered the most versatile and is the most widely used of all flooring materials. It combines beauty, warmth, some resilience, resistance to indentation, durability, availability, and ease of installation. The quiet harmony and beauty of wood floors provide a background for any style of furnishings, and such floors are always in good taste. A standard flooring for centuries, wood waned in popularity during the first half of the twentieth century with the popularity of wall-to-wall carpeting. Currently, however, wood floors symbolize high fashion and often are the choice of many designers and home owners. New methods of treatment have made wood a practical flooring for any and all areas of the house.

Methods of Laying Wood Floors

The three basic methods of laying wood floors are **strips, planks,** and ***parquetry.*** In the first method, strips of wood, usually about 2½ in. wide with ***tongue and groove,*** are nailed in place. In the plank method, the planks may be uniform or ***random,*** varying in width from 3 in. to 7 in. Some have square edges; others are tongue and groove. The parquetry method makes use of short lengths of boards, arranging them in various designs such as checkerboard and herringbone. For ease of installation and economy, 9- to 12-in. squares are assembled at the factory.

Wood Veneer

Sometimes a thin layer of hardwood is veneered to a less expensive wood, such as prefabricated parquet squares veneered and finished at the factory. These veneers are less expensive than solid wood, but they will not hold up as well under heavy wear. Sometimes thin layers of wood are laminated to backing,

PATTERNS OF HARD FLOORS

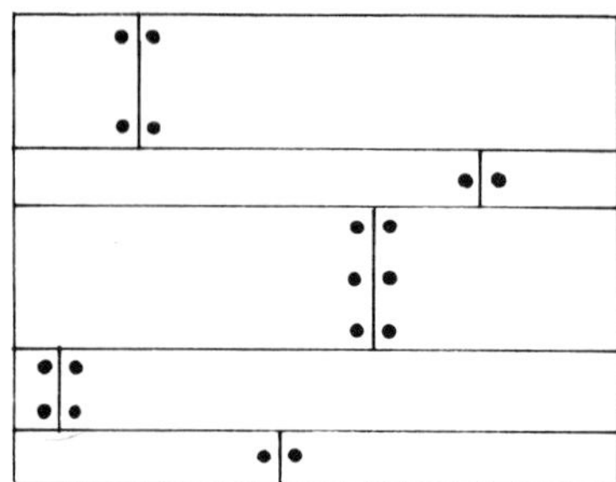

Random Plank

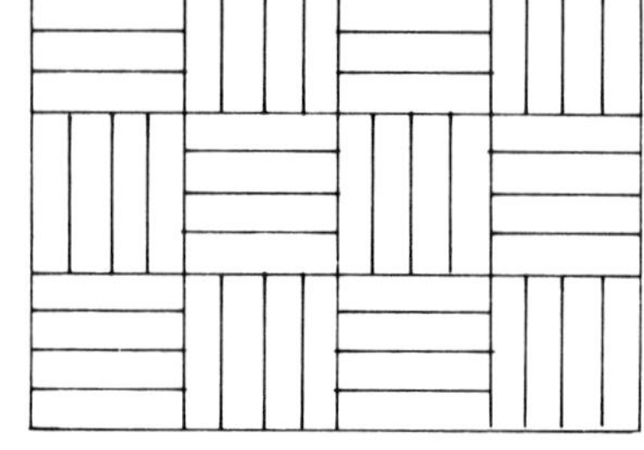

Checkerboard Parquet

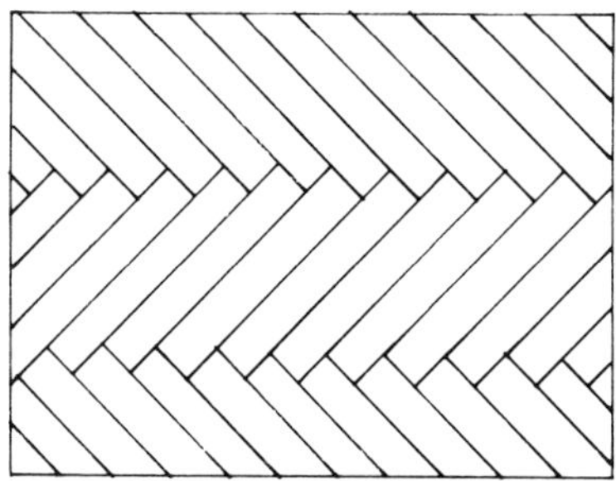

Herringbone Parquet

Figure 7.12 The warmth and versatility of a wood floor are evident in the contemporary Elliot house by Moore, Grover, and Harper. The wood is laid in vertical strips, making a pleasing transition from room to room. Both traditional and modern furniture are at home on a wood floor. *(Photograph by Norman McGrath.)*

Figure 7.13 In a smaller space, narrow oak strips are laid diagonally in an eating space. Wood is durable and easy to keep up—an ideal selection for flooring in an eating area. *(Photograph by Mark Allen.)*

Figure 7.14 This exquisite parquet wood floor adds distinction to the room and is a Marie Antoinette pattern copied from a section of the famous Versailles Palace floor. It is available from the factory in either prefinished or unfinished squares. *(Courtesy of the Chickasaw Brand Hardwood Flooring/Memphis Hardwood Flooring Company.)*

making it durable and more resilient. Hardwood veneer is placed under a surface of vinyl sheeting to protect it from moisture, wear, and household chemicals. The veneer is backed with aluminum, vinyl, and asbestos to assure a permanent, moisture-free bond to almost any subfloor. This veneer is available in a variety of woods and is generally maintained the same way as vinyl.

Plastic- (Acrylic-) Impregnated Wood Floors

Acrylic-wood flooring is a development in which real wood is impregnated with a liquid plastic hardened throughout the pore structure by irradiation. The result is a floor with the warmth of wood and remarkable durability tough enough to withstand the heaviest foot traffic. It is available in 12-in.-square prefinished parquet tiles, 5⁄16-in. thick, and comes in a variety of tones. Installation cost is comparable to that for other high-quality materials like terrazzo. Acrylic-wood flooring is an answer to the increasing demand for flooring with a natural mellow look that is durable and requires little maintenance. Because of its physical characteristics, acrylic-wood flooring is finding increased acceptance among designers as an alternative to natural untreated wood and other hard-surface flooring materials, particularly in high-traffic areas.

Particle Board

Particle board is made of pressed sawdust and small wood chips. It is most often used for subflooring.

Stained Wood Floors

Wood can exhibit a bright new alternative look in flooring. Wood flooring need not be only in familiar tones of natural wood but may also be as varied in color as fabric. Colored stain may be applied in basically the same way as natural finish, and the natural grain of the wood is not impaired. Some color tones emphasize the pattern in the wood and may even produce a three-dimensional effect. This effect can be achieved by a **stain and sealer** method, in which only the surface is stained and then sealed with polyurethane, or the **stain wax** method, in which the stain penetrates into the wood, leaving a wax residue on the surface. When the latter process is repeated and the wood is thoroughly rubbed, the surface has a soft, protective ***patina.*** Preparation, application, and maintenance of wood with color stain is the same as for natural stain. Some currently popular stains give wood a ***bleached*** effect, which can be obtained by applying certain light stains like platinum.

Figure 7.15 The soft shadings, tonal qualities, and precise definition of this inlaid vinyl flooring results in versatility, beauty, and practicality. *(Design by La Mesa, courtesy of Congoleum Ultraflor Imperial sheet vinyl flooring.)*

Stenciled and Painted Wood Floors

Stenciling, a process of applying paint through a stencil, was used by our forebears as a substitute for expensive carpets. Today, stenciled floors are still an attractive alternative. Stencil designs come in a variety of patterns and sizes and can provide an effective handcrafted look to a room.

Resilient Flooring—Vinyl

The development of vinyl for floor use is in large measure responsible for the new interest in hard floor coverings. The effects that can and are being produced in vinyl are limitless. Vinyl can be clear or vividly colored, translucent or opaque, textured or satin smooth. It comes in 6- and 12-ft **sheets** and **tiles,** or in a **can.** Vinyl can be informal or formal. Resilient hard-surface vinyl floors were once used only for kitchens, utility rooms, and bathrooms, but their present-day elegance has admitted them into any room of the house. Small patterns mask tracking and spillage, pebble vinyls achieve a natural stone effect, and embossed patterns are reminiscent of Old World designs such as Moorish tile, travertine, and marble. An all-purpose vinyl in sheet or tile requires no adhesive. A conductive tile is made especially for hospitals and chemical and electronic laboratories as a safety measure to protect against the hazard of static electricity. A foam-cushion backing makes it possible to have a practical vinyl surface with the luxurious feel of carpet.

One drawback might include the negative appearance vinyl can have when simulating a natural material. Also, when the surface is textured with grooves, cleaning is a problem.

Figure 7.16 Vinyl flooring is versatile and lends itself to a variety of configurations, colors, patterns, and textures. The flooring shown here has a "Stripwood" pattern in a striking effect. *(Courtesy of Azrock Floor Products.)*

same carpet carried throughout the living areas of the home will (6) serve as a transition from room to room, providing a feeling of unity. An art rug may serve as the room's focal point.

Quality of Soft Floor Coverings

Quality in carpeting is dependent on four ingredients: (1) the **type and grade of fiber,** (2) the **depth of pile,** (3) the **density of pile,** and (4) the **construction.**

Fiber. Over the years, virtually every fiber has been used in carpets. Today, however, about 90 percent of all carpeting sold in the United States is composed of synthetic fibers. During the past two decades, the field has narrowed down to five principal fibers: **nylon, acrylic, polyester, olefin,** and **wool.** Each of these fibers has outstanding qualities accounting for its success, but all have other supporting qualities. Fibers are often blended to bring out the best characteristics of each. To affect quality, at least 20 percent of one fiber must be present. The carpet label provides the percentage by weight of the fibers.

- *Nylon* is the single most important synthetic fiber, accounting for about 90 percent of carpeting sold today. Nylon has excellent abrasion resistance; resists crushing and matting; and reduces static electricity, *pilling,* and fuzzing. It repels soil and cleans well, particularly in spot cleaning for stains. It is nonallergenic and is mold-, mildew-, and mothproof. Improvements in methods of construction and adaptations to fashion trends have contributed to its effective use. When combined with polyester, the two complementary fibers' specific strengths offset their respective weaknesses. Antron and Anso are new fourth-generation nylon fibers that have excellent performance features and exceptional soil and stain resistance.
- *Acrylic* is much like wool in appearance. Its outstanding characteristic is solution dyeability. Resistance to abrasion and soiling is good. It cleans exceptionally well and has good crush resistance, but it is susceptible to some pilling. Orlon and Acrilan are some popular trade names.
- *Polyester* is an exceptionally soft fiber offering good abrasion resistance. It combines the look and feel of wool with a durability approaching that of nylon. Stain and soil resistance are good, and it is easily cleaned. Although polyester has great bulk and bounce, it has a tendency toward crushing and pilling. Trade names include Fortrel, Kodel, and Dacron.
- *Olefin* is another fiber of the 1960s. Polypropylene is a specific type of olefin and is the best known. It is predominant in needle-punch carpets, which are especially popular for kitchen and indoor-outdoor carpets. Ease of care and a nonabsorbent nature are its outstanding characteristics. Most stains lie on the surface, making it the easiest fiber to clean. Wearing qualities are comparable to nylon, and it is completely colorfast. During the past decade improvements have been made in color and design, which had been limited in the past. Resilience can be controlled by construction. Polyethylene is also a specific olefin. Herculon is one popular trade name.
- *Wool* is the luxury fiber and has long been regarded as the top carpet fiber, possessing all of the most desirable characteristics. Other fibers express their aesthetic qualities in relation to how nearly they resemble wool.

  Great resilience accounts for the vital quality of wool in retaining its appearance. Wool has warmth, a dull matte look, durability, and soil resistance. It takes colors beautifully, cleans well, and when cared for, keeps its new look for years. Although relatively more expensive than synthetic fibers, natural wool maintains its prestigious position in the carpet field.
- *Cotton* Although not as durable or resilient as wool and synthetic fibers, cotton is soft, takes dye very well, and is less expensive. It is used most often for flat woven area rugs like dhurries from India. Often, cotton strips are braided into rugs and used in informal settings.
- *Sisal, jute, and hemp* and other grasses are inexpensive floor coverings generally limited to area or room-size rugs. These fibers can be woven into simple or intricate designs and are often made in sections and attached. Although they provide a nice natural look, they are not as comfortable underfoot. These cellulosic fibers are used most often in tropical climates. Japanese tatami mats are made from grasses; however, they are flammable and not durable.

Each company producing these fibers has developed variants adding to the fibers' practical and aesthetic qualities, such as better soil resistance, less static, more dyeing possibilities, more bulk, and more luster. Since each manufacturer has a need to use a special name to designate its product in the carpet industry, a myriad of trade names are on the market. The generic name is therefore the key to determining fiber content and the qualities desired by the consumer.

Depth and Density of Pile. Pile depth and density will affect carpet wear. Because deeper pile or a density of pile requires more yarn, it will be more durable. Density—the number of threads per square inch—can be examined by bending back a piece of carpet. If wide spaces are between the threads or if wide gaps are between rows and large amounts of backing show, the carpet probably will not wear well. With the current direction for shorter clipped carpets, density is especially important.

Construction Methods. Because of many new technical developments, the old and well-known weaves no longer account for the bulk of present-day carpets. Most carpets on the market today are tufted, with woven, needle-punched, knitted, and flocked carpets accounting for the remainder. Methods of construction include the following:

- *Tufting* accounts for approximately 90 percent of all carpet construction today. Based on the principle of the sewing machine, this method involves the insertion of thousands of threaded needles into a backing material. Heavy latex coating is applied to the backing to anchor the tufts permanently. Some have a double backing for greater strength. Although tufted carpets are generally made in solid colors, new advances in dyeing technology make it possible to produce multicolor effects. Pattern attachments produce textural effects.
- *Weaving* was once extremely important. As recently as 1951, woven carpets accounted for 90 percent of all broadloom produced. This amount was cut to less than 10 percent during the early seventies. The three types of woven carpets are (1) ***Wilton,*** (2) ***Axminster,*** and (3) ***Velvet.*** The *Wilton* carpet takes its name from the town in England where it was first made in 1740. It is woven on a loom with a special Jacquard attachment by which the yarns are carried along the background of the carpet until they are drawn to the surface to form loops. After more than 200 years, the Wilton carpet is still regarded as a standard of high quality. The *Axminster* carpet also derives its name from the town in England where it was first manufactured in 1755. Originally a hand-knotted carpet, it is now made on a specialized American loom in which yarns are set in a crosswise row, permitting each tuft to be controlled individually. This process makes possible an almost unlimited combination of colors and patterns. *Velvet,* the simplest form of carpet weaving, is traditionally a smooth-surface pile, cut or uncut in a solid color. The pile loops of velvet carpet are woven over long wires extending the full length of the carpet.

THREE LEADING CARPETS

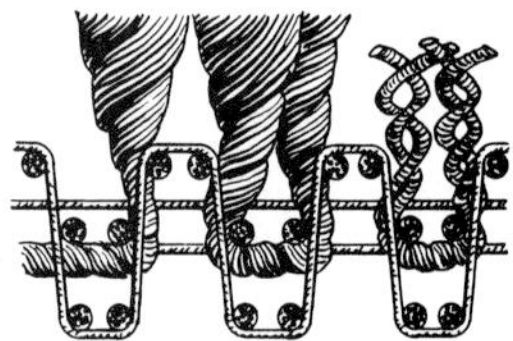

Axminster carpet. Top diagram shows different colored yarns. Bottom diagram shows use of curled down yarns for multilevel effect in face of carpet. (*Courtesy of James Lees and Sons Company.*)

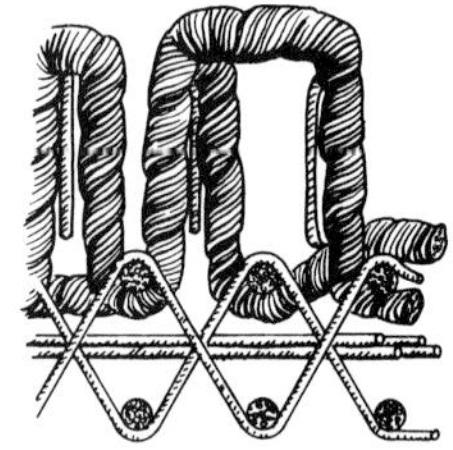

Wilton carpet (loop pile). Pile is woven over strips of metal, which are removed during weaving process.

Velvet carpet (cut pile). Backing of jute and cotton holds pile yarn in place.

- *Needle-punch* construction until recently has been used almost entirely for indoor–outdoor carpet. In this process an assembly of corded fiber webs is compacted and held together by felting needles that mechanically interlock the fibers. The back is coated with latex or other weather-resistant materials. A wide variety of textures is possible by this method, and the carpet sells at a low cost.
- *Flocked* carpets have short clipped fibers providing the appearance of velour. They may be produced by three basic methods: by beater bars, by spraying, and by an electrostatic method—the latter accounting for most flocked carpets. In this process, chopped fibers introduced into an electrostatic field become charged and then projected toward a backing fabric coated with adhesive, where they become vertically embedded.
- *Braiding* rugs by hand using small scraps of fabric—often from old clothing or bedding—dates back many centuries. The

braids are sewn together to form a rug. Today braided rugs are both handcrafted and machine-made.

- *Hooking* also dates back many centuries and today is still a method of construction often preferred by those who enjoy handcrafted products. Hooked rugs are made by forcing pile yarns through a backing (usually wool), allowing the craftsworker to create any design or color combination. Scandinavian rya rugs are one type of hooked rug.

The performance of a carpet is also dependent on the **degree of twist** and the **heat setting of the fiber.** A tight twist helps the fiber spring back under crushing foot traffic, and proper heat setting prevents unraveling.

Carpet Backings. The unseen part of a carpet—the backing—is important. A good foundation prevents stretching, buckling, and shrinking. The backing yarns should be firmly woven. Jute, the most widely used fiber, is strong but may mildew and is therefore not suitable for use where floors may be damp, such as in some basements or outdoors. Polypropylene resists mildew, is also strong, and may give better service where dampness is a problem. Tufted carpets should have a secondary backing applied for extra strength. It may be jute, polypropylene, rubber, or vinyl. All but jute and high-density rubber are placed on carpet for outdoor use.

Style Characteristics of Carpets

Before a carpet is selected, the surface texture should be considered. Definite style characteristics may be chosen within the categories of **cut pile** or **uncut loop pile,** with a variety of lengths determining the texture and design. When the area to be carpeted has been studied, the consumer can then select from the numerous styles available the one most appropriate for his or her needs. The following are the surface characteristics produced in most fibers.

- *Level-loop pile* has looped tufts all the same height. This low-cost carpet often has a foam or rubber backing and is usually used for kitchens and bathrooms, and in commercial settings.
- *Plush,* often known as velvet carpet, has a dense upright and evenly cut pile under 1 in. in height. The luxurious carpet is enhanced by highlights and shadings, which provide an extra dimension. Plush carpets are generally more appropriate for formal areas.
- *Tip* or *random shear* has both cut and uncut pile. Random or tip shear is similar to multilevel loop, except the highest loops are sheared, providing a simple patterned effect.
- *Multilevel loop* surfaces have loops at several different heights. This carpet is practical, hides footprints, and masks spots and soiling. *Tweeds* are of this type—looped with a decided texture, often with a high–low pile of multicolored yarns.
- *Embossed* carpets are woven with high and low pile. The pile may be all loop, all cut, or a combination. This carpet style is one of the most popular.
- *Sculptured* carpet is one in which part of the surface has been cut away to form a pattern, or the pattern itself has been cut away from the background. This carpet style is often custom-made and more expensive.
- *Frieze* has a tightly twisted yarn, giving a rough, nubby appearance. Friezes are available in light and hard twists. Hard twists lie flat, will keep a fresh appearance, and are less likely to show signs of wear.
- *Splush* is a term used to describe carpets with a pile height between shag and plush. It has a

CARPET CHARACTERISTICS

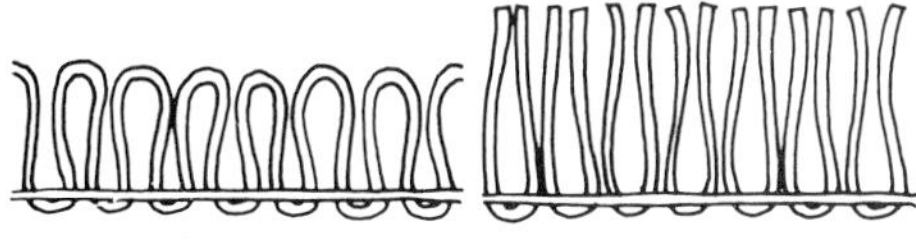

Level loop   Cut or plush

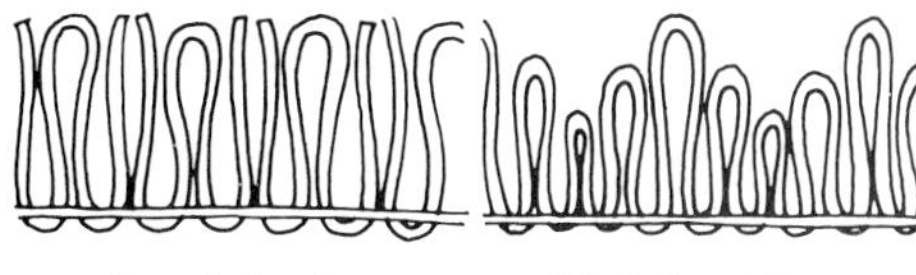

Level tip shear   Multilevel loop

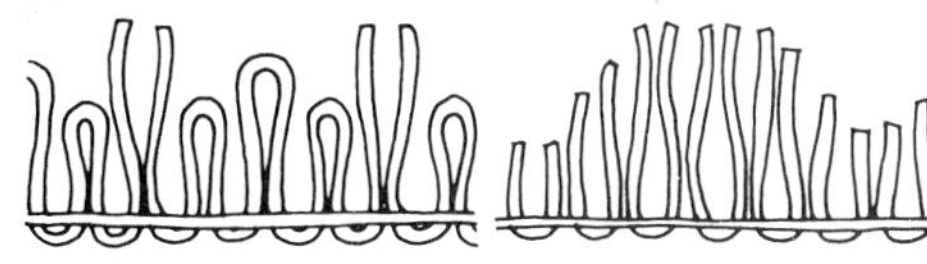

Random shear   Sculptured

more textured surface compared to plush.

- *Shag* carpets have pile yarns that are more than 1 in. in height, may be looped or uncut, and provide an informal look. Shags have generally lost favor, and very few are made today.
- *Saxony* is a combination of plush and short shag, twisted and heat set under high temperature and pressure, producing a deep, rich surface.
- *Flat-woven* cellulosic fiber rugs are machine-made of coarse flax fiber, paper pulp or "kraft" fiber, sisal, hemp, and various other grasses and rushes. They come in 1-ft squares to be sewn together or in full-sized rugs. Fiber rugs are usually in natural colors but are sometimes dyed. Popular in warm climates, they also provide inexpensive year-round floor coverings in many contemporary settings. Other flat-woven styles include dhurries from India, Navajo rugs from America, and Rollikans from Scandinavia.
- *Patterned* carpets of all kinds are on the market today and are gaining in popularity. A printing process, basically a screen-printing technique, has contributed to the interest in patterned floors. At first simple geometrics, printed designs are now numerous and highly refined for any type of decor. Patterned carpets are also being produced by standard methods—particularly Axminster—and are becoming a fashion item in residential and commercial interiors.

Figure 7.18 Often designers create custom rugs and carpets to suit the tastes and needs of a particular client. In this dining room, a room-size rug was ordered in specific colors of pink, blue-green, and cream to define the area and unify the scheme. *(Courtesy of Dan River/Wunda Weve.)*

Carpets for Specific Needs

Fortified with information about quality and style characteristics of carpets, the consumer can make an evaluation of individual needs. Following are some helpful suggestions.

- **Room size** is important. Where space is limited, wall-to-wall carpets in solid colors or overall texture will give a feeling of spaciousness. Large patterns tend to fill up space and are usually better reserved for more spacious areas.
- For **heavy-traffic areas** such as family rooms, stairways, and passageways, it is wise to select a good-quality carpet that wears well and is crush and soil resistant.
- **Furniture style** is a consideration. The carpet can aid in expressing the character of the furniture, whether traditional or modern, formal or casual. If carefully chosen, carpet can coordinate all furnishings of the room and provide unity.
- A room's particular **lighting situation** must be evaluated. A sunny room may call for a carpet in cool colors or deep shades. For a northern exposure or dark room, one of the warm

stain resistent wool carpet is Best

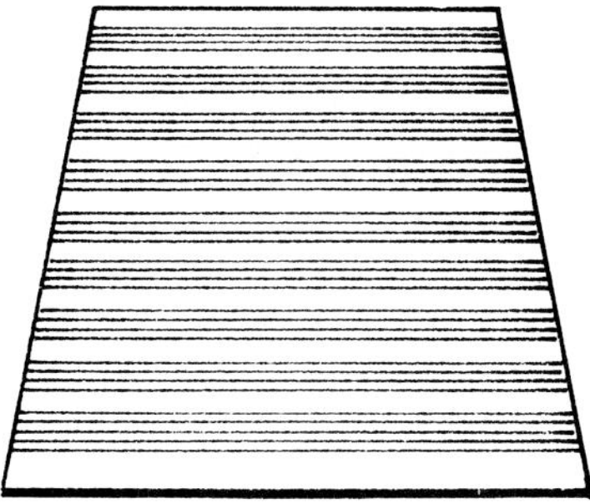

Wider

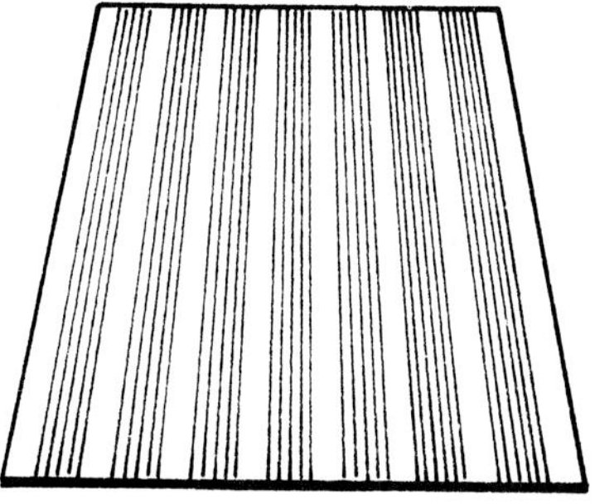

Longer

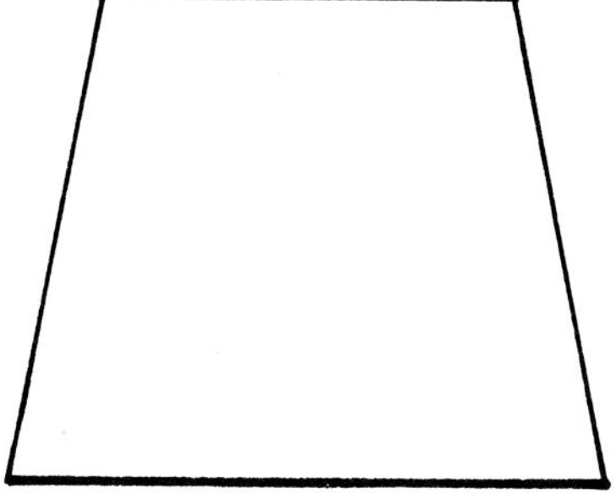

Larger

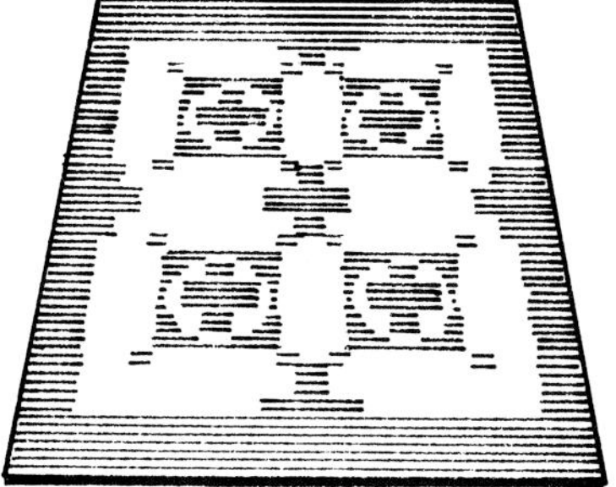

Smaller

Carpet can change the apparent size and proportion of a room.

Figure 7.19 The felted and uniquely textured carpet in natural shades flecked with color and blended with stretch wool, and the wool upholstery in fluid gem tones and classic designs, are equally appropriate for home or office. *(Courtesy of the Wool Bureau.)*

colors in lighter tones may be a better choice. Also, certain fibers, style characteristics, and textures of carpet absorb and reflect light in a different manner.

- **Color** is of vital importance because the floor is the largest usable area of the room, is the least-often changed, and is the background for all other furnishings. **Personal taste** can be the determining factor, but much thought and experimenting with samples will help make the decision a wiser one. A neutral, medium-colored carpet will show dirt less than a darker or a very light color.
- If the carpet selected has a

Figure 7.20 A richly colored Oriental rug in a contemporary eclectic setting in Connecticut is placed at a diagonal, defining the arrangement of furnishings. The placement of an exquisitely patterned Oriental rug in a clean structural background can enhance each by sheer contrast, bringing out the finest qualities of both. *(Photograph by Norman McGrath.)*

definite **pattern,** then walls, drapery, and upholstery tend to be complemented when plain colors or unobtrusive patterns are employed. Carpets with a plain overall effect permit a wider choice of furnishings.

- **Upkeep and maintenance** are a determining factor when selecting a carpet. Carpets that resist soil and are easy to clean cut down on labor and costs, thus keeping their attractive appearance for longer periods. (See pp. 206–207 for further considerations when selecting a carpet.)

Rug and Carpet Sizes

Size is another consideration in selecting a carpet or rug. For convenience, the terms *rug* and *carpet* are often used interchangeably, although technically they are not the same. (1) A **carpet** is a floor covering made in strips and often attached to the floor. Carpeting is woven in widths from 27 in.- to 18-ft-wide widths known as broadloom. Strips can be seamed or taped together and thus can cover great areas. A piece of carpet can be used as a rug. (2) A **rug** is a floor covering made in one piece, often with its own delineating border and usually not intended to cover the entire floor.

- *Wall-to-wall carpeting* has some distinct advantages: it creates continuity within a room or from room to room, makes

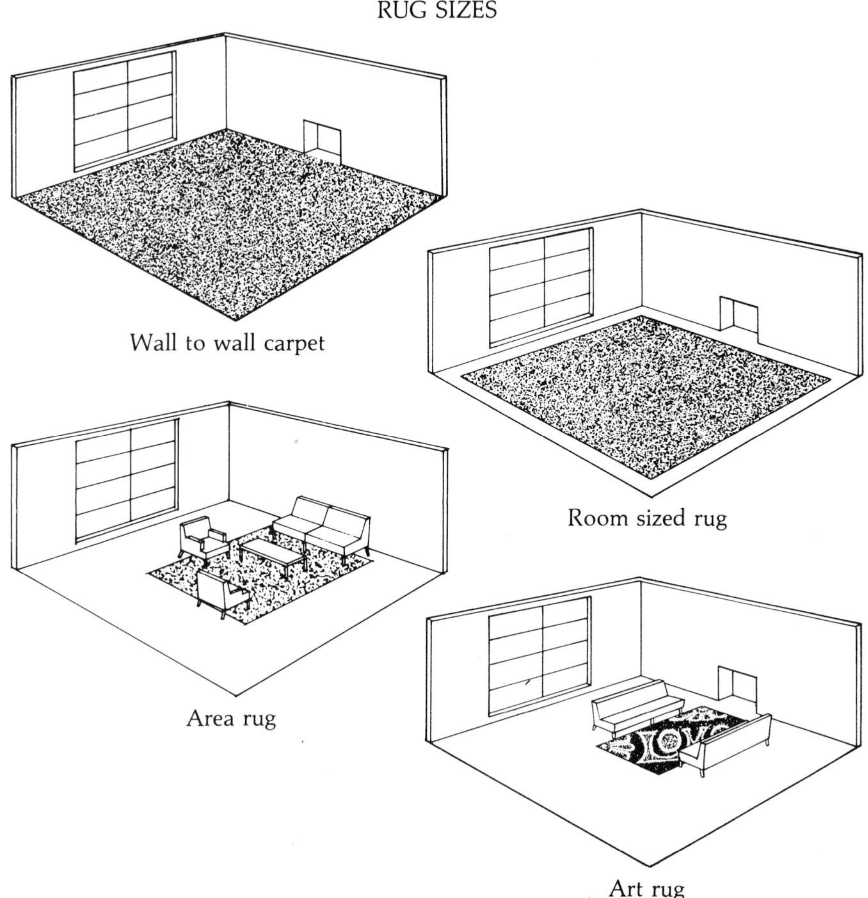

Figure 7.21 Wall-to-wall carpeting in a rust brown color depicting the design of quarry tile unifies the various arrangements of furnishings. The carpeting gives interest to the room and softness under foot. *(Courtesy of Gayl Baddeley/Associates.)*

rooms look larger, adds warmth and a feeling of luxury, requires only one cleaning process, and provides maximum safety from accidents. This carpeting treatment also has some disadvantages: it must be cleaned on the floor, it cannot be turned for even wear, and only part can be salvaged if moved.

- A *room-sized rug* is one that comes within a few inches or even a foot or so of the walls, leaving a marginal strip of floor exposed. Standard-sized rugs will fit most rooms, the 9-by-12-ft rug probably being the most common. The room-sized rug has most of the advantages that wall-to-wall carpeting has, plus some extra benefits. It can be turned for even distribution of wear and removed for cleaning. Two processes, however, are necessary for complete cleaning—one for the rug and the other for the exposed flooring material around it, usually wood.
- An *area rug* does not cover the entire floor but is used to define an area of a room according to its function. The rug should, however, be large enough to accommodate all the furniture used in the area grouping. The appropriateness of the size depends on the room in which it is used. For example, in a large room a 9-by-12-ft rug might be considered an area rug. This type of rug is versatile and may easily be changed for different grouping arrangements or moved to a different room of the house.
- An *art rug,* which is usually smaller than an area rug, is generally handcrafted and used as an accent or treated as a focal point. This rug is often placed so that furniture does not encroach on it, enabling it to be admired like a piece of art on

Figure 7.22 Two large Oriental rugs are used to help define the space and furnishings from one seating area into another at the Governor's Mansion in Salt Lake City. The rugs contribute to the total design concept with skillful use of coordinating colors, textures, and fabrics. *(Courtesy of Gayl Baddeley/Associates.)*

the floor. Usually patterned, it may be modern or traditional, such as a fine Oriental, an eighteenth-century needlepoint, an Indian dhurrie rug, or a custom-made modern design. Often an art rug functions as an area rug.

- *Scatter* or *throw* rugs are smaller rugs often used as an accent or as protection for a spot that receives hard wear.

Carpet Underlay and Installation

Before a carpet is laid, a pad or cushion is installed directly on the hard floor surface. Every carpet requires a good underlay, which provides tremendous value for the initial cost. Cushioning improves and helps to maintain the appearance of the carpet; enhances the resiliency, which assists in preventing pile matting; and prolongs the life of the carpet from 50 to 75 percent. It also absorbs noise and creates a feeling of luxury. Even low and moderately priced carpet, when laid over a good pad, will take on the feeling of cushioned elegance. Carpet is usually professionally installed by stretching the rug to the wall edges and attaching it to tacked strips secured at the perimeter of the room. Occasionally the carpet is glued to the floor.

On the market today are six basic types of carpet underlay:

- *Solid foam* underlays are made of prime urethane. They are firm, resilient, durable, and not affected by heat or moisture. Their cost is higher than bonded foam.
- *Bonded foam* underlays are made of reconstituted urethane and are usually 9/16 in. thick. They are not affected by heat or cold, go on almost any surface, hold up well, and are moderately priced. This type of padding accounts for the highest percentage of underlay sold.
- *Waffle sponge* is made of natural or synthetic rubber with a variety of fabric backings. This type of pad may deteriorate in the presence of heat or moisture.
- *Flat sponge rubber* is made of natural or synthetic rubber with a variety of finishes and fabric backings. This type is used less than foam.
- *Fiber* cushion underlays are made of jute, animal hair, rubber-coated jute, or combinations of plain or rubber-coated jute with animal hair. This type of pad is firm and extremely durable, but high cost limits its volume of sale.
- *Carpet with attached cushioning* accounts for a low percentage (approximately 20 percent) of all carpet sold today. This type of carpet can easily be picked up and relaid—a feature popular for those who move often or want to rotate a carpet to other areas of the home.

From this array of carpet cushioning, the choice should be based on individual needs, taking into consideration the condition of the floor, the amount of traffic, the function of the area to be covered, and the carpet being used.

When all necessary information is at hand and the consumer is ready to make a carpet purchase, some recommendations may be considered.

1. Generally avoid "package deals." Package deals with costs of carpet, installation, and padding lumped together are seldom a bargain in view of long-term quality.
2. Patronize a reputable dealer—one that will stand behind the product.
3. Take home a sample of the carpet. Observe it at home under all types of lighting conditions, both natural and artificial.
4. Select a dependable carpet brand. A label on the carpet

provides the name of an established manufacturer, which is an assurance of obtaining good value in the price range selected. Also, the label gives valuable information on the fiber content.

5. The finest quality the budget will allow is the best carpet investment.

Carpet Care

Soil-hiding fibers and special protective treatments help, but proper care is the surest way of keeping a carpet bright and beautiful. Regular vacuuming is essential. Heavy traffic areas need light vacuuming each day to maintain brightness and texture by removing surface soil and dirt. Thorough vacuuming once a week is desirable for most areas. Spills should be removed immediately to prevent permanent damage. Carpet retailers can provide consumer brochures containing detailed information on carpet maintenance.

Handmade Rugs

Oriental Rugs

The making of Oriental rugs is a great art. Appreciated by discriminating people the world over, Oriental rugs have been coveted possessions for hundreds of years.

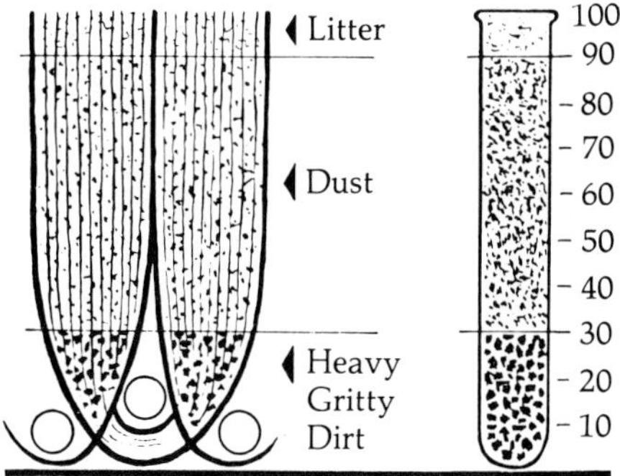

Test tube shows proportion of dirt by weight in an average carpet. *(Courtesy of Hoover Company.)*

PRINCIPAL KNOTS USED IN MAKING ORIENTAL RUGS

Ghiordes or Turkish knot, used in Turkey and throughout Asia Minor

Sehna or Persian knot, used in many parts of Iran

During the eighteenth and nineteenth centuries, rugs from China and the Near East were in great demand among well-to-do Americans who wanted such rugs to adorn their great Georgian and Federal-period mansions. Not until late in the nineteenth century, however, were they imported in great numbers.

With the advent of wall-to-wall carpeting, Oriental rugs went out of fashion in America, but during the past few decades they have been rediscovered and are again desirable for contemporary use, regardless of style. For example, Oriental rugs are perfectly at home in a seventeenth-century saltbox or a modern twentieth-century home. To meet the current demand, American manufacturers are duplicating authentic Oriental designs in loom-woven rugs retailing at a fraction of the cost of the handmade ones. These rugs are called "Oriental design rugs" to distinguish them from the hand-loomed rugs made in the Orient and called "Oriental rugs."

The great majority of Oriental rugs imported into America have come from **Persia (Iran)** and **Turkey.** Rugs brought from the Orient to America before 1905 were made primarily for local consumption rather than for export trade. They were of varying proportions and sizes, and some extremely large ones were made for the floors of palaces and homes of the wealthy. In the homes of peasants, rugs comprised the principal item of furnishings. They were used for bed coverings, wall hangings, room dividers, and storage bags as well as floor coverings.

These rugs are made by **hand tying** a knot in each weft thread as it crosses the warp. The knot is either the **Ghiordes,** or Turkish, or the **Sehna,** or Persian type, depending on the area in which it is made. Rugs are frequently made by members of a family who use the same pattern generation after generation. The name of the particular rug is usually that of the family or is one taken from the name of the village or area in which it was made.

The beauty of an Oriental rug

depends on (1) the **quality of the wool fiber** (a few are made of silk), (2) the **fineness of the weave,** (3) the **intricacy of the design,** and (4) the **mellowness of color.** Design motifs range from simple geometrics to the most intricate of patterns combining flowers, trees, birds, and animals; and sometimes they have become so stylized through the years that the original source is uncertain. The mellow patina and soft color of the early imports—so highly prized by Americans—was a result of years of constant use and often of exposure to light, sun, and sometimes sand and rain. Today, a light lime wash is often given the rug to provide this mellow look.

By the early part of the twentieth century, the supply of valuable old rugs was becoming scarce. New ones were being produced, but since Americans preferred the soft colors of the old ones to the vivid tones of fresh vegetable dyes, a way had to be found to produce the "old" look. To accomplish this, plants were set up around New York City for chemically bleaching new rugs after they arrived in this country. Rugs were bleached, retouched by a special painting process, and finally run through bar rollers that gave them a high glossy finish. This process necessarily damaged the rug and lessened the wearing quality. Fortunately, the high cost of the procedure soon made it prohibitive. Since about 1955, most Oriental rugs have been given only a light lime wash, either before they leave the country in which they are made or after they arrive in this country. This wash produces a mellow look and does little harm to the rug.

Oriental rugs are classified as **antique, semiantique,** or **modern.** A rug 50 years old is usually considered an antique. Semiantique rugs are slightly newer but have a natural patina acquired through gentle use. Modern Orientals, which may employ traditional or new designs, are those made in the Orient within the past 10 years. Age alone, however, does not make a rug valuable. Certain rugs that were originally coarse and poorly made generally are not valuable at any time, but good ones are always considered valuable.

The study of Oriental rugs can be a lifelong pursuit, given the myriad types with distinct design origins from different areas, towns, tribes, and families. A logical beginning is to become familiar with the three Oriental rugs from the Near East that are particularly pleasing to American tastes—the **Kirman, Sarouk,** and **Tekke,** commonly called **Bokhara.**

- A top-grade *Kirman* is among the most costly of Oriental rugs. The most familiar type is one with a central medallion surrounded by a plain ground with a wide border of intricate design. Sometimes the entire ground is filled with delicate blooms. This rug is one of the few Orientals with an ivory ground.
- The predominant colors in the *Sarouk* are exotic-jewel tones of red, rose, and deep blue, with black and ivory as accent colors. Although the pattern is predominantly floral, it does feature some geometric devices. The Sarouk may also have a vibrant medallion outlined in dark colors. The pile is usually heavy.
- *Bokhara (Tekke)* rugs, originally from Turkistan, are made in many Middle Eastern countries. The background of the Bokhara may be red, cream, or blue, but the predominant color is always red. The easily recognizable design is made up of octagons or polygons called **guls** (roses), which are repeated uniformly about the field. When the guls are quartered by narrow

Figure 7.23 The most familiar of the Kirman designs: an open ground, a wide, uneven border, and a medallion center. *(Courtesy of Karastan Rug Mills.)*

Figure 7.24 This Sarouk rug is made in Iran. The all-over floral with rose or red ground is typical. *(Courtesy of Chas. W. Jacobsen.)*

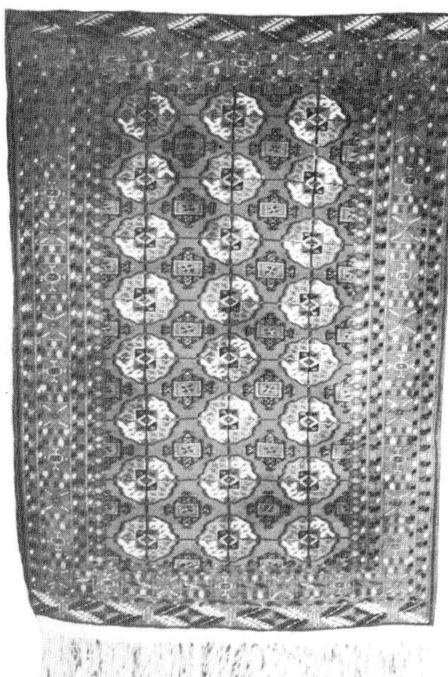

Figure 7.25 This Tekke-Turkoman (Bokhara) is made in central Asia. The straight line of geometric forms is typical. The ground is usually red. *(Courtesy of Chas. W. Jacobsen.)*

Figure 7.26 A Chinese design rug in the Bengali design. *(Courtesy of Stark Carpet Corporation.)*

lines running the length and width of the field, the design is popularly called **Royal Bokhara.**

Other well-known rugs from Iran include (1) the **Siraz,** which usually has a geometric pattern on red and blue; (2) the **Saraband,** with a field that is commonly red, covered with a palm-leaf design; (3) the **Isfahan,** one of the rarest and oldest of all antique rugs featuring a colorful floral pattern around a central medallion; (4) the **Hamadan** (the largest rug-producing section of Iran), usually featuring a stylized motif in the corners employing red, chestnut, and blue colors; (5) the **Kashan,** with intricate floral patterns, inspiring its name, "heavenly rug"; (6) the **Herez,** which has bold geometric designs with a medallion and ivory corners; (7) the **Nain,** probably the finest carpet woven in Iran today, with intricate floral designs; and (8) the **Qum,** an exceptionally fine rug, with the paisley motif most commonly employed.

Although Persia has been the primary source of these rugs, Oriental rugs have been made for centuries throughout the Middle East from Turkey and the Caucasus to India, China, and Japan.

Oriental Rugs from China. The art of rug making has been practiced in China for over 12 centuries. The oldest known rugs were from the T'ang dynasty (A.D. 618–906). The oldest existing rug dates from the Ming dynasty (A.D. 1368–1644). Early designs were taken from ancient Chinese silk weaving and are symbolic of ancestor worship. Ancient symbols, of which there are over 100, fall into a number of categories. Consumers and designers can easily recognize Chinese rugs today by the following characteristics:

- *Colors* employed for Chinese rugs are most typically blue and white (often used for the field), with yellow-orange, red-orange, gold, and cream also used in various combinations.
- *Geometric designs* are used primarily as border ornamentations. The Chinese T, key, or fret designs are the most familiar. The circle with a square in the center and two curved cells within a circle, symbolizing male and female, are common motifs.
- *Religious symbols* are commonly used, including the **dragon,** which symbolizes God and emperor, and **waves** and **closed bands** (eternity). Among the mythological symbols are the **lion** (authority), **horse** (strength), **fish** (abundance), and **stag** and **crane** (longevity).
- *Flowers* most commonly used are the **lotus** (purity), **peony** (prosperity), and **chrysanthemum** (fidelity).

Chinese rugs are made from complete paper models, and the design is outlined on a cotton warp. The pile is higher than with rugs made in the Near East, and designs are sculptured by clipping the yarns along the contour of the pattern.

Rugs made in eastern China usually have all-over patterns reflecting the Near Eastern influence. The two most familiar Chinese rugs are (1) the **Mandarin,** which has no border, an open ground, and a different asymmetrical floral spray in each corner, and (2) the **Peking,** which has a wide border, similar corner motifs, and a round cental medallion. Peking design rugs made in India are called **Bengali.**

Few rugs were made in China after the Second Sino-Japanese War (1937–1945), but after World War II, production increased and some Chinese rugs were exported indirectly from the mainland. Since the opening of trade with China, rugs are once again being exported directly, but most Chinese-style rugs found today come from Japan and India.

Oriental Rugs from India. Today many rugs of excellent quality are handmade in India for export to Europe and America. Rugs employing old and authentic designs from China, Iran, Turkey, and France are made from top-quality wool, mostly from New Zealand, and sell at moderate prices. Rugs imported into America from India come under several trade names.

- *Benares* rugs have a 100 percent wool nap, usually in natural colors with an ivory or cream ground.
- *Indo-Shahs* are some of the most common of the India-made rugs. The field is usually beige or pastel with designs in deep royal blue, aquamarine, green, or gold. Indo-Shahs are made in French **Aubusson** or **Savonnerie** designs or in old **Chinese** patterns.
- *China* rugs are among the finest of the India rugs woven today. The designs are mostly French.
- *Bengali* is a Chinese design. A center medallion is typical, and blue usually predominates.
- *Pakistani* rugs are made in West Pakistan and are of fine quality. Designs are traditional Turkoman and come in a wide color range. The best known is the **Mari-Bukaro** (**Bokhara,** or **Tekke**).

In addition to the heavy deep-pile rugs just listed, many finely woven Indian rugs are made in traditional Persian and Turkoman designs.

- *Kashmir Aubussons* are the flat-stitched tapestry Aubusson rugs employing authentic French designs.

Figure 7.27 This Numdah rug is made of rough felt with wool embroidery in the tree of life design. *(Photograph by Mark K. Allen.)*

- *Numdah* rugs, used in India for centuries, have been imported into the United States for many years and recently have had a revival in popularity. This rug is an informal type made of felt, with the wool surface traditionally enriched with bird and floral motifs worked with a long, open stitch. The tree of life design is one of the most familiar being used; others have been modernized. Colors are in rich combinations of greens, blues, reds, and yellows on a natural ground. Numdahs are most often used for wall hangings or accent rugs and are effective in almost any informal room.
- *Dhurries* are flat-weave rugs handwoven in India (see Figure 7.28). They are tightly woven in wool or cotton and incorporate both stylized and geometric designs. Colors are mostly pastels and medium tones on a natural field. Dhurries are currently much in vogue in American homes.

French Rugs

Two French-style carpets have been produced with little interruption since the seventeenth century: the ***Savonnerie*** and the ***Aubusson.***

- *Savonnerie* is a pile carpet made by hand with knotted stitches in the manner of Eastern Orientals but with French patterns. The Savonnerie factory, established in France in 1663 by **Louis XIV,** was an outgrowth of a workshop founded earlier in the ***Louvre.*** Although it was the first factory to produce tapestry-like carpets, it is best known for its velvety pile carpets, usually made in strong colors on a dark ground with elaborate designs sometimes taken from formal French gardens. Early Savonneries were made primarily for royal families of France and often bore the emblem of the king or prince for whom they were made. During the reign of kings Louis XIV, XV, and XVI, these rugs added warmth and splendor to the magnificent rooms of Versailles, Fontainebleau, and other great palaces and châteaux. Rugs of this type are still being produced.
- *Aubusson* rugs are a distinctive type. The exact date and circumstance of the establishment of the Aubusson factory are uncertain. During the late seventeenth century, however, when the upper classes of France became interested in beautifying their homes, long-established, privately owned workshops at Aubusson strove to imitate the weaving being done at Savonnerie and Gobelins to meet the new demand. Some of the oldest Aubusson rugs have an Oriental flavor, but later ones follow the French textile designs employing small-scaled stylized floral themes. Colors are usually soft, muted pastels,

Figure 7.28 An Indian dhurrie rug, designed with the "tree of life" motif, provides a complementary background for Le Corbusier's classic leather and tubular steel Grand Confort chairs. *(Courtesy of Patterson, Flynn & Martin/Jaime-Ardiles Arce.)*

Figure 7.29 The French Savonnerie is a velvety pile carpet, typically with intricate French designs on a dark ground. *(Courtesy of Stark Carpet Corporation.)*

giving a faded effect. These carpets are made in the tapestry weave but are somewhat less refined than the tapestries inspiring them. Although these rugs are no longer produced at Aubusson, the name persists to designate the type of carpet rather than the name of the factory.

Moroccan Rugs

The Moroccan is a type of Oriental rug made primarily in northwest Africa. The character of the rug has changed little in 1,000 years. Its distinctive informality has made it a great favorite in contemporary decor. Moroccan rugs are of two basic types: the **Berber** and the **Rabat.**

- *Berber* rugs are the traditional types made primarily by Berber tribes in the Atlas Mountains. The designs are abstract and geometric. Some are primitive, often of natural wool color with simple black or brown design; others are vividly colored. Top-

Figure 7.30 Aubusson rugs are made of tapestry weave, usually with French designs in pastel colors. *(Courtesy of Stark Carpet Corporation.)*

Figure 7.31 North Africa is the source of this Moroccan rug commonly called Berber. *(Courtesy of Ernest Tregavowan.)*

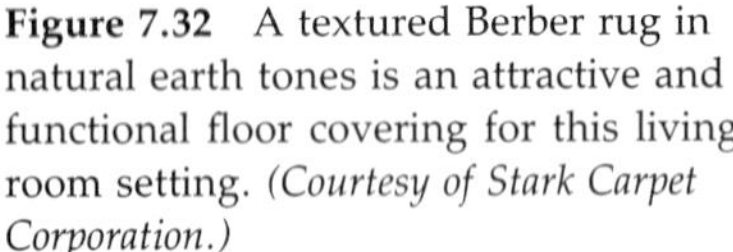

Figure 7.32 A textured Berber rug in natural earth tones is an attractive and functional floor covering for this living room setting. *(Courtesy of Stark Carpet Corporation.)*

quality carpets referred to as Berbers are being made today by leading American companies. They are usually in natural colors and may be plain or have geometric designs. Berbers are particularly in demand for contemporary homes.

- *Rabat* rugs are made mostly in factories in larger population centers. The designs show an oriental influence introduced into Morocco in the eighteenth century.

In 1938, a law was passed in Morocco prohibiting machine-made rugs. The law's intent was to safeguard employment for some 100,000 artisans and their families and to preserve the character of the handmade product. To ensure continuity in rug making, the government set up schools for girls between the ages of 9 and 15, in which the art of carpet weaving was taught. These *centres d'apprentissage* are located in the sultan's palace in Tangiers, a part of the picturesque Casbah.

The Spanish Matrimonia

The **Spanish Matrimonia,** the traditional bridal gift in Spain, is the fringed, bold-figured **Manta** rug. Woven on the Jacquard loom, these rugs have subtle shadings, a handcrafted-like texture, and a three-dimensional quality. The Spaniards' legendary love of color is typified in the bright color combinations. Patterns are inspired by medieval motifs, classic Aubussons, Far East Orientals, mythical figures, the tree of life, and ornate ***arabesques.*** Adaptations of these rugs are being made today and are particularly appropriate for homes built in the Spanish tradition.

The Navajo Rug

The **Navajo rug** is a handwoven rug or blanket made by the Navajo Indians in the Southwest. Those of finest quality are made of wool and colored with vegetable dyes. Designs are usually geometric with frequent zigzag, ***chevron,*** and diamond motifs combined with stripes. Quaint representations of birds, animals, and human figures are sometimes used. A remarkable similarity exists between the geo-

Figure 7.33 This Navajo rug is characteristic of much of the art of the North American Indian and is similar to Peruvian rugs. *(Photograph by Mark K. Allen.)*

Figure 7.34 A similarity is often present in folk rugs from remote areas. The Inca Indian influence that is evident in this rug from Peru bears a striking resemblance to rugs from eastern Turkey. *(Courtesy of Ernest Tregavowan.)*

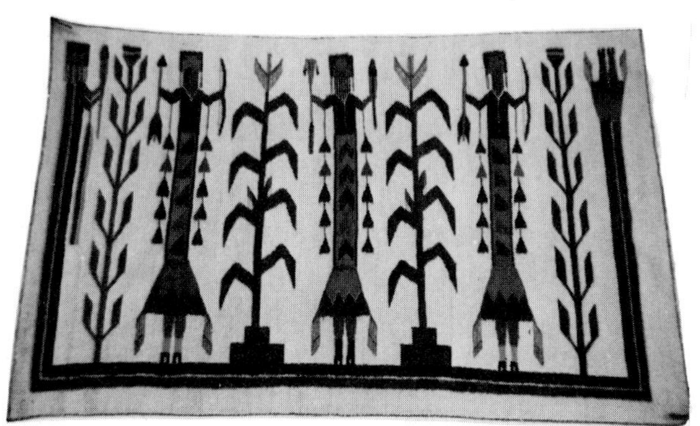

Figure 7.35 The Yeibechai (Yei) is a ceremonial rug made by the Navajo Indians of North America. Representations of animals and humans are found in folk art the world over. *(Photograph by Mark K. Allen.)*

Figure 7.36 A contemporary Danish rya rug with shaggy pile and a multicolored abstract design. *(Photograph by August Anselon.)*

metric designs of these rugs and designs of many made in the Caucasus Mountains and in Peru. Navajo rugs do not have a pile and are usually only large enough for accent or art rugs. They are especially appropriate in houses with a Southwest look. Adobe houses are particularly enhanced by Navajo rugs.

The Rya Rug

Rya is a name derived from an old Norse word meaning "rough." This hand-hooked rug is a traditional import from Scandinavia, where they have been used for centuries. The Rya is a high-pile shag rug combining a blend of multicolored yarns forced into a wool backing with a rug hook. The pile yarns are cut at an angle and at various heights, providing the "shaggy" appearance. Motifs are drawn especially from nature, including the pine cone, tree, leaf, skeleton of a leaf, forest, waves of the ocean, raindrops, stylized flowers, and animals including the reindeer, turkey, and pigeon. Geometric designs of all types are also employed, often combined with stylized themes from nature. Rya rugs are ideally suited for use as area or art rugs in many contemporary settings.

Rag Rugs

Rag rugs were one of the first floor coverings made by American colonists. Scraps of cotton, linen, or wool were cut in narrow strips and then sewn together to form long strands woven in a plain weave on a cotton or linen warp. Through ingenious methods, rags were turned into colorful rugs—a craft still practiced.

Figure 7.37 A braided rug can be used in any setting where a country look is desired.

Braided Rugs

Braided rugs were originally made in homes from scraps of clothing and blankets. They are still a favorite for rooms with a provincial atmosphere, especially in Early American and Country French rooms. Strips of rags are stitched together (on the bias), then braided into long ropes, which are either sewn or woven together in round or oval shapes. Varying bands of color can create colorful effects, adding a warm informality to a room. Rugs of this type are also produced commercially at reasonable cost.

Hooked Rugs

Hooked rugs have been familiar to Americans since the late seventeenth century, and during the nineteenth century rug hooking became a highly developed art. Although generally thought of as native to America, hooked rugs were previously made in England, Scandinavia (Rya rugs are a type of hooked rug), and other European countries. These rugs are made by hooking colored rags or yarns through a tightly stretched piece of burlap, canvas, or wool to form a pile that may be cut or left in loops. The foundation fabric and the type of material used for filling determine the degree of durability. Designs and color combinations are limitless.

Needlepoint Rugs

Needlepoint rugs were originally made by embroidering with wool yarn on a heavy net canvas. Designs range from simple to highly complex floral motifs in a wide array of colors. A popular floor covering during the nineteenth century, needlepoint rugs (now mostly machine-made) are again finding favor with Americans today.

Similarity in Folk Rugs

A striking similarity in appearance exists among folk rugs from most countries of the world. This similarity exists because primitive people most often use (1) **simple geometric designs adapted from nature,** (2) **quaint representations of human and animal forms,** (3) **colors that are invariably those of natural wools or vegetable dyes,** and (4) **construction that is done by hand on simple looms.** Whether these rugs are made by Berber tribes of North Africa, peasants in the highlands of Greece, or Navajo Indians on the western reservations of North America, they have a feeling of kinship and may be used together to add charm to rooms with an informal atmosphere.

Walls and Wall Treatments

The background elements of every room are important factors in setting and maintaining the decorative scheme. Walls, floors, ceilings, windows, doors, and fireplaces are all part of the room's enclosure and are rarely hidden, except in small areas. Although these background elements provide a setting for furniture and fabrics, their most important function is to provide a background for people.

Walls **occupy the largest area** of a room, **define its size and shape,** and **serve purposes of both function and beauty.** Functionally, walls provide protection and privacy from the exterior surroundings and create interior areas of various shapes and sizes for particular activities. Walls also provide space for plumbing pipes and electrical and telephone wires, as well as insulation against heat and cold. Aesthetically, they contribute significantly not only to the success of a room but also to its general atmosphere and personality. Some walls emphasize openness and informality; others stress protection and formality.

Traditionally, walls were stationary ceiling supports, and rooms were usually square or oblong. The design of today's walls not only includes traditional approaches but also employs other innovations, including

- Freestanding walls that are nonsupportive, allowing free placement within interior spaces. They may stop short of the ceiling, providing privacy but permitting the flow of air and light from one area to another.
- Materials used on exterior walls carried into the interior and left exposed can form the room's architectural background. This arrangement accentuates the flow of space from the outside to the inside.
- Walls may be of glass or plastic and slide into sockets or fold like accordians.
- Walls can function as wall systems allowing storage or display space. Walls may also be integrated with attached built-in furniture.
- Walls may be cut out in various shapes and sizes, allowing a visual link to the next living space.

The materials available for wall treatments today are varied and plentiful. Each type has advantages and disadvantages with regard to appearance, cost, upkeep, noise, insulation, and longevity. Wall materials should be appropriate for the particular home. Some wall treatments are extremely versatile, and others generally belong to certain moods and period styles. Materials for wall backgrounds should have appropriate textures and colors suitable for the occupant's life-style and the mood, theme, and style of the home.

When wall materials are selected, beauty, function, economy, and character—the goals of successful design—ought to be considered. Before deciding what wall material is appropriate, some basic questions include the following:

- Should walls be *emphasized or unobtrusive*? If active walls are planned, the treatment can be stronger—especially colors, textures, and patterns. If walls will take a passive role, a simple treatment is preferable.
- Will a *formal or informal* mood dominate? Walls can be elegant or casual, supporting the feeling desired. Rough or smooth textures and combinations of these should be considered.
- What is the *scale* of the room and furnishings? Wall treatment should relate in scale to enhance all interior components. For example, bold, rough concrete is not generally at home in a small-scaled space.
- Do walls need to have *acoustical properties*? Certain wall materials may be more suitable for warm or cold climates.
- Is *light reflection or absorption* required of a particular wall treatment?
- Is the wall material supportive of the home's *style and character*?
- What are the *maintenance properties* of the wall material in terms of upkeep and cost?
- Does the wall material need to be *durable* for its particular function?

Nonresilient (or Rigid) Wall Coverings

Table 7.3 contains a list of the most frequently used nonresilient wall coverings, plus information on their general characteristics, fire ratings, insulation properties, uses, and care. The most common rigid wall treatments include the following:

- *Plaster* is the simplest and most versatile of all wall treatments (see Figure 7.38). Plaster is a thick mixture of gypsum and water combined with lime and sand. This mixture must be applied to a metal lattice, a special hardboard, or any rough masonry surface. Plaster has been used for centuries, but today the cost makes it prohibitive for most housing.
- *Wallboard* may be a **gypsum plasterboard** or **pressed wood.** Gypsum plasterboard—called dry-wall construction—is the most common and is used extensively for walls in today's homes. Plasterboard and pressed wood are inexpensive wallboard treatments and come in 4-by-8-ft panels which are secured to the structure's vertical wood stud supports. Wallboard provides insulation against heat, cold, and noise and when painted produces a variety of effects from rough to smooth. Rough plaster-like walls are appropriate for informal rooms and some period rooms such as Spanish-style ones. If painted the right color, smooth plaster

TABLE 7.3 *Nonresilient wall coverings*

MATERIAL	GENERAL CHARACTERISTICS AND COST	FINISHES	FIRE RATING	INSULATION PROPERTIES	USES AND CARE
Brick (fired clay)	Solid and durable Variety of sizes, shapes, and colors Old, natural brick has feeling of warmth May be laid in regular or varied patterns Pleasant texture High cost	No finish necessary May be painted or waxed	Fireproof	Reflects noise Conducts heat and cold	Interior and exterior walls Appropriate for large- or small-scaled rooms in a wide range of styles, and for fireplace facings and hearths Little or no upkeep
Concrete blocks (lightweight aggregate)	Substantial, cold, regular shape, large scale, textured Moderate cost	No finish necessary May be painted Waterproofing necessary for exterior	Fireproof	Fair insulator	Interior or exterior walls; fireplace facings Best when used in large-scaled rooms Lacks domestic warmth Little or no maintenance
Ceramic tile (clay)	Comes in variety of shapes, sizes, colors, and patterns, and in pregrouted sheets Desirable aesthetic quality Durable, resists water and stains, but may crack or break Moderately high cost	No finish necessary	Fireproof	Reflects noise Poor insulator	Bathrooms, kitchens, utility rooms Particularly appropriate for dados in Spanish and Mexican rooms Becoming more widely used Minimum upkeep
Fiberglass (panels)	Translucent panels of reinforced fiberglass Most often ribbed or corrugated Also available in flat sheets and in several thicknesses Comes translucent, white, or colored; may simulate brick, stone, or wood Moderate cost	No finish necessary	Fireproof	Good insulator	Room dividers, folding screens, tub enclosures, translucent lighting panels for ceilings, built-ins, and sliding doors Easy upkeep
Glass (architectural)	Can be clear, rubbed, corrugated, pebbled, frosted, colored, and curved Metal mesh core will prevent breakage and will add to attractiveness May be tempered Moderately high cost	No finish necessary	Fireproof	Poor insulator	Sliding doors, screens, room dividers, clinical purposes, numerous other uses Mirror can usually expand space and add dramatic element to room One-way glass has many functional uses
Glass (block)	Excellent light transmission High-impact strength	No finish necessary	Fireproof	Solid glass blocks conduct heat Blocks with hollow air centers Good insulators	Suitable to lighten most dark areas Easy upkeep
Metal (panels and tiles)	Stainless steel, plain, or grained—not reflective finish Serviceable, sturdy, not affected by acid, steam, or alkalies Solid copper: eye appeal May be plain, hammered, or antiqued Sealed to prevent tarnish or corrosion	Factory finished with grain, or enameled in variety of colors	Fire resistant	Reflects heat	Kitchens, bathrooms, utility rooms, and wherever sturdy wall is desired Numerous functional and decorative uses Easy maintenance

TABLE 7.3, CONTINUED

MATERIAL	GENERAL CHARACTERISTICS AND COST	FINISHES	FIRE RATING	INSULATION PROPERTIES	USES AND CARE
	Aluminum glazes: solid aluminum coated with permanent vitreous glaze of porcelain, enamel, or epoxy enamel Sturdy, easy to maintain Lightweight and strong, but subject to dents that are difficult to repair Tends to have commercial effect Moderate cost				
Plaster and stucco	Smooth or textured, no seams or joints Easy to change Tends to chip and crack Moderately low cost	Paint, paper, or fabric	Fireproof	Special types have good insulation against noise	Most versatile of all wall treatments Appropriate for any room and any style Washable
Plastic (tiles)	Durable, rigid, thin, lightweight, variety of colors Simulates ceramic tile Decreasing in use Low cost	None	Poor	Poor insulator	Kitchens, bathrooms, utility rooms Excellent do-it-yourself item Easy upkeep
Plastic (sheets)	Durable, resilient Comes in variety of colors, patterns, and textures Moderately high cost	No finish necessary	Poor Some do not burn but emit noxious gas	Poor insulator	Wherever durable, resilient walls are needed Resists stains and cuts Easy maintenance
Stone	Great beauty If covering too large an area, may appear cold, depending on color Natural colors and textures Feeling of strength and durability Improves with age High cost	Waterproofing sometimes required	Fireproof	Poor insulator Reflects sound	Fireplace surround or entire wall No upkeep
Wallboard (gypsum)	Surface may be finished in attractive colors and patterns, or imprinted with wood-grain appearance Lowest cost	Same as plaster: paint, paper, or fabric	Fire resistant	Excellent insulator	In any room in which low cost is primary consideration Care depends on finish
Wallboard (plastic laminate)	Extremely durable Surface of laminate similar to plastic counter top Photo process can produce textured appearance, wood grains, colors, or patterns Matte or shiny surface High cost	Finished at factory Needs no additional finish	Smokes and melts	Reflects noise Fairly good insulator, depending on density and thickness	Hard-use areas of house (e.g., family rooms, children's rooms, basements) Resists stains and moisture Scratches are irreparable Wash with damp cloth
Wallboard hardboard (pressed wood)	Extremely durable, dent resistant, low cost, many wood grains and colors Wood grain applied via high-fidelity photo process Factory coated, virtually indestructible, easily installed Also available in embossed and textured surfaces simulating fabrics Moderate cost	May be stained, painted, or waxed	Surface melts Pressed wood burns	Reflects noise Insulation depends on thickness of pressed wood	In any area in which wood paneling of low cost and durability is required Wash with damp cloth

(continued)

TABLE 7.3, CONTINUED

MATERIAL	GENERAL CHARACTERISTICS AND COST	FINISHES	FIRE RATING	INSULATION PROPERTIES	USES AND CARE
Wood (solid)	Natural grain throughout Comes in variety of natural grains from rough barn wood to rich grains for formal rooms Can be installed tongue and groove, plain edged, flush joint, or grooved Natural colors vary, but may be stained any color Subject to denting, but can be refinished indefinitely High cost	Needs protective finish to seal against stains and water	Susceptible to burning	Good insulator and noise reducer	Depending of type of wood and method of installation, will go in any room—period or modern Beauty improves with age and care Dust only
Wood (plywood)	Thin surface of wood veneer bonded to rugged and inexpensive panel backing Appears much like solid wood, but less expensive Comes in sheets 4 ft by 8 ft for easy installation May or may not have vertical grooves Moderately high cost	Same as solid wood	Susceptible to burning	Good insulator and noise reducer	Same as solid wood

Figure 7.38 A plaster wall is one of the most versatile types of wall surfaces, allowing the designer freedom to create almost any style. White plaster walls in this room sharpen the darker values and patterns found in the furniture, accessories, ceiling beams, and fireplace. *(Courtesy of Ethan Allen.)*

can be used in any style room and with any style furniture. Because of this, the plain wall is considered the safest background treatment to use in rooms in which furnishings may likely be changed from time to time. Also **plastic laminate wallboards** are available in a wide range of colors and simulate a variety of textures.

- *Wood* walls have been a favorite background treatment for centuries. Wood applied to walls may be boards, panels, or even shingles. **Boards** can be of any wood type, cut in various widths, stained any color, and laid vertically, horizontally, or diagonally. They can be joined with tongue-in-groove, butted, or beveled edges. A wide variety of wood sheet **panels,** some with thin veneers, are also available with numerous finishes, colors, and styles and are considerably less expensive. Exterior **shingles** are also cur-

Figure 7.39 For centuries, carved wood paneling was considered one of the most rich and elegant wall treatments. The wood wall in this room is typical of the English Tudor period and continues to be used to convey authenticity of the style. *(Courtesy of Stuart Designs, London.)*

Figure 7.40 In a modern home, wood planks are lined up vertically on the walls and also used for flooring and ceiling treatment, making an excellent background for furnishings and accessories. *(Courtesy of Ron Molen, architect.)*

rently available for interior use and are suitable for informal settings or places where moisture is a problem.

Wood moldings of all types, including those used for dados, wainscotting, window and door trims, cornices, and fireplace trims, are often used to enhance backgrounds. Available are stock moldings that, when applied, give the impression of a dado, cornice, ***boiserie,*** or complete period paneling.

- *Masonry* used for walls includes brick, tile, concrete block, and stone. **Brick,** which has been used since the time of the ancient Babylonians and pharaohs, has a timeless quality of warmth and adaptability. Its natural

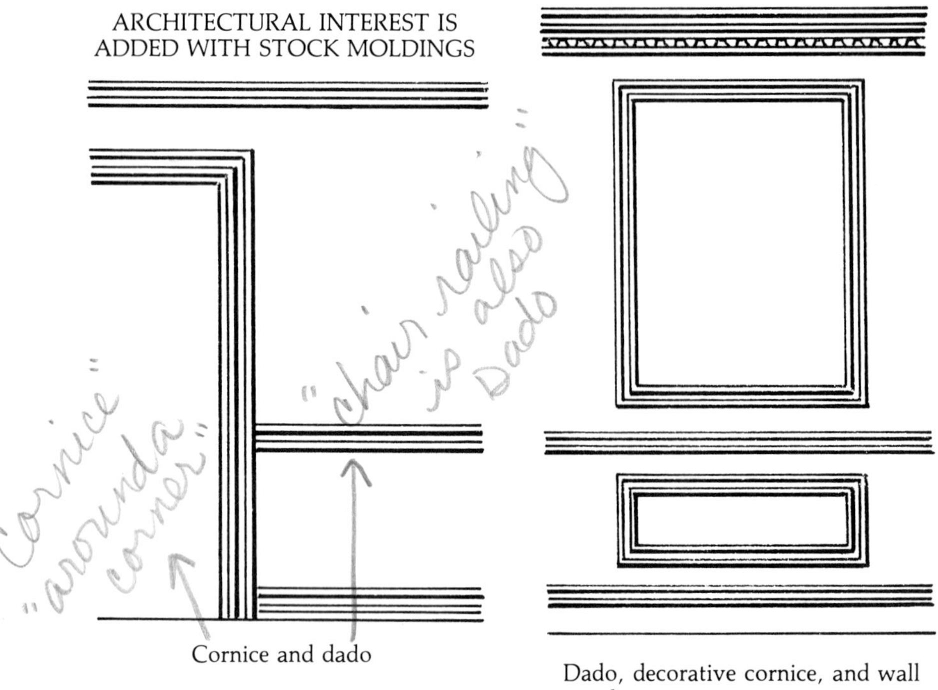

Figure 7.41 This traditional sunburst design can add formality to a front door. It is sturdy, lightweight, and easily installed. *(Courtesy of Focal Point.)*

Figure 7.42 This exquisite *fretwork* cornice, made of amazingly tough, lightweight modern material, is molded directly from notable wood or plaster originals. Through a precise process, architectural enrichment is produced in authentic detail for any style. *(Courtesy of Focal Point.)*

Figure 7.43 Brick walls shape space with a fluid quality that echoes the pattern in the brick floor. *(Photograph by Stanley F. MacBean.)*

Figure 7.44 Durable and attractive ceramic tiles line the walls, steps, and shower of this bath. The off-white tiles are accented with tile borders in a blue and brown geometric design. *(Courtesy of Arizona Tile.)*

look is equally at home in traditional or modern settings. **Ceramic tile,** available in many shapes, sizes, colors, patterns, and finishes, can be used for almost any style and room. Ceramic tile continues to be popular for use in kitchens and bathrooms. **Concrete block** is strong in texture and can be used for both interior and exterior walls. It comes in many variations and generally provides an informal and modern feeling. **Stone** includes a vast variety of types, textures, and colors, including marble, travertine, slate, fieldstone, flagstone, and quartzite. Some stones like marble can provide a formal and elegant look, and some like fieldstone can give an informal and casual feeling. Stone is popularly used for fireplaces but in contemporary homes is

Figure 7.45 A stone wall is an extremely durable wall treatment, and each stone has its own unique properties. Designed for a private residence in a ski resort area, a powerful gray stone wall fireplace rises two stories and dominates the other textures and forms in the room. *(Photograph by Lincoln Allen, Salt Lake City, Utah.)*

Figure 7.46 Marble is one of the most elegant and luxurious stones used for a wall treatment. It provides a lavish and formal mood to this bathroom. *(Photograph by Tim Street-Porter.)*

Figure 7.47 (*Left*) This A.S.I.D. award-winning dressing/exercise area in a private residence demonstrates the dazzling effect of covering all wall surfaces with mirrors. The mirrors reflect images repeatedly, giving an added dimension to the room. *(Courtesy of PPG Industries, Inc.) (Top)* A wall of mirrors in this bath adds luxury and depth. *(Courtesy of Gayl Baddeley/Associates.)*

widely used for walls as well. (See Table 7.1 on floor coverings for additional characteristics, pages 192–193.)

- *Mirrors* have the ability to expand an area visually—an advantage in today's diminished living spaces. Mirrors are available in large sheets and precut panels ready to install, and they can cover an entire wall or be spaced on a wall for function or aesthetic appeal. Mirrors also have great light-reflecting qualities.

Figure 7.48 Glass block walls, popular during the Art Deco period, are again in style. They can be used effectively in either commercial or residential design. (*Left*) A backdrop of glass bricks allows sunlight to fill the room and enhances the white Italian ceramic tiles in this luxurious private bath by designer Leona Hirschkorn. *(Courtesy of Hastings Tile & Il Bagno Collection.) (Right)* A glass block wall partition provides an interesting textural effect and introduces the seating area in a contract project. *(Courtesy of Pittsburgh Corning Corporation.)*

Paints and Finishes

To change the character of a room quickly and with a minimum of expense, nothing works like paint. Of all wall treatments, paint is the easiest to apply. It is made to adhere to any surface and is appropriate for any room or any style. Improvements in manufacturing have produced paints that are easy to apply, have little or no odor, dry quickly, and can be washed. Some paints resist rust, sun, and fire. Water-based paints are easy to apply, and cleanup after their application is no problem. Paints come in numerous colors, producing unlimited shades, tones, and tints. A painted wall surface can be smooth or given a variety of textures by use of a stiff brush, sponge, or special roller. A bonus with textured surfaces is a muffling of sound. Paint used on the exterior needs to be weather resistant and heavier than interior paint. Paints are made from a vast array of synthetic and natural materials. Types of paints and finishes include the following:

- *Alkyd paint* has virtually replaced oil paints. It is resin enamel that is fast drying, leaves no brush or roller marks, resists yellowing, and cleans better than latex. One coat, depending on the color, is generally sufficient. It is produced in high-gloss, semigloss, and matte finishes. Alkyd enamels are solvent mixed and must be thinned with turpentine or solvent. They are recommended for plaster or plasterboard, woodwork, and wood siding and are probably the best for metal.
- *Acrylic paint* is a water-based synthetic resin paint. The more acrylic the paint contains, the better it is. Acrylic is extremely durable, odorless, easily applied, quick drying, and washable. Some acrylic paints resemble baked-on enamel and are almost impervious to damage.
- *Latex* is a type of acrylic. It is a water-mixed paint, so cleanup is easy. Rollers, brushes, and drippings can be washed with water. Latex leaves no overlap marks and dries quickly, and the characteristic odor fades quickly. Latex enamel, however, shows brush marks more readily than alkyd does. A difference between indoor and outdoor latex is that outdoor latex "breathes," thus allowing moisture to escape, which eliminates blistering. Latex paints are recommended for plaster or plasterboard, masonry, wood siding, ***acoustical tile,*** and metal. Since latex includes several varieties, a choice should be made from familiar and reputable brand names.
- *Enamel* is a special type of paint similar to oil paint and made with varnish or lacquer. Its finish is exceptionally hard and durable and is available in high-gloss, semigloss, and matte types.
- *Epoxy paint* is prepared in two ways. The first is ready mixed in a single can. The second type is a two-stage finish, or catalyzed epoxy, which, when used as directed, puts a tilelike coating on almost any surface. Once it hardens, this coating can be scratched, struck, or marked with crayon or pencil and still be washed back to a high gloss. Epoxies may be used on such surfaces as worn laundry tubs, basement walls, shower stalls, and swimming pools.
- *Varnish* is a word sometimes used as a generic name for all clear resinous finishes. A resin is a natural or synthetic substance that, when dissolved in a suitable solvent, leaves a hard glossy film. Natural resins are the saps of certain trees or deposits of insects that feed on the sap. Synthetic resins are also available. Varnish is made from natural resins with alcohol or a drying oil and volatile thinners and dryers. It is usually a transparent coating and is commonly used on wood to protect the surface and allow the natural grain to show through. Some varnishes have a colorant added to darken the wood, but the result is usually less satisfactory than when the staining is done before the clear varnish is applied. Varnish comes in high-gloss or matte finishes.
- *Shellac* is a protective coating similar to varnish. It is made of a resinous substance called lac, which is deposited on trees in India and the Far East. Its solvent is alcohol. Shellac dries more quickly than varnish but is less durable and is subject to water spots. Clear shellac does not discolor when applied to a light-colored surface.
- *Lacquer* is a superior, quick-drying varnishlike finish made from resin from an Asiatic sumac (Chinese or Japanese lacquer) or from a synthetic nitro-cellulose resin. The finish ranges from high gloss to matte and comes in white, black, brown, or beige.
- *Polyurethane* is a varnishlike finish that provides exceptionally tough plastic surface coating. It comes in high- or medium-gloss or matte finish. It is an excellent protective surface for hardwood floors in heavy-traffic areas and walls where moisture is a problem. Polyurethane is also used to protect furniture surfaces and wood paneling.
- *Stain* penetrates wood pores and contains various colorants

that can enhance the natural color or give the wood a different color. Care must be taken to make sample tests before staining begins, because woods react differently to the same stain.

- *Sealers and fillers* are special substances used as preparatory bases for new surfaces to ensure a more professional finish.

Other treatments are also available.

- *Stenciling,* or painted patterns, can be added to walls to provide interest and style. Applying paint through a **stencil** provides interest and style to many rooms. It is especially popular for rooms with an informal or country look. Stenciling designs can be purchased or personally created with countless possibilities.
- *Metal* such as stainless steel, copper, and aluminum is available in sheets and tiles. Finishes either are smooth and shiny or have a brushed surface. The latter has easier upkeep. Use of metal for interior walls should be planned with discretion because of its strong textural qualities.
- *Plastics* are available in either sheets or tiles in a wide range of colors and styles. They are easy to clean and are completely waterproof, making them an excellent choice for bathrooms, kitchens, and utility rooms.

Resilient (or Flexible) Wall Coverings

Wallpaper

Decorative paper as a wall covering has played an important role in enhancing interiors since the late sixteenth century in Europe and early colonial times in America. Although wallpapers have been more fashionable during some periods than others, they have always been esteemed by discriminating individuals as a valuable tool in transforming the visual aspect of interior space.

History

A brief historic review regarding wallpaper can aid in providing an appreciation and understanding of its development and use.

- Hand-painted wallpapers are known to have been made as early as 200 B.C. in **China,** where they were used for decorating tombs.
- An early example of decorative paper found in **England** was a fragment of crude brown paper adhered to a beam in the master's lodge, Christ College, Cambridge. One side of the paper was hand blocked with an English coat of arms, a Tudor rose, and large-scaled flowers. On the reverse side, dated 1509, was printed a proclamation announcing the accession of Henry VIII.
- The first manufacture of wallpaper on an organized basis was in **France** toward the close of the sixteenth century. The first papers were painted in a marbleized effect—a design copied from imported Persian papers—and made for facing book covers and lining boxes. These were called **domino papers,** and the group of artisans who produced them were called **dominotiers.**
- Other groups in France were soon organized to fill the growing demand for decorative papers, and when Henry IV granted a charter in 1599 to the **Guild of Paperhangers,** the wallpaper industry had arrived.
- The introduction of **flocked papers** during the early seventeenth century made it possible for people to simulate the elegant damasks used in homes of the wealthy.
- Two events occurring during the latter half of the seventeenth century added momentum to the wallpaper industry: the establishment of **trade with East India,** bringing the Oriental influence into western Europe, and a **new printing method developed by Jean Papillon.**
- For the first time, a wallpaper was produced that could be matched to make the pattern continuous around the room. Thus, Jean Papillon became known as the **father of wallpaper** as we know it today. His skillful use of ***chinoiserie*** design, together with this new method of application, produced a style much in demand for the decoration of great houses all over Europe.
- Through the works of **Baptiste Reveillon** in France and **John Baptiste Jackson** in England, **pictorial murals** became popular in these two countries during the latter half of the eighteenth century.
- During the second quarter of the nineteenth century, **copper rollers** turned by a rotary machine were first invented in northern England.
- During the eighteenth century in America, hand-painted papers from China were much in vogue for the great Georgian mansions being built along the Atlantic seacoast. **Carrington House** in Providence, Rhode Island, was one of the first firms in America to supply hand-painted papers. The high cost of imported papers—not only from China but also France and England—prohibited their common use.
- In an attempt to make these

highly prized wall coverings available to everyone, **Plunket Fleeson** in 1739 established his Philadelphia factory for printing wallpapers. This endeavor met with only moderate success due to high operation costs.

- Although wallpaper was frequently used during the nineteenth century, it was not until the **Industrial Revolution,** when quantity replaced quality, that the wallpaper industry flourished in America.
- With the advent of the **modern style** of architecture and home furnishings early in the twentieth century, wallpaper went out of fashion and plain walls were more in vogue. Late in the 1930s, wallpaper again became fashionable, and when the industry developed a new method of silk-screen printing that produced papers of high quality at affordable prices, the demand multiplied. Since that time, the wallpaper industry has grown at an unprecedented rate.

Methods of Producing Wallpaper

The three most common methods of producing wall coverings today are **roller printing, hand blocking,** and **silk-screen printing. Embossed** and **flocked** wall coverings are additional processes resulting in unique surface qualities. **Roller printing** is the most common process in use today and is the least expensive. This method is a cylinder process in which each color is applied in rapid succession. **Hand blocking** is a process in which each color is applied separately after the preceding one is dry. This method is slower and more costly than the roller method. **Silk-screen printing** is a more complicated process in which a wooden or metal frame tightly stretches a silk, nylon, or metal screen made for each color of the pattern. The frame is the full-sized pattern repeat. Portions of the pattern not to be printed are heavily varnished or bleached out. Each repeat is made by applying pigment, which seeps through the screens as it is pushed across by a squeegee implement edged with rubber. Each color is allowed to dry before the next frame is printed. This method produces a high-quality wall covering at reasonable cost.

Embossed paper is made by a machine process producing high and low surface effects. This method is used where texture and three-dimensional effects are desirable. Wall coverings of this type may simulate brick or stone with surprising realism. **Flocked paper** is produced by a method in which the design motif is outlined and covered with a glue or an adhesive material. A fine wool-like fuzz is then blown onto it, producing a surface resembling cut velvet.

Vinyl-Coated Coverings

For today's practical interior designer, numerous flexible wall coverings are available that have been treated with varying thicknesses of vinyl and made to simulate any type of wall covering—nonresilient or resilient. They may be washable or scrubbable; are waterproof, highly durable, and stain resistant; and can be used on nearly any type of wall and for any style. Vinyl wall coverings are applied using the same method appropriate for wallpaper.

The following are the most common vinyl wall coverings:

- *Vinyl-protected* wall covering is ordinary wallpaper with a coating of vinyl plastic to make it washable.
- *Vinyl-latex* wall covering is a paper impregnated with vinyl, laminated to lightweight fabric or paper, then vinyl coated. The thickness of the vinyl may vary. This process produces a durable wall covering that is scrubbable.
- *Coated fabric* is a wall covering with a woven cotton backing treated with an oil or plastic coating before the design is applied. This durable, tough, scrubbable material is ideal for kitchens and bathrooms.
- *Plastic foam* is a soft, flexible material available in rolls, squares, or rectangles. Its special properties are that it absorbs sound and insulates and is soil and stain resistant. It is easy to clean with soap and water. Although more expensive than some wall coverings, plastic foam is ideal for apartments with thin walls or television rooms. This type of wall covering is particularly used in commercial and institutional settings. Foam coverings come in solid colors, embossed patterns, or large scenic designs.

Common Wallpaper Terms

Following are the most commonly used wallpaper terms.

Washable Usually refers to a wall covering that may be washed with lukewarm mild suds, but not scrubbed excessively.

Scrubbable Refers to a wall covering more resistant to rubbing than washable types. Stains such as crayon marks can generally be removed from scrubbable wallpaper with cleaning agents recommended by the manufacturer or with soap and water.

Pretrimmed Refers to rolls of wallpaper from which the selvage has been trimmed.

Semitrimmed Means the selvage has been trimmed from only one edge of the wallpaper.

Prepasted Paper that has had paste applied during the manufacturing process. Detailed instructions for hanging are usually included. Generally, prepasted paper is soaked in water and applied to the wall while wet.

Single roll Wallpaper is always priced by the single roll, but usually is sold by the double or triple roll. Regardless of width, a single roll contains 36 sq. ft.

Double and triple roll Regardless of width, a double roll contains approximately 72 sq. ft., and a triple roll contains 108 sq. ft. Generally, 18-in. and 20-in. wallpapers come in triple rolls. Double or triple rolls are used to minimize waste when cutting wallpaper into strips.

Fabric Wall Coverings

Fabric for walls is by no means a new idea. Fabric gave warmth to stone-walled rooms during the medieval and Renaissance periods. During the fifteenth and sixteenth centuries, walls in wealthy Europeans' houses were covered with tapestries and leather. In the seventeenth century, velvets, brocades, and damasks were used; and in many well-preserved palaces and châteaux, the fabric on the walls remains beautiful. Fabric-covered walls can provide rich pattern and a depth of texture.

Today, fabrics of many varieties are being used on walls. The best choice, except when using the shirred method of application, is a medium-weight, closely woven fabric such as sailcloth, ticking, Indian head, or glazed chintz for an informal look and tapestry, brocade, and damask for a formal appearance. Some fabrics come prepared for pasting on walls and are laminated to a paper backing. All-over, nondirectional patterns are easy to use because they require no matching. When a repeat pattern is used, allowance for matching must be made just as for wallpaper.

- The **shirring method** is the simplest way to cover a wall with fabric. The effect is pleasant, and the fabric is easy to take down and clean. Cut-to-fit rods are fastened just above the baseboard and near the ceiling. Single lengths of fabric are cut with a 4-in. allowance, top and bottom, for headings. The fabric is gathered the same as for sash curtains.
- The **double-face masking tape** method is not permanent, because masking tape will dry out in time. Fabric is prepared by sewing together and pressing seams. The tape is placed around the edges of the wall, then the outer coat is peeled off. The fabric is applied first at the top and bottom, then at the sides. The straight grain of the fabric should be kept vertical.
- The **Velcro method** is similar to the masking tape method, except that one side of the Velcro tape is stitched along the edges of the fabric, then attached to the other side of the tape, which has been placed around the edges of the wall.
- In the **staple method,** the fabric is prepared as in the masking tape method. The top is stapled first, then the bottom, and the sides last. Exposed staples may be concealed with braid or molding.
- The **paste method** is the most professional looking and most permanent method, but it requires special care and a set of wallpaper tools. The wall is prepared by a coat of liquid sealing or sizing to fill the pores in the wall surface. When the lengths of fabric are ready to be applied, a second coat of sealing is painted on the first section, and the first strip of fabric is positioned like wallpaper. The same procedure is then followed for the remaining strips. When the job is completed, the fabric dries overnight and then is sprayed with a protective material.

Whichever method is used for application, the room will be enhanced if the fabric is carefully chosen following many of the considerations for wallpaper described on page 227.

Other Resilient Wall Coverings

Japanese grass cloth or **hemp** is made from grass grown in Japan. The grasses are gathered with crude implements, then carried to the village, where they are boiled and allowed to ferment in the hot sun. The grasses are then washed in sparkling streams, and the outer cover is removed and dried in warm breezes and later inspected. Next follows the meticulous arranging, cutting, and knotting of fibers to appropriate lengths for skeining in preparation for hand looms. Stray strands and knots are snipped, then woven and pasted to the grass cloth. Finally, the grass cloth is hand stained or left natural, then packed and shipped. Flexible, long-lasting, and easy to care for, grass cloth provides suitable backgrounds for a variety of styles. Colored grass cloth, however, does not hold color well. Other woven reeds such as **sisal** can provide handsome and practical wall coverings.

Wood veneer with fabric backing, another method of "papering" walls, produces a true wood surface and, once adhered to the wall, is difficult to distinguish from solid wood. One advantage over wood paneling is that this material can fit around corners or curves. It is available in sheets up to 24 in. wide and 12 ft long. The cost, however, is high.

Real leather tile, made of top-grain cowhide, provides a soft, warm, rich surface. It comes in a variety of fast colors to blend with traditional or modern decor. The leather is permanently bonded to an aluminum tile base with preapplied adhesive for easy installation. It is highly resistant to scuffing, and the only maintenance required is an occasional washing with mild soap and water. Leather can effectively be used above a dado, on walls in a family room or den, and wherever a durable leather-textured wall surface is desired. Leather tile in **suede** is also available on a custom-ordered basis. The depth of the brushed nap provides an interesting texture, but its high cost limits extensive use.

Cork is a moderately priced textured material producing a warm atmosphere in natural colors of brown. It is particularly adaptable for studies and rooms in which sound insulation is important. Unless plastic impregnated, cork is not suitable for bathrooms, kitchens, and other hard-use areas.

Today's flexible wall coverings, both rigid and nonrigid, have much variety, beauty, and practicality. Patterns, colors, styles, and surface effects are unlimited and at the disposal of both the professional and nonprofessional designer for use in both residential and contract projects.

Decorative and Functional Values of Wallpaper and Other Resilient Wall Coverings

Applying wall coverings is perhaps the surest means of completely changing the atmosphere of a room. Through appropriate selection, wall coverings have numerous qualities; for example, they

- Bring **beauty, charm,** and **interest** into an otherwise uninteresting room.
- **Add architectural detail.** Many wallpapers simulate architectural features such as pilasters, cornices, dadoes, and latticework.
- Establish the **period or theme** for the room's design. ***Documentary*** wallpapers and fabrics that authentically reproduce motifs and colors used during a particular period are available.
- **Set the mood** of the room: **formal** and unrestrained or **informal** and lively.
- Supply an **effective background** for display with a blended or contrasting effect.
- Provide a **dramatic focus** by the use of a striking mural or pattern.

Figure 7.49 A documentary wallpaper establishes an authentic feeling of the period and changes the visual aspect of the room. *(From the Winterthur Museum Collection, courtesy of Van Luit and Company.)*

Figure 7.50 Sparsely and densely designed floral patterns in variations of blues, pinks, purples, and greens on a cream ground come together in Greeff's Pick-a-Flower Collection. The wallpaper and fabrics are well suited for a light country feeling. *(Courtesy of Greeff Fabrics.)*

Figure 7.51 A cream and brown quaint all-over patterned wallpaper in this bath creates a light and unobtrusive background for accessories, cabinets, and fittings. *(Courtesy of Gayl Baddeley/Associates.)*

Figure 7.52 Coordinated wallpaper and fabrics in cream and dark blue small prints fashion a room of serene beauty. *(Courtesy of the Warner Company.)*

Plain, light walls give a feeling of spaciousness but may lack interest.

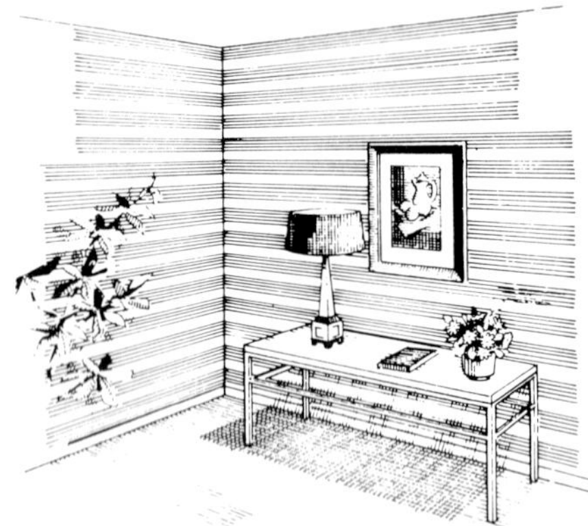

Horizontal lines make a high room seem lower.

Vertical lines make a room appear higher.

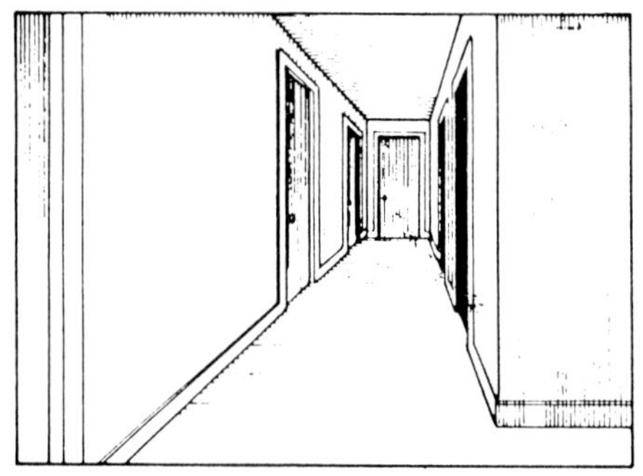

A scenic paper with a third dimension can add perspective and create the illusion of space.

- **Change the visual aspect** of a room by the skillful use of ***trompe l'oeil.***
- **Conceal architectural defects or damaged walls.** (A small all-over pattern works well for this task.)
- **Change the apparent size and proportion** of a room (i.e., make it appear larger, smaller, higher, or lower). A pattern with a three-dimensional effect can achieve spaciousness, and a bold pattern in advancing colors can make the room seem smaller. Using a vertical stripe or running the wall covering onto the ceiling about 12 to 18 in., especially if the ceiling is coved, can make a room look higher. Use of horizontal lines or dropping of the ceiling covering down onto the wall can make a ceiling look lower.
- **Bring harmony** into a room by the use of a wall covering that will unify the different components of the room.
- Wallpaper is **low in cost, easy to apply,** and **relatively easy to clean.**
- Wall coverings are **flexible** and can be used in any room of the house.

Ceilings

The ceiling—the largest unused area of a room—has been given special attention for hundreds of years. The designs of ceilings in palatial interiors during the Renaissance were magnificently ***coffered,*** inlaid, ***frescoed,*** and adorned with decorative plaster. Ceilings during the settlement period in America were usually low and plain with supportive beams. During the Georgian, Federal, Greek Revival, and Victorian periods, ceilings were generally not as ornately designed as in earlier periods in Europe, but they ranged from simple applied decoration to elegantly adorned surfaces. Since the early decades of the twentieth century, the design potential of the ceiling was generally neglected. Today, however, the ceiling is once again being brought into focus. Older, ornate ceilings are being restored, and new ones are often designed in dramatic and innovative ways. **Functions** of the ceiling include (1) protection from the elements, (2) insulation for heating and cooling, (3) a source for artificial lighting (and in some cases, natural lighting when skylights are employed), and (4) an important element in establishing the character and atmosphere of a room. If a ceiling is much above or below the average main-floor height of 8 ft,

The use of vertical space is dramatized in this architect's drawing of the interior of a solar house. Space is maximized by exposing all levels to the high gable ceilings and to the informal garden room. *(Courtesy of Timberpeg.)*

it will tend to alter the general feeling of the room. A high ceiling will emphasize space and tend to create a feeling of dignity and formality. A low ceiling, which decreases space, can produce a warm, informal atmosphere.

Making Ceilings Appear Higher or Lower

Ceilings may be made to appear higher to suit a preference for a more spacious feeling or lower to provide a cozy, intimate atmosphere. A number of methods are commonly employed to achieve this goal. For **height** one can

1. Run the wall color or covering

Figure 7.53 A pyramidal ceiling skylight runs the length of this private residence designed by architect Eduard Dreier, allowing light to flood all the major living and dining spaces, as well as providing powerful design interest. *(Courtesy of Gayl Baddeley/Associates.)*

Wallpaper extended beyond the walls and into coved ceilings gives the appearance of greater height.

a short distance onto the ceiling, especially when the corners are ***coved*** (where walls and ceiling are joined by a curve instead of a right angle). This treatment causes the eye to move upward and makes the ceilings appear higher.

2. Use a light color on a ceiling.
3. Use a predominance of vertical lines in the architecture of the room and in the decorative elements, like a patterned wallpaper.
4. Add a skylight to open up space.
5. Use diagonal beams, which draw the eye upward, to make gabled ceilings appear even higher.

For a **lower ceiling** one can

1. Paint it a dark color or use a patterned wall covering.
2. Extend the color or covering down onto the wall a short distance (dropped ceilings), where a border or a small molding may be used. As attention moves upward, it stops at the molding and the ceiling seems to begin at that point. In this way, the ceiling can be psychologically lowered as much as 3 ft.

Angled beams draw the eye upward and expand space.

Figure 7.54 Architect Ron Molen has created a triangular wood unit complete with lighting and suspended it from the ceiling over the bed. The strong form helps define the sleeping area and reinstates the lines of the triangular wood ceiling above. *(Courtesy of Ron Molen, architect.)*

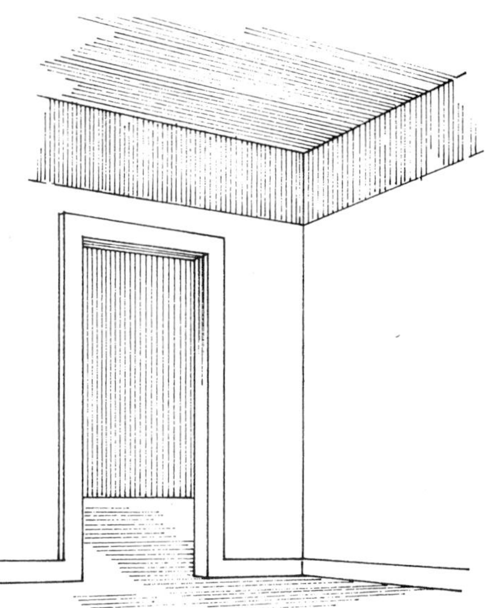

A dark paint on the ceiling or a wall covering coming down on the wall makes a ceiling appear lower.

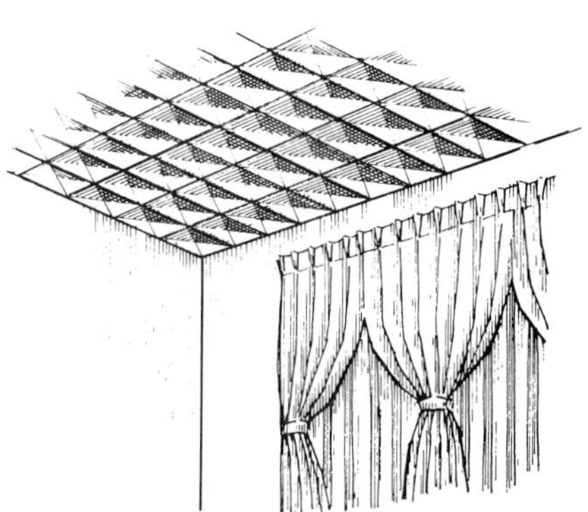

A patterned ceiling appears to advance and seems lower.

3. Use a predominance of horizontal lines in the room's architecture and decorative elements.
4. Use wood ceilings and horizontal beams, particularly when in natural wood or painted a bold or dark color.

In recent years, changing architectural styles have produced exhilarating ceiling designs, which add new dimensions to interior spaces, often by incorporating a variety of high and low ceilings within a private residence or commercial setting. A concern for energy efficiency has also determined to some extent the height of ceilings.

Types of Ceilings

Ceiling designs can be distinguished according to various structural forms and the placement or direction employed.

- The **flat ceiling** is usually plastered, painted, or covered with wood strips. The **flat-beamed** ceiling is one in which the structural beams are exposed or lightweight beams have been applied.
- The **shed** or **lean-to** ceiling rises diagonally to one side in a single slope. A room with this ceiling

Figure 7.55 In this double-pitched ceiling, dark beams against white draw attention upward and expand vertical space. *(Courtesy of Timberpeg.)*

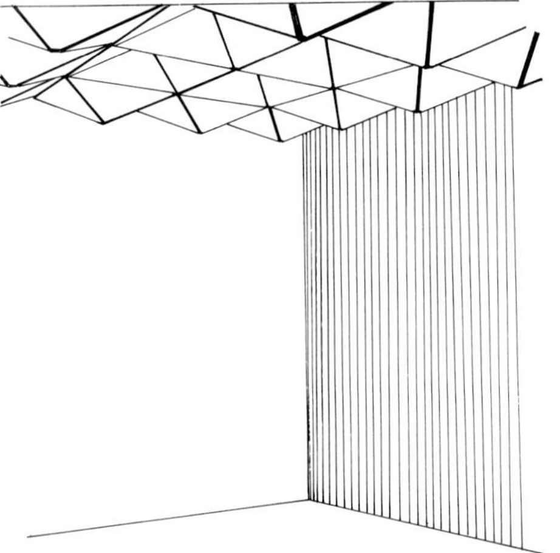

Sculptured ceiling

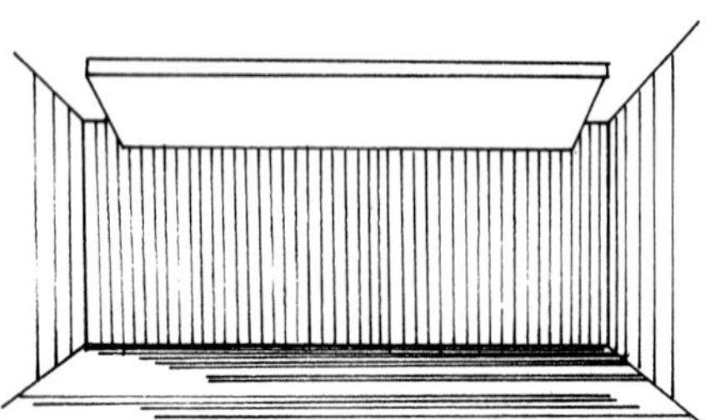

Dropped ceiling

requires particular care in arrangement of furnishings to achieve a comfortable balance.

- The **gabled, double-pitched,** or **cathedral** ceiling expands vertical space, especially when beams extend upwards. If beams are placed horizontally, the room's length is emphasized.
- The **sculptured,** custom-designed ceiling is not created as an unobtrusive background but calls attention to itself as the room's focal point. Sometimes designed in highly dramatic and unique ways, sculptured ceilings follow no set pattern and usually require ample space for construction and effect.
- The **coved** ceiling is one in which the ceiling and wall flow into each other by means of a curved surface in place of right angles. Sometimes the perimeter is prepared to accommodate recessed lighting, allowing light to shine upward on the ceiling surface.
- **Vaulted and domed** ceilings are arched structures as opposed to flat planes—and, in a way, a complete extension of the coved ceiling.
- **Coffered** ceilings, popular in past centuries, are constructed of wooden members in a grid manner, often with moldings and sunken decorative panels.
- The **dropped** ceiling is one in which a portion or the entire area of a ceiling is lowered below the main structure. This type of ceiling can define an area of a room (such as in a dining area in a dual-purpose

Figure 7.56 To give the illusion of endless space, designer Harry Stein has painted the beams and part of the ceiling black and strategically placed numerous lamps. Other sections of the ceiling are mirrored, adding to the effect of depth in this New York penthouse. *(Photograph by Norman McGrath.)*

room), provide indirect lighting, and add an element of interest to a living space.

Types of Ceiling Materials

To satisfy the demands of contemporary architecture, new ceiling materials are being developed and old ones being revived. Following are some of the most common ceiling materials employed today:

- **Plaster and wallboard** are the most common materials used for ceilings today. They are appropriate for any type of room, inexpensive, and easily applied, creating a unified background with the walls. The finished surface may be smooth, textured, wallpapered, or painted. Sometimes a plastered ceiling is stenciled or has applied decoration or moldings. Flat paint is usually preferable for ceilings, with high gloss reserved for special purposes.
- **Tiles** for ceilings come in a wide variety of materials, colors, and patterns. Many have acoustical properties for absorbing noise. Others have a foil backing, which cuts down on air-conditioning and heating costs. An easy method of installation for do-it-yourselfers employs metal tracks and clips, which have replaced the unwieldy furring wood strips previously used. Tiles can also be suspended from a supportive gridwork to create a three-dimensional effect.
- **Glass or plastic panels,** which can be transluscent or transparent, are sometimes employed in ceilings to provide overhead

Figure 7.57 In a private residence, the glass walls and ceiling open up the interior to a sweeping mountain view. *(Courtesy of Gayl Baddeley/Associates.)*

light—either natural daylight or recessed artificial light. Overall illumination may be provided, and striking lighting effects from high-up windows can be achieved. Skylight views can also add a new dimension.

- **Stamped metal** ceilings were popular during the nineteenth century and are again being made today. These ceilings are used primarily in the restoration and construction of Victorian buildings. This treatment involves stamping or pressing designs onto metal panels, providing a unique embossed effect.
- **Fabric,** although not commonly used, can be stretched, shirred, or pasted (like wallpaper) to the ceiling surface. The softness of fabric provides a comfortable and warm feeling, and when used as a repeating fabric in the room, can unify the interior.
- **Wood** employed for ceilings, either in strips, panels, beams, or planks, can provide a warm and inviting atmosphere. Wood ceilings, because of their visual weight, tend to lower the ceiling and may create a feeling of heaviness unless the ceiling is of above-average height. Often wood is combined with plaster for ceiling treatment; for example, wood beams can stretch across a plastered ceiling. Wood can be left natural, stained, or painted. Where natural beams are not feasible, ceiling beams of polyurethane (which simulate hand-carved wood to a remarkable degree) can be glued to a regular ceiling.

Insulating Against Noise and Heat Loss

A major challenge facing architects and builders today is combating noise. With the steady increase of disturbing sounds in metropolitan areas caused by such things as traffic, construction, street repairs, helicopters, and jets, as well as the increase of interior noise from televisions, appliances, electronic equipment, and other sources, a pressing need in both commercial and residential construction is to insulate against noise.

New materials and building techniques are being used to remedy the problem. Sound is being muffled by an increase in the mass and density of sound-deadening materials. In masonry construction, the space between units is filled with insulation. Where formerly 2-by-4-in. studs were standard, 2-by-6-in. studs are now used to allow for more insulation. Where double studding is employed, an air space in between the partitions is used in addition to insulating batts. Interior walls are often made by a series of slats, with spaces between filled with sound-absorbing materials. A finished wall material made of woven reeds, such as sisal, can be adhered to rigid insulation, thus providing a durable and attractive surface while adding to noise absorption.

In double ceilings, where one ceiling is above another, the lower one is suspended by means of clips so that the plasterboard is not attached directly to the joints, thus leaving a space for insulation materials. Floors are often given a deadening coat of plaster or a coat of lightweight concrete.

With energy conservation a major concern in today's housing, the use of solar energy is increasing substantially. In addition, architects and builders are employing a variety of means to control heat loss. Windows are given ***double*** and ***triple glazing.*** Extra-thick insulating batts are used, and extra foam is blown between partitions and ceilings. Although used to deaden sounds, insulation also helps immeasurably in avoiding heat loss. Thermobreak weather stripping is used around doors and windows, which separates the metal by nonconductive nylon or neoprene and prevents heat from escaping. Orienting a building to take the best advantage of the climate can save energy. Windows on the sunny side can absorb heat that can be stored for later use. Well-insulated walls on the cold side preserve heat.

Chapter Eight

Windows, Doors, Stairways, and Fireplaces

Although glass walls were known to the ancient Egyptians and Romans, historically **windows** were merely small cutouts in the walls of a house known as the **"wind's eye"** to permit smoke to escape, let in fresh air, and allow protective glimpses of the outside. Over the years, many types of windows have been planned as an integral part of the structural design. Although window treatments change with style trends, they are enhanced when attuned to the architectural spirit of the structure, both exterior and interior.

Doors originally were purely functional, used only for necessary passage. In modern times they have assumed different forms with varying degrees of design importance and traffic control.

Windows

The window is an important architectural and decorative element in a room, and its enhancement has been a major consideration for centuries. Traditionally, windows were often symmetrically placed in the facade of the house, with small panes as the norm.

With the development of modern architecture and technology, great changes were made and new types of window openings were introduced and planned as integral parts of the basic design. Window placement and design, or ***fenestration,*** today can be either symmetrical or asymmetrical, and frequently openings of unusual shapes are employed. Many types of windows unknown only a few decades ago are now common. Windows like the glass wall, corner windows, sliding glass doors, the straight or slanting clerestory,and the peaked two-story window are now as familiar as the double-hung or casement types standard for so many years.

The three primary functions of windows are (1) to **admit light,** (2) to **provide ventilation,** and (3) to **enhance visual communication.** Even

Figure 8.1 Architect Eduard Dreier has designed a soaring stone and metal fireplace that functions as a welcoming and stunning focal point in this living room. Large angled windows allow sunlight to stream into the interior spaces. *(Courtesy of Eduard Dreier and Guy Dreier Associates.)*

though light and air can now be controlled, and windows are not absolutely necessary, planning a house without windows seems inconceivable. As efficient as modern technology is, no substitutes exist for fresh air, natural light, and an outdoor view to create a psychological association with the outdoors and provide a sense of well-being.

The window is a conspicuous element in both the exterior and interior design of a house. As a source of interior light, the window is the first point to which the eye is drawn during the daytime, and at night a lighted window is the first thing seen from the outside.

Unfortunately, window openings are not always planned with indoor function in mind. Good planning can be ensured if an alert home owner or interior designer works closely with the architect. For example, a window originally pushed into a corner—a placement that creates a problem for decorating—can easily be relocated on the plans of the house.

Considerations in the Approach to Window Treatment

It is helpful to approach the location, design, and treatment of any window with a number of primary considerations:

- Should the *architectural background* of the room against which the window will be seen and placement in the wall in relation to the other architectural features of the room be emphasized, blended into the background, or camouflaged?
- The *type of window* selected can determine the treatment.
- Does the *outside view* need to be brought into focus or blocked out? For example, is the view that of a public thoroughfare, the neighbor's barbecue, a private garden, or a distant vista?
- Does *privacy* need to be created? Even if it does not, consider the cold, black appearance at night if a large expanse of glass is present.
- Is *light* excessive or insufficient? What is the window size? Glare can often be eliminated when windows are well arranged and designed. What is the exposure? Northern light will be cool, and too much southern or western light can fade and damage furnishings.
- Window type and design can be a factor in the *furniture arrangement*. If there are many openings, for example, it may be difficult to arrange furnishings effectively.
- Is there a *wind problem*? If so, how can protection against wind be arranged?
- Is traffic or other *noise* a problem? Many window treatments can help muffle sounds.
- Window treatments can be an important factor in *conserving energy* and cutting heating and cooling bills.
- Is the window *stationary or movable*? The treatment needs to accommodate the window's function.

Types of Windows

The three general classifications of windows are (1) **movable,** (2) **stationary,** and (3) a **combination of movable and stationary.** All three types are available in standardized sizes. Glass panes may be supported by wood, metal, or plastic, each of which has particular advantages and disadvantages. Wood shrinks, swells, requires a protective finish, and is the most expensive. It discourages moisture condensation, however, and emits less heat than metal. Metal is strong and does not shrink or swell perceptibly. Except for aluminum and stainless steel, however, it requires protective paint and causes moisture condensation in cold weather. Newer metal windows have a plastic thermal break built in to eliminate excessive heat loss and condensation. Plastic is stable and resists heat and cold.

Movable Windows

Movable windows are made to open to permit ventilation. The following are some of the most common:

- *Double-hung windows* are made up of two ***sashes*** that may be raised or lowered to provide 50 percent ventilation. They are simple and inexpensive.

Double-hung

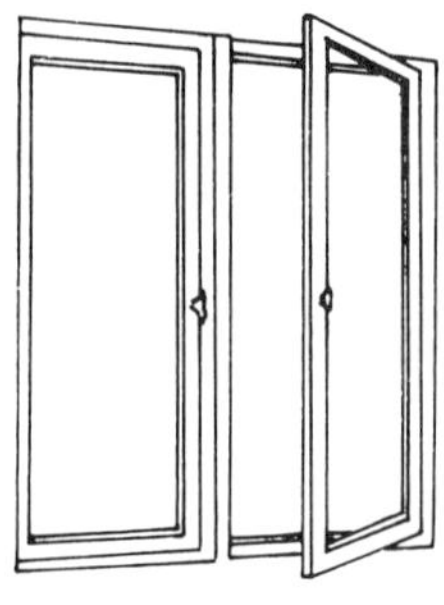

In-swinging casements

- *Casements* may swing inward or outward and permit up to 100 percent ventilation. Those that swing outward present no draping problem but can create a potential hazard outside. In-swinging casements must have special treatment. Valances must be hung high enough to clear the window. Side draperies should be out on the walls or hung on swinging-arm rods. Sheers on sash rods attached to top and bottom function well.
- *Ranch or strip windows* are wide and shallow. They are set far enough above the floor to allow furniture to be set against the wall, but they are not ceiling high.
- *Horizontal sliding windows* may be made up of two sliding panes or a large stationary central pane with a sliding pane on either side.

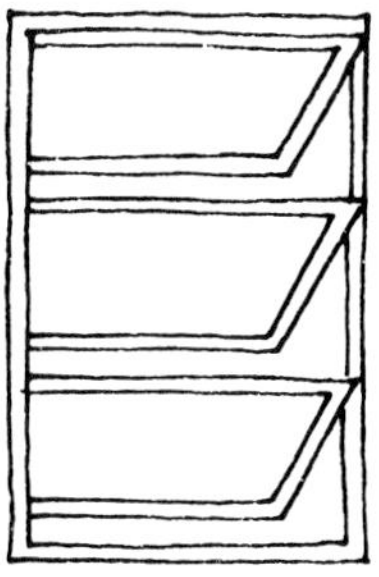

Awning or louvered

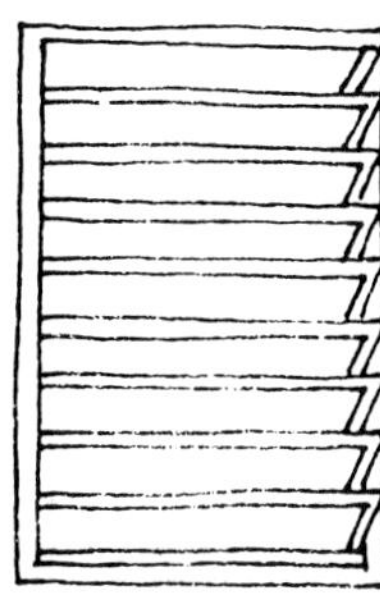

Jalousie

- *Awning (or louvered) and jalousie windows* consist of strips of glass, hinged at the top or bottom and opening outward or inward. Strips in jalousie are narrower than with the awning type. Both allow for draft-free ventilation control.
- *Single-pivoting sash windows* are raised for ventilation by means of side mechanisms. These windows are most often used as skylights or in light wells.
- *French doors* are paired doors of glass. Since they are basically enlarged casement windows to walk through, they can be treated in the same manner. Draperies and cornices should clear the operating portion of the door. ***Louvers,*** or slatted panels, are a popular alternative. Whatever the treatment, it should conform to the other windows in the room.

Stationary Windows

Stationary windows are built as an **integral part of the wall construction** and require no special framing. They may be plain glass or nonglare. Where large areas of glass are used, thermopanes or triple-glaze and nonshatter glass is advised. Some common stationary windows are picture windows, window walls, bows, bays, and clerestory.

- The *stationary window wall* is a common feature of today's contemporary homes and may extend from floor to ceiling or begin a short distance above the floor. The window wall is expensive, requiring double or triple glaze for energy conservation. Some disadvantages of the window wall are that (1) it may not allow enough privacy, (2) it may let in excessive light that can create a glare and fade furnishings, (3) the expanse of a black area at night is uninviting,

Strip

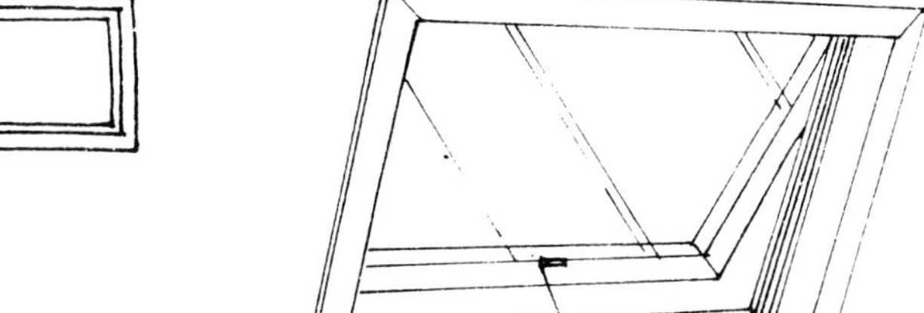

Single pivoting pane

Glass wall with sliding door

French doors

Figure 8.2 Architecturally fixed windows extend outward from the wall, providing a more prominent outside view from the reception area for Ivory & Company. The gleaming pyramidal metal ceiling adds a unique dimension. *(Courtesy of Gayl Baddeley/Associates.)*

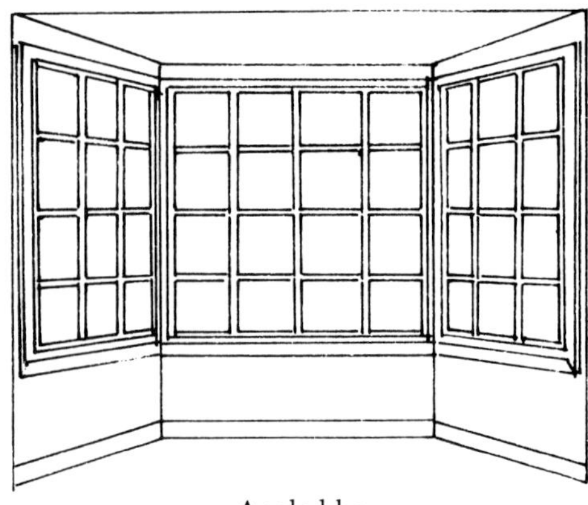

Angled bay

Bow bay

Figure 8.3 In the Kleiser Penthouse, Piano Factory in New York City, designed by Harry Stein, the solarium has a stationary ceiling of windows and window walls that are mostly permanently fixed, commanding a panoramic view of the city. *(Photograph by Norman McGrath.)*

(4) the window wall requires large quantities of drapery or other treatment, and (5) the arrangement of furniture may be more difficult. All of these disadvantages, however, may be offset by the pleasure derived from the close relationship this type of window provides with the outdoors.

- The *angled bay window* is a large projecting window that is angled.
- The *bay bow window* is a smooth, sweeping curve of multipanes.

Combination of Movable and Stationary Windows

Two popular windows composed of both movable and stationary parts are the following.

- The *picture window* is a large

Picture

Corner

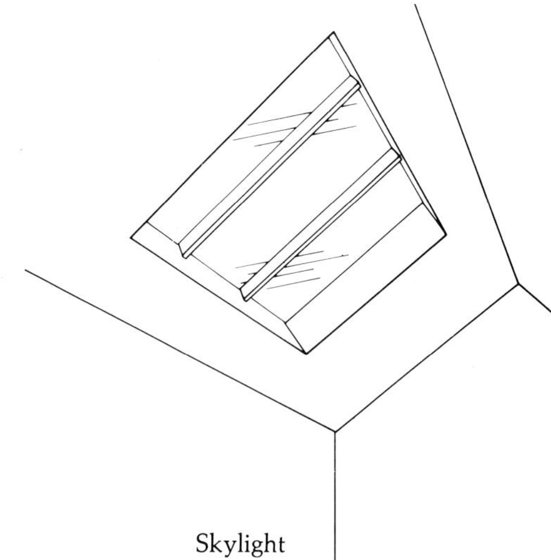

Skylight

Double

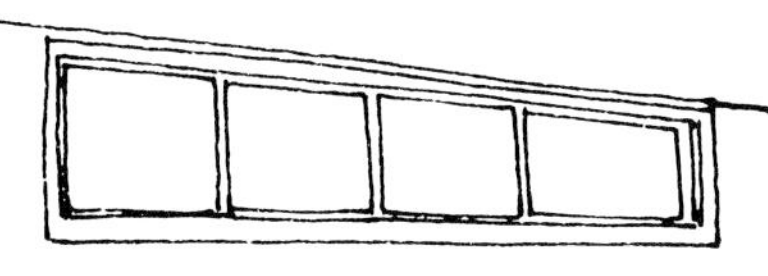

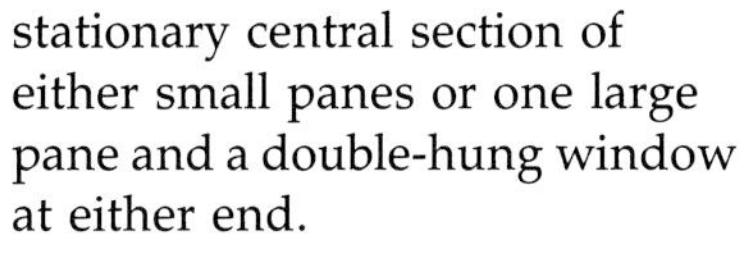

Clerestory

stationary central section of either small panes or one large pane and a double-hung window at either end.

- The *angle bay* can be made up of three or more windows that angle out of the room. The central pane may be stationary and the side ones movable.

Other Common Window Types

- The *single window* may be standard size, high and narrow, or a small cutout in the wall.
- *Double and multiple windows* refer to identical windows placed side by side. They may be separated by a strip of wall or only by their abutting window frames. Unifying them is usually the main objective.
- The *corner window* consists of two windows that meet, or almost meet in a corner. Corner windows can be thought of as double windows and treated accordingly.
- *Clerestory windows* may be straight or slanting windows set at the ceiling or high in a wall between two roof levels. They are usually left bare.

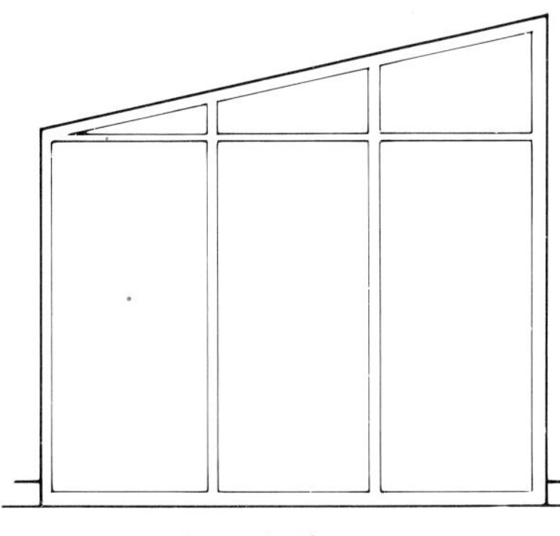

Slanted Clerestory

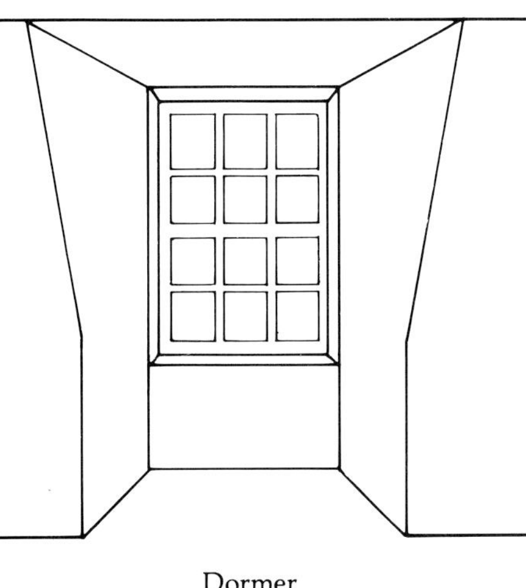

Dormer

- *Dormer windows* are vertical windows that project from an alcove in the roof, usually filling the entire space.
- *Skylights* may be single or grouped panels of clear or translucent glass or plastic, either flat or domed, and fixed or movable for ventilation (see Figure 8.3). Entire skylight ceilings in kitchens, laundries, and bathrooms have the special advantage of providing adequate daylight for inside rooms. In small areas, light from above can expand visual space and make the sky and greenery of trees part of a room. Skylights have the unique ability to bring a new dimension into a room by highlighting elements previously ignored. The skylight window has a number of disadvantages, however, including problems with water seepage, insulation, and cleaning. Also, it presents a security problem unless protected by safety-wired glass.

Figure 8.4 An arched window type in this kitchen is broken with a puffy balloon Roman treatment. The circular line of the window lends variety to the angularity of the tile and cabinets. *(Courtesy of American Olean Tile.)*

Figure 8.5 Light filters through a stained glass window reflecting a design reminiscent of the Art Nouveau style. *(Courtesy of Sonya Jacobs/The Stock Market.)*

Arched

- *Arched windows* are those in which the upper part of a rectangular opening is topped by an arch. This window type can be effective when either treated or untreated.
- *Beveled and stained glass* is being used in many homes today—both for modern and traditional styles (see Figure 8.5). Beveled glass refers to the angle ground into the edge of plate glass, reflecting the light in colorful ways. Stained glass is the art of arranging colorful pieces of glass into a pattern. Pieces of beveled or stained glass are joined by zinc, lead, or copper to bond the design. Today, stock beveled and stained glass is available for doors, windows, sidelights, transoms (small windows placed over doorways or above larger windows), and skylights. Used for the latter, it brings a brilliant glow into a room. The private craftsworker can provide custom designing for individual needs and style preferences.

Window Terminology

A knowledge of window terminology is essential to determine the type of treatment to be employed.

The Window Itself

The *casing* is that part of the window fitting into the wall. The *frame* is the wide molding covering the casing and framing the glass. The *sash* refers to the part that holds the glass. *Mullions* are the horizontal bars separating the glass panes. *Muntins* are the vertical bars separating the glass panes. These last two terms are frequently used interchangeably. The *sill* is the narrow shelf at the bottom of the frame. The *apron* is the part of the frame beneath the sill. The *return* is the distance from the end of the outside drapery rod to the wall, which should allow room for undercurtains but generally ought not to exceed 6½ in. (see illustration).

Window Hardware

Functional. Purely functional hardware is inconspicuous and includes the following types. *Sash rods* are flat rods attached close to the sash, often both top and bottom, on which curtains are shirred. *Extension rods* are used for stationary curtains and drapery. They extend to various lengths and are available in single and double sets. *Traverse rods* operate on a pulley system. Available as either one- or two-way types, they are used for drawing curtains and drapery. *Spring tension rods* fit inside the casing. *Swinging rods* are mounted on a mechanism that permits the rod to swing backward. These rods are suitable for in-swinging casements, dormers, and French doors. *Extender rods* extend outward to support stationary drapery beyond the window. *Ceiling tracks* with concealed drawing mechanisms are particularly popular in contemporary rooms. Small

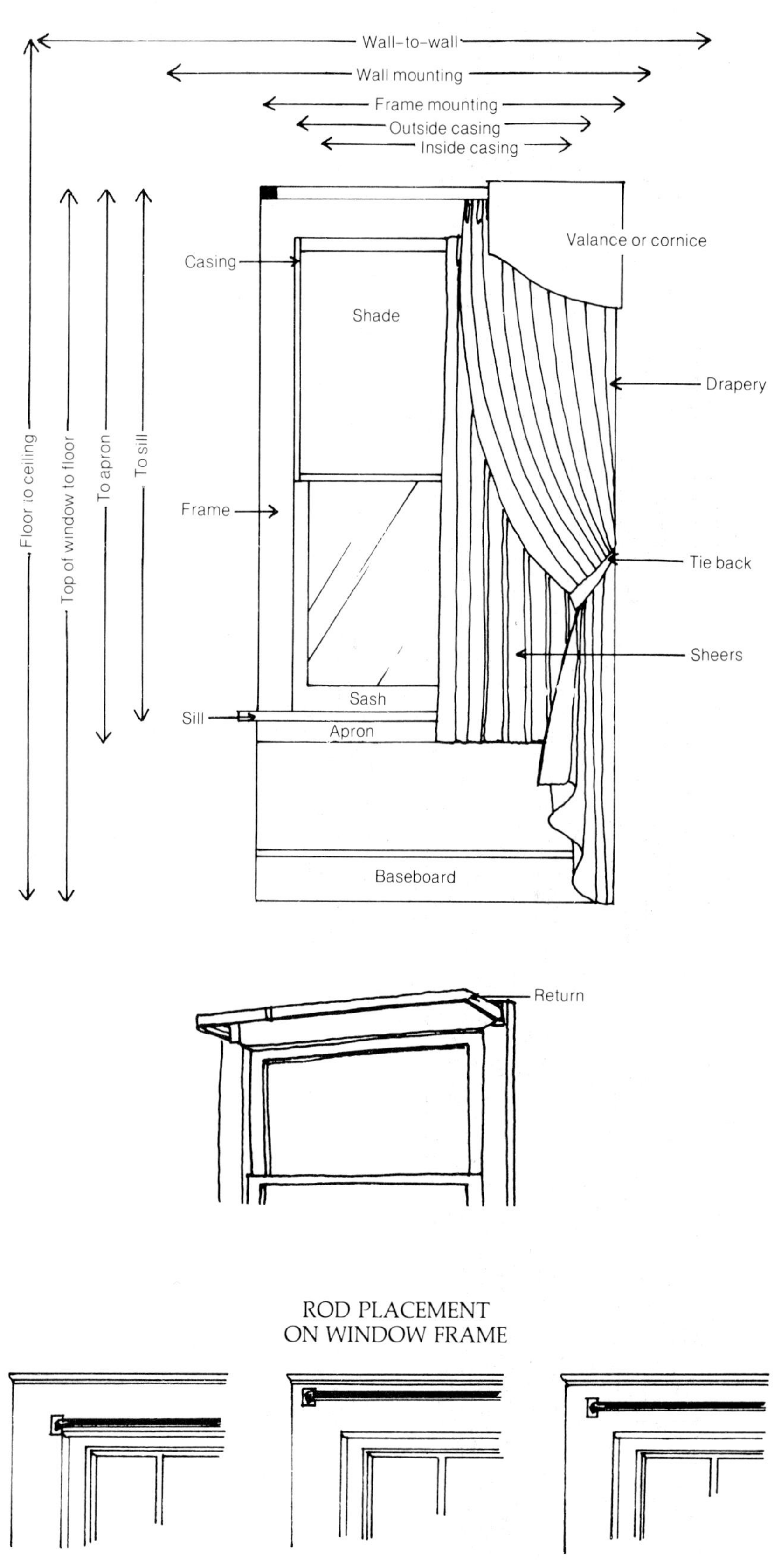

CURTAIN AND DRAPERY RODS

Single curtain rod

Double curtain rod

Single traverse rod

Double traverse rod

Valance rod kit

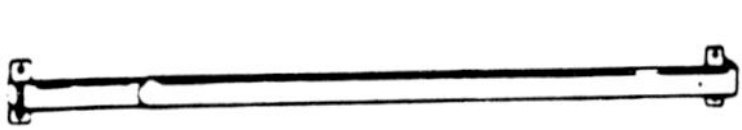
Sash rod

Corner curtain rod

Cafe rod

Curved curtain rod

Traverse-plain rod set

Spring tension rod

Swinging rod

Bay window curtain rod

Decorative traverse rod

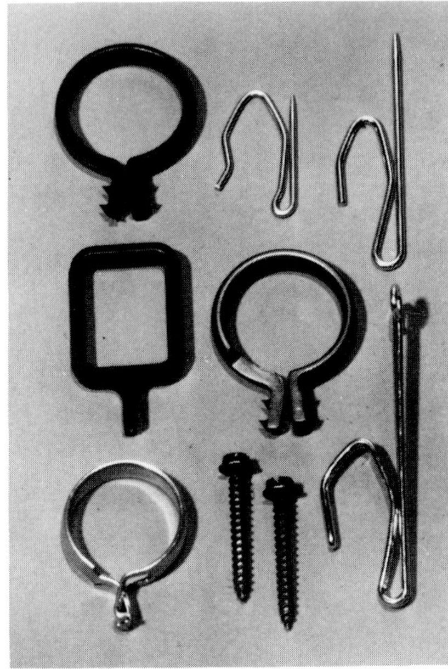
Figure 8.6 Hooks, rings, and screws for drapery. *(Courtesy of Kirsch Company.)*

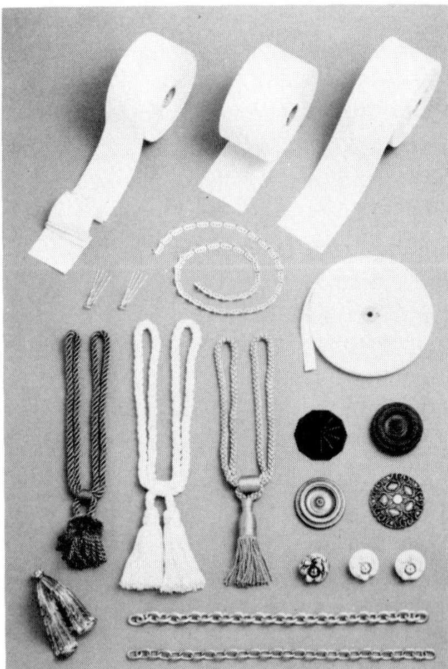
Figure 8.7 Some necessary tapes, as well as decorative hardware including cord and tassel tiebacks, and metal chain, leaf, and rosette holdbacks. *(Courtesy of Kirsch Company.)*

accessories such as hooks, rings, ring slides, brackets, and draw cords are all part of the unseen draw-drapery system.

Decorative. Decorative hardware is functional but also provides decorative accessories for the rooms. Rods may be wood (natural wood, stained, or painted), or metal, such as pewter, brass (shiny or in antique finish), chrome, bronze, or wrought iron. Decorative hardware is equipped with a variety of *finials* or other decorative features to accommodate any style. Draperies are suspended on rings and may be cord operated or hand drawn. In the latter case, rings should be loose. Metal holdbacks that conform to the style of rods can do much to add a finishing touch.

Curtain and Drapery Embellishment

The *heading* is the pleating or gathering at the top of curtains and draperies that forms the fold (providing the beauty of arrangement and fullness for drawing). Headings are made in a number of ways. (1) *French* or *pinch pleats* make up the most common type of heading. They are made by stitching together, about 3 in. from the top, three small pleats. The pleats, which are spaced 3½ to 4 in. apart, are held upright by an interlining of buckram. (2) *Ripplefold* is a simple method of creating gentle, undulating folds by means of a compact track containing snap carriers (see Figure 8.3). Folds are made from flat panels of fabric and are identical on both sides. (3) *Accordian folds* are made by a combination of a compact track with snap carriers and a nylon heading tape. Trimly tailored pleats form architectural-like folds. (4) *Easypleats* are made by a special tape attached to the inside top of the drapery. When pleater hooks are inserted in ready-made pockets, folds are automatically formed. (5) *Shirred headings* are most often used on kitchen, bedroom, and bathroom curtains. They are made by stitching a pocket approximately 1½ in. from the top, in which the rod is inserted. By means of a series of additional pockets under the main rod pocket, gathered by inserting tape, a puffy look can be created.

Tiebacks or **holdbacks** hold back stationary draperies, come in a wide variety of materials and styles, and may be cords, tassels,

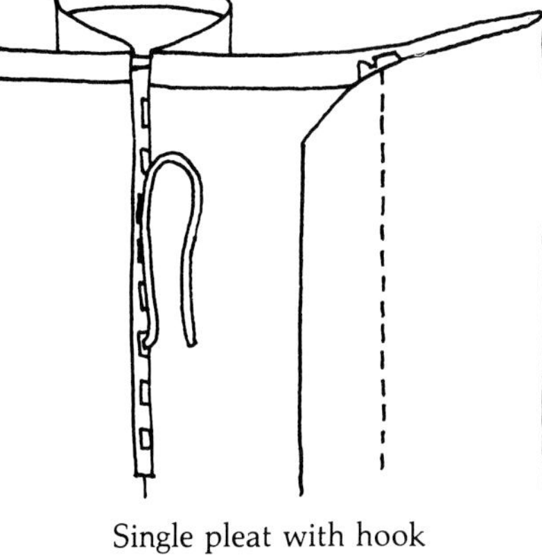

Single pleat with hook

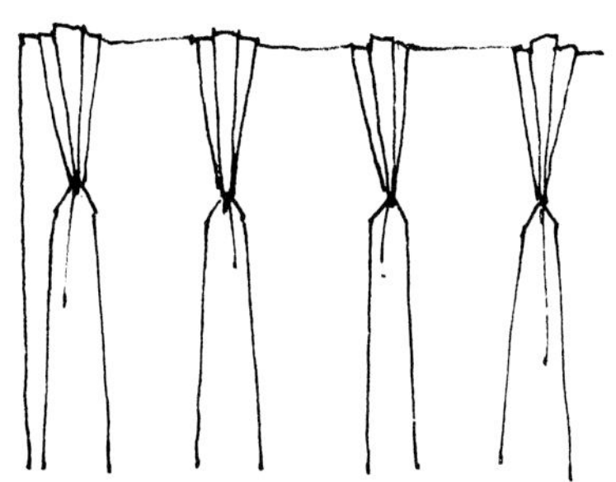

Pinch pleat detail

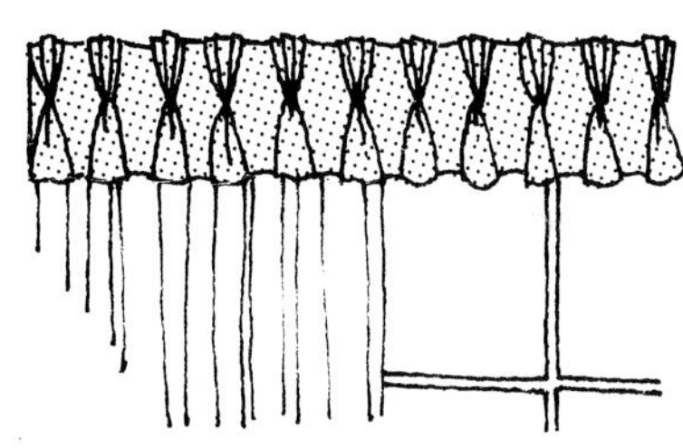

Valance with pinched pleats

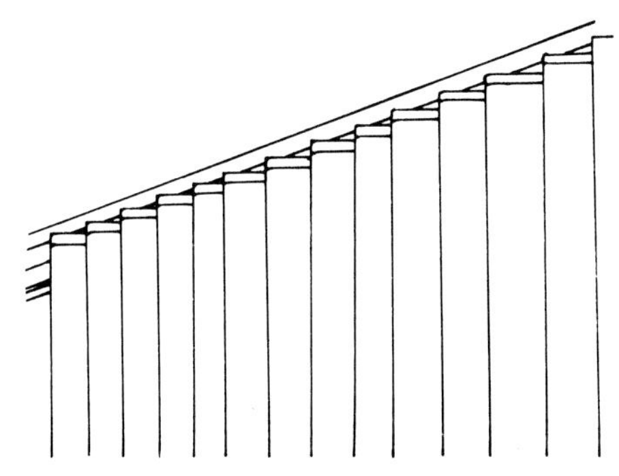

Ripplefold

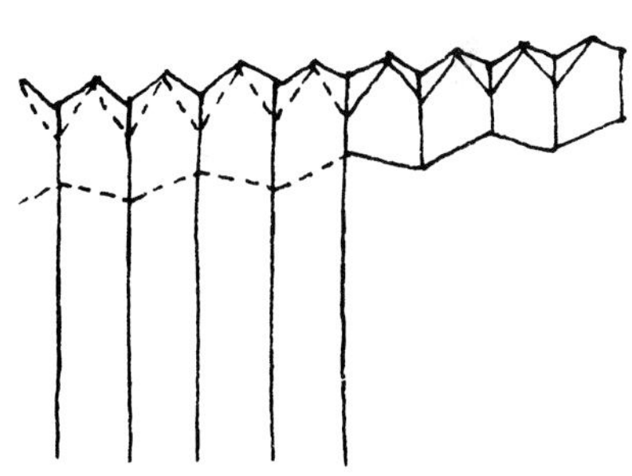

Accordian pleat

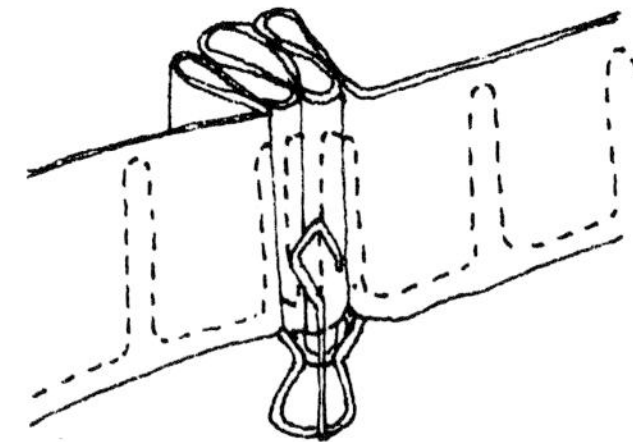

Easy pleats made with heading tape and hook

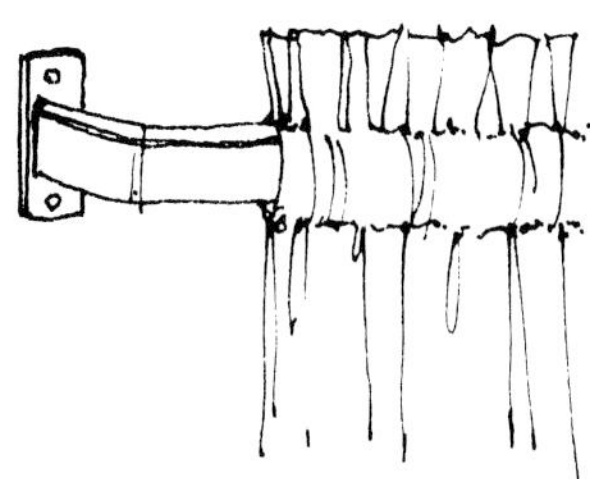

Shirred curtain on single rod

metal, wood, or matching or contrasting fabric. The point at which designers often tie back drapery is somewhere between one-half and one-third from the bottom—employing the proportions of the golden mean (see p. 112). **Trimmings** continue to be fashionable and can give a finished look to draperies, cornices, and valances. Trimmings include a vast array of fringes, braids, edgings, cords, and tassels (see Figure 8.7).

Types of Window Treatments

Today a great freedom exists in window decoration. Windows that are too big or little, too high or low, too many or few, badly proportioned, or out of balance need not be a problem. A window treatment is available for every window. The first step is to visualize the room's desired elevations, then proceed to achieve that goal. A window that is an architectural liability can often be turned into an asset.

Changing a window treatment can give a room a completely new look and need not strain the budget. Through the use of an effective window treatment, a room can take on interest and beauty, and many decorating problems can be solved. For example, small windows can be made to appear larger; low windows, higher; or awkward, unnecessary windows, inconspicuous.

With today's flexible interior design, window treatments have no absolutes. As living spaces become smaller, however, the tendency is toward simplicity. Bare windows and simple, unobtrusive treatments are increasingly in use, because they can visually expand space. When deciding on a window treatment, it is wise to keep in mind the principles of design, particularly proportion and scale.

Armed with these considerations, deciding on appropriate window treatments from the almost unlimited options available can be a pleasurable experience. Window treatments fall into two categories: (1) **soft** and (2) **hard.** Following are the most common types in use today.

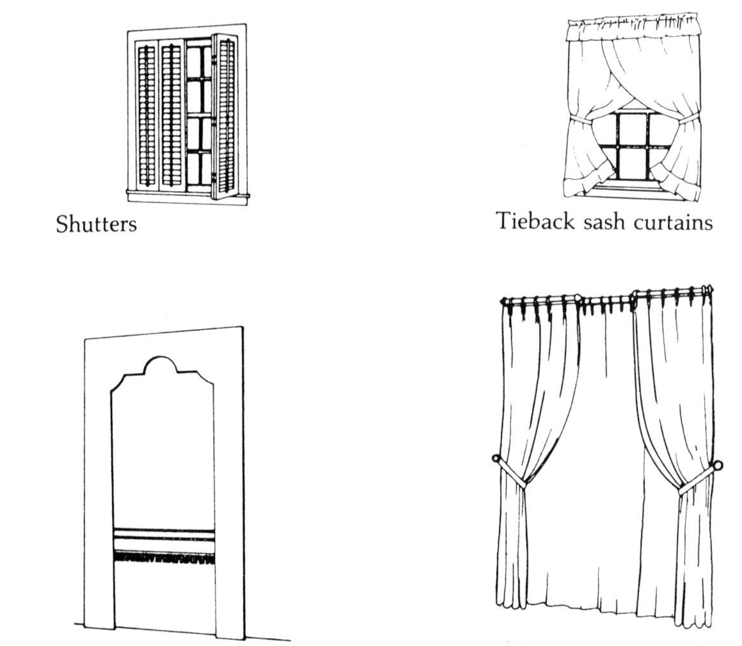
Shutters
Tieback sash curtains
Lambrequin
Tieback draperies and sheers

One window—four ways

Soft Window Treatments—Curtains and Draperies

- *Glass curtains or sheers* are used primarily to diffuse light and provide daytime privacy. They may be hung permanently

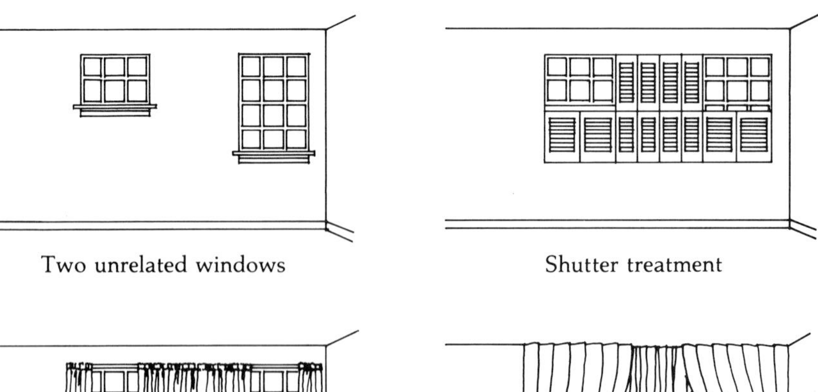
Two unrelated windows
Shutter treatment

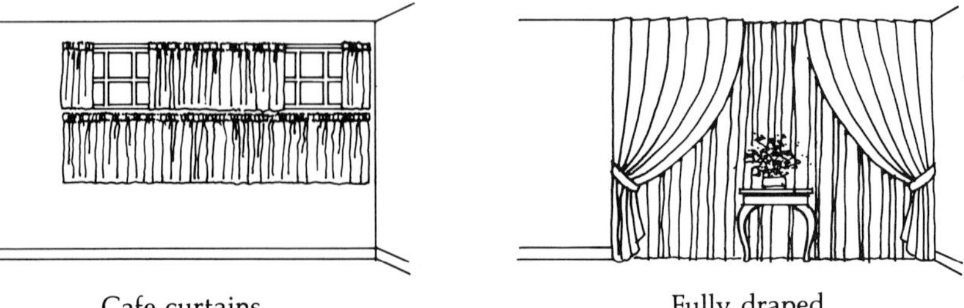
Cafe curtains
Fully draped

Three ways to handle a window problem

Figure 8.8 Subtle custom hand-woven window coverings of natural flax enhance the lovely garden view while softly filtering the sunlight. The permanently fixed tieback draperies bring definition and graceful lines in The Garden Pavilion Restaurant at the Century Plaza Hotel in Los Angeles. *(Courtesy of Conrad Imports, Incorporated. Photograph by Fritz Taggart.)*

Figure 8.9 Combined with traditional tieback draperies and a valance, loosely woven casement curtains allow some light to filter through the window.

against the glass or drawn back. Much of their beauty and efficiency is dependent on their fullness, most often three times the width of the window. When nighttime privacy is desired, sheers can be combined with draw draperies, blinds, or underdraws.

- *Semisheers or casements* (sometimes used interchangeably with sheers) are generally of a loosely woven fabric and are heavier than a sheer. They are most often used singly and drawn to control light and provide nighttime privacy. Semisheers that allow some light are the most common choice for large areas of glass.
- *Side draperies* are stationary at the sides of the window. (Draperies are usually of a heavier fabric than curtains, but the terms are interchangeable.) Side draperies may be hung straight or tied back, and their principle purpose is to bring beauty and style into the room. For daytime privacy, sheers may be combined, and for nighttime privacy and warmth, underdraws, louver blinds, or roller shades may be added.
- *Draw draperies* are made to draw over the window to control light, heat, and cold and provide privacy. They hang straight and may be used alone or combined with other curtains, blinds, or shades. For example, with a combination of draw sheers and draw drapery—the most common usage—the view can be exposed and light, sound, heat, cold, and privacy can be controlled effectively. Curtains and drapery are most often hung to one of three lengths: (1) the sill, (2) the bottom of the apron, or (3) the floor.
- *Sash curtains* are usually sheer and are hung close to the glass. They are shirred at the top and

CURTAIN AND DRAPERY LENGTHS
Sheers
Stationary drapery sheers and shade
Draw drapery and sheers
To floor (desirable)
To sill (desirable)
To bottom of apron (desirable)
Between apron and floor (not desirable)

Figure 8.10 The stationary glass wall looks onto an enclosed garden, which contributes to expanding the space. Draperies are hung on a two-way traverse rod, allowing the occupants to control the varying needs for daylight, privacy, and insulation against heat and cold. *(Courtesy of Kirsch Company.)*

Figure 8.11 A country kitchen is wrapped with documentary fabrics and wallcoverings in light and dark greens on a white ground. A coordinated decorative fabric is used from the café curtain and cascading valance overhead. *(Courtesy of Greeff Fabrics.)*

often to the bottom on sash rods. These curtains are used on many window types and doors with glass inserts.

- *Café curtains and tiers* are any curtain hung over the lower part of the window. Usually used for privacy, they may draw or be stationary. Two or more tiers are often hung to cover the entire window, in which case the rods are concealed. Café curtains may be complete in themselves or teamed with draw or side draperies.
- The *valance* is generally a pleated, gathered, or draped soft treatment across the window top. It is used solely for appearance, not changing the function of the drapery. The valance may match the side or draw draperies and is often shaped by a stiff interlining. If the fabric is patterned, the shape of the valance looks best when it conforms to that pattern. If the fabric is plain, the valance should run the same direction as the drap-

Sash curtains

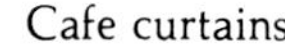

Cafe curtains

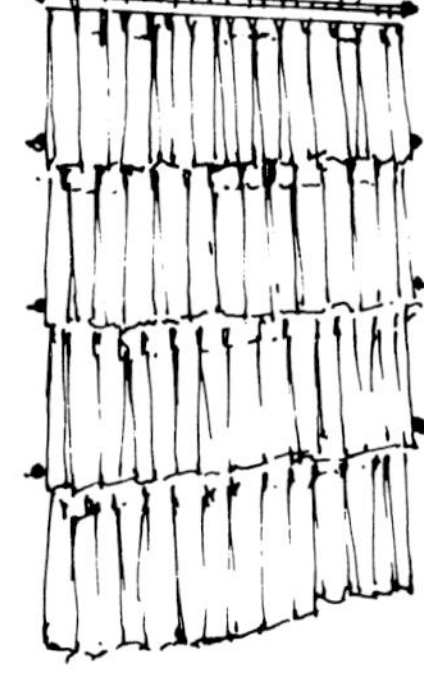

Tiered curtains

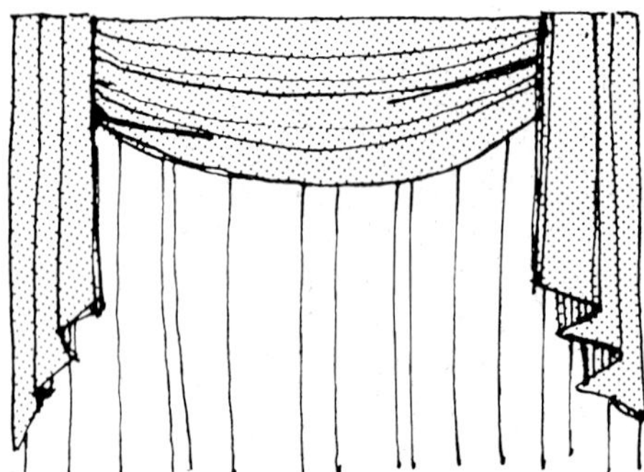

Festoon, or swag, and jabot

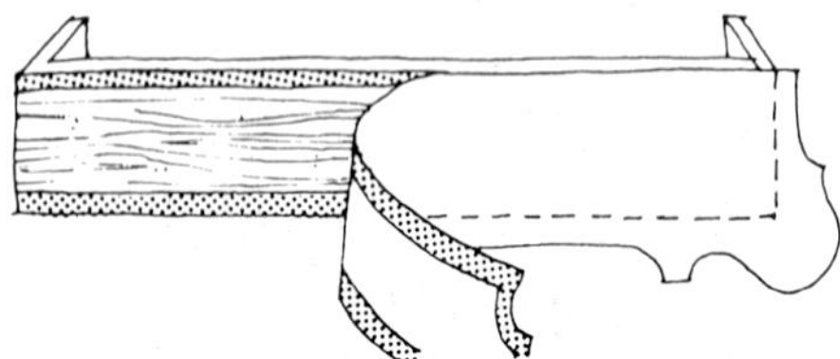

Cornice

Figure 8.12 A rose pattern covers the walls and is used for a traditional tieback drapery treatment over sheers. The arrangement is finished at the top with a pleated and staggered valance and rigid cornice. *(Courtesy of Van Luit.)*

ery. A valance screens hardware and gives the drapery a finished look. It can appear to extend the height and width of a window and unify windows of different sizes, thus altering the room's visual proportions. A ***swag*** is a type of valance treatment employing fabric draped over the top of the window and tapered at the sides. A ***jabot*** drapes down from the corners of the swag. It is usually pleated and may be of varying lengths. Swags and jabots may be hung over sheers, drapery, blinds, or shades or at the top of bare windows. A ***festoon*** is a single draped member of a swag.

- *Cornices* are generally made of wood, metal, or other hard material and are placed at the top of the window treatment. They may be stained, painted, or covered with a fabric. Cornices and valances should have sufficient return to allow for draperies underneath.
- *Lambrequins* are similar to cornices, but they also have a rigid treatment that extends vertically down both sides of the window. Lambrequins can be painted or covered with wallpaper or fabric and used with or without draperies or curtains. They provide a tailored look and can effectively unify a room. (See page 248.)
- *Fabric panels* are flat panels of fabric attached to sliders in a multichannel track with Velcro nylon fastening tape. When covering the window, panels reveal the full dimension of the fabric; when drawn back, they conveniently fold against the wall. When a tailored look is preferred, panels of fabric that slide on a track can often be the solution.
- **Ruffled tiebacks** are used mostly in kitchens, bathrooms, or other informal settings. They are usually made of light, sheer

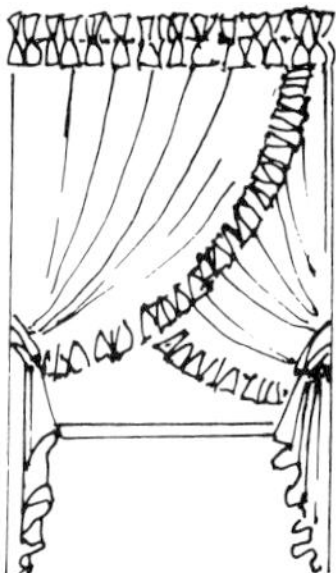

Ruffled Tiebacks

fabrics trimmed with a ruffle and shirred to a rod at the top of the window.

- *Ready-mades* are curtains and draperies made to standard length and available in most drapery departments. Although often less full than custom-made curtains and draperies, ready-mades often have effects that belie their modest cost.
- *Drapery lining* serves several functions: Windows are viewed from two perspectives: outside and inside. Drapery lining provides a uniform and attractive view from the outside, covering patterns and colors seen most effectively from only an interior perspective. Usually a plain off-white lining will make windows unobtrusive. When several windows face the street, an attempt to coordinate their appearance through the use of drapery lining is desirable—especially for windows on the same level. Drapery lining also provides additional insulation from heat and cold, protects the drapery, and adds a graceful draping quality.

Figure 8.13 In this glass-walled seashore home, miniblinds control the light without obstructing the view. Skylights are left bare. *(Photograph by Leland Lee, courtesy of Levalor Lorentzen Company.)*

Hard Window Treatments

- *Venetian blinds* were used in ancient times and later in Colonial America and during the Art Deco period for purely functional purposes. Today, modern adaptations of this blind have again become popular window treatments in both traditional- and contemporary-style homes. In most cases, venetian blinds are constructed of aluminum, stainless steel, plastic, or wooden slats. These horizontally, or sometimes vertically, arranged strips can adjust precisely for light and privacy.
- *Miniblinds* or louvers are made on the same principle of venetian blinds, but the metal or plastic slats are narrow, creating a sleek, trim look (see Figure 8.13). Miniblinds are lightweight and come complete, requiring no supplementary hardware. A wide range of colors are available, and miniblinds are treated

Mini shades

Figure 8.14a Sill-length vertical blinds add architectural interest, provide privacy, and control light. Dramatic lighting illuminates the bookshelf below the sill. *(Courtesy of Levalor Lorentzen Company.)*

Figure 8.14b Vertical blinds provide an efficient and simple window treatment supportive of the modern style employed in this bedroom. *(Courtesy of Juan Montoya Design Corporation.)*

on both sides. Used alone, they can add sophistication to the most formal interior and be at home in the most modest room. Miniblinds can be combined with a wide range of draw and side draperies for a more traditional look. The blinds are a little difficult to dust and clean.

- *Vertical blinds,* also based on the design of venetian blinds, are made of vertical strips that pivot at the top or at the top and bottom. When drawn, the strips overlap to provide maximum privacy and light control. Vertical blinds may have a different color on each side and may also be covered with wallpaper or fabric.
- The *roller shade,* an old favorite, is an effective and inexpensive window treatment. It may be installed between window casings or on the outside of the frame. The most common material is vinyl, which is available in a variety of weights and usually in white or off-white. Originally thought of as purely functional, the simple roller shade can be laminated with fabric and trimmed in a variety of ways and has assumed a role of decorative importance. When hung in a bottom-up manner, it is especially effective for privacy. Roller shades may be light filtering or room darkening, depending on the thickness of the material employed. They are easy to maintain, and they insulate against heat and cold. **Window quilts** or **thermal shades** are made of additional layers of fabric, often have a decorative stitched pattern, and provide extra insulation.
- *Roman shades* have a flat surface when extended down. When drawn upwards by a cord, the surface overlaps in horizontal folds made possible by a precreased rigid lining or by rings (or ring tape) and cords attached to the back of the shade. Roman

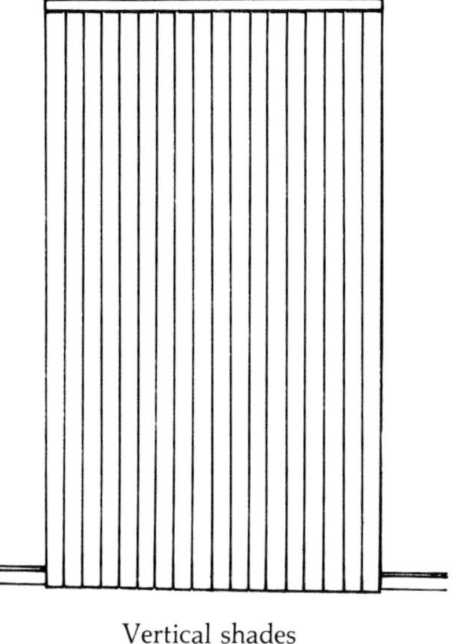

Vertical shades

Figure 8.15 Balloon shade made of permanently pleated polyester has an ethereal appearance. *(Courtesy of Jack Lenor Larsen.)*

Figure 8.16 Three separate roman shades in a plain dark pink fabric are trimmed with a stripe pattern and complement a blue and pink paisley and striped fabric on the sofa (a fabric derived from an 1870s man's dressing gown). *(Courtesy of Greeff Fabrics.)*

TYPES OF ROMAN SHADES

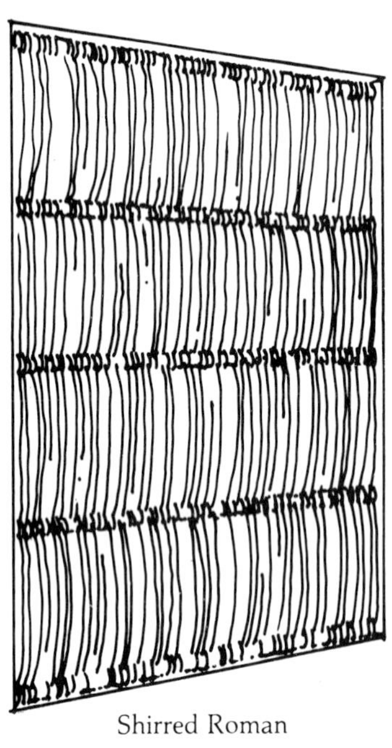

Shirred Roman

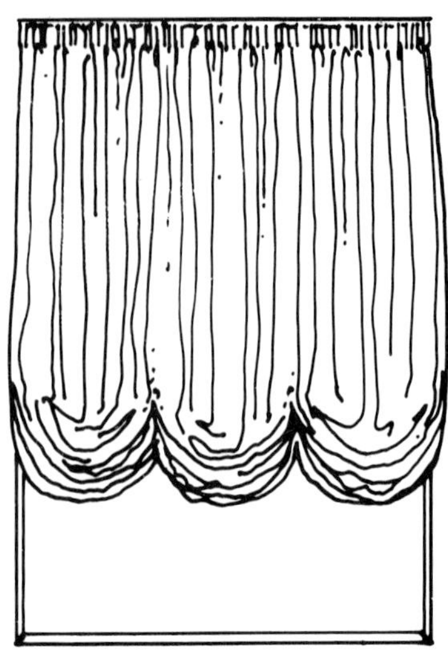

Shirred Balloon

Flat Roman

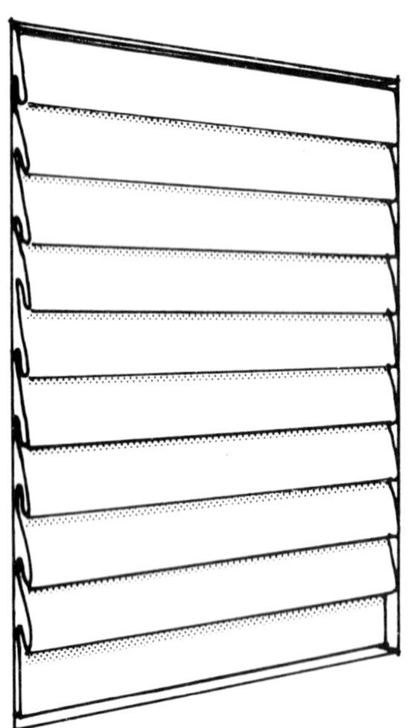

Soft Pleated Roman

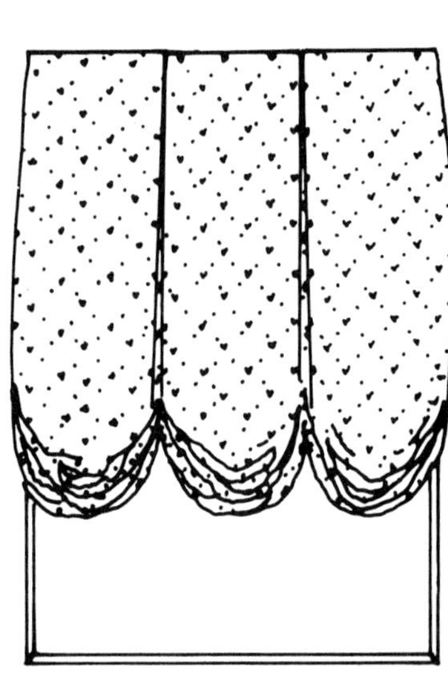

Balloon Roman

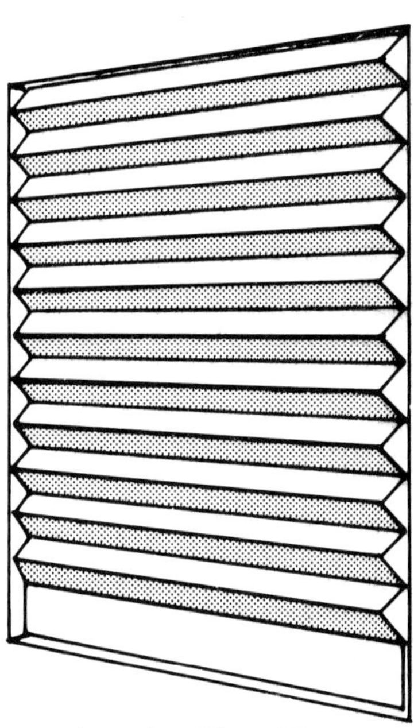

Accordian-Pleated Roman

shades come in six basic treatments: (1) **flat Roman,** (2) **shirred Roman,** (3) **balloon,** (4) **shirred balloon,** (5) **soft-pleated Roman,** and (6) **accordian-pleated Roman.** (See illustration.)

- *Austrian shades* consist of rows of lightweight fabric seamed in such a way that they fall into deep scallops. The shade is operated by a draw cord and is similar in design to the shirred balloon Roman.
- *Woven split-wood and bamboo blinds* employ slats of wood interwoven with colored or plain yarn. Woven split-wood and bamboo shades allow some light, and their warm natural texture is appropriate for most informal rooms. They may be used alone or combined with draperies, but they are inadvisable on large windows because

Figure 8.17 A valance with a bamboo pole over the wood slat sunshades gives a tailored finish to the window treatment and provides a subtle background for other furnishings. *(Courtesy of Conrad Imports, Inc.)*

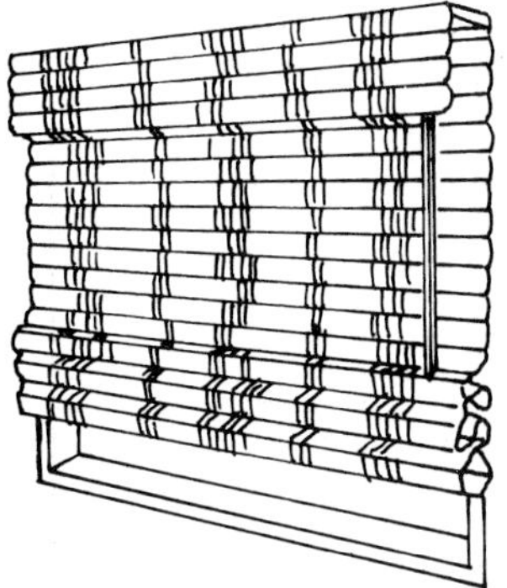

Woven wood Roman shade

of their weight. This type of shade is raised by rolling or pleating.

- *Shutters* have been used since ancient times and continue to be a popular window treatment. They can substitute for drapery, be adjusted for light and air, and are remarkably versatile. Shutters come in

Figure 8.18 Ever-versatile and timeless, shutters are suitable in any style of decor and on any window. In this contemporary setting in a mountain residence, they cover almost the entire expanse of a two-story window. The shutters can be opened to the light or closed to shut out heat, cold, and light. *(Photograph by Mark Allen.)*

Figure 8.19 Shutters can also function as doors. In this private residence, a wall of flexible shutter doors opens onto a large terrace and view. These shutter doors can also be shut for privacy and insulation. *(Courtesy of Gayl Baddeley/Associates.)*

Figure 8.20 Custom-made shutters are fitted to a large arched window with a fan-shaped arrangement at the top providing an effective and functional decorative window treatment. *(Courtesy of Kirkwood Shutters, Phoenix, AZ.)*

standard sizes and can be custom-made to fit any window. Light colors are more practical, because dark colors show dust more readily.

- *Screens and grills* can work wonders for windows. Widely used in Spain and the Middle East for centuries, the pierced or grillwork screen can be an exotic window treatment and has become popular in America. Privacy can be secured while light is filtered through, creating an atmosphere of uncluttered appeal. A screen can conceal an unsightly view, a group of poorly designed windows, an architectural defect, or a windowless wall. With rice-paper panes, shoji screens, either sliding or stationary, may be used to establish an Oriental theme.
- *Plants* can successfully be used in lieu of other window treatments (see Figure 8.22). Hung at varying heights and placed on pedestals or the floor, plants can form a bower of greenery that will soften hard-edged architecture, filter the light, and afford privacy, depending on the number of plants used. The built-out window can become a greenhouse and can use passive solar energy.
- *Bare windows* are sometimes beautiful in and of themselves, and concealing them in layers of drapery can be a mistake. Triple glazing can help control energy, and if privacy is not a problem, the maximum benefit from nature can be obtained by leav-

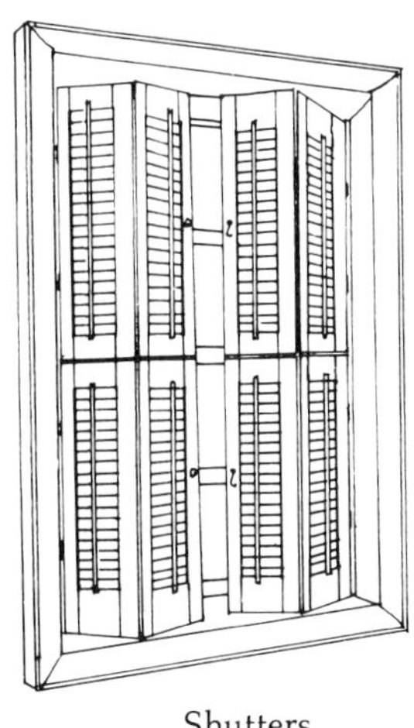

Shutters

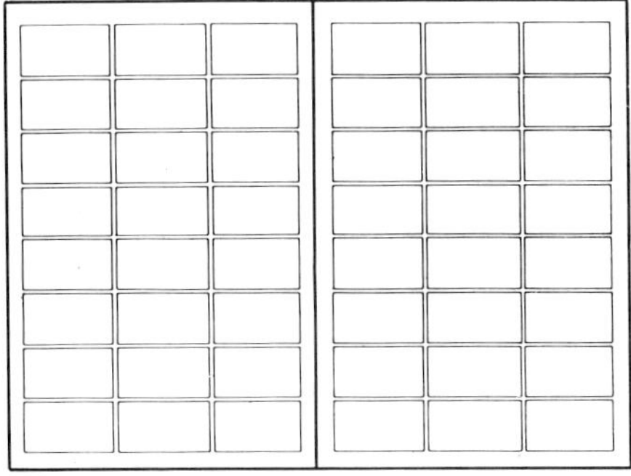

Shoji screen

Figure 8.21 Beautiful windows speak for themselves, and in this setting need no drapery or blinds. Graceful plants provide a pleasing contrast to hard edges. White wall, wood floor, and a dhurrie rug complete the background for the handmade furniture in this striking contemporary room. *(Courtesy of the McGuire Company.)*

Figure 8.22 Architecturally fixed windows are untreated, allowing the residents to look out on a tropical garden. Window frames are painted white, matching the white painted rafters and beams of the ceiling. Peach walls and peach and gray fabric on the rattan sofa and chairs enhance the effect. *(Courtesy of Whitecraft Rattan, Inc.)*

ing the window bare. Miniblinds with outside control can be used on the exterior or between double-paned windows.

Windows and Window Treatments That Conserve Energy

With the current energy consciousness of the American public, ways to insulate windows from seasonal elements are of major concern. Manufacturers are making multiple-glazed windows with a special antireflective coating to direct the sun's heating energy inward. Set in wooden frames, these windows are attractive and highly energy efficient. Curtain and drapery manufacturers are producing a variety of insulators for windows to save energy, such as double-woven multilayered fabrics that trap warm air in the room and insulated drapery and linings that insulate against heat and cold, thus cutting down on utility bills.

Generally, natural materials do the finest job of insulating. The more yarn used in the fabric, the tighter the weave, the bulkier the material, and the fuller the drapery, the more air it will trap. Layered window treatments are effective insulators. One efficient combination is woven wooden shades placed near the glass, with drawn sheers and lined draw draperies. To trap cold or hot air, the sides of the drapery may be anchored to the window frame or wall by two-faced fabric tape. Other effective energy-saving window treatments are quilted blinds, lambrequins and cornices sealed at the top and sides, and window shades equipped with side channels to seal the cracks, which can be operated by a mechanical device. Edge sealing is the most critical point for effective energy saving in window treatments.

Rapid changes occurring in housing and technology and the long-range need for energy conservation continue to affect the design and treatment of windows.

Doors

Although similar in function to windows, doors have distinctive qualities. For example, doors

- Are an essential part of a room's architectural background.
- Allow passage into the house and from one room to another.
- Can, by their location, control the flow of traffic.
- Can, by their location, preclude the arrangement of furniture.
- Provide privacy or a two-way view, depending on their structural materials.
- Can allow ventilation.
- Help control temperature.
- Provide sound barriers.
- Provide safety and security.

The main entrance door is generally the most important element and focal point in the facade of the house. Over the years this door has been given special attention. Traditional paneled period doors and leaded glass panels continue to find favor. Many exterior and interior contemporary doors are plain and flush, sheathed on both sides with plywood. Metal interior doors with insulating cores are effective in saving energy and are being used increasingly.

Figure 8.23 A custom-designed wood door by architect Ron Molen in a vertical design and arrangement creates an inviting entrance into a commercial eating space. *(Courtesy of Ron Molen, architect.)*

Figure 8.24 Exquisitely designed beveled glass lends distinction to a window or an entrance door, and combines the protection of insulated glass with the appearance of antique leading. *(Courtesy of Weather Shield Manufacturing.)*

Types of Doors

The three basic types of doors are (1) **swinging,** (2) **folding,** and (3) **sliding.** They may be constructed of a variety of materials such as wood, aluminum, plastic, and glass or a combination of a number of these, depending on design, location, and function.

- *Swinging* doors are most commonly used. They are easy to install and operate and are available in standard sizes. They may be **single** or **double hinged** at one side. Most doors are single hinged and swing one way only; the double-hinged door swings both ways. The latter is convenient for use between kitchens and dining rooms. A swinging door placed near a corner, with the arc swinging toward the adjacent wall, preserves wall space and directs traffic along the side of the room. **French doors** are pairs of glass-paned single-hinged swinging doors that open the same way, leading to a private outside area or used between rooms. The **Dutch door** is a single-hinged door divided horizontally, making it possible to have ventilation and visual communication from the upper area while the lower half is closed.
- *Folding* doors are a practical solution to saving space. They are available in sizes from a single door to a full wall divider, and they may be attached at both top and bottom or at the top only. Made in a wide variety of styles (such as louvered) and materials (including plastic and fiberglass), they are flexible and relatively inexpensive.
- *Sliding* doors used on the exterior may be part of a glass wall or installed in pairs that slide one behind the other. They are popular in contemporary houses

BASIC DOOR TYPES

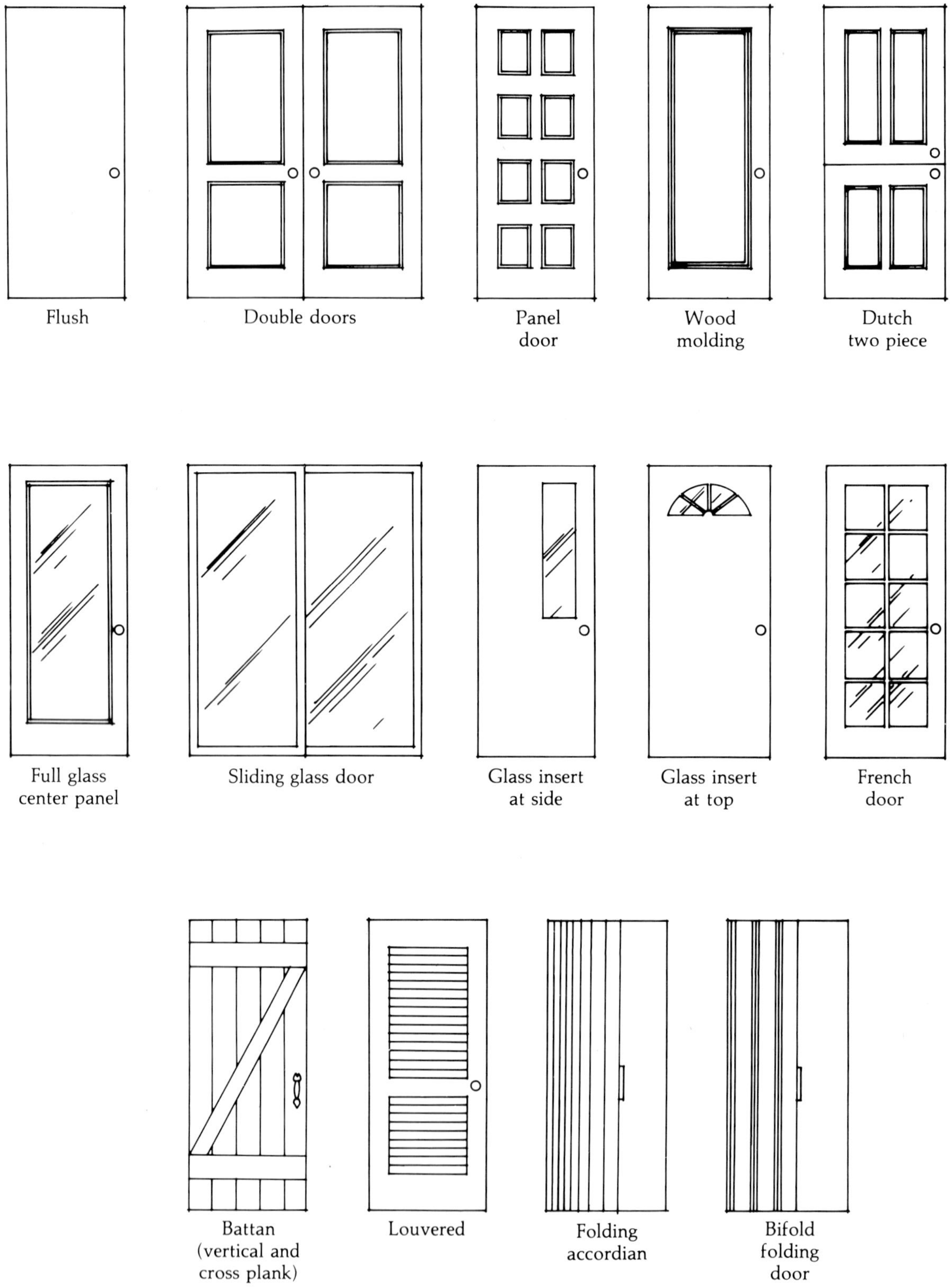

Flush

Double doors

Panel door

Wood molding

Dutch two piece

Full glass center panel

Sliding glass door

Glass insert at side

Glass insert at top

French door

Battan (vertical and cross plank)

Louvered

Folding accordian

Bifold folding door

in making the patio or garden a visual part of the living area. Sliding-glass doors can be a safety hazard when safety glass is not employed in the construction.

Interior sliding doors usually slide into a pocket installed in the wall. Although not as flexible as folding doors, sliding doors are great space savers and can provide complete or partial privacy, depending on the materials used. The traditional Japanese shoji sliding panel is at home in both traditional and modern interiors, serving multiple uses.

Placement of Doors

If doors are well placed to preserve wall space and direct traffic in the most efficient manner, they present no problem. If a room has a surplus of doors, it may be necessary to camouflage them. One possibility is to cover the door with paint or paper it the same as the wall. Another option is to remove the hinges and fill the opening with shelves for books and small art objects. For a number of reasons, relocating a door is sometimes possible and desirable, and the expense may be worth it.

Treatment of Doors

The treatment of doors depends on the design and style of the room. Doors are often painted to blend with the walls, or wood doors may be stained or left natural. If a door has a particularly good design, painting it a contrasting color may aid in the room's decoration. When walls are paneled, doors may conform to the walls or be painted in a contrasting color. In adapting to the prevailing emphasis on height, many of today's doors are dramatically tall, sometimes fitting into arched openings.

Stairways

Stairways are repeating strips of flooring rising in an upward direction that may be free-standing or attached to one or two walls. Basically, stairways consist of the **tread** (horizontal member of the step), **riser** (the vertical support), and a protective **railing.** In the past, stairways in simple homes were merely functional, allowing the occupant to travel from one floor to another. In palatial settings stairways became extravagant features, often employing marble or wood with elaborately carved balustrades and columns. Tremendous possibilities exist today for the design of stairways. Often the architect will exploit the stairway's sculptural potential, resulting in dramatic and often sweeping forms—especially when the stairway is a freestanding design.

Not only are stairways visually important, but the designer needs to consider the safety and functional aspects as well; for example:

- The depth of a **tread** should accommodate the entire length of the foot, and a measurement of 11 in. is generally employed. Often a tread is carpeted for additional safety, because hard surface materials can be a hazard. When treads are tapered

SIZES OF STAIRWELLS, RISERS AND TREADS

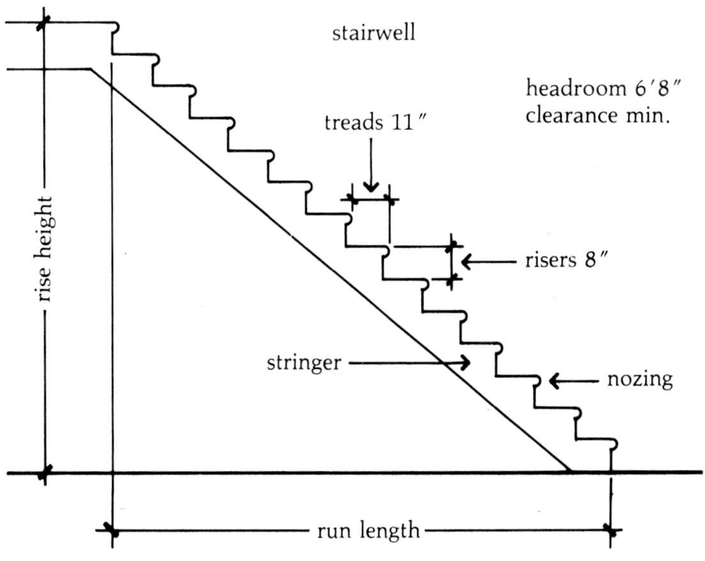

ariel view down

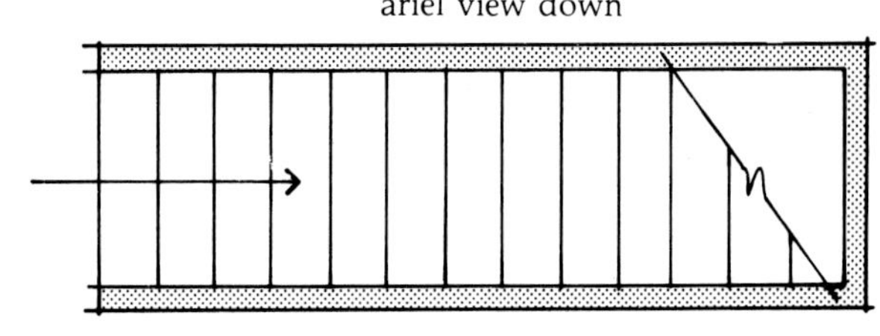

Figure 8.25 A handsomely carved wood balustrade and staircase in an old traditional English style are inviting and serviceable. *(Courtesy of Stuart Designs, England.)*

Figure 8.26 This exquisite and welcoming circular staircase is custom made by expert craftspeople in the classical traditional style. Carved vertical supports are painted white and capped with a dark stained wood railing which matches the wood step. *(Courtesy of Driwood Moulding Company.)*

Figure 8.27 A bold structural white staircase is finished with an upright wood railing and seems to float above the large space. The dominating staircase is further emphasized against a wall of soaring windows. *(Courtesy of Eduard Dreier, architect, and Guy Dreier Associates.)*

on a curving staircase, caution should be taken to ensure that the small end of the tread is wide enough for safe use.

- The vertical distance between each tread is the **riser.** Eight in. is usually the maximum height for comfort.
- A **handrail** is a necessary feature for occupants of all ages.
- **Headroom clearance** should be planned for the top and bottom of the staircase; 6 ft 8 in. is considered a minimum clearance.
- Treads and risers should be **consistent in size.** Varying sizes on the same staircase is a danger—the traveler expects and needs each step to be the same height and depth.

Fireplaces

Fireplaces have served an important functional role through the centuries as a source of warmth and a convenience for cooking meals. In simple homes it was especially the focus of the home and a place where the family congregated. In today's homes the fireplace is generally a visual luxury and may serve primarily as a room's focal point. Studies show that very few fireplaces are lit at all and then only when the climate is cool. When a fire is burning in the fireplace, the heat it generates is most often not adequate to warm an entire room unless planned with energy-efficiency features. Additionally, fireplaces are expensive and hard to clean after use, and they require space for fuel storage.

The fireplace, in spite of these drawbacks, remains a symbol of "hearth and home." American architect Frank Lloyd Wright felt that the fireplace was the "heart of the home" and built wings extending outwards from this point. Still considered a desirable and satisfying asset, fireplaces in residential living spaces can add to a home's market value.

A fire burning in a fireplace seems to draw people into a room emphasized by the flame's flickering movement, vibrant color, crackling sound, and warmth. When planning a fireplace, one needs to consider additional criteria.

- The *location* of a fireplace within the home and room requires functional and visual planning. Most homes today have one fireplace, most often located either in the living or family room. Sometimes more than one fireplace may be featured in a single dwelling. Dining rooms, kitchens, recreation rooms, and master bedrooms are also popular spaces for a fireplace. *Place-*

Figure 8.28 The dynamic freestanding fireplace in this Cleveland home, designed by Stanley Jay Friedman, acts both as a principal focus in the space and as a major divider between the seating and dining spaces. *(Courtesy of Stanley Jay Friedman. Photograph by Peter Vitale.)*

Figure 8.29 The custom-designed fireplace in the library of the Elliot House, created by Moore, Grover, and Harper, rises along with the bookshelves and ceiling. All components are constructed of smoothly finished wood strips laid in horizontal bands and accented with curling forms. *(Photograph by Norman McGrath.)*

ment within a particular living space varies in the contemporary home, whether traditional or modern in design. A fireplace may be centered on a wall, placed in a corner (popular in the southwestern adobe home), situated asymmetrically, or made a freestanding unit away from the wall (typical in Scandinavian homes). A fireplace may even function as a wall divider between two living areas.

- The *size* of the fireplace within a certain living space is often flexible. Small fireplaces can possess a certain charm and appeal. Although not occupying a major portion of the room, an average- or medium-sized fireplace can be a focal point without overwhelming a room, and a very large fireplace can be a dramatic feature. Also, a fireplace may be flush against the wall or extend outwards from a few inches to a number of feet, and the opening may be small or large enough for a person to step inside. The appropriate size of a fireplace may usually be determined after considering the *scale and proportion* of a space in order to provide a harmonious continuity within the home.
- The *style* of a fireplace generally falls into two categories: (1) **traditional** or (2) **modern.** Traditional styles for fireplace design continue in popularity, providing charm and a feeling of authenticity. Great variety of design and style is prevalent in modern homes, and often fireplaces are custom designed for a particular space. Also, a fireplace may soar vertically or horizontally, or circular forms may be emphasized. The fireplace may or may not have a mantel, the hearth may be on the floor or raised, and the fireplace may be set against the wall or project outwards from a few inches to a number of feet. The style of a fireplace is generally most successful when it complements the room's furnishings and background.

Figure 8.30 When a room has a fireplace, it usually commands attention, and other furnishings are planned to be subordinate. In this casual southwestern room, the sofa, rug, and tile flooring direct the eye toward the fireplace, which features strong horizontal and square forms that project outward from the face. *(Courtesy of American Olean Tile.)*

With the high cost of heating, the wood-burning stove has become popular across the country and is available in a large range of styles. Tile stoves, descended from the beautiful alpine Kachelofen heaters of Europe, which can be traced back almost six centuries, are being manufactured today. They come in a variety of styles and provide economical ceramic radiant heat.

- *Materials.* The most common materials employed for fireplace construction include

Brick, available in many sizes,

textures, and colors and laid in simple or intricate arrangements;

Stone of all types (marble, travertine, terrazzo, quartzite, fieldstone, granite, etc.);

Wood of all varieties, either in strips (laid in numerous patterns and directions), panels, planks, or elaborately carved members;

Facings of **plaster** or **stucco,** painted or left plain;

Concrete, plain or with exposed aggregate accents;

Tile in a variety of colors, textures, and patterns (occasionally employed).

Often fireplace design includes combinations of these materials. For example, a stone fireplace may have a handsome wood mantel, or a plastered fireplace may be outlined around the opening with colorfully patterned tile.

- *Construction.* Fireplaces should be constructed with adequate *safety, functional,* and *maintenance* features. A fireplace should draw properly, incorporate fireproof materials, and be constructed so that ashes can be conveniently removed. Firescreens—usually glass or wire mesh—can be built-in or freestanding and can help contain flying sparks from a burning fire. The concern for *energy conservation* has prompted new fireplace construction, allowing more efficient use of fuel and heat output. One popular choice is the freestanding metal stove.

  Construction may incorporate the fireplace as part of the total wall composition by using shelves or built-in furnishings, extending the fireplace material the full length and height of the wall, or constructing it independently. Consideration of the scale and proportion of the room, the style, the materials to be employed, and the effect and function desired can help one determine the most appropriate construction for a particular living space.

ASSIGNMENT

Using Plate 11 in the Student Work Packet, carefully examine the window at the top of the page and design an appropriate treatment for each of the following three conditions:

1. The window has an unsightly view, but it must provide light during the daytime. Since the room is near a public highway, it must have day- and nighttime privacy as well as noise control.

2. The window has a pleasant view onto a private enclosed garden, but it needs nighttime privacy and energy control.

3. The window has a dramatic hilltop vista both night and day. Privacy is not a problem. Since the window faces west, however, faded furnishings and energy conservation are major considerations.

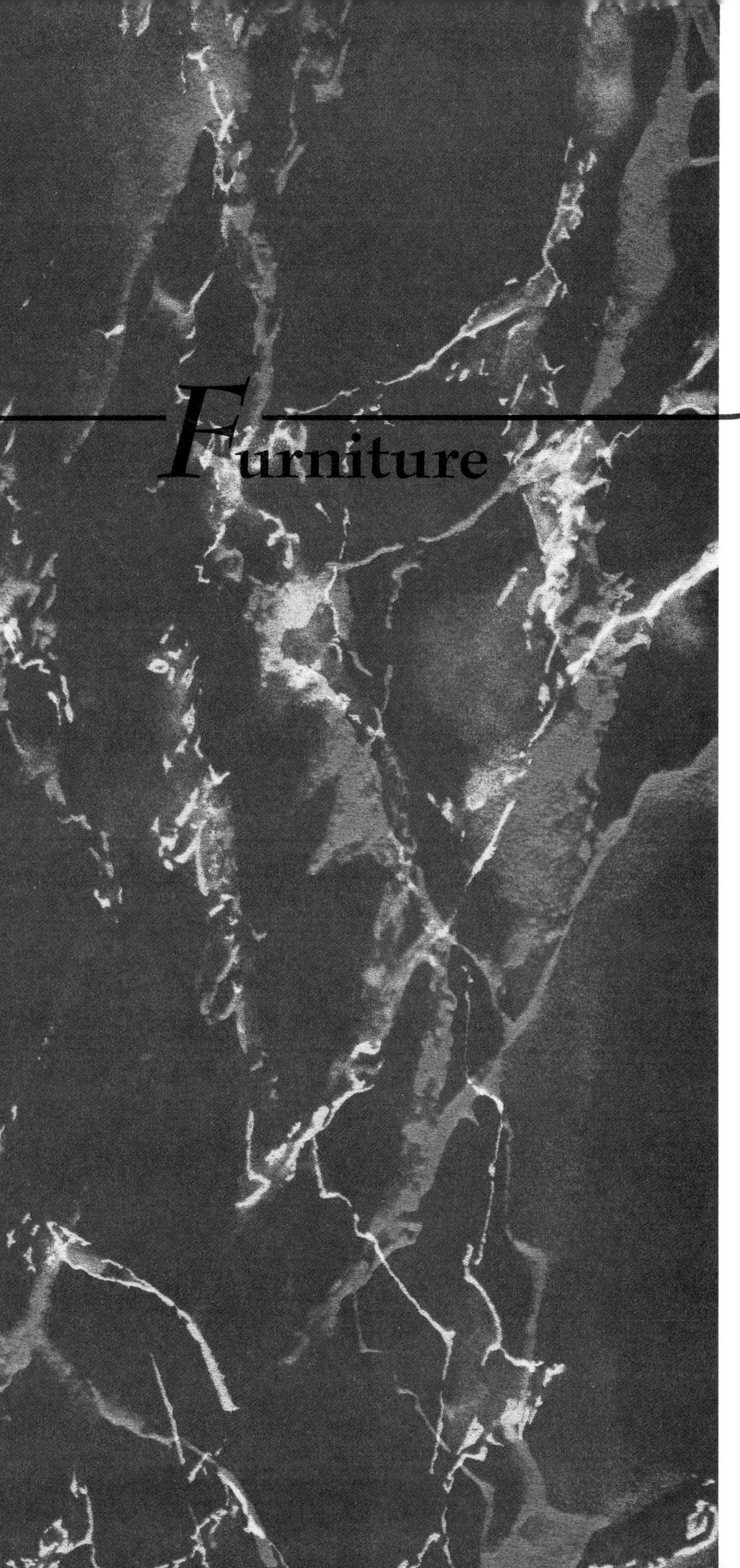

Chapter Nine

Furniture

(continued)

Quality of Construction and Materials

Wood
Metal
Synthetic Materials

Upholstered Furniture

Upholstery Fabrics

Intelligent Shopping

Care of Fine Furniture

Fashion and fads in home furnishings come and go. With each change of fashion, only a few select items survive, while others become dated and fall by the wayside. Over time, the good elements of each period will be updated by new components, but the basic character and design will remain the same. Being able to discriminate between long-lasting and faddish designs is the goal of a wise consumer.

Before Buying Furniture

Furnishing a home can be a rewarding experience. The pride of ownership adds a new dimension. Initial purchases, when well selected, can last a lifetime. Careful study and planning can enable the consumer to make wise decisions. This approach requires time and effort but pays long-term dividends. Acquiring a knowledge of the principles of design and of what goes into the making of a fine piece of furniture aids the consumer in the selection process.

Seldom does the consumer decorate a first living space with a specific style of furniture in mind, and this may not be as important as having a **long-range plan** before purchasing a piece. A preferred **general theme** like informal modern or formal traditional can be developed over a long period, with each furniture piece supporting the initial idea. Usually, simple and well-designed pieces can be blended into a definite scheme later on. Buying a roomful of "economy furniture" should generally be avoided. At best it will be mediocre and will likely be dated in a few years. Instead, one good piece of furniture is a wise start, combined with an assortment of temporary items artfully retrieved from a variety of sources.

A first piece might be a basic article, like a chest or cabinet, that will serve many functions over the years. Other essential pieces include a bed, tables, chairs, and other seating and storage units. If one piece is chosen at a time with the overall plan in mind, rooms will likely have more appeal

Figure 9.1 The design of this eclectic living room includes a Near Eastern Kilim rug, an Etruscan table, Louis XV chairs, contemporary sofas, and Oriental accessories providing a harmonious blending of many styles. *(Photograph by Alex Groves.)*

and personality. The temptation to purchase something momentarily appealing or a so-called bargain that is in no way related to other furnishings should be resisted. No matter what the cost, if a piece of furniture does not meet individual needs and does not seem right in the room, it is not a bargain at any price. If a piece of furniture is well designed initially, it will always be good.

Furniture Selection

Today the market abounds with furniture of many types, styles, and prices, allowing the consumer to make a selection appropriate to a particular life-style and to fulfill particular needs. Furniture-marketing methods often present furniture in **suites, groups,** and **collections.** A *suite* of furniture consists of pieces designed to be used together in a specific room. All pieces share a common design, are priced as a unit, and often cannot be purchased separately. A *furniture group* is a large ensemble or collection coordinated by the same design. A group may include suites for bedrooms, dining, and living rooms. A danger is that a look-alike design may become monotonous. A *collection* has a look of individuality and usually is in the higher-priced market. The impression is one of a mixture of pieces thoughtfully collected over a period of time. Designs are not the same, but the pieces appear compatible. Most professionals prefer to select well-designed pieces from various sources that harmoniously relate but have a distinct character of their own. Wise furniture purchases are dependent on a number of basic considerations, including

- **Function and utility.** Furniture should satisfy human requirements for physical comfort and function for specific needs. A chair, for example should be selected with use in mind. Such questions as (1) how and where will it be used? (2) who will use it? (3) what space will be required? (4) how durable must the piece be? and (5) what maintenance is necessary? are essential inquiries before one purchases the piece.
- **Available space.** Since space is generally limited in today's homes, the space required for a particular piece is of special importance. For example, lightly scaled furniture with superfluous designs eliminated and built-in units help conserve space.
- **Economy.** The consumer's budget is a necessary consideration when planning and furnishing a home. Good quality and design are a wise investment and, if carefully selected, can be obtained at reasonable cost.
- **Aesthetic appeal.** Often the initial impression—the beauty of a furniture piece—provides aesthetic appeal in the home. Aesthetic appeal is a matter of personal taste and is purely subjective. An acquaintance with the principles of design, however, helps provide the consumer with a knowledgeable background on which to make a discriminating choice.
- **Individuality and character.** These are the unique aspects that draw the consumer to a particular piece and seem to contribute personality to the owner's private living spaces.

Types of Furniture

Study of the development of furniture through the centuries reveals that human beings first created crude, but somewhat functional, pieces. As time passed, a refinement process occurred, and furniture became an important art form. By the time of the ancient civilizations of Egypt, Mesopotamia, Greece, and Rome, furniture was elegantly formed and decorated, satisfying the need for both function and beauty. For centuries after development of these early cultures, various styles evolved that proved to have a lasting influence on following generations, especially the English and French designs. However, basic furniture types remained fairly constant with the exception of built-ins and modular units that would emerge on a grand scale during the twentieth century. Furniture types prevalent in today's homes include the following:

- **Chairs.** For centuries people have been fascinated by the design potential of the seating unit. Human beings use chairs every day of their lives for a variety of functions, and their importance as essential pieces of furniture is unquestionable.

Figure 9.2 This popular traditional Provincial French chair is based on the Louis XV Style.

Furniture Identification:
Seating Pieces and Beds

Furniture Identification:
Tables, Case Furniture, Desks, Beds, and Pianos

Figure 9.3 One of the most important of all traditional chairs is the Queen Anne armchair.

Figure 9.4 An Early American ladder-back armchair constructed of wood with a rush seat.

Figure 9.5 The classic eighteenth-century English Chippendale ladderback side chair.

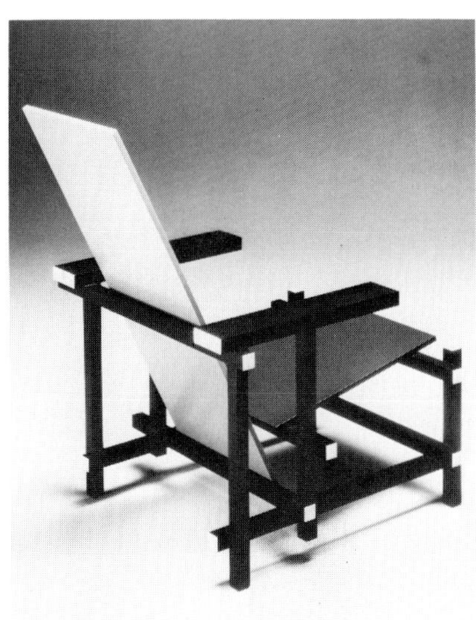

Figure 9.6 One of the finest examples of furniture from De Stijl (see Chapter 2) is the Red/Blue chair (1918), designed in Holland by Gerrit Rietveld. It is constructed of wood in an abstract arrangement and painted red, blue, yellow, and black. *(Courtesy of Atelier International.)*

Figure 9.7 Finnish designer Alvar Aalto designed this cantilevered laminated birch chair with a seat and back of webbing. It is an excellent example of Scandinavian modern furniture design. *(Courtesy of ICF.)*

Figure 9.8 The famous Pedestal chair, designed by Eero Saarinen in 1967, has a molded plastic and fiberglass seating shell with an aluminum base. *(Courtesy of Knoll International.)*

Figure 9.9 The "Ribbon" Chair 582, created by French designer Pierre Paulin in 1965, is constructed of a tubular metal frame that is covered with a tension-held rubber sheet and then upholstered. *(Courtesy of Artifort.)*

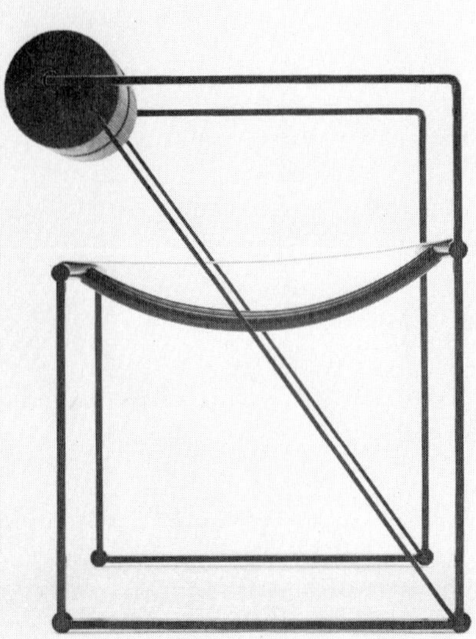

Figure 9.10 The Seconda armchair (1982), designed by Swiss architect Mario Botta, is constructed of perforated sheet metal with a backrest of polyurethane. *(Courtesy of ICF.)*

Some considerations for chair design include the following: (1) The height, depth, and width should comfortably accommodate the human form. (2) An adjustable chair can give flexible service. (3) ***Ergonomic*** designs, based on extensive anthropometric studies, are available for maximum comfort. (4) Chairs of varying sizes are available, ranging from simple and lightly scaled side chairs to oversized upholstered lounge chairs. (5) Materials generally employed include wood, metal, plastic, leather, and textiles. (6) Styles from all periods are available to suit any taste (see p. 280). (7) A chair is on the market to satisfy every possible function—whether for relaxation or work. Generally, a variety of chair sizes and designs are required for numerous functions within one home.

- **Sofas.** Sofas are long upholstered seating units accommodating more than one person, and through the ages particular terms have been associated with certain designs. **Lawson** is a popular type with armrests lower than the back support. The most common *sofas,* a familiar term for most seating of this type, include the following: (1) the **couch,** a long upholstered unit with a low back and one endpiece; (2) the **davenport,** originally a small writing desk named after its designer, is often used today to define a convertible sofa; (3) the **tuxedo,** a completely upholstered piece with armrests the same height as the back; (4) the **divan,** a low couch without arms or back units, derived from stacked rugs used in Turkey for seating purposes; (5) the **loveseat,** a smaller sofa created for seating two persons; (6) the **settee,** a lightly scaled piece, often with some upholstered sections; (7) **settles,** completely constructed of wood with very high backs, originally used in early American homes to retain heat from fireplaces; (8) **dual-purpose sofas,** which can be used for both sleeping and seating (**studios, sofa-beds,** and **convertible sofas** fall into this category); and (9) **modular and sectional sofas,** which have been popular in recent years.

- **Tables.** (1) Dining and kitchen tables, (2) coffee tables, (3) end or occasional tables, (4) game tables, and (5) desks are all functional furniture pieces used in the home to serve various needs. Tables should be sturdy, strong, and durable and of a usable size and shape. The height should be adequate and comfortable for the intended function.

- **Beds.** The best set of mattress and springs the buyer can afford is a wise investment, because much of the occupant's general health and feeling of well-being are dependent on the quality of sleep. Individual preferences for sleeping comfort vary. A bed may be (1) built-in,

Figure 9.11 The lines and form of this classic contemporary upholstered sofa have a timeless appeal and can be incorporated into any decor. *(Courtesy of Thayer Coggin.)*

Figure 9.12 When Le Corbusier designed the Grand Confort Collection in 1928, he eliminated the traditional construction of an upholstered piece and used a light support of tubular steel for loose cushions. *(Courtesy of Atelier International.)*

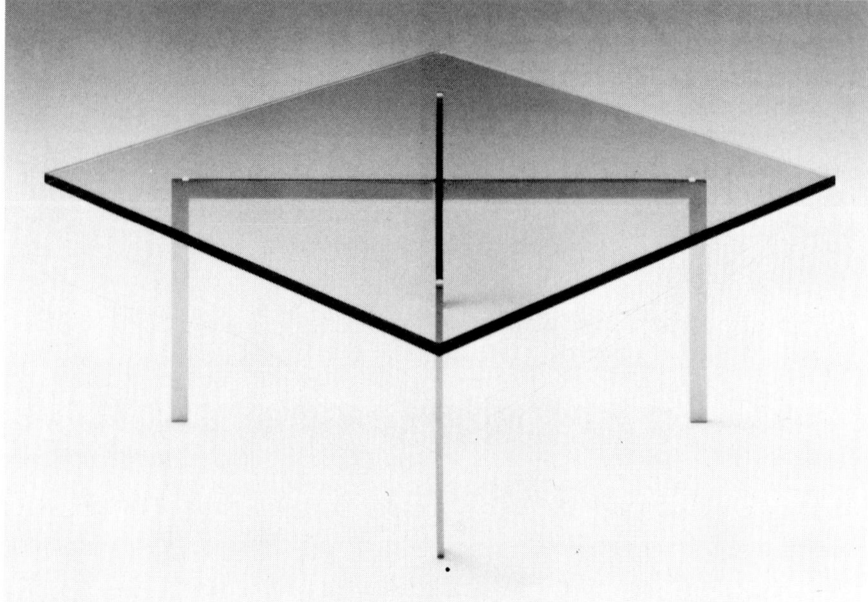

Figure 9.13 The classic Barcelona table, designed by Mies van der Rohe in 1929, has a chrome X-shaped base topped with a slab of glass and is used as a coffee table in a formal or informal setting. *(Courtesy of Knoll International.)*

Figure 9.14 A combination bed and storage unit. An island bed with a storage headboard, flanking armoires, a lighted canopy, and mirror. *(Courtesy of Henredon.)*

(2) freestanding, (3) a dual-purpose piece, (4) a fold-down-from-the-wall type, (5) a bunk bed, (6) a waterbed, or (7) a trundle bed.

- **Storage.** Many innovative pieces designed for functional storage are available on the market to help alleviate the problems of small living spaces. Convenient and efficient storage is required in many rooms of the house for various items. **Chests, cupboards, hutches, china cabinets,** and **shelves** are the common furniture pieces to provide storage space.
- **Built-in and modular units.** Built-in furnishings may function as seating, tables, beds, and storage space and are an integral part of the wall construction. They have the advantage of providing architectural unity and a more spacious feeling. A drawback can be the inability to move the components. Modular units are flexible pieces that can be arranged in a variety of compositions, providing great flexibility.

Figure 9.15 A traditional casepiece with drawers and a writing and display section used effectively in an entry. *(Courtesy of Drexel.)*

Figure 9.16 A modern casepiece, Sideboard 2, designed by Charles Rennie Mackintosh at the turn of the century, was put in production in 1974. The piece, made of ebonized wood and contrasted with pearlized and stained glass, can be used for a variety of functions. *(Courtesy of Atelier International.)*

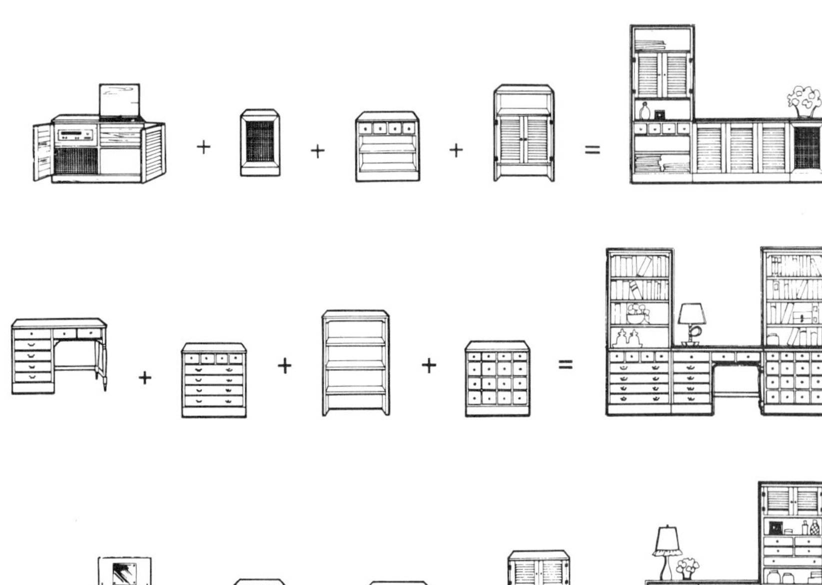

Custom wall units may be purchased one piece at a time, used for a variety of purposes in different rooms of the house, or assembled into a single wall composition. *(Courtesy of Ethan Allen Treasury.)*

Basic Furniture Styles

Throughout history, the diversity of world cultures has found expression in many directions, including the way people have lived in their homes and the furnishings with which they surrounded themselves. Invariably the most basic piece of furniture in all Western countries has been the "seat." Differences in designs for seating pieces and other items of furniture, as well as the decorative arts, were the result of a number of factors including climate, politics, religion, and customs, which varied from one country to another.

Interest in America's cultural heritage has grown in recent years, and a concern for historic homes has come into focus, with furniture being an important element. Today few restraints are imposed on how furniture is combined, and the alternatives are many. Effectively integrating the past with the present, however, requires pertinent information. Although a complete understanding of period styles is not necessary to create an attractive home, some basic knowledge of historic furnishings can deepen the aesthetic appreciation of our design heritage, broaden individual concepts of interior design, and foster creative energies. A working knowledge of the most commonly used styles of furniture, both traditional and modern, is essential to the interior designer. For the consumer interested in designing a home, this knowledge will instill a more confident design ability, provide a basis for making valid choices, and possibly be the source of a gratifying long-term interest in and appreciation for present and past styles.

In the belief that a detailed consideration of furniture styles is beyond the scope of a beginning course in interior design, an effort has been made to characterize briefly the furniture styles that have had the greatest impact on Americans. These styles are correlated and presented in sequence with the homes presented in Chapters 1 and 2 for easy cross-referencing.

The Spanish Styles

The Spanish settlers built their private and public buildings primarily in what is now New Mexico and California during the seventeenth to nineteenth centuries. The **Spanish Mission** or **Colonial, Southwest Adobe, Monterey,** and **California ranch** architectural styles reflect the basic Spanish heritage in the United States, with each having distinctive regional differences in both construction, style, and furniture design. The Spanish adapted their homes and other buildings to existing cultural and geographical conditions but still reflected their own unique Spanish background.

The California Mission/Colonial Style (circa Eighteenth Century to the Present). During the eighteenth century, when the Spanish were colonizing what is now the state of California, a string of Catholic missions were built up the California coast, introducing characteristics of architecture based on prototypes in Spain. Furniture was often brought to America from Spain and was regarded as highly treasured pieces. Other furniture was copied from original Spanish designs. The Mexican influence was also incorporated into the Spanish Mission or Colonial Style.

- **General Characteristics:** Heavily proportioned, strong, and sturdy furnishings reflecting the cultures of Spain and Mexico. Moorish influence from Spain. Furnishings often painted. Strong use of geometric designs. Use of spindles, finials, and grilles. Walnut and oak popular woods employed—usually stained dark. Scrolled Spanish foot. Nails and joinings frankly exposed. (Some nailheads of brass and iron often had patterns.) Furniture often ornamented with silver and other metals.

Principal Furniture Types—Most Typical Pieces

- *Seating:* Chairs often accented with heavy metal nailheads and ironwork. Ladderback chairs topped with hoods and finials. Tooled leather chairs. Vigorous use of geometric designs, lattice, and turned spindles. **Shepherd's chair.** Leather upholstered bench.
- *Casepieces:* The *varguena* (a cabinet-desk with a fall front) an essential Spanish piece. Cupboard or *trastero* with grille doors and geometric carvings.
- *Tables:* Heavily carved **trestle** table with iron ***stretchers.*** Legs straight or splayed outwards.
- *Beds:* Carved spindle arrangement topped with finials typical.

- **Fabrics:** Leather, often embossed or painted. Velvets and tapestries for formal look. Wool, leather, and rush for informal furnishings. Colors in strong chroma (see Chapter 5). Motifs drawn from Spain and Mexico.
- **Accessories:** Wrought-iron chandeliers, candlesticks, and sconces. Tinware, often with a perforated design. Hand-painted Mexican tile and pottery. Christian religious relics. Mirrors with ironwork or heavily carved wooden frames.

SPANISH
(Colonial/Mission Style)

Ladderback

Leather seated chair

Shepherds' chair

Highback chair

Spanish foot

Leather upholstered bench

Trestle table

Vargueno

Brass nailhead

Nailhead

Cupboard or Trastero

Panelled door

Moorish arch

Spanish tile

Headboard with finials

Filigree pineapple sconce

Bull's-eye mirror (Moorish)

The Southwest Adobe (circa Seventeenth to Twentieth Century) and the Santa Fe Styles (circa 1920s to present). When the Spanish settled in the area that is now New Mexico and parts of Arizona, they built their homes based on pueblo dwellings of the native Indians living in these regions. However, they incorporated Spanish furniture designs that were familiar and more practical for their own particular life-style. The result of blending the Spanish and Indian cultures was a unique and influential design direction known as the Southwest Adobe Style. Furnishings for Southwest Adobe homes were basically the same as for houses found in the Spanish Mission and Colonial homes—furnishings reflecting Spanish and Mexican influences. A strong Indian influence was also incorporated. Later, when settlers arrived in the area from the eastern colonies, they brought English furniture for use in the Southwest Adobe home. In the 1920s, 1930s, and 1940s, a fresh style, based on original Southwest Adobe interiors and furnishings, was developed primarily by easterners vacationing or living in Santa Fe, a popular tourist resort of the twentieth century. Each contributed characteristics that gradually developed into a distinctive and highly sophisticated style. This popular updated interior treatment, known as the **Santa Fe Style,** utilizes modern interpretations of furnishings, colors, fabrics, and accessories and has become a popular design approach of the past several decades.

- **General Characteristics:** Simple and functional pieces, often crudely fashioned, typical. (General characteristics similar to Spanish Mission and Colonial Style furnishings.) Furnishings set against irregular and molded adobe stuccoed walls. Santa Fe Style features eclectic look which includes European antiques with Southwestern American handicrafts and art, providing a fresh, contemporary look.

Principal Furniture Types—Most Typical Pieces

- *Seating:* Chairs with spindle backs, rush-bottom seats. Simple lodgepole pine furniture currently popular in the Santa Fe Style. Equipale leather and wood chair. Carved colonial bench.
- *Casepieces:* Storage pieces with perforated tin design insets. Large cupboard, *trastero,* often painted and with lattice design. Stars-and-stripes cupboard typical. Mexican cupboard. Geometrically carved grain chest. High cupboard with spindle forms. Chest on curved legs.
- *Tables:* Equipale leather and wood drum table (leather stretched and laced over a circular form). Trestle table. Simple table with carved apron.
- *Beds:* Carved colonial bed. Lodgepole pine bed often used for the Santa Fe Style.

- **Fabrics:** Informal fabrics. Wool and cotton textiles. Geometric designs. Indian influence. Embroidery. Southwest Adobe interiors may feature brilliant colors. Santa Fe Style most often utilizes warm desert colors, including sage greens, peaches, pinks, blue-greens, tans, corals, and purples. White. Black in small amounts.
- **Accessories:** Handcrafted Spanish, Indian, and Mexican arts—especially geometrically designed Navajo rugs and blankets (see p. 212). Tinware. Indian pottery and baskets. Hand-painted Mexican pottery, mirrors, sconces, and tile. Indian, Mexican, and Spanish religious relics. Iron, wood, or clay candlesticks. Cactus plants. Accessories displayed in *nichos* (niches built into the wall). Handcrafted stylized animals. Kachina (Indian) dolls. Any accessory reflecting the New Mexican life-style (i.e., boots, skulls of animals, wagon wheels, farm tools, and cooking utensils). Items fashioned of silver. Colorfully painted undulating wooden snakes. Accessories highly individualistic, with unexpected combinations of items evident in the Santa Fe Style.

Spanish Monterey and California Ranch Styles. Typical furnishings for these two styles (see Chapter 1) are similar to those found in the Spanish Mission or Colonial Style. The Spanish Monterey Style typically includes eighteenth-century English furniture blending with the Spanish influences, which often provides a more formal aspect.

Seventeenth- and Eighteenth-Century Country Style (Early American Furnishings)

An informal provincial style emerged in America during the settlement period in the seventeenth and eighteenth centuries and became popularly known as Early American. Architecture and furnishings reflected the colonists' English, Dutch, Swedish, and German heritage. (See Chapter 1 for additional information on seventeenth-century homes in America.)

Many furnishings were brought on ships from the native country or authentically reproduced in the new land. The English colonies were dominant, and their furniture clearly is expressive of the Gothic, Elizabethan, Jacobean, and William and Mary heritage. Some of these original furnishings have had a continued appeal for Americans through the centuries.

- **General Characteristics:** Informal country or village look.

SPANISH
(The Santa Fe Style)
Carved wooden armchair
Lodge pole pine chair
Carved wooden armchair
Equipale leather and wood chair
Carved geometric design bench
Carved bench with Southwest motifs
Drum table
Equipale leather and wood table
Carved table with splayed legs
Cabinet with wood lattice and carved geometric design (trastero)
Cabinet with perforated tin panels
Cabinet with hood and spindles
Hutch with hood and spindles
Carved and painted headboard
Lodge pole pine bed
Mirror with perforated tin frame
Indian basket and wool rug
Iron candlestand
Religious relic

Simple handcrafted furnishings. Pine, maple, oak, cherry, and hickory wood most common types used. Utilitarian pieces.

Principal Furniture Types—Most Typical Pieces

- *Seating:* **Brewster chair:** developed by early Pilgrims. Has numerous turned spindles, a wood seat, and heavily turned posts. **Bannister-back chairs** similar in design, most often with split spindles. **Wainscot chair:** a wood paneled chair of English and French influence during the sixteenth and seventeenth centuries; originally an addition of a seat to the wooden wall paneling or wainscot. **Ladder-back chairs** have a back with horizontal slats in a ladder arrangement; popular since time of the Pilgrims. **Carver chair** (circa 1660), named for the first governor of Massachusetts Bay colony; three or five turned spindles in back, rush seat, finials, and a variety of turnings. **Jacobean chair** (circa 1660): high back, finials, and wide, carved front stretcher; back panel and seat usually leather; later version had a cane back. **William and Mary wing back:** first luxurious upholstered chair in colonies; crested top rail and gracefully rolled arms. Early ***cabriole leg*** joined by turned stretchers. Spanish (paintbrush) feet. **Windsor chairs** have a wood frame with a turned spindle back, a thick saddle-shaped seat, and splayed legs. Originated in England during the early eighteenth century. **Hitchcock chair:** although of a later period (early 1800s), this chair, with a unique gold stencil of fruit and flowers, often employed in contemporary homes to provide an early American look. **Joint stool** wood seating; baluster-turned legs joined by stretchers; some had wide overhang tops that doubled as tables. **Benches,** called forms, made in varying lengths for different functions. **Settles:** benches with high backs, usually plain and made of pine; helped shield against drafts. **Jacobean day bed,** with typical turnings, a prized possession.
- *Casepieces:* **Court cupboard:** influenced by English Tudor designs; a large and handsomely carved cupboard, often with large, bulbous forms showing the Elizabethan influence. **Hadley chest:** first discovered in Hadley, Massachusetts; displays tulips carved over front rails. (Chests assumed regional forms.) **Sunflower chest** common in colonial Connecticut, with either carved or painted sunflower motifs and split spindles showing Jacobean influences. **Hutch:** an open cabinet for china storage. **Corner cupboard** fits into a corner and is curved or diagonal; prominent in eighteenth-century America. **Slant-top desk:** shape derived from early Bible boxes; slant top served for reading and writing; a forerunner of future desks. **William and Mary highboy and lowboy:** highboy is a chest of drawers supported on various number of legs following Flemish forms; lowboy is a table with two to four drawers. **William and Mary double-hooded desk:** high desk topped with two hoods symbolizing the joint reign of King William and Queen Mary of England at the end of the seventeenth century. **Dry sink:** a cabinet to hold a pitcher and wash basin.
- *Tables:* **Trestle table:** a medieval table characterized by trestle or splayed leg supports; various styles based on this original type emerged in America. **Gateleg table:** large or small table with hinged legs supporting the drop leaves. **Butterfly gate leg:** hinged legs in the shape of butterfly wings. **Candle stand:** small pedestal table, often with three legs. **Table chair** could be manipulated for use as a table or chair.
- *Beds:* Simple frame. Often large and hand carved. **Trundle bed:** a low bed made to slip under the regular bed during the day. **Cradles:** handcrafted of pine or oak with deep sides and often a hood for warmth.

- **Fabrics:** Fabrics made on looms. Homespun wool. Some cotton. Natural dyes employed. Coverlets for beds. Needlework of all types. Rugs made from fabric scraps. Imported printed cottons with quaint motifs.
- **Accessories:** Quaint pictures, often of family members. Utilitarian items of silver, pewter, iron, tin, brass, and copper. Simple pottery, often hand-painted. Items of wood including churns, bowls, buckets, kegs, dippers, boxes for spices, spoons, doughboxes, and other household articles. Candles and holders. ***Betty lamp.*** Freestanding and wall clocks after about 1720. Schoolhouse clock a favorite. The courting mirror presented to a prospective bride. Square mirrors, often with William and Mary–type cresting.

Early and Late Georgian (circa 1700–1790)

As Americans prospered and began to live a more leisurely life-style, homes and furnishings reflected eighteenth-century England and became more formal and refined than those of the earlier settlement period. Commonly known as Georgian, the style was named after Kings George I, II, and III of England, whose reigns dated from 1714 to 1795 (see Chapter 1, pp.

EARLY AMERICAN
(17th and 18th Century Country Style—Part 1)

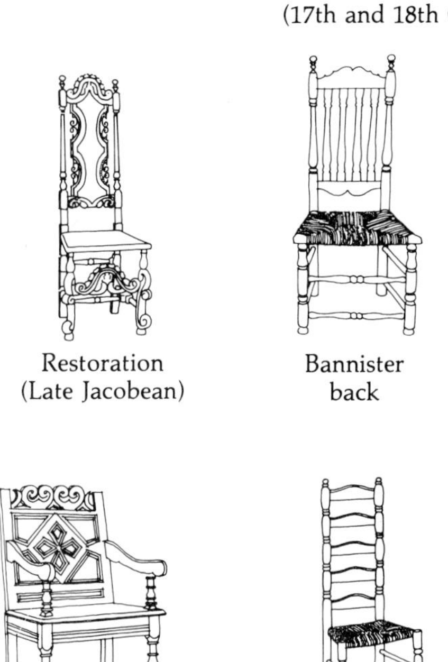

Restoration (Late Jacobean)

Bannister back

Carver

Brewster

Jacobean wainscot

Slatback (ladderback)

Windsor

Hitchcock

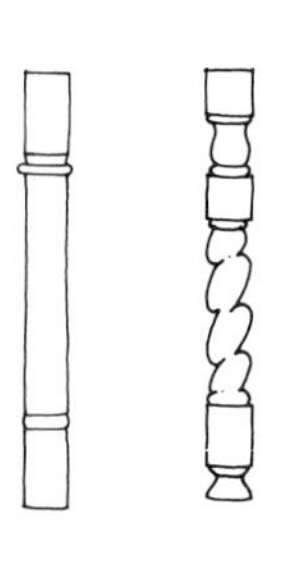

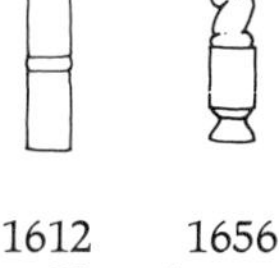

1612 1656
Chair legs

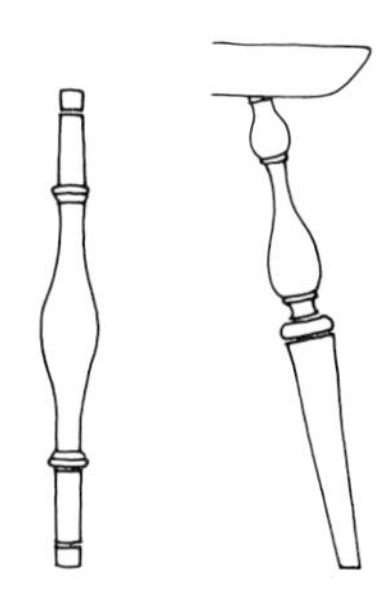

American Windsor turnings

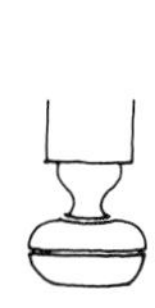

Bun foot

Joint stool

Cricket stool

Jacobean daybed

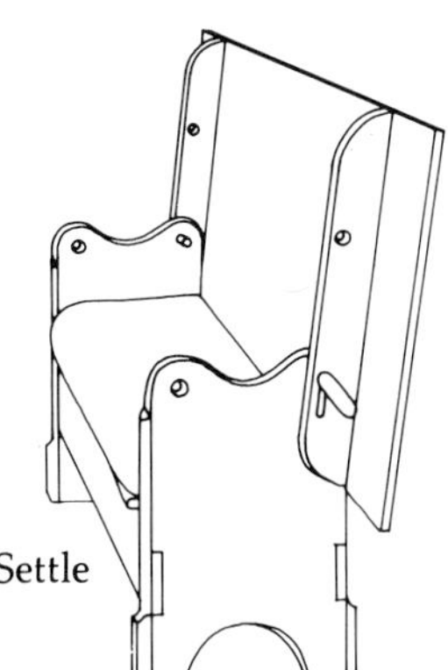

Settle

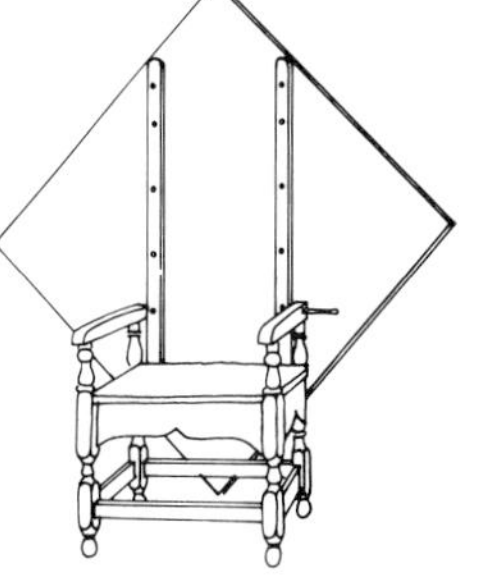

Table chair

EARLY AMERICAN
(17th and 18th Century Country Style—Part 2)

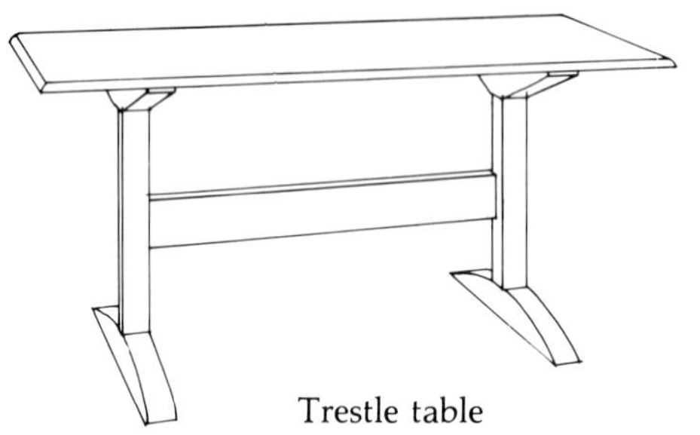
Trestle table

Butterfly table

Dry sink

Court cupboard

Sunflower chest

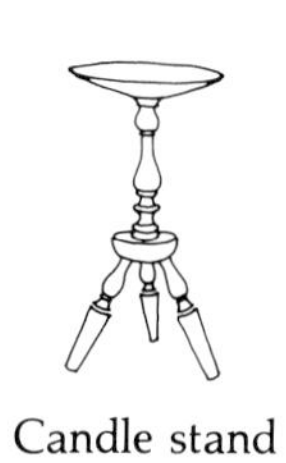
Candle stand

Slant-top desk

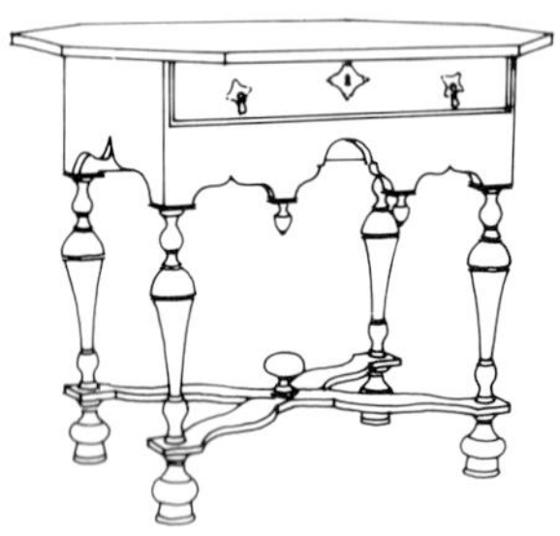
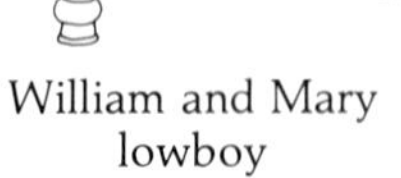
William and Mary lowboy

William and Mary highboy

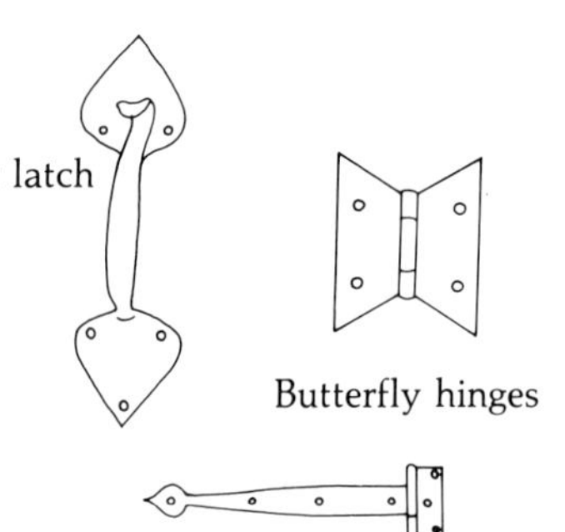
Heart latch

Butterfly hinges

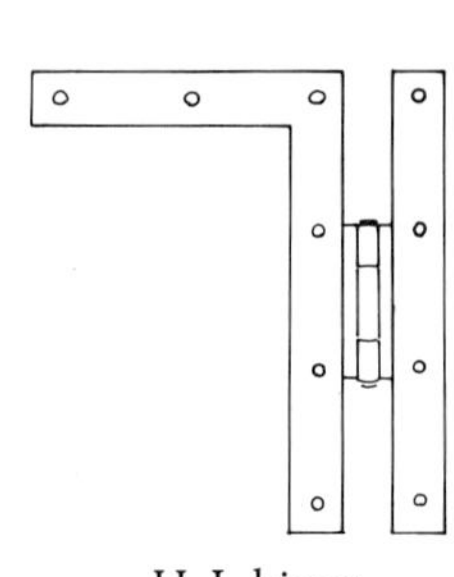
H–L hinge

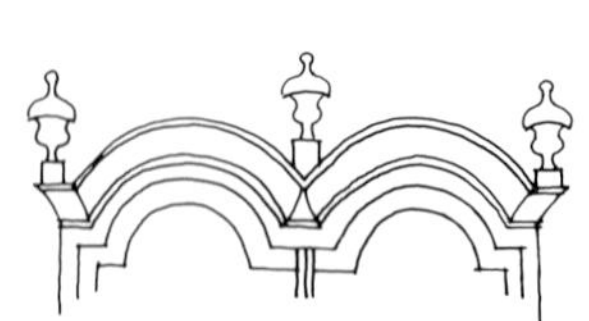
Double-hooded pediment

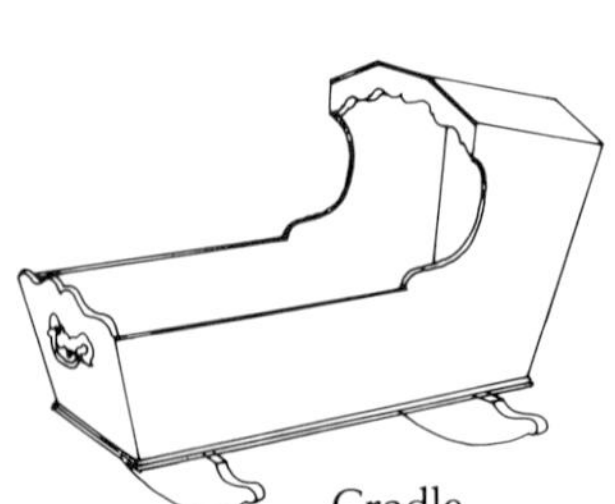
Cradle

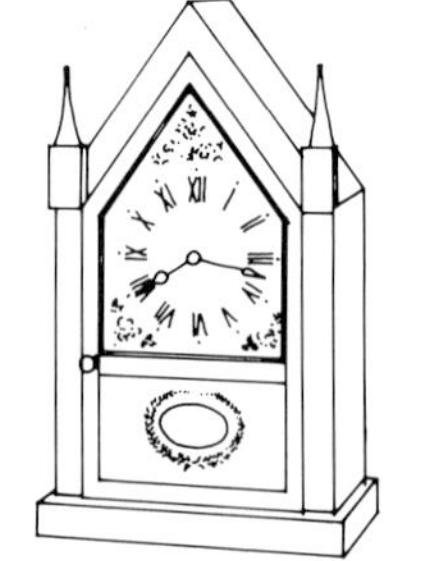
School House clock

Courting mirror

17–22). The style known as **Queen Anne,** named after the queen who reigned from 1702 to 1714, was introduced around 1700 and marked the beginning of a new and elegant style in American furniture design. It was uniquely based on the curve and assumed a grace and refinement formerly unknown in English furniture. The **Early Georgian period** began in the early 1700s and continued until about 1745, the year that introduced on a grand scale **Thomas Chippendale's** more heavy and masculine furniture. The Queen Anne Style had an immediate and lasting influence on Americans, who found in its timeless and versatile design a practicality that combined well with most styles. **Early Queen Anne** was less formal and ornate, with more simple forms employed. Later, the **Queen Anne Style** became more decorative and elegant and was employed in a more dignified setting.

Chippendale furniture (produced in England in the eighteenth century during the "Golden Age" of great cabinetmakers) graced the Georgian mansions of a new affluent society in America during the mid- and late eighteenth century. Thomas Chippendale (1718–1779) wrote *The Gentleman and Cabinet-Makers Director* in 1754, which had a tremendous influence on other cabinetmakers, who widely copied his designs. Chippendale furniture, therefore, was a product of a "school" rather than the work of a single man, and it incorporates designs from Queen Anne, Gothic, French, Adam, and Chinese styles. It uses both straight and curved lines and is large in scale, sturdy, and elegant. The use of Chippendale furniture generally marks the introduction of the **Late Georgian Style,** although Queen Anne furniture designs continued to be popular. Both Queen Anne and Chippendale furniture took on distinct regional differences in the colonies. Today, both styles are often appropriately combined when designing the Georgian Style.

Queen Anne Furniture (circa Early 1700s–1745)

- **General Characteristics:** Based on the cyma (S) curve. Graceful and dainty. May be formal and elegant or informal and simple,

Figure 9.17 Comfortable eighteenth-century English Queen Anne wingback host chairs with Queen Anne fiddleback chairs surround the traditional dining table. An element of surprise is the addition of a modern abstract painting. *(Courtesy of Armstrong World Industries.)*

QUEEN ANNE
(Georgian Period)
Wingback
Armchair
Fiddleback
Side Chair c. 1705
Fiddleback
Side Chair c. 1710
Stool
Drake
Pad
Club
Spanish
Late Queen Anne
Settee c. 1715
Claw & Ball
Slipper
Bracket
Tea Table
Highboy
Lowboy
Butterfly Hardware
Mirror
c. 1700
Mirror
c. 1720
Tall Case Clock

depending on upholstery employed. Use of mahogany. Introduction of lacquering an important innovation. The **scallop-shell motif** most typical and particularly employed for chairs, tables, secretaries, mirrors, and other pieces. Simple butterfly-shaped metal hardware.

Principal Furniture Types—Most Typical Pieces

- *Seating:* The **fiddleback side chair** is the most popular piece, distinguished by its unique fiddleback slat with the cyma-curve top rail and ***cabriole leg*** design (a leg shaped in a double curve with a swelling of the upper part). Use of the **pad** or **club foot.** ***Claw and ball foot*** employed late in Queen Anne period. **Wing chair,** an upholstered lounge chair with upper side units or "wings," developed about 1750. The **round-about chair** much in vogue. **Sofa** with high curved back.
- *Casepieces:* The **highboy** is tall chest of drawers arranged in two sections supported by turned or cabriole legs; **lowboy** is a low table with small drawers supported by turned or cabriole legs.
- *Tables:* **Tea table** is a delicate, small table supported on slender cabriole legs. **Tilt-top table** with a central pedestal and the **dropleaf table** popular pieces.

- **Fabrics:** Elegant formal damasks, velvets, taffetas, and brocades. For a less formal effect, a light background chintz with flower motifs popular. Also, simple cotton and wool fabrics. Colors: red, gold, muted green, and blue most common.
- **Accessories:** Oriental rugs. Oriental porcelain vases. Baroque brass or bronze chandeliers. Mirrors had tall vertical frame with characteristic S-curved top, often lacquered. Tall case clock (c. 1720) often lacquered.

CHIPPENDALE FURNITURE (CIRCA 1745–1790)

- **General Characteristics:** Sturdy and elegant, with vigorous carving in high relief. More masculine in form than Queen Anne. Mahogany almost exclusively used, with secondary woods utilized for accents. Ornate metal butterfly, stirrup, and ring hardware.

Principal Furniture Types—Most Typical Pieces

- *Seating:* **Yokeback** chair construction with upturned "shoulder" ends typical. Side chairs employ influence of rococo, Gothic, Chinese, and Adam designs. Modified and more ornate versions of Queen Anne. **Pierced ladderback chair.** Claw-and-ball foot. Cabriole leg with acanthus leaf or shell motif. Straight **Marborough leg** often employed. **Camelback sofa** with distinctive hump or humps on backrest unit. **Wing chair** similar to Queen Anne wing chair, but more masculine form; wings larger and flared. Marborough leg most typical.
- *Casepieces:* **Highboys, lowboys,** and **chest on chest** important casepieces. **Secretary** with ***bracket*** supports typical. Elaborate carvings. ***Breakfront cabinet*** with a projecting center section flanked with two side panels. **Kneehole desk** an important piece—sometimes massive. Casepieces often topped with carved ***finials*** and ***broken*** and ***scrolled pediments.*** Bracket supports, often with ***fret*** designs.
- *Tables:* **Piecrust tilt-top table** a favorite piece. **Folding card table.**
- *Beds:* The **Chinese Chippendale** style, with dramatic use of fret motif one of the most favored bed designs.
- **Fabrics:** Formal damasks particularly used; also brocades, taffetas, and velvets. Rich gold, yellow, deep red, blue, and "Williamsburg green" typical colors employed.
- **Accessories:** Chippendale-styled mirrors. Baroque brass or bronze chandeliers. Oriental rugs and porcelain. Wall sconces. Tall, elegantly carved case clocks.

The Neoclassic Period (circa 1790–1845) (Early Federal; Late Federal, Early American Empire, and Regency; Greek Revival or Late American Empire)

The last decade of the eighteenth century and first four decades of the nineteenth century were characterized by Neoclassicism. The Neoclassic Period is divided into three overlapping but identifiable subperiods: (1) the **Early Federal Period** (circa 1790–1804); (2) the **Late Federal, Early American Empire,** and **Regency Period** (circa 1804–1825); and (3) the **Greek Revival** or **Late American Empire Period** (circa 1825–1845).

Early Federal Period (circa 1790–1804). Furniture in America from about 1790 to 1804, known as Federal, was distinguished by light forms and straight lines, with some semicircular and elliptical curves. After the Revolutionary War, when Americans were weary of English domination in architecture and furnishings, Americans looked to France, Italy, and Greece for inspiration. Ironically, the Federal Period was dominated by the styles of English cabinetmakers **George Hepplewhite** (d. 1786), **Thomas Sheraton** (1751–1806), and

CHIPPENDALE
(Georgian Period)

HEPPLEWHITE
(Federal/Neoclassic Period)

SHERATON
(Federal/Neoclassic Period)
Chair Back
French Bracket Foot
Sheraton/
Hepplewhite
Side Chair
Sheraton Leg
Martha Washington
Chair
Armchair
Sofa
Chest with
French Bracket
Tambour
Table
Pembroke Table
Pedestal Table
Splayed leg
Architectural
Mirror
Sheraton Sideboard
Extension Table

the **Brothers Adam** (**Robert,** 1728–1792, and **James,** 1730–1794), whose designs grew out of classicism and the Louis XVI taste. The Adam influence in America, however, was seen more in interior architecture than in furnishings. These new styles were more delicate than Queen Anne and Chippendale, and the emphasis was on color and surface decoration rather than form. Dining-room furniture in the new style was particularly popular because the smaller scale made it suitable for most homes. During the Early Federal Period, America produced its most famous cabinetmaker, **Duncan Phyfe** (1768–1854).

In the Early Federal Period, monumental casepieces of the Chippendale Period were replaced by lighter forms. The highboy, lowboy, and cabriole leg went out of style. There were a number of innovations: the buffet; the china cabinet; the dining-room extension table; the ***tambour front*** secretary or desk, with a flexible shutter made of thin wood strips on canvas or linen; the ***Martha Washington chair,*** called a "Lolling chair"; and numerous small tables for a variety of functions—the sewing-bag table being a notable example.

The designs of Hepplewhite and Sheraton were freely exchanged, and frequently a furniture item would incorporate designs of both. For example, a chair may have had a Sheraton-styled back and Hepplewhite-styled legs and been labeled either Sheraton, Hepplewhite, or both—Hepplewhite/Sheraton. Some features were consistently employed by both styles such as the ***French bracket foot,*** oval and round hardware, and ***crossbanding*** (the practice of veneering small sections of lighter wood opposite to the grain of the wood surface). Stretchers were rarely employed by either.

In spite of the similarities and overlapping designs, Hepplewhite and Sheraton furniture had distinctive characteristics.

Hepplewhite Furniture

- **General Characteristics:** Hepplewhite furniture was a bridge between the Chippendale Style and the Neoclassic Style. This can be seen in the use of a modified Chippendale scroll on casepieces and mirrors, the camelback sofa, and the serpentine front. Typical Hepplewhite leg straight, square, tapered, and either plain or fluted, and it terminates with or without a ***spade foot.*** Use of inlay—especially the eagle, ***paterae,*** and bellflower motifs. Brass ring hardware. Glass and china knobs a later feature.

Principal Furniture Types—Most Typical Pieces

- *Seating:* Chair backs in the form of shields, hearts, or ovals, with the honeysuckle, shell of flowers, and ***Prince of Wales plume*** favored motifs. Sofas have upholstered curved or camel backs with arms that flare back from the seat. **Windsor chair** modified, and the **rocking chair** came into favor during the first quarter of the eighteenth century. (Note: The Windsor chair today is more associated with the Early Settlement period. See p. 8.)
- *Casepieces:* **Sideboard** among most important pieces, supported on six legs with concave front ends. **Tambour secretaries** an innovation, often displaying scroll pediments. **China cabinets** and **bookcases** popular. **Chests** had straight or serpentine fronts. (Hepplewhite employed crossbanding in straight lines on casepieces.)
- *Tables:* **Dining tables** given special importance. Usually oval with typical straight supports. ***Pembroke*** tables with drop leaves either oval or serpentine. ***Pier table*** and **sewing-bag table** with typical legs well-known pieces.
- *Beds:* **Four-poster bed** with high, slender, fluted or spiralled posts.

- **Fabrics:** Formal and elegant damasks, velvets, brocades, and taffetas. Fabrics and wallpapers with French and classical themes in pastel colors, particularly soft blues and greens.
- **Accessories:** Mirrors strongly influenced by Adam and Chippendale. Mirrors often convex, with the eagle motif. (The eagle, America's new official national emblem, a favorite motif.) Elegant crystal chandeliers. Wedgwood china and medallions. Oriental or French rugs. Intricate stitchery crafts. Tall, slender clock cases. Two especially popular clocks were the "pillar and scroll" shelf clock and the Willard banjo clock. Fine silver and glass accessories.

Sheraton Furniture

- **General Characteristics:** Dominance of straight lines. Simplicity of design. Graceful and well proportioned. Influenced primarily by the Brothers Adam, Hepplewhite, and Louis XVI Style in France. Employed classical motifs such as the urn, festoons, swags, scrolls, pendant flowers, rosettes, and oval paterae. Arabesques and other motifs painted on furniture were a later feature. Typical Sheraton leg is straight, tapered, and reeded and terminates in a ***thimble foot.***

Principal Furniture Types—Most Typical Pieces

- *Seating:* Chair backs square, but in a variety of designs with or without arms. Sofas have carved wood railing across the back, and armrest extends straight above the leg, leaving an opening between the armrest and upholstery. Sofas sometimes extremely long.

- *Casepieces:* **Chests** have bowed fronts. **Buffets** have convex front ends. **Secretaries** have finials, often in the form of an urn. (Sheraton employed oval crossbanding on his casepieces.)
- *Tables:* **Dining tables** typically supported on two or more columns with three or four splayed reeded legs. Numerous **small tables** with straight or pedestal supports. **Sofa table** an innovation. Many **dual-purpose tables.**
- *Beds:* **Four poster** topped by a canopy or terminating in a carved vase. Sheraton was first to design **twin beds.**

- **Fabrics:** (See Hepplewhite.)
- **Accessories:** Mirrors architectural in form with gilt frame consisting of side colonnette supports. Some were horizontal, made in three sections to hang over the mantel. Some combined features of Hepplewhite and Sheraton. (See Hepplewhite.)

Duncan Phyfe

Among the many fine cabinetmakers of whom New York and other design centers boasted, the most famous was Duncan Phyfe. Phyfe maintained his New York workshop from 1795 to 1847. The enormous furniture output of those years falls into two periods: (1) his early (and many critics considered his best) work inspired by Adam, Hepplewhite, and Sheraton, with some Regency features and (2) his later work influenced by French Empire styles. Phyfe more than any other is credited with having established the Empire Style in America. His designs during the Greek Revival period followed the current fashion and were heavy and massive but usually had a monumental grace.

Although Phyfe's work covered a wide range of styles, his name is associated more with Regency than any other, and his furniture was called New York Regency. He is the only American to whom is attributed a "period furniture style."

- **General Characteristics (Early Duncan Phyfe Furniture)** Strikingly fine proportions. Clean, simple lines with freehand curves. Structural soundness. Restraint in the use of ornamentation, which consists of turning, fluting, reeding, and ***foliate carving.*** Principal motifs were the lyre, palm leaves, holly, laurel, small acanthus, lion's heads, medallions, wheat, and swags. Some early pieces so similar to Sheraton's that they could be mistaken for reproductions.

Principal Furniture Types—Most Typical Pieces

- *Seating:* Low backs rolled over top rail. Back panels have cross splat or cane. The lyre is distinctive. Seats are of the ***slip type.*** Legs are straight and reeded or ***saber-shaped,*** ending in animal paws. Some chairs have ***curule-shaped*** supports reminiscent of Pompeii. Early sofas followed Sheraton design. Phyfe sofas have a reeded front rail in sleigh form, often with the lyre motif. Feet are reeded, curule, or ***cornucopia. Récamier sofa*** followed lines of the French Empire Style.
- *Tables:* Numerous tables designed for a variety of functions. Some of most popular include the ***console,*** a simple pedestal supported on splayed legs; ***card table,*** with a folding top; ***library table,*** long and narrow with drop leaves supported on ends by lyres or columns; and the ***dining table.*** (Phyfe is credited with having invented the accordian extension table.)

- **Fabrics:** Similar to Hepplewhite and Sheraton.
- **Accessories:** One of the best known Phyfe accessories is the ***cheval,*** a full-figure-length mirror mounted on trestles swinging from vertical posts.

Late Federal, Early American Empire, and Regency Period (circa 1804–1825). Furniture of the second phase of the Neoclassic period in America, from about 1804 to 1825, is referred to in style as Late Federal, Early Empire, or Regency Style, because it was marked by the continuing Federal period in America, the Napoleonic period in France, and the Regency period in England. Furniture manufacturing was dominated in America by Duncan Phyfe, who developed furniture along the lines of English Regency and French Empire Styles, although other notable cabinetmakers of the period included Charles-Honore Lannuier and Joseph Meeks of New York, Samuel McIntire in Salem, and John Seymour in Boston.

Ancient motifs from Rome, Greece, and Egypt, particularly favored by Napoleon, were combined to create a new style. Napoleon actually dictated the new style to classic artist **Jacques-Louis David** (1748–1825) and decorators **Percier** and **Fontaine.**

A renewed interest in the "Golden Age" of ancient Grecian and Roman architecture influenced designers to build magnificent temple mansions employing the Three Orders of Architecture for both exterior and interior treatment in America. The **English Regency Period** (the time of George IV's Regency) flourished during this period, with furniture interpreted in more delicate terms. Leaders in England were **Thomas Hope**

DUNCAN PHYFE
(Federal, American Empire, and Regency)

Curule form chair

Ancient Grecian sabre leg chair

Side chair with sabre leg

Lyre back chair

Sofa with cornucopia legs

Window bench

Card table

Library table

Accordion extension table

Cheval glass with column supports

Lyre motif

Cornucopia legs

Lion's paw foot with caster

Lion's head pull

AMERICAN EMPIRE

Klismos Chair

Scroll Chair (animal legs)

Recamier (Cornucopia leg)

Settee

Pier Table

Table (falcon support)

Caryatid Support

Buffet (Paw foot)

Sleigh Bed (Egyptian column)

Girandole Mirror (Bull's eye)

Banjo Clock

Acanthus leaf carving

(1770–1831) and **Thomas Sheraton.** ***Biedermeir furniture*** in Germany was an extreme simplification of the style.

- **General Characteristics:** Concepts of the French Empire and English Regency Styles were transplanted to America through periodicals published abroad and sent to the New Republic and by imported pieces that were copied. Furnishings generally heavy, massive, and masculine. Supports included lion-paw feet and figural elements of swans and dolphins. Large areas of plain veneer appeared. Many surfaces enhanced with classical ormolu mounts and brass inlay. Typical motifs: the lyre, honeysuckle, cornucopia, honey bee, laurel wreaths, swags, festoons, crowns, torches, animal forms, and ***caryatids.***

  Furniture made early in the period was well designed and expertly finished; but after the second decade of the nineteenth century, both design and workmanship deteriorated, and heavy, ostentatious furniture became the vogue. Dominant woods: rosewood, mahogany, and ebony.

Principal Furniture Types—Most Typical Pieces

- *Seating:* Grecian Klismos chair, Roman curule, or X-based chairs dominant. Some chairs had heavy scrolls with winged or caryatid supports. Popular Boston rocker became higher, with broad top rail. Window bench in vogue. Many interpretations of the Grecian couch. Récamier similar to the Roman couch.
- *Casepieces:* Heavy sideboards supported on short legs with brass lion-paw feet and lion-mask pulls. Wardrobe introduced.
- *Tables:* French-styled **pier table** (a side table with mirror backdrop) assumed extraordinary designs. Small tables designed to serve multiple purposes.
- *Beds:* **Sleigh bed** was introduced.
- **Fabrics:** Elegant damasks, brocades, and velvets. Green, yellow, red, gold, and blue in strong chroma. Also white and black. Motifs drawn from ancient Egypt, Greece, and Rome.
- **Accessories:** Include the well-known "banjo" clock. The "bull's-eye" rounded mirror with convex or concave glass, often surmounted by an eagle, continued to be popular. ***Torchère lamps.*** Harp and lyre. Crystal and oil-vessel chandeliers. Ceiling fan (***punkah***) used in Southern United States. Ormolu decorations applied to furnishings. Pier mirrors with column frames. Bowls supported by a columned base. Other accessories reflecting Egyptian, Roman, and Grecian themes.

The Greek Revival Period (circa 1825–1845). The third phase of the Neoclassic Style in America is known as Greek Revival or Late American Empire. Duncan Phyfe, who continued to produce furniture until 1847, followed the fashion trends but was more restrained than most cabinetmakers of the day, among whom were Forbes & Son, Thomas Astens, and Joseph Meeks of New York; Antoine Gabriel Quervelle and the Loud Brothers of Philadelphia (the latter made pianos); and William Hancock of Boston. All these designers worked in distinct regional styles during the 1820s and 1830s.

- **General Characteristics:** Furniture of the Greek Revival Style bold and monumental in character, following the taste of England and France. Many pieces heavier versions of the Empire Style. After 1820, furniture showed definite American divergence from English tradition. Supports became large animal-paw feet with hairy shanks combined with a profusion of deep, heavy carving of acanthus leaves, cornucopias, plumes, and diamond-patterned pineapple motifs and ormolu. Legs had ornate turnings and twisted reeding. Swan and dolphin favorite decorations.

  In late 1830s carving superseded by plain surfaces and simple lines—known as "pillar and scroll." Highly figured veneers standard as surface features. Darkened mahogany surfaces lavishly gilded, painted, and stenciled with abstract linear patterns, Greek ***anthemia,*** and large fruit and floral motifs.

Principal Furniture Types—Most Typical Pieces

- *Seating:* **Gondola** reflecting the French Restoration Style. Heavily scrolled and profusely carved sofas.
- *Casepieces:* Enormous **wardrobe** with plain wood doors and stencil trim a typical piece.
- *Tables:* **Pier table** of extraordinary design. Pedestal or pillar table of plain design. **Table** with pineapple-motif pedestal and splayed, hairy legs with bold acanthus design. Pillar pedestal **card table.**

- **Fabrics:** Increased use of cotton. Continued popularity of elegant fabrics. Horsehair often used for seat upholstery. Stripes became broader, in contrasting colors. Fabrics printed with bold medallions on an open ground with borders of anthemia and Greek key patterns popular. Colors strong, with golden yellow and crimson red being favorites.

GREEK REVIVAL
(The Neoclassic Period)

- **Accessories:** American manufacturers at Boston and Sandwich, Massachusetts, produced fine glass that was pierced, cut, and colored. Silver tea sets, porcelain, and stoneware also of American make. Oil-burning lighting devices decorated in classical or rococo designs. Dolphin-shaped glass candlesticks and ***hurricane glass*** over candles. Brass fireplace and lighting fixtures.

The French Styles in America (Late Eighteenth Century to Present)

Homes built by French settlers during the eighteenth century in America (described in Chapter 1) had a particular influence on domestic architecture and furnishings based on eighteenth-century French styles that has continued into the twentieth century.

When **Louis XIV** (1643–1715) finished his magnificent palace of **Versailles** outside of Paris, European designers began imitating the grandeur of its interiors and furnishings. But the extravagant style of Louis XIV had little impact on America. It was under the reign of his grandson, Louis XV (1715–1774), that the ***rococo*** style emerged—a style enthusiastically embraced in America and still widely imitated. This ornately curved style was influenced by **Madame du Pompadour** and then **Madame du Barry,** who lived at the palace of Versailles and helped promote the feminine and delicate style. After Louis XV's death, the reign of **Louis XVI** (1774–1793) marked a significant change in French design. With the discovery of Pompeii and a renewed interest in Classicism, the new style employed the use of straight lines and classical motifs. Both the Louis XV and XVI Styles reflected the love of luxury, extravagance, beauty, and frivolity—which paved the way to the French Revolution.

The Empire Style (1804–1815) was so called because of the association with the French emperor Napoleon. The Empire Style was a return to the classic lines of the ancient Greek, Roman, and Egyptian prototypes. This style had an important influence on American furniture design in the early and late American Empire periods (circa 1804–1845).

Furniture of the Louis XV period was later simplified by those who did not live at the court. They produced an extremely popular and versatile style that Europeans and Americans have termed ***Provincial French,*** which may be successfully dressed up or down. The choice of fabrics employed often determines the degree of formality. Excellent reproductions of these exquisite styles, along with the more informal interpretations, are currently being produced by manufacturers, sometimes with a surprising degree of authenticity.

Country French is the most rustic and informal style from France. Its charm results from incorporating handcrafted furniture and accessories reflecting the distinctive flavor of the French countryside.

Italian Provincial is a term coined by Tom Kindel, of the American firm Kindel Furniture Co., after a decade of assembling a choice collection of furniture designed in Italy and France during the latter half of the eighteenth century. Italian Provincial has much in common with the Louis XVI Style but is much more restrained and characterized by dignified simplicity. This style has had limited use in the United States.

Louis XV Style (1715–1774)

- **General Characteristics:** Elegant, graceful, and elaborately carved. Strong feminine influence. Dainty and more lightly scaled than Louis XIV. Free-form style employed. Asymmetrical decoration typical. Court French Louis XV employs gilded, painted, and ***chinoiserie lacquered*** surfaces. A variety of local and imported woods employed. Exotic woods especially used for ***marquetry.*** Lavish use of ormolu mounts.

Principal Furniture Types—Most Typical Pieces

- *Seating:* ***Fauteuil*** (open-arm chair) and ***bergère*** (closed-arm chair), with or without wings, classic pieces. Both employ the curved ***cabriole leg*** and upturned ***dolphin nose foot.*** Extended ***chaise longue*** is luxurious piece. Fashionable ***marquise*** was an extra-wide bergère. Chairs typically made for variety of functions. **Sofas** and **day beds** assumed various forms. ***Canape sofa*** had unbroken back and inward-curving ends. **Stools** followed typical curved lines.
- *Casepieces:* **Commode** (chest of drawers)—often with a marble top—most characteristic piece. Chinese themes and gilded, lacquered, and painted finishes typical. ***Armoire*** (large upright storage piece) with flowing carved decoration an essential item. ***Secretaire*** and ***console*** are also well-known casepieces. Small **lady's writing desk** one of most appealing innovations of eighteenth century.
- *Tables:* Tables to meet all needs designed employing typical curved lines, treatments, and motifs popular in the Louis XV Style. One of most important was **bureau plat** (a large table-desk).
- *Beds:* Lavishly carved and draped canopy bed of the Louis XIV period remained fashionable in palaces, but began to be replaced by the ***alcove bed.***
- **Fabrics:** Formal and elegant. Tapestries, cut velvets, brocatelles. Brocades and silks often with small patterns. Asymmetri-

LOUIS XV
(The French Style)

cally arranged flowers and flowing ribbons popular motifs. Colors in soft pastels, gold, green, Venetian blue, and peach.

- **Accessories:** Aubusson, Savonnerie, or Oriental rugs (see Chapter 7). Elaborate crystal chandeliers. Asymmetrical candle holders and wall ***sconces.*** Clocks with swirling metal designs in the Louix XV expression. Mirrors small with ornate frames. Perforated metal and other elaborately treated firescreens. Oil paintings in ornate gold frames. French and Oriental porcelains. Busts of royalty and nobility.

Louis XVI Style (1774–1793)

- **General Characteristics:** Distinguished by renewed interest in architectural forms and ornament of ancient Greece and Rome—in particular, discovery of the ancient city of Pompeii, which had been covered by volcanic ash for centuries. Strict adherence to rectangular forms and straight lines replaced flowing free forms of previous style. Feminine influence at court continued with Louis XVI's queen, Marie Antoinette, who supported Neoclassicism. Furnishings had finishes often painted and gilded in pale colors. Exquisitely finished wood employed—especially mahogany, rosewood, and exotic woods for expanded marquetry. Ormolu continued in use with designs assuming classical forms. Laurel and acanthus, rosettes, wreaths, festoons, lyres, swans, urns, ribbons (the love knot), egg and dart, bound arrows, and animals were important motifs. Carving simple and more delicate. Inset of porcelain plaques became popular in fine furniture. ***Gesso*** work applied to furniture, then painted.

Principal Furniture Types—Most Typical Pieces

- *Seating:* **Fauteuil** and **bergère** chairs characterized by use of straight lines. Most distinguishing feature of Louix XVI furniture: the supports, which are clearly seen in seating pieces. Legs straight and tapered—either square or round with vertical or spiral reeding or fluting terminating in a slender thimblelike shape—often surmounted by a square block enclosing a carved rosette. Sofas or **canapes** followed form of chairs. Backs of chairs and sofas straight or oval. Innovation called the ***confident*** was large canape with seat added at each end. **Day beds** popular. **Benches** long and narrow. **Stools** followed form of chairs.
- *Casepieces:* **Desks, commodes, cabinets,** and **secretaries** with floral decorations; stone, wood, and porcelain inlays; ormolu mounts; ***galleries;*** and brass or gilt moldings. **Armoire** with straight forms. Roll-top desk very popular. Small drop-leaf desks made in great numbers.
- *Tables:* **Bureau plat** remained a favorite. The **console,** a decorative table to go against the wall, and the **console-buffet,** used as a serving table for the dining room, both well-known pieces. **Dining table** became a necessity because, for first time, rooms specified for dining. Numerous small tables designed; among most important was the ***bouillotte***—a small circular gaming table with a metal gallery edge and the ***gueridon*** for candles and small articles. Marble tops typical.
- *Beds:* For most beds, head and foot boards of the same height, following the characteristic designs of chair backs. These were frequently placed in alcoves with the long side against the wall. Favored bed of Marie Antoinette was the **"angel" bed,** with a much shortened canopy or ***lambrequin*** that supported lavish hangings.

- **Fabrics:** Formal silks, damasks, velvets, and tapestries. Colors in soft pale colors. Motifs drawn from classical Greece and Rome. Bouquets and baskets of flowers and the love knot with flowing ribbon motif especially popular. Small floral prints alternating with stripes—one of most typical designs. ***Toile de Jouy*** (cotton or linen with pastoral and ancient classical scenes) employed for a less formal feeling.

- **Accessories:** Elegant and formal accessories of gold gilt. Mirrors architectural and rectangular. Frames painted and gilded. ***Trumeau*** usually had upper section painted with Sèvres vases and delicate scrolls. Sconces and candelabra with urns, festoons, columns, and other classical motifs. Ormolu clocks for mantels and hanging clocks of gilt bronze surmounted by a fluttering bow fashionable. Elaborate fireplace accessories. Exquisite crystal chandeliers. Aubusson, Savonnerie, and Oriental rugs. French masters' oil paintings in ornate gold frames. Busts of royalty and nobility often sculpted in marble.

Provincial French and Country French

- **General Characteristics:** Furnishings influenced by the Court styles of Kings Louis XIV, XV, and XVI but expressed in simpler, more affordable expressions. Simple, unadorned surfaces. Furniture designed for family functions rather than court life. Pieces ranged from expensive furnishings (mostly

LOUIS XVI
(The French Style)

PROVINCIAL FRENCH

associated with the Provincial French Style, which flourished primarily in Paris) to inexpensive furnishings (mostly associated with the Country French Style popular in the country provinces), with regional and social-economic differences. Oak, walnut, and fruitwood most-used woods. Louis XV Style emerged as most prominent influence for Provincial French furniture. Country French distinguished by homemade crafted pieces. Distinctively charming and homey. Sturdy ***distressed*** furniture influenced by Louis XIV. Rural and rustic feeling, with both straight and curved lines employed.

Principal Furniture Types—Most Typical Pieces

- *Seating:* Ladder-back chair with a rush seat and ***salamander*** back. Simplified version of the Louis XV fauteuil typical of the Provincial French Style. Stool with a rush seat popular in the Country French Style.
- *Casepieces:* Simplified Louis XV **commode, buffet,** and **armoire** most important pieces. **Hutch** (open cupboard) and **cupboards** with "chicken wire" grills.
- *Tables:* Long, end, and other functional tables in Louis XV Style. Small **breading table** for bread making an important item.
- *Beds:* Closed bed or ***lit clos*** (with draw curtains for warmth) an essential piece in the Country French home.

- **Fabrics:** Formal Provincial French fabrics include velvets, tapestries, damasks, and silks often employing motifs popular at court. Cottons, wool, and linen used for informal Provincial French and Country French. Toile de Jouy one of the most distinctive fabrics employed to establish either style approach. Plaids, checks, stripes, and small, quaint prints. Colors: red, blue, white, and apple green especially dominant.
- **Accessories:** For a formal Provincial French direction, accessories similar to the Louis XV and XVI Styles typical. Among informal accessories, both decorative and utilitarian items including the ***panetière*** (bread box) and items of pewter, copper, wood, and painted tin. ***Primitive paintings, silhouettes,*** brightly painted pottery, and pictures of song birds. ***Tole lamps.***

French Empire (circa 1804–1815)

- **General Characteristics:** Empire furniture characterized by massiveness, bisymmetry, and rectangularity emphasized by rigid edges and right angles, with function and comfort sacrificed for show. Most furniture an adaptation of preexisting types. Mahogany was most preferred, with ebony, rosewood, and other exotic woods also highly prized. Large veneered surfaces replaced marquetry and lacquer. Most furniture supports were caryatids, but other common props were sphinxes and Egyptian busts. Elaborate ormolu mounts used in profusion. Dominant motif was capital letter *N* enclosed in a laurel wreath tied with a bow of ribbon. Other motifs—the imperial eagle, military symbols, and Egyptian and classical Grecian and Roman themes.

Principal Furniture Types—Most Typical Pieces

- *Seating:* Chairs marked by broad, simple lines—both straight and curved. Back legs usually straight, with front legs straight, saber, or in form of a winged lion. ***Gondola chair,*** with back curved downward to form the arm, a great favorite. **Side chair** made without arms to accommodate soldier's saber. ***Meridienne,*** a small sofa or day bed with one end higher than the other, in fashion. ***Reclining couch*** with flaring swan-neck end pieces named for the famous Madame Récamier. **X-stool** in great demand, since only those of rank permitted to sit on chairs before the emperor.
- *Casepieces:* Casepieces massive and elaborately decorated with ormolu. Fashionable **commode** has oblong marble top resting on a square or octagonal base (plinth) and was flanked by caryatids enriched with ormolu. **Sideboard** with cupboard below popular. **Bookcases** enormous. **Fall-front secretary** and **roll-top desk** followed prevailing style but had a number of adaptations.

- *Tables:* **Circular** or **octagonal tables** made in wide diversity of types to serve particular needs. **Dining tables** round and massive, supported by columns, classical figures, or animals. **Bureau plat** continued to be popular. Most essential piece of Empire furniture was **console**—placed against wall, had a rectangular or semicircular top and was supported by a variety of typical supports; back panel was often a mirror. Numerous side tables and center tables of varying sizes. Three-legged ***tripod*** popular. ***Lavabo***—a tripod with a porcelain wash basin—was an innovation. **Bouillotte** and **gueridon** common. Tall **pedestals** to support statues and vases popular. **Toilet tables** came into use.
- *Beds:* Heavy and majestic beds designed to be placed lengthwise against the wall. **Boat-bed,** with head and foot the same height and connected by a segmental

FRENCH EMPIRE

line, was characteristic. **Tent** or **field bed** (a tribute to Napoleon) was a four-poster with a canopy resembling a tent.

- **Fabrics:** Silks lavishly employed for furnishings. (The silk industry was revolutionized in 1801 by the invention of the Jacquard loom.) Taffetas, damasks, satins, brocades, and velvets in high demand. Fabrics typically had open ground with Empire motifs of contrasting colors. Brilliant green (Empire green) was favored color, along with gold, red, crimson, blue, black, and white. Popular motifs were letter *N* in a laurel wreath, bees, stars, swans, and eagles. Also, motifs drawn from ancient Egypt, Greece, and Rome, including the fret, honeysuckle, vase forms, anthemion, caryatids, heads of Apollo, and heads of horses and rams.
- **Accessories:** For the most part, accessories represented adjuncts of the Napoleonic reign or items of classical or Egyptian origin. Psyche was a large swinging mirror enclosed in a rectangular frame supported by two columns—always richly decorated. Dressing-table mirrors and portable mirrors were designed especially for ladies. Clocks of the pendulum type produced in abundance. Clocks usually rested on marble bases incorporated into a group of mythological figures, often covered by a glass dome. Sèvres porcelain pieces bearing Empire designs, Greek vases, bronze table lamps, busts, statues, and engravings of Napoleon's family and officers were displayed in profusion.

Victorian Furniture (circa 1840–1900)

Queen Victoria reigned in England from 1837 to 1901, and during this period a variety of architectural styles and furnishings were designed bearing her name (see Chapter 1). During the Victorian Era, imitations of furniture styles of the past were interpreted in various manifestations in America. These primarily included **Gothic, rococo,** and a concurrent concept called **Renaissance Revival** Style, which was typified by massive forms and deeply carved ornamentation. Merging into the Renaissance Revival Style was the regeneration of the **Louis XVI** Style (see pp. 301–302). This trend was introduced into America by the Paris–New York firms of Rinquet Le Prince and Marsotte. Their furniture followed late-eighteenth-century French precedents in both form and ornament and reached the height of American popularity in the 1860s.

Two names that stand out as predominant in America during the Victorian Era are New York–based **John Belter** (1804–1863), whose rococo style dominated the mid-nineteenth century and the English designer **Charles Eastlake** (1836–1906), whose "Reform" furniture was popular from the 1870s through 1890s. Eastlake's furniture was principally drawn from Gothic and Renaissance themes. He wrote his influential *Hints on Household Taste* in 1868.

Much Victorian furniture, which for so long was maligned and considered no better than junk, is now sought after as valuable antiques. Many Victorian-furniture admirers are enthusiastically restoring, refinishing, and reintroducing these treasured pieces. After moving from the parlor to attic to junkyard to antiques shops, Victorian furniture has returned to use in contemporary homes.

Victorian furniture today has been greatly moderated from the stereotype of a century ago. Both young and old are finding that nineteenth-century furniture is a good mixer and, to the surprise of many, is often at its best in a modern structural setting.

BELTER ROCOCO, EASTLAKE GOTHIC/RENAISSANCE, AND CLASSIC VICTORIAN (CIRCA 1840–1900)

- **General Characteristics:** Elaborate adaptations of **French Rococo, Second Empire, Neoclassic, Gothic, Renaissance, Oriental, Elizabethan,** and **Jacobean** prototypes were designed during the Victorian Era. Usually, particular styles of furnishings were fashioned to complement their Victorian architectural counterparts. However, drawing from the numerous furniture styles of the Victorian Era, which varied from region to region, three styles consistently can be identified as those most popularly associated with the period and considered collector's pieces today:

1. **Belter Rococo.** Although Victorian furniture was a mix of many stylistic influences, the image most commonly evoked by Americans is the lavish Belter or Victorian Rococo parlor with its florid walls and carpets, marble-topped tables, and excessively carved suites adapted from the Louis XV Style. Lest the room seem bare, accessories of all types were placed on every surface and hung on all available wall space. Woods most commonly used for Victorian Rococo furniture were walnut, rosewood, and mahogany.
2. The **Eastlake** or **Gothic/Renaissance** parlor laden with furniture and accessories recalling Renaissance and Gothic forms was also one of the most popular Victorian styles. This direction employed more lightly scaled and simplified machine-made furniture having basically rectilinear forms with incised, carved, and turned design applications. Many American cabinetmakers adapted and

VICTORIAN
(Belter Rococo)

VICTORIAN
(Eastlake–Renaissance)

Tufted Side Chair
Turned straight leg

Eastlake Chair

Walnut Settee

Renaissance Revival
sofa with cresting

Pedestal

Side Table
Incised decoration

Dresser

Wooten Patent Desk
Eastlake influence

Detail

Eastlake Bed

modified the designs of Eastlake for use in American Victorian homes. Oak was the most typicial wood used for Eastlake furniture.

3. Regeneration of the **Louis XVI** or **Classic Victorian** Style followed the other two previous styles in popularity. Furniture was simple in expression, delicately scaled and decorated, borrowing themes from the French Louix XVI period.

Principal Furniture Types—Most Typical Pieces

- *Seating:* **Belter "lady's and gentleman's"** chairs showing rococo influence. Elaborately carved **high-back** side chair. **Balloon-back** chair in Louis XV Style. ***Vis-à-vis*** sofa allowing occupants to face in opposite directions. Carved rosewood ***crested*** sofa. **Classic** Victorian chair. **Renaissance Revival** sofa with gilt incised lines, cresting, and turned legs. Walnut Eastlake ***settee*** and chair. **Gothic "rose window"** chair.
- *Casepieces:* Laminated round ***bureau*** (dresser). Belter rosewood **console** with ***étagère.*** Eastlake dresser with simple chest of drawers and rectangular mirror design. **Wooten patent desk** displaying influence of Eastlake with incising, short spindles, and characteristic cresting.
- *Tables:* Rococo rosewood and Eastlake center tables. Eastlake side table with incised decoration. Tall Eastlake-style pedestal stand.
- *Beds:* Carved and laminated Belter rosewood bed. Massive and lavishly carved Eastlake Renaissance bed. Iron or brass bed with Gothic arch design.

- **Fabrics:** Formal brocades, plush velvet, lace, and damasks. Use of black horsehair upholstery. Large and small patterns profusely employed, with flower, foliage, and fruit motifs most common. Use of gold fringe. Colors: deep red, dark pinks, mauves, purples, golds, browns, and dark greens.
- **Accessories:** Gilt pier mirror. ***Whatnot*** shelves laden with ***bric-a-brac.*** Small bronze statuary. Dried flowers under glass domes. Patterned rugs and carpets. Collections of all types displayed. Electrified gasolier chandeliers (often formed of brass or wrought iron). Tinted and painted glass lamps. Silhouette and charcoal portraits. Currier and Ives prints. ***Blackamoor statutes.*** Picture viewer for ***daguerreotype*** photographs prominently displayed on a tabletop.

General Classification of Furniture Styles

A clarification of the terms ***antique, reproduction, adaptation,*** and ***period style*** or ***traditional,*** can aid the consumer when purchasing furniture.

Antique. A piece of furniture or work of art that, according to United States law, must be at least 100 years old.

Reproduction. A copy of an original. Some reproductions are done so meticulously that only the well-trained eye can detect the difference, yet some modern reproductions are far from exact copies.

Adaptation. A piece in which only some elements from the original have been adapted to a contemporary design.

Period style. A term used to designate a single item or a complete interior, including the architectural background, furniture, and decorative arts prevalent in a specific country or a particular time in history. This style is often referred to as ***traditional.***

Furniture styles typically fall into two general categories: (1) **period** or **traditional** (see p. 320) and (2) **modern** or **contemporary.**

Contemporary and Modern Furnishings

Contemporary. Current styles are called ***contemporary,*** often referring to eclectic designs that to some degree have been adapted from historical or modern influences. For example, "classic contemporary" is a modified historical style marked by a fresh interpretation suitable for today's home. Many furniture manufacturers employ authentic motifs and carvings. The grace and dignity of Old World artistry is combined with contemporary originality to produce fine furniture that has timeless beauty and appeal. Additionally, these furnishings are produced employing the latest advancements in technology and materials, making them sturdy and durable.

Modern. At any time in history when a new art form emerges that breaks all ties with previous design forms—whether in music, architecture, or furniture—it is referred to as "modern." Today's modern furniture design is principally an expression of the twentieth century and aptly suggests the tempo of modern Americans. The roots of modernism can be traced to the Industrial Revolution in Europe. With the invention of new materials and technology, a fresh approach to furnishings gradually emerged. (See Chapter 2 for an outline of the development of modern architecture and design.) Since the early twentieth century, modern design has gone through many stages, each contributing something of lasting value. Some furniture designs of the modern period have become twentieth-century classics. Since a complete study of the development of modern furniture is beyond the scope of this introductory text, only a brief outline of the major design directions and contributors is presented—basic material of interest and value to both the consumer and beginning interior designer. The following discussion complements the discussion of modern architecture in Chapter 2.

- *Earliest modern furniture.* As early as 1840, **Michael Thonet** developed his process for bending wood—a process still employed by manufacturers today. His **bentwood rocker** and **Vienna café** chair remain classic pieces.
- *The Arts and Crafts Movement in England and America* (latter half of the nineteenth century) was a revolt against machine-made products and a movement advocating a return to handcrafted furnishings. Inspiration was drawn from medieval and Gothic prototypes. Oak was the most common wood used. Furniture was simple, sturdy, and structural. Leading furniture designers included

  England: **William Morris,** founder of the movement; **Charles Eastlake; Edward W. Godwin; Philip Webb; Ernest Gimson;** and **Charles F. A. Voysey,** all of whom created simple handcrafted furniture considered early expressions of modernism.

  America: **Gustav Stickley, Frank Lloyd Wright, Henry Hobson Richardson,** and **Charles and Henry Greene** designed handcrafted structural furniture based on their own distinctive interpretations of the movement.

  Furniture of the Arts and Crafts Movement in the United States is also known as ***Mission*** Style.
- *Art Nouveau* (circa 1890–1910). A decorative style based on nature—especially the lines found in nature—flourished primarily in Europe and America. Art Nouveau motifs include flowers, meandering vines, the female form, reptiles, waves of the ocean, the sinuous whiplash line, and flowing forms of all types. Leading contributors included

  France: When **Samuel Bing** opened his Paris studio, La Maison de l'Art Nouveau, in 1895, the style was officially named. **Hector Guimard, Emile Gallé,** and **Louis Majorelle** were known for their exquisite and elegant furniture.

  Belgium: **Henri van de Velde,** considered the spokesman for the style, opened his own furniture studio in Brussels.

  England: **Arthur Heygate Mackmurdo** and **Charles F. A. Voysey** created furniture in a more conservative and symmetrical manner, typical of the English approach.

  Spain: **Antoni Gaudi,** considered the most "wild and imaginative" of all the Art Nouveau designers, was known for his sculptural and expressive furnishings.

  Germany: **Richard Riemerschmid** designed simple interpretations of the new style. In Germany and Austria the style was known as ***Jugendstijl.***

  Finland: **Eliel Saarinen,** whose **White Collection** is well known, is considered the father of modern architecture in Finland.

  Scotland: One of the most outstanding designers of the period was **Charles Rennie Mackintosh** in Glasgow. His designs are an interesting paradox, and his creations included pink and white Art Nouveau furniture and extraordinary "perpendicular" furniture. The latter furnishings were geometric compositions with tall, straight chair backs—significant contributions to the modern movement. Classic pieces include the **Argyle, Hill House,** and **Willow chairs.**

  America: Prominent New York designer **Louis Comfort Tiffany** designed superb stained-glass lamps and other furnishings considered collector's items today.
- *The Secession* (circa 1897–1903) was an artistic movement that "seceded" from historical styles. The movement's focus was primarily in Vienna, Austria. Leaders included **Otto Wagner, Adolf Loos, Josef Maria Olbrich,** and **Josef Hoffmann.** Hoffmann's furniture has had a long-lasting influence on the design world. His classic pieces include the **Fledermaus, Prague,** and **Haus Koller chairs** designed during the first decade of the century. The ***Wiener Werkstatte*** (studio), formed by Hoffmann in 1903, was an offshoot of the Secession and provided a setting where a more geometric and structural design approach was fostered.
- *De Stijl* (1917–circa 1932) was a new radical style that emerged in Holland in 1917. The group adhered to strict design principles they called ***neoplasticism:*** (1) only red, yellow, blue, white, gray, and black were employed; and all creations (2) had to be

EARLY MODERN FURNITURE
(Thonet, Arts & Crafts, & Art Nouveau)

Bentwood Rocker
Michael Thonet

Vienna Cafe
Michael Thonet

Morris Chair
Phillip Webb

Eastlake Chest

Godwin cabinet

Voysey Chair

Stickley Chair

Robie Chair
Frank Lloyd Wright

Cathedra Chair
H.H. Richardson

Greene & Greene
Armchair

Adirondack Chair
Am. Arts & Crafts

Art Nouveau Chair
Hector Guimard

Art Nouveau Chair
Emile Galle

EARLY MODERN FURNITURE
(Art Nouveau, Secession, & De Stijl)

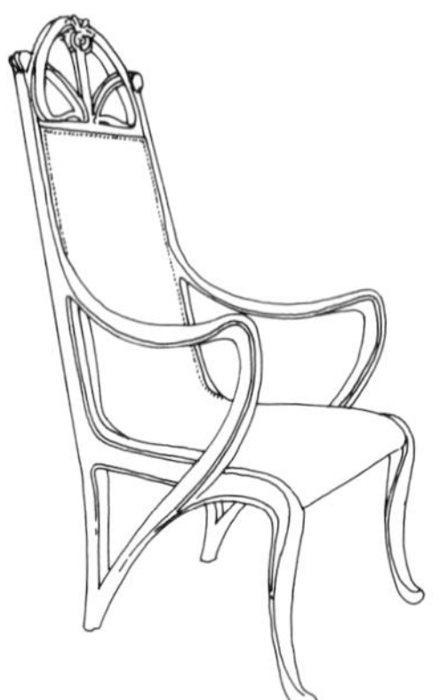
Art Nouveau Chair
Louis Majorelle

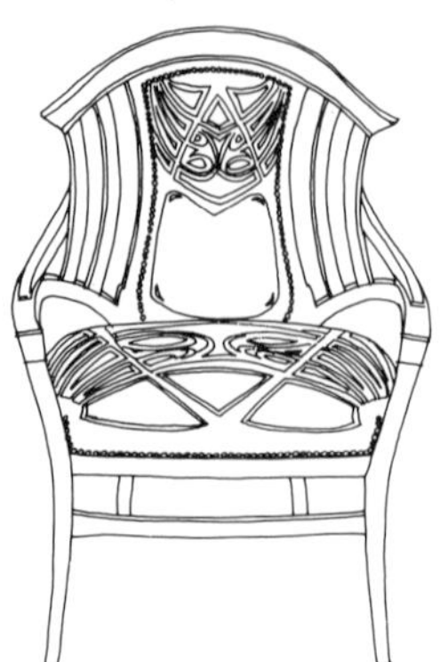
Art Nouveau Chair
Henri Van de Velde

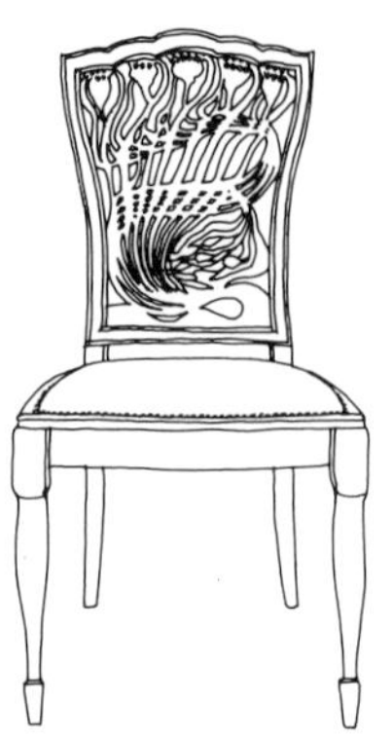
Art Nouveau Chair
Arthur Mackmurdo

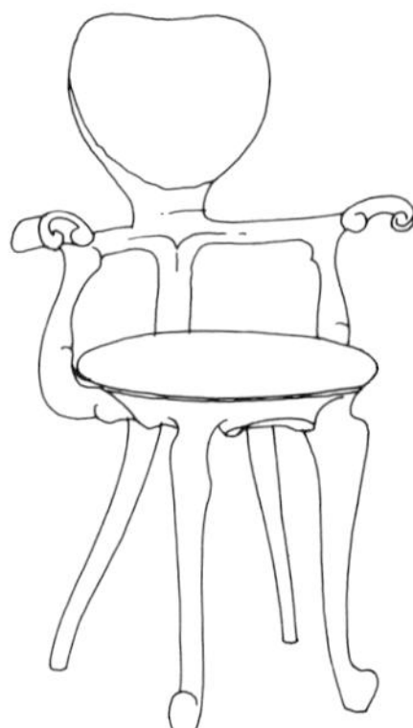
Art Nouveau Chair
Antoni Gaudi

White Collection
Eliel Saarinen

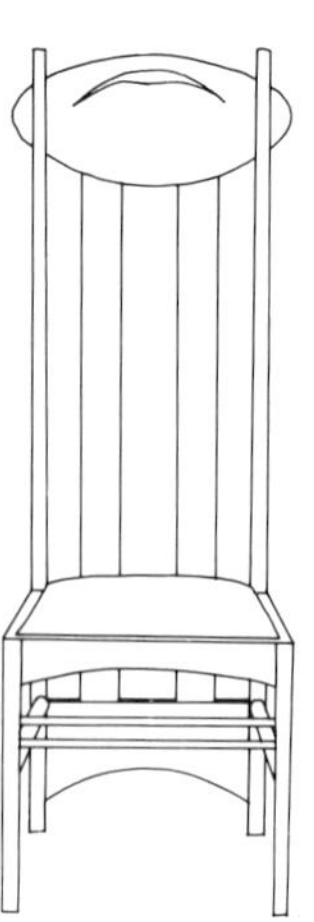
Argyle Chair
C.R. Mackintosh

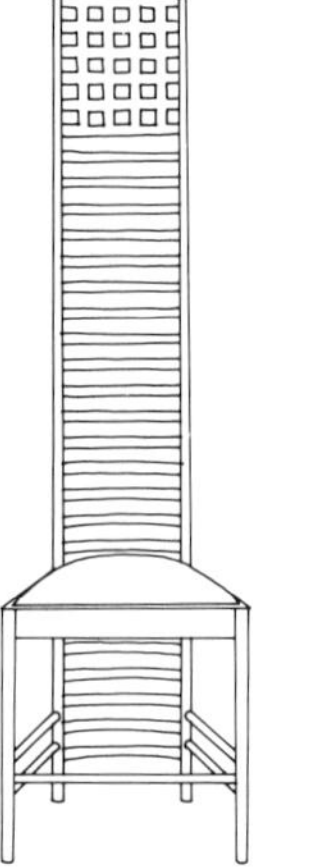
Hill Chair
C.R. Mackintosh

Secession Stool
Otto Wagner

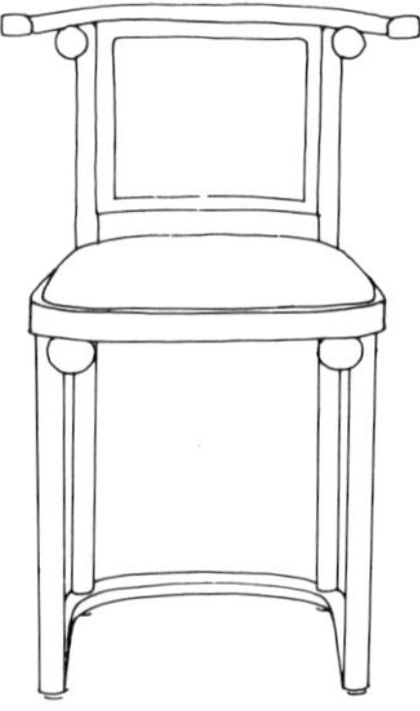
Fledermaus Chair
Josef Hoffmann

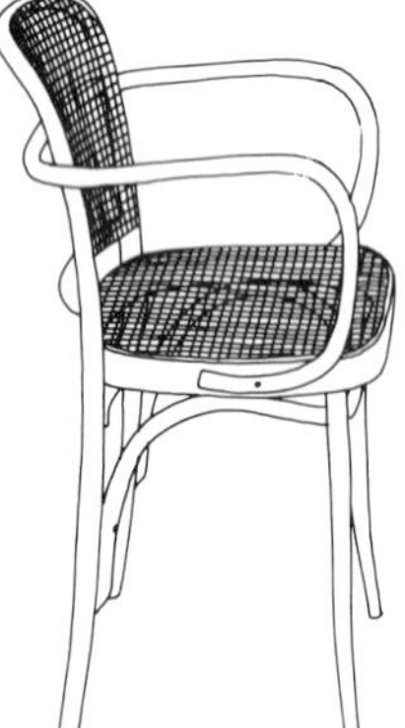
Prague Chair
Josef Hoffmann

Haus Koller Chair
Josef Hoffmann

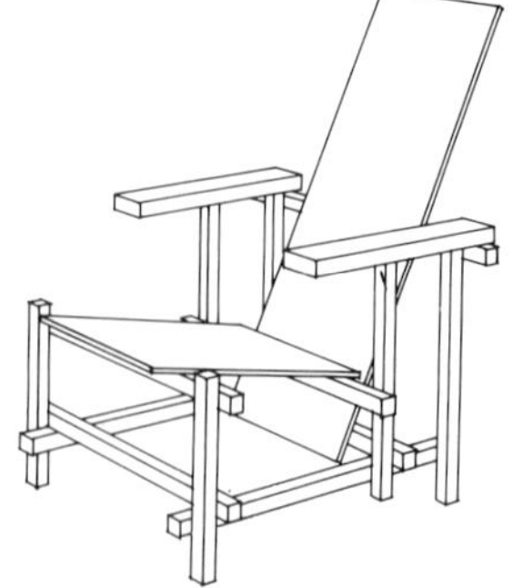
Red/Blue Chair
Gerrit Rietveld

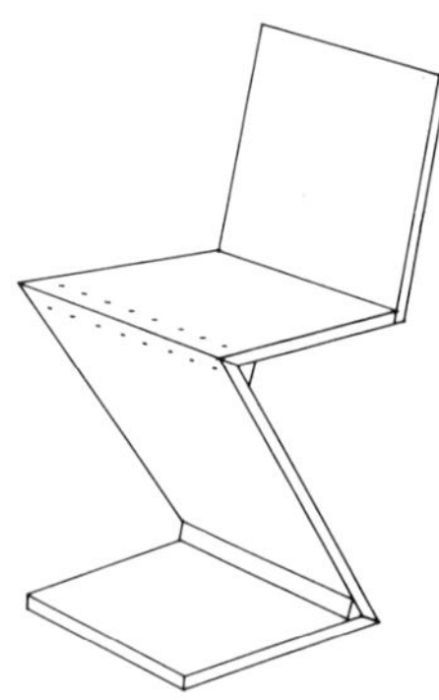
Zig-Zag Chair
Gerrit Rietveld

abstract; (3) have smooth, shiny surfaces; and (4) be composed of only right angles. Leaders included the painter **Piet Mondrian; Theo van Doesburg,** the founder; and **Gerrit Rietveld,** whose furniture pieces are well-known classics. Outstanding are the **Red/Blue** (1918) and **Zig-zag** (1934) **chairs.**

- *The Bauhaus (1919–1933) and International Style.* The focal point of modern design from 1919 to 1933 was the **Bauhaus** in Weimar, Germany. Its philosophy—that aesthetically pleasing objects could be created by mechanical means—was the impetus for the Bauhaus. At the Bauhaus, an experimental design school, two great furniture pioneers, **Marcel Breuer** and **Ludwig Mies van der Rohe,** developed the cantilever chair and tubular steel for furniture construction. Classics include Marcel Breuer's **Wassily lounge** (1925) and **Cesca chair** (1928) and Mies van der Rohe's **Barcelona Collection** (1929) and **Brno chair** (1930).

  Le Corbusier, who worked out of his studio in Paris, is considered a master of the ***International Style.*** His classics include the **Petit** and **Grand Confort** (1928) and **Pony chaise lounge** (1929). Other designers of note in Paris were **Eileen Gray,** who designed the **Transat chair** (1927), and **Robert Mallet-Stevens,** whose **Mallet-Stevens stacking chair** (1928) is particularly popular.

- *Art Deco* (circa 1909–1940) was a decorative style that flourished in Europe and America principally between World War I and World War II. The term *Art Deco* was derived from the great **Paris Exposition in 1925**—the **Exposition des Arts Decoratifs.** Inspiration for the new style was drawn from many sources, including the glamour of the movies and stage, jazz music, African art, ancient Egyptian, Assyrian and Aztec Indian cultures, new technology, the Bauhaus and International Style, the skyscraper, a sophisticated new society, the fashion world, and other inspirations. Motifs include the zigzag; lightning flash; pyramid; Egyptian themes, including the sunburst and palm tree; the peacock; stylized flowers and animals; and numerous geometric shapes. For furniture design, many types of new materials were employed, and old materials were used in refreshing new ways. Some outstanding designers and classics of the period are

  France: **Jacques-Emile Ruhlmann,** whose elegant and expensive furniture was widely imitated.

  America: **Frank Lloyd Wright's imperial chair** (1920) is a classic. **Paul Frankl,** known for his **skyscraper furniture,** and **Donald Deskey,** designer of the furnishings for Radio City Music Hall in New York, are influential furniture designers of the style. **Eliel Saarinen,** the prominent Finnish designer, moved to America in 1922 and soon became director of the prestigious design school Cranbrook Academy, in Michigan. His best-known classics of this period include the **Cranbrook sidechair** (1929) and the **Blue Collection** (1929).

- *The 1930s* witnessed the contribution of a number of designers from various countries whose classics are still widely recognized. These include (1) Spain's **Salvador Dali,** designer of the surrealistic **Mae West Lips chair** (1936, revived by the Italians as the **Marilyn** in 1972); (2) Denmark's **Kaare Klint,** who designed the **Deck chair** (1933); (3) England's **T. H. Robsjohn-Gibbings,** critic, historian, and designer who revived the classic **Klismos chair** (1936) of ancient Greece; and (4) Argentina's design team of **Bonet, Kurchan,** and **Hardoy,** creators of the famous **Butterfly chair** (1938).

- *Postwar Scandinavia.* After World War II, the Scandinavian countries developed furniture of exceptional quality and design. Classic pieces and designers include

  Finland: **Alvar Aalto** designed a series of lightly scaled laminated bentwood designs. **Eero Aarnio** exploited new forms and materials, as expressed in his **Globe** (1966) and **Gyro** (1968) **chairs.**

  Denmark: **Hans Wegner** is known for his expert craftsmanship and beauty of form and materials. His outstanding classics include **"The chair"** (1949), **Peacock chair** (1947), and **Chair 24** (1950). **Arne Jacobsen** is known for his sculptural **Egg** and **Swan chairs** (1958) and his **Series 7 Group** (1955). **Poul Kjaerholm** preferred combining natural materials with metal. His outstanding classics are **Chair 22** (1956) and **Chair 20** (1968). **Vernor Panton,** who currently works out of Switzerland, is renowned for his work in molded plastic. His **Panton Stacking Chair** (1960–1968) is a landmark piece. Currently, a new generation of Scandinavian designers continue to uphold the high standards of design, craftsmanship, and technology set by previous masters.

- *Postwar America.* After World War II, America emerged as a world leader in furniture design, led by **Charles Eames** and **Eero**

MODERN FURNITURE
(Bauhaus/International Style)

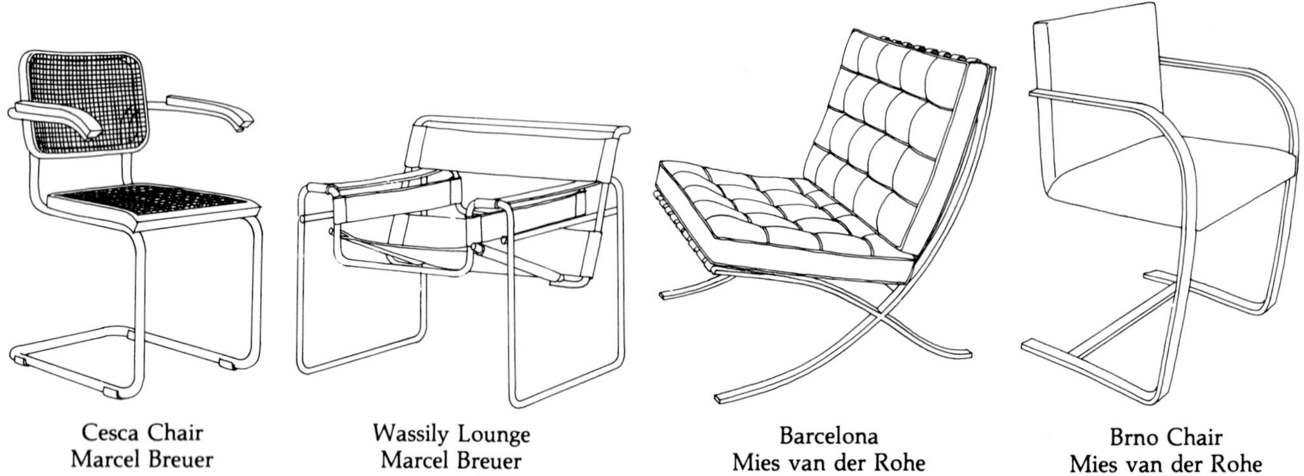

Cesca Chair
Marcel Breuer

Wassily Lounge
Marcel Breuer

Barcelona
Mies van der Rohe

Brno Chair
Mies van der Rohe

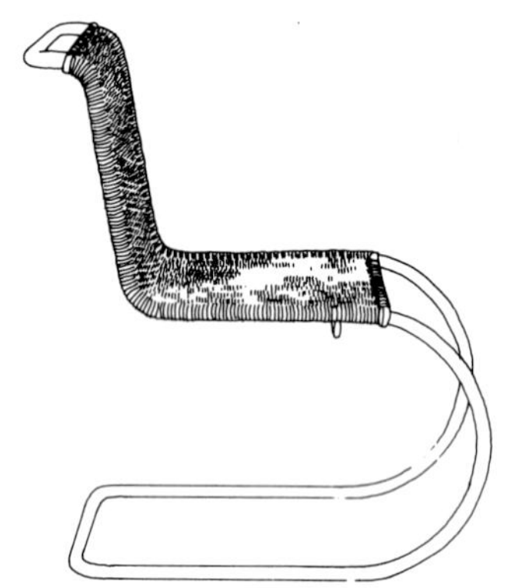

MR Chair
Mies van der Rohe

Grand Confort
Le Corbusier

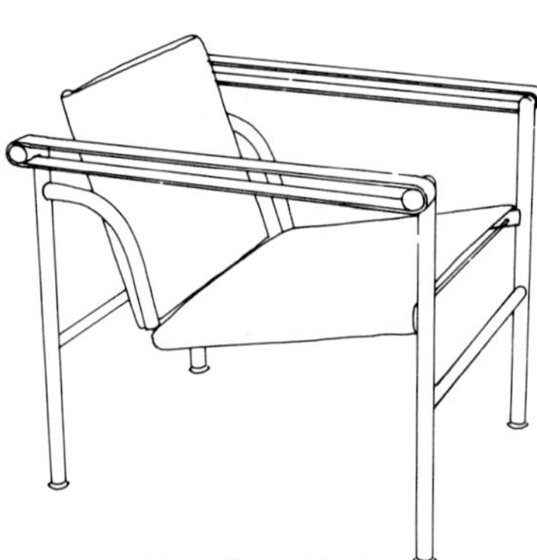

Basculant Chair
Le Corbusier

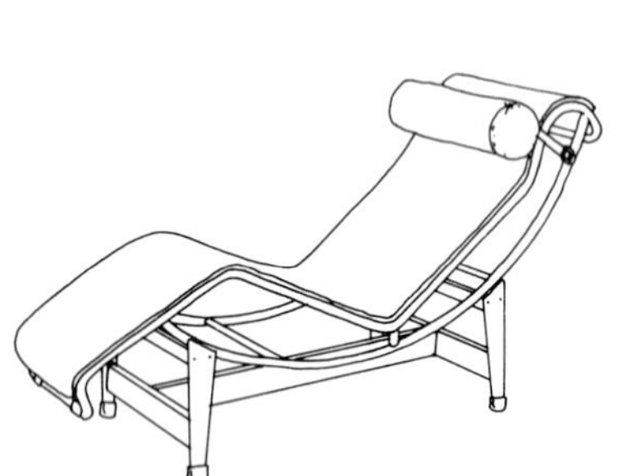

"Pony" Chaise
Le Corbusier

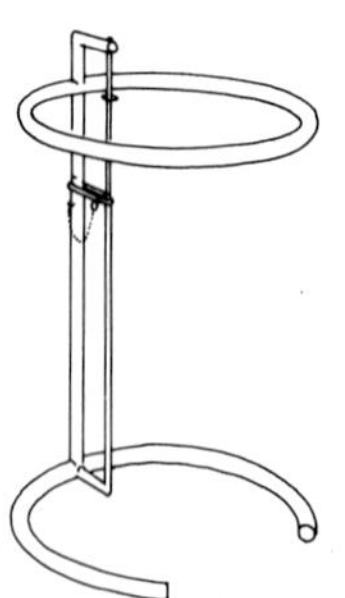

Smoking Table
Eileen Gray

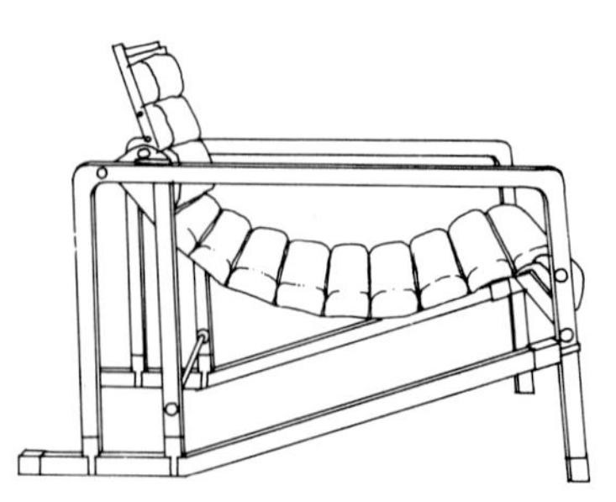

Transat Lounge
Eileen Gray

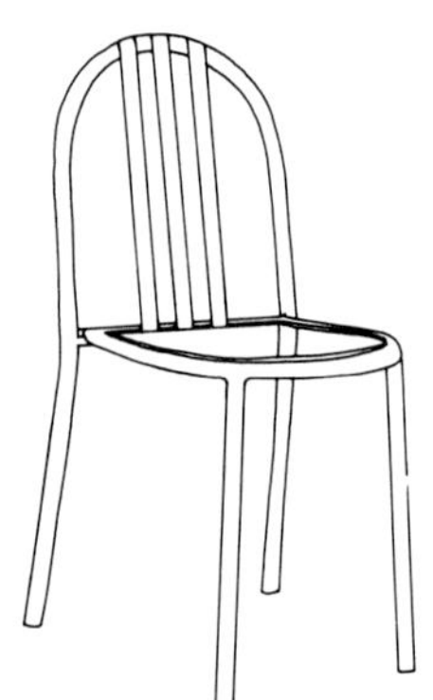

Stacking Chair
Robert Maillet-Stevens

MODERN FURNITURE
(Art Deco & 1930s)

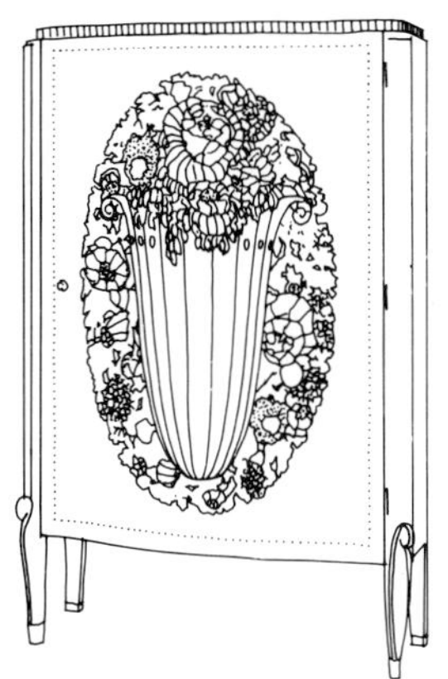
Art Deco Cabinet
Jacques-Emile Ruhlmann

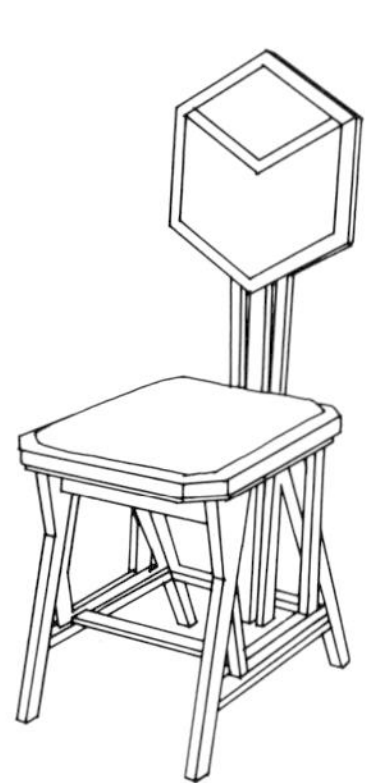
Imperial Chair
Frank Lloyd Wright

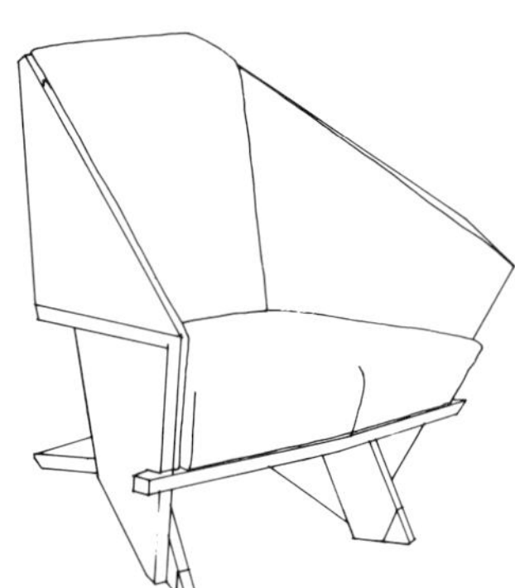
Taliesin Lounge
Frank Lloyd Wright

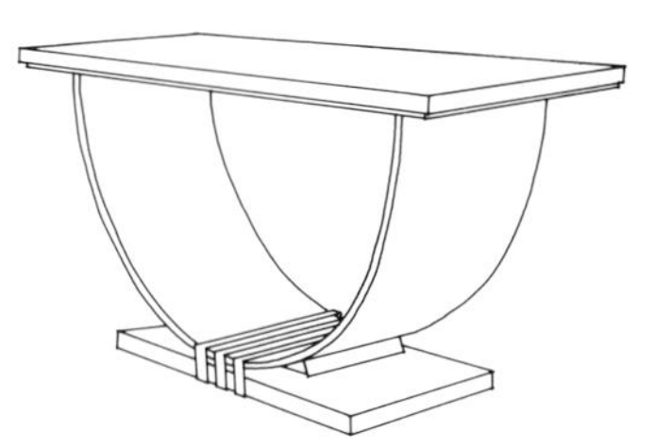
Art Deco Table
Donald Deskey

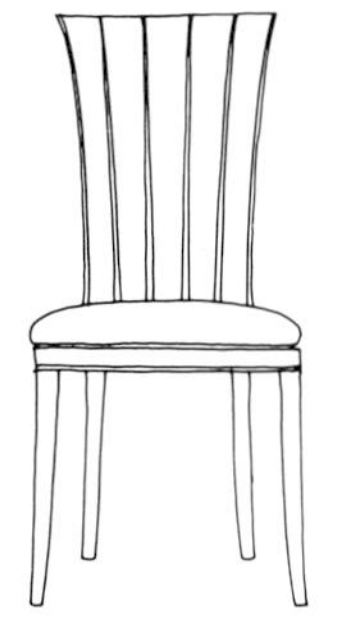
Cranbrook Chair
Eliel Saarinen

Blue Collection
Eliel Saarinen

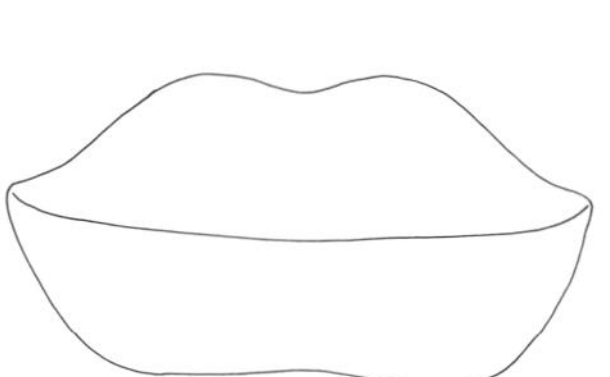
"Lips" or "Marilyn" Lounge
Salvador Dali/Studio 65

Deck Chair
Kaare Klint

Klismos Chair
T.H. Robsjohn-Gibbings

Butterfly Chair
Bonet, Kurchan & Hardoy

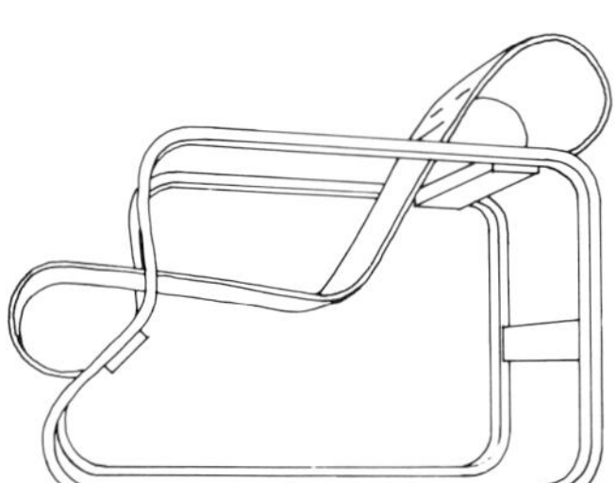
Paimio (Scroll) Chair
Alvar Aalto

CLASSIC MODERN FURNITURE
(Postwar Period – 1950s)

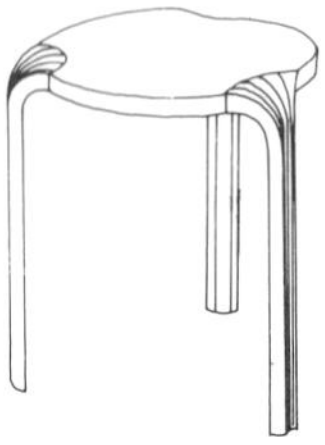

Aalto stool
Scandinavia

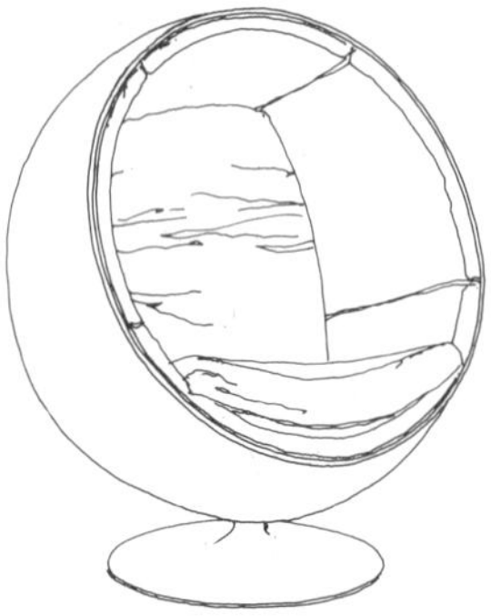

Globe chair
Eero Aarnio
Scandinavia

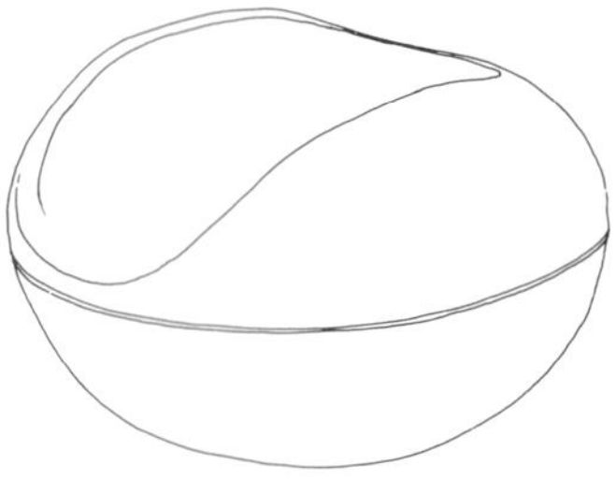

Gyro
Eero Aarnio
Scandinavia

"The Chair"
Hans Wegner
Scandinavia

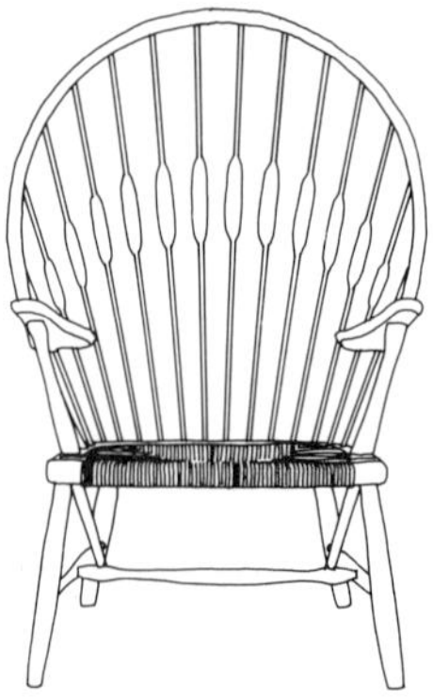

Peacock chair
Hans Wegner
Scandinavia

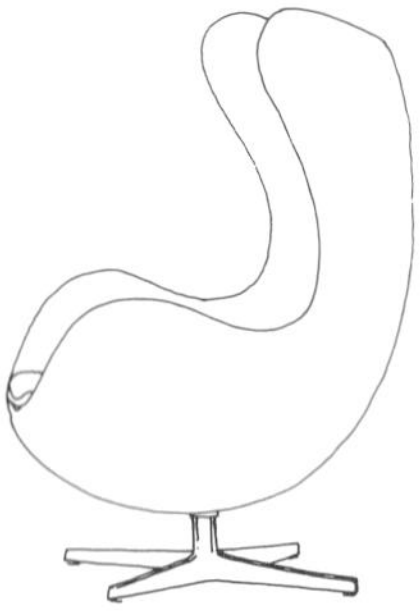

Egg chair
Arne Jaconsen
Scandinavia

Chair 22
Poul Kjaerholm
Scandinavia

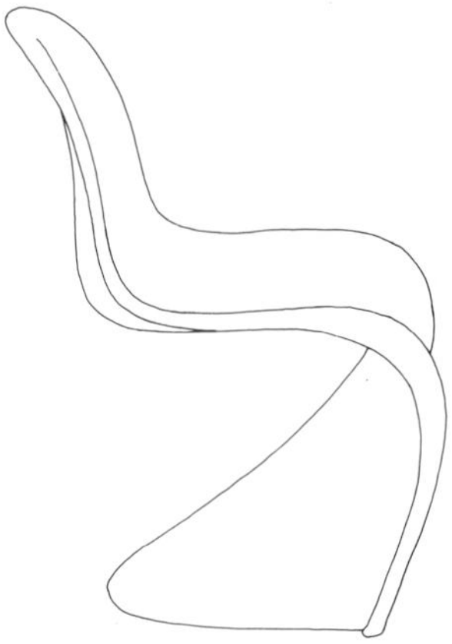

Panton Stacking Chair
Vernor Panton
Scandinavia

Eames Lounge
Charles Eames
U.S.A.

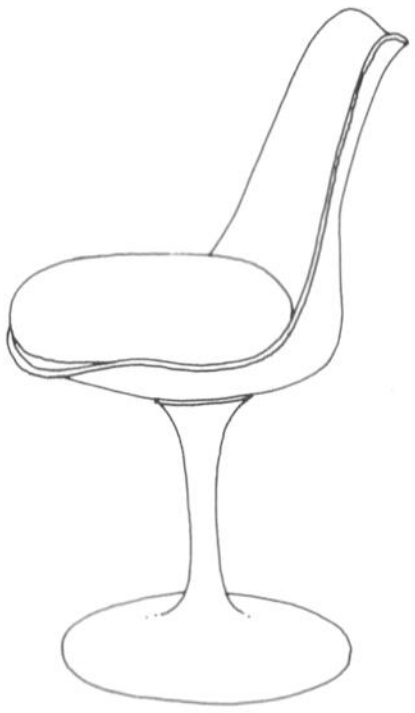

Tulip/Pedestal
Eero Saarinen
U.S.A.

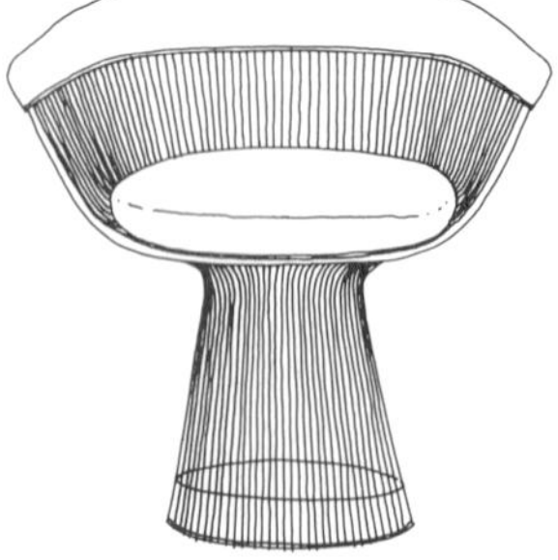

Wire chair
Warren Platner
U.S.A.

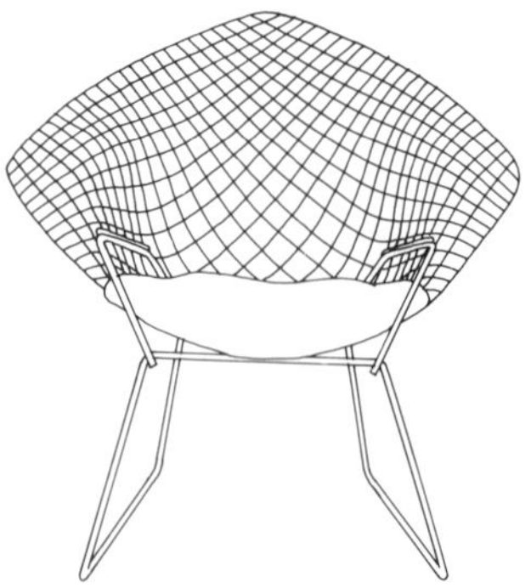

Diamond chair
Harry Bertoia
U.S.A.

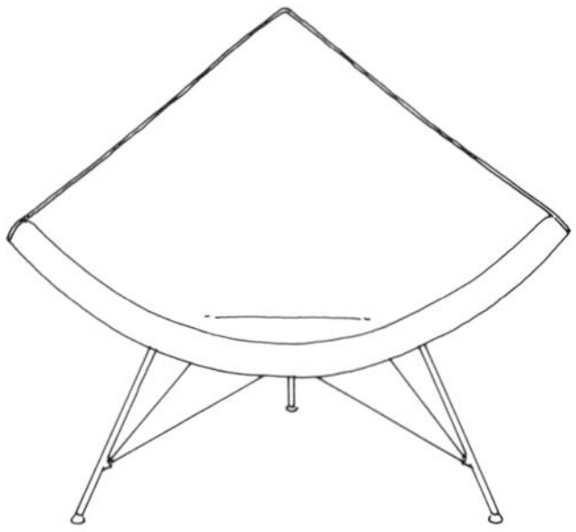

Coconut chair
George Nelson
U.S.A.

Saarinen. Eames and Saarinen were responsible for many innovations in furniture design, including molded fiberglass and plywood creations. Eames's classic pieces include the **Eames Lounge Chair 670** (1956), **DAR Shell chair** (1950), and the **Aluminum Group** (1958). The **Tulip Pedestal Group** (1957) is considered Saarinen's most important furniture design. Other important designers and classics are **Harry Bertoia,** known for his **Wire Collection** (1951); **Warren Platner,** who also developed an important **Wire Collection** (1966); and **George Nelson,** who created the **Coconut chair** (1956).

- *Italian Design.* Influenced by the Bauhaus and International Style, Italian designers attracted world attention after World War II for their innovative use of materials and technology. Pioneer designer **Gio Ponti** created his classic **Superleggera chair** in 1957. **Joe Colombo** was particularly noted for his plastic designs including the **Elda chair** (1965) and **Colombo chair** (1967). **Vico Magistretti** is another prominent Italian designer responsible for numerous classics. Two of his best known are the **Selene** (1961) and **Maralunga** (1973). Other outstanding classics from Italy include the **Plia chair** (1969), by **Giancarlo Piretti;** the **Soriana Collection** (1970), by **Tobia and Afra Scarpa;** the **Sacco** (1969), by **Design Studio;** and the **Cab chair** (1977) by **Mario Bellini.**
- *Other Postwar contributions* include the sculptural furniture of **Pierre Paulin** in France and Pedro Freideberg in Mexico. Paulin's best-known classic is the **Ribbon Chair** (1965). **Pop furniture** was created by numerous designers, especially during the 1960s. Representative of this style is the **Hand chair** (1963) designed by Pedro Freideberg.
- *The Handcraft Revival* began at the end of the 1970s in England and America, inspired by the ideals of William Morris and the Arts and Crafts Movement in England during the latter half of the nineteenth century. Furniture is beautifully handcrafted and finished. Some classic pieces and designers are the **Ebony Gothic chair** (1978), by **John Makepeace** in England; **Rocking Chairs** (1970s and 1980s), by **Sam Maloof** in California; and **Bench with Horses** (1979), by **Judy Kensley McKie** in Boston. Currently the Handcraft Revival is a strong design direction.
- *Furniture of the 1980s.* During the 1980s various design directions emerged, many of them extensions or reinterpretations of previous modern styles. Of particular note are the following.

1. **Handcraft Revival** (just described).
2. **High-Tech** furniture employs the most advanced scientific and industrial techniques and materials.
3. **Post-Modern** is a prominent direction in both architecture and furniture design distinguished by a freer spirit of expression. Primarily rejecting the austere International Style, Post-Modern designers are historically aware and sensitive to new modern concepts expressed through strong form and subtle colors. Outstanding leaders of this style are **Michael Graves,** whose **Graves armchair** (1982) is a classic example, and **Robert Venturi,** designer of the popular **Venturi Collection** (1980s)—a series of chairs borrowing styles of the past interpreted in extraordinary ways.
4. **Classic Modern** brings styles of the past into the twentieth century, adapted in elegant and simplified terms. The **Grande Flute chairs** (1985), by the late New York interior designer **Angelo Donghia,** are based on eighteenth-century Louis XVI chairs and are typical of this trend.
5. **Ergonomic** furniture is created with a concern for human comfort and efficiency. **Niels Diffrient's Jefferson chair** (1985) is a superb example. It has adjustable angles for maximum comfort and function and is named after one of President Thomas Jefferson's chairs of similar design.
6. **Memphis** is an avant-garde group of about 20 international designers assembled in 1981 by Italian-based **Ettore Sottsass, Jr.** Named after Memphis, the hometown of Elvis Presley and the ancient city of Memphis in Egypt, the Memphis design group was encouraged by Sottsass to employ complete freedom of expression with an emphasis on style, color, and form. Sottsass's colorful **Carlton bookshelf/room divider** (1981) is a much publicized piece. **Michele de Lucchi's First chair** (1983), with its circular composition, is another piece that has received international recognition.
7. **Art Furniture** is furniture created by artists as a piece for "art's sake." This new design approach is expressed individualistically by various artists, each creating a completely unique piece or collection. These pieces may or may not be functional or comfortable. Some pieces of furniture that have received national acclaim are **Queen Anne, Queen Anne** (1981), by **Terence** and **Laura Main,** and **Nothing Continues to Happen** (1981), by **Howard Meister.**

CLASSIC MODERN FURNITURE
(1950s to 1970s)
Superleggera
Gio Ponti
Italy
Elda chair
Joe Colombo
Italy
Maralunga
Vico Magistretti
Italy
Plia chair
Carlo Piretti
Italy
Soriana
Tobia &
Afra Scarpa
Italy
Sacco
Design Studio
Italy
Cab
Mario Bellini
Italy
Ribbon chair
Pierre Paulin
France
Batting Joe Lounge
Design Studio-Italy
Pop Furniture
Hand chair
Pedro Freideberg
Pop Furniture
Mexico
Ebony Gothic chair
John Makepeace
Craft Revival
Rocking chair
Sam Maloof
Craft Revival
Horses bench
Judy K. McKie
Craft Revival
Atlantis
Wendell Castle
Crafts Revival

CLASSIC MODERN FURNITURE
(1980 s)

Graves chair
Post-modern

Venturi chair
Post-modern

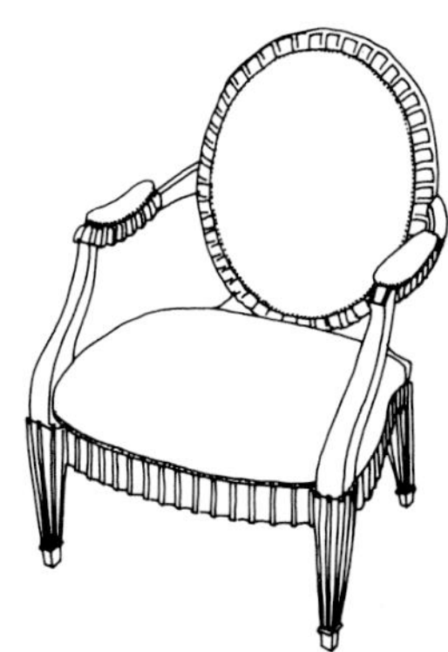
Grand Flute
Angelo Donghia
Classic Modern

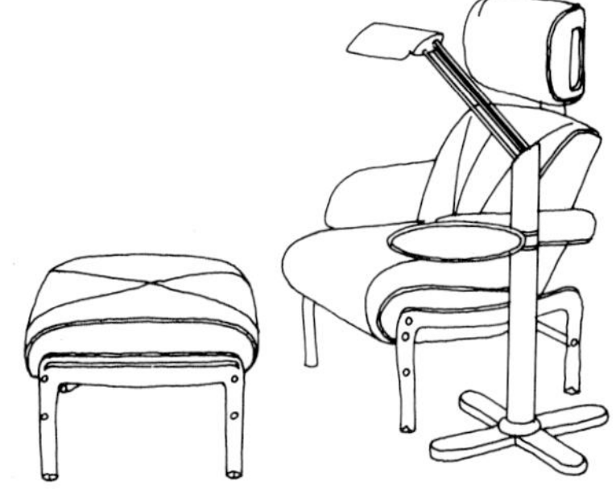
Jefferson chair
Niels Diffrient
Ergonomic

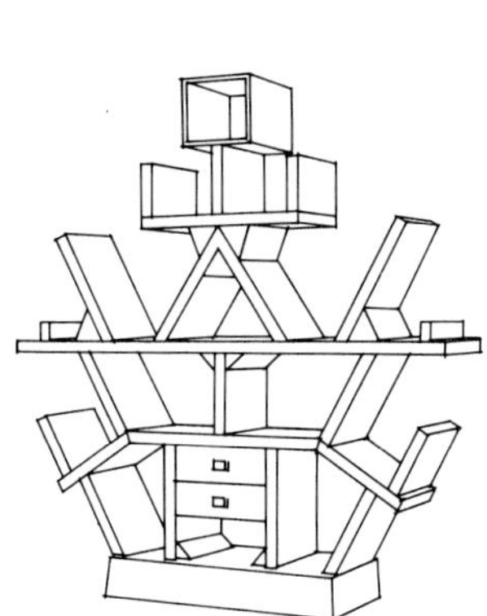
Carlton Bookcase
Ettore Sottsass, Jr.
Memphis style

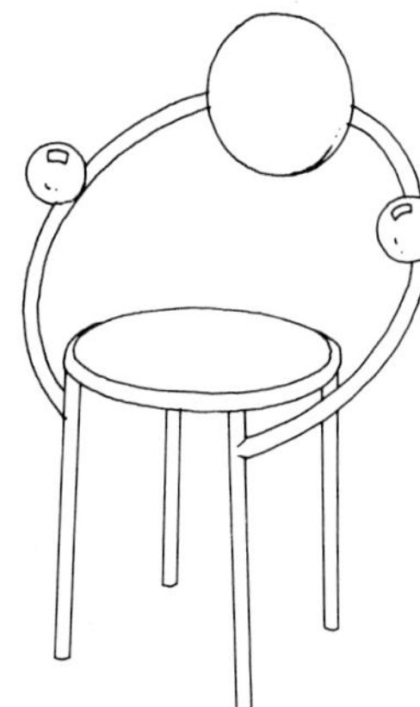
First chair
Michele de Lucci
Memphis style

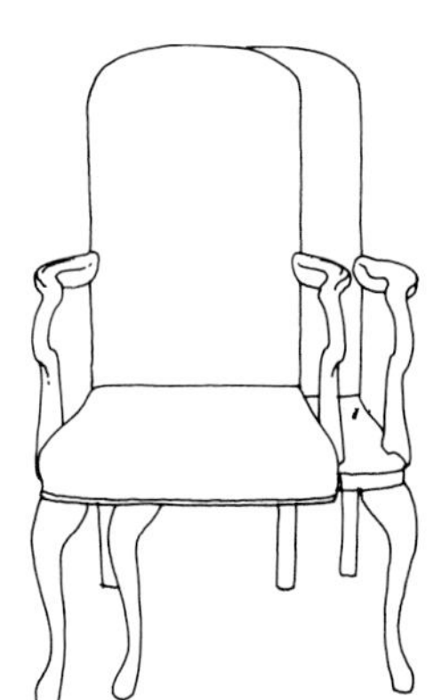
Queen Anne, Queen Anne
Terence & Laura Main
Art Furniture

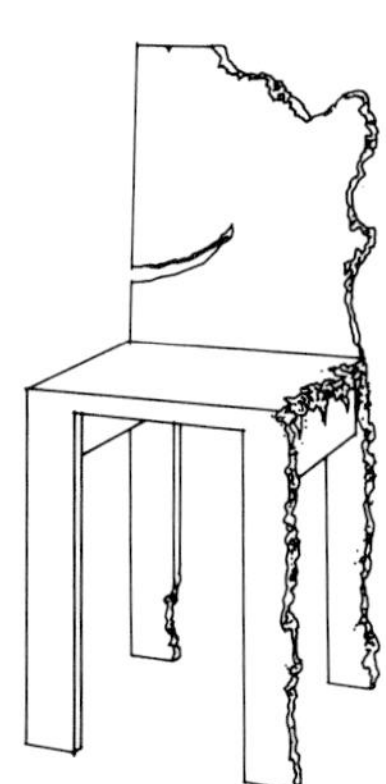
Nothing Continues
to Happen Chair
Howard Meister
Art Furniture

Richard III Chair
Philippe Starok
France

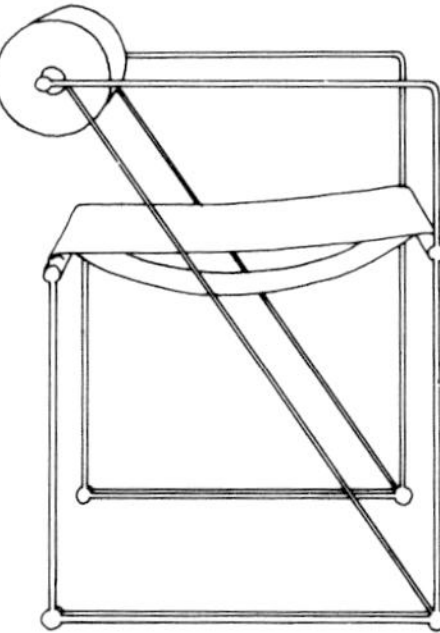
Seconda chair
Mario Botta
Italy

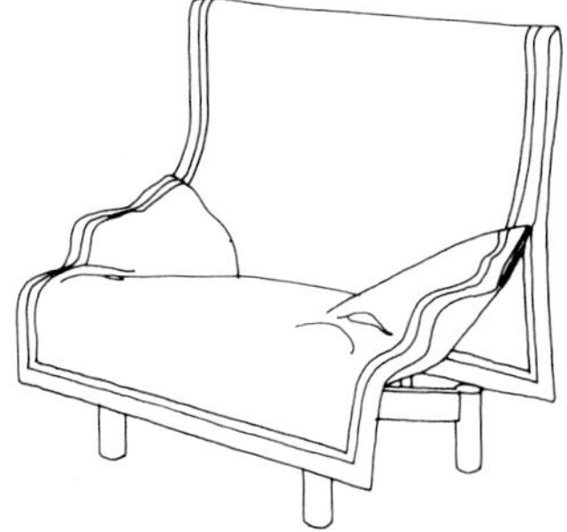
Sindbad
Vico Magistretti
Italy

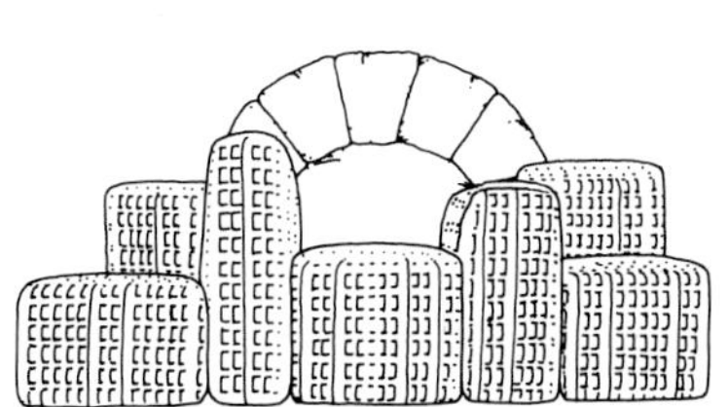
Sunset in New York
Gaetano Pesce
Italy

8. **Individualists.** A number of individualistic designers have created outstanding classic furnishings during the past decade that have gained international recognition. Although this list is extensive, a few are particularly outstanding. **Philippe Starck** in France has created unusual pieces of furniture derived from many sources. His **Richard III chair** (1980s) is representative. Swiss architect and furniture designer **Mario Botta** has designed a series of unique furniture pieces. The **87 Seconda** (1982) is one of his best-known works. Italian designers **Vico Magistretti** and **Gaetano Pesce** continue as leaders in the design field in Italy today. Magistretti's **Sindbad chair** (1980s), and Pesce's **Sunset in New York** (1980) are good examples.

American Oriental Style

The Oriental influence, particularly from China and Japan, is part of America's early tradition, since it was known to our ancestors in Europe. Furnishings and accessories inspired by Oriental motifs have remained popular in the twentieth century in the United States. Principles and elements of Japanese architecture, which include the predominance of the horizontal line, the use of natural materials, asymmetry, open planning, simplicity, and the absence of ornamentation, were used by Frank Lloyd Wright in his buildings and are an integral part of the **Japanese** and **Organic Modern-style** houses in America today.

The interior of the Japanese house is open and uncluttered; wood floors have tatami mats; ceilings are beamed or modular; walls are plain; and shoji screens, often used for both walls and windows, open onto gardens. Furniture is sparse, usually in a natural finish and built low. Basic pieces include a low table, a chest, and ***zabuton*** (pillows) for seating.

Design influences from **China** have had their greatest impact for American designers in the field of furniture and accessories. Manufacturers in the United States have borrowed freely from both Japan and China to create "Oriental" furniture collections. Following are some of the most recognizable features of Oriental furnishings found in American homes.

From Japan

- Simple unembellished furniture, usually in a natural finish
- Low tables
- Zabuton or pillows often stacked on floor
- ***Tansu*** (Oriental chest) with brass hardware typical
- Incorporation of shibui color schemes and philosophies (see Chapter 5)
- Only a few treasured items displayed (see following list)

From China

- More decorative furnishings employing certain motifs (to be described). A vast selection of pieces for many functions are manufactured.
- *Finishes:* Lacquered finishes in black, red-orange, gold, and green popular. ***Tortoise shell*** (a mottled effect). Painted Oriental scenes, motifs, and figures on furniture surfaces. Highly polished natural finishes.
- *Colors:* Those from China, brighter. Especially employed are blue, white, red, red-orange, gold, yellow-gold, and jade green.

Typical Forms, Motifs, and Accessories from Japan and China

- *Forms:* ***"Monkey paw"*** legs (slight turning inwards). ***"Elephant leg"*** (slight swelling and splaying outwards). ***Pagoda*** forms. ***Fret design.*** **Chest-on-chest** arrangements with a slight separation between pieces.
- *Motifs:* Bamboo, chrysanthemum (most popular flower), and cherry blossoms; asymmetrical pine branch; fret design; mandarin duck and heron; the horse, tiger, dragon, and fish; Oriental figures, parasols, and pagodas; Mt. Fuji and floating clouds. Many motifs associated with the Japanese and Chinese cultures.
- *Accessories:* ***Bonsai*** plants, Oriental figures, ***calligraphy, coromandel screen*** (freestanding decorative multipaneled screen), wall-hung multipaneled screen, Chinese porcelain vases (particularly **"Ginger jar"** vases), Chinese rugs (usually employing combinations of blue, white, red-orange, and gold), ***Temple foo dogs,*** brass hardware, statues of Oriental gods and goddesses and animals (mentioned under motifs), simple flower arrangements called ***ikebana,*** pieces made of jade and ivory, the hanging scroll (often with calligraphy forms), wood carvings, lacquerware, and, occasionally, Oriental fans and kimonos.

Style Selection

Considering the numerous styles available, making a selection can be simplified by determining the general feeling desired. The approaches fall into five basic categories: (1) **informal provincial,** (2) **formal traditional,** (3) **informal modern,** (4) **formal modern,** and (5) **eclectic.**

ORIENTAL FURNITURE

Figure 9.18 Many rooms today are enhanced by including both modern and traditional aspects. In this room, a modern architectural background dominates, with furnishings that include modern wicker furniture, a modern table and accessories, with updated French dining chairs. *(Courtesy of Gayl Baddeley/Associates.)*

Deciding on one of these style directions can help the consumer and designer achieve a compatible, functional, and aesthetically satisfying environment.

- *Informal Provincial.* This is generally a handcrafted, simple, and casual look. To achieve this informality, one ethnic style or combined furnishings from many country sources may be used, as long as the feeling is one of unpretentious homeyness. Whether part of the architectural background, movable furniture, or arts and crafts, informal provincial furnishings from the same country or many countries generally share a natural affinity and combine well. The term *country look* became popular during the early sixties. Shortly thereafter it became a catchall term for almost anything from rustic to manor. Today, however, it has become a viable style. The look is cloistered, comfortable, and rustic and may incorporate furniture from a number of countries as long as designs are rooted in the past and have an aura of charm and informality. Styles most commonly employed in America providing this feeling are **Early American** (seventeenth and eighteenth century), **Country English** (often simplified **Georgian**), **Country Provincial French,** and **Spanish.** Also appropriate are **Dutch, Swedish,** and **German** furnishings.
- *Formal Traditional.* The term *traditional* may refer to interior furnishings from any country so long as they are of the more formal styles. Many of the

favorite traditional designs come from the eighteenth century, an age of great prosperity and a flourishing of the arts in the Western world. The furniture styles of this period from both France and England have been great favorites with many Americans who enjoy their warmth, grace, and elegance. Some of these styles have been adapted and scaled to meet present-day requirements without losing their true character. Styles appropriate for a formal traditional look include **Early and Late Georgian** (Queen Anne and Chippendale furniture), **Federal** (Hepplewhite, Sheraton, and Adam furniture), **Court French** (Louis XV and XVI), **Empire and Greek Revival** (Duncan Phyfe furniture), **English Regency** (Hope and Sheraton furniture), and **Victorian** (Belter and Eastlake).

- *Informal Modern.* Numerous types and styles of "Modern" furniture are available on the market, drawing principally from European, Oriental, and American designers (see pp. 309–320). When an informal modern setting is preferred, generally casual fabrics with a matte finish, simple materials, and unpretentious accessories will provide the result. Almost all modern styles lend themselves to being incorporated into an informal look depending on these qualities. Informal modern furniture styles particularly suitable for this direction include the **Santa Fe Style, Scandinavian,** modern furniture inspired by **Japanese** prototypes, and the **Handcraft Revival.** Other modern styles including the **Secession, De Stijl, Bauhaus** and **International Style, Post-Modern, Italian,** and other modern styles of furniture can generally be designed in either an informal or formal manner, depending on the supportive treatment.
- *Formal Modern.* A formal modern environment can be created by employing elegant, sophisticated, and refined architectural backgrounds, accessories, and fabrics (often with a shiny surface). **Art Nouveau, Art Deco, Classic Modern,** and **Post-Modern** furniture are particularly well suited for a formal setting. **Italian, Secession, Wiener Werkstatte, De Stijl, Bauhaus** and the **International** Style furniture may be very formal and sophisticated, depending on supportive elements. **Modern Oriental** is often used in a formal manner.
- *Eclectic or Mixing Styles.* Today, fewer consumers than before buy matched items of furniture, and there is no longer a trend to maintain the same style of furniture throughout the house or even throughout the same room. The eclectic look—which is a mixing rather than a matching one—is in vogue. Eclectic does not mean a hodgepodge, however. Pieces should be related in scale and chosen with a final goal in mind. Success is more surely achieved if a common theme runs through the entire scheme—some element that ties the pieces together. For example, to achieve the provincial look, informality is the key and all country furniture, regardless of the source, is generally compatible. For a formal traditional look, dignity is the key, and refined pieces of almost any style can be combined with pleasant results. The modern look often allows for more daring and imagination.

Whatever the general theme of a room, it ought not dominate and thereby create a feeling of monotony. Interest can often be brought into a room by the unexpected. For example, a pair of Victorian chairs placed in a modern setting will bring some-

Figure 9.19 An eclectic design combines good design from many sources. In this living room, French, Oriental, and Modern styles are particularly prevalent. *(Courtesy of Gayl Baddeley/Associates.)*

Figure 9.20 The eclectic approach is achieved in this living room by combining French Louis XV chairs and a French rug with an Oriental end table and modern twentieth-century furnishings. *(Courtesy of Esto Photographics Inc.)*

thing special to the room. A modern sofa can give a period room a fresh, updated look. The clean sweep of modern decor may serve as the most effective background for a highly prized antique.

Today, more than ever before, consumers are taking a sophisticated look at furnishings of the past and present and finding new ways to use them. The discovery is being made that much can be borrowed from furnishings of the past to enrich present-day living and that furnishings from the present can add new life to the old. As new domestic and foreign influences come along, each can be adapted to meet current needs without discarding everything from another period.

Quality of Construction and Materials

The quality of construction and craftsmanship are often readily apparent. Through a knowledge of what constitutes quality in these areas, one can be assured of getting well-made furniture. Some of the construction features that can be discerned are the following.

- All sections of furniture must be **firmly joined** and secure.
- Furniture should be **well proportioned and comfortable.** The consumer can sit on a piece to be assured of the comfort of a chair or sofa. The depth of the seat and height of the back and arms should be checked. If a lounge chair is being chosen for a particular person, it is wise to have that person try it out.
- A well-constructed chest, chair, or table will **remain rigid and sturdy** when an attempt is made to rock it.
- A fine-quality **finish** will be smooth and evenly applied, with no spotting, sticky areas, running, or buildup of coats. Good wood furniture has a mellow patina resulting only from much rubbing, a practice requiring time and effort and therefore adding to the total cost. Finishes make woods highly resistant to marks from glasses, spills, scratches, and abrasions. Even cigarette burns are no longer the catastrophe they once were. These wonder-

working finishes are often completely invisible and let the beauty of the wood grain and color shine through. A qualified salesperson can explain the type of finish on the furniture being considered for purchase. Poorly constructed furniture often has a hard shine produced by varnish, which may cover inferior wood but will quickly reveal scratches.

- **Back panels** should be recessed and smoothly finished.
- **Movable units** like drawers and door panels must be durable and easily operated. Drawer runners are best when made of metal, plastic, or durable hardwood. Well-made drawers have solid sides, three-ply nonwarp bottoms that are sanded and sealed against snags, have dovetail joints, and are separated by dust barriers.
- **Leg and base supports** should be particularly sturdy with a durable finish because they take much abuse.
- Furniture with **flat areas** like tables, cabinets, and desk tops is best constructed of a durable material in order to maintain its function and appearance adequately. Although some materials are practical, each may have a particular hazard; for example, marble may stain, glass may break, plastic may chip, and hardwood may scratch.
- **Furniture edges,** found on tables and other pieces, are especially susceptible to damage and wear. Rounded edges, reinforced strips, and edges made of solid hardwood are practical and help ease the problem.

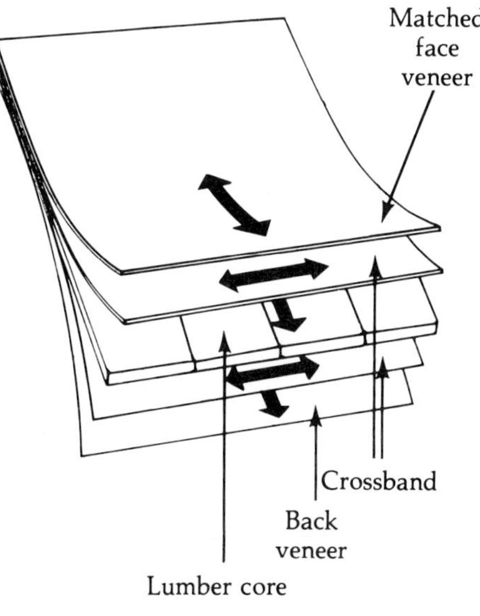

Veneering

Wood

Wood, the major material employed for furniture construction, is better appreciated through an understanding of wood terms: ***solid, genuine,*** and ***veneer.*** When a piece of furniture is marked **solid,** this indicates that it is made from solid hardwood. The label **genuine** shows that the furniture is made of a single hardwood, with veneer on flat surfaces and solid structural parts such as the legs. **Veneer** is a thin layer of finishing wood applied to the body of a less refined wood. Some people still cling to the old notion that furniture with veneer is of inferior quality. The contrary, however, is true. With advanced methods of cutting and laminating veneers, a piece of veneered furniture today can be stronger and more resistant to warping than a solid piece. Only veneering permits the beautiful effects achieved by the different methods of matching wood grains.

Furniture is made from both hard and soft woods. **Hardwoods** come from **deciduous trees** (those that drop their leaves), such as oak and maple. Hardwoods are more durable and dent resistant than softwoods, and they are more costly. Hardwoods are generally more attractive than softwoods and often are preferred for fine furniture. **Softwoods** come from **coniferous trees** (those with needles that are mostly green the year round), such as pine and spruce. Softwoods are used for less expensive furniture and are also used in combination with hardwoods. The woods most widely used in furniture construction today are pine, birch, maple, oak, cherry, walnut, mahogany, beech, pecan, and teak (see "Color in Wood," Chapter 5). Labels describing the finish such as "fruit wood finish" or "walnut finish" refer to the color only, not to the species of wood used. Each wood has its own special properties; and when selecting a type for a particular furniture piece, one should be certain that the wood is properly dried and well suited for its intended construction, purpose, finish, size, and style. Also, the wood selected must be resistant to warping, splitting, swelling, and shrinking.

Quality furniture is made from leaf-bearing trees, called hardwoods (right). Less expensive furniture is made from needled or evergreen trees, called softwoods (left).

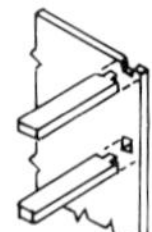

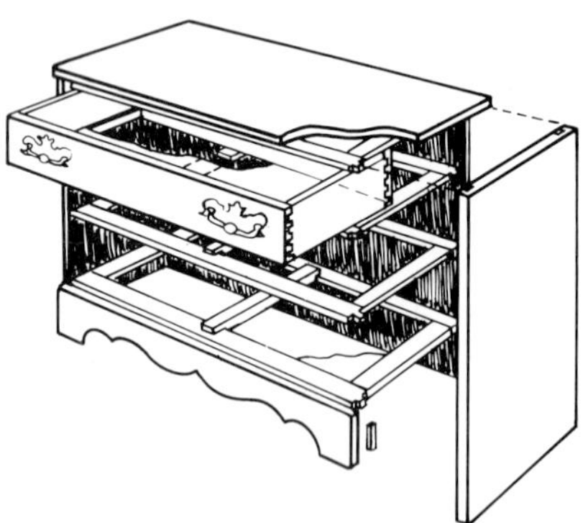

Inner characteristics of furniture determine durability: selected hardwoods; mortise and tenon joints; heavy-duty center drawer guides; drawers dovetailed front and back; durable dust panels between drawers; durable drawer bottoms held rigidly in grooves; strong casebacks recessed into ends; well-mounted top and sides; drawer interiors sanded and sealed. *(Courtesy of Stanley Furniture.)*

TABLE 9.1 *Most common wood types*

WOOD TYPE	CHARACTERISTICS	USES IN HOME
Acacia	Hardwood. Light brown.	Furniture. Woodwork. Often used for religious decorations
Alder	A light, weak wood. White to light browns.	Furniture. Framing.
Ash	A blond hardwood. Texture resembles oak. Relatively inexpensive.	Cabinetry and furniture. Furniture framing. Flooring.
Bamboo	A tropical tubular woody plant with a raised joint.	Popular for Oriental-style furniture. Decorative accessories.
Beech	A blond hardwood. Fine grain texture. Strong.	Informal furniture. Popular in Scandinavia. Flooring.
Birch	Subtle wavy grain. Hard and durable. Takes stains well, or beautiful in natural finish.	Furniture. Popular in Scandinavia. Flooring, doors, cabinetry.
Cedar	Reddish-brown, often with yellow streaks. Soft. Lightweight. Strong odor. Moth repellent.	Closet lining, chests. Informal furniture. Shingles. Siding. Paneling.
Cherry	Reddish-brown hardwood. Resembles mahogany. Durable. Strong.	Used in small quantities. Inlay and marquetry work. Popular for Early American furniture.
Cypress	Color varies. Usually from light yellow to darkish-brown. Soft. Warp resistant. Inexpensive. Weathers to a silver gray.	Particularly used as a finish wood. Outside finish work. Doors, shingles, siding. Some informal furniture.
Ebony	Exquisite dark heartwood with brownish-black streaks. Ebony sometimes red or green. Hard and heavy.	Modern and Oriental furniture. Inlay and marquetry designs.
Elm	Light brown with gray overtones. Takes stain well. Slight undulating grain. Hard and heavy.	Particularly used for veneers. Furniture. Interior finish work.
Fir	Strong and durable. Wavy grain. Takes stain well. Resembles pine.	Plywood and laminated sheets. Cabinetry. Trim pieces. Inexpensive furniture.
Gum	Reddish-brown. Medium hard. Resembles mahogany. Interesting grains.	Veneers. Doors. Interior trim. Furniture parts.
Mahogany	Reddish or reddish-golden brown with fine grain. Can be beautifully finished.	Fine expensive furniture. Especially popular for Queen Anne, Chippendale, and other 18th century furniture. Paneling and cabinetwork.

The **quality and type of wood joinings** indicate the durability and aesthetic quality of a piece. The most common construction methods for joining wood are the following.

- **Mortise and tenon:** The mortise (hole) joins with a piece that has a projecting piece (tenon).
- **Dowel:** Rounded dowels (pegs) join into corresponding holes.
- **Miter:** Edges are cut at a 45-degree angle and may have a supportive strip straddling the joint.
- **Dovetail:** A splaying dovetail form fits into grooves of the same size and form. This type of joint is found on fine furniture.
- **Tongue and groove:** Tongue and groove forms extend the entire width of the piece.
- **Rabbeted or rebated:** One edge has a groove cut the entire width to accommodate a straight-edged piece.
- **Butt:** This type is not used for fine furniture. It is sometimes found on inexpensive furniture, but it must have cross-supports or corner blocks.

Metal

Metal used as a material for furniture was known in **ancient civilizations.** Bronze and iron were particularly used by the Egyptians, Assyrians, Greeks, and Romans for chairs, lamps, accent pieces on furniture, table bases, and other small furnishings. During the **Middle Ages** and **Renaissance,** exqui-

TABLE 9.1 *(Continued)*

WOOD TYPE	CHARACTERISTICS	USES IN HOME
Maple	White to pale yellowish-brown. Fine grain. Hard and heavy. Resembles birch. Relatively inexpensive.	Informal furniture. Popular for Early American Style. Flooring. Cabinetwork.
Oak	White oak is light to golden brown. Red oak has pinkish tones. Straight to strong wavy grain. Hard and durable.	Most important wood for furniture, trim, and cabinetwork. Quarter sawn (straight grain) usually preferred for fine furniture and paneling.
Pecan	White to reddish brown. Refined grain, often with darkish streaks. Hard, strong, and heavy.	Fine furniture. Furniture parts. Cabinetwork, paneling, and trim.
Pine	Off-white to pale yellow. Soft. Not strong. Lightweight. Inexpensive. Close grain with occasional wavy grain.	Flooring, doors, trim. Informal furniture, particularly Early American or provincial furniture and paneling. Cabinetwork.
Poplar	Off-white to yellowish brown. Softwood. Lightweight. Subtle straight grain. Inexpensive.	Informal furniture. Works well painted. Trim, cabinetwork, and exterior siding.
Rattan	A jungle vine from the Orient. Pale yellow to light brown. Soft and pliable.	Informal furniture with Oriental feeling. Can be nicely painted and stained.
Redwood	Uniform red color. Grays when exposed to weather. Available in large planks.	Exterior finishes. Beams, paneling, etc. Cabinetwork. Outdoor furniture.
Rosewood	Fine textured reddish-brown hardwood with black streaks. Beautiful when highly polished.	Popular for fine 18th century furniture. Inlay designs. Danish Modern furniture.
Satinwood	Pale blond color with smooth satin finish. Unique grain. Expensive.	Fine furniture and finish work. Inlay and parquetry designs.
Teak	Yellow to reddish-brown with fine black streaks. Strong and durable. Beautiful with oiled finish.	Popularly used for Oriental and Danish designed furniture. Decorative and functional accessories.
Walnut	Light to dark golden brown. A variety of beautiful grains. Hard, strong, and durable. Expensive.	Used for fine furniture in many styles. Especially used during 18th century Queen Anne period, called the "Age of Walnut." Paneling.
Yew	Dark reddish-brown hardwood particularly found in England. Close grained.	Cabinetwork and some furniture.

Mortise and tenon

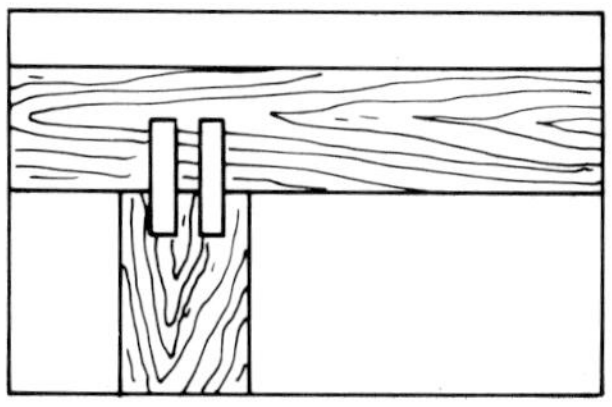

Dowel

Miter

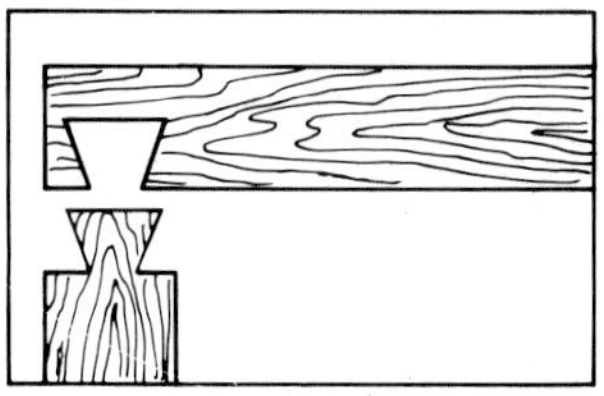

Dovetail

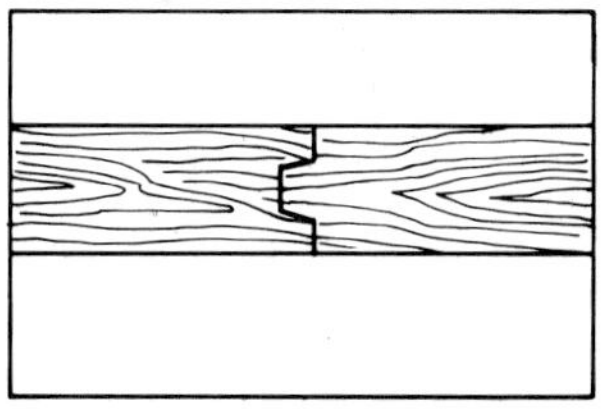

Tongue and groove

sitely wrought iron and other metals were used for many furnishings and also for ornamental supports, hinges, bands, handles, and locks. In the **eighteenth century,** metals were especially employed for accenting fine furniture. By the **Victorian** and **Industrial Revolution periods,** iron and brass beds (particularly popular) and iron furniture of all types were produced for indoor and outdoor use. With the advent of the **Bauhaus** and other **modern movements** since the turn of the century, new uses for metal have been developed, like tubular steel, sheet-metal, chrome-plated steel, wire, steel with baked-on enamel, and small and large metal rods and pipes for furniture construction. **Considerations for selecting metal furniture include the following:**

- Metal can be shaped in many forms and be riveted, bolted, and welded, providing great flexibility of design.
- The most common metals used for furniture construction include

brass, bronze, iron, steel, and aluminum.

- A wide range of finishes are available today including shiny, dull, striated, and textured in numerous ways. Steel with baked-on enamel in many colors is available.
- Metal is relatively inexpensive, strong, durable, and cool to the touch.
- Some metal furniture is lightweight and transportable.
- Care should be taken that the metal is rustproof.
- If damaged, repairs can be costly.

Synthetic Materials

Man-made products for furniture construction have revolutionized the design field. Now synthetic materials are used for almost all furniture types and in numerous ways. Basically, synthetic materials are employed in six ways: (1) **lamination and bonding agents,** for example, adhering plywoods, veneers, and wood chips; (2) **molded furniture,** employed either as a part of or as an entire piece; (3) **functional hardwood parts** and **decorative accent pieces;** (4) **finishes** of all types like paints and lacquers; (5) **upholstery** fabrics including vinyls, nylons, polyesters, acrylics, and so on (see Chapter 6); and (6) **upholstery fillers** (see next section on Upholstered Furniture).

Key considerations when selecting synthetic products for furnishings are as follows.

- Synthetics can be molded into many sizes and forms, and their use for residential and contract furnishings is unlimited.
- Synthetic materials are available in a wide range of colors, textures, and patterns. Lucite and Plexiglas have transparent and translucent properties.
- Synthetics are durable and easy to keep clean.
- Synthetics, when well designed, mix well with other furnishings and can successfully combine with other materials for furniture pieces.
- Foamed plastics have revolutionized furniture construction, allowing more lightly scaled furniture designs.
- Some synthetics may dull over time, break, or scratch and are very difficult to repair. Also, some synthetic materials are flammable.

Upholstered Furniture

Upholstered furniture was known in **ancient civilizations** when fabric—especially animal skins, rush, or leather—was simply stretched over a sturdy frame. Seats and backs with fabric stretched over a frame are still used for lightweight pieces today. During the **Renaissance** simple padding or cushions were placed on top of the stretched fabric. Later, fabrics were used to cover the cushion and stretched fabric. By the **sixteenth century** padding made of horsehair, feathers, wool, and down made cushions even deeper and more comfortable. In the **eighteenth century** springs were introduced and modern upholstery had arrived. Little change occurred in upholstery construction until the introduction of synthetics **during the 1930s,** which had a tremendous impact on the furniture industry. Upholstered furniture today is basically of two types: (1) **overstuffed**—referring to furniture that has padding or stuffing attached over the frame—and (2) an **exposed frame with partially exposed sections.** Hidden beneath the cover of upholstered furniture are the elements that should produce durability, comfort, and quality. Upholstered furniture is composed of the following.

- **Frame.** A good frame is constructed of kiln-dried hardwood such as maple, poplar, oak,

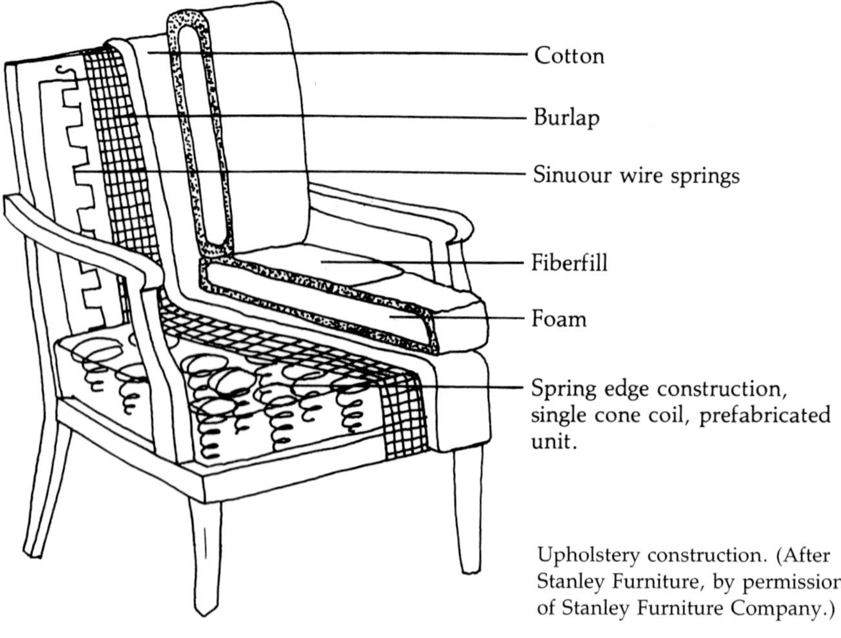

Upholstery construction. (After Stanley Furniture, by permission of Stanley Furniture Company.)

ash, birch, or elm. (Softwoods tend to split.) The wood frame should be firmly assembled and usually joined by double dowels that are spiral grooved and then glued. Reinforcement braces of metal or wood blocks should be glued and screwed to the corners. Nails are never used for good-quality furniture. Frames may also be of synthetics, metals, wicker, or rattan.

- **Webbing.** Generally of linen, jute, plastic, or rubber, this is arranged in a basket weave and used on the frame to provide support for the springs and cushioning. Good-quality webbing measures 3 to 4 in. in width.

- **Springs.** The spring construction may be of either sinuous wire or coils. The sinuous wire is simpler and by some criteria better. It is particularly desirable for slimline modern furniture and light-seated occasional chairs. The cone coil comes in both single and double cone. The **single-cone coil** is a prefabricated unit for standard styles. It is an all-wire unit with coils tied to each other and attached to top and bottom border wires. **Double-cone coils** are mounted and affixed on a resilient base such as strips of webbing or metal, and are hand tied at the top to prevent slipping. This construction provides maximum comfort and is used in more expensive deep-seated upholstery. Fine-quality springs have individual coil springs contained in a muslin. **Burlap** is used to protect and cover springs.

- **Filling, stuffing,** or **padding** materials of various types and qualities are used for cushioning, either alone or in combination. These materials—but not the qualities—are listed on the label. In the past, long curled hair, cotton, moss, or kapok was used. Today, the most commonly used fillings include the following:

1. **Polyester** is lightweight, resilient, and odorless, and it resists mildew and moths. It may be used alone or combined with cores of foam or innersprings. Polyester fillings are often wrapped with Dacron.
2. **Foam rubber** or **Latex** (looks like well-beaten egg whites with tiny holes close together) is used in solid sections and is durable and resilient and holds its shape well. It may deteriorate over time if it is not of good quality.
3. **Polyurethane foam** is more suitably used today than foam rubber and is highly resilient. Along with polyester, it is the most used filler. Polyurethane is often wrapped with polyester for use on fine furniture. It resists liquids, moths, and mildew.
4. **Down** or **feathers** are soft but require frequent plumping up to maintain shape. This filling is generally reserved for back cushions only.
5. **Rubberized fibers** such as sisal, which have less resiliency than the previously mentioned filling materials, are used in moderately priced furniture.
6. **Shredded fibers** from natural sources such as some leaves are generally used in low-priced furniture.
7. **Cotton** is occasionally used for small pieces.

Muslin used as covering over the filling material is always employed on fine-quality furniture to prevent seepage and facilitate movement. **Cotton felt** is used to protect springs and other filling materials, and it is used alone on inexpensive furniture.

- **Fabric** is employed last of all to cover all the construction of the piece, and it should be professionally finished. Seat and back **cushions and pillows,** filled with the materials just mentioned, may be added to complement the furniture's style. They may be fastened or movable, depending on the style and preferred degree of flexibility. Cushioning should be comfortable, resilient, and able to take hard usage, and it should stay in place. Since new materials are being added continually and older ones being improved, some important questions are, What kind of cushioning does the chair or sofa have? Will it retain its shape? Can it be cleaned? Is it odorless and nonallergenic?

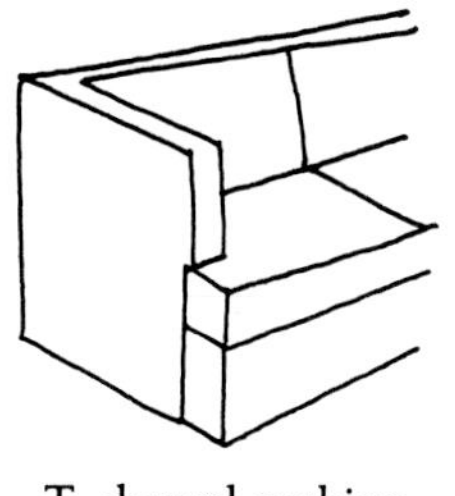

T-shaped cushion

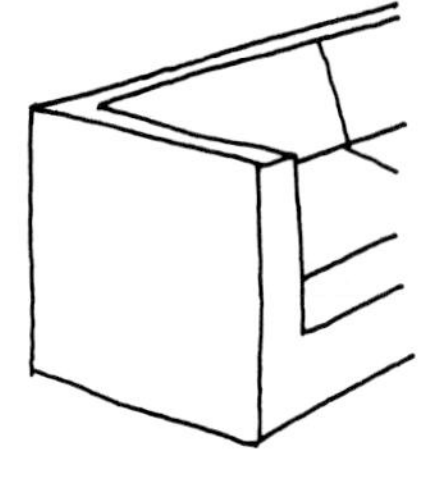
Square cushion

Slip seat

Upholstery Fabrics

In the purchase of upholstered furniture, fabric is usually the first consideration, because it is an important step in interior design and an expression of personality and individual taste. In selecting the fabric, **use** is generally the determining factor. Selecting suitable upholstery fabric involves many considerations and questions such as the following.

1. What type of **fiber and weave** are employed, and how **durable** is the fabric? An upholstery fabric, for example, will last longer if the warp and fill are the same weight and tightly woven (see Chapter 6 for fiber information).
2. Is the fabric **attractive** and **comfortable** to the touch?
3. Is a **pattern or plain** fabric preferred? Fabrics with small overall patterns tend to show soil less than solid colors. If a pattern is used, is it in scale with the room, and does it support the style?
4. Is the fabric **suitable for its intended function**? For example, will the upholstery be used by active children in a family room or by a single professional in a seldom-used area?
5. Is the fabric the best quality the **budget** will allow, considering long-term wear and maintenance? It is usually not advisable to buy expensive fabric for cheap furniture and fabric of less quality for exquisite and fine furniture; fabric and furniture should generally be in the same price category.
6. What **maintenance** process is necessary? Does the particular upholstery fabric require a **water- and soil-repellent finish** like Scotchguard or Zepel? This process is best when the fabric is treated at the factory rather than after it has been cut.
7. Does the upholstery fabric fit the **style, mood,** and **character** of the room? Is the fabric formal or informal? Does it seem to conform to the life-style of the occupants and complement the environment?

Additionally, the quality of upholstery construction is readily apparent, because the consumer can inspect the finished product firsthand. In selecting a piece of upholstered furniture, the following criteria are essential.

- **Precise tailoring** is necessary for a well-finished appearance. Seams, welts, and cording should be smooth, straight, and firmly sewn. Hems and pleats should hang evenly, with no loose threads.
- Large **patterns,** when employed, should be carefully centered and matched on each cushion and skirt.
- When fabrics are **quilted,** close, secure stitching will prevent snagging.
- **Cushions** should fit snuggly.
- If **zippers** are used, they must be sewn straight with no puckering, and they must operate easily.
- When fabric has a **nap,** it should only run in one direction.
- Fabric should be **smoothly stretched** over the frame with no buckling.
- **Back panels** should be firmly and neatly tacked or stitched.
- **Exposed wood parts** should be of hardwood and be well finished.

Intelligent Shopping

Following are suggested guidelines to aid the consumer in making the best purchase decision.

- The **quality of construction, materials,** and **finishes** ranges from poor to excellent and often is dependent on the integrity of the manufacturer and the word of the salesperson. A good manufacturer takes great pride in the skilled workmanship that goes into the product, because the company's reputation depends on it. A reliable merchant will honestly evaluate the quality of merchandise offered to the patron or client. Patronizing a reputable and dependable home furnishings or design firm is a wise investment.
- When selecting furniture, **style names** should generally not completely govern a decision. They can, however, serve as guidelines. The consumer should determine what features distinguish one style from another, what mood is created by each, and which styles can and cannot be used together compatibly.
- The buyer should learn what constitutes a **genuine antique,** a **reproduction,** and an **adaptation** (see p. 309). Becoming familiar with various **furniture types** can help the consumer make an intelligent choice suitable for functional and aesthetic needs.
- The consumer must **discriminate** between fine furniture and faddish, elaborate, or overly ornate furniture. Although the much-publicized warehouse operations have a preponderance of poor to mediocre furniture, good design can be found there at reasonable prices by shopping with a trained eye.
- **Design or style** is a personal consideration, and the design of furniture is usually chosen on the basis of **individual taste.** If taste is formed on an understanding of the **general principles of design,** and if **suitability** and **comfort** are kept in mind,

each furniture purchase should be satisfactory. In general, simple, unadorned items are wise purchases. They will likely be a better value than ornate pieces. Purchasing cheap imitations of more costly hand-carved items should be avoided. The **consumer** should know what is good design and what is right for individual needs. If a piece of furniture does not have personal appeal, the buyer should not be pressured into a purchase—no matter how popular the style.

- Good design is not necessarily expensive, and well-designed furniture is available at modest prices. **Available budget** can be widely invested in quality and good but simple design. Makers of fine furniture have often pointed out that only the rich can afford to buy cheap furniture—cheap furniture is not a good investment.
- Since purchasing furniture involves a **long-term investment,** it is generally wise to take the time necessary to shop for the best furniture addition—one piece at a time.

Care of Fine Furniture

Elementary as it sounds, regular **dusting and polishing** are the best guardians of the beauty of a fine furniture finish. Grandma with her feather duster understood the secret of preventing the accumulation of surface soil, often abrasive and harmful to a carefully rubbed finish. Today excellent waxes and polishes, if used regularly, can deepen the luster and clarity of fine wood finishes as they maintain an important protective film. Accidents will occur, and for the treatment of these, the following suggestions are presented, courtesy of Ethan Allen, Baumritter Corporation.

Minor scratches. A wax stick in a matching color can be used to fill the scratch. Wax sticks are inexpensive and are usually available at paint, hardware, or furniture stores. The wax should be rubbed in well, then the furniture wiped with a soft, dry cloth, followed by an application of polish.

White spots—cause unknown. The blemish can be rubbed with cigar or cigarette ashes, using a cloth dipped in wash, lubricating oil, vegetable shortening, lard, or salad oil. The area should be wiped off immediately and rewaxed with polish.

Alcohol spots. Method A—The spot can be rubbed with a finger dipped in paste wax, silver polish, linseed oil, or moistened cigar ash. The area should be rewaxed with polish. Method B—On some finishes a quick application of ammonia will do the trick. A few drops should be placed on a damp cloth and rubbed on the spot. An application of polish should follow immediately.

Watermarks. Marks or rings from wet glasses are common on tables, especially if these surfaces have not been waxed. Wax cannot prevent damage when liquids are allowed to stand on the finish indefinitely. The wax will, however, keep liquid from being absorbed immediately, thus allowing time for the liquid to be wiped up before it damages the finish. If watermarks appear, the following methods should be tried. Method A—Wax or polish should be applied with fine 3/0 steel wool, rubbing lightly. Method B—A clean, thick blotter should be placed over the ring and pressed with a warm (not hot) iron. The process can be repeated until the ring disappears.

Candle wax. An ice cube should be held on the wax for a few seconds to harden it, but melted ice must be wiped up immediately. As much wax as can be removed with the fingers should be crumbled off, then the area can be scraped gently with a dull knife. A brisk rub with a clean cloth saturated with liquid wax is the next step. The area may then be wiped dry with a clean cloth. The process can be repeated until the mark disappears.

Milk spots. When milk or foods containing milk or cream are allowed to remain on furniture, the effect of the lactic acid is like that of a mild paint or varnish remover. The spilled food should be wiped up as quickly as possible. If spots show, they can be cleaned with wax. Then the procedure for alcohol spots should be followed.

ASSIGNMENT

Visit a wide range of furniture stores, from the economy-priced factory outlets to the most prestigious showrooms, and make the following observations:

1. Compare the quality of design and craftsmanship and the prices. Make notes of findings at different price levels.
2. Observe room setups for the overall effect, then make a detailed examination of the floor coverings, wall and window treatments, individual pieces of furniture, and accessories. Identify various furniture styles.
3. Feel the wood and inspect the upholstery and drapery fabrics. The furnishings that appeal repeatedly will help determine personal preferences.
4. Submit a paper including information gleaned from the preceding criteria.

Furniture and Wall Arrangement

Chapter Ten

Furniture

Wall Composition

MODERN ART

The arrangement of furnishings in a room constitutes a composition in spatial design and, if successful, incorporates certain artistic principles and elements. Since a room is planned for particular people and their unique way of living, however, furnishing a room can wisely be approached from a practical, commonsense point of view, employing the principles of design merely as guidelines.

Furniture

Spatial Design in Floor Composition

New economic standards, contemporary trends in architecture, new furniture styles, and changes in manner of living that place an emphasis on different **activities within the home** all influence the use of space, not only throughout the house as a whole but also within individual rooms.

With the increase in building costs, **space is at a premium,** and its distribution within the home has changed to meet today's needs. During the early years of the century, the parlor was a small, often austere room used only for special occasions. The dining room was the gathering place for families three times a day, and the kitchen was big and homey—the heart of the home. In the late twenties, open planning became the vogue, with the entrance way, living room, dining room, and often the kitchen as one open space, with areas of activity defined by rugs and furniture placement and through the use of color and fabric. The past decade has seen a return to more privacy but with an easy feeling of flexibility. Little need exists for the parlor today, although a living room off bounds to household activities is once again in demand. The dining room

Figure 10.1 The spacious dimensions of this living area in a Cleveland residence designed by Stanley Jay Friedman allow the accommodation of a number of comfortable seating areas. Large sofas and lounge chairs contribute to a warm and inviting atmosphere. *(Courtesy of Stanley Jay Friedman. Photograph by Peter Vitale.)*

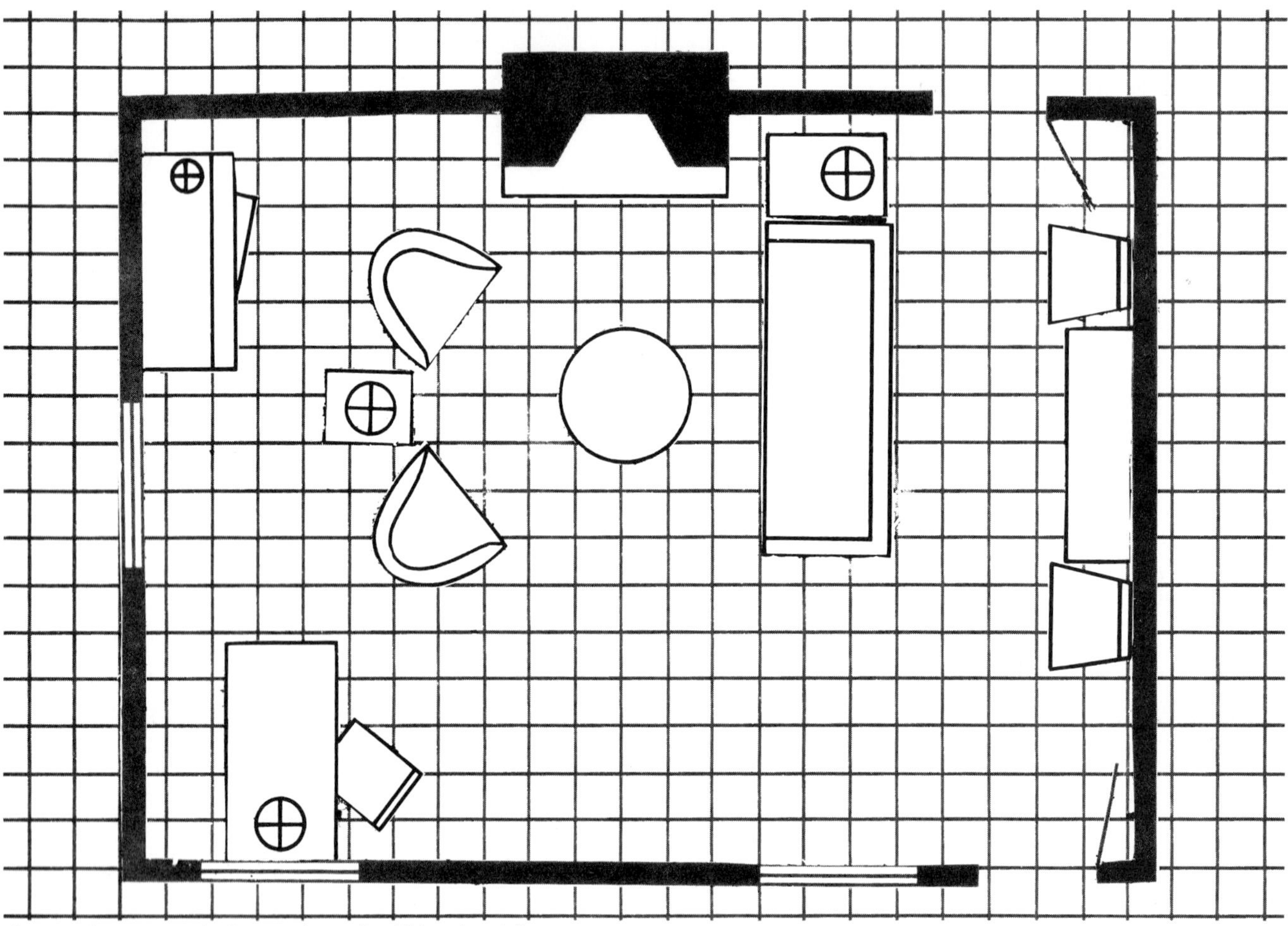

A room drawn to scale. Large pieces should be placed first.

is back, but it is smaller and is used as a dual-purpose space, since three-times-a-day togetherness is seldom possible. The kitchen, expanded into a family room, has again taken on the main burden of household living.

The key word today in furniture arrangement for every room is **efficiency.** Strict adherence to any set of rules will most likely be inappropriate in furnishing today's home. When arranging furniture in any room of the house, **first priority should be given to the household and its life-style.** Beauty and good design are important, but comfort and convenience are the most essential. A room can be pleasant in appearance but impractical for living.

In spite of the differences in life-styles, **room-furnishing procedures and guidelines** can provide assistance.

Room-Furnishing Procedure

In thinking through and carrying out the furnishing of a room, the following suggestions may be useful:

- Seldom should a room be furnished all at once; it should grow according to a **well-organized plan.** Whether the room is being furnished for the first time or is undergoing some minor modifications, the mood and function of the room should be determined. Once the completed room has been visualized, furnishings can be purchased with more confidence. Avoiding inappropriate or faddish furnishings will help maintain a unified atmosphere and outcome. No room, however, must adhere so rigidly to a theme that it becomes monotonous or does not allow for new expressions. Achieving **harmony with variety** is a wise final goal.
- The room's **size, shape, assets, and possibilities** should be assessed. After the room assets, defects, and potential have been studied, the following questions may be asked: (1) Are the dimensions of the room pleasing, or will altering the apparent height, width, or length be necessary? (2) Are the openings well placed for balance and convenience? (3) Are there jogs, niches, or other features to be minimized or emphasized,

or would the addition of some architectural feature add interest? (4) Would built-in furniture be effective? (5) Will it be necessary to redirect traffic? (6) What is the light exposure? (7) How much will the quality and quantity of light affect the choice of colors and furnishings?

- A **floor plan drawn to scale** can aid one in determining furniture placement within a space. Generally, graph paper using a measurement of ¼ in. equaling 1 ft is preferable for use in residential design. Commercial space planning usually requires a smaller scale to accommodate larger spaces. The drawn plan indicates the exact position of all architectural features such as doors, windows, radiators, heat vents, and electrical outlets. **Traffic lanes** (lanes in which traffic must pass from one door to another, one room to another, and around furnishings and activity centers) should be clearly marked. Experiments with different furniture arrangements can be made within the area drawn. Through the use of ***furniture templates,*** pieces can be moved around until the desired functional and decorative effects are achieved. Although this procedure may not be the complete solution to furniture arrangement, moving templates around on paper is much simpler than pushing heavy pieces around the room, and it can save time and energy.

TRAFFIC

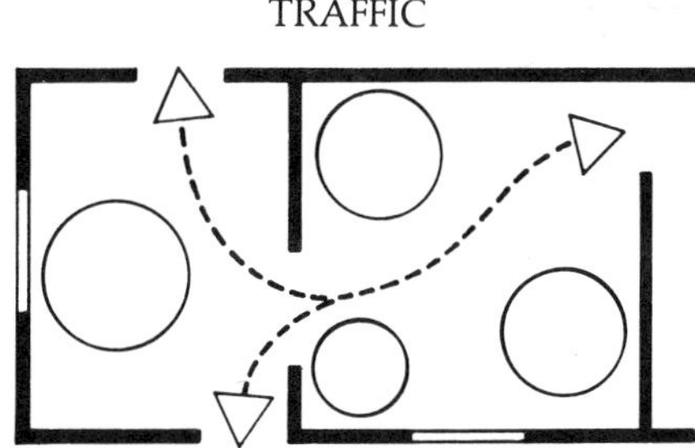

Traffic lanes and areas of activity should be indicated.

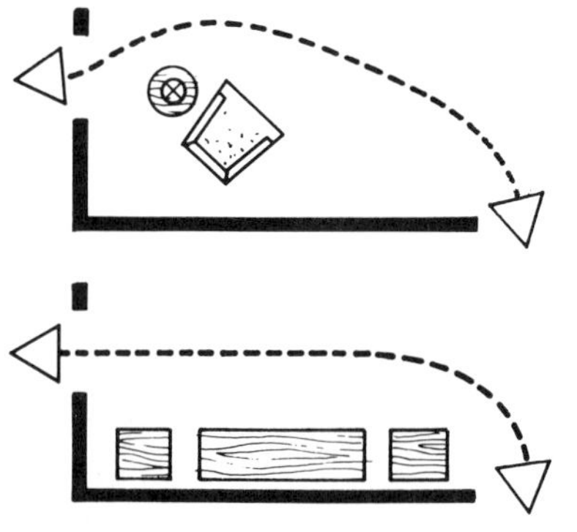

Blocking doorways should be avoided.

Guidelines in Furniture Arrangement

- Each room should be planned with function in mind, and **furniture should be grouped for function.** A decision should be made on who will use the room and for what purpose. For example, a principal living room area may be arranged with comfortable sofas, chairs, tables, and lamps that are conveniently placed, providing a pleasant area for conversation to flow. Generally, furniture arranged for conversation is placed between 8 to 10 ft apart. A spotty arrangement of furnishings seldom meets the criterion for efficient function as a grouping of serviceable pieces.
- Furniture should be arranged to accommodate necessary **major and minor traffic lanes.** Space should be allocated for occupants to move about easily from room to room and within the space itself.
- **Adequate clearance** between furnishings is essential; for example, occupants need leg room and enough space to conveniently get into and out of dining chairs around a table. Sensibly placed furnishings will help occupants avoid bumping

Figure 10.2 A circular sofa nicely conforms to the architectural background and functions as the principal seating area around a grand piano. *(Courtesy of Gayl Baddeley/Associates.)*

into corners or barriers providing efficient movement and access to furnishings.

- Determining the room's **focal point** is an important part of the planning process. The center of interest may be a painting, a large piece of furniture, a panoramic view from the window, or a fireplace. Once this decision is made, the center of interest can be emphasized by arranging other furnishings in a supportive manner.
- **Large furnishings** usually work best when placed first in the room and parallel to the wall, except in particular cases when a room lends itself to a diagonal arrangement. A large reclining chair can be pleasing and inviting when placed at an angle. Pushing large pieces tightly into a corner or close against floor-to-ceiling windows should be avoided.
- It is wise to keep furnishings in **scale** with the room. The overall dimensions and architectural background can determine the size and general feeling of the furnishings so that they complement the room.
- Space for **traffic** is an essential requirement. Doorways should be free. Major traffic lanes, unobstructed by furniture, allow occupants to circulate freely within a space. Generally, major traffic lanes require 6 ft and minor lanes 4 ft. Redirecting traffic is sometimes necessary. This can be accomplished by skillful furniture placement and

Figure 10.3 An inviting and comfortable furniture grouping is placed around a large fireplace in this living room primarily functioning for relaxation and conversation. Lighting is placed for convenience and aesthetic pleasure. *(Courtesy of Ralph Edwards, architect.)*

Figure 10.4 Furniture arrangement can support the room's focal point. In this Post-Modern living room designed by Michael Graves, the fireplace dominates the large space. The placement of classic Villa Gallia chairs, designed by the Secessionist Josef Hoffmann at the turn of the century, complements the fireplace wall. *(Photograph by William Taylor.)*

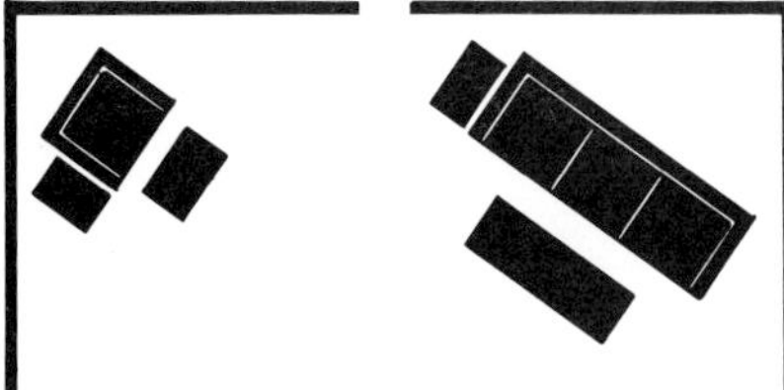

A large chair is often better across a corner.
Except in specific cases, a sofa or straight-wall piece of furniture should generally not cross a corner.

In some cases, a sofa may cross a corner. This room arrangement is pleasant.

TRAFFIC SHOULD BE REDIRECTED WHEN NECESSARY.

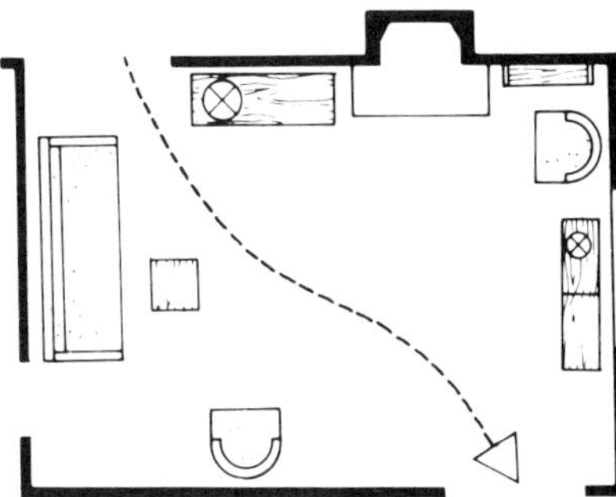

This arrangement should be changed

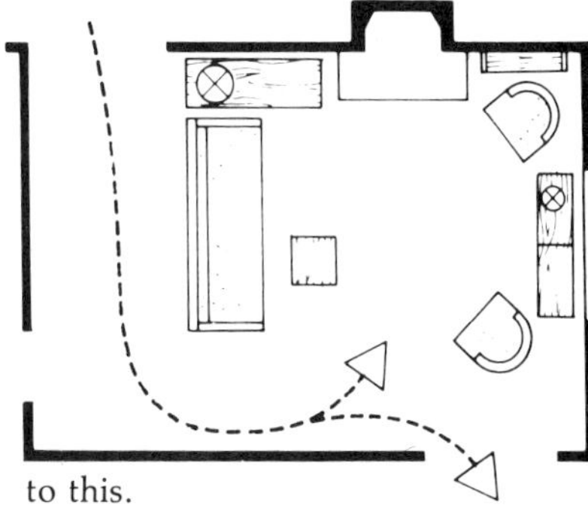

to this.

the use of screens, dividers, and plants.

- Furnishings should be arranged to give the room a **sense of equilibrium.** Opposite walls, when balanced, will help provide harmony and rest. Furniture should be pleasantly distributed around the room, considering size, color, texture, and form. For example, placing all heavy pieces of furniture at one end of the room would create an unharmonious feeling of imbalance. When neither architectural features nor furniture distribution can create this sense, it may be achieved through the knowledgeable use of color, fabrics, and accessories. Arrangement of the heaviest furniture along the highest wall in rooms with slanting ceilings will help in obtaining balance.
- A good **balance of high and low and angular and rounded furniture** will help establish interest and variety. When furniture is all or predominantly low, the feeling of height may be created by incorporating shelves, mirrors, pictures, and hangings into a grouping.
- **Architectural and mechanical features** are an important concern when planning furnishings. Nothing should interfere with

Figure 10.5 A combination of high and low pieces in this room adds interest and balance. The mahogany four-poster bed is placed against the largest wall in the room and becomes the room's central focus. Heights of the highboy, chair, end tables, bench, and lamps provide a pleasing variety. *(Courtesy of Henredon.)*

In a room with a slanted ceiling the heaviest furniture grouping should be against the highest wall.

Figure 10.6 A decorative chandelier placed over the dining table illuminates the area and adds beauty to the room. Uplighters under plants in the corner distribute the lighting and provide a dramatic accent. *(Courtesy of Gayl Baddeley/ Associates.)*

Figure 10.7 Artfully arranged paintings, books, candles, porcelain, and other accessories reflect the owner's interests and taste. French doors open into a garden with whimsical animal statues placed on the lawn. *(Photograph by Alex Groves.)*

the opening of windows, swinging of doors, or functioning of heating or air-conditioning devices. Lamps placed near electrical outlets will be convenient for use.

- **Underfurnishing a room** is often more attractive than overcrowding. Having some empty spaces between groupings helps give an uncluttered effect. An occasional open space or empty corner may enhance a room and give the occupants breathing space. On the other hand, an underfurnished room may be too stark and uninviting. Either extreme should generally be avoided.
- Rarely is a piece of furniture complete in itself, because it calls for **related pieces for function, comfort, or both.** For example, a desk needs a chair, a piano needs a bench, and a lounge chair and sofa require a table to accommodate such useful items as glasses, ash trays, magazines, and lighting.
- Since most groupings need **lighting,** the appropriate lamp or lighting fixture should be chosen to provide adequate light for the particular purpose. It is necessary for lighting fixtures and electrical outlets to be indicated on the floor plan.
- The **placement of accessories** usually comes last and can pull other furnishings together, establish the mood and style of the room, and reflect the occupant's personal taste. Considerable flexibility is possible here, and it is generally necessary to experiment with placement after major and minor furnishings are in position to determine the most satisfying arrangement (see Chapter 11).

Planning a room that is **functional, comfortable, conveniently arranged,** and **aesthetically appealing** is the ultimate goal in spatial planning.

Spatial Planning for Rooms of Various Shapes

- *The square or nearly square* room is considered one of the least pleasing in proportion. To give the room a new dimension, the principles and elements of design can be applied. Some suggestions are as follows: (1) Two opposite walls may be expanded by using a light, receding color, and a darker tone on the two remaining walls will pull them in (see Chapter

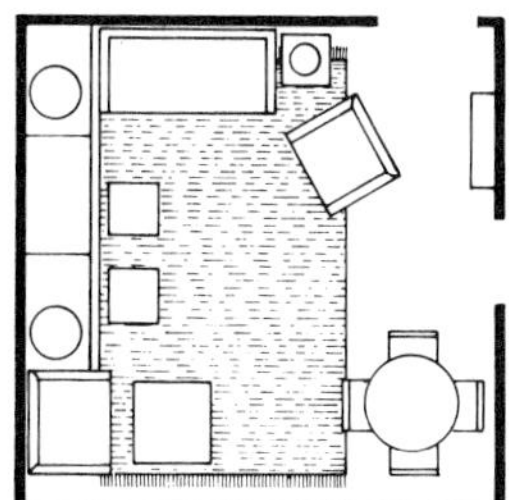

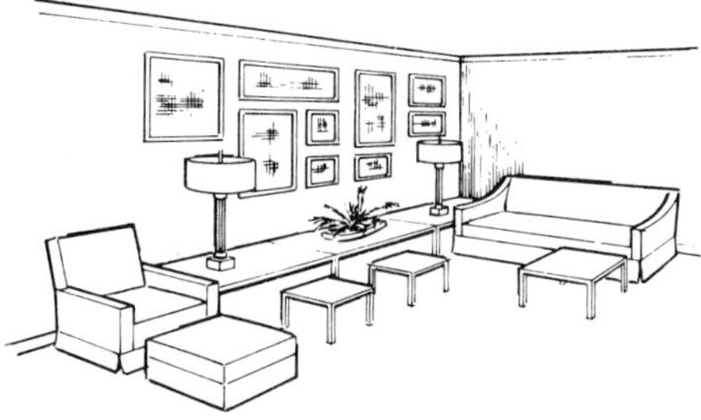

Skillfully planned furniture arrangements change the apparent proportion of a square room.

5). (2) One wall can be "extended" by running bookshelves the entire length. (3) An area rug the full length of the room, but less than the width, can be placed with the long side parallel to the bookshelves. (4) Furniture can be arranged to create a rectangular effect. The wall opposite the bookshelves should have some interest to provide weight and pull it in, and this treatment can make a room seem rectangular. These are only a few of the ways in which the proportions of a square room may be altered (see illustration).

- *The rectangular room,* if well proportioned, is the easiest room to arrange. Comfort, convenience, and beauty should be the main concerns.
- *The long, narrow room* may present a problem, but knowledgeable use of a few principles of optical illusion can modify the apparent proportions of the room. First, the activity centers should be determined. Then, if the goal is to maintain the visual appearance of one large, flexible room, the furniture that stands out from the wall can be kept low. If the goal is to make separate compartments,

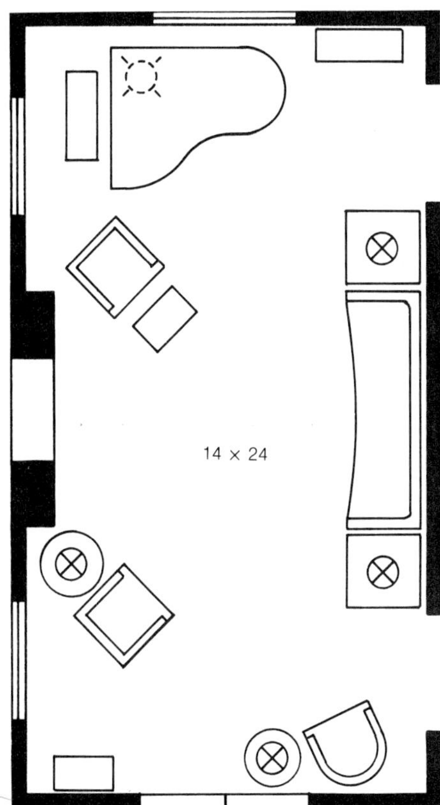

The rectangular room, if well proportioned, is the easiest room to arrange.

Figure 10.8 A long, narrow room is transformed into an inviting and interesting seating and entertainment center through the ingenious placement of furniture and accessories. The ceiling is treated with undulating neutral forms which help direct the eye toward the painting and built-in seating. *(Photograph by Norman McGrath.)*

some high pieces can be used as dividers. Furniture at right angles to the long wall will cut the length. Sectional furniture may turn a corner to create a cross-room grouping (see illustration). Rugs can be used to define areas and preferably are placed at right angles to the long wall. Dividers and screens can create activity centers that will cut the length of the room. Ceiling fixtures hung low will draw groupings together. A platform partition that creates a new level at one end of the room can shorten the room's appearance. Color can work magic if used skillfully. Light colors expand space, and dark colors reduce space. Distinct changes of color for large areas such as a dining area will further alter the apparent room dimensions.

- *The L-shaped room* lends itself naturally to a division of activities, particularly living and dining. Area rugs, dividers, and furniture placement can easily create livable space in the L-shaped room.
- *The room with a jog* need not be a problem. The offset area can be used in such a way that it becomes a feature of and asset to the room.

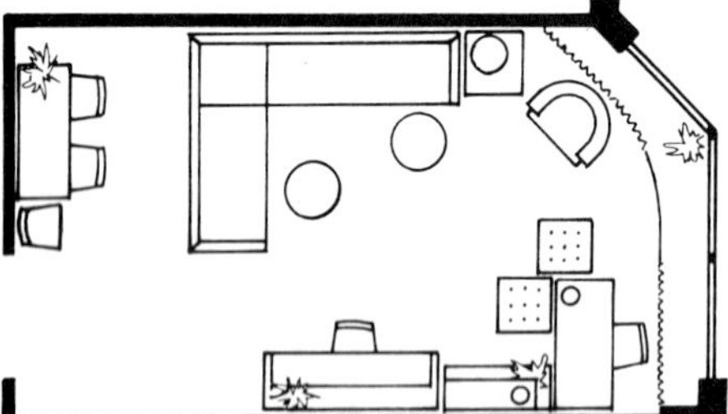

Principles of optical illusion alter the apparent proportions of a long, narrow room. The curved line of drapery, the angled sofa, and the desk placed at a right angle to the long wall make the room seem wider.

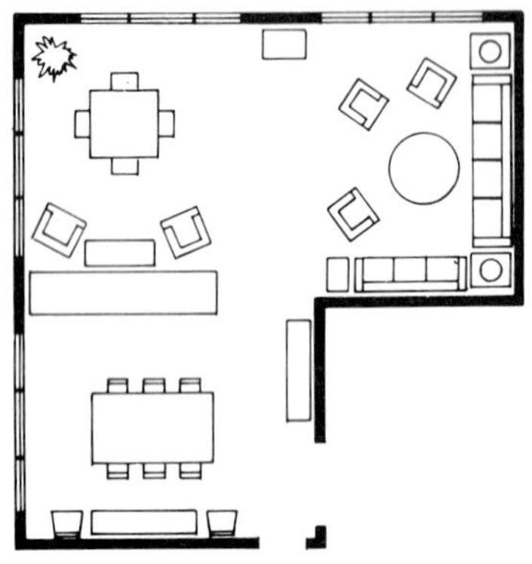

A divider provides storage and privacy in an L-shaped room.

Space Planning for Specific Rooms

Each room of the house presents a unique problem according to its function. Since the functions of different rooms vary greatly, each room should be considered separately.

The Entrance Hall

An entry is a passageway and should not be cluttered. Empty space permitting an **easy flow of traffic** is essential. The size of the room will necessarily determine the amount and scale of the furniture that should be placed against the wall. If space permits, an entrance can accommodate all or some of the following pieces: a bench, a console or narrow table, a mirror, lighting, a coat rack, and accessories (see Chapter 11).

During the past three decades, many houses were built without an entrance hall. In houses where the front door opens directly into the living room, a usually desirable plan is to create an unobstructed entrance to redirect traffic and provide some privacy. This arrangement may be accomplished in a number of ways, depending on the space available, the placement of the door, and the arrangement of the rooms to be reached.

A successful way to set off an entrance is by the use of a built-in or freestanding storage wall. This wall will require slightly more room than a screen or a single wall divider, but it has important advantages. If space is available, a deeper storage wall may provide closet space for outer garments on one side and open shelves for books or display on all or part of the opposite side. The storage divider can be planned with numerous combinations, depending on personal needs, and it may be a decorative as well as functional element in the home.

Where space does not permit a heavy divider, a screen, either freestanding, with a track, or with a panel attached to the wall and the remaining panels free-swinging, may serve as a partial divider. In a small room where any type of divider would cut needed space, the furniture may be arranged to redirect traffic by turning a sofa, a piano, or chairs toward the room and at right angles to the door, leaving a passageway for traffic. Such devices can provide limited privacy and create the feeling of an entrance way (see illustration).

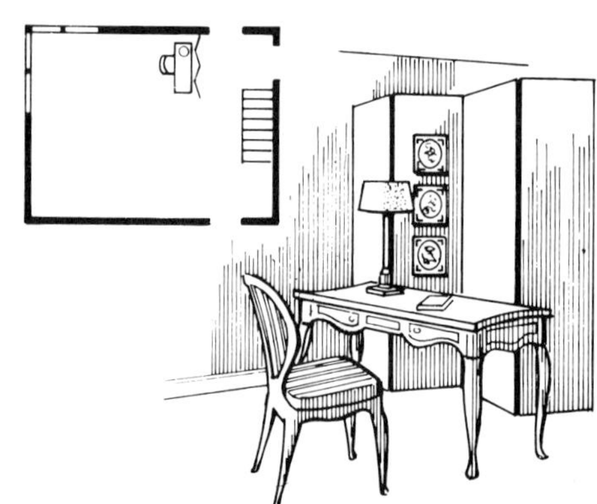

A standing screen creates a foyer and a backdrop for a desk.

The Living Room

The conversation area is the most important group in the living room and usually enhances and is combined with the focal point. In some cases the conversation area itself is the focal point of the room. Most important to keep in mind when **planning the conversation area** is its function—to provide an intimate grouping, out of the line of traffic, in which people can hear and be heard in a relaxed atmosphere. The optimum distance across this area is between 8 and 10 ft. Plans can be made for enlarging a conversation area by including occasional chairs that have been located at convenient points.

Built-in seating is usually not as comfortable or flexible as movable sofas and chairs, which may be regrouped for more intimate occasions or opened out to invite more participants. The **sunken conversation "pit"** has had some popularity, but it can be restrictive. It may serve nicely as a supplementary area where space will allow, but it is usually not preferred for the principal conversation area of a living room.

Bringing furniture out and away from the walls in a room is more conducive to intimate conver-

LIVING ROOM
14X24
FOUR ARRANGEMENTS

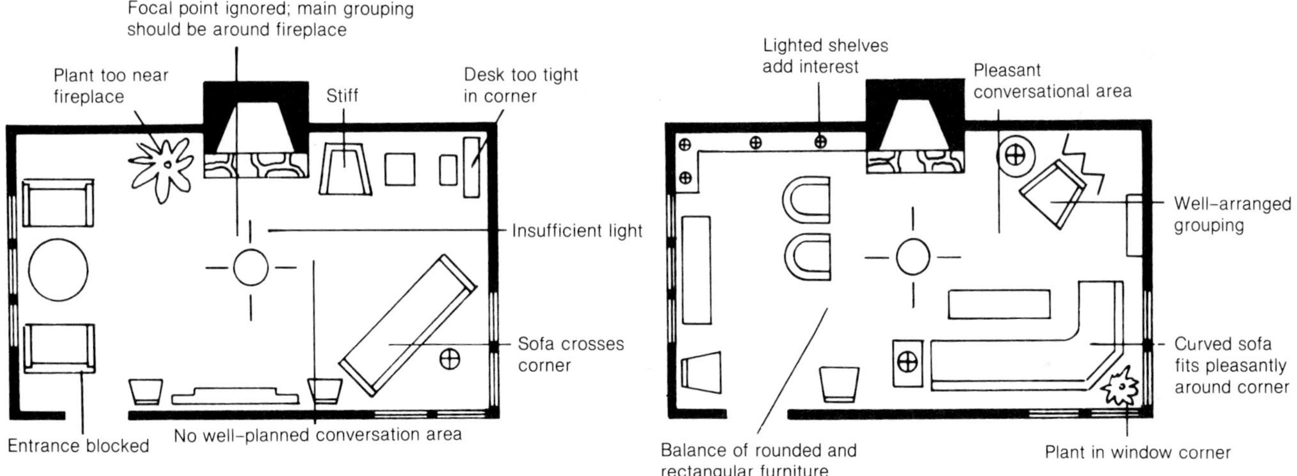

(1) poorly arranged room

(2) well-arranged room

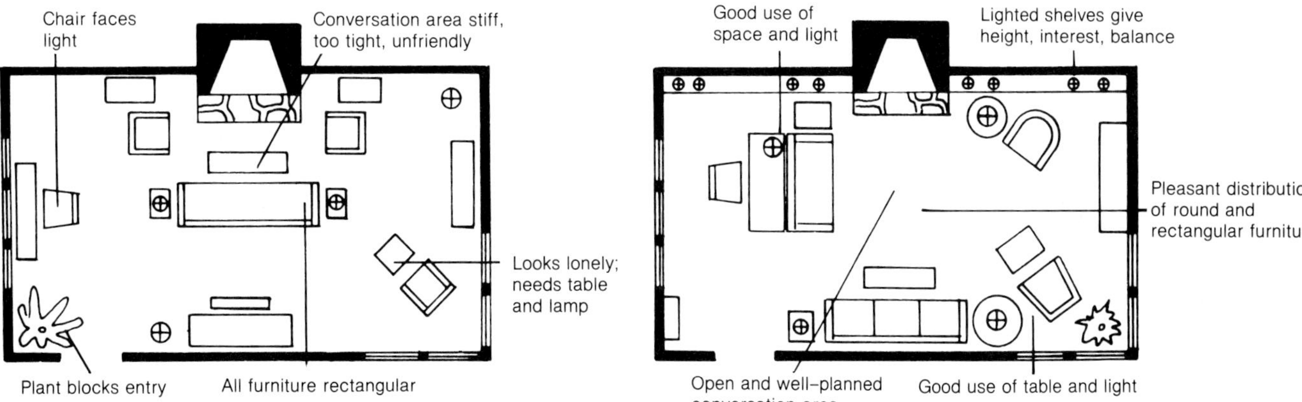

(3) poorly arranged room

(4) well-arranged room

Figure 10.9 When well integrated into a corner grouping, the sofa need not be placed parallel to the wall. In this room, the corner space behind the sofa accommodates triangular tables and secondary seating, resulting in an ingenious overall arrangement. *(Courtesy of Michael G. Merle Associates.)*

A corner arrangement need not be placed against the wall.

SIX BASIC CONVERSATION GROUPINGS

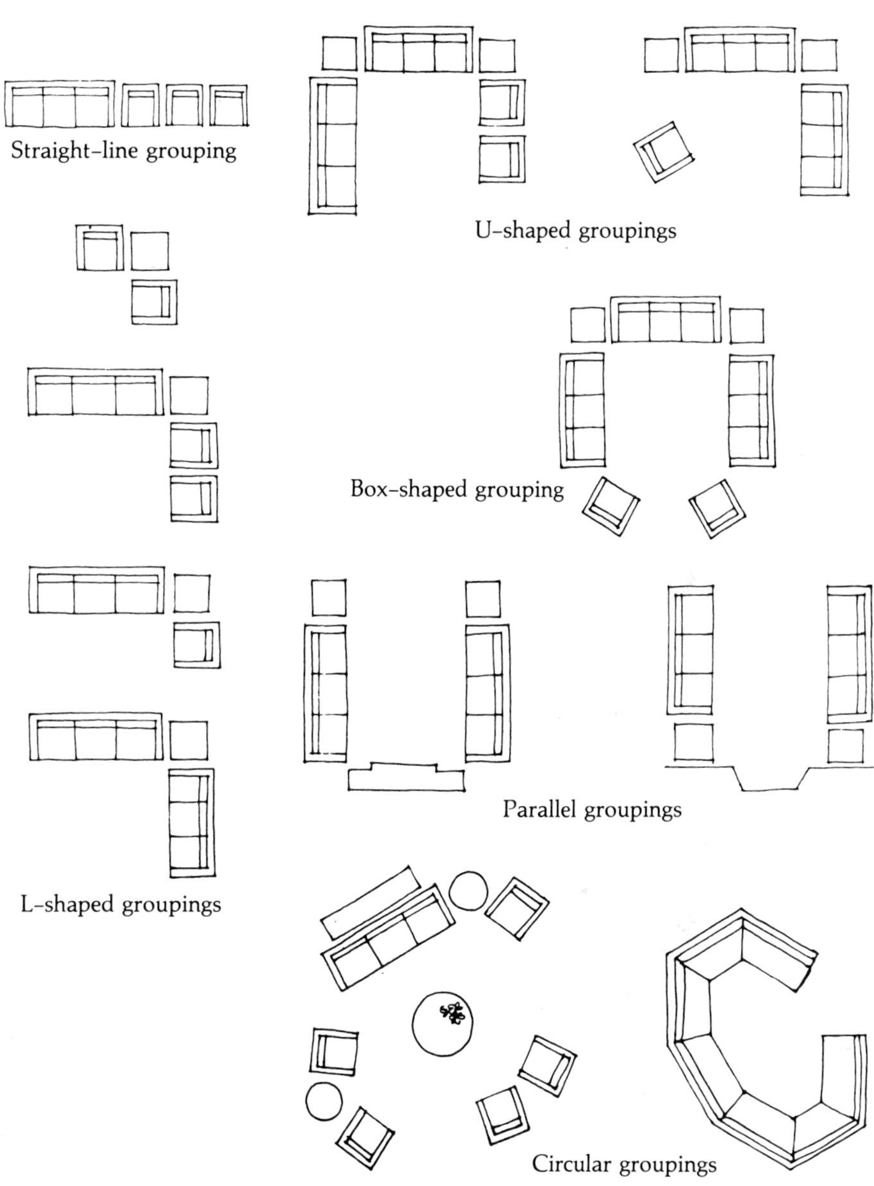

sation than furniture placed directly against the walls. An **angled or slightly curved sofa** lends itself to easy conversation more than a long, straight one does, and a comfortable corner is satisfying. The curve of a sectional sofa is invariably occupied first, just as the corner table in a restaurant is the most popular. A **comfortable corner arrangement** in a room is an invitation to quiet repose for all who enter. Whether an actual corner is invitingly arranged, a pillowed window seat is used, or a cornered sectional seating arrangement is placed free of the walls, an inviting corner is a wise addition in any living room.

A current solution to providing a flexible seating arrangement is movable **modular furniture.** Two or three separate pieces that fit together may be purchased at once; others can be added later. Modular furniture can be arranged in a variety of placements depending on space and the number of pieces.

The Basic Conversation Groupings (see illustration):

1. The *straight-line grouping* is ideal for public places but is not conducive to intimate conversation.
2. The L-*shaped grouping* is good for conversation and lends itself to both large and small areas.
3. The U-*shaped grouping* is comfortable and attractive but requires considerable space.
4. The *box-shaped grouping* is popular where space is ample. Allowance should be made for a sufficient opening to present an inviting aspect.
5. The *parallel grouping* emphasizes an existing focal point such as a fireplace or a special wall feature and provides a pleasant arrangement for conversation.
6. The *circular grouping* may encompass an entire room or an area of a large room. This arrangement can be intimate and inviting, because it provides an enveloping seating element.

To assure that household members and guests enjoy good conver-

A pair of chairs flank a small table.

Chairs in a corner for privacy

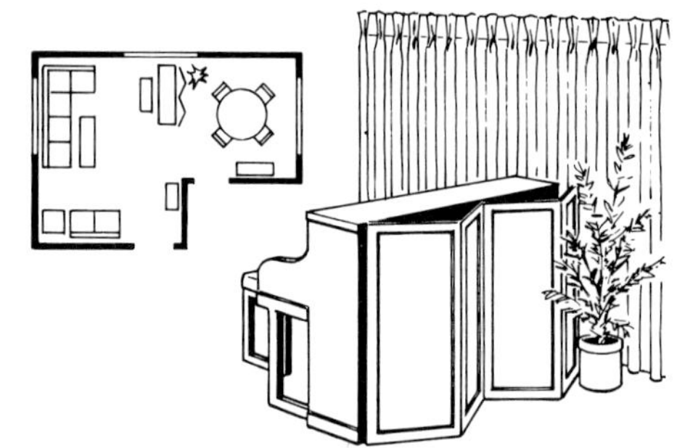

An upright piano may serve as a partial room divider.

sation, the best possible environment should be provided. Soft, low-level **lighting** provides a feeling of intimacy to a conversation area; however, this does not mean the area should be in semidarkness. People need to see the features of those with whom they are talking. A low-hanging light can pull a grouping together and serve for reading when turned to its maximum power. **Mirrors** hung where people talking can look up and see themselves is inadvisable because it is distracting and may be annoying.

Comfortable **living room chairs** of various types and sizes can provide flexibility. Since human beings are built differently, what is comfortable for one person may be uncomfortable for another. Rigidly placed chairs can make the guest believe that altering the placement would be a major calamity. Suitable tables placed conveniently near lounge chairs and sofas provide surfaces to hold lamps and small items such as books, magazines, and light refreshments.

The **use of pairs** can enhance the living room in many ways. Identical items can be a unifying factor and hence an asset to a room. They can give balance and pull together unrelated furniture. A pair of chairs can create a conversation grouping in a number of ways: angled about a table to give an intimate corner feeling, placed on either side of a fireplace, or placed side by side to balance a sofa on the opposite side. Where space is adequate, a pair of love seats or sofas may be used in place of single chairs. Identical tables placed at each end of a sofa have always been a popular arrangement in American homes. Placing them in front of a sofa is a flexible substitute for a standard coffee table. Two similar chests placed on either side of a doorway or a fireplace will enhance almost any room. Pairs of lamps, candelabra, or wall accessories can have a pleasing effect. The use of pairs when carried to an extreme, however, can be detrimental to an interior treatment.

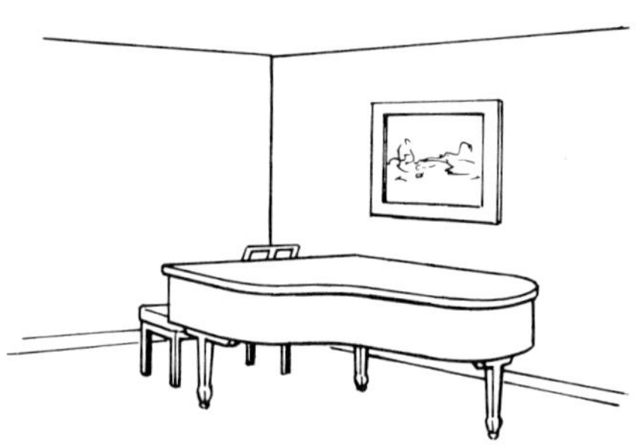

The straight side of a grand piano should be parallel to the wall.

Finding the right wall space for a **piano** is often a problem. Direct sunlight and changes in climate can have a damaging effect on a piano, limiting possible placement within the room. An **upright piano** can be placed against a wall or at right angles to the wall with other appropriate furnishings concealing the backside. A piano placed at right angles to the wall may also function as a room divider. A **grand piano** may be more difficult to place in the average room because of its size, and the straight side should in most cases be parallel to the wall. A bay window furnishes a beautiful setting for a grand piano if temperature and light conditions permit. In a large room a grand piano may be placed to form a room divider. Whatever the location, the pianist should face the room.

In the living room, most **tables** are used where a functional need exists, including **end tables** and **coffee tables.** The scale, shape, and height of each table should be right for the purpose and size of the chair or sofa it accompanies. ***Console tables*** can be decorative as well as functional and when combined with a mirror or picture are an asset to almost any room. The **writing table** or **desk** may be placed flush or with its short end against the wall and thus contribute to the attractiveness of the room. When the desk is placed in front of a window, the chair should be placed behind it, facing away from the light.

Large case or wall pieces are usually located to provide the room with a feeling of balance. If the area is small, careful planning is necessary to place the large piece where it will be most functional and will complement the wall space.

Dining Room

The scale of the room can help determine the size of the furniture for use in the dining room. Furniture arrangement seldom presents much choice in this room. (1) The **table** is usually placed in the center of the room under an architecturally fixed (2) **lighting source** with (3) a **chest** or **buffet** for storage against the longest wall and (4) a **small serving piece** near the kitchen door. If the room is large enough, a high piece such as a **breakfront** or **china cabinet** can provide space for display and add dignity as well. **Corner cupboards** are often the answer for storage and display in smaller rooms. (5) **Chairs** generally work best when not too wide across the front. The unnecessary width takes up too much room around the table. Where space is limited, a **round or oval table** will allow more

Figure 10.10 In a traditional country eating area with a fireplace, the dining table is surrounded by four Windsor chairs on three sides and a Windsor bench on the other long side. An oversized plaid rug gives definition to the grouping. *(Courtesy of Ethan Allen.)*

TYPICAL DINING
TABLE ARRANGEMENTS

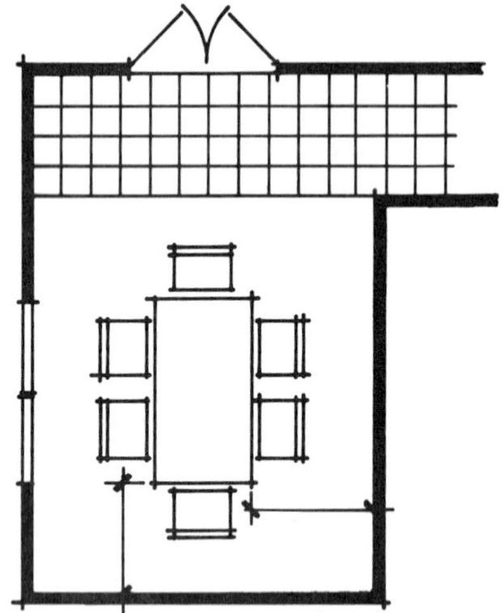

A rectangular table with six chairs placed in the room's center requires ample space for clearance

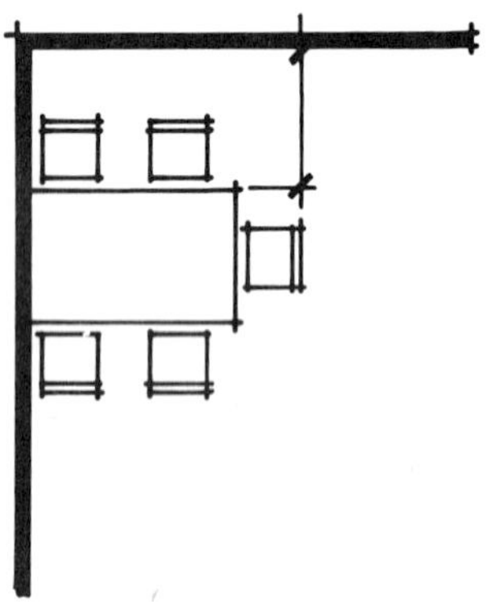

A rectangular table with one end placed against the wall accommodates seven chairs with even less space required

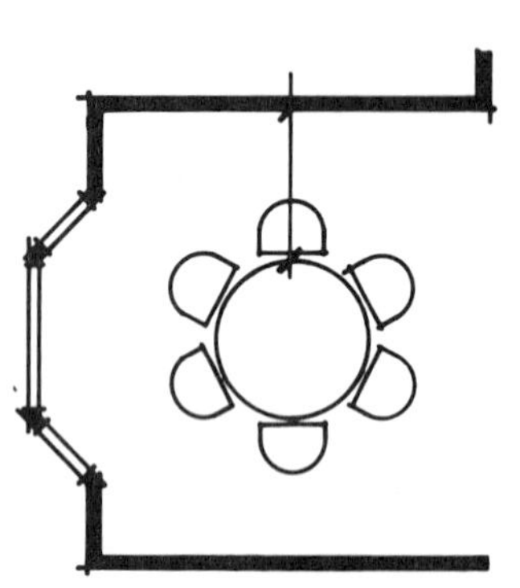

A round table placed in the room's center accommodates six chairs with less space requirements

room for passage and seat occupants more easily than a **rectangular table** of the same width and length. If the dining area is small, one option is to use a dropleaf table that, when not in use, may be closed and placed against the wall along with a wall-hung shelf for serving.

Occupants need adequate space for a pleasurable and convenient dining experience. Getting into a chair at the table requires about 2 ft. Assisting someone in seating requires about 4½ ft.

Family Room

The family room in the American home is probably the most used room of the house and one where family members congregate around an entertainment center, read, converse, play games, and often entertain. More than in any other area of the house, the arrangement of furniture is of utmost importance to accommodate and permit easy adjustment for various activities. Use, convenience, and practicality are guiding principles in arranging furnishings. (1) **Seating** for conversation incorporates similar solutions and requirements covered for this activity in the living room (see p. 337). When television viewing is an important activity, seating should be planned for easy viewing. Additional flexible seating for various activities can be included where space permits. (2) A number of **tables** can add to the occupants' comfort, including a large coffee table to accommodate beverages and food and side tables for lighting and other necessary items. (3) Convenient and adequate **lighting** is essential in a family room and must be comfortable and flexible enough to accommodate all activities (see Chapter 4). (4) An **audio-visual entertainment system** has become an important addition to the family room during recent decades, and special planning is necessary for placing a television set, movie screen, stereo, or complete entertainment center to take best advantage of possible space. (5) Family rooms may also serve as an area for quiet games. A **game table** can be incorporated into the space, when available. When space is limited, games can be played on kitchen or dining tables in other areas of the home.

Bedrooms

Since furniture arrangement in a bedroom is usually more limited than in other rooms, carefully planned space is especially important. Before furniture placement begins, a decision should be made on the purposes the room will serve in addition to sleeping. (1) Because of size, the **bed** will occupy the dominant place in the room, and seldom is there more than one wall large enough to accommodate it. Once the bed is established, traffic lanes should be planned, with careful attention given to nighttime walking. The foot of the bed is often a good place for a **storage chest** or **narrow bench.** In children's rooms, bunk beds or trundle beds can often solve a space problem when a room must serve two or more occupants. (2) **Built-in units or tables** placed at the sides of a bed are essential to accommodate necessary items. (3) **Lighting** should be conveniently located next to the bed and by additional functional areas. (4) Windows should be kept free of furnishings to facilitate **ventilation** and **light.** (5) Space permitting, **seating,** such as a small bench, side chair, lounge chair, or chaise lounge, is a practical and comfortable addition in a bedroom. The foot of the bed is often a good place for a long, narrow bench. (6) **Chests, built-ins, chests of drawers,** and other **casepieces** are essential furnishings in a bedroom for clothing **storage.** Built-in under-the-bed drawers can convert unused space into storage. (7) A **mirror** is a

Figure 10.11 In this master bedroom, the bed is arranged to take advantage of a view of Lake Tahoe and a television wall unit. The back wall and over-the-bed ceiling section are covered in a light blue fabric to match the bedspread. *(Courtesy of Eduard Dreier, architect, and Guy Dreier, Associates.)*

necessary furnishing and can either be adhered to sliding closet doors, be freestanding, or be attached to walls or furniture.

In arranging furniture throughout the home, guidelines can be applied with a good measure of common sense. (See Chapter 11 for furnishing all areas of the house.)

Making the Most of Space with Furniture

Making a Small Room Appear Larger

Through the adroit use of the principles and elements of design, a small room may be transformed and made to appear much larger than it is. The room should first be examined carefully, and traffic lanes should be defined. Then, beginning with the backgrounds, space-making principles can be applied to expand the room. The results of studied efforts in creating the feeling of space may be amazing.

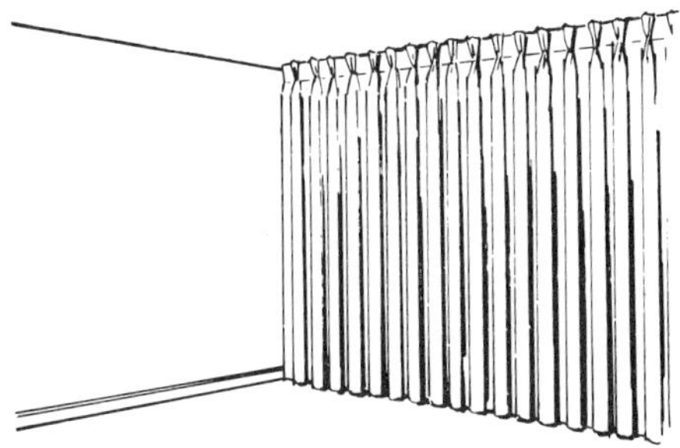

Plain, light walls and blended wall-to-wall and floor-to-ceiling drapery expand space.

Furniture

- **Small-scaled furniture** can be accommodated more readily in a small space than large-scaled pieces—but a dollhouse effect should be avoided.
- **Casepieces supported on legs** rather than those flush to the floor will allow additional space.
- **High, shallow pieces** for storage and display extend the eye upwards, and the depth keeps furniture from added extension into the room.
- **Tables and other furnishings with rounded corners** take up less space.

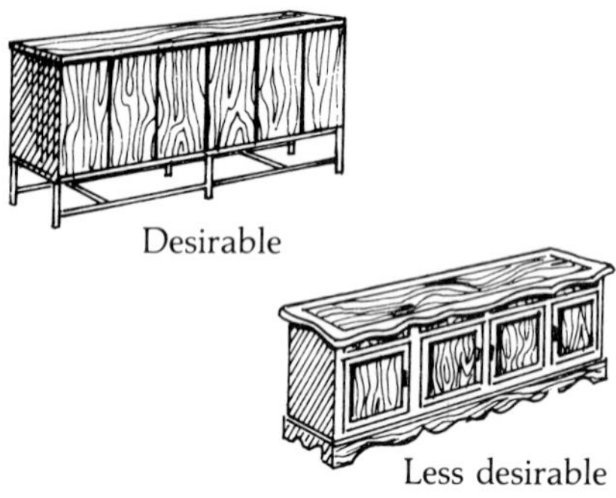

Desirable

Less desirable

Desirable

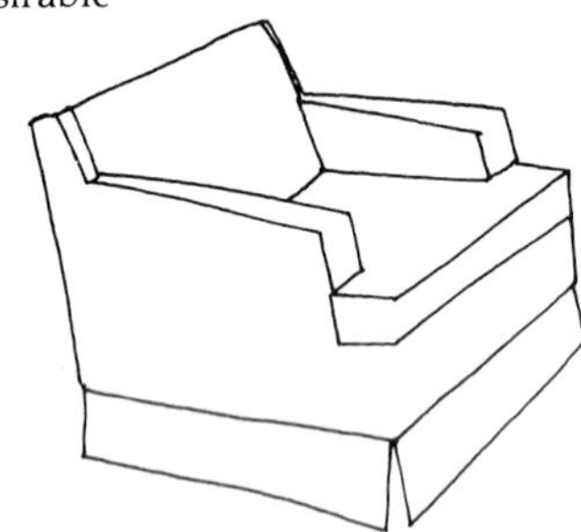

Less desirable

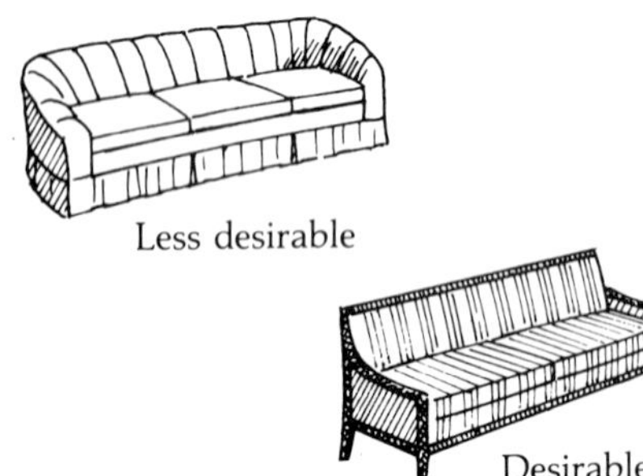

Less desirable

Desirable

- **Clear glass or plastic tops** allow the eye to see additional space.
- Chairs and other furnishings with **see-through backs** or **backs and sides of caning** or of **clear plastic** help to provide a sense of more space.

A wall-hung shelf with rounded corners takes little space.

- **Furnishings with no arms** free up space.
- Upholstered pieces covered in a **plain** or a **small all-over patterned fabric** blended to the room's background provide visual space. Repeating the same fabric on other pieces will help unify furniture and will have a space-making effect.
- **Upholstery** that is neatly **tailored** and **without skirts** will provide an uncluttered look.
- **Furniture aligned against walls** will leave the center of the room free.
- If extended to the ceiling, **shelves** and **high storage units attached to walls** will visually add height and if terminated approximately 1 ft from the floor, will allow the perimeter of the room to be seen, adding to the space. Smaller units such as serving tables, consoles, ***buffets,*** and desks can also be wall hung, eliminating the need for space-using legs.

Lighting

- Light **cast on ceilings** or on the **upper part of the wall or drapery** will direct the eye upwards.
- Lamps with **inconspicuous shades** that provide indirect lighting help conserve space.
- **Uplighters** placed at key points on the floor around the perimeter of the room add to the illusion of height and space.

Accessories

- **Clutter should be avoided.** Rather than being scattered about the room, items used sparingly and in a well-organized way will enhance the space.
- With skill, **a few bold accessories** can give a sophisticated feeling without visually eliminating space.
- **Mirrors** strategically placed can reflect a wall, the outdoors, or a particular area, thus multiplying space.
- A few **plants,** generally small-leaved ones, can give an airy feeling.

For additional space-saving techniques, see the section in Chapter 4 on space (page 97).

Making a Large Room Appear Smaller

The challenge of making a big room livable is not a common one. When it does occur, the following are some suggestions for selecting and arranging furniture to provide a comfortable human dimension.

- The most important consideration is **scale.** Massive furniture, overscaled patterns, and large pictures can be employed.
- All furnishings, however, need not be massive. After large pieces have established the broad outlines of the room, lighter pieces can be used to complete the groupings.
- Too little furniture in a big room can result in a cold, uninviting interior, and too much furniture may give a feeling of clutter. More important than quantity, however, is the **arrangement.**

Figure 10.12 Arranging furniture and accessories in a large room presents a unique challenge. In this spacious living room, two large sofas, a coffee table, and a love seat are easily accommodated. An area rug helps define the principal conversation area. The room gains interest through the use of large-scale accessories. *(Courtesy of Gayl Baddeley/ Associates.)*

The best technique is to plan separate areas of different sizes. Some may be small and intimate; others, more open. ***Occasional chairs*** may be moved from one group to another, thus forming a link between groupings.

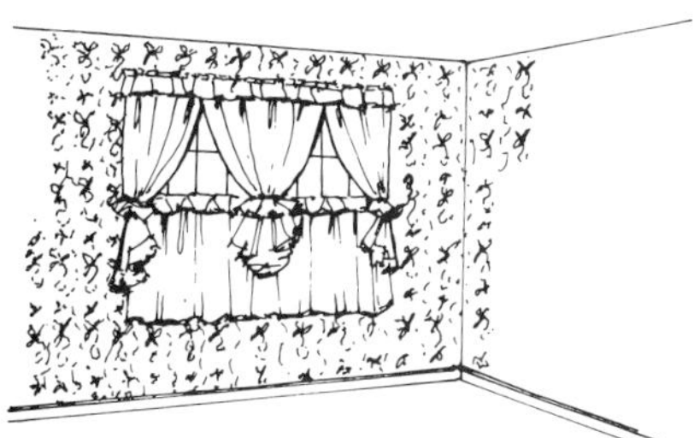

Patterned walls and ruffled curtains seem to fill up a room.

- All furniture used in the middle of a room should look attractive from all angles. A **sofa-back table** is a versatile and attractive piece to serve two areas.
- A few empty spaces in a large room can be pleasant. A room that looks as though it could use one more item has a certain appeal. One writer referred to this as "the charm of the incomplete."

Wall Composition

A floor is on a horizontal plane, and its composition is primarily one of furniture arrangement. A wall is on a **vertical plane** limited by ceiling, floor, corners, and other permanent **architectural features** such as doors, windows, mantels, and paneling. Because the wall is viewed from a different angle, **movable items** such as hanging and portable lamps and pieces of furniture seen in relationship to the wall are part of the complete com-

Figure 10.13 Two walls in this modern space, designed by Robert Brain, are arranged in different approaches. A close grouping of pictures of various sizes lines the wall adjacent to the long dining table. The large wall behind the sofa is emphasized with one magnificent abstract oil painting. *(Courtesy of Robert Brain, designer.)*

position. If architectural features are not well planned, a designer can disguise or emphasize whatever will enhance the total wall composition. If **ceilings** are below standard height (8 ft), any horizontal division of the wall should be avoided, since this will tend to make the ceiling seem lower. Instead, vertical lines can be emphasized to add height. If ceilings are too high, they may be made to appear lower by emphasizing horizontal lines.

Each **wall elevation in a room** should be considered individually, and each composition should present a pleasing effect suitable to the style and mood of the room.

Application of the principles and elements of design is helpful when selecting and arranging items for a wall composition.

- The **scale relationship** among the individual items, and between the overall composition and the room, should seem right. The placement of items against the wall and the **proportion of the wall** to be covered should be carefully planned in a manner complementary to the complete composition.
- A pleasant feeling of **balance** should be present (see Chapter 4). If the overall composition is one of asymmetry, it will most often remain interesting under constant viewing longer

Bisymmetrical balance may become monotonous.

Asymmetrical balance will remain interesting longer.

than if it is bisymmetrical. Some formal balance, however, can bring unity into the arrangement.

- **Straight lines** are enhanced when **curved lines** are introduced. A composition can be enhanced by a pleasing **juxtaposition of rectangular, square, circular, and oval shapes.** Variety with a sense of unity is an important goal when combining various lines and shapes.
- **Uneven numbers** often make a more pleasant and interesting composition than even numbers.

No specific rules of measurement are available by which to produce a perfect composition. That intangible quality of taste or judgment must therefore be employed, resulting in a wall composition that is easy to live with, is complementary to the architectural background and style, and is visually pleasing.

Two-Dimensional Art

The need to add some form of visual interest to walls of a dwelling has existed for centuries. From prehistoric animal paintings on the walls of caves to arrangements of pictures in homes of the twentieth century, art has been some measure of human nature. Artwork selected for a home reveals much about the owner's personality and individual taste. Watercolors, paintings, prints, posters, and other two-dimensional artworks are favorite items employed for wall compositions. Following are considerations when selecting and arranging two-dimensional art for a wall composition.

- The **frame** is extremely important. A picture worth displaying is worthy of framing appropriately. A picture can be enhanced or destroyed by the way it is framed. Achieving the most pleasing result possible can be a complex task, but with a little study and observation it can be accomplished. Some pictures do not call for a frame and are complete without one. Frames

Figure 10.14 One small wall of a kitchen area has a composition of shelves with dishes and other functional items openly displayed and combined with a tile-faced hood and counter backdrop. *(Courtesy of Arizona Tile.)*

Figure 10.15 A wall composition designed to project a country look is covered with a quaint all-over pattern topped with a coordinating border with space above for a white painted molding shelf deep enough to display dishes, sculpture, and a painting. A hutch with accessories and a small tree planting complete the arrangement. *(Courtesy of Country Life Designs.)*

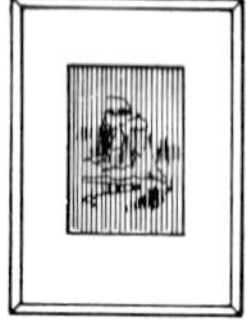
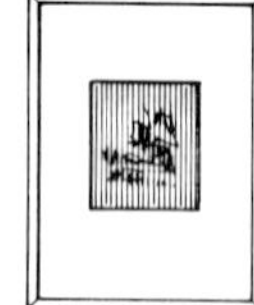
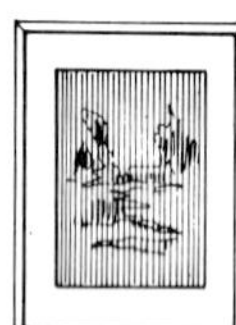

Pictures of different sizes can be unified by the use of mats and similar frames.

are available in many materials, including wood of all types, metals, enamels, paints, and gilded surfaces, and they may also be structurally or decoratively designed. When a frame is selected, it generally should not dominate the artwork but complement the subject, style, and feeling of the picture. Often traditional oil paintings are framed in heavy and ornately carved frames, and simple etchings and watercolors in lighter and narrower frames. Many two-dimensional artworks are enhanced by a **mat,** which will make the picture larger and can make a nice transition between the picture and the wall.

- When a picture is selected for a composition, the **texture** of the wall should be compatible with the art piece.
- Pictures can be **hung individually or in groupings,** but whatever alternative is selected, it should **relate to the sofa, chairs, tables, or other furnishings that constitute part of the total wall composition.** Usually a picture relates best to the composition when not "floating" alone on the wall. A table, console, or other furnishing

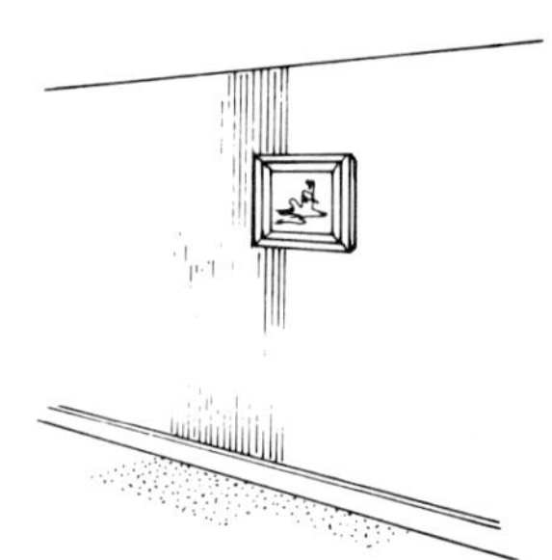

The picture seems to float when not anchored.

PICTURE ARRANGEMENT

Picture is too small for the chest.

Picture is too large for the chest.

Picture is a pleasing proportion for the chest.

beneath the picture can stabilize the artwork.

- When arranging art groupings, **positive areas** are the actual spaces filled with the two-dimensional artwork, and **negative spaces** are the areas in between these pieces. Regardless of shape and size, each picture hung should have a pleasing space surrounding it in relationship to the adjoining picture.
- When a single picture is used on a wall, it usually works best when **hung at eye level,** but **artwork hung at unusual levels** can be sophisticated and appealing.
- Wall art can provide the room's **focal point,** with furnishings arranged to support this emphasis.
- A picture hung above a chair or sofa should be placed high enough so the head of the seated person does not touch the frame: approximately 6 to 8 in. will **provide sufficient clearance.** Additionally, pictures are seen and appreciated when not obstructed by lamps, flower arrangements, or other accessories.
- **To assemble an arrangement** of a two-dimensional art composition, a large sheet of brown paper the size of the area to be covered can be used. The paper is laid on the floor, and pictures and other objects are arranged on it until the final composition is created. Each object can then be traced around the perimeter, and a point can be marked where it will be hung on the wall. The paper can then be held up against the wall with marks made where nails or hooks will go. The pictures can then be easily hung in the planned arrangement.
- Pictures look best when **hung flat against the wall** with nails and hooks securely attached and cords and wires concealed.

Bouquet obstructs the mirror.

Bouquet forms a link with mirror and container.

Asymmetrical

Bisymmetrical

Figure 10.16 Storage wall planning and organization are combined in creating a center for storage display and versatile use. The drop-down table folds up when not in use to provide extra floor space and to mask unsightly storage. *(Courtesy of Interliebke.)*

Storage Units

A storage unit partially or completely covering a wall and extending from floor to ceiling, containing both open shelves and closed units, will occupy little space, provide abundant storage, and be an important architectural feature in the room. The unit can incorporate books, pictures, mirrors, and other diversified objects, as well as the television. When artfully planned and arranged into a harmonious composition, the storage wall can be a masterpiece of design and color and may even form the room's focal point.

Since walls of a room form the background not only for furniture but for people, the final effect usually works best when not an obstructive one. With this in mind, and with an acute awareness of the importance of the relationship of form, space, line, texture, and color, a successful wall composition can be achieved.

ASSIGNMENT 1

Carefully observe and analyze wall arrangements in magazines, studio setups, and homes. On graph paper, do some experimenting with various wall compositions until you believe that you have developed some skill. Then put your skill to a test by arranging the walls in a room of your choosing. The challenge may have rewarding results.

The specific class assignment is left to the discretion of the instructor.

ASSIGNMENT 2

In the following assignment, you are given an opportunity to apply the principles and guidelines of floor composition discussed in the chapter. Study the four living room arrangements in the Student Work Packet.

This assignment includes plans for five rooms, templates, and graph paper. Examine each of the empty rooms to determine its assets and defects. Rooms 1 and 2 present particular problems that need to be resolved. Decide on the functions of each and the areas of activity. Experiment on the graph paper until you have found a satisfactory arrangement for each room. Then arrange the templates to take the best advantage of space in creating pleasant, functional rooms. Follow the procedures as outlined in the chapter.

The completed rooms should be checked with the 12 items on the checklist on page 358. Room arrangements will be evaluated according to this list.

The following is a list of the *minimum clearances* for placement of furniture:

LIVING ROOM	
Traffic path—major	4 ft to 6 ft
Traffic path—minor	1 ft, 4 in. to 4 ft
Foot room between sofa or chair and edge of coffee table top	1 ft to 15 in.
Floor space in front of chair for feet and legs	1 ft, 6 in. to 2 ft, 6 in.
Chair or bench space in front of desk or piano	3 ft
DINING ROOM	
Space for occupied chairs	1 ft, 6 in. to 1 ft, 10 in.
Space to get into chairs	1 ft, 10 in. to 3 ft
Space for person to assist in seating	4 ft, 6 in.
Traffic path around table and occupied chairs	1 ft, 6 in. to 2 ft
KITCHEN	
Working space in front of cabinets	2 ft to 6 ft
Counter space between equipment	3 ft to 5 ft
Ventilation for attachments in back of some appliances	3 in. to 5 in.
BEDROOM	
Space for making bed	1 ft, 6 in. to 2 ft
Space between twin beds	1 ft, 6 in. to 2 ft, 4 in.
Space in front of chest of drawers	3 ft
Space in front of dresser	3 ft to 4 ft (both directions)
BATHROOM	
Space between front of tub and opposite wall	2 ft, 6 in. to 3 ft, 6 in.
Space in front of toilet	1 ft, 6 in. to 2 ft
Space at sides of toilet	1 ft to 1 ft, 6 in.
Space between fronts of fixtures	2 ft to 3 ft

CHECKLIST FOR ARRANGING FURNITURE

1. Are traffic lanes neatly marked and left free? Mark the major traffic lanes in red. (These are the lanes leading from one door to another.)

2. Where the outside door opens directly into the living room, has an entranceway been created that provides some privacy, particularly for the main conversation area?

3. Has one well-chosen center of interest been made the important, yet not completely dominating, focal point in the room? Is this grouping comfortably and conveniently arranged, out of the line of traffic, yet open enough to be inviting?

4. Are other areas of activity clearly defined, conveniently located, and artistically arranged with all necessary items?

5. In dual-purpose living–dining rooms, has a screen, a divider, or an effective furniture arrangement been employed to provide some privacy or adequate division of space?

6. Large pieces of furniture:

- □ Is each piece placed to take the best advantage of space and not pushed tightly into a corner?
- □ Is each piece placed parallel to the wall (with the possible exception of a lounge chair), unless the major seating arrangement is based on a diagonal plan?
- □ Does a large piece block a window?
- □ Where windows go near to the floor, are large pieces placed out far enough to allow passage behind?
- □ Where a grand piano is used, is the straight side parallel to and nearest the wall?

7. Does the room have a sense of balance?

- □ Do opposite walls seem the same?
- □ Are high and low pieces pleasingly distributed?
- □ Are round and rectangular pieces pleasingly distributed?

8. Are occasional chairs placed at convenient points to be moved easily into various groupings?

9. Is lighting adequate and conveniently located? Are all electrical outlets indicated?

10. Does each living room have a feeling of comfort and interest, with a variety of activity areas for music, reading, writing, and conversation, without being crowded or cluttered? Are dining areas arranged for convenience? Are bedrooms furnished to make the best use of space, with room for nighttime walking?

11. Is there a feeling of unity?

12. Is each room's composition done with professional neatness?

Chapter Eleven

Unifying the Interior Environment

Thinking Through an Interior Design Project

Specific Areas

The Front Door
The Entrance Hall
The Living Room
The Dining Room
The Family Room
The Entertainment, Recreation, and Educational Centers
The Kitchen
The Utility Areas
The Master Bedroom
The Bathroom
The Child's Room

Planning for the Handicapped and Elderly

Decorative and Functional Accessories

Screens
Pictures and Paintings
Sculpture
Books
Mirrors
Lamps
Clocks
Flowers, Foliage, and Plants
Crafts as Accessories
Finishing Touches

Anyone who has ever gone house hunting need not be reminded of the frustration experienced while traveling from one unfurnished apartment or house to another. Too often the places desired are too expensive or are so badly planned or so run-down that it is difficult to visualize the empty spaces as comfortably designed rooms. Because prospective home owners have trouble visualizing the completed product when looking at empty rooms, real estate agents invariably urge home owners to continue living in their homes while selling them. In areas of tract houses, where identical homes are for sale, the more attractively designed homes consistently bring a higher price than those not as appealing, even though the buyer knows the furnishings will not remain in the house.

Thinking Through an Interior Design Project

How does the homeowner go about thinking through the numerous problems involved in making a home out of empty walled-in spaces? Of primary importance are intelligent study and insight and an accumulation of information about design principles, floor plans, colors, fabrics, materials for backgrounds, furniture selection and arrangement, and intelligent shopping. Also important is courage—courage to heed personal convictions regardless of outside pressures to follow current fads. Creative ideas that have accumulated over a period of time and from innumerable sources are necessary as well. Thomas Carlyle once said, "He is most creative who adapts from the greatest number of sources." Carlyle's statement is particularly true when applied to the design process. Interior design is usually most successful when it proceeds slowly according to a well-organized plan, not when it is finished all at once. Designing an interior is an ongoing process and should be based on individual or household needs and kept within a given budget.

Figure 11.1 In a Brooklyn home, designer Stanley Jay Friedman has incorporated Oriental accessories and artfully placed lighting to unify the sophisticated design. *(Courtesy of Stanley Jay Friedman. Photograph by Peter Vitale.)*

Figure 11.2 A custom-designed wood door by the architect effectively introduces this modern glass, wood, stone, and metal home. *(Courtesy of Eduard Dreier, architect, and Guy Dreier Associates.)*

Figure 11.3 The entry of the same home pictured in Figure 11.2 makes a striking architectural impression with fenestration that allows natural light to flood the area. *(Courtesy of Eduard Dreier, architect, and Guy Dreier Associates. Photograph by Richard Springgate.)*

Specific Areas

A specific mood generally seems to be appropriate for each area of the house, but this necessarily varies with individual households. Also, as space becomes tighter, daily functions will increasingly be combined in multipurpose rooms. The following suggestions may be helpful in establishing the mood of specific areas of the house.

The Front Door

The front door can visually be the most interesting architectural exterior feature of the house, often providing the focal point. It can create the image or style the owner wishes to convey. Whether the doorway is to be a vivid focal point or blended into the facade of the house, knowledge of color, texture, and style can help achieve the objective. Standard doors of every period and style are available today. If the current door is a good style but dull, it can be remodeled with molding strips, stained glass, pilasters, a cornice, a pediment, or a modern treatment. Old hardware can be replaced (the market abounds in all types); ornamental ironwork can be refinished; and shutters, side lanterns, or overhead lighting can be added. Whether the scheme is quiet or daring, painting alone (an inexpensive solution) can work magic. When the door itself is completed, final touches might include a group of potted plants, a pair of urns, a bench, or a sculpture.

The Entrance Hall

Homes of the past almost always had an entrance hall. The earliest seventeenth-century houses in New England had a tiny entrance from which the narrow stairway ascended to the attic. Later the entrance and stairway became the focal point of the house. With the advent of open planning, this room was generally abandoned, with the front door opening directly

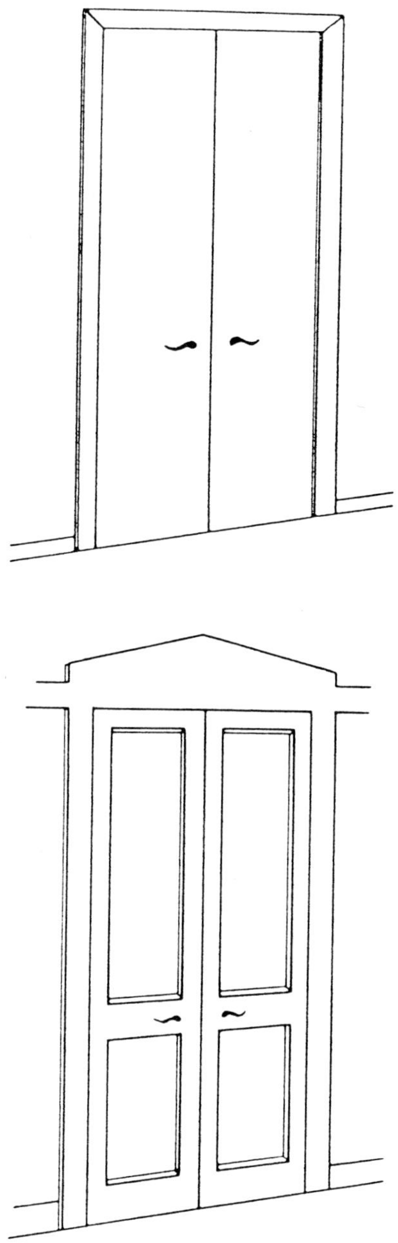
Stock moldings can change the aspect of a door either inside or out.

into the living room. Some points to consider include the following.

- An entrance hall—no matter how small—can direct **traffic** throughout the house and is an excellent use of space.
- Whatever the **general style or theme** of the house, the entrance hall is a good place to enhance it. The entrance hall can not only establish the character and mood of the home but also leave a lasting impression on all who enter. With the new materials available today, a room can be formal, even luxurious in feeling, yet also take the wear and tear of daily living.
- An entrance with a shoe-box look can benefit from some architectural interest if a traditional look is preferred. Lumber companies have a wealth of stock moldings and paneling from which to choose. The entrance is also an excellent place to use an attractive wall covering. If the entrance is narrow, walls can be pushed out by the use of a mural with a three-dimensional effect that leads the eye into a distant scene or with artfully placed mirrors. When decorative paper is used, a dado can help take the wear off the lower part of the wall.
- An important point to remember when selecting the **floor covering** is that the entrance is a passageway and must take traffic. One of the hard-surface materials such as wood, brick, tile, terrazzo, travertine, or other types of stone will provide a lifetime floor and be easy to maintain. A well-anchored area or throw rug can add warmth and serve as a color transition with adjoining rooms.
- **Scale** and the **amount of furniture** used in the entrance hall will be determined by the size of the room and available wall space. Wall space is usually large enough only for the necessities: a chair to sit on, a small table, and effective lighting. A bench may substitute for both the chair and table. Where space is limited, a wall-supported shallow and rounded console is an excellent choice and will seem to take up no space. A mirror is important in this area. In addition to providing its functional purpose, it will expand space. Bookshelves, art, plants, and other accessories can add warmth and a humanizing touch.

The Living Room

If the living room lives up to its name, it will provide for all household members and guests as well. A trend that began in the 1950s relegates most family activities to a separate family room and reinstates the more formal parlor—but without using that name. With today's dwindling space, however, this arrangement is not always possible and activities are often combined. Where two living areas are permitted, the living room usually takes on a more formal appearance. In planning the living room, a realization that more people share this area than any other room in the house is helpful. Following are some general considerations when planning the living room:

- The **transition from the entry** is important. The general feeling of the entrance way should flow easily into the living room with a pleasant transition of color. If walls of the entrance are papered, keeping the living room walls plain, either painted or paneled, is usually advisable. Sometimes a paper coordinated with that in the entry can be used.
- The interior of the living room is often successful when designed gradually, beginning with the **backgrounds.** Use and personal choice will determine the type of floor coverings, as well as the wall, ceiling, and fireplace (if one exists) treatments. Since the more formal living area is generally designed for relaxation, neutralized and

Figure 11.4 Italian designer Vico Magistretti's famous Sindbad chairs and modern uplighting are inviting and creative additions to a traditional architectural background. This eclectic look is currently considered one of the most flexible design directions. *(Photography by Norman McGrath.)*

simple backgrounds are a popular choice.

- The **style and mood determined for the furnishings** (Chapters 9 and 10) can vary widely. Generally, furnishings are selected from traditional or modern styles employing either formal or informal looks. Eclectic furnishings continue to be popular. **Arrangement of furnishings** (Chapter 10) can be functional as well as aesthetically pleasing.
- **Backgrounds** in a living room help determine the total design approach. Walls may be simply painted or elaborately paneled and papered; floors can be hard, soft, or a combination; and ceilings may be structural or decorative. A decision can be made determined by personal preferences for style, materials, and the general feeling of formality or informality desired (see Chapters 7 and 8).
- Well-planned **lighting** to aesthetically and functionally support the living room's design is essential (see Chapter 4).
- A well-planned **purchasing procedure** is needed. Rarely is a home furnished by purchasing everything new. Working with existing pieces is the usual procedure. First, an inventory is important. If new furniture is needed, one piece purchased at a time and then lived with a while before purchasing another piece will enable the owner to find pleasure with each new addition, and the final result will likely be more gratifying. Furniture is arranged according

Figure 11.5 In this contemporary living room the furniture is arranged for comfort and conversation around a large coffee table and fireplace. Pools of light accent the art objects and provide a warm ambience. *(Photograph by John Rees.)*

to existing space, functional needs, and visual satisfaction (see Chapters 9 and 10).

- According to personal preference, backgrounds can be enlivened by colorful **fabrics** or kept in a more restrained atmosphere by the use of soft, neutral tones. Usually, fabrics for the largest areas are selected first, then secondary and accent fabrics. The mood of the room will be to a large extent established by the fabrics selected and the way they are used. To assure satisfaction, no decisions should be made until these fabrics have been observed in the room during daytime and in artificial light at nighttime.
- Particular attention to the **window type and its treatment** will enhance the living room, considering the total architectural composition, natural lighting, location, furniture arrangement, the need for privacy, the window's view, and the room's style and mood (see Chapter 8).
- Effective **fireplace treatment** can be a welcoming, attractive, and unifying element in the living room (see Chapter 7).

The Dining Room

At the turn of the century, the dining room was often a big and somber room with a massive table and sideboard, a chandelier, and heavily shrouded windows. Family members gathered here three times a day in a congenial atmosphere and learned manners and the art of conversation.

After World War I, dining rooms generally lost favor and were not considered a necessity. Open planning blended kitchen, dining, and living areas into one, and as a result, family dining around a table in many homes went out of fashion. A trend in the 1960s was a renewed interest in the dining room. Home owners discovered how important this room was to family life. "As you eat, so will your guests love and remember you" goes an old Roman saying. To this may well be added, "So also will your children remember you."

Figure 11.6 The warmth of wood, architecturally fixed lighting, furniture placed for function, a few well-chosen accessories, and easy upkeep are features of this inviting modern dining room. *(Courtesy of Ron Molen, architect.)*

- Friendly gatherings in this room inevitably involve eating. Whether the food consists of hors d'oeuvres around a coffee table, a buffet supper, or a sit-down meal, efficient space planning for the room's **function** will contribute to the success of the event. The dining room, which can serve many functions, need not be formal, but privacy from the front door and distance from the clutter of the kitchen are highly desirable. In the dining room plan, unobtrusive colors or wallpapers help facilitate the use of a variety of table settings. In a more traditional setting, a dado will protect the wall from chair bumps and finger marks.
- Practical hard and soft **floor coverings** function well for household use and maintenance. Carpets and rugs for this purpose can be selected that shed dirt and clean well. A patterned carpet or rug is a particularly good choice, since it will conceal spots. Hard-surface materials are available on the market for any decor. A combination of a hard-surface material with a rug under the dining table is an effective treatment.
- Keeping the dining room in the same basic **theme and mood** as the living room is wise and makes a pleasing transition.
- **Furniture** generally works best when suitably scaled to the room. The practical pedestal-base table gives maximum knee room, and round and oval tables make it easier to squeeze in an extra guest. Two-arm chairs, or host chairs, add dignity and can serve as occasional chairs in the living room. If the dining room is spacious, a large cabinet with shelves for china and glass and drawers for linens and silver is a handsome addition. If space is limited, a shallow chest or a wall-hung shelf for serving can suffice.
- Flexible approaches to this **space** exists. If the dining room is an alcove, part of a living room or multipurpose area, a number of treatments are available to set it apart. Walls may be papered or painted a different but coordinated color. Freestanding screens, a plant grouping, or an area rug can help define the space. Tables that convert to different sizes and heights and thus do double duty are useful here. These and many other devices may give the dining

Figure 11.7 An eating area need not be large to be inviting. This tiny space has all the attributes necessary for pleasant and intimate dining. *(Courtesy of Pier 1 Imports.)*

room a feeling of importance and privacy.

- Some type of artificial **lighting** over the table is needed for functional purposes. Traditionally, period chandeliers of all styles and materials are hung directly over the table. Modern treatments may incorporate unusual or other unique lighting methods, including architecturally built-in or custom-designed fixtures. The height from the table top to the bottom of the lighting fixture varies with taste, but a general trend allows the fixture to hang lower than in the past but still not interfere with the dining room's function. Additional lighting in the dining room is preferred by designers including lit china closets, uplighters in corners, spotlights on accessories, and other pleasant and supportive lighting treatments.

- Because the main function of the dining room is to serve as the setting for meals, familiarity with the basic facts about **table settings**—silver, china, stoneware, glassware, and other materials—is important for the designer, whether professional or nonprofessional.

  Silver, china, and glassware are sure to be among the most-used items of all home furnishings. Tableware and accessories are available in any color, design, or quality. Tableware can be mixed or matched, complemented or contrasted.

  The following is a list of significant terms pertaining to table settings. Understanding these terms can help determine appropriate usage.

Bisque. Fired, unglazed clayware.

Bone china. A fine-quality porcelain made only in England, where the bone-ash clay is preferred.

Chased. Hand decorated with cutting tools.

China or **porcelain.** Two interchangeable terms, applying only to fine, nonporous, translucent wares that have been fired at extremely high heat. They are hard and sturdy, despite their delicate appearance. Originally made only in China, fine porcelains are now manufactured in the United States and Europe.

Crackle. A purposeful and controlled crazing that is protected by an overglaze: a decorative effect.

Crazing. A cracking in the glaze—historically, a sign of poor quality.

Crystal. Refers to the colorless, sparkling quality of good glass.

Dirilyte. Gold plated.

Earthenware. Made of whiter, more refined clay than pottery and fired at a higher heat. It is less porous and therefore sturdier than pottery. Earthenware has many grades and qualities. Some of it is fine in texture, weight, and glaze, and some of it is ovenproof.

Embossed. Decorated by die impressions.

Engraved. Hand decorated with cutting tools.

Etched. Decorated by chemical applications.

Faience. An ornamented French pottery.

Flat silver. Eating utensils: spoons, knives, forks, and servers. Flat silver may be sterling or plate.

Gadroon edge. The word *gadroon* means "half an almond" and refers to a decoration of Arabic origin. It is the oldest and most frequently used border motif for silver.

Glass. A hard substance, usually brittle and transparent, composed chiefly of silicates and an alkali fused at a high temperature.

Glaze. A thick, glasslike coating, baked into the clay body to give a smooth, highly polished finish.

Hammered silver. A procedure for hand decorating sterling hollowware.

Hand-blown glass. Air blown into a bubble of molten glass, which is then shaped by hand as it cools. Used in making fine stemware.

Hand-pressed glass. Molten glass pressed into a mold, where it is shaped and patterned at the same time. Used for intricate shapes and decorations in glass.

Handwrought silver. Completely hand shaped and decorated. The term is often incorrectly applied today, since some of the steps are usually done by machine.

Hollowware. Dishes and decorative items: bowls, pitchers, trays, coffeepots, teapots, candelabra, and so on. Hollowware may be sterling or plate.

Lead or flint glass. Clear and sparkling glass, with a brilliant resonance or ring when struck.

Majolica. A tin-glazed pottery made in Italy.

Opaque. Nontranslucent, as earthenware or pottery.

Open stock. Refers to patterns or styles that may be purchased by the piece rather than by the complete set. Open stock does not mean that the pattern will always be available for replacement or additions.

Oxidized. Chemically darkened to highlight the beauty and detail of ornamentation.

Patina. The soft, lustrous finish that comes with usage.

Place setting. Refers to the assorted items in one pattern that may be desired or needed for each person at the table.

Pottery. Porous and the least sturdy of baked clay products. Because it is fired (baked) at such low heat and often unglazed or unevenly glazed, it chips and breaks easily.

Pure (fine) silver. What the name implies. In its pure form, silver is too soft and pliable for practical use.

Rock crystal. A semiprecious stone. A misleading term, for it is commonly used by today's manufacturers to denote a polished cutting on high-quality glass.

Sheffield plate. The first substitute for sterling. The Sheffield method of fusing silver over copper went out of use in about 1840 when the silver-plating process was discovered. True Sheffield is rarely found today except in museums.

Silver plate. Pure silver coating on a base-metal shape (nickel silver for flatware, nickel silver or copper for hollowware). The cost and quality of silver plate vary with the thickness of the silver coating and the degree of finish given the base-metal form before coating.

Sterling (solid) silver. A combination of 92.5 parts pure silver with 7.5 parts alloy, usually copper. These proportions are fixed by law and are true of any silver that is stamped "sterling." The cost and quality of sterling vary with the weight or amount of silver used and the intricacy of design.

Stoneware. A hard and heavy ware made of unrefined, heat-resistant clays.

Terra-cotta. Unglazed pottery made of red or yellow clays.

Translucent. Allowing light to pass through, though not transparent. Another identifying quality of true china.

The Family Room

The family room came into being during the 1950s. A successful family room takes into account the tastes, interests, and activities of all household members. This room may take many forms, depending on the individual household, but the main objective of a successful family room is to provide a flexible area to serve many purposes. The atmosphere of the family room works well when it is one of comfortable intimacy, planned for easy upkeep. Activities vary according to the household, but most family

Figure 11.8 An eclectic family room combines an informal plaid rug, comfortable overstuffed leather sofas, antiques, interesting accessories, and a large, soaring fireplace to offer the residents an inviting area for casual living. *(Courtesy of Aldo Bussio. Photograph by John Rees.)*

rooms require a suitable area to snack, talk, watch television, read, and listen to music. A fireplace is an added attraction around which to gather with family and friends.

- If a household is active, durable and easily cleaned **backgrounds** are advisable. For **walls,** wood paneling, scrubbable wallpapers, stone, and simple painted surfaces are popular choices. **Flooring materials** are dependent on the room's use, but generally hard or soft coverings are sensibly selected for comfort and easy maintenance (see Chapter 7). Area or room-sized rugs are practical in households where the room also serves as a recreation area, and they may be easily removed.
- **Fabrics** are practical when they are durable, easy to clean, and stain resistant. Vinyl upholstery is especially preferred for use in family rooms and is available in a wide range of colors, patterns, and textures. Tightly woven fabrics are more durable than loosely woven pieces (see Chapter 6).
- Sturdy and comfortable **furniture** is practical, and easily movable pieces offer flexibility for rearranging on a moment's notice. Pieces of furniture that can serve a dual role are particularly serviceable. For example, a sofa can serve as a bed for an overnight guest, low tables can double as stools for seating, and tables that can be raised and lowered may serve for coffee tables, games, and eating. A great variety of dual-purpose furniture is available today to fill individual needs.
- Of all rooms in the house, the family room probably needs the most well-planned **storage** to take care of all items used in this area, such as a card table, folding chairs, games, records, video tapes, books, or a movie screen and projector. With the advent of numerous new and flexible storage units, otherwise dull rooms can be given new interest. Shelves can be added almost anywhere—between, over, and around windows or walls; under a stairway; around and behind a doorway; and flanking a fireplace. Freestanding walls, built-ins, or wall systems may be set up to provide floor-to-ceiling banks of drawers, cabinets, and shelves. If a smooth facade is desired, storage may be concealed behind plain or louvered doors in keeping with the other woodwork in the room. Open shelves hung from wall strips of metal or wood are probably the most flexible storage, because they can be adjusted and readjusted for height and length to accommodate a variety of items. These may be freestanding and placed

Figure 11.9 In this award-winning entry in the "Design with Mirrors Competition," the living area and family center of a condominium are unified through functionally arranged lighting and furnishings (including the television set), placed to take advantage of a lake view. *(Courtesy of PPG Industries, Inc.)*

against the wall or serve as a room divider.

- In today's family room, the **television** and video-tape machine are generally standard equipment. Many of the new television designs provide a large screen and minimal cabinetry, resulting in greater flexibility for combining the television with other furnishings in the home environment. The television may be housed in many ways. The most common is placing it in or on a horizontal chest or stand. Or it may be part of a larger system also holding a stereo, a video-tape machine (VCR), video tapes, and records—often with counter space above. Locating the television in a central section of a wall of built-ins is an excellent way to incorporate and unify this piece with other furnishings. It may be placed in a fireplace wall niche to take advantage of the furniture arrangement for convenient viewing. Whichever method is chosen, the television unit should be placed so that it functions efficiently, allowing many individuals to enjoy television viewing comfortably.
- **General lighting** is usually desirable in the family room, as well as area lighting for specific activities. Carefully planned lighting, located according to individual needs, will meet requirements for such activities as reading, television viewing, playing of games, and conversation (see Chapter 4).
- A current trend in location of rooms merges the family room and kitchen into one big room for cooking, informal dining,

Figure 11.10 In this spacious entertainment center, a pool table, comfortable furniture, a game table, and a bar are conveniently arranged with adequate lighting. *(Courtesy of Gayl Baddeley/Associates.)*

and many household activities. Family rooms function nicely when located where there is easy access to the outside and the kitchen and away from the bedroom wing. Ideally, the room design successfully fills current needs and can easily be changed as the household status changes.

The Entertainment, Recreation, and Educational Centers

The current "video revolution" is having a major impact on the lives and living environments of individuals of all ages. In the fifties, the television was often in a small, comfortable room called a den. In the sixties, the color television with its hi-fi components made its appearance in the family room. In the seventies, the television with its expanded equipment was often housed in the media room. Currently there is an increasing return to the home for entertainment. With the vast array of new electronic products for the home now on the market, new design problems have arisen, and new design solutions are being explored. These products include the home computer with its many hardware and software components, video-cassette recorders, video discs, cable and portable cameras, video-game consoles, and satellite receivers. Integrating these products into the home so they will best serve the household and still preserve the domestic environment presents a challenge to the interior designer, both professional and nonprofessional. A primary concern is securing adequate space within the home to house this equipment efficiently. To meet this challenge, entertainment and educational centers are being designed for electronic equipment in the home to enhance the quality of living.

- The **area** in which the **entertainment center** is located should be planned with **practicality** in mind, since it will most likely have continual use. Combining it with space for other recreational activities is logical. Often the question is, where can this space be found? A close examination may reveal underused space. The attic may have wasted space that can be put to good use. The basement may have possibilities, and noise is muffled in a downstairs location. The garage may be converted into a recreation center and the roof extended for a carport. An extra room that is already finished may be available after some minor shifting. Adding a new room is another, but more costly, possibility. Space problems involving location for the educational center may also exist and can be explored in a similar manner.

- The **background treatment for the entertainment center** can make a big difference. Once the space is decided on, planning should start from the **floor** upwards. Since traffic and wear will be heavy, a good-quality heavy-duty flooring is practical. A carpet that can be rolled up for various activities gives versatility. Sturdy **wall treatments** with easy upkeep are a wise selection.
- A high priority is **where to place the entertainment center;** other furnishings can then be placed for function. Considering flexibility, easily movable pieces are a good choice. To promote social interaction, lounge chairs and sofas should be comfortable and conveniently arranged. Covering them with vinyl or other durable and cleanable fabrics is a must.
- **Supportive furnishings—tables,** especially cocktail and game tables—are functional additions to recreation and game centers. To avoid breakage and scratches, sturdy tables with durable finishes are practical. A **billiard or Ping-Pong table** will encourage competitive activity and development of skills. Comfortable, durable, and easily cleaned **seating** adds to the occupants' enjoyment, and a variety of possibilities are available to the consumer (see Chapter 9). An upright **piano** or a player piano can give hours of pleasure.
- A recreation or entertainment center can be enhanced by a **fireplace** with a wide hearth. If an architecturally fixed fireplace does not exist, freestanding models in many styles and materials are readily available.
- **Additional items** can add a great deal. A pull-down **screen** to show home movies and slides can be installed permanently at low cost. **Extra folding chairs** are often needed. For example, canvas ***director's chairs*** are inexpensive, can be colorful, and are easily brought out of storage to handle a crowd. Large **floor cushions** can also invite informality and relaxation. A **bar** can be a popular gathering spot for family and friends.
- **Lighting** that is inviting and functional is an important part of the planning process for a successful recreation and entertainment room. For example, lighting over a billiard table, around a bar, and close to the seating and entertainment center adds to the occupants' ability to use these facilities in a comfortable and pleasant manner. Lighting in an educational center is primarily geared for function and should be efficient and comfortable.
- **Flexibility** is valuable. Recreation centers can be planned not only to encourage activities with household members alone but also to broaden involvement with school, church or synagogue, and community affairs. A room that is always open and ready for a committee meeting, a video game, or a rehearsal will surely become a focal point for gatherings of all ages. What better use could be made of space?

The Kitchen

Today's kitchens are no longer the antiseptic centers for preparing meals they once were, and they have once again become the hub of the home—an area where food preparation, serving, eating, and other activities take place. A recent study revealed that the kitchen has also become an area for socializing and relaxing with friends in a weekday or weekend retreat atmosphere. There is a demand for flexible kitchens geared both for those who hate to cook and might order food brought in, and for those who love to create culinary masterpieces. Architects and builders have responded to current lifestyles and requests for more efficient and multipurpose kitchen spaces. Unifying the kitchen involves a number of considerations and decisions.

- **Shape.** A kitchen arrangement employing the most ideal shape (usually the U shape, L shape, peninsula, or island) will determine the location of work centers, accommodate physical limitations, and facilitate everyday household activities that are carried out spontaneously (see Chapter 3).
- **Kitchen–family room arrangement.** When the kitchen connects with an informal family room, a pleasant transition of color, floor, and wall treatment will create a unified environment.
- **Kitchen storage.** Storage should be adequate and efficiently located for all essential items. Receptacles for trash and big broom closets are desirable. A pantry storage space, where

Figure 11.11 An ideal kitchen that combines the functions of food preparation, dining, and living, but with a well-defined area for each. The contemporary cabinets set the tone for the decor. The tile floor is the principal unifying element. The island work center with cooktop range and ventilating hood dominates the whole. *(Courtesy of Armstrong World Industries.)*

Figure 11.12 This country kitchen, with its warmth of natural wood, quarry tiles, drying herbs, and the aroma of freshly baked bread, provides a pleasant retreat from worldly pressures. *(Courtesy of Allmilmo Corporation.)*

practical, is an added convenience.

- **Style.** Ready-made cabinets with a variety of colors and surfaces, such as plastic laminates, are at the disposal of those who prefer a kitchen with a sleek modern look. For those who enjoy a traditional style, finely crafted custom-made wood cabinets are available with new sealers and finishes that protect the wood. Also, wood cabinets can be fashioned in modern designs. Whatever style of kitchen cabinets selected, durability and cleanability of all materials should be considered.
- **Materials.** Today's market abounds with both new and old materials for floors, walls, counter tops, and furniture coverings that are easy to clean and maintain and that resist heavy wear. From the vast array of available products, a selection can be made that best serves individual needs. (Materials available for walls, floors, and counter tops, along with their characteristics, uses, treatment, and care are discussed in Chapter 7). Having an efficient kitchen involves keeping up to date on new materials. Almost every month new materials invade the retail market. Before making an investment, however, it is wise to make certain that all new items have been tried, treated, and found to live up to the claims made for them.
- **Accessories.** Whatever the basic style of a kitchen—traditional or modern, formal or informal—it should provide personal enjoyment. Accessories, both functional and decorative, unify the kitchen and provide visual pleasure. Posters, pictures, baskets, candles, pottery, plants, cookware, and dishes can be artistically displayed. Utilitarian items like knife holders, salt and pepper shakers, serving trays, containers with often-used utensils, hot-plate holders, cookbooks, and paper-towel dispensers, for example, can be attractive as well as conveniently placed for use (see section on accessories in Chapter 11).

The Utility Areas

Function, convenience, and transition are major considerations with utility areas. Areas for laundry and sewing or other work areas can be unified into the total design scheme through simple means. If located close to the kitchen, the same floor covering can extend into the utility area. A complementary wall treatment can make the utility area a pleasant work space; many designers use an unobtrusive wallpaper treatment here. A few well-chosen accessories, either utilitarian or decorative, can also provide a pleasant working atmosphere (see Chapter 3 for information on space planning in the utility area).

The Master Bedroom

Because it is so personal and private, the process of designing the master bedroom is different from that for any other room in the house. Traffic and wear and tear need not be of concern here. The main consideration should be 24-hour comfort. Comfort does not require a large room, but it does require organization of space and imagination. It is important to keep in mind that the master bedroom is a room usually shared by a couple. Each occupant should have input as to personal preferences for furniture style, colors, fabrics, and general mood of the room.

- The popular king- or queen-sized **bed** is no innovation of the twentieth century. The oversized bed was well known in Tudor England. The famous ***Bed of Ware*** measured 12 ft square and could—and often did—accommodate four couples at the same time. It is now in the Victoria and Albert Museum in London. The canopied bed is also no newcomer to this century. The Crusaders returning from the East introduced it to England and France, and its popularity has never ceased.

  Sleeping grandly has been the custom of kings and queens throughout history. Tutankhamen, the Pharaoh of Egypt during the fourteenth century B.C., slept on a bed of gold. The bed, however, reached its heyday in the seventeenth century, which was called "the century of magnificent beds." Louis XIV is reputed to have had over 400 beds, all lavishly draped and some inlaid with precious stones. The custom of kings holding council while lying on a sumptuous bed was common practice, and women at the court of ***Versailles*** received their friends while elegantly ensconced in bed.

  As the predominant feature of the room, the bed is the focal point and demands special attention. No definite rules govern the choosing of a bed. The choice may be a canopy bed, a sturdy four-poster, a sleek chrome or simple bamboo type, or a popular brass frame or no frame at all. A few personal luxuries, such as a warm throw to curl up in, attractive sheets and blankets, and a comfortable backrest for reading can add much to the feeling of personal well-being.

- Before the actual interior design begins, **purposes** the room will serve, other than repose, should be decided. A bedroom and study can be a pleasant combination, and bookshelves will be

Figure 11.13 A sophisticated bed with mirrored ceiling has a soft quilted white bedspread and is flanked by comfortable seating upholstered in the same fabric. Textures of wood and wicker combine nicely. A wall of shutter doors open to a lush mountain view for the enjoyment of the occupants. *(Courtesy of Gayl Baddeley/ Associates.)*

Figure 11.14 A spacious traditionally designed master bedroom offers a pleasant retreat for the inhabitants. A comfortable four-poster bed, Traditional wingback chair, large windows, and fireplace add to the room's warmth. *(Photograph by Tim Street-Porter.)*

convenient and lend warmth. Comfortable chairs invite relaxation. If space permits, a luxurious chaise may substitute for one of the chairs. Essential items are bedside tables or built-ins containing drawers or shelves with moisture-proof surfaces and large enough to provide spaces for necessary items such as a telephone, clock, or lamp (unless overhead architectural lighting is provided). Mirrors on the wall or on closet doors both expand space and function for dressing purposes.

- **Lighting,** both portable and architecturally fixed, needs to be adequate for dressing, reading, or relaxing. An abundance of lighting types—modern or traditional, informal or formal—is available to support the selected style (see lighting section in Chapter 4).
- A luxurious element in the room is **fabric.** It can add softness and color and set whatever mood is desired. For normal use, a bedspread that is too delicate is not a wise choice. The market offers attractive bedspreads that are durable and do not wrinkle or show soil easily. Draw draperies, window blinds, or shades keep morning light out when necessary.
- Individual preferences and lifestyle can be guides for establishing the **style and mood** and for furnishing this most personal room. Generally, the goal is to achieve a pleasant and inviting mood of relaxation and comfort. Numerous furniture companies offer a wide range of both traditional and modern styles in many colors and finishes. Sometimes custom-made pieces or architecturally built in furnishings are preferred for individual needs. Furniture, colors, fabrics, and accessories can all be selected by the occupants to support the desired outcome.

The Bathroom

Since the beginning of the twentieth century, the bathroom has undergone many changes. From being one large family room at the end of the hall, it became a personal adjunct to the bedroom and as such became smaller and took on a utilitarian look. Then, in the following decades, color became the vogue. Appearing in all the so-called decorator colors were new paints, wallpapers, floors, towels, and even plumbing fixtures. In the sixties, white fixtures again became the fashion, but the bathroom itself took on an aura of elegance and became a glamour room in the American home.

No longer does the bathroom serve purely functional needs. Today, function and luxury are combined, and the room once hidden behind closed doors is frequently exposed to sky, garden, terrace, and in some instances to other rooms of the house, with screens or sliding-glass doors for privacy. What was once a small, sterile room has become a powder room, dressing room, and even sitting room.

- **Fixtures and their arrangement** in the bathroom have kept

Figure 11.15 Fixtures and accessories in this bath combine to create an unusual look, from custom-built architectural elements like the columns and cabinetry to the lavatory fitted with elegant fixtures. A tile floor is striking and easy to care for. Recessed lighting is efficient and unobtrusive. *(Courtesy of Kohler Company.)*

Figure 11.16 An efficient his-and-her bathroom with two sinks, separate toilet compartments, and no-wax floor. The bathroom is all white except for the blue fixtures, rose towels, green ferns in the wicker basket, and the fig tree. The skylight in the sloping ceiling and sliding glass doors admit ample light. Folding louvered doors provide privacy. *(Courtesy of Armstrong World Industries.)*

abreast of the trend. Recalling the splendor of Rome, **tubs** may be sunken and deep enough for standing. Also popular today are larger tubs, often with water-massage elements. Tubs may be conveniently located in almost any place in the bathroom including the center of the room. They are also available in all shapes, designs, colors, and sizes and with built-in seats. Sometimes tubs are placed beside large windows to take advantage of a view. Beautiful new manufactured or hand-carved **basins** are made of marble, onyx, china, or other materials. They may have baked-in or hand-painted traditional or contemporary motifs to set the theme of the room. Similar motifs are often coordinated for use on the **toilet** or **bidet.**

- Manufacturers have coordinated **accessories** in many materials and styles including shower curtains, towels, towel bars, soap dishes, mirrors, faucets, and other decorative and functional items. These accessories exhibit personal taste and help unify the bathroom and its relationship to other rooms. Personally selected accessories like pictures, sculpture, pottery, and other items acquired through the years are also effective in this area.
- For the household bathroom, **easy upkeep** is of major importance. The market offers scrubbable vinyls, tile, and other **background materials** for every purpose, which are readily available in numerous colors and patterns (see Chapter 7). If carpet is the choice, one that resists spots and cleans easily is a must. One of the most enduring materials for bathrooms through the years has been tile, which remains popular.
- Ample **storage** in the bathroom for such items as towels, medicines, and grooming and cleaning aids is essential. A place for soiled clothing is also an advantage. Storage can be built-in shelves and cabinets or free-standing or wall-hung units placed for convenience. Storage can also be attractive, for example, when items like towels, soap, and other utilitarian items are nicely arranged on shelves.
- Good natural and artificial **lighting** is a requisite in the bathroom. Effective lighting around mirrors used for makeup and grooming needs is essential. Additionally, mirrors can double light and visually expand existing space. General lighting needs should also be planned.

The Child's Room

Home is a place where a child develops personal goals and values, learns to respect the privacy of others, and develops an appreciation for good books, art, and music. We may never know how much the houses we live in contribute to the growth of children, but a well-planned physical environment can help guide their emotional development. Often the simplest things in a house make the biggest difference. If traffic lanes are thoughtfully arranged, harmful results from unnecessary nagging may be avoided. If the child is provided a private retreat, no matter how small, it will contribute to a

Figure 11.17 A small, well-planned space can be the private realm of a teenager. This bedroom features a built-in bed above an enclosed closet and storage space, with areas planned to display personal accessories. Surfaces are warm, inviting, and easy to care for. A table for study and hobbies is an essential item. *(Courtesy of Ron Molen, architect.)*

Figure 11.18 A child's room can be whimsical and delightful without sacrificing efficiency, comfort, and safety. The design focus is a painted wall depicting a landscape and hot-air balloons in a lavendar, blue, and cinnamon brown color scheme which is repeated on the roller shade. *(Courtesy of Kirsch.)*

feeling of self-esteem and well-being and can be an invaluable gift. Individual members of a household have differing concepts of personal environment, and perhaps what fills the needs for one does not necessarily fill the needs of another.

- A child's room can be a **private world** and ought to be respected as such by other members of the household. The room harbors pets and friends and is a place to store, display, and hide things. It is a place to read, work at hobbies, snack, and dream.
- A child's room requires good **storage,** adequate **lighting,** a **desk** for study, a comfortable **bed,** and **space for play.** The design can be planned with the child's input so the room will have personality. The smallest space, if skillfully planned and arranged, can meet these needs. For the young child, safety with simple, sturdy, small-scaled furniture is a paramount concern. If furniture for the nursery is wisely chosen, it can be converted to serve changing needs as the child grows. For example, a low chest of drawers can serve as a changing table for an infant and later be used for storage for a child of any age. An infant's wardrobe may become a bookcase later on.
- Since the daily habits and interests of children during their developing years vary widely, their needs may be best served by creating **personal environments** in which they spend their private lives and express their personality. With long-range planning and frequent modifications, a child's room can serve from toddler to teenage years. As the child grows and changes, so should the room. Individual needs can determine what changes should be made and when, but the maturing child requires ongoing alteration of an older physical environment.
- Almost any informal room that serves many needs can benefit from some type of bulletin board or **display space** where the child can exhibit schoolwork, photographs, and other prized possessions.
- Durable and cleanable **backgrounds**—wallpaper, fabrics, floor coverings, and furniture—can be chosen wisely with the child's individual taste in mind.
- As the child grows older, his or her interests will invariably change; and an awareness of current trends, as well as a knowledge of traditional and contemporary styles, will enable the child to select furnishings that are particularly and personally appealing. The child will undoubtedly take pride in helping create a private environment that reflects his or her personality—an environment that can function at an optimum level.

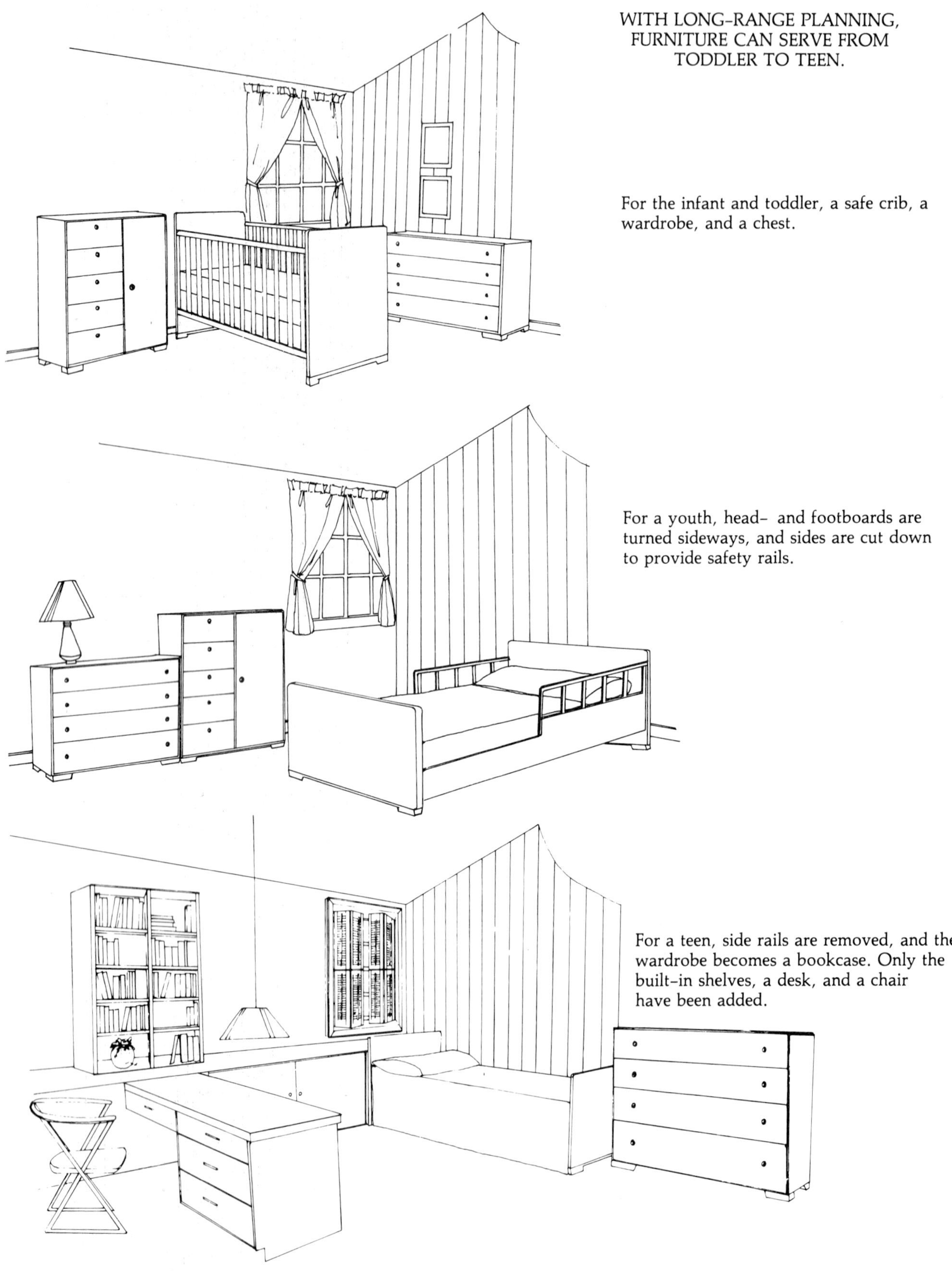

WITH LONG-RANGE PLANNING, FURNITURE CAN SERVE FROM TODDLER TO TEEN.

For the infant and toddler, a safe crib, a wardrobe, and a chest.

For a youth, head- and footboards are turned sideways, and sides are cut down to provide safety rails.

For a teen, side rails are removed, and the wardrobe becomes a bookcase. Only the built-in shelves, a desk, and a chair have been added.

Figure 11.19 A refreshing bedroom for a child or teen that incorporates beauty and comfort. The bedspread, drapery fabric, and coordinated wallpaper depict a red tulip motif delicately arranged on a white ground. Bed, woodwork, and furniture are painted white. *(Courtesy of Warner Company.)*

Planning for the Handicapped and Elderly

Handicapped and elderly individuals are often part of a household and in many cases may be the only occupant in the living space. Some individuals may be temporarily or permanently confined to a wheelchair or be partially or completely ambulatory. Some elderly persons may not be physically handicapped or impaired but may also need a home that functions particularly well for convenience, safety, and security. Sensitive designers are aware of these special considerations and requirements that can contribute to a positive, safe, and pleasant environment for those with particular needs. Some criteria include the following:

- The home should be **free of architectural barriers** so that those who may be using a wheelchair, crutches, or a walker can easily circulate throughout various areas. If possible, a plan without stairs can be selected so all facilities are on one floor. Open planning is a wise choice. Traffic lanes should be kept clear and be well planned. Doors should be at least 32 in. wide with easy-to-turn knobs.
- **Bathrooms and fixtures** must be conveniently and safely located with ample room for manipulating a wheelchair. Grab bars conveniently positioned to walls by the tub and toilet will provide added safety. Tubs should have flat, nonslip bottoms. Faucets should have temperature controls. Wall-hung toilets and showers without curbs are preferred.
- **Clearances** between furnishings in all rooms of the house should be adequate to accommodate a wheelchair or walker. Traffic lanes must be kept free of clutter and be wide enough for easy movement. (Charts for the handicapped are available listing sufficient clearances for all facilities throughout the home.)
- **Easy access to garage and outdoor areas** is of utmost importance.
- **Lighting** throughout the home should be located with access to switches, controls, and outlets. Switches should be 3 ft high and outlets 1 ft 3 in. high. Pull-down lighting fixtures are an added convenience.
- **Floor coverings** in hard, smooth surfaces that are slip resistant work most efficiently for safe and easy movement. If carpet is used, a dense, short pile works best. Generally, area and throw rugs should be avoided. Thresholds should be flat.
- The **kitchen,** an area especially susceptible to accidents, should be arranged with heights, clearances, and other measurements planned for convenience and safety. Dishes, cooking utensils, and other items should be within easy reach. Working surfaces that pull out and storage areas with open and revolving shelves are an asset. A front-loading dishwasher and washer/dryer, an upright refrigerator, and an oven with front controls are convenient. There should be easy access to the sink and faucets.
- **Climate-control boxes** should be approximately 2 to 4 ft in height.

Decorative and Functional Accessories

Accessories add the finishing touches to a room—the "icing on the cake"—reflecting personal taste and individuality. An accessory may be almost anything from a ***Coromandel screen*** to a door knocker and be a powerful tool in establishing the design theme. An object need not be used just to fill up space. A safe rule to follow is if the item is neither useful, beautiful, nor meaningful to the owner, it has no place in the home. If an article does not meet at least one of these criteria, a prudent decision might be to leave the space empty.

Among the many accessories that complete a room and give a desirable lived-in feeling are **screens, pictures** and **paintings, sculpture, mirrors, lamps, books, clocks, flowers** and **foliage, metal work, candles, ceramics** and other **crafts** as well as **drapery rods, fireplace tools, tiebacks,** and **hardware.** Most homes are enriched by the employment of both decorative and functional accessories. Decorative accessories provide no other value than the pleasure derived from aesthetic qualities. Functional accessories serve some utilitarian purpose but may also become an interesting display item. Whether functional or purely decorative, each accessory can contribute to the enhancement of an interior if chosen with care and discrimination.

Screens

One graceful means of individualizing an environment is through the use of a freestanding screen. A wide variety of screens in numerous styles and materials are on the market today. The versatile shutter screen with movable louvres and mirror screens may be used almost anywhere. Wood frames containing light-filtering materials such as caning, pierced metal, or filigree, which come in a wide assortment of designs from geometrics to exotic arabesques, are available. A decorative screen may give an architectural quality to a room, set or enhance

A filigreed screen can be both beautiful and functional.

the room's decor, provide a backdrop for a furniture grouping, substitute for side drapery, or serve as the room's focal point.

In addition to its decorative values, a screen may serve many functional purposes. It can be the primary multipurpose item in the home, usually easily moved from one room to another. It can (1) set off an entrance where the front door opens directly into the living room, (2) act as a divider between a living and dining area, (3) close off a kitchen, (4) set off a private area by making a room within a room, (5) redirect traffic when strategically placed, (6) extend the apparent size of a room by replacing a door with an airy see-through effect, (7) control the flow of air and the direction of light, (8) camouflage an old-fashioned radiator or air-conditioning unit, and (9) conceal storage. Whatever the theme of the room, a well-designed screen used in the right place can provide a valuable asset.

A screen can provide a backdrop for a furniture grouping.

Figure 11.20 The Oriental Coromandel screen provides an effective backdrop in this elegant dining room. The Oriental blue and white porcelain bowl is perfectly complemented by the glass table top. The large hurricane lamps and graceful mirror add to the room's success. *(Courtesy of Gayl Baddeley/Associates.)*

Pictures and Paintings

Pictures and paintings are the most personal items in a home and when effectively displayed can contribute much to a room's appeal and distinctiveness. Two-dimensional art consists of a variety of works in many different mediums. These include (1) original pigment **paintings** of oil, tempera, acrylic, or water colors; (2) pencil, ink, charcoal, or crayon **drawings;** (3) limited **prints** that are reproduced directly from the original work and numbered and signed by the artist; (4) mass-produced **reproductions** of artwork, particularly of paintings and drawings (this type of art is generally considered in poor taste, but can be effective when one has a limited budget); (5) **posters,** originally called "poor man's art" at the turn of the century, are available at minimal cost and can depict any work of art or an advertisement for a museum, an area, or an exhibit (they are usually considered a low-budget accessory but are often seen in fine contemporary settings); and (6) professional **photographs** have become popular artistic accessories for the home. Family photographs can also add a personal touch and are particularly effective when displayed in private areas of the home.

Figure 11.21 An orderly and traditional display of accessories is evident in this country eclectic room. The pictures are arranged symmetrically and function as the focal point. Baskets, plants, a flower arrangement, candles and holders, a plaid rug, a pillow, lamps, and a shawl restate the room's design theme. *(Courtesy of Deulofeu-Wilson.)*

Frames and mats can enhance or take away from two-dimensional artwork. The market abounds in frames of all types, from elegant wood or gilded frames to simple enamel or chrome frames. Whatever frame is selected, it should be supportive of the colors, textures, and theme of the artwork. Occasionally, a painting works best when no frame is employed at all. Mats, often combined with glass, are generally used for drawings, prints, photographs, and watercolors. Oils are not covered with glass. A mat works best when it does not detract from the work, but complements the medium, colors, and subject. Often posters work well sandwiched between two pieces of glass or plastic with clip supports.

In general, pictures are most effective when they are in keeping with the **style and mood of the room.** Sometimes, however, the opposite may be true. For example, a modern painting in a traditional room or a traditional painting in a modern room can add a variety the interior may need. (For picture arranging and hanging, see "Wall Compositions" in Chapter 10.)

Sculpture

Three-dimensional works of art can be treasured accessories in the home. Sculpture is expressed in many mediums, including metals, marble and other stone, wood, and clay and can be modern or traditional in style.

Placement often depends on the size of the piece. If small, the piece may be best displayed on a shelf, mantel, or tabletop. If the sculpture is large, it can dominate an area or provide a focal point. A pedestal may be used for both small and large sculpture to provide more prominence and importance for the piece. Lighting that spots the artwork can especially give visual interest.

Books

Books can do more than anything—except people—to add friendliness to a home. Cicero said, "A room without books is a body without a soul." Usually no room has a mood that would preclude books nor a color scheme so complete it cannot benefit from the warm tones and textures of books. Bookshelves can go in almost any room in the house, require little space, and create a warm, friendly atmosphere. They can be planned in the initial design of the house or added later. The living room, family room, and study are excellent areas to hold a multiplying collection of books for the entire household. Children need bookshelves in their rooms at a height easily reached. Other bedrooms can accommodate shelves where space permits—usually close to the bed for nighttime reading. Kitchens need handy shelves for reference books and cookbooks. In the absence of preplanning for

Figure 11.22 Unexpected accessories like giant herons and a large umbrella can add drama and interest in a designer's showroom. The basket of tall reeds and the basket stuffed with plants are also effective eyecatchers. *(Courtesy of Gayl Baddeley/Associates.)*

Shelves can be built around a window to fill the entire wall. Storage is a bonus.

A doorway framed with books is a valuable addition to a room.

Use wasted space under a staircase.

Make a headboard or a room divider for books.

Create an entranceway with bookshelves.

Figure 11.23 The architectural treatment of wood, brick, and pebble concrete is an effective background for display of books, pottery, paintings, weavings, and rugs. The items are arranged for maximum enjoyment in this informal modern decor. *(Courtesy of Ron Molen, architect.)*

A mirror in a corner can give an illusion of space and increase the light supply.

bookshelves, they can be fitted under stairways, into niches or odd corners, and around doors and windows to employ unused space. A room divider can hold books on one or both sides. Books, like flowers, are never out of place, and like friends, people need them always close at hand.

Mirrors

Distinct in their inherent beauty, mirrors are a decorative and functional medium in today's homes and a helpful tool for the interior designer. Mirrors are available in almost any size and in frames to fit any decor. Through decorative know-how, mirrors can be used to (1) add beauty, (2) multiply space, (3) conceal unattractive structural features, (4) distribute and double light, (5) brighten dark areas, and (6) bring life into an otherwise drab room. Because of their myriad uses, mirrors have steadily increased in popularity through the years and today play a virtually indispensable role in all styles of interiors.

Lamps

The lamp is an important element of beauty and purpose both during the daytime and at night, providing light when needed and functioning as an accessory at all times. Lamps that are carefully chosen for a **specific room, style, mood, location,** or **purpose** can be a great contributing element. Lamps are available in a wide range of styles—traditional and modern, decorative or structural, and with or without a shade. Also, lamps employing numerous materials are available on the market. Some popular base materials include ceramics, metals of all types, wood, and stone.

Generally, lamps work best when the design is simple and unobtrusive (see Chapter 4, "Artificial Lighting").

Clocks

Clocks have long been important accessories in the home. From the handsome grandfather clock to the old-fashioned ***wag-on-the-wall*** to the contemporary streamlined clock, they not only serve a necessary function but also add an important decorative touch to any room, because by their very nature they attract attention. **Style preference** and **available space** are important considerations when selecting an appropriate clock. Naturally, it must be placed where it can be seen easily.

Flowers, Foliage, and Plants

- **Fresh flowers.** Of all accessories making up the final touches of a home, almost nothing can duplicate the effect of fresh flowers. A bouquet of live foliage and flowers can greatly enhance a room, adding a special warmth and attraction. The extra effort that fresh arrangements require reflects the personal taste of the occupants. During all seasons, flowers and foliage of some type are almost always near at hand. With a little imagination they can be arranged and displayed in a manner that adds life, interest, and beauty to an interior space. The sophisticated beauty of the rose, either in a full bouquet or standing along in a graceful bud vase, is well known, but a lovely arrangement of a variety of small and large flowers, branches, and foliage can also enhance a room. Since flowers come in a variety of species, colors, and sizes, limitless possibilities exist. The **art of flower arrangement** can be learned in a formal classroom setting or acquired by observation and experience through the years. Three popular basic flower-arranging styles and approaches include (1) **Oriental *(ikebana),*** (2) **traditional,** and (3) **contemporary freestyle.** The **container** for fresh flowers contributes to the total success of the arrangement and generally works best when the texture, pattern, and size are complementary. Glass, metal, porcelain, pottery, and baskets are some of the most commonly employed containers and can be effectively combined with traditional or modern furnishings.

  Both beginner and expert can discover continuing satisfaction in the gentle art of flower arranging. Combining new materials and finding creative ways of arranging familiar materials present an ongoing challenge.

- **Plants.** Living plants are usually generously placed around living spaces, contributing to the total design scheme and helping to bring something of the outdoors into the interior spaces. Since living plants are generally a permanent accessory in the home, they should be selected

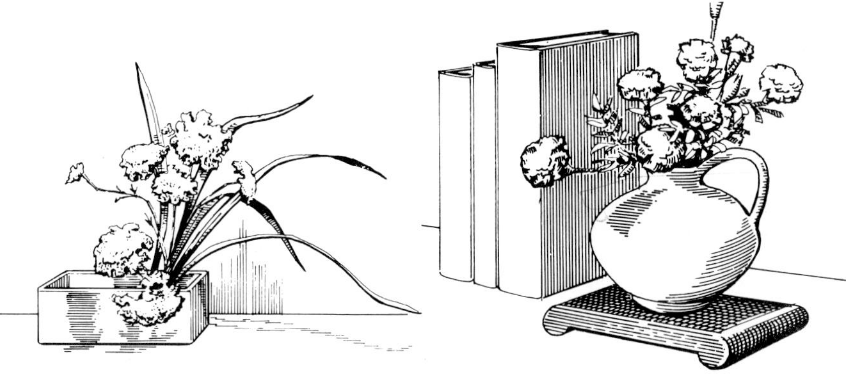

Queen Anne's lace is attractive in a flat container.

A bouquet need not be large. Tuck a small one near some books.

Daisies look at home in a simple basket.

In this arrangement of leaves and berries, the large leaves interestingly face in several directions.

Figure 11.24 A soaring cactus plant in the corner, a rugged log stump table, an animal skin rug, and an old metal bucket planter and end table all convey the informal style popular in the western United States. *(Courtesy of The Naturalist.)*

A window greenhouse

with care. Numerous varieties are available on the market, which sometimes complicate the selection process. Personal preference for **texture, form, color,** and **size** is a consideration, as well as the special **care requirements** for light, water, and temperature for a particular plant. A plant may **function** as part of a focal point, soften rigid architectural features, complement an arrangement of other accessories, or be an inviting addition in itself. A plant can be enriched by its **container** (see preceding section on flower containers).

- **Dried arrangements.** Dried flowers, weeds, branches, pods, and other foliage types are often arranged as alternatives to fresh plants and flowers. They have the advantage of being permanent and require no upkeep other than dusting. Dried arrangements can be particularly attractive when placed in a well-designed container. For example, tall branches of corkscrew willow can be complemented when placed in a handsomely thrown piece of pottery. Although many designers will select living plants and flowers over dry arrangements, when artfully composed, dried flowers, weeds, and other foliage can function as a well-appreciated accessory.

- **Silk flowers and foliage.** Today there is a growing demand for flowers, foliage, and plants made of silk and other fibers. Like dried arrangements, they are permanent and require only occasional dusting. Well-made silk flowers, foliage, and plants have been developed to an amazing degree of naturalism. Many commercial and institutional organizations have elected to use these arrangements because of the easy upkeep and single investment. Some designers arrange dried flowers and foliage with silk flowers to provide a more natural effect. There are still many designers and homemakers who prefer to use only fresh flowers and plants because of their natural appeal.

Crafts as Accessories

Accessories, both utilitarian and decorative in value, have been manually fashioned since the dawn of civilization. With the advancement of the modern movement, handcrafted items have become valued possessions. During the late 1970s, the **Handcraft Revival** emerged in the United States and England and has remained popular as a strong design direction. This movement, which advocates handcrafted pieces over machine-made products, has greatly contributed to a new appreciation for handcrafted items in many mediums. For centuries **fine art** has generally been held in higher esteem than the **applied arts,** but this is no longer the case. The demand for handcrafted items has become an important trend of our times, and these often are more expensive than machine-made products. Following are some artistic accessories particularly favored for both residential and contract design:

- **Ceramics.** Accessories of clay have been created since the beginning of time and include **sculpture, dishes, bowls, platters, pots,** and **tile.** Clay comes in a variety of types ranging from coarse to fine and in a wide variety of colors that affect the final product. In addition, the artisan may create a unique ceramic piece by applying a wide variety of ornamentation, colors, textures, and shapes. The result may be a ceramic piece that is formal, informal, decorative, structural, modern, or traditional. Ceramics fall into four basic categories: (1) **porcelain,** (2) **china,** (3) **earthenware,** and (4) **stoneware** (see pp. 367 and 368).
- **Glass.** Accessories formed of glass are highly flexible items for use in the home and include vases, dishes, bowls, and sculpture. **Hand-blown glass** has been a popular art for centuries, and exquisite pieces from many countries, each with its own design approach, have been widely appreciated in American homes. Modern designs have been pioneered, most notably by the Italians and Scandinavians, who continue to fashion beautiful and unique pieces. Glass can be **etched, colored, enameled, cut,** and **engraved. Leaded stained glass,** an artistic composition of small pieces of colored glass held together by lead, has also been known through the ages, particularly during the Gothic period when stained glass was employed for extraordinary windows. Today, stained glass can be employed for window and door panels, hung at a window, or designed as a freestanding piece of art.
- **Weaving and other fabric art.** The art of weaving has been known in almost every country of the world, and each has developed distinctive cultural designs. Most weavers through the centuries have employed a simple hand loom, wool yarns, natural dyes, and simple designs. During the twentieth century, and especially at the Bauhaus in Germany during the 1920s, new designs and approaches were fostered in this medium (see Chapter 2). Today, weaving and other art compositions employing fabrics and fibers are regarded as highly valued works of art and make a beautiful accessory in both private and public settings. Combined with imagination, new yarns, colors, and other innovations make weaving and fabric-art designs limitless.
- **Basketry.** The art of basket weaving has changed little since ancient times; however, today's designers have further developed this art by introducing new approaches in color use, form, pattern, and style. Traditional baskets created by particular cultures, like the Navajo Indian tribes, display distinctive characteristics and style that are highly valued. Almost any home, especially an informal environment, can be enhanced by the use of baskets, which may either stand alone, be part of a grouping, or function as containers for flowers and plants.
- **Pillows.** Pillows as accessories add a touch of warmth and human comfort, helping to soften the hard lines of architecture and furnishings. They are available in a wide variety of colors and may be patterned or plain. Handcrafted pillows may be intricately stitched, woven, or created by other forms of

Figure 11.25 A country look is established through the use of pillows covered in quaint prints, the paintings, porcelain rabbits, and baskets of flowers. The accessories contribute to the enjoyment and style of the room. *(Courtesy of Country Life Designs.)*

Figure 11.26 A leather-covered built-in sofa surrounds an antique Danish table. The contrast of light against dark sharpens the accessories used, including pillows, pottery, sculpture, and rugs, creating an inviting and comfortable atmosphere in this basement family room. *(Photograph by Mark Allen.)*

Figure 11.27 A small entry makes a grand impression and an excellent introduction to the home through the use of accessories including a graceful wood swan, large flower arrangement, decorative mirror, and large basket full of tall, narrow cuttings. *(Courtesy of Gayl Baddeley/Associates.)*

fabric art. Pillows are most often found on sofas, beds, and chairs and sometimes on the floor.

- **Handcrafted and custom-designed rugs.** (See Chapter 7.)
- **Wood crafts.** Wood carving is another art that has survived through the ages and continues today as a medium for highly prized decorative and structural accessories. Items carved of wood and used as accessories in the home include sculpture and statuary—either traditional or modern, bowls, vases, picture and mirror frames, lamp bases, clocks, and candle holders.
- **Metal works.** Bronze, brass, silver, pewter, iron, aluminum, steel, chromium, tin, and copper are some of the most popular metals employed for accessories. Sculpture, statuary, pots, bowls, vases, plates, platters, candle holders, fire tools, decorative and functional hardware, and other items can be beautifully fashioned from metal, often providing the right textural touch to a room.
- **Candles.** Originally employed for purely functional purposes, handcrafted candles today have become a highly intricate art form. Candles are created in any color and in a wide range of textures and forms suitable for both traditional and modern settings. Candles are often used

for decorative accents in the interior and, when lit, provide a warm, inviting element in the private or public environment.

Finishing Touches

The finishing touches added to an interior scheme can be like pieces of fine jewelry and give a personal and final stamp of approval to a room.

- **Hardware.** A contemporary room can be made strikingly modern and a traditional room can take on historical authenticity through the discriminating use of small details such as door knockers, doorknobs, switch plates, curtain rods, and tiebacks. Drawer pulls, ***escutcheons,*** and hinges can give a piece of furniture a definite feeling for any period. Whether the style is authentic Early American, graceful Georgian, elegant French, refined Classical, romantic Spanish, exotic Oriental, or sleek Modern, the right hardware can convey the appropriate mood.
- **Placement and background.** The desire to display one's prized possessions is universal, and the challenge is to arrange these treasured objects into a composition of uncluttered beauty. If items collected are worth acquiring, they are worth displaying. The secret lies in training the eye to see beauty in color, form, and space relationships when grouping the items in an artistic arrangement. By themselves, small things may be insignificant, but through skillful arrangement, even the simplest items can take on special meaning. When grouping small objects, one should keep in mind that they are not seen in and of themselves but against a background of walls and furniture, which can be considered part of the arrangement. As the designer brings together various items, an awareness of their relationship to each other is important. Perhaps a grouping of round objects of varying sizes is pleasing, but adding a rectangle can provide a different perspective. In an arrangement with three elements—a horizontal piece, a higher intermediate piece, and a tall vertical piece—the eye will move from the low horizontal to the high vertical, providing a pleasant sense of transition. This rhythm is seen in nature when the eye observes the earth, flowering plants and towering trees, which direct the sight still higher. A common color subtly running through each element can add unity to an arrangement.
- **Experiment.** Experimentation with accessories can aid in creating the desired outcome. Items for functional or decorative use in all areas of the home can add visual pleasure when displayed alone or grouped with an aesthetic eye—often after the process of experimentation has taken place. Books can be combined with an occasional figurine, a small painting, a trophy, or any small article. A plant sprawling over the edge of a shelf to a lower level will provide an interesting effect. Experimenting with combinations of accessories and their placement within the interior space is a valuable learning process.

If the designer believes a room lacks character, a search can be made until the right elements are discovered. Anything that is used should be in keeping with the quality that has been established in the home and either strengthen the chosen theme or, by contrast, add a touch of excitement. Leaving a little empty space need not be of concern—there is often a "charm in the incomplete."

FINISHING TOUCHES

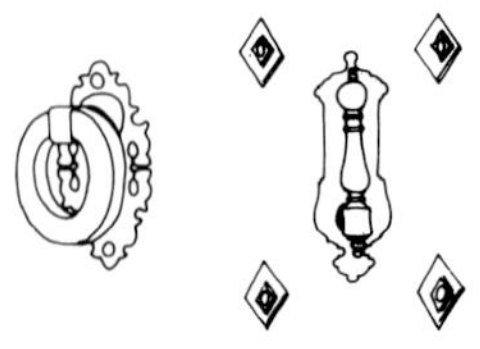

Door knockers

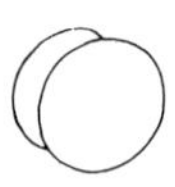

Doorknobs

Drawer pulls

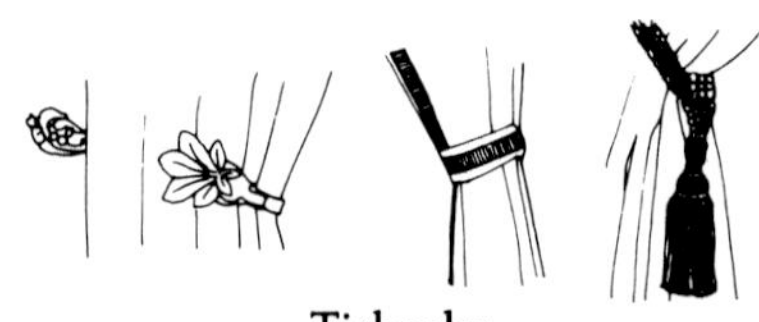

Tiebacks

Interior Design as a Career

Chapter Twelve

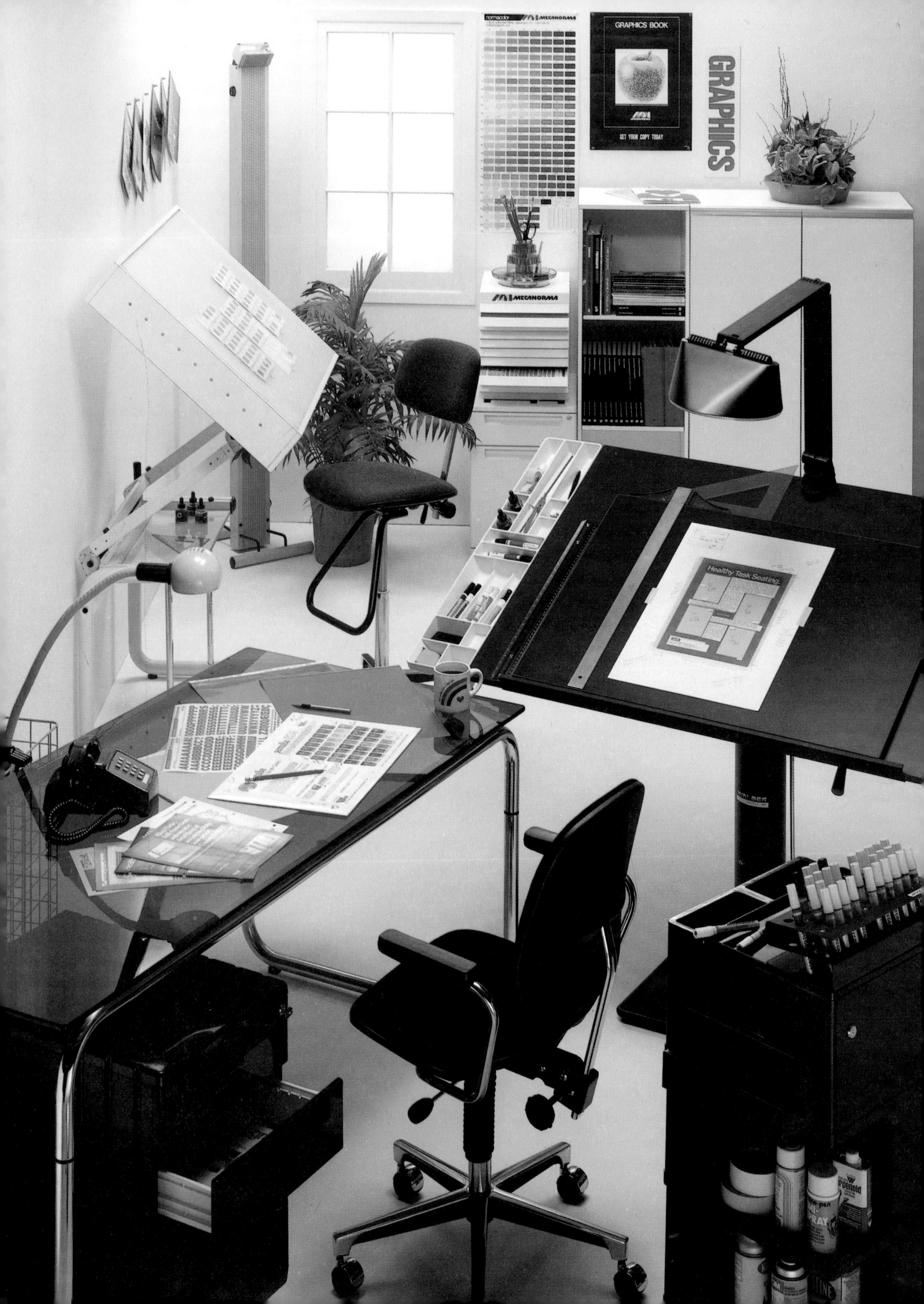

normacolor
MECANORMA
GRAPHICS BOOK
GET YOUR COPY TODAY
GRAPHICS
MECANORMA
Healthy Task Seating.

The following definition of an interior designer was formulated by the National Council for Interior Design Qualifications (NCIDQ) and has been endorsed by the American Society of Interior Designers (ASID), the Foundation for Interior Design Education Research (FIDER), and the Interior Design Educators Council, Inc. (IDEC).

The professional interior designer is a person qualified by education, experience, and examination, who

1. Identifies, researches, and creatively solves problems pertaining to the function and quality of the interior environment

2. performs services relative to interior spaces, including programming, design analysis, space planning, and aesthetics using specialized knowledge of interior construction, building codes, equipment, materials, and furnishings, and

3. prepares all drawings and documents relative to the design of interior spaces in order to enhance and protect the health, safety, and welfare of the public.

History of the Interior Design Profession

Figure 12.1 The professional designer requires a functional workspace with necessary equipment for both residential and contract projects. *(Photograph courtesy of Martin Instrument Company.)*

The profession of interior design, as a separate and distinctive career direction as just described, is a relatively new profession that evolved primarily during the latter half of the nineteenth century and the early decades of the twentieth century, then fully emerged in the decades following World War II. Interiors designed prior to the establishment of the profession as we know it today were executed primarily by furniture designers, painters, sculptors, architects, and others active in the decorative arts. Some major developments instrumental in establishing the profession of interior design include the following.

- **Authors, moralists, and other early advocates of good design** were deeply interested in the relationship of human comfort and well-being incorporated with the effective use of sound principles of design. The development of interior design in America was influenced by the writings and sermons of many individuals and by various publications, including (1) **William Morris** and the **Arts and Crafts Movement** (1860s) in England, who advocated "good design for everyone"; (2) English author and moralist **Charles Eastlake,** who in 1868 wrote *Hints on Household Taste,* one of the first books on interior decoration; (3) American Arts and Crafts Movement leader **Gustav Stickley,** who published *The Craftsman* (turn of the century) illustrating numerous articles on home design; (4) various late-nineteenth-century publications such as *Godey's Lady's Book, Harper's New Monthly, Harper's Bazaar,* and *Ladies Home Journal,* which advocated more tasteful interiors; (5) **Edith Wharton** and **Ogden Codman,** who in the 1890s wrote a book called *The Decoration of Houses,* which was intended to show that the purpose of interior decoration was to bring out the proportions of a well-designed room (This book was reluctantly published in 1907—the publishers were not certain the public would be interested in such a topic.); (6) **Candace Wheeler,** who in 1890 published an article entitled "Interior Decoration as a Profession for Women"; (7) **W. C. Gannet,** who wrote a privately printed series of essays called ***"The House Beautiful,"*** from which the publication of a magazine of the same title derived its impetus and was first published in 1896. Soon, other home-decorating periodicals appeared on the market.
- At the turn of the century and on into the next decades, **architects** like **Frank Lloyd Wright, the Greene & Greene Bros.,** and other progressive designers both in America and Europe saw the need to integrate the exterior of a structure with the interior spaces and furnishings. Most often the architects themselves assumed this responsibility.
- The impact of **social and economic growth** on interior design was an important factor for the development of the profession. During the past century, America has become one of the most prosperous nations in the world, and as a result, the profession of interior design found a prominent place in society. Americans demanded more efficient and aesthetically pleasing private and public environments—and were willing to support a new profession that would implement that desire.
- **"America's first interior decorator"** had a great influence. Although there were many relatively unknown decorating shops and private decorators in

Figure 12.2 Elsie de Wolfe, considered America's first professional interior designer, believed the home should express the good taste of the owner. In her own dining room in New York City, 1896, traditional furnishings (which she preferred) have been carefully selected and coordinated. *(Photograph from the Byron Collection, The Museum of the City of New York.)*

America and Europe at the turn of the century, one of the most famous individuals to offer interior decorating services to the public was New York actress **Elsie de Wolfe.** With her expert knowledge of French furniture and antiques, she felt confident that she had a unique, marketable service to offer the public. In 1901, Elsie de Wolfe set herself up in business as "America's first interior decorator." Through her efforts, along with the work of other women during this period, including **Syrie Maugham** and **Nancy McClelland,** the profession of interior decorating was established. These female interior decorators became known as **"the ladies of good taste."** Other well-known pioneer interior decorators followed—both women and men who promoted the new profession.

- The **establishment of professional interior design societies** began in the 1930s and gave credibility to the new vocation. For decades, the accepted term for the profession was ***interior decorator,*** a term the professional societies felt implied only dealing with the superficial embellishment of the interior. The term ***interior designer*** soon replaced the old term and implied a well-trained professional who understands and applies highly technical skills (see p. 395).
- **The profession today** is growing and changing. Prior to World War II, the profession of interior design was relatively limited to selecting fabrics, furnishings, and background materials for the home. Since the 1950s, however, there has been a great demand for both residential and contract designers who are well trained and qualified in executing all aspects of interior planning and sales.

The Classifications of Interior Design

Interior design has become such a multifaceted field that many designers choose to specialize in one of the following areas in order to develop and concentrate their expertise. Basic options are classified into the following two types.

- *Residential interior design* refers to the design of an entire private residence, apartment, condominium, or parts of one, in which the client is to be the user or occupant.
- *Nonresidential design,* also referred to as *contract design,*

Figure 12.3 Residential design—the design of private living space—is one of the two major directions for the professional interior designer. Prominent designer John Saladino worked closely with the client to create a composition that would be functional, livable, and aesthetically suitable. *(Photograph by Peter Margonelli.)*

Figure 12.4 Many interior designers deal largely with contract projects. All furnishings, lighting, and details were planned for this large commercial concern by trained professionals who were sensitive to the architectural background. *(Courtesy of Gayl Baddeley/Associates.)*

encompasses the design of public interior environments including financial, medical, and educational institutions, museums, restaurants, governmental and recreational facilities, offices, hotels, motels, retail establishments, theaters, and other public settings.

- Additional areas of *specialization* in which an interior designer may elect to concentrate include furniture, lighting, fabric design, color consulting, interior photography, design journalism, or product representation for a manufacturer (see p. 403, "Opportunities for Interior Designers").

The Responsibilities of an Interior Designer

The professional interior designer is

- Required to be proficient in the planning, designing, and implementing of residential and nonresidential design.
- Qualified to coordinate all elements of design to create functional and aesthetically pleasing living and working environments that fulfill the total needs of the client or user.
- Trained to make the most of space. Living and working space is diminishing in size because of increased building costs, and the designer therefore has the challenge to use every square foot to the best advantage.
- Qualified to work with an architect from the initial planning stages of an environment to

completion, working from empty space until the last interior detail is in place and the client is satisfied.

- Knowledgeable about and able to appropriately integrate period and contemporary styles of architecture, furniture, and decorative arts.
- Knowledgeable about furniture materials and construction, and has the creative ability to custom design furnishings such as case goods and redesign or add architectural elements such as wood trim, doors, and mantels.
- Concerned not only with the immediate effect but also with the construction, durability, and maintenance of fabrics and finishes. A designer is also well qualified to select and employ fabrics and textiles for the best performance and appearance as applied to all aspects of an interior, including floor, wall, window, and upholstery treatments.
- Knowledgeable about lighting and its effect on interior colors, finishes, and spaces.
- Familiar with a broad range of products and services, and must have a good working relationship with those professionals who provide the products and services to assure that ordering, shipping, delivery, and installations go smoothly.
- Able to draw upon reliable sources to complete a design project, including manufacturers, cabinetmakers, artisans such as upholsterers and refinishers, and professionals in workrooms, antique shops, showrooms, and auction rooms. These sources can be invaluable to the client, because access to some high-quality merchandise, labor, and services is available only through professionals.
- Responsible for the completed project and willing to see that any flaws in quality or craftsmanship are corrected.
- A good visual and oral communicator. One of the many requisites to a successful design is a sound designer-client-resource relationship.
- Able to incorporate artistry and expertise with the client's purposes and objectives within the bounds of good taste.
- An effective salesperson, for without this element, the interior design profession would not exist.
- Other valuable personal attributes include enthusiasm, imagination, curiosity, perceptual skills, sociability, keen insight regarding people, respect for time commitments, and organizational and record-keeping skills.

Working Procedures for the Professional Interior Designer

Establishment of a successful working procedure, combined with creative design solutions and the satisfaction of the client, is the goal of a professional interior designer. Although it is not the intent of this book to cover the entire working procedure for the designer, the following is an outline of the basic logical steps or elements involved:

- **A suitable workspace.** Designers require a suitable workplace with a desk and chair set up for drawing and planning. Good lighting and storage are also essential, along with all necessary equipment to accomplish the task.
- **The program.** The designer and client should have a project agreement with common goals in mind. The program helps determine this designer/client understanding. A program may be set up for a small residential job or a large commercial project. It involves developing a step-by-step working procedure, taking into account all needs of the consumer. Information is obtained concerning such criteria as space allocation, intended function, furnishings, and special requirements. All information is then evaluated.
- **Presentation to the client.** After the program information has been collected and evaluated, it is presented to the client for approval. At this point projected budget and design solutions may be agreed upon.
- **First-step drawings.** In this initial stage the designer makes preliminary sketches and drawings indicating space allocations, interior architecture, and furnishings. Involving clients in this process is usually optimal, but the client's final approval is necessary.
- **Final detailed drawings.** These are completed during this stage. Renderings, elevations, and often perspectives are professionally executed.
- **Presentation to the client for final approval.** Finished professional drawings and specifications are presented to the client before proceeding to the next step.
- **Blueprints or "construction drawings."** These are made to determine the actual working procedures and cost. At this stage the designer works with architects, contractors, electricians, plumbers, and all those connected with the construction and technical aspects such as air conditioning, heating, wiring, safety, and acoustics. Also, at this point the designer begins color scheming and planning for required furnishings.

Figure 12.5a Interior designers are often required to draw a rendering of the proposed interior for the client. This perspective of a living room was executed by designer Jennifer Budd to present the design concept to the client. *(Courtesy of Jennifer Budd, designer.)*

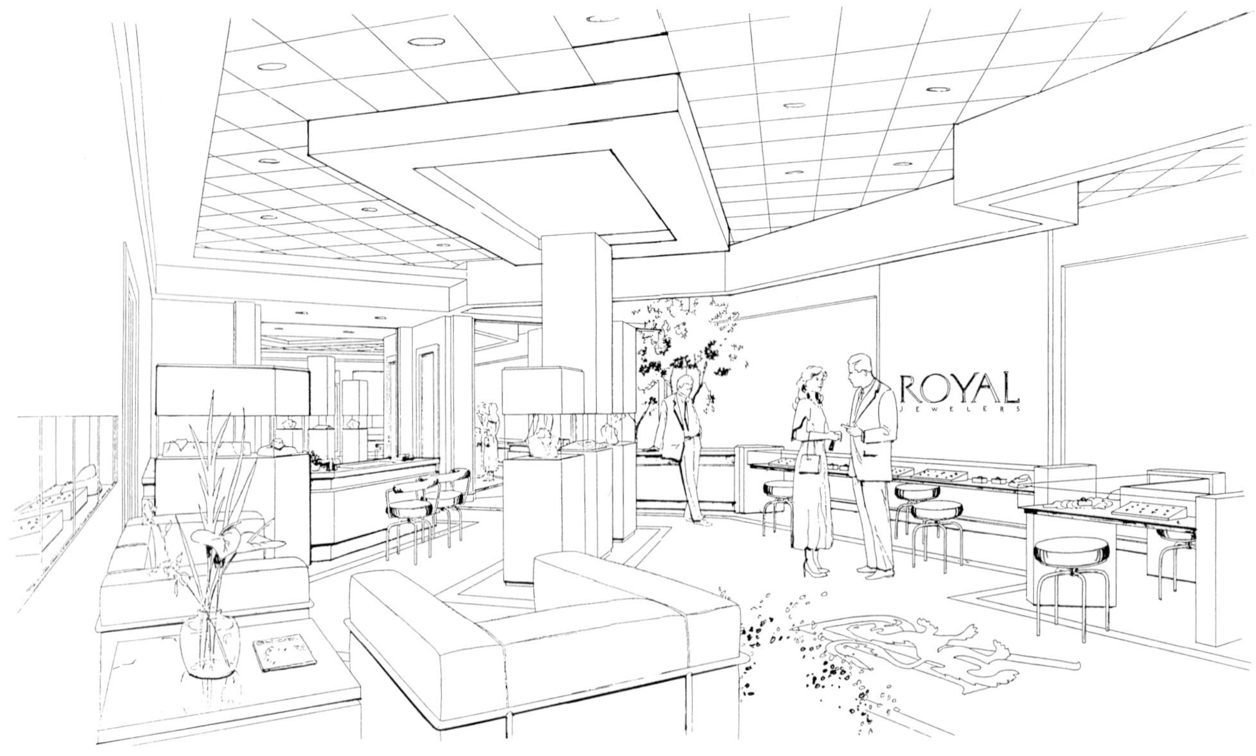

Figure 12.5b An effective contract rendering executed by designer Robert Olson for a jewelry firm helps the client visualize the completed project. *(Courtesy of Robert Olson, designer.)*

Figure 12.6 Designers Jodee Glazier and Dale Brown rendered this award-winning contract design of a large banking facility for a student project. *(Photograph courtesy of Jodee Glazier and Dale Brown, Alpine Sun Design.)*

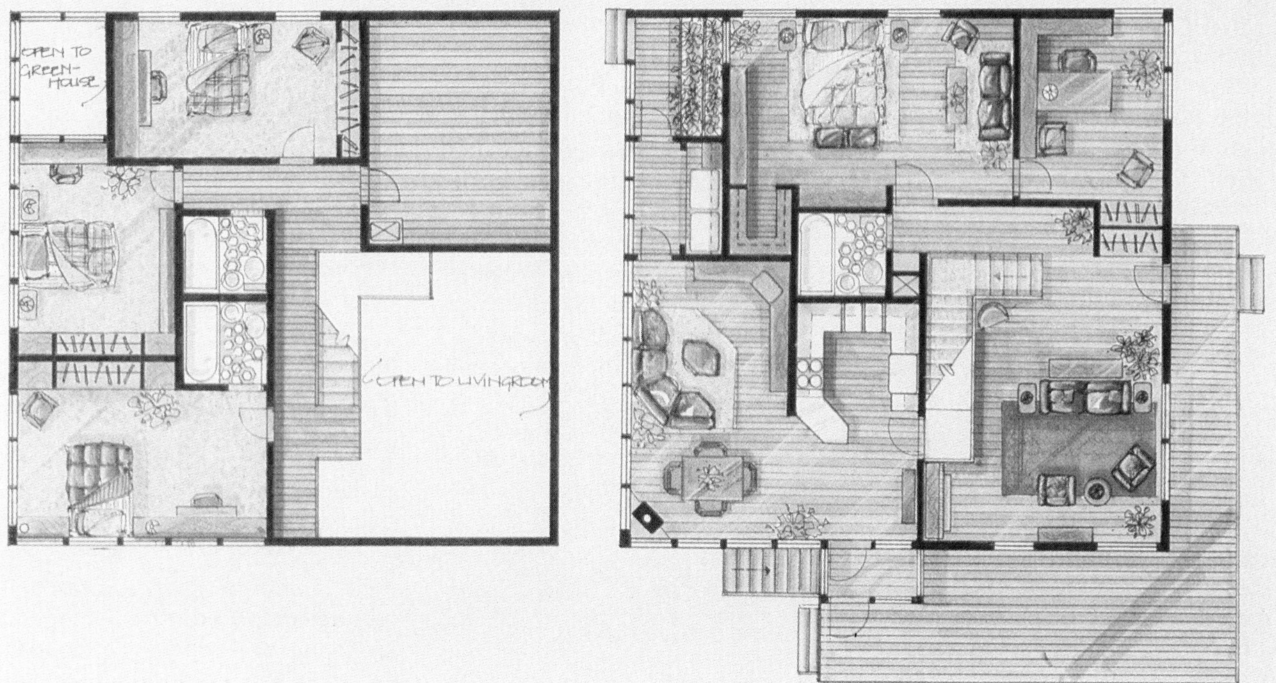

Figure 12.7 Drafting floor plans is a primary responsibility for the professional interior designer. This floor plan allows the client to visualize the space and furniture placement. *(Courtesy of Jennifer Budd, designer.)*

Figure 12.8 Often architects and designers are required to build a working model of a residential or contract project to present to the client and aid in the designing and building process. This model, created by architect Eduard Dreier, was built to scale to identify all details of the project including integration to the site. *(Courtesy of Eduard Dreier, architect.)*

- **Estimates and bids.** After blueprints or construction drawings are completed, the designer submits them to contractors for estimates and bids. Usually the job is awarded to the lowest bidder. Sometimes the project is completed on a cost-plus basis rather than on a predetermined price agreement.
- **Scheduling of the project.** The designer now schedules the final project with the contractor and others involved in the actual working process.
- **Purchase of necessary materials.** The designer acquires all materials needed for the completion of the project—a process requiring a sound professional business background. Selections must be made, purchase orders filled out, and delivery dates determined. Coordinating these aspects of the design process is necessary to ensure an effective project-completion goal.
- **Supervision of all major aspects of the design project.** Supervision is a necessary step in which the designer checks to see that all specifications are accurate and well executed.
- **Supervision of the final details.** Arranging furniture, pictures, lamps, and other accessories until all furnishings are in place is the last stage of the working procedure. It is an essential step in the satisfactory completion of the job. Often the professional designer will **follow up** or **evaluate** the project at a later date to determine the success of the design solutions.

Preparing for a Career in Interior Design

Deciding on a career is a searching process requiring careful examination and evaluation of one's interests and capabilities as well as one's inadequacies. Creativity, sensitivity to the environment, and interest in America's cultural heritage and ancestral homes as well as today's contemporary design are all necessary traits for an individual who is seriously pursuing a career in interior design. A designer is also concerned with improving the quality of personal environments, work spaces, institutional and recreational environments.

One of the initial steps toward becoming a professional interior designer is to successfully complete an interior design program at a college, university, or design school (preferably a FIDER-accredited educational facility) (see chart) where students are educated and trained in such areas as

- Visual, written, verbal, and graphic communication skills, as well as drafting skills and preparation of a portfolio.
- Theory, elements, and principles of design.
- Development of knowledge about building and interior support systems and codes, textiles, lighting, materials, and barrier-free design.
- Programming and planning, interior component selection, furniture layout, space planning, and cost estimates.
- History of art, architecture, and interiors.
- Business practices and principles.
- Human factors and ergonomics.
- Product design and construction.

Most interior design programs require students to participate in an internship or in work-study courses as part of the requirements for graduation. Internship programs vary somewhat in different schools, but all have the same objective,

The Foundation for Interior Design Education Research (FIDER) Recognizes Three Types of Undergraduate Programs:

Baccalaureate Degree	Certificate or Diploma Programs	Certificate Programs
—four years —intensive training —interior design major —see curriculum outlined in text	—three years —intensive training —usually specialized design schools that require prerequisite training in liberal arts	—two years —emphasis is technical for interior design aides —usually offered at community, junior, or technical colleges

which is to enable the student to experience firsthand the professional business world prior to graduation by combining classroom theory with practice. Students work in the interior design area of a reputable business establishment during the summer months or part-time during the school year or both. Some schools give college credits, and the monetary agreement, if any, is arranged between the student and the firm.

Internship experience is invaluable to the student. By becoming actively involved in the real world of interior design, students

- Experience operational procedures, policies, and various phases of design, such as client-designer relationships; learn about interactions of designers within a firm; and observe and participate in design from concept to implementation.
- Learn to be open to new and different attitudes and perspectives in all aspects of design.
- Learn more about themselves in terms of potential future desires and goals as a professional interior designer.
- In general, students receive valuable experience that can be entered on a job resumé for use after graduation.

Information on and locations of schools offering interior design programs can be obtained from local libraries or from the Foundation for Interior Design Education Research (FIDER), Room 1501, 322 8th Avenue, New York, NY 10001.

The interior design profession offers a rewarding career for well-trained, dedicated individuals.

Opportunities for Interior Designers

As the demand for quality housing and commercial facilities rises, the interior designer is finding more and more opportunities for creative job opportunities. They are now perceived as important in the design process and are employed by many offices and businesses in architecture-related fields. Interior designers are being sought by industry, which has become aware of interior designers' buying power, and manufacturers are turning to the design community for advice in product development.

Major design trade centers can now be found in New York, Texas, California, and Illinois. One of the most notable trade centers for residential furniture is in High Point, North Carolina. Surveys have shown that interior designers' activities in both residential and contract design have significantly expanded since 1980. An increasing source of clients is the growing segment of the population made up of families with two wage earners, who, because of limited time, are turning to professional interior designers to carry out the time-consuming project of home planning and interior design.

Some **residential and contract career opportunities** open to professional interior designers include the following:

- An **independent residential or contract interior designer** may be the head or a member of a design firm or decorating studio, may own a small specialty shop, or may even work out of a home making purchases from a wide range of sources. The independent interior designer will go to a client's home or office, appraise the job, work out floor plans, assist in selecting and arranging furniture, assemble color schemes, place orders, and supervise the job until its completion.
- Many **department and furniture stores** are staffed with interior designers, drafters, buyers, and other design-related personnel. These designers follow the same procedure as the independent designer and offer a number of advantages as well: (1) a limited amount of free advice is available, (2) payments for all purchases and services can be made on the store's payment plan, and (3) store merchandise may be moderately priced due to the quantity purchased by the store.

  In smaller stores, decorating and design services are usually more limited. The designer may or may not be a trained professional and may not be permitted to go to the client's home or office. Also, only merchandise carried by the store may be sold. Each store establishes its own policies; therefore, services may vary.

- A **renderer,** who prepares realistic, three-dimensional drawings and illustrations of a designer's concept for an interior, can work as an independent designer or for architectural and design firms. A **drafter** prepares precise mechanical drawings for architects, designers, builders, and furnishing manufacturers.
- A **set designer** works on television, theater, and movie productions or creates complete room displays for department stores, furniture companies, and manufacturers for advertising purposes.
- A **commercial-contract designer** works for a design company, architectural firm, or corporation performing any of a variety of tasks such as space planning, drafting, and specifying and purchasing furnishings and materials in volume for installation in hotels, apartments, schools, health care facilities, and other public settings.
- A design specialist may focus on **historic preservation and restoration**—an important and growing design direction today.
- Interior designers can be involved with **transportation**—designing interiors of planes, ships, trains, mobile homes, and other transportation projects.
- **Kitchen designers** are trained experts who help clients create the most efficient and functional kitchen space to fulfill particular needs.
- A **wholesale market representative** sells interior design-related merchandise in quantity to retail establishments.
- **Lighting design specialists** are particularly in demand today for contract projects.
- Designers may specialize in **color consulting** to aid clients in both residential and contract programs.
- A **design journalist or photographer** completes work for newspapers, magazines, or publishers on a variety of timely aspects of interior design.
- A designer may be involved in creating interiors for **model homes** and **model rooms** and designs for **display settings.**
- An **interior design educator** is generally employed by a state or privately supported school system on a secondary, junior college, or university level. Interior design schools also require qualified instructors.

This list outlines the major employment opportunities open to the trained interior designer. Other challenging opportunities are developing in government, business, and industry, where the diverse skills of design professionals are considered essential to long-range planning and product development. Experienced, professional interior designers are currently serving in key positions with large corporations in industry, manufacturing, transportation, communications, recreation, computer-aided design, and many other areas. Designers are now members of state and federal governments. A market is rapidly evolving in some of the developing countries, such as the wealthy Persian Gulf region of the Middle East. In 1981, Saudi Arabia held its first International Exhibition of Interior Design. This new development affords unlimited possibilities and opportunities for American interior designers.

The Computer: Applications for Interior Design

Interior design deals with many elements in order to present a pleasing and precise solution. Many hours are spent consulting plans, sketches, fabrics, and materials. The use of the computer in the design field has made this consultation time more effective, thorough, and efficient.

Available to the interior designer are computer-generated representations of exteriors and interiors of the project, showing shape, surface textures, light and shadow, mass or plane, and lighting models. With a palette of several hundred colors, the computer allows the user to create and manipulate the design in numerous ways and experiment with color schemes and structural changes. Such a "walk-through" can be invaluable in evaluating the design and pinpointing problem areas. Some major tasks computers are capable of handling include

1. **Expediting routine office tasks** such as filing, bookkeeping, billing, purchase orders, and other clerical duties.
2. **Drafting and perspective drawing.** Computer-aided design programs (CAD) completely eliminate the need for manual drawing, although most architectural firms use the CAD systems for redrawing and ideation. Floor plans, perspectives, elevations, and full-color renderings of furniture and architecture can be produced in a fraction of the time it takes to produce them by hand. A normal job requiring 160 drawing hours for a draftsman can be completed in 4.5 hours by a computer.
3. **Aiding in the planning process**

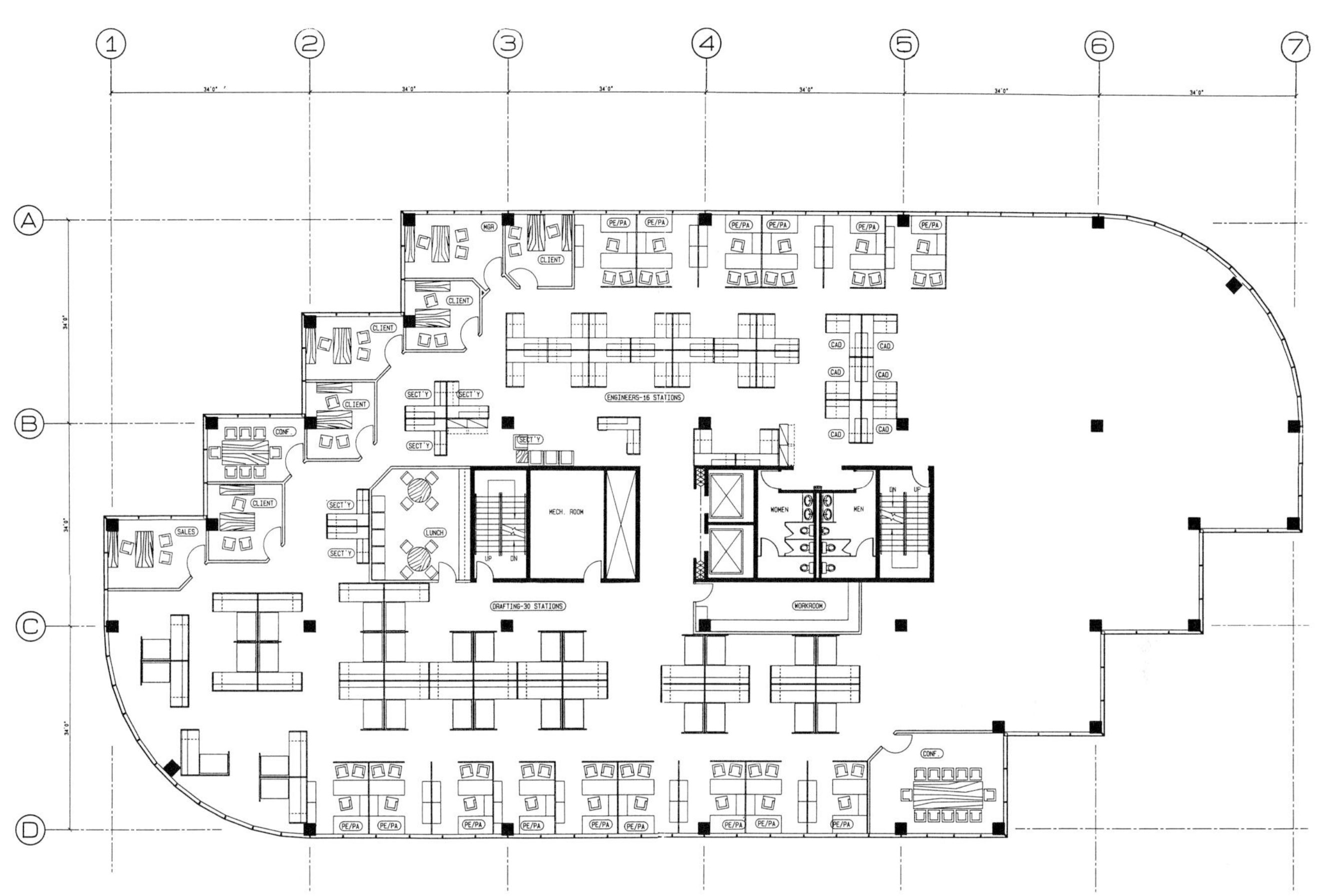

Figure 12.9 With the aid of a computer designers can create any floor plan concept and configuration indicating specific details such as wall partitions, doors, stairways, windows, columns, lighting, and furnishings. *(Courtesy of Valentiner Jones, architects/Drawn by Bill Hall.)*

Figure 12.10 Computer-graphic techniques provide numerous opportunities for the interior designer to manipulate forms within a space until a desirable solution is created. *(Courtesy of Henry Christiansen, civil engineer.)*

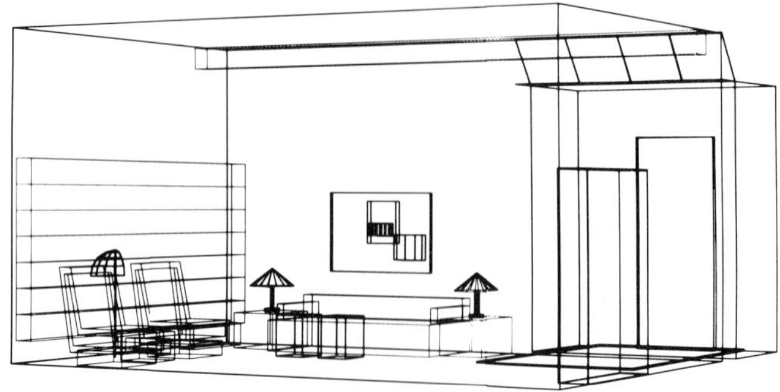

Figure 12.11 A computer-aided perspective design depicts a seating area with all intersecting lines needed to execute the illustration. The computer allows the designer to explore numerous possibilities for a particular space. *(Courtesy of Larry Cindrich, designer.)*

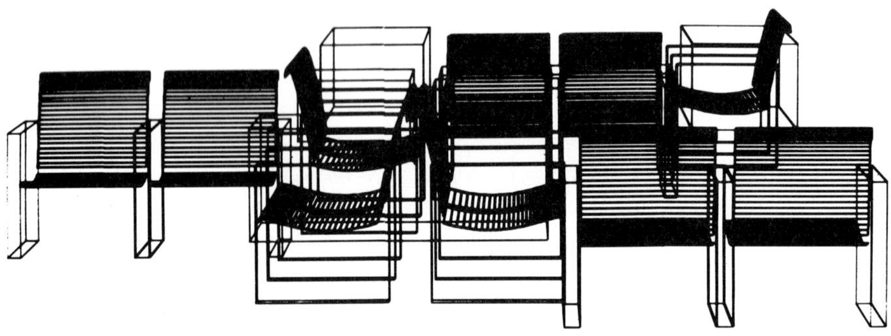

Figure 12.12 The computer can also be used to develop 3-D forms for a single piece of furniture and further convey how that piece can be utilized in multiple units used in varied arrangements. *(Courtesy of Larry Cindrich, designer.)*

with data banks of information readily available. Because all information used in the design process is filed in the computer's memory system, it is retrievable. Specification lists and facilities reports can be accessed as detailed printouts, which accurately list all the components in any design on file. The program keeps track of all data, drawing figures and point allocations automatically so that the user does not have to keep records of items. When the data are retrieved, the computer can display on the screen or page an area as large as the floor plan of an entire building or as minute as a single pencil on a desktop—or any area in between.

4. **Estimating costs.** With cost information stored in the computer's memory, the task of projecting plan proposals into cost estimates is relatively simple.
5. **Preparing specifications,** which can be an effortless task. The computer is capable of storing suppliers' catalog data including prices and other valuable information, facilitating efficient preparation for project specifications. Manufacturers can supply electronic images of their products that can be introduced in plans and perspective drawings.
6. **Communicating.** Computers have the capability of rapidly and accurately communicating information between architects, builders, and designers through an efficient computer network system.
7. **Ordering.** Orders for required furnishings can be placed directly through the computer to the manufacturer.

Computer programs typically come to the user with a basic working capacity. The user may augment a particular program by purchasing specialty packages that adapt the system to the efficient processing of a specific area, such as interior design. In time, the designer can create a personalized library of software programs that are peculiar to his or her discipline. Standard graphic items include typical floor-plan symbols such as wall types, windows, doors, cabinetry, and popular furniture types.

As the computer becomes more adapted to usage within the design world, many new innovations are being developed that make the work of the designer and architect more efficient. One such invention has been developed by the architectural firm of Skidmore, Owings, and Merrill (SOM). The architects of SOM have devised a CAD-CAM (computer-aided design and computer-aided manufacturing) program in order to create models of buildings already designed and recorded in the computer. They use a laser cutter to cut out parts needed to construct a model for presentation to their clients. Because of the cutting ability and exactness of the laser, the models are more accurate in scale and more cost efficient. The investment for the development of the laser cutter was approximately $35,000, whereas the price for each model cut by hand would cost approximately $70,000. It reduces the time for model making from days of tedious work to hours. To the interior designer, a CAD system can be what the bulldozer is to the user of a shovel. It permits each user to get the job done more quickly and efficiently and less expensively. It strips tedium away and allows the computer and designer to work in concert, with each doing what it or the user does best.

Being relatively new within the design realm, computers have both pros and cons for use in architecture and interior design. Although the computer reduces labor costs, enhances efficiencies, expands visualization, and eliminates repetitive work for draftsmen and designers, initial expenses in investment, training time for employees, and software management are sometimes problem areas. Although computer application has generally been most efficient in major firms that have literally hundreds of projects at a time, smaller computers with higher capabilities are now available for use in smaller firms. Many small firms are also taking advantage of opportunities to connect into a centralized equipment system, which are often offered by larger manufacturing firms or by other individual services. With constant advancements in computer equipment and techniques, training design students is an ongoing process, and it is often necessary for the new employee to receive updated training for the first few weeks on the job.

Professional Interior Design Societies

- *The American Society of Interior Designers (ASID)* is a professional international organization established to enact and maintain standards of excellence to enhance the growing recognition of interior design as a profession. It was formed in 1975 through the consolidation of the American Institute of Interior Designers (AID) and the National Society of Interior Designers (NSID), but its roots date back half a century to the founding of AID in 1931. ASID is the largest organization of interior designers in the world, representing over 20,000 members in the United States as well as abroad. It represents interior design as a profession dedicated to serving people, and it provides a forum for its thousands of talented members to bring their differing points of view into harmony to promote unified action. ASID fosters the development and improvement of interior design practice through a variety of activities and programs that reflect a broad spectrum of professional concerns, ranging from interior design to community service workshops. During the 1990s, ASID plans to take a leadership role in historic interior design to take advantage of the boom in restoration of historic buildings.

  Over 150 **student chapters** of ASID (American Society of Interior Designers) are in colleges across the country, and current student membership is approximately 7,400. The society's educational program includes seminars, show-house tours, lectures, access to designers and restricted design centers, and opportunities to participate in national student competitions. Of particular importance to members is the fact that upon graduation they are eligible to advance automatically to associate membership in the society.

  The advancement to professional membership is earned after an applicant fulfills the practical-experience requirements and completes the **National Council for Interior Design Qualification (NCIDQ)** exam. Professional members are distinguished by the letters *ASID* beside their name, which serve as a symbol of professional excellence. The national ASID headquarters is located at 1430 Broadway, New York, NY 10018.

- *The Institute of Business Designers (IBD)* is an internationally established organization dedicated to the professional designer whose major field is commercial and institutional interiors and products. This includes designers responsible for offices; hotels; hospitals and health care facilities; and other institutions such as stores, schools, theaters, and banks.

  The institute is dedicated to exploring new directions in design, expanding the influence of the designer and supplementing the formal education of its members. To accomplish this, IBD is actively involved in design research, continuing education, and student design education programs. The institute also sponsors major design competitions.

As with ASID, IBD has various membership categories and requirements for membership, including education, experience, and the NCIDQ examination. Information regarding this organization can be obtained by writing to the IBD national office, 1155 Merchandise Mart, Chicago, IL 60654.

- *The Interior Design Society (IDS),* another national organization, is a relative newcomer to the profession. Organized in 1973, IDS is steadily growing across the country, with over 25 chapters and some 1,500 members. The society, which is an arm of the **National Home Furnishings Association,** provides its members with a variety of sales aids and educational programs, as well as the professional recognition they deserve as retail designers. The headquarters is at 406 Merchandise Mart, Chicago, IL 60654.
- *The Interior Design Educators Council, Inc. (IDEC),* incorporated in 1967, is dedicated to the development of interior design education. Its purpose is to strive to improve the teaching of interior design and, through this, the professional level of interior design practice. The IDEC program is concerned with establishing and strengthening the lines of communication among individual educators, educational institutes, and organizations concerned with interior design. It is an international organization and an associate member of the **International Federation of Interior Designers (IFID).** During its brief history, IDEC has been a catalyst for change and a strong contributor to most of the major accomplishments that have made the profession of interior design what it is today. Every teacher of interior design can benefit from membership in this organization. Information about IDEC can be obtained by writing IDEC, Box 8744, Richmond, VA 23226.
- One purpose of the *National Council for Interior Design Qualifications (NCIDQ)* is to establish a professional level of competence for interior designers so that they may better serve the public. Level of competence is determined through the formulation and administration of a relevant examination that qualifies the individual designer. Another purpose of NCIDQ is to investigate the advantages and disadvantages of pursuing legal registration or certification of the profession.

The incorporation charter of the council provides membership for professional design organizations only; it offers no provisions for membership to individuals. All council member organizations require the NCIDQ exam as a prerequisite for professional membership. Nonaffiliated interior designers who have the required education and experience may apply directly to NCIDQ to take the exam.

The examination, offered twice a year at various locations around the country, consists of two parts given on two consecutive days. The first part—the academic section—tests the candidate's knowledge in such areas as history, modern design, technical information, business practices, and ethics. The second part is a 10-hr design problem testing the candidate's ability to arrive at a conceptual solution to a realistic design problem. The problem requires a design concept statement, space planning, furniture selection and arrangement, interior surfaces, interior systems, presentation skills, and project specifications. Information about the council can be obtained by writing to NCIDQ, 118 East 25th Street, New York, NY 10010.

Other professional organizations that may be of interest are the following:

Environmental Design Research Association, Inc.
L'Enfant Plaza Station
P.O. Box 23129
Washington, DC 20024

Foundation for Interior Design Education Research
242 West 27th Street, Suite 6B
New York, NY 10001
(212) 929–8366

Interior Designers of Canada
168 Bedford Road
Toronto
Canada M5R 2K9

Getting That First Job

How is that important first job obtained? First, carefully designing and planning strategies for obtaining a job are often a full-time project. Reading trade journals, newsletters, and periodicals dealing with the field of interior design is a good start. Every available source of information, including visits to offices of agencies and professional organizations, can be explored.

Before going to the first interview, the prospective professional interior designer is advised to

- Examine personal needs, assets, and weaknesses. Salary requirements and corresponding responsibilities for that salary should be determined. Does the aspiring professional know what is desired now and in the future? Is the resumé a full and honest representation? Does it say too little or too much? Is the ***portfolio*** a true reflection of the best professional and creative work?
- Examine personal appearance carefully and objectively. The importance of personal appear-

ance and presentation cannot be overemphasized. Being well groomed and appropriately dressed, standing straight, and sitting properly are all important. First impressions are lasting. It is wise to approach the potential employer with a positive state of mind. The applicant should be polite, articulate, straightforward, honest, and self-confident, but without arrogance. It is helpful to point out one's training, skills, and genuine desire to be of service to the company. A job seeker should take every opportunity for an interview; and personal technique will most likely be improved each time.

Attaining Visibility

A question facing every new interior designer is, How am I going to become known in the design field? To answer this question, a few suggestions may be helpful to the novice designer:

- Be proud of and enthusiastic about the profession. Let others be aware of this. Believe in yourself and in what you are doing. Before asking the public to believe in you, you must believe in yourself.
- Put your profession within reach of everyone in the community. Offer to give lectures for your firm. Contact local societies, clubs, and charities who may be interested in a lecture or slide presentation. Set up an adult education class through local high schools or colleges.
- Write articles for local newspapers. Express stimulating ideas. A good place to start might be an article on children's rooms, because these rooms quickly capture the public's interest.
- Contact key employees at local radio stations. They may be interested in presenting a series of daytime lectures on practical interior design problems.
- Show courtesy and concern for every client encountered, regardless of whether or not a contract is secured.
- Become involved in preservation and restoration efforts. If no preservation society exists in the community, the opportunity may be there to organize one. Nearly every town has some building worth preserving. Being responsible for putting a structure on the National Register of Historic Places can bring prestige, visibility, and a sense of pride to the community.
- Participate in national and local professional interior design or related organizations.

The Interior Designer's Challenge for the Future

In light of the impact professional design and designers have on the economic, social, cultural, and environmental life of our nation, the challenge for the interior designer as a protector of the human environment in the final decade of the twentieth century is significant. Perhaps the first challenge and major responsibility is to design for people. Many designers are concerned primarily with the big commercial jobs that offer visible recognition. These types of jobs are most assuredly desirable and essential, but until people take precedence over buildings, the interior design profession will not have met its most important obligation: *to improve the quality of life for everyone.* To accomplish this, the interior designer must heighten the awareness on all levels of society of the many ways in which interior designers can affect the living and working environment.

In today's cost-inflated world, profound **social and economic changes** are occurring that present new challenges requiring immediate attention. About 20 years ago, energy was inexpensive and abundant, and home owners took it for granted. Today, energy conservation must be a part of design consciousness in all aspects of housing, both the exterior and the interior. Ever-rising cost and the change in the size and composition of families, along with their increasing mobility, present a whole new range of problems, of which one of the most crucial is space. During the 1980s a 60 percent cost increase occurred in small houses for "empty-nesters," childless couples, and single-parent families, with a large percentage of the population being forced to live in small spaces of different types. Many home owners are redesigning current facilities rather than building larger quarters. A shift from the group-oriented society of the 1960s to a concern for personal fulfillment is seen in the enlargement of home entertainment centers such as wet bars, hot tubs, wide video screens, and health and fitness centers.

Technology is rapidly making inroads in residential designs. The burgeoning **computer market** and its corresponding technologies such as home computers, along with modified use of media equipment, specialized sound systems, and television apparatus, are making a direct impact on the interior design industry. These technologies also present new problems to the designers, who must integrate the necessary machinery into personal living spaces without sacrificing the essential character of the home environment.

Another challenge to the interior designer is **preservation and restoration.** The awakening to the preservation of America's cultural heritage has prompted many people to buy and restore older homes. Long-standing but well-constructed buildings of all styles are being recycled to serve a wide range of commercial and public needs.

Despite the accomplishments of the preservation movement in America in recent years, the focus has been on exterior architecture rather than on interiors, which imposes a responsibility on the interior designer to broaden understanding and appreciation of the homes in which American ancestors lived out their lives. These homes provide a living record of social and cultural history and afford a base for authentic restoration and preservation. To bring about a fuller knowledge and understanding of the living past, the Educational Foundation of ASID is undertaking a research task with a "Significant Interiors" survey, which reaches across the country.

The requirement that today's interior designer stay up to date in the profession is no small order. In our rapidly changing world, some estimate that the amount of information doubles every four years, putting excessive demands on professionals in every field of endeavor. As design has become more demanding and technical, specialists have emerged to take over in areas where the interior designer requires particular expertise, such as in lighting, drafting, and computer design.

As a practicing professional, the interior designer is compelled to **keep abreast of the field through a continuing educational process** in order to serve both contract and residential clients adequately. The interior designer must also remember that each job and client is unique. It is imperative to be careful and responsible with the client's funds, maintain integrity, and conscientiously lead and educate—not dictate. Although the ultimate goal is to support human values, family life, and society as a whole, the designer also has a responsibility to industry and the quality of life in a working environment.

The future will present many new conditions demanding innovative design solutions. Constant recycling and renovation of the environment are necessary to meet changing human needs. The shifting of population centers will bring about growth in some existing towns and communities and the development of new ones, which will require new ecological designs. By the turn of the century, it is predicted that artificial space habitats for human beings may exist. It is possible that technology may already be in place to implement such dramatic changes, but will interior designers be creatively and psychologically prepared?

All of this does not mean designers need to submit unquestioningly to the trends and fashions of the future. Designers must be masters of change, not blind followers. The future can be built on the appreciation of and dedication to preserving the best of the past and combining it with the finest of the present. Designers should constantly and consistently reexamine old and eternal values. Environments may change, but the human needs, desires, and aspirations that have endured since the beginning of civilization will most likely remain the same. The challenge for the designers of the future is to meet the demands of current and future technological advances while addressing functional and aesthetic needs of society. In view of current and future challenges in residential and contract design, the services of interior designers are invaluable now and will be in demand even more in the future.

Bibliography

Albers, Ann. *Weaving.* Middletown, Conn.: Wesleyan University Press, 1965.

Albers, Josef. *Interaction of Color.* New Haven, Conn.: Yale University Press, 1975.

Alexander, Harold. *Design: Criteria for Decisions.* New York: Macmillan, 1976.

Alexander, Patsy. *Textile Fabrics and Their Selection.* Boston: Houghton Mifflin, 1976.

American National Standard Specifications for Making Buildings and Facilities Accessible to and Usable by Physically Handicapped People, ANSI A117.1–1980. New York: American National Standards Institute, 1980.

Aronson, Joseph. *The Encyclopedia of Furniture.* 3d ed. New York: Crown, 1965.

Ball, Victoria Kloss. *Architecture and Interior Design: Europe and America from the Colonial Era to Today.* 2 vols. New York: Wiley, 1980.

———. *The Art of Interior Design.* 2d ed. New York: Wiley, 1982.

Ballast, David Kent. *Practical Guide to Computer Applications for Architecture and Design.* Englewood Cliffs, N.J.: Prentice-Hall, 1986.

Barrows, Claire M. *Living Walls.* New York: Wallcoverings Council, 1968.

———. *New Decorating Book.* New York: Better Homes & Gardens, 1982.

Battersby, Martin, et al. (illus.) *History of Furniture.* New York: Morrow, 1976.

Bayley, Stephen (ed.). *Conran Directory of Design.* New York: Random House, Villard Books, 1985.

Bennett, Corwin. *Spaces for People.* Englewood Cliffs, N.J.: Prentice-Hall, 1977.

Bevlin, Marjorie Elliott. *Design through Discovery.* New York: Holt, Rinehart & Winston, 1955.

Birrell, Verla. *The Textile Arts.* New York: Harper & Brothers, 1959.

Birren, Faber. *Color and Human Response.* New York: Van Nostrand Reinhold, 1978.

———. *Light, Color, and Environment.* New York: Van Nostrand Reinhold, 1969.

Blake, Jill. *Color and Pattern in the Home.* New York: Quick Fox, 1978.

Boger, Louise Ade. *Furniture, Past and Present.* Garden City, N.Y.: Doubleday, 1966.

Boyce, Charles. *Dictionary of Furniture.* New York: Roundtable Press, 1985.

Bradford, Barbara Taylor. *How to Solve Your Decorating Problems.* New York: Simon & Schuster, 1976.

Brett, James. *The Kitchen: 100 Solutions to Design Problems.* New York: Whitney Library of Design, 1977.

Brown, Erica. *Sixty Years of Interior Design.* New York: Viking Press, 1982.

Bush, Donald J. *The Streamlined Decade.* New York: George Braziller, 1975.

Cheatham, Frank R., Jane Hart Cheatham, and Sheryl A. Haler. *Design Concepts and Applications.* Englewood Cliffs, N.J.: Prentice-Hall, 1983.

Clark, Robert Judson (ed.). *Arts and Crafts Movement in America, 1876–1916.* Princeton, N.J.: Princeton University Press, 1972.

Cobb, Hubbard H. *How to Paint Anything: The Complete Guide to Painting and Refinishing.* New York: Macmillan, 1972.

Conran, Terance. *The Bed and Bath Book.* New York: Crown, 1978.

———. *The House Book.* New York: Crown, 1976.

———. *New House Book.* New York: Random House, Villard Books, 1985.

Copplestone, Trewin (ed.). *World Architecture.* London: Hamlyn, 1963.

D'Arcy, Barbara. *Bloomingdales Book of Home Decorating.* New York: Harper & Row, 1973.

Debaigts, Jacques. *Interiors for Old Houses.* New York: Van Nostrand Reinhold, 1973.

De Sausmarez, Maurice. *Basic Design: The Dynamics of Visual Form.* New York: Van Nostrand Reinhold, 1983.

Design Criteria for Lighting Interior Living Spaces. New York: Illuminating Engineering Society of North America, 1980.

Diamonstein, Barbaralee. *Interior Design.* New York: Rizzoli International, 1982.

Diflow, Donna. *How to Buy Furniture.* New York: Macmillan, 1972.

Downer, Marion. *Discovering Design.* New York: Lothrop, Lee & Shepard, 1963.

Eiland, Murray L. *Oriental Rugs: A Comprehensive Study.* Greenwich, Conn.: New York Graphic Society, 1973.

Emery, Marc. *Furniture by Architects.* New York: Harry N. Abrams, 1983.

Emmerling, Mary Ellisor. *American Country.* New York: Clarkson N. Potter, 1980.

Evans, Ralph M. *An Introduction to Color.* New York: Wiley, 1959.

Faulkner, Ray and Sarah, and LuAnn Nissen. *Inside Today's Home.* 5th ed. New York: Holt, Rinehart & Winston, 1986.

Faulkner, Sarah. *Planning a Home.* New York: Holt, Rinehart & Winston, 1979.

Fehrman, Cherie, and Kenneth Fehrman. *Post-War Interior Design, 1945–1960.* New York: Van Nostrand Reinhold, 1986.

Ferebee, Ann. *A History of Design from the Victorian Era to the Present.* New York: Van Nostrand Reinhold, 1970.

Fetterman, Elsie, and Charles Klamkin. *Consumer Education in Practice.* New York: Wiley, 1976.

Fitch, James Marston. *American Building.* 2d ed. Boston: Houghton Mifflin, 1966.

Fitzgerald, Oscar P. *Three Centuries of American Furniture.* Englewood Cliffs, N.J.: Prentice-Hall, 1982.

Foley, Mary Mix. *The American House.* New York: Harper & Row, 1980.

Friedmann, Arnold, John F. Pile, and Forrest Wilson. *Interior Design: An Introduction to Architectural Interiors.* 3d ed. New York: Elsevier, 1982.

Furuta, Tok. *Interior Landscaping.* Reston, Va.: Reston Pub. Co., 1983.

Gains, Patricia Ellisior. *Fabric Decoration Book.* New York: Morrow, 1975.

Garner, Philippe. *Contemporary Decorative Arts.* New York: Facts on File, 1980.

———. *Twentieth-Century Furniture.* New York: Van Nostrand Reinhold, 1980.

Gaynor, Elizabeth. *Scandinavia Living Design.* New York: Stewart, Tabori & Chang, 1987.

General Electric. *The Light Book.* Cleveland, Ohio: Nela Park, 1981.

Gilliat, Mary. *Kitchen and Dining Rooms.* New York: Viking Press, 1970.

Gilliat, Mary, and Douglas Baker. *Lighting Your Home: A Practical Guide.* New York: Pantheon, 1979.

Grillo, Paul Jacques. *What Is Design?* Chicago: Paul Theobold, 1962.

Gutman, Robert (ed.). *People and Buildings.* New York: Basic Books, 1972.

Halse, Albert O. *The Use of Color in Interiors.* 2d ed. New York: McGraw-Hill, 1978.

Hanks, David A. *Innovative Furniture in America from 1800 to the Present.* New York: Horizon, 1981.

Hardingham, Martin. *The Fabric Catalog.* New York: Simon & Schuster, Pocket Books, 1978.

Harness, S., and J. Groom. *Building without Barriers for the Disabled.* New York: Whitney Library of Design, 1976.

Hartwigsen, Gail Lynn. *Design Concepts: A Basic Guidebook.* Boston: Allyn & Bacon, 1980.

Helick, Martin R. *Varieties of Human Habitation.* Cambridge: MIT Press, 1970.

Hepburn, Andrew H. *Great Houses of American History.* New York: Bramhall House, 1972.

Hicks, David. *Style and Design.* Boston: Little, Brown, 1987.

Hitchcock, Henry-Russell, and Philip Johnson. *The International Style.* (1932, Reprint). New York: Norton, 1966.

Hoffman, Hubert. *Row Houses and Chester Houses: An International Survey.* New York: Praeger, 1967.

Hollen, Norman, and Jane Saddler. *Textiles.* New York: Macmillan, 1964.

Horn, Richard. *Memphis: Objects, Furniture, and Patterns.* Philadelphia: Rushing Press, 1985.

Itten, Johannes. *The Art of Color.* New York: Van Nostrand Reinhold, 1973.

———. *Design and Form: The Basic Course at the Bauhaus.* New York: Van Nostrand Reinhold, 1964.

Jackman, Dianne R., and Mary K. Dixon. Winnipeg: Peguis, 1984.

Jacobson, Charles W. *Check Points on How to Buy Oriental Rugs.* Rutland, Vt.: Charles E. Tuttle, 1969.

Jaffe, Hans L. C. *De Stijl.* New York: Harry N. Abrams, 1967.

Jencks, Charles, and William Chaitkin. *Architecture Today.* New York: Harry N. Abrams, 1982.

Jordan, R. Furneaux. *A Concise History of Western Architecture.* London: Thames & Hudson, 1969.

Joseph, Marjory L. *Essentials of Textiles.* 3d ed. New York: Holt, Rinehart & Winston, 1984.

Kahlenberg, Mary Hunt, and Anthony Berlant. *Navajo Blanket.* New York: Praeger, 1972.

Keiser, Marjorie Branin. *Housing: An Environment for Living.* New York: Macmillan, 1978.

Kira, Alexander. *The Bathroom.* New York: Viking Press, 1976.

Kleeman, Walter B. *The Challenge of Interior Design.* New York: Van Nostrand Reinhold, 1981.

Klein, Dan. *Art Deco.* New York: Crown, 1974.

Kopp, Joel, and Kate Kopp. *American Hooked and Sewn Rugs.* New York: Dutton, 1975.

Kostof, Spiro. *History of Architecture.* New York: Oxford University Press, 1985.

Kron, Joan, and Suzanne Slesin. *High Tech: The Industrial Style and Source Book for the Home.* New York: Clarkson N. Potter, 1978.

Kuppers, Harold. *Color: Origins, Systems, Uses.* New York: Van Nostrand Reinhold, 1973.

Larsen, Jack Lenor, and Jeanne Weeks. *Fabrics for Interiors.* New York: Van Nostrand Reinhold, 1975.

Lewis, Ethel. *Romance of Textiles.* New York: Macmillan, 1937.

Libby, William Charles. *Color and the Structural Sense.* Englewood Cliffs, N.J.: Prentice-Hall, 1974.

Lightolier. *The Light Book.* Jersey City, N.J.: Lightolier, 1981.

Liman, Ellen. *Money Saver's Guide to Decorating.* New York: Macmillan, 1972.

Lucie-Smith, Edward. *Furniture: A Concise History.* London: Thames & Hudson, 1985.

Maass, John. *The Victorian Home in America.* New York: Hawthorn, 1972.

Mackay, James. *Turn-of-the-Century Antiques: An Encyclopedia.* New York: Dutton, 1974.

Magnani, Franco (ed.). *Interiors for Today.* New York: Whitney Library of Design, 1975.

Mang, Karl. *History of Modern Furniture.* New York: Harry N. Abrams, 1979.

Marsh, Betty. *All about Furniture.* High Point, N.C.: Southern Furniture Manufacturers, 1969.

Mather, Christine, and Sharon Woods. *Santa Fe Style.* New York: Rizzoli International, 1986.

Mazzurco, Philip. *Bath Design.* New York: Whitney Library of Design, 1986.

McCorquodale, Charles. *A History of Interior Decoration.* New York: Vendome Press, 1983.

McFadden, David. *Scandinavian Modern Design.* New York: Harry N. Abrams, 1982.

Meadmore, Clement. *The Modern Chair.* New York: Van Nostrand Reinhold, 1975.

Meeks, Carol. *Housing.* Englewood Cliffs, N.J.: Prentice-Hall, 1980.

Minimum Guidelines and Requirements for Accessible Design. Washington D.C.: U.S. Architectural & Transportation Barriers Compliance Board, 1982.

Molesworth, H. D., and John Kenworthy-Browne. *Three Centuries of Furniture in Color.* New York: Viking Press, 1972.

Money Management Institute. *Your Home Furnishings Dollar.* Chicago: Household Finance Corp., 1973.

Munsell, Albert H. *A Color Notation.* 10th ed. Baltimore: Munsell Color Company, 1954.

Naar, Jon, and Molly Siple. *Living in One Room.* New York: Random House, 1976.

Naylor, Gillian. *The Bauhaus.* New York: Dutton, 1968.

Nicholson, Arnold. *American Houses in History.* New York: Viking Press, 1965.

Nuckolls, James L. *Interior Lighting for Environmental Designers.* New York: Wiley, 1976.

Page, Marian. *Furniture Designed by Architects.* New York: Whitney Library of Design, 1980.

Panero, Julius, and Martin Zelnick. *Human Dimensions and Interior Space.* New York: Whitney Library of Design, 1979.

Papanek, Victor. *Design for Human Scale.* New York: Van Nostrand Reinhold, 1983.

Pevsner, Nikolaus. *Pioneers of Modern Design from William Morris to Walter Gropius.* 2d ed. New York: Museum of Modern Art, 1975.

Phillips, Derek. *Lighting in Architectural Design.* New York: Holt, Rinehart & Winston, 1968.

Pierson, William H., Jr. *American Buildings and Their Architects: The Colonial and Neoclassical Styles.* New York: Doubleday, 1970.

Pile, John F. *Interior Design.* Englewood Cliffs, N.J.: Prentice-Hall; New York: Harry N. Abrams, Inc., 1988.

Plumb, Barbara. *Young Designs in Color.* New York: Viking Press, 1972.

Pomada, Elizabeth, and Michael Larsen. *Painted Ladies: San Francisco's Resplendent Victorians.* New York: Dutton, 1978.

Pool, Mary Jane, and Caroline Seebohm (eds.). *20th Century Decorating, Architecture and Gardens: 80 Years of Ideas and Pleasure from House and Garden.* New York: Holt, Rinehart & Winston, 1980.

Pratt, Richard. *The Golden Treasury of Early American Houses.* New York: Harrison House, 1967.

Praz, Mario. *An Illustrated History of Furnishings.* New York: George Braziller, 1964.

Proshansky, Harold M., et al. (eds.). *Environmental Psychology: Man and His Physical Setting.* New York: Holt, Rinehart & Winston, 1970.

Radford, Penny. *Designer's Guide to Surfaces and Finishes.* New York: Watson-Guptill, 1984.

Radice, Barbara. *Memphis.* New York: Rizzoli International, 1984.

Riggs, J. Rosemary. *Materials and Components of Interior Design.* Reston, Va.: Reston Pub. Co., 1985.

Rogers, Meyric R. *American Interior Design.* New York: Bonanza Books, 1947.

Rooney, William F. *Practical Guide to Home Lighting.* New York: Van Nostrand Reinhold, 1980.

Russell, Frank, Philippe Garner, and John Read. *A Century of Chair Design.* New York: Rizzoli International, 1980.

Schlosser, Ignace. *The Book of Rugs.* New York: Bonanza Books, 1958.

Schofield, Maria (ed.). *Decorative Art in Modern Interiors, 1974/75.* New York: Viking Press, 1974.

Scully, Vincent J., Jr. *Modern Architecture.* Rev. ed. New York: Braziller, 1974.

Sharpe, Deborah T. *The Psychology of Color and Design.* Chicago: Nelson-Hall, 1975.

Siegel, Harry. *Business Guide for Interior Designers.* New York: Whitney Library of Design, 1976.

Siegel, Harry, and Alan Siegel. *A Guide to Business Principles and Practices for Interior Designers.* Rev. ed. New York: Whitney Library of Design, 1982.

Sinclair, Peg B. *Victorious Victorians: A Guide to the Major Architectural Styles.* New York: Holt, Rinehart & Winston, 1985.

Smith, C. Ray. *A History of Interior Design in 20th Century America.* New York: Harper & Row, 1987.

Smith, S. Jane. *Elsie de Wolfe: A Life in the High Style.* New York: Atheneum, 1982.

Sommer, Robert. *Design Awareness.* Corte Madera, Calif.: Rinehart Press, 1972.

Stimpson, Miriam. *Modern Furniture Classics.* New York: Whitney Library of Design, 1987.

St. Marie, Satenig S. *Homes Are for People.* New York: Wiley, 1973.

Sulahria, Julie, and Ruby Diamond. *Inside Design: Creating Your Environment.* San Francisco: Canfield Press, 1977.

Tate, Allen, and C. Ray Smith. *Interior Design in the 20th Century.* New York: Harper & Row, 1986.

Taylor, Lucy D. *Know Your Fabrics.* New York: Wiley, 1956.

Textile Handbook. 4th ed. Washington, D.C.: American Home Economics Assn., 1970.

Trachtenberg, Marvin, and Isabelle Hyman. *Architecture from Prehistory to Post-Modernism.* New York: Harry N. Abrams, 1986.

Verity, Enid. *Color Observed.* New York: Van Nostrand Reinhold, 1982.

Wanscher, Ole. *The Art of Furniture.* New York: Reinhold Pub. Corp., 1967.

Warren, Geoffrey. *Art Nouveau Style.* London: Octopus, 1972.

Watson, Sir Francis. *The History of Furniture.* London: Orbio, 1982.

Weale, Mary Jo, et al. *Environmental Interiors.* New York: Macmillan, 1982.

White, Wilson H. *Cluster Development.* New York: American Conservation Assn., 1964.

Whiton, Sherrill. *Interior Design and Decoration.* 4th ed. Philadelphia: J. P. Lippincott, 1974.

Wiffen, Marcus, and Frederick Koeper. *American Architecture, 1607–1976.* 2 vols. Cambridge, Mass.: MIT Press, 1981.

Wills, Royal, of Barry Associates. *More Houses for Good Living.* New York: Architectural Book Publishing, 1968.

Wilson, Jose, and Arthur Leaman. *Color in Decoration.* New York: Van Nostrand Reinhold, 1971.

Wingate, Isabel B., Karen Gillespie, and Betty Mildram. *Know Your Merchandise for Retailers and Consumers.* 4th ed. New York: McGraw-Hill, 1975.

Wise, Herbert. *Kitchen Detail.* New York: Quick Fox, 1980.

Wright, Frank Lloyd. *The Natural House.* New York: Bramhall House, 1954.

Zelanski, Paul, and Mary Pat Fisher. *Design: Principles and Problems.* New York: Holt, Rinehart & Winston, 1984.

Selected Periodicals

Abitare

Americana

American Craft

American Home

Antiques Magazine

Apartment Life

Architectural Digest

Better Homes & Gardens

Budget Decorating

Design and Environment

The Designer Magazine

Designers West

Domus

Home

House and Garden

House Beautiful

Interior Design

Interiors

Metropolis

Metropolitan Home

1001 Decorating Ideas Home Library

Southern Accents

Waverly's Easy-to-Do Decorating

Woman's Day Service Series

Other Readings

Current *catalogs and brochures* are published and made available by major manufacturers of fabrics, wallpaper, wall paneling, hard floor coverings, carpets, and furniture.

How-to booklets on every phase of building, remodeling, and interior design are available to both the professional and nonprofessional and are advertised in current periodicals.

Glossary

achromatic Without chroma—a color scheme employing white, black, or gray.

acoustical plaster A plaster containing sound-absorbent ingredients.

acoustical tile A tile especially constructed to absorb and control transmission of sound.

acoustics In design, the study of sound, including its properties and successful adaptation in a human environment.

acrylics Strong, flexible, and transparent plastics that can be formed into any shape; used for many types of furnishings. Lucite and Plexiglas are common trade names.

active solar system Architectural systems particularly designed to collect and distribute solar heat, often requiring additional supportive energy.

adaptation The modification of an item to make it fit more perfectly under conditions of its current environment. In furniture design, an adaptation indicates that only some elements of the original have been adapted to the present design.

adaptive reuse Historical structures recycled for current use.

additive color Mixing or adding primary hues, through the use of either dyes and pigments or lighting.

adobe brick A brick of sun-dried earth and straw; most often used in the Southwest adobe–style dwelling.

aesthetic Pertaining to the beauty found in nature or an artistic composition.

affinity Relationship, attraction, kinship.

ambient light A term interchangeable with *general lighting;* lighting that provides overall illumination.

American Society of Interior Designers (ASID) The principal professional international organization of interior designers established to enact and maintain standards of excellence in the field.

antebellum Existing before the Civil War.

anthropometrics The science of measuring the dimensions and functions of the human body and applying the results to the total design approach, ultimately providing human comfort and well-being.

antique A work of art, piece of furniture, or decorative object made at a much earlier period than the present, often at least 100 years old; according to U.S. customs laws, an item made before 1830.

arabesque A leaf-and-scroll pattern with stems rising from a root or other motif branching in spiral form; usually in a vertical panel.

arcade A series of adjoining arches with their supporting columns on piers.

arcaded panel A panel with a field depicting two dwarf columns supporting an arch.

architrave A horizontal member located above the column and capital in classical architecture.

armoire The French term for a tall cupboard or wardrobe with doors.

Art Deco A term derived from the 1925 Paris exhibition called "Les Expositions des Arts Decoratifs"; known during the period as Moderne or Modernistic. This stylistic movement emerged during the pre–World War I era and generally ended before the outbreak of World War II and encompassed architecture, furniture, and the decorative arts.

artificial lighting Manufactured lighting produced in three ways: (1) combustion, (2) incandescence, and (3) fluorescence.

Art Nouveau A modern stylistic movement based on the flowing lines of nature that flourished principally in Europe and the United States circa 1890–1910.

Arts and Crafts Movement Founded by William Morris and others in England (circa 1860), this artistic movement was inspired by the honest craftsmanship of the medieval and Renaissance periods whose purpose was to create good design in all mediums. Known as one of the first important modern movements, its influence in handcrafted items is still prevalent today.

ashlar Square or rectangular blocks of stone masonry used in the construction of a building.

atrium plan A floor plan in which all major rooms open onto a central atrium or court that may be open or enclosed in glass.

authentic Conforming to an original so as to reproduce essential features.

awning window Windows with a hinge at the top allowing the window to swing outwards. (Occasionally the window is hinged at the bottom.)

Axminster Named after a town in England, this carpet construction has a cut wool pile and jute back. Now made on a special American loom, the yarns are set in a crosswise row, permitting each tuft to be controlled individually and allowing almost unlimited combinations of colors and patterns.

balcony A projecting platform from the exterior or interior wall of a structure enclosed by a railing.

ballast An electrical transformer that converts current necessary for fluorescent lighting.

balloon-frame construction A type of construction employing a simple and economical skeletal frame and used most often for small wood houses with closely placed supportive elements with spaces in between for wiring, plumbing, and insulation.

baluster A turned, upright support of a rail, as in the railing of a staircase.

balustrade A row of balusters topped by a rail.

banquette An upholstered bench seating piece.

Baroque A powerful and imaginative art and design direction circa seventeenth and eighteenth centuries characterized by elaborate and massive decorative elements; a reaction against the severe classic style.

baseboard A strip of molding attached at the bottom of the wall along the floor's edge.

bas-relief A type of decoration in which the design is slightly raised from the surface or background.

batik A process of decorating fabric by wax coating the parts not to be dyed. After the fabric is dyed, the wax is removed.

batten A long strip of wood employed to cover the joint between two larger wood strips.

Bauhaus A school of art and architecture in Weimar (and later Dessau), East Germany, from 1919–1933, founded by Walter Gropius for the purpose of uniting art and industry; considered the most influential element in the promotion of modern design and the International Style of architecture.

bay window An angled window that projects outwards from the wall surface.

bead-and-reel A convex classical Greek molding, with disks singly or in pairs, alternating with oblong beads.

beam A horizontal timber or metal bar supported on vertical posts, used to support a roof or ceiling.

bentwood A process of bending narrow strips of wood into various artistic forms; developed primarily by Austrian designer Michael Thonet during the latter half of the eighteenth century.

bevel The edge of any flat surface that has been cut at a slant to the main surface.

bidet A water-cleansing fixture used by adults after the toilet facility.

blueprint A photographic print, formerly white lines on a bright blue ground, used for copying architectural plans. The standard today is blue lines on a white ground.

board-and-batten construction Construction employing wide upright boards placed side by side with joints covered by *battens.*

boiserie A French word generally used to designate carved wood paneling.

bow windows A semicurved window that projects outwards from the wall surface.

breakfront A large cabinet or bookcase, with a center section projecting beyond the flanking end sections.

broadloom Carpet strips woven in 36-in. strips.

buffet A cabinet for holding dining room accessories and from which food may be served.

burl A strong irregularity in the wood grain providing an interesting design and color; often used for veneering in furniture.

burnish To make brown or lustrous by rubbing.

cabriole leg A furniture leg support designed in the form of a conventionalized animal leg with knee, ankle, and foot creating a double curve or S shape.

calendering A finishing process employed for fabrics where the textile is pressed between rollers.

candela In lighting, the unit of measure of *candlepower.*

candlepower A measurement of light intensity equal to the luminosity of a candle.

caning Flexible rattan or cane woven in open mesh for chairbacks, seats, and other furniture members.

canister A small box or case used for holding tea, coffee, flour, salt, or sugar. Early imported canisters were prized household items.

cantilever A projecting beam or furniture member supported at one end only.

captain's walk A balustraded observation platform built atop the roof of a coastal dwelling, providing an unobstructed view of the sea; also called a widow's walk (most often found on Georgian and Federal homes).

carmine A rich crimson or scarlet; red hue in high saturation.

carpet A flat woven or pile fiber floor covering most often sold by the yard and laid on the entire floor surface. Today the term often refers to any rug or carpet size.

casement window A window hinged on one side only, allowing it to swing inwards or outwards.

casepiece A general term applied to furniture storage pieces that have no upholstered components.

ceramics Decorative or functional items fashioned from clay and fired (or baked) in a kiln.

chair rail See *dado*

chaise longue A French term for a lounge chair (with or without arms) with an extended seat providing leg support for the occupant.

chandelier A lighting fixture suspended from the ceiling with branches to support candles or electric lamps.

château A castle or large country house in France.

chevron A repeating V shape or "zigzag" motif consisting of diagonal bars meeting at a point.

chinoiserie (French) Refers to Chinese designs, which were popularly employed during the eighteenth century on European furniture.

chroma The purity or saturation of a color.

circa Approximately.

circulation The traffic patterns of occupants within an interior space—particularly important when planning rooms, stairways, hallways, etc.

clapboard A horizontal overlapping of thin wood boards used for the exterior sheathing of structures; popularly employed for seventeenth- and eighteenth-century Colonial style homes.

classic A term applied to a work of art recognized as a standard of value and excellence.

classical A term relating to the arts of ancient Greece or Rome—especially designs created during the "Golden Age."

clerestory Windows placed at the top of a structure's wall allowing extra light; first built by the ancient Romans for churches and palaces.

closed plan An architectural floor plan in which interior space is divided into separate rooms.

cluster planning A method of arranging concentrated dwelling units, usually low-rise and either separate or attached, to take advantage of communal open spaces.

coffered ceiling Ornamental sunken panels between beams employed for a flat, vaulted, or domed ceiling providing a three-dimensional effect.

Colonial A term loosely used in referring to the 200-yr period that includes the settlement of the early colonies in America through the Federal period (circa 1607–1835). According to some authorities, however, nothing after 1776 is rightfully Colonial.

colonnade Columns arranged in a straight or curved row, often supporting an entablature.

colonnette A miniature colonnade used for decoration.

commode A French term referring to a low chest supported on legs with drawers.

common denominator A common multiple or an element common to all items to which it pertains.

condominium A multiunit structure, such as an apartment house, in which each unit is individually owned. Maintenance and services are provided but are paid for by the residents.

conduction heater A method of heating employing a radiator that circulates hot water or steam, providing warm air within a space.

console table A table designed to be fixed on a wall; sometimes supported by two front legs.

contemporary design Living or occurring at the same period of time. In furniture the term commonly refers to a modified type of modern or updated traditional design.

convection heating A method of heating employing a furnace that forces warm air through registers that are placed throughout the living spaces.

Corinthian The most ornate of the three Greek orders, characterized by its capital of small volutes (spiral, scroll-shaped ornaments) and acanthus leaves.

cornice A horizontal and projecting member that crowns an architectural composition; a molding on a wall near the ceiling or under the eaves of the roof. Cornice board is a molding used with drapery instead of a valance.

Coromandel screen A large freestanding paneled screen with Oriental designs, originally imported from the Coromandel Coast of India.

Cotswold An area of rolling green hills and limestone outcroppings, mainly in Gloucestershire, England. The region is famous for picturesque stone houses called Cotswolds.

coved ceiling A ceiling that meets the wall by means of a concave curve rather than a right angle.

credenza A long, table-height cupboard with drawers and doors. Popular during the Italian Renaissance; today, a low storage unit with doors and often drawers.

crown molding The uppermost molding.

cruciform A cross-shape form.

crystal The finest quality of lead glass.

cupola A small structure built on top of a roof for a lookout or to provide interior lighting; commonly used in Georgian, Federal, and Victorian structures.

cyma curve A double curve formed by the union of a concave and convex line.

dado The lower part of an interior wall when treated in a different manner from the wall above; usually defined by a molding called a dado cap or chair railing.

day-bed An extended type of couch or chair that can be converted for use as a bed.

De Stijl A Dutch art and design movement from 1917–1929 characterized by abstract forms, right angles, smooth shiny surfaces, and the use of primary colors plus black, white, and gray; helped pioneer Modernism.

distressed Refers to a surface treatment found on antique reproductions when the furniture is intentionally damaged to provide an aged appearance.

dormer A window in a small gablelike projection built out from a sloping roof.

double glazing A process of hermetically sealing two sheets of glass together with air trapped between. This type of glass provides efficient insulation against heat and cold.

double-hung window A window divided into two sections, one lowering from the top, and the other rising from the bottom.

dovecote Originally, a small, compartmented, raised house or box, used for housing domestic pigeons; eventually became a roof type.

dovetail joint A type of wood joint used in furniture construction consisting of two slotted fan-shaped pieces that interlock.

dowel A round wood peg. Often used for furniture joinery, the peg is inserted into a cavity of the same size.

dower chest A chest to hold items for a prospective bride; used by most civilizations. In early Pennsylvania it was the dower chest and took on distinctive characteristics.

downlight Recessed or ceiling-mounted architectural lighting with lamps that direct the light downwards.

Dresden Fine porcelain made in Meissen, near Dresden, East Germany. Established 1710–1720, the factory produced some of the most famous china in Europe.

drill A twill cotton in a stout weave, often used as fabric backing for walls.

drop-leaf table A table with one or two hinged members that can drop to the sides or be supported to provide a larger tabletop surface.

dropped ceiling A ceiling that is placed lower than the regular height of a particular space. Often ceilings are deliberately dropped by various means and materials when too high for personal preference or function.

Dutch door A single-hinged door divided horizontally so each section can be opened independently.

earthenware Objects made of a coarse brown or red clay. After firing, earthenware is porous and nondurable, unless treated with a glazed finish.

eave A protecting lower edge of a roof which overhangs the walls of a building.

eclecticism Mixing furnishings or borrowing styles from various sources and periods with an eye to compatibility.

egg-and-dart A classical Greek molding consisting of ovoid (egg-shaped) forms alternating with dartlike designs.

electromagnet A core of magnetic material surrounded by a coil of wire through which an electric current is passed to magnetize the core.

ell A wing or extension placed at a right angle to the structure.

elliptical fanlight A fan-shaped window that topped the central doorways of Federal-period houses in America.

entablature The upper part of a wall usually supported by columns or pilasters and in classical orders consisting of the *architrave, frieze,* and *cornice.*

epergne A tiered centerpiece.

ergonomics A relatively new science with a goal to provide a comfortable relationship between human beings and their environment (especially the working environment), through the study of body mechanics and sensory performance.

escutcheon In hardware, it refers to a shaped plate for a keyhole or a metal fitting to which a handle or knob is attached.

étagère A series of shelves supported by vertical supports; used chiefly for display.

etching A design produced on an etched plate or an impression taken in ink from an etched plate.

eyeball In lighting, a ceiling-mounted or recessed incandescent fixture with a pivoting spherical lamp that can be maneuvered to direct the light where desired.

facade Refers to the exterior front of a building, either decorative or structural.

Federal period The political, social, and decorative formation era in America following the Revolutionary War (circa 1790–1825).

felting A process of matting fibers into a fabric.

fenestration The placement, type, and design of windows and other openings found on a building.

festoon A carved, molded, or painted classical ornament representing a decorative chain, swag, or strip.

fiber A natural or synthetic substance processed into a thread or yarn of continuous length.

fiberglass Glass fibers that reinforce various plastics; often used for furniture, furniture parts, or skylights.

filament A threadlike conductor (as of carbon or metal) that is rendered incandescent (brilliant) by the passage of an electric current.

finial An upright ornament that forms the upper extremity of an architectural detail, a piece of furniture, or an accessory.

flatware Knives, forks, and spoons.

Flemish Relating to or characteristic of the Low Countries, now Belgium and the Netherlands.

flocking A process employed for duplicating the effect of velvet fabrics on wallpaper in which fibers are applied to an adhesive. A type of carpet also involves this process.

fluorescent lighting Artificial light produced when a gaseous mixture of mercury and argon, sealed within a glass tube that is lined with a fluorescent coating, is activated by an electrical current.

fluting Parallel concave grooves commonly used on the shafts of columns.

foil Anything that serves, by contrast of color, pattern, texture, or other elements, to adorn or set off another thing to advantage; also a wallpaper with the appearance of a thin sheet of metal; a background.

footcandle An international unit of light measurement. It is the illumination at a 1-ft distance from the light of one candle. The intensity of light is calculated in footcandles.

footlambert In lighting, the unit of measure for reflected light.

Foundation for Interior Design Education Research (FIDER) The national accrediting organization for interior design educational programs.

French doors Paired, single-hinged doors of paned glass—a walk-through window—which swings either inwards or outwards.

fresco The art of painting on moist lime plaster with water-based pigments.

fretwork Interlaced ornamental work either perforated or cut in low relief, usually in geometric patterns; also, tracery of glazed doors and windows.

frieze The horizontal decorative section found between the *architrave* and the *cornice* in classical architecture.

FRP Thin translucent sheets of reinforced fiberglass plastic, sometimes employed for patio roofing, furniture, and wall panels.

fusuma screen A sliding movable screen used in Japanese houses as a partition to define space.

gable The end portion of a building formed by the roof coming together at the top.

gallery A miniature railing placed along the edge of a tabletop or shelf.

gambrel roof A roof made from two lengths of lumber, the upper one being flatter and the lower one a steeper slope.

generic A term pertaining to the characteristics of a particular type or class of fibers.

geodesic dome A triangular patterned dome held together by a self-supporting network of rods and covered with a variety of materials—usually a plastic membrane or glass. The geodesic dome was developed by Richard Buckminster Fuller, an American architect and engineer.

Georgian An English architectural and furniture style popular during the reigns of George I, II, and III in

England (circa 1714–1790) and copied by Americans; furniture included the styles of Queen Anne, Chippendale, Hepplewhite, and Sheraton.

glass block Hollow glass forms in a variety of sizes and textures used in building construction to emit light.

Gothic Refers to the period from approximately 1160 to 1530 A.D., in which the ecclesiastical architecture dominated all the arts. The Gothic arch and vault were the most significant design contributions.

grain Refers to the vertical configurations or textural (coarse or fine) features of wood.

Greek Revival The third and final phase (circa 1825–1845) of the Neoclassic style in America in which bold and monumental characteristics were related to the early forms of Greece and Rome.

grout A mortar (generally of cement), used to set tiles or fill in cavities.

half-timber construction Construction of timber frame, with the spaces filled with masonry or lath and plaster.

hand or ***handle*** The feel or drape of fabric.

hemp A tough fiber from an Asiatic herb.

henequen A sisal fiber related to maguey found chiefly in Yucatan.

highboy A tall chest of drawers supported on tall legs and divided horizontally into two sections; particularly popular during the Georgian period.

High Tech A current design expression developed during the late 1970s employing industrial components and the latest technology, providing a streamlined and mechanical appearance.

hip roof A roof with sloping ends and sloping sides.

Hitchcock chair An American chair (1820–1850) named for Lambert Hitchcock of Connecticut. It derives from a Sheraton "fancy" chair and is often black with stenciled fruit and flower motifs.

hutch An informal chest or cabinet common to many countries, which came to America from England. The type most commonly used has bottom doors and open upper shelves.

HVAC Indication for heating, ventilating, and air-conditioning systems.

incandescent lighting Light produced by heating a tungsten filament sealed in a light bulb.

indigenous Inherent; native to or living naturally in a country.

indigo A blue dye obtained from several lands but now chiefly made synthetically.

inlay Pieces of stone, wood, shell, metal, or ivory arranged in a design composition and set into another piece of wood or other material for a decorative effect.

insulation The use of nonconductors between the inside and outside of a structure or between materials to prevent the transfer of sound, heat, cold, or electricity.

intensity See *chroma*

Interior Design Educators Council (IDEC) A society formed for interior design educators.

International Style A style of architecture based on the Bauhaus and principles of other leading modernists. Developed during the first two decades of the twentieth century, the style is simple, structural, and functional.

Ionic The second Greek order designated by the four spiral volutes of its capital.

Italianate Name given to one of the main styles of American Victorian architecture. It embodied many features of the Italian villa and remained in vogue for almost 100 years (circa 1830s–1920s).

Jacobean From the Latin *Jacobus* (James); the general term for English furniture styles from circa 1603–1688. Jacobean was the prototype of most furniture made by the early colonists in New England during the seventeenth and early eighteenth centuries.

Jacquard A loom apparatus for weaving fabrics of intricate weaves and patterns; invented in France in 1801 by Charles Marie Jacquard.

jalousie window A window made of narrow horizontal and overlapping adjustable glass louvers that control ventilation and light.

kapok A mass of silky fibers from the ceiba tree; used for filling cushions.

kiln A furnace or oven employed for firing ceramics.

knot Wood with a distinctive oval or round feature in the grain. Knots, which were originally avoided, are often chosen today for their effect.

lambrequin An ornamental window treatment, usually in the form of a wooden frame across the top and down the sides of the window, either painted or covered with fabric. Common in French country houses.

laminate The binding of layers of wood together. In paneling, several layers are laid alternately across the grain for strength and durability. For decorative purposes, a thin layer of fine wood (veneer) is glued to the surface of the basic wood; a process also used for plastics.

lamp The light source (base and bulb or tube) of artificial lighting.

lath Thin strips of wood or a metal mesh attached to the structural frame of a building to support plaster, tile, reinforced concrete, or other material.

lathe A machine used to turn wood or metal into various shapes.

leno A loose, open weave with warp yarns wound in half twists around each other, alternating in position on each row.

lintel The horizontal beam or component that spans the area between openings such as columns, windows, and doors.

louver A slatted panel (usually wood) for controlling the flow of air and the radiation of light; most often used as a window treatment.

lowboy A low chest of drawers supported on legs; particularly associated with the Georgian style.

lumen A quantitative unit for measuring light output.

luminaire A complete light fixture including the lamp and all supportive elements.

luminescence Commonly referred to as fluorescence.

madder A Eurasian herb with a root that produces a red dye.

maguey A fleshy-leaved Mexican agave plant that produces a liquid and a fiber from which rope, rugs, and other items are made.

mansard roof A roof having two slopes on all sides, the lower one steeper than the upper one.

marquetry A decorative inlay design glued into furniture and floors employing a variety of woods or other materials.

masonry The structural construction of a building employing brick, stone, concrete blocks, tile, or other materials adhered with mortar.

matte A dull finish.

medieval Refers to the Middle Ages—a turbulent time that followed the decline of the Roman Empire and extended to the Renaissance, covering roughly 1,000 years (circa 500 to 1500 A.D.).

melamine An extremely durable opaque or translucent plastic used most often for dinnerware and counter tops; well-known trade names include Formica and Melmac.

memorabilia Items worthy of remembrance or preservation.

miter Joining two members of material at a 45-degree angle to form a corner.

mode A prevailing fashion or style.

modular Constructed with standardized units or modules.

module One in a series of standardized units to be integrated together, such as building construction units or a set of furniture.

molding An architectural wood strip, usually decorative, that projects from the ceiling or wall surface; may also be of metal, plaster, or plastic.

mordant Any substance that serves to produce a fixed color in a textile fiber, leather, or other similar material.

mortise and tenon A type of joint used in furniture construction with a projecting tenon that fits into the mortise or cavity.

mottle A dripped or irregular color.

mullion A horizontal member dividing glazed doors, windows, or bookcases.

muntin A vertical bar dividing the panes of a window, door, or bookcase. *Muntin* is often used interchangeably with *mullion.*

National Council for Interior Design Qualification (NCIDQ) An official body for testing professional interior design competencies and establishing guidelines for legal licensing.

Neoclassic Revivals simulating the ancient classical designs of Greece and Rome, such as Louix XVI, Adam, Directoire, and Empire styles.

newel post The main post at the foot of a stairway.

nosing The projecting edge at the top of a stair's riser.

open plan A floor plan with a minimum of fixed partitions, allowing space to flow from one area to another.

orientation Placement or arrangement of various elements such as buildings, windows, rooms, or furnishings in relation to points on the compass or other elements.

Palladianism Relating to a classical style in architecture based on the works of Andrea Palladio (1518–1580), the most copied of all Italian architects.

Palladian window A window consisting of three vertical parts with the central section higher than the flanking ones and surmounted by a fanlight. This window was a popular feature in the Palladian style of architecture in England in the seventeenth century and in America in the eighteenth century.

panetière A decorative French bread box with open spindles.

parapet A low wall or protective railing at the edge of a roof or platform.

parchment Animal skin prepared for writing or a superior paper made in imitation of parchment; sometimes used on furniture.

parquetry A mosaic of wood laid in geometric patterns.

passive solar system A system of collecting, storing, and distributing solar heat by employing elements of the structure such as glassed-in porches oriented to the sun.

patina A mellow surface often developed with age.

patio (Spanish) A courtyard.

pavilion A part of a building projecting from the main structure.

pedestal A support at the base of a column; any base or foundation on which to display an art object.

pediment A triangular architectural structure above a portico, window, or door.

pendant An object suspended from above.

pendant chandelier A light suspended from the ceiling with a single fixture.

perimeter lighting Lighting that follows the outer boundary of a room.

period style A term used to designate a single item or a complete interior including the architectural background, furniture, and decorative arts prevalent in a specific country at a particular time in history.

pilaster An upright rectangular projection or partial column fixed to a wall, architecturally treated as a column.

pilling Describes fiber that works out of the yarn structure and makes little balls on the surface of a carpet or fabric.

pitched roof A sloping roof—either a low or high pitch.

plan A drawn arrangement of elements in a structure indicating walls, rooms, spaces, and so forth shown from floor level.

plywood A process of laminating layers of wood with alternating grain direction. Usually the top layer or *veneer* is of a finer quality; used for furniture and paneling.

polyurethane A group of plastics characterized by light weight and flexibility and varying in density, hardness, and resilience.

Pompeii A city of Italy buried in 79 A.D. by the ash of Mount Vesuvius and excavated in the eighteenth century. The great interest it aroused in the classical arts inaugurated the classic revival.

portfolio A flexible case used by designers containing renderings, pictures, and other design-related projects.

portico A projection from the main structure of a building over the front entrance supported by columns often capped by a pediment.

Post-Modernism A new direction of modern architecture that for the most part rejects the philosophies of the Bauhaus; freely borrows from the past, but extremely reinterpreted and updated.

prefabricated (prefab) Mass produced in standardized modules or parts for later assembly at the factory or building site.

primitive painting Refers to many American paintings done in the late seventeenth and early eighteenth centuries by untrained artists. The style is peculiar and unlifelike, and all such works have a remarkable similarity that is easily distinguishable.

program The first step in a design project, involving a verbal outline of goals, requirements, and plans.

prototype An original from which another item is modeled.

proxemics A study developed especially during the 1980s concerned with the relationship of human psychological aspects to personal space needs.

Pueblo One of the Indian tribes of New Mexico; an Indian village built in the form of commercial houses.

quoin A solid exterior angle on a building distinguished from the adjoining surface by material, color, size, or projection.

ranch style Also known as a California ranch or rambler home; a ground-hugging single-level plan with a low-pitched overhanging roof supported by posts.

random plank Wood planks laid in a manner disregarding the width of individual boards.

reeding A small convex molding—the reverse of fluting; used on columns, pilasters, and furniture.

Renaissance A period in Europe after the medieval and Gothic periods. Beginning in Italy in the fourteenth century, it was marked by a humanistic and classical period in which an unprecedented flourishing of the arts occurred.

replica An accurate reproduction.

repoussé Relief work done on metal, created by hammering the material on the reverse side.

reproduction A precise duplication of a historic style; a replica.

riser The upright member between two stair treads.

Rococo A phase of European art that had its roots in the late Italian Renaissance but developed in France during the reign of Louis XV in the first half of the eighteenth century. It was an extravagant style using symmetry, shells, rocks, and all manner of elaborate decoration.

Romanesque An architectural style popular in Europe from circa 800–1150; use of the semicircular arch, massive rusticated stone, and the horizontal line; revived during the late nineteenth century in Europe and America.

salamander-back chair A ladder-back chair in which each crossbar resembles two salamanders; a fitting piece for Country French. The salamander was the symbol of Francis I, king of France.

sash The framework (in a window or door) in which the glass is set. It may constitute a movable part.

sconce A lighting fixture secured to the wall.

shade A color that has been darkened by adding black; a low value.

shoji A basic element of a Japanese house, it is made of panes of rice paper and wooden mullions and used as an exterior window. Shoji panels are also employed as wall partitions and freestanding screens.

sisal A strong, durable white fiber derived from the leaves of a West Indian agave; usually woven as a floor covering.

soffit A lower section of a ceiling; area underneath this section.

spectral Pertaining to or made by the spectrum.

standard milled items Items of various kinds (e.g., doors, door frames, windows, window frames, and mantels) made in standard sizes in large quantities in the factory, thus making the cost much less than for custom-made items.

stepped gable A gable in which the sides ascend to the peak in steps; a style brought to America by the Dutch.

stretcher The horizontal supportive crosspiece spanning the area between the legs of a chair or table.

stringcourse A narrow horizontal band placed on the exterior of the Georgian house between the first and the second floors.

swag A festoon of flowers, fruit, or drapery.

synthetic Something artificial simulating the genuine piece.

tambour The front of a piece of furniture made with strips of wood attached to fabric and adjusted on a track, allowing it to open and close.

task light Efficient and functional lighting especially designed for various types of work or tasks.

tatami mat A soft straw mat, approximately 3 ft by 6 ft by 1½ in., which is the basic element of the Japanese house and serves as a unit of measurement. It is the basis of organization and determines the size and proportion of all spaces. The dark lines of its binding form an overall grid pattern, according to which rooms are sized.

templates Small patterns of furniture (either to cut or trace) used as guides in planning rooms.

terrace Usually refers to a relatively level paved area adjoining a building.

thermoplastic Any plastic material that softens with heat and hardens when cooled. Examples include vinyls and acrylics.

tint A color that is lightened by adding white; a high value.

toile de Jouy Fabric made at Jouy, France, by Oberkampf in the late eighteenth and early nineteenth centuries; usually printed on cotton using only one color (red most favorite) on a natural ground. Rural French and Chinese scenic designs are the most characteristic.

tone A neutralized hue produced by adding gray or the color's complement.

tongue-and-groove joint The rib on one edge of a board is made to fit into a corresponding groove in the edge of another board to make a flush joint.

tracery Decorative carved stone or wood openwork in the head of a Gothic window.

traditional style An inherited style of beliefs, customs, architecture, or furnishings. "Traditional" in home furnishings usually refers to styles in the English tradition.

tread The horizontal section of a stair.

trompe l'oeil French expression meaning "to fool the eye"; a term applied to wall decoration such as wallpaper showing bookshelves full of books, cupboards with dishes of fruit, and so on, in remarkably realistic renderings.

Tudor The name of the ruling house of England from 1485 to 1603.

Tudor arch A low or flattened elliptical arch.

tungsten-halogen lamp A highly efficient incandescent light source (also known as a quartz lamp) employing tubes, bulbs, or reflectors.

turning See *lathe*

valance A short decorative fabric treatment at the top of a window that conceals drapery, curtains, and often lighting.

value The lightness or darkness of a color, ranging on a scale from white to black.

veneer Thin sheets of wood or other material (usually of a finer quality) used as a top surface over other more ordinary materials such as plywood.

veranda An open galley or portico (usually roofed) attached to the exterior of a building.

Versailles The magnificent baroque palace built by Louis XIV in the late seventeenth century outside of Paris.

villa (Italian) A large residential structure.

visual weight A visual (not necessarily actual) weight impression of a space and its components depending on various design elements including color, texture, light, and pattern.

wag-on-the-wall One of the earliest clocks used in New England, characterized by an unenclosed, freeswinging pendulum.

wall sconce An ornamental wall bracket to hold candles or electric bulbs.

work triangle The work pattern in a kitchen connecting the three basic elements of sink, refrigerator, and stove.

Index

Industrial age –